CULTURAL SURVEYS

of

PANAMA — NICARAGUA — GUATEMALA

EL SALVADOR — HONDURAS

by

Richard N. Adams

Pan American Sanitary Bureau, World Health Organization, 1957

Republished by Blaine Ethridge — Books, Detroit, Michigan, 1976

This book is a photographic facsimile of a copy in the Memorial Library of the University of Wisconsin, Madison.

**Library of Congress
Cataloging in Publication Data**

Adams, Richard Newbold, 1924-
    Cultural surveys of Panama-Nicaragua-Guatemala-El Salvador-Honduras.

    Reprint of the 1957 edition published by the Pan American Sanitary Bureau, Washington, which was issued as No. 33 of its Scientific Publications.
    Includes bibliographies.
    1. Central America. I. Title. II. Series: Pan American Health Organization. Publicaciones científicas; no. 33.
[F1428.A3 1976]   301.29'728   76-41776
ISBN 0-87917-056-5

TABLE OF CONTENTS

	Page
Part One—Background and Methods	1
Part Two—Panama	27
Part Three—Nicaragua	147
Part Four—Guatemala	261
Part Five—El Salvador	413
Part Six—Honduras	523

Part One

BACKGROUND AND METHODS[1]

[1] I wish to thank Judith Freedman and Ruben Reina for suggestions for the clarification of this background report.

I. THE PROBLEM OF AREA KNOWLEDGE

The Second World War sharply focused the fact that our knowledge of the general cultural, social, and economic nature of many of the world's populations was grossly unsatisfactory. Areal knowledge was a subject of limited interest prior to the war, and concern in the matter was generated principally by theoretical problems. One of the earliest and most extensive area study programs was the work of the Carnegie Institute of Washington in the Mayan area of Mexico and Central America. The present Human Relations Area Files also originated through theoretical concerns for cross cultural comparison.[2] Knowledge of an area for the sake of that knowledge and its potential usefulness in the solution of as yet unformulated problems evidently did not seem important until the practical issues of the war revealed them.

Interest in area studies rose rapidly during the war and in the immediate post-war years.[3] As the importance of such knowledge became clear, various approaches were made to solve the problem of how to get such knowledge. These may be classified into four major types: (1) *compilations*, including those of both old and new materials; (2) *random individual studies* of regions unknown systematically, usually done through community studies; (3) *coordinated field studies* of specifically delimited regions, including those carried on specifically for academic interest and those concerned with programs of application; and (4) *regional and national surveys*.

For Latin America the compilations were the first answer to the problem. The Strategic Index of the Americas was set up at Yale University as one means of compiling available data; work began with the assembling of published and manuscript materials, the translation of those of particular value, and the indexing by subject of all material. This project was never brought anywhere near completion. A more successful attempt, but much more specialized, was the *Handbook of South American Indians*, the first volume of which appeared in 1946.[4] The *Handbook* limited itself to Indian cultures, both contemporary and historical, and tried to provide summaries of the available knowledge concerning these cultures. Of particular note was the fact that much new material was included. Such encyclopedic compilations as the *Handbook* are extremely useful, not only for the information they make available, but because they require that the compilers reformulate the data in the light of new findings and concepts.

With all their advantages and usefulness, compilations are limited by the material which may be available. A further step in the solution of the problem of how to gain areal knowledge was the encouraging or sponsoring of further studies in those regions where knowledge was especially deficient. An important organization which furthered such work was the Institute of Social Anthropology of the Smithsonian Institution. At the time that such work was being fomented,

---
[2] Murdock and others, 1950, p. xii.
[3] See Steward, 1950, for a discussion of the development of these studies.
[4] Steward, 1946–50.

the community study, as a general technique of approach, was very popular and frequently was the main technique used. Scattered community studies played an important role in our developing understanding of the nature of the modern cultures of Latin America. They also proved to be an important step in clarifying the nature of the field work necessary for areal knowledge. Since such studies were usually in regions unknown from the point of view of systematic study, the descriptive data they provided were important additions to knowledge; inevitably, however, the problem of generalization arose. To what degree was a given community representative or illustrative of a specific region or country? Obviously a single community can tell us much about a region, but to evaluate what it has to say, one must know much more than merely the data available about that community alone. Community studies were especially valuable when they were the first done within a given culture area or subarea. After one such good study was available, area knowledge became a problem of figuring out how much of the culture and social forms of the community were applicable to other towns and communities and what variations may have existed. The usual community study, by itself, does not provide this information.

The disadvantages of community studies from the point of view of regional knowledge were considerably lessened by the development of coordinated regional study programs. These programs varied in their complexity and relative coverage, but they may be classified under two general types: those intended to solve theoretical, areal, or historical problems; and those designed as forerunners or part of practical improvement projects. Among theoretically oriented projects may be mentioned the Tarascan program, the Viru Valley project, and the Puerto Rican study.[5] These projects were important because they brought together various specialists and attempted to coordinate their efforts towards the better understanding of a single region. The precise definition of the region varied from case to case. In the Viru Valley and Puerto Rican projects, obvious natural boundaries formed the limits of study; in the Tarascan project, the population considered as Tarascan Indian was the defined subject.

Community studies intentionally formed the major part of the ethnographical portions of these projects because such an approach was understandable and traditional. It must be noted, however, that surveys, in some form, were also made as part of these efforts. Steward reports that a survey was made in order to determine the principal regions of the island of Puerto Rico, and these regions, based on land use and ownership forms, were critical in the selection of communities for intensive study.[6] The Tarascan program also did a certain amount of survey work on specific topics.

The second type of coordinated regional program is that which is a prelude to an action program. This type of program has become increasingly common in recent years, usually sponsored by national governments either with or without international agency assistance. Its importance in the present context is that it has tended to bring into play a number of techniques which are usually not used by anthropologists. Principal among these are survey and question-

---

[5] See Steward, 1950. [6] Steward, 1950, p. 137.

naire methods. While anthropologists have used these, they have seldom been leaders in their improvements as techniques, and they have often avoided them entirely. When knowledge is desired concerning a large universe, however, the usual anthropological techniques are simply not adequate and recourse must be made to others.

Survey work in the field of areal knowledge has usually been more characterized by rural sociological techniques than by a cultural approach.[7] This approach has been important in drawing together some of the available population data, and providing descriptions of social institutions and non-cultural aspects of living such as ecology, national economy, geography, etc.

The ethnographic or social anthropological survey has never been highly developed. It has usually consisted of the student involved looking briefly into various subjects which were of interest to him, defining the area of coverage by convenience and in accordance with these interests, and seldom adhering to any method, either well formulated or not. Nevertheless, with all the drawbacks which such an approach suggests, such surveys have been very useful. The only published anthropological regional survey with which I am familiar is that by Tschopik, Muelle, and Escobar.[8] Somewhat different in objective are the two surveys carried out by the Carnegie Institution of Washington personnel as part of their Maya program.[9]

These surveys have usually consisted of brief visits to a number of different communities, gathering information on various subjects, and then writing up the data in a fairly descriptive and impressionistic way with little analysis. The degree to which the data is subjected to analysis varies with the preferences of the authors. Surveys such as this should not be confused with the much more intensive reports which form the body of the *Ethnographic Survey of Africa*; these studies are actually much more akin to compilations, such as the *Handbook of South American Indians*.

II. AREAL KNOWLEDGE OF CENTRAL AMERICA

When I started working with the World Health Organization in Central America in 1953, the paucity of systematic knowledge of the region was a severe barrier to applied work. In the two previous years I had done field work in Guatemala, El Salvador, and Costa Rica, and had formed some general ideas of the general culture, but I felt completely inadequate to act as a consultant in the region without more systematic knowledge. Indeed, anyone coming to work in Central America was faced with the same problem. While some specific studies had been done, even these were rarely available to the person working in the region. At the time the surveys were initiated, in February of 1953, the following was the general status of our systematic knowledge of the region:

(1) There were scattered intensive studies and some regional surveys of the

---

[7] See, for example, T. Lynn Smith's *Brazil: People and Institutions*, Baton Rouge, 1954; Loomis, et al., *Turrialba*, Glencoe, 1954.

[8] Tschopik, 1947.   [9] Goubaud, Rosales, and Tax, 1944; Redfield and Tax, 1947.

Mayan Indians of Guatemala. Relatively speaking, we had greater systematic knowledge about the Guatemalan Indian than about any other socio-cultural population with the exception of the Cuna Indians of Panama.

(2) There were some studies, published, in microfilm, and in manuscript, of the cultural differences and relationships between the Guatemalan Indians and Ladinos (people of Spanish-American culture) in specific communities. Other similar field studies were under way. The work available was that of Tax, Redfield, Siegel, Gillin, and Tumin; the work in progress was that of Ewald and King.

(3) There were scattered studies of the Honduran, Nicaraguan, and Panamanian Indians. Only the Cuna of Panama, the Boruca of Costa Rica and the Black Carib of British Honduras have witnessed intensive recent study with published results.

(4) There were available (either published or as manuscripts in restricted circulation) a number of studies of the *Meseta Central* population of Costa Rica, and at least one more was underway by Goldkind.

(5) There were various historical observations by travellers and students throughout the region which threw much light on the cultural status of various localities at periods from between 30 to 400 years ago.

With the exception of the historical material and the studies of the Ladino-Indian relations, the socio-cultural groups which may be said to be represented (although in no way fully or adequately described) by previous work include a population of about 2,200,000 as follows: Guatemalan Mayan Indian, 1,500,000; scattered lowland Indians, 100,000; Costa Rica *meseta central* Spanish Americans, 600,000.

These figures, estimated from the 1950 Census, included both rural and town dwelling populations. The total population of Central America at this time was approximately 9,000,000, of which between six and seven million could easily be classified as rural. This meant that not only the majority of the Central Americans, but the Ladinos, the culturally dominant and fastest growing group, were almost unrepresented by systematic study. The importance of knowing something about the Central American population is obvious when we look at the United Nations' forecast of population growth: from the figure of 8,856,000 in 1950, it is estimated that the population will grow to somewhere between 16,000,000 and 21,500,000 in 1980.[10]

Of the four major ways of filling the gap in our knowledge concerning Central America, only one, the survey, was really open for my use. A compilation, by itself, of previous materials would have been next to useless since there were few pertinent studies upon which to draw. A single community study would give us little areal knowledge; the coordinated study project might have been a good solution had there been nine other trained specialists besides myself, and enough time and money. So circumstances required that we survey, or drop the whole matter.

I had already given some thought to the problem of how to do this work, and

---

[10] United Nations, 1954.

had decided that a general survey, done along stricter methodological lines than has at times been the case, would be the most rapid way of gaining an area picture. Harry Tschopik and I had discussed the possibility of undertaking such a survey jointly, but had conceived of it more in terms of the survey which Muelle, Escobar, and he had made in Peru, and one which Tschopik and I had carried on in Costa Rica in 1952. The Costa Rica survey was a brief study of eight communities which were chosen on the basis of major regions previously delineated after conversations with persons conversant with Costa Rica. With the possibility of extending such surveys to all of Central America, the general approach used on the Costa Rican survey seemed to place the cart before the horse; we defined our areas and then selected towns. In a survey, we should, instead, pick our towns on a more random basis, and then define our areas on the basis of knowledge gained from the town visits, combined with other information which might be available. It was planned particularly to lean heavily on available population reports from the census bureaus. I have been impressed with the degree to which population data have been omitted from such general studies, and how much social and cultural information is extractable from them.

It should be pointed out that the surveys, as conceived, were not in any way intended to be substitutes for intensive studies. Rather, they were the only practical means available for accomplishing the general goal. They can be considered as complements to intensive studies, but the latter will always be necessary for the solution of many particular problems.

The Spanish-American culture of Central America was taken as the special focus of the surveys. While there are other cultural components of great importance, there were both practical and theoretical reasons for focusing on this group in particular. More specifically, the focus was to be on the countryman culture of the Spanish-American. By countrymen, we mean the inhabitants of rural areas and small towns; for practical purposes, this includes just about the entire population of the Central American countries outside of the national and provincial capitals. The concept of countryman, itself, includes Indians and non-Indians, peasants and farm laborers, farmer and shopkeeper, etc; it only becomes more specific when some specific restriction is made. The Spanish-American countrymen of Central America compose the largest single cultural population in the entire area. This population is larger in numbers than either the non-Spanish speaking group or the Spanish speaking urban groups. The rationale of studying this group in particular was the reverse of that which has motivated many studies of refugees or survival groups. Our interest was focused on the Spanish-American countryman group precisely because it is the largest and the fastest growing group in the region. The fact of rapid growth, and the consequence in the fields of both rural and urban growth, the depletion of natural resources, and the national economic and political development, make the countryman culture of tremendous importance; and as was already indicated, it is probably the group about which we know systematically the least.

The countryman culture is also of importance on the theoretical side. There has developed in recent years concepts of "mestizo," "creole," "modern Latin American," and "emergent middle class" culture.[11] Given the fact that rural peoples, in Central America at least, include the vast majority of the population, knowledge of this population will clarify and evaluate present concepts of this emergent culture. Furthermore, the concept of the culture area in the past has been used mainly in relation to cultures whose histories survive in legend, as archaeological remains, or not at all. Where it has been applied to contemporary societies, it has been extremely general, such as Steward's fourfold division of cultures of South America, or Herskovits' early culture area delineation of Africa. As a result, it has not often been possible in the past to evaluate the historical processes by which a culture area comes into being. Since the countrymen cultures have developed during the historical period, the delineation of the cultures in terms of culture areas should make it possible to further our understanding of the processes involved in the historical emergence of a culture area and throw light on the nature of the appearance of subareas or regions.

Geographically, the limits of the study were set to include the five countries of Central America and Panama. Panama was included because although historically it has been considered as a part of South America, in recent years its size and location has led it to strengthen its relations with the Central American neighbors. The comparable size of the Central American countries permitted the same general plan of work to be applied to each; such a plan would have to be altered considerably if the work were to be extended to the larger countries to the north and south.

As a part of the general surveys, I intended to revisit Costa Rica and fill in the gaps in the subject matter and regions omitted in the survey which Tschopik and I made in 1952. Unfortunately, this proved impossible because, as an employee of the World Health Organization, it was incumbent on me to work through the national Director General of Public Health, and the Costa Rican Director General refused permission to do the work. I wish it to be clear that the omission of Costa Rica from the survey series was in no way due to any desire on my part that it be omitted. Central America as a whole has many local variations, and it is important that Costa Rica be considered in the Central American context. It is unfortunate that the study was prohibited. Fortunately, the material gathered in the earlier survey, the really excellent census data made available by the Costa Rican Census Bureau, and the scattered studies now available in various forms by other social scientists makes it possible to draw some conclusions concerning the distribution of cultures in Costa Rica.

III. THE GENERAL PROCEDURE OF THE SURVEY

The planning of the survey involved various problems. In the first place, account had to be taken of many aspects of living, both cultural and non-cultural.

---

[11] Gillin has written a good deal on the subject of modern Latin American culture. For a fairly full account, see Gillin, 1949 and a recent work, Gillin, 1953. See also the report of the Committee on Latin American Anthropology, 1949.

Even though my orientation was towards anthropology and the concept of culture, a practical survey cannot rely on a free floating culture concept, but must be firmly based in such issues as size and characteristics of the population, the ecological situation, and easily observable culture traits. Furthermore, I was strongly of the opinion that while a survey was the best way for a lone individual to get the general picture, there were reasons not to spend an excessive amount of time on the overall task. A survey of this type, depending as it would upon peculiar techniques, must involve the accumulation of some erroneous information, and to spend an excessive amount of time in getting such information would not be reasonable.

The survey is based on a premise which, although not scientifically demonstrated, has been noted by many people in the course of their field work. This is that it is possible under average field conditions to gain a great deal of information concerning the society and culture of a community from one or a limited number of informants in a matter of a few hours. The things one learns in the course of such initial interviews are the obvious characteristics of the population, the things which most inhabitants would know from merely being participants in the social order. Following the collection of this easily obtainable and obvious information, there is a period of some confusion and waiting while the worker begins to locate channels of information which will lead him deeper into the culture and along the intricate paths of the social organization to provide him with a less superficial view of the culture. The surveys were based on the idea that initial information is of considerable importance when little is known about a community or the culture of the region of which it is a part. Although such information is bound to contain errors, there is so much valuable information involved that many generalizations may be made with reasonable security if the data are combined and checked against each other as well as other data which may be available.

The general steps involved in the survey work were as follows.

A general survey schedule was prepared in the form of a small handbook and a food checklist was elaborated (see Appendix). The schedule was to be used as a reminder list for me in the course of the interview; it was not a fixed list, every point of which had to be covered, but a set of general subjects with specific reminders of critical or possibly critical items. As the survey field work was carried on, some of the subjects originally on the list were omitted because they seemed to be of little importance or because there was consistent difficulty on gaining information on them. Since the survey was frankly exploratory, I often allowed the informants to digress if they were providing information on some subject which was especially interesting. I felt the uncovering of general patterns to be of equal importance to the gathering of specific data for inter-community comparisons. The surveys were in no way intended to be definitive.

The original survey schedule was elaborated on the basis of my own experience in the region and the studies which were available from the work of others. It is probably of some worth to note that it would be difficult for a person who was a complete neophyte to an area to prepare such a list effectively.

Each country was to be surveyed separately. This was necessary from a practical point of view, due to problems of crossing borders, working through national health authorities, and in dealing with nationally gathered census materials. Theoretically, also, the nation in Central America was as good a framework within which to work as any which presented itself. Prior to the survey in each country a visit of a few days to a week was paid to the national capital; during this period the necessary formalities for carrying on the surveys were taken care of, letters of introduction to municipal and other local authorities were provided by the local health officials, and visits were paid to appropriate governmental and private agencies in order to obtain copies of publications which would be of use in the studies. Conversations were held with people who it was thought could provide information on road conditions and travel facilities in general and wherever possible, with persons who were familiar with various regions of the country. On the basis of these general data, a rough preliminary itinerary was prepared and later the survey itself was carried out.

The decision as to the number of towns to be visited and the selection of the towns was fairly arbitrary. Three factors were considered: the geographical size of the country; the size of the total population; and a general time limit of five weeks for the field work in any one country. Between fifteen and thirty towns were selected but not infrequently problems of transportation or other factors dictated changes in the original itinerary. With a few exceptions, towns which were capitals of departments or provinces were not selected. The choice was among the municipal capitals and villages. Regions which, according to published census reports, were extremely underpopulated were omitted almost entirely since it was felt that the nature of the survey would not produce useful information from such regions, and it was from the more heavily populated areas that information was particularly needed. As a result, the Petén in Guatemala, the Department of Colón in Honduras, the Department of Zelaya in Nicaragua, and the provinces of Darién and Bocas del Toro in Panama were entirely excluded from the field survey work.

Travel in all countries except Guatemala was made possible through the courtesy of local or national agencies, or was by means of standard local transport forms. The latter included buses, trains, horses and mules, boats, airplanes, and by foot. Acknowledgement is made in each of the country monographs for aid in this matter.

When arriving in a community, if I planned further travel for the same day, I went immediately to the municipal building and spoke with the mayor or his representative, explained my mission, and solicited his aid. Notes were taken openly in front of the informants except on some of the later surveys when a wire recorder was used. In the latter case, it was explained that the interview was being recorded. Whenever it was planned to spend the night in the community, arrangements for sleeping were usually made prior to undertaking the interviewing. During the interview the schedule would be covered first, and the food checklist would be done last.

Upon completion of the survey, the notes were taken back to my office in

Guatemala where I classified them in accordance with a simple subject index (see Appendix, Part III). The material was then typed up by community and subject on separate cards and filed under the appropriate headings. In this way it was possible to analyze the comparable material from each town.

The original plan for presentation of the final reports was as follows. A single monograph was to be prepared on each country. These country monographs were to contain the following general materials:

A. A general description of the Spanish-American countryman culture, divided into chapters concerning various subjects. The typical chapters appearing are as follows: A summary of relevant census data; Land, Labor, and Agriculture; Production, Transport, and Commerce; The Domestic Scene; Family and *Compadrazgo*; General Social Structure; Local Political Organization; Religious Activities; Patterns of Sickness and Curing.

B. A general discussion of the numbers and locations of Indian and other important non-Spanish-American groups of the country. When communities of these peoples were included on the survey, a description is provided of the general culture.

C. A brief description is provided of each community visited on the survey.

D. Usually some concluding comments on materials which I found to be of particular interest.

In addition to these data, most of the monographs have appended descriptions which were prepared by other field workers, and which they kindly contributed in order to make more knowledge available on the groups involved. Doris Stone contributed descriptions of Matagalpa and Torrupan Indians to the Nicaragua and Honduras volumes, Ofelia Hooper contributed critical comments concerning the Panama data, and Edwin James' study of cases of sickness and curing in a Salvadorean community accompanies that monograph.

It was originally planned that following the country monographs, a single summary monograph, drawing the materials together for Central America as a whole, would be prepared. Whether or not this is done is as yet undecided.

In the country monographs a résumé of the material collected on foods was included only in the first two. I later felt that this information was probably so inferior to that being accumulated by the Institute of Nutrition of Central America and Panama that it was not worthwhile dealing with it in any great degree.

IV. THE RATIONALE OF USING OUTCAST TECHNIQUES

From the description of the general approach to the survey field work it is obvious that I had recourse to a number of techniques which have generally been outcast from proper ethnological circles. In order to visit between fifteen and thirty towns in each of the countries, to allow for travel time and the inevitable delays which accompany any piece of field work, the most time which could be allocated to actual systematic collection of data in any specific locale was about half a day. In practice, three to five hours were spent on each interview when one person was interviewing, and two hours on those occasions when two field workers were on hand or when the wire recorder was used. In spite of the fact that a considerable range of data was to be covered, time would not permit the use of numerous informants. It was decided to rely generally on one or a small group of informants. In order to obtain a good informant in the quickest possible time and to have some assurance that he would be available for the two to five hours necessary to get the required information, it was planned to utilize the auspices of the various local civil authorities, or if it seemed wiser, local medical or school personnel. These persons were to serve to locate informants for us. In order to gain comparable information on each community, it was necessary to rely on the survey form and to utilize direct and sometimes leading questions. Little time was available for observation or indirect questioning.

Social scientists and others who have had experience in interviewing and social research will immediately be aware of the heresies involved in this situation. Among others: a single informant was to be used to provide information on the culture and society of an entire community, and in some cases, of the surrounding countryside as well; no time was allowed for the anthropologist to select this informant himself; a minimum of time was allowed for the anthropologist to establish rapport with the informant; the great majority of the information was to be gained through direct and leading questions; and practically no time could be devoted to checking on the information given by the informant.

There is no debating the fact that the use of such methods was bound to bring errors into the results of the surveys. The question was, however, not whether errors would enter the results, but whether the ultimate value of the results of the survey would be so reduced by such errors that the surveys themselves would not be economically worthwhile. At the time of writing, four of the five country monographs have been returned by readers to whom they were sent for critical inspection as to general accuracy of portrayal of the regions under consideration; in all cases, the readers, who were familiar with the countries in question, have found the reports to be satisfactory. Obviously they could not check on the accuracy of much of the detail, but the general picture drawn was meaningful to them. There are various reasons why the use of these outcast techniques have not invalidated the results of the surveys.

(1) The subject matter of the survey included mainly superficial information concerning a community and its way of life. Most of the subjects were chosen so that almost anyone, aside from the village idiot, could have known whether or not the traits discussed were common or not. Certain information which would have been difficult to gather without more refined techniques (such as referring to a specialist) was elicited, but the great majority of the subjects would have been obvious elements in the community life if present. Consequently, a single fairly good informant was able to provide information on most of the subjects. Since few of the subjects covered were things which were expected to pose threats for the informants, intentional lying was not anticipated. However, if an informant did lie, there were few ways to check it.

(2) In most (perhaps all) Latin American countries the village and town

political structure is the lower part of a hierarchial, pyramidal, national authority structure. Whether the local people like a specific town mayor or not, he is nevertheless the mayor and not only the local governing authority but also the representative of the national government. Most of the townspeople are accustomed to being called to the townhall to be present on official business. Using a letter from the national director-general of public health of the country as an introduction to the mayor, we were rarely greeted in anything but a cordial manner in the some 105 towns visited in the course of the survey. Some officials were brighter than others, some less motivated to help, but all consistently put themselves at our service for the work. In a sense, then, the specific local authority structure of the area studied was an important factor in the successful use of the techniques employed. I would not imagine such immediate positive response from many of the small rural communities in the central midwest of the United States, for example, where local authority is locally vested and not responsible to state or national authority.

(3) The approach used with the mayor or local authority was to give a brief explanation of what we wanted (not going into detail unless it was requested): a) We wished to talk with a mature, adult, male, member of the community, a person who was born there and had spent the better part of his life there. Our reason for this specification was that we wanted to know things which were fairly common in the life of a community member, but which a person recently in from the outside might not be too familiar with. b) We preferred a person who was familiar with farming since many of our questions had to do with agriculture. c) The conversation would last some hours so we wanted someone who was not immediately occupied in other work and who would have the time to spend with us. As to where the interview was held, we showed no preference except that it should be where we could talk without having to shout over other noise. As a result, it was usually held in some part of the townhall building or in the home of the informant.

(4) Since we started the discussion out on general environment and communication facilities, and moved on from there to agricultural affairs, it permitted the informant to discuss something which was of common knowledge. It was usually possible within the first half hour to detect if the informant was grossly unsuited to provide us with the information desired. If this was the case, he would be dismissed with thanks, and we would then ask the mayor for someone else, explaining that for some reasons (the reasons used varied with the situation) we wanted someone else. Not infrequently in laying the problem before the mayor he offered to give us the information himself. In this case, and sometimes in other cases as well, a few other people would gather around for varying lengths of time and offer their opinions on the answers to some of the questions. After a few experiences of this nature, we usually tried in one way or another to restrict the group to three at the most, preferably two, and even more preferably one. These group sessions lost a great deal of time through reminiscing. It gradually became clear that with more people present, less information was gained. Not infrequently, we would be getting rather good data from a single informant

when a group would gather; the informant then frequently became embarrassed, his answers would grow shorter, and he began relying on the other informants; occasionally a dispute would start over some minor point and the informant would "clam-up" entirely.

(5) In view of the manner of obtaining their help, it was not expected that informants would be entirely at ease. This, however, rarely developed into a real problem. Usually, it was possible to detect early in the interview whether the informant was very uncomfortable; when such was the case, he was told that if he had something else he should be doing, we did not want to interrupt his own work. On these occasions, if the informant desired, he could take advantage of the break, excuse himself, and we would again go to the mayor and ask for someone else.

(6) Needless to say, the statuses of the informant provided a constant bias in the information. Experience on the survey, and our increasing knowledge of the class structure of the various countries, permitted us to detect some of these biases, and to use them to advantage to obtain class attitudes. In any particular town, we had the bias of the particular informant, but taking all the towns in general within any given region, we usually had various class points of view expressed and this permitted a certain amount of crude interpolation. The fact that our informants were usually men meant that data from the woman's culture and the woman's point of view was usually lacking. The same deficiency was true for many other statuses.

(7) The use of leading questions at times brought answers that we felt were either not adequate or not true; in such situations, attempts were made to check the particular subject matter again with the mayor or some other person after the interview terminated. In any case, a note was made together with the statement that (for whatever reason) it was not considered by the note-taker to be satisfactory. Many of the questions were checked through internal crossing of questions. At different stages in the interview, for example, we would ask how they carried in the crops, where they stored them, where they sold them, which they used; these various questions on crops often brought out apparent inconsistencies between the descriptions provided and made possible "internal checking" within the interview situation.

(8) Since a survey schedule was used, the order of the subjects was approximately the same for each interview. This order, it developed, had some disadvantages; where these became very obvious, we shifted the order of the subjects. In general, we did not change the form of the schedule. We preferred to make no basic change for two reasons. First we were not sure that we could find a better order without a great deal of experimentation, and we did not wish to use the surveys for such experiments. Second, in the process of interviewing, we would often pick up new items of information; by adhering to the same order, the survey form would suggest these items to us when carrying on the interview in subsequent towns. In shifting the order of the subjects, we would have lost the advantage of this very useful memory aid. Since the surveys were in great

part exploratory, it was very important to check new information in succeeding towns.

(9) Since the same material was covered in each survey site, it frequently became evident that the reported absence of a certain trait in a specific community was not certain in the light of information from surrounding towns. If a trait was reported from all the towns, except one, within a single region, there were two possibilities: a) the trait was actually absent from that town, and the town then provided an exception to the general regional picture, in which case from the general point of view, it was not too important; or b) the information was wrong, and the town actually had the trait, in which case the general regional picture was still satisfactory. Another way of checking such information in a town, when it was reported that a trait was absent, was to ask the informant if he had heard of the presence of the trait in other communities (specifically some of the communities in which a survey had already been made). If he said he had, then it suggested that he was aware what the trait was, and his statement of its absence may have been correct. It was also soon determined that this reasoning did not necessarily apply to certain subjects, principal among which was witchcraft. The attribution of witchcraft to other towns, but the denial of its presence by an informant in his own town, was a fairly common pattern to emerge from the survey.

(10) Aside from the fact that some informants were not extremely good, did not know some of the materials covered, and that some of the information required the expression of generalizations, the main problem encountered in the course of the surveys was interview fatigue. It was appreciated prior to the initiation of the work that more than two hours of interviewing will generate fatigue in both the interviewer and the informant. Insofar as it was necessary for me to do all the interviewing, there was no way to avoid this and to cover the geographical territory which was desired. Two things happened to alleviate this situation to some degree. On some portions of the survey I was joined by other interviewers who were able to cover some of the subjects with a separate informant, or who were able to check the same subjects with a different informant. On the last two surveys I had at my disposal a small battery operated wire recorder which permitted the interview to be carried on in a much shorter time, usually not over two hours; I would then copy the data down in the evening. There is little doubt that writing down the data at the time of the interview increases the interview time considerably.

These factors served to mitigate to a great degree the faults which would have otherwise greatly weakened the usefulness of the techniques used. There is no doubt in my mind that there are errors in the information collected, and that many of these have escaped detection in the final analyses. As was mentioned earlier, however, the question is not one of whether there are some errors, but whether the material is unsafe to use because of that. The value of any specific technique must be judged in terms of the type of information or results which one is trying to obtain. This is obvious in the case of such diverse techniques and goals as are involved in economic studies and basic personality studies. When a technique is once used and proved to be unsatisfactory for the study in which it is employed, it is thrown out or changed. There is a tendency, however, to leave such techniques without further analysis. An anthropology student commented to me that anthropological techniques had become "so refined" that such a crude approach as the community study is outmoded! The obvious retort to this is, "Outmoded for what?" The community study has served an important function in expanding our knowledge about contemporary cultures, and on the basis of experience, will continue to serve an important function in future studies. The fact that it has proven unsuccessful to meet all the tasks set before it does not mean that it is not very useful for some of them. The same may be said for the dependence upon a single informant and the other aspects of the techniques used in the present study. If one is aware of the limitations of a technique, he may then be the judge of whether it will serve or not.

It is interesting to note that the techniques used in the present surveys have frequently been used, only in a much cruder form, for gaining much important information. A person who is concentrating his work in one community or within a restricted region will often spot questions during short visits to other regions to determine to what degree certain findings are present elsewhere. A number of well-known Latin American specialists have commented to me that they always find the conversations of taxicab drivers and shoe shine boys most helpful in this regard. One may read in a report that ". . . trait X what was of importance in Peru has also been reported from Panama and the writer found it in north Chile." The phrases "reported from" and "found in" are often dependent upon spot checks or brief inquiries made by the student or someone else. The information gained casually from taxi drivers is frequently trusted because they participate in the culture in question and if they know the trait, it is significant.

Basically, the surveys in this series are aimed at unfolding a general, regional picture, not at providing intensive insights into the culture of the peoples concerned. In fact, however, the repetition of certain responses in many communities within a given culture region is itself indicative of the importance of some traits, and a survey can actually provide us with a dimension which is completely prohibited to the persons concentrating in a single community.

REFERENCES

Committee on Latin American Anthropology of the National Research Council
    1949 "Research Needs in the Field of Modern Latin American Culture," *American Anthropologist*, Vol. 51, No. 1, pp. 149–154.
Gillin, John
    1949 "Mestizo America," in *Most of the World*, edited by Ralph Linton, pp. 159–226. New York.
    1953 "Latin America," in *Approaches to Community Development*, edited by Phillips Roupp, pp. 331–344, The Hague, 1953.
Goubaud, A., Rosales, J. de D, and Tax, Sol
    1944 "Reconnaissance of Northern Guatemala," *Microfilm Collection of Manuscripts*

  on Middle American Cultural Anthropology. No. 17, University of Chicago, Chicago.
Murdock, George P., Ford, Clelland S., and others
  1950 "Outline of Cultural Materials. 3rd Revised Edition." *Behavior Science Outlines, Vol. 1.* Human Relations Area Files, Inc. New Haven.
Redfield, Robert, and Tax, Sol
  1947 "April is this Afternoon: Report of a 3-Day Survey by Robert Redfield and Sol Tax in Eastern Guatemala," *Microfilm Collection of Manuscripts on Middle American Cultural Anthropology, No. 19,* University of Chicago, Chicago.
Steward, Julian H. (editor)
  1946–50 *Handbook of South American Indians,* Bureau of American Ethnology, Bulletin 143. 6 Vols.
Steward, Julian H.
  1950 "Area Research: Theory and Practice," *Social Science Research Council, Bulletin 63.* New York
Tschopik, Harry
  1947 "Highland Communities of Central Peru," *Institute of Social Anthropology,* Publication No. 5, Smithsonian Institution, Washington.
United Nations
  1954 "The Population of Central America (including Mexico), 1950–1980," *Population Studies,* No. 16. New York.

Appendix

THE SCHEDULE AND CLASSIFICATION INDEX USED IN THE SURVEY

  In order to carry out the survey and obtain comparable information, the following survey schedules were utilized. Part I consists of a check list of certain plants, foods, animals hunted, etc., items concerning which information could be had through a simple positive or negative response. This check list was mimeographed and filled out with the informant in each community. Part II, the major body of the survey, is again a check list, but was used as a basis for discussion with the informant and provided the writer with a means of remembering the various items on which information was needed. A single copy of it was prepared in a small booklet and the writer referred to it during the course of his conversation with the informant. Some of the material, that marked with an (x), was not included in each survey. Data was at times not pertinent, such as in cases of descriptions of landscape where geographical studies have been carried on, or elaborate local government in a scattered *caserio.* Sometimes the informant proved a blank on certain subjects such as local curing practices. And at times the survey had to be cut short.
  Upon completion of a survey, the material was classified in accordance with the simplified Classification Index which is included as Part III of this appendix. It was typed on 5 x 8" cards, and subsequent reports were made by study of the material thus classified.

Part I

Check List

Community .... Informant ....
Depar't. .... Worker ....
Country .... Date ....

Crops produced	Crops produced (Cont'd)	Vegetables	Foods and drinks (x)
corn	coffee	zanahoria	chicha-maiz
frijoles	wheat	rábanos	chicha
squash (ayote)	barley	cebolla	coconut
cacao	oats	ajo	corn and honey
sweet cassava (yuca)	hotóes	repollo	palm wine
bitter cassava	achiote	lechuga	mamey wine
chili	maizillo	remolacha	atol
pineapple	haba	nabo	coffee
avocado	garbanzo	apio	cacao
papaya	lenteja	coliflor	manioc
zapote	cereza	bruselas	beans
coconut	ciruela	tomatoes	eggs
tobacco	manzana	strawberries	goats milk
potato	guayaba		cow's milk
cotton	gengibre	**Agricultural tools**	rice
camote		coa	tamales
gourds	**Weapons used**	barreta	tortillas
maguey (juice)	rifle	azadón	chile
maguey (fiber)	escopeta	arado	Main dishes:
coca	arco y flecha	machete	
mamey	honda (sling)	hacha	**Animals hunted**
plantain	venablo (javelin)	adz	venado
banana	throwing stick		saino
ñame	trampas	**Domesticated animals**	iguana
rice	blowgun		armadillo
sugar cane		ganado	cerdo silvestre
pejibaye palm		bueyes	pisotes
sandía		caballos	conejos
bitter oranges		mulas	tepezcuinte
oranges		burros	pájaros
limas		gallinas	pesca (list)
limones		jolote (turkey)	
mandarinas		patos	**Fishing equipment**
mangos		cerdos	
fruta pan		cabros	line
guanábana		ovejas	bait
tuna (cactus)		conejos	redes
toronja		palomas	trampas
gandul		abejas (bees)	dynamite
		loros	weirs
		perros	

0: Absent   1: very important   X: used   3: rarely used

Part II

Environment
    land formation
    altitude
    flora coverage (x)
    water sources; annual variation
    mineral sources (x)
        clays
    climate
        rainfall
        fog
        seasons
    fauna (x)
    insects; seasonal variation (x)
    soils
        rocky, sandy, clay, organic matter

Transportation access
    roads, conditions thereof
    river
    air
    time required to reach community

Communication
    telegraph
    mail service
    runner
    telephone
    newspapers

Local transportation forms
    animals (specify)
    walking
    carts: yoke
            wheels
            manner of directing
    buses
    trucks
    air service
    tump line
    human yoke
    canoe, raft, dugout
    paddles, poles, sails

Settlement pattern
    dispersion of dwellings
    map of town (x)
    relative location and access of public buildings:
        church
        municipal offices
        slaughterhouse
        hospital
        market
    nearby populated areas
    relative location of:
        stores
        rivers
        bridges
        houses or residential areas
        water sources: wells, springs
        haciendas or industries

Public building construction
    describe construction of public buildings

Local government
    local hierarchy
    personnel, titles, functions
    length of office
    extent of local authority
    mode of obtaining office

Public works
    roads
    cemeteries
    bridges
    sponsoring: local, national, private

Agencies of national government
    extension work
        agricultural
        public health, sanitation
        cultural missions
    tax collecting
    military conscription (x)
    labor conscription
    schools
        number of grades
        ages of students (x)
        most children attend?
        extra-curricular activities
            garden, domestic animals, clubs
        committee of parents

participation of parents
maestro a local man?
maestro usually present?
how many maestros?
many children seek higher education?

Are there municipal archives?
where are they located?
of what do they consist?

What is territorial demarcation of town?

Town traditions
as to origin of town
origin of population
colonial historical events
republican historical events
does a town monograph exist?

Demographic data available locally

Agricultural information
(*In addition to the check list on food products*)

Tools: how are they obtained?
    how are they made?
    any parts made locally?
    how are they utilized?
Sugar press:
    pole-in-hole type
    hand turned
    animal powered
Woods: any woods preferable for particular products?
Herbs: list herbs used medicinally and how they are used?
Hunting methods:
    in groups? individually?
    use of animals?
Poisons: vegetable, animal, mineral?
    how prepared?
    how utilized?
Fishing methods:
    in groups? individually?

Specific agricultural traits

Division of labor by sex in:
    cleaning land

planting
cultivation
harvest
rituals for crops
carrying crops
seasons for planting and harvesting?
fields lie fallow for what period?
how long are fields used? for different crops
irrigation used? type of system
terraces used?
fertilizing used?
techniques used to get rain or good crops
crop pests; how combatted
what determines time of planting and harvesting?
methods of threshing

Land ownership and usufruct
rent
free usufruct
ownership
property in trees

Patterns of labor
work: individually
    with relatives (which?)
    with neighbors (which?)
    in groups (at what times?)
    exchange labor
    partidario
    as mozo, peón
work on haciendas, fincas
    seasonal? permanent?
    what types of work?
sindicatos, or guilds?
migratory labor? when?

Household characteristics
plan of house: physical arrangement
sleeping accommodations:
    platform bed
    hammock
    ground mat
    materials used, construction
stools, benches, chairs
tables, shelves, hanging shelves
methods of construction, materials

kitchen
  types of containers:
    pottery, gourd, metal, china, bamboo, wooden, leather
  stove type (plan)
  storage methods
    gross storage
    storage of small items
    storage of perishables
    water storage
  fuel types; storage
  food tongs (to remove food from fire) (x)
  flat hanging basket
  comal
  basket strainer (x)
  gourd strainer (x)
  fire fan
  grinding stone: (3 legs, 4 legs, worked, crude)
  pilón
  corn preparation materials: lime, ashes
  method of grinding corn
  drums:
    hide; tongue type
  use of skins
  use of bark, or bark cloth
  baskets: where made?
  hammocks:
    string (where made)
    cloth
  ladder (single pole type?)

Outbuildings

trojes
latrines
casa de santos
animal shelters
sweat baths (x)
ovens
field rain shelters (x)

House construction

floor plan
roof shape
materials:
  framework
  walls
  roof
  internal partitions
  floor
  binding
location of fire
windows, shutters
doors
corridors
use of: stone, clay adobe, woods, grasses, reeds, tile, metal
tree houses
location of:
  house in domestic compound
  walls or fences
  gates
  corral areas
  animal shelters
  well
  open spaces
  latrine

Food and drink (x)

(*The following information should be gathered with respect to the most important foods and the other items listed below*)

source of materials (x)
form of exploitation (x)
tools used in exploitation and preparation
techniques used in preparation
how consumed

chicha, corn, rice, beans
fermented drinks

Sanitary facilities

disposal of: excrement
    urine
    garbage
    water waste
    animal wastes

Local products

is there work in or specialists in:
  housebuilding
  boat or canoe building
  cart or sugar-press building
  coffins
  other wood-working

pottery
  (describe)
weaving
  (describe)
leather tanning
leather products
tile making
starch making
clothes for women
clothes for men
clothes for children
mask making or other paraphernalia
string and fiber weaving
string and fiber preparation
spinning
gourds and calabazas
furniture
beadwork; lacework
exploitation of salt
tobacco
cigars
natural dyes
  shellfish purple
  vegetable
  mineral
hats
iron working; blacksmithing
pictographs
rubber collecting
rubber processing
preparation of foods for sale:
  coffee
  cacao
  rice
  sugar
  panela
  corn

Clothing (x)
hats
footwear
designs and styles
belts
hair styles
ornaments: for wrist, finger, head, ears, nose, neck, legs
man's dress
woman's dress
children's dress

Social organization
residential geneologies (x)
post-marital residence
evidence of dominance of one sex (x)
extended family
  relatives nearby?
  relatives live in home?
inheritance pattern: land, animals, personal goods, houses
incest restrictions
  degree of distance of prohibited marriage
  with compadres or their children
kinship terminology (x)
family active unit in:
  agricultural work
  trading
  religious activities
  political activity
compadre structure
  baptism, marriage, confirmation, other?
  mutual help or respect between compadres
  same or different persons for different events?
  same person for siblings?
  class difference between compadres?
do relatives participate in:
  economic work
  marriages
  funerals
  trading trips
non-local personnel important in social organization:
  school teacher
  government agents
  political leaders
  traders
  religious personnel

Class/caste structure
ethnic based endogomous groups
wealth based differences
time of arrival differences
racial based groups
language differences as basis
political differences as basis
characteristics which distinguish the classes

Territorial organization
  urban subdivisions:
    barrios, cantones, etc.
  rural subdivisions:
    cantones, caseríos, aldeas
  functions of subdivisions:
    political differences
    economic differences
    ethnic differences
    religious differences
    specialties
    wealth
  environmental differences in distinct territories
  intra-divisional attitudes and feelings:
    unity, competition, hate
  map

Life cycle
  birth
  puberty (x)
  marriage
  death
  child's death
  do women attend funerals?
  age groupings—status differentiation (x)
  sex groupings—status differentiation (x)

Voluntary associations
  secular
    sports
    sociedades pro-civic groups
      patronato escolar
      junta de educación
    fraternity type organization
    occupational groups (guilds, unions)
    funeral societies
    work groups
  clique groups
  religious groups
    cofradías, sociedades
    church committee
    informal groups: novena, rosario
    pilgrimage groups
    protestant groups

Leadership
  who are leaders: elders, political men, religious men, wealthy men, women, curers, midwives, professionals
  leading groups: cliques
  evidence of conflict for leadership
  hereditary leadership

Trade and commerce
  markets and fairs
    if one locally, then:
      how often?
      how big?
      region represented?
      major products
      time of day?
      modes of transport
      civic control
      entertainment elements
      eating facilities
      map
  other markets:
    when, times of day?
    travel, and transport
    products carried there
    products purchased there
  travelling vendors
    frequency
    origin
    products
    mode of travel
  stores
    number; description; principal products; region served

Hacienda economy
  important?
  types of haciendas and fincas
  resident or absentee landowners
  proportion of population implicated
  main times of work
  organized labor
  benefits offered by haciendas

Industry or mining
  do the people participate in any industrial or mining work?

Recreation and diversion
  recreation related to:
    work
    markets
    religious celebrations / activities

civic functions
domestic activities
leisure time spent:
  games (football, basketball, baseball)
  horseplay
  travelling to centers for entertainment
  gambling
  bars, cantinas
  movies
  cockfights, bullfights
  serenading
  rubber ball
  volador
  see-saw
  children's games (wax, marbles)

Musical instruments

drum (type?)
flute
harp
modern: string, woodwind, brass

Religious organization

church organization
  clergy: local, or when and where do they come from?
  quality of clergy
  lay employees of church
  laymen act in capacity of clergy?
  instruction in doctrine: by whom? how often?
  description of church and equipment
principal saints, manner of celebrating them
public fiestas
  what are important fiestas?
  how are they sponsored?
  activities:
    misas
    processions
    dances (social? special?)
      masked or costumed dances?
    visiting
    eating and drinking?
    games
  are fiestas related to:
    harvest?
    planting?
    rain?
    sicknesses?
    hunting or fishing activities?
    visited by outsiders?
    what region represented?
    some fiestas new?
    known fiestas which have disappeared?
family religious activities
  cuadros, images
  rosarios, novenas?
  prayer sessions?
  inheritance of family saint?
voluntary groups:
  what type of organization
  for what purposes
  how financed
  class, neighborhood, family or ethnic participation?
  how many such groups?
  which sex is more active?

Protestant activities

missionaries
local church and/or congregation
proportion of local population
history of church in community
relations with catholics

Evidences of the supernatural (x)

shrines
crosses
witchcraft
curanderos (parchero)
spiritualists
charms
siguanava
llorona
cadejo
duendes
guardians
nagual

Sickness and curing

susto
aire, mal aire, viento
frío, calentura
cleansing the stomach
  (use of *purgas*)
empacho

pasmo
sol
luna
phases of the moon
para pecados
pujo
soul loss
mollera
bilis
estirón de las venas
ataque de espíritus
hijillo
brujería, hechizos
molestation by the dead

what are the most common diseases in the community?
materials and methods of curing (x)
   eggs
   herbs
   animals
   flowers
   prepared foods
   sucking
   blowing
   rubbing
   pills
   injections
   powders
   salves
   santiguar
   massage
   geophagy
are there curing specialists?
   parteras
   curanderos
   farmacéuticos
   padroneros
   enfermeras
   doctores
   sanitarios
what are the causes of: (x)
   paludismo
   tifus
   tos
   lombrices
   tuberculosis
   disentería
   diarrea
   mal de orina
   susto
   granos

Part III

Classification Index

A   Environment (incl. information on water sources; maps)
B   Demography, Physical Anthropology
C   History and Language
D   Settlement Pattern
E   Travel, Transport, Communication, Power Facilities
F   Productive Economy

   F1 Agriculture, Aboriculture, Floriculture
   F2 Livestock
   F3 Hunting, Fishing
   F4 Gathering
   F5 Hand Industries and Exploitations
   F6 Labor, Patterns of work inside community
   F7 Labor, Migratory
   F8 Land Usufruct, Ownership, etc.

G   Domestic Economy

   G1 Shelter

    G2 Furnishings
    G3 Kitchen
    G4 Food
    G5 Clothing

H Commercial Economy, Marketing, Service Industries
I Local and National Government
J Family, Kin, *Compadre*, Residence
K Non-governmental territorial and voluntary associations
L Class, Caste, Clique, Ethnic Groupings, Leadership
M Religious Structure and Activities
O Non-religious Supernatural Beliefs and Activities
P Medical and Sanitary Beliefs and Practices
Q Life Cycle, Socialization, Daily Cycle
R Education, Extension and Welfare Activities
S Recreation, Diversions, Disputes not connected with property
T Impressions, Attitudes, Ethos, Trends of Change, Focus of Culture
U Notes on Field Work Techniques, Methodology, Informants, etc.

Part Two

PANAMA

WITH APPENDED NOTES BY OFELIA HOOPER

1953

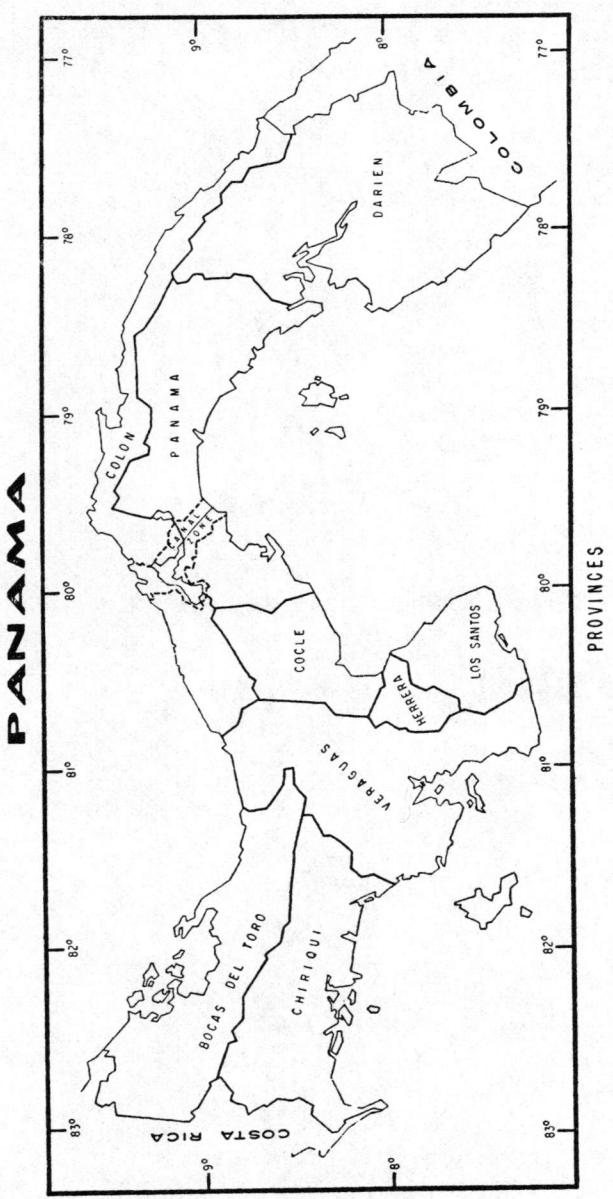

INTRODUCTION

This report is the first in a series which is intended to provide a picture of the territorial delineation of contemporary culture areas in Central America and a preliminary description of the Spanish-speaking rural cultures of the various countries. The general nature of the surveys on which these reports are based is described in Part One of this series. Since the field surveys and analyses thereof are being done during a limited period of time, certain problems arise in some of the surveys which can only be corrected in later ones. This, the Panama survey, was the first field survey in the present series to be completed. Prior to the analysis of the Panama material the Nicaraguan field survey was also completed. As a result, information came to light in the course of the Nicaraguan survey which could have been useful during the Panama work, but of course, it was then too late to use it to advantage.

It was hoped that the Panama material would have provided a systematic check on the impressions gained during the field work for the delineation of cultural subareas or regions within the countryman culture area. Unfortunately, upon analysis of the Panama materials, it developed that the data was not adequate to provide this check. It is hoped that this situation, which will make the Panama and possibly the Nicaragua reports deficient in one aspect which the writer considers to be of some importance, can be improved in subsequent surveys.

In the discussion to follow, certain materials have been drawn from the Panamanian census reports in order to give certain materials which are much more meaningful in statistical terms. For some of the agricultural data preliminary census reports have been used. It was felt that changes in the final census reports would not be sufficiently different to warrant waiting for the final data. The rest of the report, however, is derived from the survey except in a few cases where the work of other anthropologists and sociologists have been available for consultation.

The field work on which the report is based was carried on during the months of March and June of 1953, lasting a period of about three and one half weeks. In March the writer visited the backlands of Chorrera in the Province of Panama, and the towns of Alanje, Querévalos, and Las Lomas in Chiriquí. In June, automobile trips were made with Mr. Norman Craig to Lagarto, Chepo, and to the remaining towns in the provinces of Panama, Coclé, Herrera, and Los Santos. The trip was continued in the company of Mr. Félix Dormoí to the provinces of Veraguas and Chiriquí. It was originally planned to make trips to certain of the Spanish-speaking populations in Darién and Bocas del Toro, but the time required did not seem to warrant such visits in view of the small population involved and the nature of the survey.

The field work and report have been made possible by the cooperation and help of the following persons: Señorita Ofelia Hooper, of the Extension Service of the Panamanian Ministry of Agriculture; Dr. Angel Rubio, of the University of

Panama; Mr. Félix Dormoí, of the Health Education Section of the Ministry of Public Health; Mr. William Rost, of the Institute of Inter-American Affairs; Señoritas Carmen Miró and Ana Casis, of the Office of Statistics and Census; Dr. Albert Bissot, Director General of Public Health; the staff of the Panamerican Sanitary Bureau in Guatemala and Panama, and especially Mr. Norman Craig, who is the writer's collaborator on the present project. Transportation was made possible by the Ministry of Public Health and the Institute of Inter-American Affairs. Finally, the writer is greatly indebted to the municipal officials, school teachers, public health officers, and private citizens who acted as informants and provided him with the information on which the present report is based. In keeping with anthropological research policy, their names do not appear in the report since it is considered their privilege to be protected from criticism should the report not be received well. The first draft of the manuscript was read in part or in its entirety by Srta. Hooper, Sr. Hernán F. Porras, Dr. Douglas Stout, and Dr. John Biesanz. Many of their comments have been incorporated in the report. Due to the fact that Srta. Hooper was kind enough to submit a fairly long series of notes, the writer felt that the report would be enhanced by attaching many of them as an appendix. This has been done with the kind permission of Srta. Hooper and references are made in appropriate places in the text to them. The writer, of course, accepts all responsibility for the form and content of the report.

R. N. A.

March, 1954
Guatemala, C. A.

TABLE OF CONTENTS

Introduction.. 29
I. THE CULTURE TYPES IN PANAMA............................ 33
   1. The Indian Cultures.................................... 33
      The Indian Population.............................. 34
      The Guaymí.. 37
      The Cuna.. 42
      The Chocó... 42
      Cultural Relations between Indians and Panamanians.. 43
      Status of Our Knowledge of the Panamanian Indian Groups......... 48
   2. The Antillean Cultures................................. 49
II. THE CULTURE OF THE PANAMANIAN COUNTRYMAN.............. 51
   1. Introductory Note..................................... 51
   2. Population and Its Distribution......................... 51
   3. Land Utilization...................................... 60
   4. Agriculture... 65
   5. Other Exploitations................................... 72
   6. Home and Local Industries............................ 76
   7. Travel, Transport, and Commerce..................... 80
   8. The Domestic Establishment.......................... 83
   9. Family and *Compadre* System......................... 89
   10. Notes on the Life Cycle.............................. 92
   11. Social Structure of Town and Country................ 95
   12. Political Structure................................... 99
   13. Notes on Religion.................................... 101
   14. Ideas of Sickness and Practices of Curing............ 102
   15. Notes on the Spirit World............................ 106
   16. Recreation and Diversion............................ 106
III. COMMUNITIES INCLUDED IN THE SURVEY..................... 108
   1. Chepo and La Margarita de Chepo.................... 110
   2. Palmas Bellas.. 112
   3. The Chorrera Backlands: Corozales Afuera, Corozales Adentro, Yayas Adentro, and Zangüenga........... 114
   4. El Espino.. 116
   5. Sonadora.. 117
   6. Santo Domingo...................................... 118
   7. Los Pozos.. 120
   8. Ocú.. 121
   9. Montijo.. 124
   10. San Francisco....................................... 126
   11. Soná.. 127
   12. Corozal... 129
   13. Remedios... 129
   14. Alanje and Querévalo............................... 130

15. Las Lomas.. 132
　　　16. Dolega... 133
IV. A Commentary on the Economy and Culture of the Countrymen.... 133

References... 138
Appendix: Notes by Ofelia Hooper.. 139

I. THE CULTURE TYPES IN PANAMA

Panama has long been a transit zone. Archaeological studies have indicated that even before the Spanish conquest migrations and trade passed through this region. In both the northern Andean region and Central America have been found articles which must have originated on the other side of the isthmus. Following the conquest Panama served as the route of transfer of most of the men and supplies which went to the west coast of South and Central America, and of the riches which were sent back to the mother country. With the construction of the canal early in the present century, the route became established as one of world importance. In view of this history one would expect Panama to present a very complex cultural situation. Outside of the transit zone itself, however, it does not seem to be as complex as one would expect. The two major cities, lying at the far ends of the canal, are kaleidoscopic, but this fades out rapidly as one leaves the immediate area of the Canal.

Basically, there are four major culture types to be found in the country of Panama: the Panamanian, the Indian, the Antillean, and the North American. The main body of the present paper will be concerned with the first of these. The Indian and Antillean will be briefly treated in the pages which follow immediately. The North American culture is primarily restricted to the Canal Zone and has had surprisingly little effect on the country as a whole. The populations living in the cities of Panama and Colón have felt the North American influence, and the workers who have come in from and returned to the country side have taken a little back with them. Some retired American Canal Zone workers have moved to the Panamanian countryside, principally to Chiriquí, to live out their lives, but it is mainly in Chiriquí that they have made a mark on the local cultural picture. Since it is not the purpose of the present monograph to deal either with the urban or Canal Zone populations, they are mentioned here merely to complete the general picture of Panama before going into the specific Panamanian culture which is our subject.

1. THE INDIAN CULTURES OF PANAMA

The Indians of Panama, unlike the populations to be found in Meso-America and the Andean highlands, have retained much of their cultural individuality through retreating from the encroaching Spanish and Panamanian population. Some, particularly the San Blas Cuna, have defended their independence and social unity against attempted Spanish encroachments, while others, such as the Guaymí have depended more upon retreating to isolated regions into which the Spanish did not wish to venture. During the Colonial period, the Spanish forced population movements upon many Indians, while others voluntarily moved out of reach. During these centuries of displacement, movement, and conflict, the Indians lost much of their aboriginal culture, but resisted extensive borrowing. As the Spanish moved in and gained actual control over much of the Indian population, the long process of mestizoization which racially and culturally characterizes the countryman population of Panama today got under way.

Since the present paper has nothing new to contribute in the way of field research concerning the Indian groups, the present sections are intended merely to provide a framework and summary of information which will help orient the reader concerning the general culture area picture of Panama.

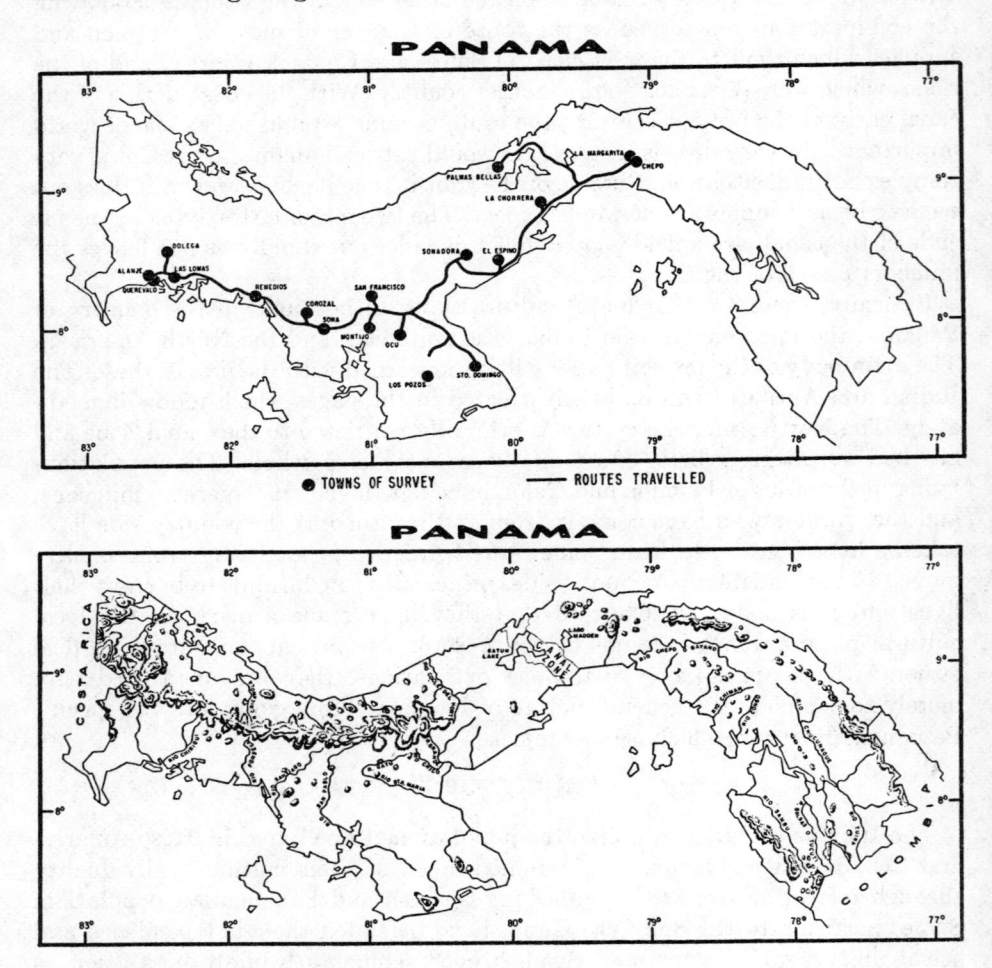

The Indian Population

The following map shows the present areas occupied by predominantly Indian groups. As elsewhere in Latin America, the areas indicated do not contain *only* Indians, but from the point of view of general culture, they may be considered to be predominantly Indian as opposed to Panamanian or Antillean.

The distribution of the total population of the Panamanian Indians according to the 1950 Census of Indians[1] is provided in Table 1. The census itself does not provide distribution of the total population in terms of the three major groups we will deal with here, but the distribution is distinct and with the aid of Table 2 it was possible to make certain adjustments to obtain approximate figures.

The largest Indian group is that which we here call the Guaymí. The figure

Table 1.—Indian population of Panama by province and district—1950 (Census 1950a)

Province and District	Total
Republic, total	48,654
Bocas del Toro, total	9,147
Bocas del Toro	766
Bastimentos	2,443
Chiriquí Grande	5,938
Colón, total	17,350
Comarca de San Blas	17,350
Chiriquí, total	14,288
Barú	64
Gualaca	321
Remedios	2,033
San Félix	2,088
San Lorenzo	3,432
Tolé	6,350
Darién, total	4,180
Chepigana	2,433
Pinogana	1,747
Panama, total	1,691
Chepo	1,651
Chimán	40
Veraguas, total	1,998
Cañazas	1,009
Las Palmas	869
Santa Fe	120

given in Table 1 actually includes some Terraba Indians as well as some which were referred to as "Talamanca" speakers. The Guaymí compose 52.3% of the entire Indian population of the country. The second most numerous group, the Cuna, compose 40.5% of the Indian population. The smallest group, the Chocó, account for the remaining 7.2%.

While this total Indian population of 48,654 is only 6% of the total population of Panama, it is 9.6 or almost 10% of the total rural population. The Indians

[1] Census, 1950a, Table 8.

comprise a significant ethnic minority within the country and particularly so when one takes into account the extensive territory they occupy.

While the 1930 and 1940 Censuses were deficient with respect to the Indian population, there are some indications that there has been a slight increase since 1930.[2] The provinces of Bocas del Toro, Veraguas and Panama saw consistent rises over the two decades, while Chiriquí saw a rise from 1930 to 1940. In Chiriquí, the 1940 census reported a 94.2% increase in Indian population over the 1930 figure; this information is hardly believable. In order for this to have occurred, it means that every woman beyond the age of puberty would have had to have during this period something over three children who survived. It seems likely that the 1930 Census may have been slightly under in its report, and that the 1940 Census was vastly over.

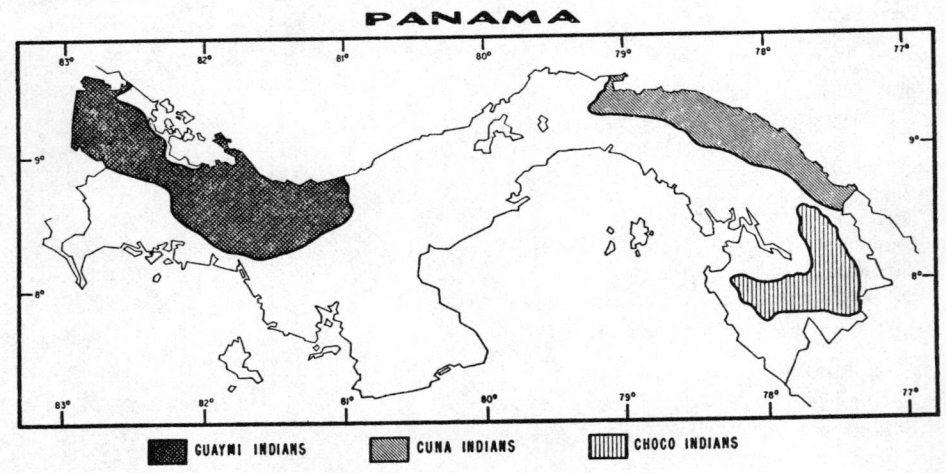

Principal Indian Areas

The Cuna population of Colón province for 1940 is reported to have been 20,831, an increase of 37.4% between 1930 and 1940. It then decreased 16.7% in the last decade. Stout, however, claims that this figure for 1940 included "4000 individuals, mostly male, in the Canal Zone, Colón, and Panama City."[3] Taking this into account, we get a rise from 15,154 to 16,831 for 1930 to 1940, and then to 17,350 for 1950. The 1930 Census reported 3,459 Indians present in Coclé, and 33 in Herrera and Los Santos. By 1940, none were reported from any of these provinces. It seems not unlikely that the persons reported as Indians in Coclé, Los Santos, and Herrera in 1930 were judged more on the basis of racial appearance than on custom. In the 1940 and 1950 Censuses only persons living under a "tribal" organization, i.e., non-civil government, were registered as Indians.

Only Darién showed a steady decline in Indian population between 1930 and 1950. While census data on race is usually quite unreliable, it can be indicative.

[2] See Census, 1950a, Table 7.   [3] Stout, 1947, p. 14, footnote 6.

The 1940 census gives the following figures for Darién: white, 193; Negro, 3,985; mestizo, 4,028; Indian, 6,651.

Considering the reports on the movement into Darién of Negroes from Colombia, and their intermarriage with the Chocó population, it seems not unlikely that this registered decline may in part be due to a negroization of this region as well as to a mestizoization.

We may conclude from this general picture that there has been a rise in the Indian population since the 1930 Census. If we take the 1930 figure at its face value, there has been an increase of 13.4 % in the Indian population between 1930 and 1950. On the other hand, for Panama as a whole, there has been in the same period an increase of 72.2 %. Consequently, even if the Indian population is increasing, it is doing so at a much slower rate than is the rest of the population of the country.

The Guaymí

The Indians of western Panama whom we here group as the Guaymí are in fact descendents of a number of different pre-conquest and colonial Indian groups. The Colonial and Republican periods of Panama history saw considerable movement of these Indians from their original homes, both forcefully and voluntarily to escape further contact with encroaching Spanish populations. The result is a poorly classified contemporary population scattered from the Pacific piedmont to the Caribbean coast.

Most of the classifications available at present are based on linguistic considerations. Those discussed by Johnson[4] and by Wassén[5] depend entirely on the analysis of the languages spoken. The classification used in the 1950 Census of Panama is also in terms of dialects, but it differs considerably from that of Johnson and Wassén. Johnson[6] provides a second classification based on habitat and cultural differences, but he is not explicit as to what criteria he used.

Linguistically, Johnson[7] follows Pinart's 1885 classification. Wassén,[8] however, believes that this must be modified. There are, according to Wassén, two basic dialect groups to be found in the Guaymí region: an *Eastern Group* and a *Western Group*. In the *Eastern Group* are those languages known as *Murire, Bukueta* (Wassén believes this to be the same group referred to as *Bogotá* by Nordenskiöld), and *Sabanero*. Wassén points out that there is some question as to whether it is merely the term the Spanish used for the *Murire-Bukueta*; Lehmann[9] evidently used the term in both contexts. Wassén's Western group include those languages known as *Valiente, Mové, Norteño,* and *Penonomeño*. As for location, Wassén says the *Eastern Group* live "chiefly in the eastern parts of the provinces Bocas del Toro and Chiriquí," and the *Western Group* live "chiefly in the central and western parts of the same provinces."[10]

Wassén's classification is fairly clear-cut but conflicts with the location which Johnson assigns to some of the groups mentioned. The *Mové*, included by Wassén in his *Western Group*, are to be found as far east as the Río Belén, the border

[4] 1948a.   [5] 1952.   [6] 1948b.   [7] 1948a.   [8] 1952.   [9] 1920.   [10] 1952, p. 277.

between Veraguas and Colón. Also, in the west, the *Murire* and the *Mové* (pertaining respectively to Wassén's *Eastern Group* and *Western Group*) "either occupy neighboring localities or else [the] representatives of one group live among the others."[11] The problem seems to be less one of proper linguistic alignment than one of deciding where these people live.

The 1950 Census of Panama has used a different linguistic classification. Leaving out of consideration seven *Valiente* reported living in Chepigana in Darién, and six Chocó Indians reported to be in Remedios, the census data on the Guaymí is given in Table 2.

It will be seen from the information of the census that the *Bogotá* and *Valiente* are located in districts which are in accord with Wassén's *Eastern* and *Western Group* classification, respectively. Wassén believes, following Pinart and Lehmann, that the term *Sabanero* refers to the groups otherwise known as *Murire* and *Bukueta*, members of his *Eastern Group*. The census, however, distributes the *Sabanero* speakers from the district of San Félix in the west to the district of Cañazas in the east. This distribution would seem to cut into Wassén's *Western Group* area. Wassén's own informant in San Félix said that the *Sabaneros* lived further east, "in the direction of Tolé." (See Appendix, #1)

To determine what dialect was spoken within a family the census takers were instructed to ask what the person called his language. It is not to be expected that such local designations would always correspond to those used by linguistic analysts, so the distinction made between *Guaymí*, *Guaymí llanero*, *Guaymí montañero*, and *Guaymí Sabanero* cannot be heavily depended upon. Before leaving the census classification there is a further point of importance. The easternmost Guaymí speakers are reported in the districts of Bastimentos in Bocas del Toro, and Cañazas in Veraguas. There are no speakers of Indian languages reported from the district of Santa Fe, the area in which, it will be remembered, Johnson reported both *Murire* and *Mové* speakers to reside. There are reported to be 78 Indians who speak Spanish in this district.

Johnson, in his description of Guaymí culture, makes another dual division of this population. "The *Guaymí* are divided into *Northern* tribes and *Southern* tribes. The former live in the Tropical Forest, and certain fundamental traits were superficially modified by it so as to contrast with the Southern tribes living in the uplands of the Pacific coast. Other differences, though appearing in minor details, appear to be more deeply rooted."[12] In the body of his description, however, Johnson speaks almost entirely of the "*Guaymí*" or the "*Southern Guaymí*," only making three references to possible variations to be found among the Northern Guaymí. This is doubtless due to the paucity of data available on the latter populations. Nevertheless, this division, made evidently on the basis of geographical zones (tropical forest as opposed to the Pacific coast uplands) and scattered information on cultural differences will probably stand up under further examination. For example, the ethnographic information published by Wassén[13] on the *Bogotá* group, visited by Nordenskiöld in 1927, points up important varia-

[11] Johnson, 1948a, p. 52. [12] Johnson, 1948b, p. 231. [13] 1952.

Table 2.—Indian population of 7 years of age and older according to language and dialect in the Republic of Panama, by province and district: Census of 1950[1]

(Reproduced by permission of the Office of Statistics and Census)

Area	Total of 7 years age or more	Total	Bogota or Bocota	Cricamola or Valiente	Chocó	Guaymí	Guaymí Llanero	Guaymí Montañero	Guaymí Sabanero	Cuna	Teribe	Spanish	Spanish in addition to an Indian language[2]
Republic, total[3].....	36,936	35,943[4]	164	180	2,682	14,801	506	677	1,558	15,224	146	959	10,367
Bocas del Toro......	6,798	6,620	164	173	0	5,748	0	0	384	0	146	178	1,178
Bastimentos......	1,764	1,684	164	0	0	1,136	0	0	384	0	0	80	614
Bocas del Toro....	597	524	0	18	0	355	0	0	0	0	146	73	274
Chiriquí Grande...	4,437	4,412	0	155	0	4,257	0	0	0	0	0	25	290
Colón..............	13,389	13,389	0	0	0	0	0	0	0	13,389	0	0	2,448
San Blas..........	13,389	13,389	0	0	0	0	0	0	0	13,389	0	0	2,448
Chiriquí...........	10,537	10,294	0	0	6	8,642	504	677	465	0	0	243	3,925
Barú.............	49	43	0	0	0	43	0	0	0	0	0	6	28
Gualaca..........	224	221	0	0	0	221	0	0	0	0	0	3	91
Remedios........	1,486	1,486	0	0	6	1,354	107	0	19	0	0	0	606
San Félix.........	1,478	1,478	0	0	0	368	323	677	110	0	0	0	446
San Lorenzo.......	2,544	2,464	0	0	0	2,439	25	0	0	0	0	80	769
Tolé.............	4,756	4,602	0	0	0	4,217	49	0	336	0	0	154	1,985
Darién.............	3,210	3,184	0	7	2,646	0	0	0	0	531	0	26	2,384
Chepigana........	1,882	1,880	0	7	1,873	0	0	0	0	0	0	2	1,657
Pinogana.........	1,328	1,304	0	0	773	0	0	0	0	531	0	24	727
Panama............	1,334	1,334	0	0	30	0	0	0	0	1,304	0	0	98
Chepo............	1,304	1,304	0	0	0	0	0	0	0	1,304	0	0	70
Chimán...........	30	30	0	0	30	0	0	0	0	0	0	0	28
Veraguas............	1,634	1,122	0	0	0	411	2	0	709	0	0	512	334
Cañazas..........	824	454	0	0	0	32	0	0	422	0	0	370	146
Las Palmas.......	732	668	0	0	0	379	2	0	287	0	0	64	188
Santa Fe..........	78	0	0	0	0	0	0	0	0	0	0	78	0

[1] The inquiry concerning Indian language referred to that regularly spoken by the family in the home and not to that which any individual may be able to speak.

[2] The inquiry was made individually of each member of the family.

[3] Includes 34 persons of the district of Bocas del Toro whose families were declared to speak English regularly.

[4] Includes 5 persons of the district of Bocas del Toro who were declared to speak Talamanca regularly.

May 13, 1953

tions from the general picture of the *Guaymí* given by Johnson based on his own field work among the southern groups.

No matter what traditional differences may ultimately be found between the Northern and Southern Guaymí, there is a mounting body of evidence that differential contact with the Panamanian and English speaking population is producing such a distinction at present. A glance at the map of the Culture Areas of Panama will show that of the three provinces in which are found the Guaymí groups, Chiriquí and Veraguas provide broad areas of contact with the Panamanian culture while Bocas del Toro is fairly restricted from such contact. Data provided by Johnson[14] and that received by the writer from local informants in Remedios, Soná, and the David region indicate that the farther one moves back from this line of contact, the more one encounters traits which are not shared with the Panamanian country dweller population.

The only quantitative indication of the degree of importance of this contact at present is that to be taken from the census figures. Table 3 gives the relevant

Table 3.—Indian bilingualism

Province	Total No. of Indians	%	Speak Indian in the home	%	Also speak Spanish	%	Speak Spanish in the home	%
Bocas del Toro....	6798	100.0	6620	97.5	1187	17.5	178	2.5
Chiriquí..........	10537	100.0	10294	97.7	3925	37.1	243	2.3
Veraguas.........	1634	100.0	1122	68.7	334	20.4	512	31.3

figures (taken from Table 2) together with relative percentages on Indian bilingualism.

The above information shows there is a considerably higher percentage of people speaking both the Indian and Spanish languages in Chiriquí than in Bocas del Toro, and a much higher percentage speaking Spanish in the home in Veraguas. Bocas del Toro has the lowest percentage of people who speak Spanish in addition to their own dialect and has about the same percentage of people who speak Spanish in the home as does Chiriquí. If we take into account the additional fact of the 34 English speakers in Bocas del Toro, we cannot escape the conclusion that the Indians of Chiriquí and Veraguas have been much more influenced by the Panamanians in this aspect of their culture than have those of Bocas del Toro.

This census information also throws light on the problem of the distribution of Indians in Veraguas today. It will be remembered that Johnson reported Guaymí as far as the Río Belén and the Río Coclé del Norte (in Colón); the census figures indicate that in the district of Sante Fe, there are no speakers of Indian languages, and only 78 people reported as being Indians. In Cañazas, the next district to the west, of the 824 people recorded as being Indian, 370 (44.9%) spoke

[14] 1948b.

Spanish in the home, and an additional 146 (17.7 %) spoke Spanish in addition to speaking the Indian dialect. As one moves yet further to the west into the districts of Las Palmas (Veraguas) and Bastimentos (Bocas del Toro) the relative amount of Spanish speakers drops considerably.

These data suggest that the rate of acculturation in the eastern end of the Guaymí area is greater than that in the center and the west. Along the southern border of the Guaymí area, particularly in Las Palmas, Tolé, Remedios, San Félix, San Lorenzo and Gualaca, acculturation seems to have been playing a supplementary role to migration. Johnson reports,[15] and it was confirmed to the writer in various conversations in Panama, that some of the Guaymí move into the zone of Panamanian political control to avoid problems they are facing in the Indian area, while others have retreated further back into the cordillera to avoid the influences and effects of contact with the Panamanians.

To summarize our present knowledge with respect to the classification of contemporary Guaymí groups, we may say that a linguistic division between an *Eastern Group* and *Western Group* has been made. At present, it is impossible to say just what the cultural significance of this dividing line may be, and it is uncertain just where this line should be placed on the map. In addition, a cultural division has been made between a *Northern Group* and a *Southern Group*, which seems to receive support by intensive studies and scattered reports stemming from short visits. This division is further strengthened by evidence of greater acculturation along the southern and south-eastern border of the Guaymí area than in the northern part. As with the east-west division, it is uncertain where the dividing line between these two groups may be.

It seems not unlikely, were a serious survey of the contemporary Guaymí area to be undertaken, that local differences might prove to be of more importance in the delineation of subareas than would the division into the *Northern* and *Southern* groups. Also, account must be taken of the political allegiance to various leaders recognized by the Guaymí themselves. This has seen many changes in recent years; one such serious conflict was witnessed by the census takers during their pre-census survey.

Within this Guaymí area there were 146 Indians which were assigned by the census to the *Terraba (Teribe)* language group and five people who were said to speak a language called *"Talamanca."* Both groups are in Bocas del Toro, and while the first is a recognized language, the term *"Talamanca"* might refer to any of the Indian languages to be found at present in eastern Costa Rica. The pre-census reports state that these *"Talamanca"* speakers were born in Costa Rica and migrated to Panama.[16] The census also records the presence of 43 Guaymí Indians in the district of Barú, Chiriquí. These people seem to be somewhat isolated from the rest of the Guaymí. Miss Miró, Director of the Census, says[17] that this population was evidently not transitory and was part of a total population which also contained countrymen.

---

[15] 1948b, p. 246. [16] See Hooper, 1952, ms. [17] In correspondence.

The Cuna[18]

The contemporary Cuna fall into two main groups: the San Blas and the mainland, but during historic times, mainly to avoid the Spanish, the greater number of them have moved out to the islands of the San Blas Archipelago. As the figures from the census indicate, the island groups are by far the most numerous today.

The contemporary mainland Cuna are found in a number of places. The principal locales in Panama are the upper Chepo (or Bayano) River and the headwaters of the Chucunaque River. "The San Blas Cuna refer to these two groups as the *Yalatola* (Mountain or South people) and *Walatola* (Curves-of-the-River people), respectively. Another group, the *Payatola* (Snake people?), lives along the Paya, Purco, and Capeti Rivers, all tributaries of the Tuira River. This group numbered 180 persons in 1953 and since then has decreased rapidly and is now almost extinct. The remnants of a fourth mainland group live at Arquia, Colombia, in the Atrato valley. They numbered about 120 in 1933. The inhabitants of Arquia and the few who, until about 1930, lived at Caiman on the eastern shore of the Gulf of Urabá are referred to by the San Blas Cuna as the *Tanakwitola* (Eastern people). The mainland groups call the San Blas Cuna, the *Telmaltola* (Sea people)."[19]

These various groups recognize their cultural affinity, but there is no supreme Cuna authority over the entire population. The same language is spoken although the Payatola group had evidently more Spanish words in their vocabulary. Table 2 shows that, of the present San Blas Cuna, 2,448 of the 13,389 people over 7 years of age in 1950, or 18.3%, speak Spanish currently in the home. Of the mountain Cuna, the Chepo people all speak the Cuna language in the home, and only 70 of 1,304, or 5.4%, also speak Spanish. From the data available, it is not possible to say whether the 727 people who speak Spanish reported from Pinogana in Darién are Chocós or Cunas. Considering the relative isolation of the Cuna location in the headwaters of the Chucunaque River, however, it seems likely that these Spanish speakers are probably Chocó.

Of the various Panamanian Indian groups, the San Blas Cuna are by far the most highly organized and have the most clearly established relations with Panamanians. This, at least, was the situation at the time Stout made his studies from 1939 to 1941. At that time, there were many Cuna who were working in Colón and the Canal Zone, and presumably, the need for labor during the war years brought many more from the San Blas area into the zone under influence of Panamanians and Americans. Just what effect this may have had on the political and social organization of the San Blas and other Cuna groups cannot be estimated without further study.

The Chocó

The Chocó are the smallest, the least known, and probably the most poorly organized of the Panamanian Indian groups. There is no evidence that there is

---

[18] The information on the Cuna is a brief summary of the material to be found in Stout, 1947.

[19] Stout, 1947, p. 13.

any recognized political system which includes the entire population, and there is evidence that a considerable portion of the population has been and is at present being amalgamated with Negroes who have moved in from Colombia. Stout states that the Chocó ". . . have been gradually spreading northward since the conquest so that they now occupy the lower courses of rivers on the south side of Darién that were once exclusively Cuna. In this movement the Chocó (and numerous Negroes as well) have been occupying areas abandoned by the Cuna in their emigration northward."[20] Recent political disturbances in Colombia have evidently increased the movement of the negro population into Darién, and there has been quite a bit of intermarriage between the Chocó and the Negroes.

It is not possible to classify subgroupings of the Chocó since there are no studies available. The census data in Table 2 indicates clearly that the majority of those included in the census spoke Spanish in addition to speaking Chocó in the home. In Chimán, 28 out of thirty were bilingual and in Chepigana 1,657 out of 1,873, or over 83% of the population, spoke both languages.

Cultural Relations Between Indians and Panamanians

The expression "cultural relations" here refers to the sharing and borrowing of cultural traits between one society and another. For our purposes, we may distinguish between two functionally distinct types of cultural relations. First, there are some traits which, once borrowed, can be reproduced or perpetuated within the borrowing society without further contact or stimulus from the lending society. The Spanish, when they came to Panama to live, took over the Indian shifting agriculture and its technology. Once this was learned, the trait could have been perpetuated in the Panamanian culture without further contact with the Indians. Similarly, once the Indians took over the raising of chickens, they needed no further stimulus from the Panamanians to retain this trait. There is a second class of traits, however, which depend upon the cultural and material resources of a particular society for their production. The *chácara*, or net carrying bag, which is standard equipment for most of the countrymen of Panama, is made principally by the Guaymí Indians and is to some degree a trait of this nature. Stout (1947, p. 23) gives a list of such traits for which the San Blas Cuna are dependent upon the Panamanian culture as producer or intermediary: "From traders are obtained iron pots, china and enamel ware, tools, fishline and hooks, shotguns, shells, powder and shot, cloth, string (for hammocks), needles and thread, soap, salt, sugar, kerosene, plug tobacco, and glass beads."

Table 4 gives a list of traits which are shared between the Panamanian countryman culture and the three major Indian cultures of the country. With a few exceptions, the traits listed are those of the first type mentioned above. Aside from the list quoted above from Stout, we have no adequate study of the commercial relations between the Panamanian Indians and the nation nor do we know the degree to which the Indians are dependent upon such trade goods for their daily living. Before looking closely at Table 4, there are a few explanations which

---
[20] 1947, p. 17.

CULTURAL SURVEYS

Table 4.—Traits shared between the Indian and *campesino* cultures of Panama

Origins
S: Spanish
N: Native
O: Other or combination

x = Present
0 = Absent
? = Possibility present
blank = No data

	Trait	Origin	Pana-manian	Guaymí (Southern)	Cuna	Chocó
Food and food products	Corn	N	x	x	x	x
	Beans	N	x	x	0	
	Lima beans	N	x	x	0	
	Yuca	N	x	x	0	x
	Papaya	N	x	x	x	
	Avocado	N	x	x	x	
	Gourds	N	x	x	x	x
	Camote	N	x	x	x	
	Coconuts	N	x	x	x	
	Pejibaye	N	x	x	?	x
	Plantains	S	x	x	x	x
	Banana	S	x	x	?	x
	Pigeon peas	S	x	x	0	
	Ñame	S	x	x	0	
	Rice	S	x	x	x	
	Yautia	N	x	x	0	
	Sugar cane	S	x	x	x	x
	Millet	S	x	x	0	
	Chicha, made by chewing	N	x	x	x	
	Collecting wild honey	N	x	x	0	x
	Palm wine	N	x	?	?	
Domesticated animals	Horses	S	x	x	0	0
	Cats	S	x	?	x	
	Dogs	O	x	x	x	x
	Pigs	S	x	?	x	x
	Chickens	S	x	x	x	x
	Ducks	O	x	?	0	x
	Cattle	S	x	x	0	
Clothing and adornment	Men's western clothing	S	x	x	x	x
	Men's decorated ceremonial clothing	O	x	x	0	
	Men's loin cloth	N	0	x	0	x
	Women's decorated daily clothing	O	x	x	x	
	Straw hats	S	x	x	0	
	Face painting	N	0	x	x	x
	Body painting	N	0	0	x	x

Table 4.—Continued

	Trait	Origin	Present distribution			
			Pana-manian	Guaymí (Southern)	Cuna	Chocó
Material traits	Machete	S	x	x	x	
	Shotgun/rifle	S	x	x	x	
	Hunting traps	N	x	x	0	
	Fishing bait and line		x	?	x	
	Fishing nets	O	x	x	x	
	Fishing traps	N	x	x	?	
	Spirit ships		0	0	x	x
	Rectangular houses	N	x	x	x	x
	Baskets	N	x	x	x	x
	Pottery	N	x	x	x	x
	Ceiling storage platform		x	x	x	
	Double headed drum	O	x	x	x	x
	Single headed drum	O	x	?	x	x
	Digging stick	N	x	x	x	
	Fishing spears	N	0	x	x	x
	Fish poisons	N	x	x	?	
	Bow and arrow	N	0	x	x	x
	Blowgun with pellets	N	0	x	0	0
	Blowgun with darts	N	0	0	x	x
	Pile dwellings	N	x	0	0	x
	Round and apsidal houses	N	x	x	0	x
	Platform beds	N	x	x	0	x
	Firefans	N	0	?	x	?
	Wooden mortar	N	x	x	x	
	Grinding stone	N	x	x	x	
	Net bags	N	x	x	?	
	Tumplines	N	x	x	x	
	Solid log stool	N	x	x	0	
	Solid stool, carved	N	0	x	x	x
	Hammocks	N	x	x	x	x
	Dugout canoe	N	x	x	x	x
	Notched log ladder	N	x	x	x	x
	Bark cloth	N	0	x	0	x
	Sewed applique work	O	0	x	x	
	Weaving	N	0	x	x	0
	Beadwork	O	0	x	?	x
Economic organization	Slash and burn, shifting agriculture	N	x	x	?	x
	Land clearing done by men	O	x	x	x	
	Planting done by women	N	x	x	0	
	Planting done by men	O	x	x	x	
	Planting and general cultivation by women	N	x	0	0	
	Women make pottery	N	x	x	x	
	Women make hammocks	N	x	x	x	
	Men make baskets	N	x	?	x	
	Men make straw hats	O	x	x	0	
	Women make straw hats	O	x	0	0	
	Group working teams	O	x	?	x	
	Private land owning	O	x	x	x	
	Communal land owning	O	x	0	x	

Table 4.—Continued

	Trait	Origin	Present distribution			
			Pana-manian	Guaymí (Southern)	Cuna	Chocó
Social organization	Monogamy standard	O	x	0	x	x
	Polygamy permitted to certain people	N	0	0	x	x
	Polygamy common	N	0	x	0	0
	Matrilineal descent	N	0	x	0	0
	Patrilineal descent	N	0	0	0	x
	Bilateral descent	O	x	0	x	0
	Matrilocal residence	N	0	?	x	0
	Patrilocal residence	N	0	0	0	x
	Neo-local residence	O	x	?	0	0
	Community leadership by election or approval	N	x	0	x	x
	Community leadership by inheritance	N	0	x	0	
	Separation of spouses frequent	O	x	x	?	
Misc.	Girl's puberty rites	N	0	0	x	x
	Boy's puberty rites	N	0	x	0	
	Girls clothed very young, boys not until later	O	x	x	x	
	Midwivery	—	x	x	x	
	Catholic religion elements	S	x	x	x	

should be made concerning it. The items on the list were taken from the studies of Johnson[21] for the Guaymí, Stout[22] for the Cuna, and Stout[23] for the Chocó. Additional points on the Guaymí are taken from the writer's notes from informants in Soná and Remedios and manuscript notes of Señorita Ofelia Hooper taken from observations of the pre-census survey of 1950. The traits selected from these descriptions were chosen on the basis of being illustrative of the sharing of culture between the Panamanians and the Indian groups, or of sharing between the Indian groups themselves. Relatively speaking, the data on the Guaymí was the fullest, while that on the Chocó was the thinnest. As a result, it is not always possible to state whether some of the traits listed are present in the cultures or not. The purpose of the table, then, is not to provide a quantitative delineation of cultural relations between these groups, but a qualitative illustration. Those large areas of the culture which are represented only slightly or not at all on the table, such as social organization, life cycle, idea, belief and value systems, are in fact those aspects in which very little is shared between the various cultures. A deeper analysis, were it possible, of these aspects of the culture of the Indian groups would probably point up more similarities than are suggested on the chart; however, it is unlikely that many more would appear between the various Indian cultures and the Panamanian culture. It should further be noted that the absence of traits like trade goods from the table does not mean that they are considered to be unimportant. Depending upon the prob-

[21] 1948b. [22] 1947. [23] 1948b.

lem at hand, they may be considerably more important than some of the traits which are included.

The most striking aspects of sharing to be noted from Table 4 is that the Panamanians seem to have incorporated many more traits of Indian culture into their way of life than the reverse. The Indians have specifically borrowed most heavily in food crops, domestic animals, and certain items of technology. The machete has probably long been of some importance, but the shotgun and rifle are fairly recent introductions, and relatively few Guaymí have them. The use of the sugar press doubtless came as part of the general sugar-cane complex. Of the two specific clothing traits mentioned on the list, the making of straw hats is reported to be a recent introduction also. The effect of the Spanish conquest and the subsequent developing contact with Panamanian culture does not show up in the table. As Steward and Stout have pointed out, the main result of this long history was a deculturation of the Indian groups; that is, they lost many of the traits which characterized them previously, but they did not automatically take on replacements from the Spanish culture. The Spanish, on the other hand, had less to lose, and much to gain by adoption of certain Indian traits to adjust to the new environment.

Many of the traits listed on Table 4 cannot be classified as being specifically of Indian or Spanish origin. In some cases, such as with domesticated dogs and ducks the trait was previously present in both cultures. In others, such as the bead work, the materials are now of western origin, but the form and meaning are contemporary Indian. In the case of hat making by men, the hats are western in origin, but among most of the Panamanian countrymen they are made by the women. The transfer into Guaymí culture was evidently made on the basis of basket working; baskets are made by men, and since hat making was a similar activity, it was turned over to the men also. Some of these traits, such as the single headed drum, may be of Antillean origin or influence. Yet other traits may be New World developments out of the Spanish-Indian combination, or due to local social situations. The separation of spouses and the degree to which children of different sexes are clothed would fall into this category.

The retention of specifically non-Spanish and non-Panamanian social and ideological organizations by the Indians is of considerable importance. Again, while the table does not show this characteristic, one need only to dip into the scant ethnological literature on these groups to realize that in the realms of beliefs and social relations, the Indians are worlds away from the Panamanian population. Yet the fact that the Panamanians base their economy on forms fundamentally similar to those employed by the Indians means that the Indians, either individually or in small groups, can convert themselves into Panamanians. It is the feeling of the present writer that such conversions will inevitably come as the pressure of Panamanian population pushes in on the Guaymí, Chocó, and the mainland Cuna. The Guaymí particularly have retained an individuality in their culture through successive withdrawals away from the gradually encroaching Panamanian population. But even now in parts of Panama the countrymen are feeling the pressure of population and are migrating to less occupied areas. From the point of view of population density, the Guaymí area and Darién are open lands. The differences in points of view between the Guaymí Indians and the Panamanian countrymen will not be bridged. This does not mean that they could not be bridged, but rather that the movement is towards the ultimate destruction of the Indian culture. Only among the San Blas Cuna have the Indians long openly defied the encroachments of the Panamanian nation and population, and under present conditions it is among these Indians that there is the greatest likelihood of a continuance of cultural individuality.

The Status of Our Knowledge of the Panamanian Indian Groups

In general, systematic knowledge on most of the Panamanian Indians is lacking. Of the three major groups, only the Cuna have received intensive study during the past three decades. The anthropologists most concerned with them have been Nordenskiöld, Wassén, Holmer, and Stout. Stout[24] provides a bibliography of most of the titles to that date, although both Wassén and Stout have published brief papers since.[25] While there is fairly adequate basic ethnological data available on this group, and historical perspective on the acculturation of the San Blas Cuna has been provided by Stout, the problems presented by public health and welfare work will demand additional research on the local social structure of any particular area which may be included in project work.

The most numerous Indians in Panama, the Guaymí and neighboring groups, have received very little systematic study. In the early 1930's, Frederick Johnson carried on two field seasons of work, evidently among the Southern Guaymí, but aside from this, most of our information comes from fairly casual observations or from sources which are more valuable for their historical information. Johnson[26] provides a bibliography of the sources he utilized in the composition of his summary of the contemporary culture of the Guaymí. Unfortunately this article, while very helpful, is the only general study which Johnson has published on his own work in the region.

Further systematic studies on the Guaymí are badly needed We know next to nothing concerning the regional variations to be found within the area, and we need contemporary functional studies to throw light on the position of this group in modern Panama. Considering the size of this group, it is surprising that so little work has been done.

Concerning the Panamanian Chocó, we have no systematic reports. Again, we must rely on casual reports and historical documents. Wassén and Nordenskiöld have published on the Chocó in Colombia, and other work has been done since that time in that region.[27] The Panamanian group, however, as Stout has indicated, has taken over many traits from the neighboring Cuna and probably present a different picture than do the Chocó to the south. The Chocó are undergoing such extensive acculturation that contemporary studies are badly needed,

---

[24] 1947, pp. 117–121.
[25] Those which have come to the writer's attention appear in numbers 16–21 of *Etnologiska Studier* (Göteborg, Sweden); also Stout, 1952.
[26] 1948b.   [27] See Stout, 1947, Bibliography.

not only from the point of view of future public welfare projects, but also from a historical point of view.

As a general reference, the Handbook of South American Indians, Volume 4 (1948) is the most satisfactory single source on Panamanian Indians. The articles on the various groups are short, but they represent a fairly adequate summary of the data available at the time of writing. In addition, Stout's 1947 publication on the Cuna provides more extensive information on the course of acculturation of that group.

2. THE ANTILLEAN CULTURES

The term "Antillean Cultures" refers to the ways of life of the recent negro migrants from the Caribbean. There are at present two main concentrations of

Table 5.[27a]—Percentages by race and province of civil population in census of 1940

	Negro	Mestizo	White	Other
Bocas del Toro	58.9%	32.4	4.4	4.3
Colón	50.1	31.4	14.8	3.7
Darién	48.1	48.7	2.3	0.9
Panama	22.5	60.1	15.7	1.7
Coclé	3.2	92.7	3.5	0.6
Chiriquí	2.5	82.6	13.3	1.6
Herrera	1.4	89.3	9.0	0.3
Veraguas	0.9	91.6	6.9	1.7
Los Santos	0.4	80.6	19.0	—
Total republic	14.6	71.8	12.2	1.4

Antilleans in Panama, one in the Canal Zone and the cities of Panama and Colón, and the other in the plantations around Puerto Armuelles. During the early part of this century, there was also such a population in Bocas del Toro. The writer has not had the opportunity to study any of the populations here discussed, and so will rely entirely on the reports of others.

It is quite recognized that the Antillean population does not include all people of negro ancestry in the country. There are many people who have racial characteristics of the Negro but who are considered to be mestizo and part of the general countryman population. The Antilleans are those who have retained much of the culture which they brought with them from the islands. While the census does not yet provide us with information on the contemporary distribution of this population, some indication of their presence may be taken from the racial data provided by the 1940 Census. It should be made clear that the use of this material does not reflect any confusion of race and culture nor any extreme faith in the quality of the 1940 Census on this point. The information is indicative, however. For comparison's sake, we give only the percentages.

Table 5 indicates that in 1940, there was still a large negro population in

---

[27a] Census, 1940, Table 17.

Bocas del Toro which had not moved out after the plantations there reduced operations because of the Panama Disease.

The Antillean populations now found in Colón and Panama first came in with the construction of the railroad. At that time and later during the Canal construction many Negroes immigrated, and with the termination of the work, remained in the two cities. This population has seen gradual augmentation by those who left Bocas del Toro, and yet others brought later to the Canal.

The Puerto Armuelles Antillean population in 1940 was small, about 900,[28] but evidently distinct since many of them were included in the census as foreigners, and most lived in the plantation.

It should be noted in passing that the large negro component reported for Darién is probably composed mainly of colonial refugee Negroes and those who have moved up from Colombia. The Darién population does not contain many Antilleans.

The concern expressed by some Panamanians against the heavy Antillean concentration in the major cities of the republic is not a reflection so much of racial prejudice as of cultural differences. The best brief studies on race relations in the urban and canal areas are to be found in the work of John Biesanz.[29] Biesanz points out that the Antillean population comes from various islands, therefore includes different dialects and does not represent a distinct or unified social group. Also, as a population in the Canal Zone, they are basically exploitable. The rejection of the urban Antilleans by Panamanians is based not so much on biological differences, but on real or imagined economic competition and cultural differences. With respect to this point, Biesanz says, "The fact that 'prohibited immigration' includes, not Negroes, but *English-speaking* Negroes, is the clue to Panama's 'race' prejudice." He goes on to point out that the Antilleans have found it difficult and not immediately necessary to take over the Panamanian culture, and they earlier preferred to retain English speaking schools. Finally, as the cultural differences between Panamanians and Antilleans disappear, the prejudice against the latter declines. A good example of this may be seen in Palmas Bellas, a rural town on the Atlantic coast west of Colón. Until ten years ago one *barrio* of the town was called "Guachapalí" or "Barrio de los Jamaicanos." Now, however, in formal recognition of the fact that the originally different populations have become assimilated, the two *barrios* are known merely as "del Norte" and "del Sur," referring to their respective positions. Perhaps the most distinct demonstration of Biesanz's conclusions is the fact that since early in the colonial epoch negro slaves were imported into Panama to carry on boat-building and field labor. The net result of this is that there are regions in the interior where the population has a high negroid component. These people are considered to be Panamanians and, aside from occasional class recognition given to generalized color differences, there is no particular prejudice shown against them because of their color.

The second group of Antilleans are to be found in the plantations at Bocas del Toro and Puerto Armuelles. The writer was not able to visit either of these areas,

---

[28] Census 1940, p. 228.   [29] 1949, 1950a, 1950b, 1951, 1953.

and so cannot make comments on the situation present. It is clear, however, that the plantation population is by no means restricted to Antilleans as both Guaymí Indians and Panamanians are employed to some extent at both places. It was reported to the writer (he cannot vouch for the truth of it) that the smallpox epidemic which hit the Guaymí in 1953 started among some Guaymí workers at Puerto Armuelles. Being frightened, they returned to the cordillera and served to carry the disease into the Indian area.

II. THE CULTURE OF THE PANAMANIAN COUNTRYMAN

1. INTRODUCTORY NOTE

The population with which the present essay is principally concerned lives between Chepo in the east and the Costa Rican border in the west, excluding the major cities of the country and the Canal Zone. To the south this population area borders on the Pacific Ocean. To the north in the Province of Colón the area borders on the Atlantic Ocean; west of Colón, it borders on the as yet not clearly defined boundary of the Guaymí Indian region. Panamanians tend to divide this area into four subregions: the area west of the Canal, Colón, the Province of Chiriquí, and the entire remainder, which is called the *Interior*.

This population is Spanish speaking, racially mixed, and predominantly rural in that they live in rural-oriented towns or in the countryside. The culture is one in which the basic economy has been drawn from the Indians, while the general orientation of the superstructure, that is, the social, ideological, and value systems, are predominantly of Spanish origin. This population we call the "countryman" population of Panama. Locally, they are sometimes referred to as Panamanians or the "civil population;" but in order to distinguish them from other elements of the population who live in a different way and have distinctive cultural traits, we prefer the term "countryman," being a direct translation of the Spanish *"campesino."*

It has been necessary to provide fairly gross coverage concerning many of the traits described in the sections to follow. There is considerable local variation from one area to the next, and wherever such distinctions have been clear, they are indicated in the description. Such local and regional variations will be of great importance in the understanding of the general cultural picture of Panama and must be taken into account if one is to focus his attention on a particular community. The object has been to describe the variations so that the reader may have an idea of the approximate limits and degree of variation to be found.

2. POPULATION AND ITS DISTRIBUTION

Panama's position as a zone of transit has frequently led to the belief that the country's population is concentrated in the area around the two major cities and the canal. Otherwise excellent commentaries on the human geography of Latin America have occasionally gone far astray in dealing with Panama.[30] The fact of the matter is that Panama as a country has a rural population which falls within the range found in the other Central American countries. Compare the results of the 1950 Censuses in Table 6.

In density Panama is also in the range of the Central American countries. Table 7 suggests that Panama is comparable to Nicaragua and Honduras in density. The same holds true for the general distribution of population in the various countries. Leaving out of the discussion El Salvador which has no

Table 6.[31]—Percentage of rural and urban population in Central American countries according to the 1950 censuses

	Rural	Urban
Guatemala	69.1%	30.9%
Honduras	69.0	31.0
Costa Rica	66.5	33.5
Nicaragua	65.0	35.0
Panama	64.1	35.9
El Salvador	63.6	36.4

Table 7.[32]—Population densities of the Central American countries according to the 1950 censuses

	Persons/Km.²
El Salvador	88.9
Guatemala	25.3
Costa Rica	15.7
Panama	10.9
Honduras	10.0
Nicaragua	8.2

Atlantic coastal zone and is generally highly populated, all the rest of the countries of Central America have certain areas of very low population. Guatemala has its Petén; Honduras, its departments of Olancho and Colón; Nicaragua, the departments of Zelaya, Río San Juan, the northern part of Jinotega, and the comarca del Cabo Gracias a Dios; and Costa Rica has large portions of the departments of Limón, Puntarenas, Alajuela, and Guanacaste.

[30] See for example, James, p. 724: "The rest [outside the canal area] of Panama is of very minor significance in a study of human geography..." James then goes on to give a brief, but badly misleading account of the distribution of population in rural Panama.

[31] It should be noted that the definition of "urban" in all countries except Panama is on the basis of the seats of municipal governments, whereas in Panama, "urban" is defined as being any community population of 1500 or larger. Data from official Census Reports.

[32] Data from Census 1950a, table 5 and from Boletín Estadístico, II Epoca No. 2, marzo y abril, de 1952, San Salvador, El Salvador, p. 26.

In Panama, the regions of low population density are Bocas del Toro, Darién, northern Veraguas, and eastern Panama. These areas of low population form three major regions: the Petén region and inland of British Honduras; the Atlantic coastal region of Honduras, Nicaragua, Costa Rica, and Panama; and eastern Panama. In the second of these regions, the area of low population extends over to the Pacific in two places, in Guanacaste and Puntarenas, as of course, it does in eastern Panama.

In common with Honduras and Nicaragua, and to a slighter degree with Costa Rica, the regions of low density of population in Panama are inhabited by ethnic groups which differ considerably from the rest of the civil population of the country. In some cases, the ethnic populations are Indian, but in others, mainly in the Atlantic coastal belt in Darién, there are strong negro compo-

Table 8.[33]—Increase of rural population in Panama by provinces, 1940 to 1950
(*These figures include the Indian population*)

Province	Rural population in 1940	Rural population in 1950	Percentage increase
Bocas del Toro	12,856	17,846	38.8
Coclé	48,999	63,315	28.6
Colón	33,726	37,940	12.5
Chiriquí	95,068	112,544	18.4
Darién	14,930	14,660	1.8
Herrera	33,328	40,325	21.0
Los Santos	45,541	56,152	23.3
Panama	48,273	73,731	52.7
Veraguas	79,330	99,075	24.9
Total	412,051	515,588	25.1

nents. Panama shares with all these countries the presence of large areas of little exploited lands and the problems of adjusting the resident ethnic populations with distinctive cultures to the demands of an expanding civil population.

Panama, in common with the rest of the countries of Central America, has seen a tremendous recent increase of population. For the country as a whole, the rural increase between 1940 and 1950 was 25.1% as compared to an increase of 37.7% in the urban areas. These figures show that although urban growth has been greater than rural growth in the corresponding period, the rural growth itself has been very great.

Except for the Province of Darién, the rural provincial growth has varied between 12 and 53%. Table 8 provides the data on each province in this respect.

Another indication of the fact that the rural growth has been considerable is to be seen by comparing the increase in the size of the districts since 1930.

Table 9 shows a decline in the number of small districts and the increase in the number of larger districts. This reveals better than gross numbers the rural

[33] Data from Census 1950a and 1940.

problem which is beginning to result from the growth of the rural population. Not only are the larger towns and cities receiving an influx of rural people, but the rural districts themselves are growing in size. To some degree, it is not that the large cities are "drawing" people from the country, as has occurred in the United States, but rather that the pressure of increasing population in certain

Table 9.[34]—Number of districts and percentage of inhabitants according to size of the districts; Panama, 1930 to 1950

Size of district by inhabitants	1930 Number of districts	1930 Percent of inhabitants	1950 Number of districts	1950 Percent of inhabitants
Less than 2,500	10	4.1	4	0.8
2,500– 4,999	23	19.3	12	5.6
5,000– 7,499	13	17.7	21	16.3
7,500– 9,999	6	11.2	6	6.7
10,000–14,999	5	12.7	10	14.9
15,000 or more	5	35.0	11	55.7

Table 10.[35]—The change between 1940 and 1950 of the relative percentage of persons classified as rural as compared with those classified as urban

Province	1940 Urban	1940 Rural	1950 Urban	1950 Rural	Change of rural percentage
Bocas del Toro	22.2	77.8	20.1	79.9	+2.1
Coclé	12.1	87.9	13.4	86.6	−1.3
Colón	56.8	43.2	58.0	42.0	−1.2
Chiriquí	14.5	85.5	18.5	81.5	−4.0
Darién	0.0	100.0	0.0	100.0	0.0
Herrera	12.6	87.4	19.5	80.5	−6.9
Los Santos	8.2	91.8	8.6	91.4	−0.4
Panama	72.1	27.9	70.3	29.7	−1.8
Veraguas	6.7	93.3	7.4	92.6	−0.7
Total republic	33.8	66.2	35.9	64.1	−2.1

parts of the country is forcing migration of the people to less populated rural regions and to the cities.

A further indication of this may be seen in the following comparison of the change from 1940 to 1950 of the relative percent of urban and rural dwellers by province.

Table 10 indicates a number of points of interest. First, the Province of Panama, which one would expect to show a relative increase of urban over rural, actually shows a relative decline in the number of urban dwellers. The

---

[34] Taken from Census 1950a, Table 6, p. 5.   [35] Data from Census 1950a and 1940.

two provinces which show a marked increase in urban over rural dwellers are Chiriquí and Herrera. This reflects in part the tremendous growth which the towns of David, Puerto Armuelles, Chitré, Pesé and some others have had during this period and since 1930. Elsewhere, La Chorrera in the Province of Panama and Santiago in Veraguas have had great increases in urban population, as have Panama City and Colón. In these regions, however, these urban increases seem to have almost been equalled by corresponding rural increases. Urban increases in the Interior of the country reflect a growing national economy in this period. The figures for Darién, which have been taken from the 1940 and 1950 Censuses, fail to note that the town of La Palma is recorded as having a population of 1,703 in 1950, and therefore could be classified as urban. If this

Table 11.[36]—Change in density of population by provinces from 1911 to 1950

Province	Area in Km²	People per Km²					Increase in density 1911–50
		1911	1920	1930	1940	1950	
Total country	74,010	4.5	6.0	6.3	8.4	10.9	6.4
Bocas del Toro	9,086	2.5	3.0	1.7	1.8	2.5	0.0
Coclé	3,807	9.2	11.9	12.7	14.6	19.2	10.0
Colón	7,279	4.4	8.0	7.9	10.7	12.4	8.0
Chiriquí	9,564	6.6	8.0	8.0	11.6	14.4	7.8
Darién	15,525	0.6	0.7	0.9	1.0	0.9	0.3
Herrera	1,470	15.7	19.7	21.1	25.9	34.1	18.4
Los Santos	3,655	8.2	9.5	11.3	13.6	16.8	8.6
Panama	11,530	5.4	8.5	9.9	15.0	21.5	16.1
Veraguas	12,094	4.9	5.5	5.8	7.0	8.8	3.9

were done, Darién would have an 11.6% urban population for that year and an 83.4% rural population.

There is a further consequence of the increase in population which should be tabulated here. This is the increase in population density which has occurred in the various provinces.

It is of interest to note in Table 11 that Herrera has not only shown the greatest increase in density, but has had the highest density of any province of Panama since the first census. Herrera, Coclé, and Los Santos have remained among the top four provinces in density during this whole period, being displaced only by the increase in population of the Province of Panama. The density of Chiriquí is relatively low since some of the province is in the Indian Culture Area and very underpopulated. The rest of Chiriquí, could an estimate be made, would probably have a density more comparable to that of Coclé.

The growth in the rural population of Panama which is demonstrated in the comparative census reports makes knowledge of this population all the more

[36] From 1950a Census, Table 4, p. 4; the calculated increases from 1911 to 1950 do not appear on the original table.

critical. The fact that this growth is occurring in the entire region of the Panamanian countryman, although in some regions more than in others, means that the future will see many changes in the ways of life of these people. Not only are some moving to the larger towns, but there is considerable movement into the yet thinly populated sections of the country. These regions are at present primarily the Provinces of Panama, the southern portion of Veraguas on the Azuero Peninsula, and Bocas del Toro. The areas of overcrowding are the eastern coast of the Azuero Peninsula, extending up into Coclé, and certain parts of Chiriquí.

In terms of climate and geography, the distribution of the Panamanian countryman population has its heaviest concentration in the region of least rainfall. The eastern Los Santos, Herrera, and Coclé coast are a region of under 60 inches of rainfall per year. The rest of the area has between 60 and 100 inches. This region of 60 to 100 inches extends from the Costa Rican border east along the Pacific coastal slope down to approximately the latitude of Jaqué. This medium rainfall region is also the savanna country of Panama. It is generally rolling and broken hills, with occasionally flat plains along the coast. It may be of some significance that the Pacific slope and coastal region to the east of the Canal Zone, while not now heavily populated, is recorded as having a climate not too dissimilar to that which the Panamanian countryman is accustomed to in the Interior. Possibilities of colonization should be explored.

The Bocas del Toro, northern Veraguas, Colón, and Darién areas of Panama are essentially humid mountain slopes and tropical rain forest. The rainfall varies from 100 inches to over 140. At present, these regions are sparsely populated, mainly with Indian groups, although the Colón coast in the immediate vicinity of the canal, and scattered to the east and west, have aggregates of non-Indian peoples. It seems likely that except where there are centers already established, this region will not be populated as rapidly as that which is more similar to the Interior.[37]

Settlers and the contemporary mestizo population in Panama have generally avoided the mountainous and the highly humid regions. The main exceptions to this have been in the coffee producing region of Chiriquí, and the Colón settlements to the east and west of the Canal.

Racially, the Panamanian countryman population varies between three extremes: Indian, negro and white. The population is in general mestizo, manifesting varying characteristics of these three types. The white population tends to be dominant among the upper class and in certain regions of the country, such as Los Santos. The negro component, stemming from the slave population brought in during the colonial period and in some places from admixtures with the Antillean populations which have come in since the beginning of the century, seems strongest in the regions immediately to the east and west of the Canal Zone, in certain places along the Coclé coast, and scattered elsewhere, such as on the Chiriquí coastal plain. The Indian component seems strongest throughout

---

[37] This data on climate and geography is taken from Rubio 1950, Sauer 1950a, and from the writer's observations.

the backlands of the Interior, in Panama, Veraguas, Coclé and Chiriquí. Table 5 provides the information recorded by the 1940 Census. The two provincial areas which are said to have the highest percentages of white population are Chiriquí and Los Santos. The major tendency in Panama, as was noted in the 1940 Census, is towards a mestizoization of the population. The meaning of the term "mestizo" in this context refers to any sort of racial mixture, not merely the white-Indian mixture to which the term usually applies.

The sex proportions are very different in the urban and rural regions.

Table 12 shows the marked proportion of women over men in urban regions, and the even more marked number of men over women in the rural regions. This variation is not so marked in comparison with the figures for the country as a whole. Nevertheless, the differences between 1940 and 1950 show a great

Table 12.[38]—Number of women per 100 men for rural and urban regions

	1911	1940	1950
Total country	93.7	94.9	96.5
Urban	—	100.9	106.9
Rural	—	91.5	91.3

Table 13.[39]—Relative change in proportions of racial components of population, 1911, 1940

	1911	1940
Mestizo	66.1%	71.8%
Negro	16.8	14.6
White	16.0	12.2
Other	1.1	1.4

increase in the proportional number of women in the urban regions, but do not show a corresponding decrease in the proportion in the rural population. The trend for the country as a whole, taking the changes between 1911, 1940 and 1950, indicate that the relative number of women is increasing.

The evident increase in the population of the country as a whole may be related to the fact that the mestizo population seems to show different characteristics than does the negro population in this respect, and the mestizo population is growing.

Table 13 shows an increase in the mestizo component of the population between 1911 and 1940. The 1940 Census shows a great divergency between the negro population and the mestizo population with respect to proportions between the sexes.

For the mestizo population as a whole, in 1940, there is almost a balance between the sexes; but for the negro population, there is a markedly higher

---
[38] Data taken from Census 1940, 1950; data on rural-urban for 1911 not given.
[39] Calculated from Census 1940, Table 16, p. 95.

number of men. Table 14 also points out that in 1940 the relatively higher number of women in the cities seems to be primarily a mestizo trait. While within the negro group, there was a much higher proportion of women in the cities than in the rural population, the actual proportion is still very much under that of the mestizos.

This relatively higher proportion of men than women in the mestizo and negro rural populations is of considerable significance. It tends to confirm reports which the writer received in the field that the women who had no adequate means of support would go to look for work in the cities. Since in the population as a whole there are fewer women than men (Table 12), it does not

Table 14.[40]—Number of women per 100 men in mestizo and negro populations, 1940

	Mestizo	Negro
Total	99.4	90.0
Urban	115.2	94.9
Rural	93.2	73.3

Table 15.[41]—Civil status, by percentage, of men and women of rural and urban populations

	Rural Men	Rural Women	Urban Men	Urban Women	Total Men	Total Women
Single	48.1	38.5	52.1	46.8	50.0	42.1
Common-law	33.1	37.4	17.9	18.8	26.8	29.2
Married	16.6	17.9	27.6	25.7	20.8	21.3
Widowed	2.3	6.0	2.0	8.1	2.2	7.0
Divorced	0.1	0.2	0.4	0.6	0.2	0.4
Total	100.0	100.0	100.0	100.0	100.0	100.0

seem demographically inevitable that there will not be enough women to go around. Instead, we must look to the social and economic organization of the country dwellers to account for this movement.

The 1940 Census provides information on the relative number of people who were single, lived in common-law marriage, were married, widowed and divorced.

Table 15 shows that there is a much higher percentage of common-law alliances among rural men and women than among the urbanites. As will be noted later in the discussion of the rural family, this may account for a certain amount of feminine emigration from the rural areas.

While there are no data available on the number of common-law marriages in 1911, a comparison is made in the 1940 Census which includes single and common-law as a single group. Table 16 shows this comparison. It is evident that

[40] Census 1940, Table 17-A.   [41] 1940 Census, Table 21.

during this time span there has been almost no change in the relative number of married people as opposed to the single and common-law people. The situation reported for 1940 can be considered to be of long standing, approximately in the proportions which are found in 1940.

Table 16.[42]—Comparison, by percentages, of civil status in 1911 and 1940

	1911 Men	1911 Women	1940 Men	1940 Women
Single	75.8	71.2	76.8	71.3
Married	21.2	20.6	20.8	21.3
Widowed	3.0	8.2	2.2	7.0
Divorced	—	—	0.2	0.4
Total	100.0	100.0	100.0	100.0

Table 17.[43]—Comparisons, by percentages, of civil status of racial groups, 1940

	Mestizo Men	Mestizo Women	Negro Men	Negro Women	White Men	White Women
Single	51.0	43.3	52.8	43.3	43.0	35.2
Common-law	30.4	32.4	23.5	25.3	18.1	18.5
Married	16.3	17.7	21.0	22.9	36.0	36.5
Widowed	2.1	6.3	2.4	8.1	2.4	9.1
Divorced	0.2	0.3	0.3	0.4	0.5	0.4
Total	100.0	100.0	100.0	100.0	100.0	100.0

Table 17a.[43a]—Comparative percentage figures on civil status by provinces, 1950

Province	Single	Married	Common-law	Other	Total
Bocas del Toro	46.8%	23.4%	24.1%	5.7%	100.0%
Coclé	46.2	16.2	32.6	5.0	100.0
Colón	43.6	26.6	22.5	7.3	100.0
Chiriquí	48.9	19.2	28.1	3.8	100.0
Darién	46.2	10.0	40.9	2.9	100.0
Herrera	44.6	25.1	25.5	4.8	100.0
Los Santos	43.4	19.8	31.3	5.5	100.0
Panama	46.8	24.8	22.6	5.8	100.0
Veraguas	46.1	17.8	31.2	4.9	100.0
Total republic	46.2%	21.9%	26.6%	5.3%	100.0%

[42] From 1940 Census, Table 21. [43] Census of 1940, Table 23. [43a] Census 1954.

It is of interest that the predominance of common-law alliances over formal marriages is evidently more characteristic of the mestizo population than either the negro or white.

Table 17 shows the varying proportions which were recorded in 1940 for these racial groups. It is of note that none of the racial groups in themselves have as high percentages of common-law marriages as are to be found in the rural population. (Compare Tables 15 and 17)

The lowest provincial figures in 1950 were Panama and Colón; but in both these provinces, the low figures are due specifically to the large urban aggregates; in the smaller towns and rural areas, the common-law union percentages are much higher, usually ranging from 35% to 50% or over.

Aside from Darién, the provinces with the relatively highest percentage of common-law unions are in the provinces of Coclé, Veraguas, and Los Santos. Herrera, which is neighbor to all these provinces, has a relative low percentage.

3. LAND UTILIZATION[44]

The predominant form of land utilization among Panama countrymen is right of usufruct. Of the 236,611.9 hectares of land in use reported by census takers (this does not include those in which there was no response), 17.9% was titled and in private hands, another 12.1% was rented, and 59.0% was under usufruct. The remaining 11.0% was mixed.[45] This 59% of the land belonged to the government, as does most of the unused land of the republic. Permission is given to use this land upon request to the local municipal authorities or through the authorities of the *caseríos*. Usually, this permission is given for two years at the most, and theoretically, it does not include the right to plant any permanent crops. All harvests are supposed to be annual. Actually, this is overlooked at times in cases such as sugar cane, bananas, and coconuts. Many of the renters of the land also plant annual crops, so taking the usufructuaries and part of the renters together we have possibly over 70% of the cultivated land under short-term, shifting, cultivation.

Table 18 shows the relative percent of each type of utilization in terms of the number of reported exploitations. The provinces of Coclé, Colón, Chiriquí, and Veraguas are all fairly similar with respect to the relative number of owned, used, rented, and mixed exploitations. Herrera and Los Santos vary markedly, however, the former in having a much higher percent of owners, and the latter in having a higher percent of renters. The Province of Panama has a slightly higher percent of both owned and rented exploitations in comparison with the major group, but lower than in either Herrera or Los Santos.

With respect to the amount of land in each province under cultivation, Table 19 supplies data on the percent of the land in each province which is in use and which is under cultivation. It will be seen from this table that the provinces which have the relatively highest percent of their land both in use and under

---

[44] It is not possible to go extensively into the subject of land usufruct and ownership in Panama. Ofelia Hooper (1945) has treated the subject in greater detail and the reader is referred to her work for additional information.   [45] Census 1950b.

cultivation are Herrera, Los Santos, and Coclé. This of course reflects the fact that except for the Province of Panama, these three provinces have the highest population density of any in Panama (see Table 11). From Table 20 it may be seen that these three provinces also have the fewest average number of hectares per exploitation of any in the country.

Heavier population and the more restricted area have produced a divergent landholding situation in Herrera and Los Santos. To this, however, must be

Table 18.[46]—Percentage of reported exploitations according to class of operator in certain provinces

Province	Land worked by:			Mixed	Total
	Owner	Usufructu-aries	Renter		
Coclé	9.4	78.2	4.8	7.6	100.0
Colón	9.1	74.3	8.8	7.8	100.0
Chiriquí	9.8	71.8	8.9	9.5	100.0
Herrera	25.8	53.2	6.7	14.3	100.0
Los Santos	11.3	57.5	18.5	12.7	100.0
Panama	12.9	67.9	10.2	9.0	100.0
Veraguas	11.0	75.2	6.1	7.7	100.0

Table 19.[47]—Percentage of area in use and under cultivation in certain provinces

	Area of province in hectares	Percent of area in use	Percent of area under cultivation
Coclé	308,700	41.1	8.95
Colón	727,900	4.8	1.9
Chiriquí	956,400	35.9	5.7
Herrera	147,000	82.7	12.6
Los Santos	365,500	44.2	7.5
Panama	1,153,000	11.8	2.6
Veraguas	1,209,400	15.0	4.5
Total republic	7,401,000	15.6	3.3

added a further fact. Herrera and Los Santos have had a more Spanish population than have the provinces of Panama, Coclé, Colon and Veraguas (Chiriquí is very much mixed). Consequently it may be that historically the western concept of ownership as opposed to mere usufruct may have taken a firmer stand in these provinces than elsewhere in the country. If we take the combined percentages of renters and owners from Table 18, we find that Herrera has 32.5%, Los Santos 29.8%, and next in descending order is Panama with 23.1%. Coclé, Colón, Chiriquí and Veraguas vary between 14.2 and 18.7%.

Of critical importance in this situation of the predominance of usufruct over

[46] Census 1950c. [47] Census 1950c, 1950d.

other forms of tenancy are the facts that the agriculture is shifting, and following from this, any given individual can handle a relatively restricted amount of land per year. Table 21 provides us with information on the relative size of the landholdings of the different types of exploitation. It will be seen from this table that the exploitations of people who own their own land tend to be larger than those who have usufruct; and those with usufruct, in turn, tend to have slightly larger holdings than do those who rent. This order doubtless reflects

Table 20.[48]—Number of cultivated hectares per exploitation in certain provinces

Province	Number of exploitations	Number of cultivated hectares per exploitation
Coclé	10,797	2.5
Colón	3,864	3.6
Chiriquí	17,338	3.1
Herrera	8,776	2.1
Los Santos	12,821	2.1
Panama	10,714	2.7
Veraguas	18,187	3.0
Total republic	85,363	2.5

Table 21.[49]—Percentage of exploitations according to size and type of operator for exploitations of over 1 hectare

Size in hectares	Owner	Usufructuary	Renters	Mixed	All exploitations
No. of exploitations	12,058	57,513	7,981	7,921	85,473
1.0– 1.9	12.9	23.6	33.0	9.5	21.8
2.0– 4.9	17.6	33.3	29.9	25.9	30.3
5.0– 9.9	18.6	20.2	14.3	22.1	19.7
10.0–19.9	19.1	12.8	12.6	19.6	14.3
20.0–49.9	18.1	7.5	7.8	14.7	9.6
50.0 and over	13.7	2.8	2.4	8.2	4.3
Total	100.0	100.0	100.0	100.0	100.0

some difference in wealth in the three types of groups. Those who have usufruct can usually work as much land as they are able, and can employ additional labor only if they have the funds to do so. The people who rent land usually must do so because in their particular region there is not enough available government land. They must pay in some manner for the right to use the land they work, and therefore, get relatively less out of it. Those who own land, on the other hand, usually can employ labor, and work larger amounts. It should be noted that Table 21 does not include any exploitations of under one hectare.[50]

[48] Census 1950d. [49] Census 1950b.
[50] Census 1950d, notes that there are some 20,000 exploitations of under one hectare in extension.

It was estimated to the writer by informants in Panama that under shifting cultivation a single man could work a hectare or more of land by himself fairly easily. A man with family presumably could work up to two or three, and with an occasional field hand, the amount again would be boosted. This generalization is fairly well supported by the figures in Table 21. About 57% of the usufructuaries work under 5 hectares of land and about 63% of the renters work this quantity. Only slightly over 30% of the owners, however, have exploitations this small.

The data gathered during the survey agree with the general picture given by the figures of the 1950 Census. In Santo Domingo it was said that people tend to consider the land their own even though they frequently do not have titles to it. The land is fenced in when necessary, and a person retains perpetual usufruct. This situation stands even though it is frequently necessary to permit a piece of land to rest 4 or 5 years before it can be cultivated again. In Los Pozos and Ocú it was reported that while there is still a certain amount of government land not utilized, much of this is quite distant from living sites and in many cases is badly broken and difficult to work. Consequently, if a person does not own land, which many do, he usually prefers to rent it than to have to make the regular trips necessary to take up free land. This situation apparently extends at least as far west as Montijo. In Soná and Corozal, however, most people were usufructuaries. There were some fairly large *haciendas*, but in general, sufficiency of land did not become a problem until one reached Chiriquí.

Along the Chiriquí coastal belt most of the land is in the hands of large cattle *haciendas* and is used for pasturage. This situation is becoming worse for the countryman due to a system of rental which is found both in Chiriquí and on the Azuero Peninsula. It is very common for a landowner to give a piece of land in rent for perhaps two years, with the only payment being that at the end of two years the renter leaves the land planted in pasturage grass and fenced in. In this way the *hacienda* owner assures himself of more pasturage land with no cash outlay on his part (see Appendix, #2). While the writer collected no information in Panama on the type of pasturage grasses most commonly used, from the situation found in certain other parts of the Pacific coastal region of Central America, it is unlikely that once a strong grass is planted, the *monte*, or weed and brush, can again take over the land. Planting in pasturage, then, usually effectively removes the land from further use by the small cultivator and practically guarantees that it will be cattle land for some time in the future. This situation has gone so far in some places, such as Remedios, that the countryman has no alternative but to work as labor on the cattle *hacienda* or to migrate to another part of the country where government lands are still available. It is a peculiar situation, in a country where under 16% of the land is in use (see Table 19) that there should be significant internal migrations in search of cultivatable lands.

Moving north and east from Herrera, the situation remains fairly difficult for the countryman. The districts of Natá and Aguadulce have large *haciendas* of sugar, while these two districts together with Penonomé and Antón have considerable cattle production. Table 22 shows that of the reported number of cattle exploitations, only 6.7% have more than 20 head of cattle. This means that where there are good sized herds of cattle, they are in the hands of relatively few producers. It is the common situation in Central America that a person cannot live off a few head of cattle. If the land is limited, the individual must depend upon agriculture and not livestock.

In the remainder of Coclé, Panamá, Veraguas, and Colón, there is still a good deal of government land available. Panama, particularly, on both sides of the canal has seen quite a bit of immigration during the recent years by countrymen from the Azuero Peninsula and the more crowded parts of Chiriquí.

Where usufruct is the most common form of land tenure, the land is usually used from one to two years. The actual duration of usage of a particular piece of land depends upon the climate, the quality of the local soil, and to some degree

Table 22.[51]—Percentage of number of reported exploitations according to the number of head of cattle
(*Based on sample of 5% of exploitations of under 100 hectares and all exploitations of over 100 hectares*)

Number of head of cattle	Number of reported exploitations
Total number	85,388
None	63.6
- 1	2.6
2- 5	12.6
6-10	8.3
11-20	6.2
21-50	4.6
Over 50	2.1
Total	100.0

upon custom. The countryman notes well the fact that a second crop off a piece of recently cleared land never produces as well as the first; consequently, he usually plans to shift his cultivations frequently. The amount of time during which the land is allowed to grow up in bush and weeds again also depends upon various factors. In general, three years seems to be the average length of time, but in some regions it rests only two, and in others up to four of five.

No matter what the laws of Panama may be with respect to usufruct, homesteading, and selling of government land, there is a great deal of variations in the countryside in knowledge of who can do what with the land. It was evident in the rural region behind Chorrera that many of the countrypeople did not know that it was possible to purchase the lands they were using. They believed that the land would remain with the government in perpetuity and that they would have continued usufruct merely by making the proper requests through the local authorities. There is no such misapprehension in Chorrera itself; there

---
[51] Census 1950c.

the writer talked with municipal officials and the method by which one can purchase any of the government lands was made quite clear. In Dolega it was said that merely staking out a piece of land, and putting up any sort of boundary marker gave the individual claim over the land forever. It was not necessary that he use the land immediately. There are many *Chiricanos* who, feeling the pressure of the expanding *haciendas* of the coastal area, are moving up into the borders of the Guaymí Indian region and staking out claims in lands which were until recently held by the Indians. This, of course, is forcing the Indians further back into the mountains and into lands which are less hospitable to agriculture.

In general, Panama is a country which has enough land. Even with the expanding population, it is in specific areas such as the eastern Azuero Peninsula, coastal Chiriquí and Coclé, that the rise in population by itself, or in combination with the existence of large *hacienda* holdings, is forcing people to work as daily labor or migrate. While the situation is not critical yet, it will become so in the future.

4. AGRICULTURE

The food crops cultivated by the Panamanian countrymen have come down to him from both the Old World and the New.

In Table 23 the foods have been divided into two groups on the basis of general importance in the economy of the countryman. In general, corn and rice are the principal crops in the agrarian economy; the tubers, yuca, yautia, and yams, form a smaller portion of the diet, but are found throughout the country in some quantity; beans are found almost everywhere although some regions show more intensive production than do others. Pigeon peas are widespread although it was reported occasionally that they were not cultivated.

The distinction made between foods of first importance and second importance is based on the amount of time which must be expended in the reproduction and importance by quantity in the diet of the people. There are many crops which are produced not only for consumption, but also as a cash crop. In this group would fall oranges and other citrus fruits, bananas and plantains, coconuts, coffee, and sugar cane. There are also a number of products which are used generally, but are not produced in any great quantity. Chili peppers and *achiote* are products of this class.

It is not the purpose of the present essay to analyze the agricultural production of either the countrymen of Panama or of the country as a whole. A study of this nature is outside the scope of the present report. Nevertheless, there are certain important agricultural characteristics of the various regions of Panama which should be taken into account in describing the agriculture. The Colón region, for example, specializes in the production of bananas and coconuts. The Province of Panama, aside from staples, produces oranges and coconuts in some quantity. Coclé continues the zone of orange production, but specializes particularly in sugar cane. Herrera and Los Santos specialize in sugar cane, avocados, chili, and tomatoes, as well as in corn, and Los Santos also has a high production of rice, beans, plantains and coconuts. Besides the staples, Veraguas produces considerable quantities of bananas, plantains, oranges, and coconuts. Chiriquí not only produces high quantities of the staples, but also has the most diversified production of any province in the country. It is among the first four provinces in the production of sugar cane, bananas, plantains, oranges, avocados, chili, tomatoes, and is in addition the main producer of potatoes, cabbages, and lettuce. Among the non-comestible crops, tobacco is produced primarily in Chiriquí and Los Santos, and a little cotton is produced through Veraguas-east Chiriquí

Table 23.[52]—List of foods of contemporary importance in agriculture of the countryman, according to source of origin

	Present in the New World at the time of conquest	Not present in the New World at the time of conquest
Foods of first importance	Corn (*maíz*) Yuca Yautia (*hotóes*) Beans (*frijoles*)	Yam (*ñame*) Rice (*arroz*) Sugar cane (*caña de azúcar*) Plantains (*plátanos*) Banana (*banana, guineo*) Pigeon peas (*gandú*)
Foods of second importance	Chili peppers (*ají*) Pineapple (*piña*) Avocados (*aguacates*) *Papaya* Coconuts (*cocos*) Sweet potato (*camote*) Tomato (*tomate*) Pejibaye (*pixbal*) Soursop (*guanábana*) Guava (*guayaba*) *Achiote*	Citric fruits Breadfruit (*fruta pan*) Coffee (*café*) Kaffir corn (*millo*) Broadbean (*haba*) Ginger (*gengibre*) *Mangos* (See Appendix, #3)

region for thread. From this, we can distinguish certain major regions by types. Chiriquí is a large producer and the most diversified. Colón specializes more in tropical products; Coclé, particularly Aguadulce and Natá, specialize in sugar cane, while western Panama and Coclé specialize in citrus fruits. Herrera and Los Santos and southern Veraguas are high in grain staples, as well as in tomatoes and sugar, and Veraguas and the rest of the Interior are relatively higher in the production of tubers (yuca and yams).[53]

Among other crops are the pejibaye palm nut. Pejibaye, pronounced *pixvá*

[52] List taken from writer's survey; identification from INCAP, 1951; sources from Sauer, 1950b; Sauer does not believe that the evidence claimed for origin of the tomato, plantain, and banana is conclusive, although the general opinion is as they are listed above. While Johnson, 1948b, p. 232, lists the *hotoe* as being of foreign origin, Sauer, 1950b, p. 511, lists it as a native American crop. The terms in parenthesis are those used in Panama. The scientific names appear in INCAP, 1951, and Sauer, 1950b.

[53] This information is taken from Census 1950d.

(*pifá* in Dolega) in the countryside, has a distribution which generally limits it to Veraguas, and to the uplands of Chiriquí, Herrera, Los Santos, Coclé and Panama. It is quite important in Colón, but not used by the Margarita people near Chepo. It is generally not used on the Chorrera-Coclé, and east Azuero coast.

Millet was reported in use by the Guaymí in eastern Chiriquí, but was reported as a countryman crop only in San Francisco. It is referred to locally as *millo*.

The basic agricultural method of the countryman is the slash-and-burn, shifting cultivation which presumably has been inherited from the Indians. The cultivation cycle usually starts in January, or even as early as December, with the cutting of the new land to be cultivated. This usually is carried on into February, varying with the locale and the individual. This process consists in felling the trees and cutting down the bush. The dead bush and trees are then left until March or April to dry, at which time they are burned. The field at time of planting is usually an area studded with stumps, and the larger trees which have not burned are scattered at odd intervals. The cleaning and burning process in some places is referred to as the *roza* (see Hooper 1945, pp. 168–172 for other terminology). In fields which are being used for the second or third year, the cleaning is much easier since it is only the year's growth of *monte*, weeds and bushes, which must be cut and burned.

Planting ordinarily begins around the time of the beginning of the rainy season in April. Even in Colón, where there is rain throughout the year, custom dictates that the corn and rice are planted at about this time. Planting of corn and tuber crops is usually done after the rains begin. It is common in some regions to plant rice an estimated two weeks before the rains start. It was said by informants that the rice needed this extra time in the ground. If they miscalculate, and the rains come unusually late, then the rice is lost and must be replanted. The amount and type of cultivation and cleaning which is done depends upon local custom and local conditions. At least one cleaning, called *deshierba* in some regions, *rastro* in others, is usually done. The time of maturation of rice and corn varies from between three and one half to five or six months. Corn is usually ready by the end of the third month or at least by the end of the fourth, but following the custom found elsewhere in Central America, much, if not most, of the corn is left to dry on the stalk until five or six months have gone by. It is then harvested and stored.

It is the custom over most of Panama to have two different plantings and harvests during the course of the year, and in some places even three. The fact that there are two or three plantings does not mean that there is a yield of two or three times the amount harvested from the first planting. Only in the production of beans are the plantings after the first larger and more important than the first. While less than 38% of the total corn production, and only 14% of the total rice production, in 1950, came from the second plantings, almost 60% of the total bean production came from harvests other than the first.[54] The different

---

[54] Census 1950d.

plantings and harvests are distinguished by different names. In Chorrera, the first is known as *del tiempo*, and the second is *de postrera;* in Ocú, they are called the *primera coa*, and *segunda coa* or *postrera*. Generally from the Azuero Peninsula to the west they are called the *roza* (since it follows the cutting and burning) and the *postrera*. In Montijo, where the three crops were reported to be used, the first two were *roza* and *postrera*, and the third was *rastrojo*. (See Appendix, # 4.)

The second planting usually follows immediately after the first harvest. If the first harvest is in August or September, then the planting will be in August, September or October. The harvests from the second grain planting usually come in December or January.

Beans in general are grown more in the mountains than on the coastal plains. It is common in some places to plant them along with the grain crops in April or May, but in other regions they are planted in October or November, usually in a field recently cleared of rice.

Mixed plantings are very common in Panama. Yuca, yams, or yautias are frequently sown together with rice or corn. The writer could find no general rule with respect to these crop mixtures. It seemed to be a matter of individual preference and perhaps local custom. When such mixed planting was done, the usual reason given was that they "grew better;" elsewhere, if asked why they did not plant mixed crops, the answer would again frequently be because they "grow better."

There is no artificial or animal fertilizer commonly used. About the only soil improvement which is practiced is to fold the rice, corn, and sometimes other dry leftovers of the yield back into the ground. Of course, the shifting agriculture itself is intended as a means by which the land regains strength, and it was reported occasionally during the survey that some people would switch a piece of land from rice to corn, or the reverse, or to some other crop, in order to permit the field to produce more. But such "crop rotation," if it can be dignified with that name, seems to be haphazard and not extensively practised. The countryman, as was mentioned earlier, is conscious that using a piece of land for too long reduces its productive capacity. While much has been written against the practice of burning of land, it still remains as the most effective technique in the hands of the countryman to accomplish an arduous task.

The countrymen cultivate a number of crops which last more than a year. Sugar cane is a two year crop at a minimum, and can produce up to four or five years under the local techniques. However, sugar cane production has been curtailed in many parts of the country by lack of buyers and processing equipment. It is mainly in Coclé, Herrera, Los Santos, and Chiriquí that production is fairly high at present. Bananas and plantains are both crops which, provided they are given a little care, will produce annually. They require a minimum of time, however, in comparison with grains, tubers, and other field crops. Coconut and pejibaye palms are frequently planted, but the writer did not have occasion to see large holdings of them. Usually they were scattered here and there; an owner had to cover a fairly large area to harvest his coconuts.

In general, the countryman finds most of the year occupied with work in the fields. The other things which must be done, production of domestic and other utilitarian implements and the selling of goods, are done in the short interim periods. This does not mean that he is constantly busy. Much depends upon the amount of land he has available and the quality of the crop he expects as to how much labor he must expend in getting enough to live on. Many must put in time as paid labor in order to earn enough.

The implements which the countryman uses in his agriculture are few. The ax and the machete are indispensable for those who must annually clear new land. For planting, the *coa*, dibble or digging stick, is used. Over most of the country, there is an alternative to the *coa*, the *chusa*, which is usually used only in the planting of rice. The difference between the two is that the *coa* has a pointed metal end while the *chusa* has a flat end, also of metal. (See Appendix, # 5) For the *deshierba*, or cleaning during the period of cultivation, a curved machete called variously *champa, mocha,* and *daga* is used in some areas. For cutting larger weeds, a hooked stick, the *garabato*, is used to gather the weeds together so that they may more easily be cut with the machete. Neither the hoe nor the wooden plough seems to be used in Panama, and the metal plough is used only on larger plantations. In the harvest of rice, a small knife is frequently used. Sometimes this is called the *uña*, since the fingernail is sometimes employed for the same purpose. In Ocú, there are two such implements, one called the *camarón* and the other the *jaiba*. The first of these is strapped in the palm of the hand, the other on the inside of the wrist. For carrying seeds when planting, the countryman usually ties a half gourd to his waist.

Agricultural work involves significant social organization forms as well as crops, implements, and climate. The countrymen have various ways of joining together to accomplish their tasks. Principally these are: employed labor; exchange labor, called *peón-por-peón;* large gatherings in exchange labor, called *peonadas;* and large gatherings to aid someone, called a *junta*. People also work individually and with members of their own family.

When labor is done individually, a man may work by himself, with some immediate male relatives, or in some areas, with his wife. In exchange labor, or the *peón-por-peón* system, a man will work for another for one day or on one piece of work; later, the other man will return the labor in quantity. Basically, the exchange labor system is looked upon as being the poor man's way of obtaining field help; he cannot afford to hire a man, so he works in exchange for one. Hence we have expressions such as, *"voy a ganar un peón"* (I am going to earn a *peón*), when one goes first to work for another; this means that the other person will owe the work of a *peón;* and the expression, *"voy a pagar un peón"* (I am going to pay a *peón*), which means that a person is going to work for another to pay off the debt of work which he owes.

Exchange labor is sometimes done with two or three people. When more are involved, it is no longer merely exchange labor, but becomes the *peonada*. In this kind of labor, up to 30 people, sometimes more, but usually less, will come to work for a man, and then the man will owe an equal amount of labor to each of the participants. The *peonada* is said to differ from the *junta* principally in that the latter involves no obligation on the part of the sponsor to return the work of the others. It was reported in Soná that the *peonada* is gradually replacing the *junta;* the latter was the older form, and usually involved many more people than the *peonada*. Also, *juntas* were held more rarely, perhaps only once a month. Today the *junta* evidently is found around Ocú and occasionally in Veraguas. The difference between a *junta* and a *peonada* makes them sometimes hard to distinguish in practice. Both, for example, may have a fiesta with music and dancing following the work. Both usually include the provision of food and drink by the sponsor. Most of the so-called *juntas* which are held today, however, would be better called *peonadas*. In some cases, they are no more than a group form of exchange labor with the sponsor responsible for no refreshments at all. In some places, the *junta* or *peonada* (in these cases it was not clear which) were held not merely with the object of getting work done, but also with the object of having the dance and general fiesta which followed. This seemed to be the case in parts of the Chorrera-Coclé region. In these cases they are held only on Saturdays which permits the participants to recover from their hangovers on the following Sunday. Saturday was said to be the principal day in the Chorrera region and in El Espino; elsewhere, it was said that such work groups met on any day of the week. (See Appendix, #6 and #7)

While no specific data was gathered on the use of special customs in connection with work groups over most of Panama, it was reported from Dolega that there are certain patterned methods of returning from work and presenting the food to the workers. Also, in some places it was reported that the working group was used only in certain kinds of labor. In El Espino, it was said that only harvests and planting were times when men worked in groups; in Querévalo, it was reported that they were used in the original cleaning of a new piece of land as well. Elsewhere a work group apparently could be used in any kind of field activity.

Only the Colón-Chepo region seems to lack the working group pattern. In both Palmas Bellas and Chepo it was reported that no *juntas* were used and that the people much preferred to employ *peones*. This situation is seeing some change, especially in the Chepo region, with the influx of people from the other parts of the Interior. The countrymen of La Margarita de Chepo, originally from the Las Tablas area, do use the *junta*.

While it is not possible at present to determine whether the *peonada* grew directly out of the exchange labor pattern or the *junta* pattern, it seems clear that today it is directly related to the fact that the countryman can often not afford to actually employ *peones*. It should be noted in passing that, except for the large old-style *juntas*, most working groups are composed of people from a neighborhood. In Yayas Adentro, back of Chorrera, there were six different neighborhood groups that usually worked separately. In Zangüenga, near Yayas Adentro, the writer found that the entire *caserío* was out on a *junta* when he visited there. The size of a given group depends upon the popularity of the sponsor, the degree to which the other men are occupied, and the strength of the working group custom in the particular area. While there are almost always some relatives involved in a working group, it is more because people tend not to move too far from their original neighborhood to live; the fact that there are relatives involved is thus a function of the fact that relatives also happen to be neighbors, not that a person will particularly look for relatives.

In preparing the food and drink for the workers at a *peonada* or *junta*, it is customary for the women of the various participants to congregate at the home of the sponsor and to aid in the preparation of the *chicha* and various foods. In some places, the women also work in the *junta* itself, but this seems to be fairly rare. It was definitely reported only from Montijo.

With respect to the division of field labor between the sexes, there is some variation over Panama. In the Colón-Chepo region, women generally are not included in the field labor; it was reported from Chepo, however, that women would aid if needed. The only other region in which they are definitely excluded from such work seems to be the east coast of the Azuero Peninsula. In this respect, the migration of people from Los Santos and Herrera to the Chepo region will probably strengthen this regional difference. In Palmas Bellas the informant stressed that locally the women did no such work, but that the *naturales* further in the backlands did have their women work in the fields. In both El Espino and Sonadora women worked regularly in the fields. El Espino presents a special situation in that many of the men spend much time fishing, making the field work by the women more necessary. In the uplands of the Azuero Peninsula and in Veraguas, the work of the women seemed to be limited to special kinds of field activities, usually revolving around rice. In Los Pozos, it was reported that they worked only in the planting and harvest of rice; in Ocú, in the harvest of rice and beans; in Soná, in the planting, cultivation and harvest of rice; and in San Francisco, in the cultivation and harvest of rice and potatoes. In Corozal (Las Palmas) it was reported that they did not work in the fields, but this may be a local variation; in Remedios, it was again reported that they worked in the fields when necessary. (See Appendix, ≠ 7)

The pattern of women working in the fields seems in part to be an inheritance from the Indian pattern. Prior to the conquest, the Indian men of Panama were usually occupied in hunting and fishing rather than in agriculture, and the cultivation was considered a woman's task. Among the Guaymí, the women still play a very active part in agriculture. It is in the two regions most removed from the former Indian way of life, the Colón-Chepo region and coastal Herrera and Los Santos, where the women do not today work in the fields. In El Espino, the fact that the men today are occupied more in fishing than in agriculture seems a straight carry-over of the Indian pattern.

There are many threats to the success of agriculture in the life of the Panama countryman. Most important among these are the possible lack of rain and the variety of insects and animals which can damage the crops. In order to assure rain, *rogativas* are held over most of the Interior. These usually consist of a mass said in church, a procession. Where there are no *rogativas*, it is usually because there is no need for them, such as in Palmas Bellas, or because there was no priest available for some years to lead them, such as was reported in

Los Pozos and Querévalo. It may be, however, that the Colón-Chepo region differs from the rest of the country in this respect also because it was reported that Chepo used to have *rogativas*, but has them no longer.

Hooper[55] has discussed the various pests which threaten the crops of the countrymen and the reader is referred to her discussion for a full account. It will suffice to mention here that there are many varieties of insects as well as wild animals and domestic cattle which provide a constant problem.

5. OTHER EXPLOITATIONS

While agriculture is the single most important subsistence activity of the countryman, there are various other ways in which he obtains enough to live on. Principal among these are the keeping of livestock, hunting, fishing, exploitation of forest products, and where possible, special exploitations such as salt and charcoal.

Table 24.[56]—Number of animals per exploitation in certain provinces

Province	Cattle	Pigs	Chickens	Ducks	Turkeys
Coclé	5.3	0.9	15.3	0.8	0.7
Colón	1.9	1.3	18.3	1.2	0.2
Chiriquí	9.4	2.0	16.5	0.4	0.2
Herrera	9.2	2.6	17.9	1.0	0.1
Los Santos	9.2	3.4	22.8	1.0	0.2
Panama	2.8	1.0	21.4	1.1	0.5
Veraguas	6.0	2.4	20.0	1.4	0.3
Total republic	5.7	2.1	19.2	1.0	0.3

Although it is very common for a person to have a few cows and pigs, by no means all the countrymen have them. Table 22 shows that the relative number of exploitations which have no cattle is over 63% of the total. Another 15.2% have five or under, and 14.5% have between 6 and 20. Only 6.7% have over 20. Since these figures do not take into account some 20,000 exploitations under one hectare in size, we may estimate that of the total, probably considerably more than 63% have no cattle.

The raising of cattle for any substantial profit requires a fairly big herd; this, both because of the capital investment and the problem of sufficient land, is beyond the reach of the countryman. The area of the country where there are larger herds of cattle (see Table 24), Chiriquí, Herrera and Los Santos, are also areas where there is a scarcity of land for the countryman. Most of the countrymen who have cattle keep them to fatten and sell.

Pigs are much less important from the point of view of the total production of the country, but are more important in the lives of the countrymen. While the slaughtering of cattle is frequently restricted in the larger towns to certain

---
[55] 1945, pp. 183–186. [56] Census, 1950d.

people, anyone can kill a pig in his back yard. As a result, it is easier to get pork into the diet than it is to get beef. In general, reports indicate that there are more people who keep pigs than keep cattle.

Chickens are ubiquitous in Panama, as in the rest of Central America. However, in certain regions there is also a fairly high percentage of turkeys. The main turkey producing region runs from the Canal Zone west to Veraguas, back from the coast. Ducks are also kept in most parts of the Interior. There are rarely any shelters for chickens; they usually roost in trees.

Perhaps the most important animal to the countrymen is the horse. *Burros* are very rare in Panama except occasionally a jackass for breeding, and mules are almost as rare. The use of mules is restricted to large *haciendas* and generally the Chiriquí region. The countryman, when he has a beast of burden, has a horse. Horses are used as a means of travel, but more important as a means of transport of products from the home to the market. They are little used in the fields since the paths are frequently not good enough, and a man can usually handle the amount he would bring in. But between the home and the market, where the distance is much greater, the horse is a valuable aid. The writer has no figures at present on the number of such horses to be found in Panama, but it was his impression that within each local community there are a few people who keep a number of animals. Most people cannot afford horses in the first place, so the person who has some rents them out for a comfortable income.

Among the less important animals, goats were reported in small quantities from Montijo, Ocú, and Santo Domingo, and pigeons were kept in various places, as were parrots. No one reported the keeping of bees, although many collected wild honey for food and medicines.

The role of hunting in the life of the countryman varies greatly from one part of the country to another. Most areas evidently provide some deer and peccary (the *"saíno,"* identified by Gilmore[57] as the collared peccary, *Tayassu tajacu*, and the *puerco de monte*), rabbits and birds. The object of the hunt is frequently to do away with crop pests as much as to get meat to eat. Hunting is usually done with a shotgun or .22 rifle. The use of the bow and arrow is restricted to Indians. Birds are frequently caught with traps, usually a basket-like fall-trap called *tapón*. It was reported in Ocú that a pitfall may be used in deer hunting, either using a hole, or building a fence in front of a small canyon, and driving the deer to jump over the fence to his death. Hunting for the larger animals is frequently done at night. The hunter will wear a miner's lamp. The hunters will also wait by a cultivated field which they know is ripe to attract deer. For hunting peccaries they may search out a bathing place, and wait in hiding for the animal to appear.

The informant in Soná reported that in the Cañazas area, both Indians and countrymen will organize fairly large hunts known as *cazar en pasadero*; the landscape in this region has frequent deep cut water courses which are filled with shrubbery and trees. Through these go deer paths, *pasaderos*. The hunters

---
[57] 1950, p. 382.

may work in groups of ten or more; some wait on the path, while the others surround the string of woods and send in dogs to scare up deer. As the deer comes down the path, he is shot. Each person in a hunt like this will receive a portion, but the person who actually shot the deer gets the best portion. The hunters are usually neighbors or relatives. Dogs are also used in hunting peccaries.

In hunting rabbits the hunter may lie in wait, or use a stockade type trap with a door triggered to the bait. This is called a *chiquero*.

To the people living in the backlands, hunting frequently is an important economic activity as well as a way to do away with plant pests. In some regions it is used as a way to get cash, since the skins can be sold if they can reach the market.

Fishing generally plays a more important role than hunting in the lives of the countrymen. It is most important to those living near the sea coast who have fairly good sized streams running through their territory. In some communities, especially those near the ocean, more fish than meat is eaten. In El Espino the men spend a good part of their time throughout the year fishing. On the Atlantic coast, *tortuga* hunting is important, particularly in June and July when the *tortugas* come in to lay their eggs.

Ocean fishing is usually done with tidal weirs or from dugouts. The tidal weir, *chiquero* (stockade), is set up near the shore; when the tide comes in, the water covers the weir, and the fish can swim over it; as the tide recedes, the fish which were swimming within the *chiquero* are caught. This was reported from Montijo. Fishing from dugouts involves the use of nets and lines. It is sometimes done at night with a light, and the fish which is attracted may be killed with a machete.

Stream fishing is done in a number of different ways. The use of gunpowder, while prohibited, nevertheless continues to be an important technique. In some areas it has been used with such effectiveness that the fish population is practically non-existent. Since gunpowder can be elaborated at home with materials bought in the towns, it is hard to effectively stop this technique. (See Appendix, #8) Fish poisons are also fairly common. In Ocú, the bark of a tree called *manglio* is used; it is dried, ground, and sprinkled in the stream. There is another tree, the *manzanillo*, which is said not to be used in some places because it is supposed to be poisonous to man as well as to the fish. In Remedios and Soná the tuber of a vine called *cabeza negra* is ground up as a poison; also the sap of the *barabas*, and a plant called *oreja de mula*, are used. (The writer did not collect specimens of these plants and so cannot provide scientific identification.)

In Soná, an interesting method called *pescar con trueno* was reported. A large stone is thrown into the river, and then another rock is thrown very forcefully on the first. The shock of the sound is said to kill or stun the fish in the immediate vicinity.

The most common kind of stream fish trap used is that called the *barbasca* (*barabasco* in Sonadora). A wall of rocks is placed across the stream with a single opening in it; on the down stream side of this opening a henequen bag, *chinchorro* or *malla*, is placed. The fish coming with the current through the opening into the bag usually cannot get out since the current is too strong. Lances, small throwing nets, and hook and line are also used in stream fishing.

Shrimp are taken from streams throughout most of the Interior in various ways. From Veraguas to the east, the *nasa*, a basket trap is used. It is a round basket, the bottom of which turns up and in, with the sticks thus turned up being sharpened, and leaving a hole of two to four inches across set in the bottom. The top is narrow, and can be tied shut. This is laid in a stream with meat bones or cooked rice in it as bait. The shrimp swim in the open bottom, and since the sticks on the side of the opening are pointed, they either get impaled on trying to get out, or cannot find the exit. When the *nasa* is removed from the stream, the top is untied, and the shrimp removed. Shrimp are also caught with the *chinchorro*, a simple cloth or sack held open at the top by a circle of vine. This is pulled through the water by hand, and the shrimp dished out. Both men and women catch shrimp in this way. It is also common to take shrimp out by hand; rocks are removed carefully, and the shrimp grabbed before they can escape.

In Ocú, Holy Week is said to be a time when the entire family will go to the streams to fish. In general, however, fishing is a man's activity, and it is specifically so where it provides an important source of food or income for the family.

The writer suspects that the importance of hunting and fishing may have been overlooked in some of the estimates which have been made concerning the life of the Panama countryman. With hunting, it is specifically in the backlands that it achieves any real economic importance, but fishing occupies some time and contributes to the diet along the entire coastal area and wherever there are streams and rivers.

The exploitation of forest products in Panama is most important in those areas where the population is as yet light. Over the greater part of the savanna of the Interior, most of the land has long since been cut over a number of times. There are relatively few stretches of virgin forest left. There are still to be seen excellent stands in Chiriquí and southern Veraguas, and of course, as one approached the Atlantic watershed and the rain forest area, the forests become at once impressive. Except in the Colón-Chepo region, however, the countryman does not have extensive forest resources to exploit for export. The trees which are felled during the clearing of land for crops could be reduced to kindling, and shipped out, but transport facilities make it a highly unprofitable source of income. It is mainly on the Atlantic coast and east of Chepo that the forests are being exploited for their woods, and in these cases the people involved spend most of their time in this activity. Platt[58] has described some phases of the economics of such free lance exploitation in the river basin of the Chagres river, east of the Canal Zone. The major stands are to be found in eastern Panama, Darién, and Bocas del Toro but we must exclude these areas from consideration in the present essay.

---

[58] 1938, pp. 21–25.

Colón and Chiriquí are both high in the production of charcoal. They account, respectively, for 26 and 61% of the total charcoal production of the country (Census, 1950d). In Palmas Bellas one carbon making center is on the east bank of the river, just in from the sea coast. The charcoal is produced entirely by the men and is done in addition to their agricultural work. It is burned in the district, but much of it is taken to Colón for sale. The technique is basically the same as found elsewhere in Central America; the wood is placed in a pit, the fire built and then covered with earth. It smolders until the wood has been converted into charcoal.

The exploitation of salt by countrymen is limited to those sea coast areas in which are found salt flats. One such region is below the town of Querévalo in Chiriquí. The people from the town go down to this area, called Barqueta, to gather salt for themselves, to sell, or barter for other products which are produced in other *caseríos* (crude sugar, cabbage, or other food products). They scrape the salt off the flats, then boil it in large iron caldrons. In the boiling, the dirt and scum comes to the top and is scraped off. As the water boils away, the salt is left in blocks. It is then wrapped in leaves of the *bijao* tree (see Appendix, #9) and carried off. When stored in the home, the salt is usually kept over the fire so that the smoke will keep it dry and hard.

6. HOME AND LOCAL INDUSTRIES

Since most countrymen work basically in a subsistence economy, they have little surplus to spend in purchasing consumer goods on the national market. The degree to which they do operate in this market, however, depends not only upon cash surplus, but also the degree to which they have been conditioned to prefer enamel or metal ware to pottery, enamel or china dishes to wooden dishes, metal spoons to wooden spoons, hand grinding machines to wooden mortars, factory produced clothing to home made clothing, etc. In turn, the degree of conditioning depends upon the history of the local area in which one lives, the commerce which it has with distant regions, its proximity to effective transportation facilities, the number of people who have lived or worked in urban centers, the Canal Zone, or other centers in which industrial goods are commonly used. Thus, the importance of home industries in the life of the countryman depends upon many factors.

The products which come from local and home industries are found in almost every phase of the countryman's life; cooking and eating utensils, agricultural implements, transport equipment, clothing, recreational equipment, and furniture are all produced by hand on the local level in many places in Panama.

A common series of products are those made of fibers, thread, cloth, bags, baskets, and hats. Spinning is still found over much of the Interior, particularly in Veraguas and in the highlands of the Azuero Peninsula. Spinning used to be much more important than now, and in earlier years there was considerable cotton produced for weaving. Now, however, very few people produce cotton; most of that which is used comes from plants which are now wild, descended from the former domesticated plants. Spinning of cotton is done by women on a simple wooden spindle with a wooden whorl. Weaving of cloth has almost completely dropped from the countryman's culture. Ocú was the only site in which informants said that it was still done. Ocú, it should be noted, is also the center of the only region in which a characteristic costume is still to be found.

The thread which is spun today is used in sewing cloth. Women in many parts of the Interior still make their own clothes, and frequently some of their husband's. As a general rule, however, except in the Ocú region, men buy their clothing and the cloth from which clothes are made is also purchased. In the towns there are usually a number of women with sewing machines who specialize as seamstresses and make clothing on order. It was reported in both Sonadora and Palmas Bellas that some men make their own clothes.

The making of straw hats is a fairly important woman's occupation in the eastern part of the interior. The hats are mainly the type referred to as the *montuna*, being part of the general classical *montuna* countryman costume. In Ocú, three types were distinguished: the *sombrero palmilla* is natural color, the *sombrero pintado* has black lines in it, and the *sombrero capacho* has woven black and white fibers. The importance of the hat industry varies over this eastern region. In some places, most of the women occupy a large part of their spare time in making hats for sale; elsewhere, they produce them principally for their families.

Around Montijo in Veraguas, the pattern of hat production begins to change. Here, and to the west, both men and women make hats, and the hat style changes. In Soná two different types were distinguished, both distinct from the *montuna* type. The *de pieza*, or "Panama" is the finer weave, usually made for sale. For local use, the *"de junco"* is made. Both the Panama and the *de junco* have a crown similar to the regular urban felt hat, not the more semi-circular crown of the *montuna*.

While woven fiber hats are more generally a part of the man's costume, many women also use them; this is particularly true of the *montuna* type.

Of greater importance than hats are baskets. Baskets are used principally for transport among the countrymen. Called *jabas* or *motetes*, the carrying basket is usually one of two types. These are made everywhere by men, usually by almost anyone who needs them. In a few places it was reported that there tended to be some specialization in their production, that those who could make them better were contracted to produce them for a buyer. These baskets have an hexagonal, open weave, and are usually between 1½ and 4 feet high. The most common type, which is found all the way from Chepo to Chiriquí, is shaped like a U; it is straight sided with a slightly rounded bottom, but can stand by itself. The other type has a short convex section spreading out from the rim, then the sides cut in concave to the flat base.

In addition to these large carrying baskets, the writer encountered the use of wide fiber, tightly woven twill baskets in the Chorrera area. One, with a generally cylindrical shape, 4" in diameter by 7" deep, was used to strain *chicha*, the other, squared, 6" on a side and also 7" deep was used to carry seed during planting. To what degree these types are found elsewhere was not determined.

Besides baskets, there are various other woven products. Over most of the Interior the countrymen use net bags, *chácaras*, which are made by the Guaymí Indians. In Dolega, these bags are also made by the countrymen. Hammocks are made in various places, as are *petates* (straw mats). It was reported in Dolega that these fiber products used to be more generalized in their production than now; the tendency seems to have been for fewer people to make them, and that these people make them for sale. In Sonadora it was reported that various vegetable dyes are used in the coloring of some of these woven products.

Wood products play a critical role in the countryman's daily life. In almost every reported case, items of wood are made by men. Most men can make certain household items: the *pilón*, or large wooden mortar; *bateas*, or general flat utility trays; stools; and in certain areas they make spoons, forks, plates, mixers (*batidores*) and leather-seated chairs (*taburetes*). In some places the fabrication of these goods tends to be done by certain persons who specialize in their production. Carpenters are to be found almost everywhere. They make furniture, coffins, dugout canoes and in some places, ox carts. While the mortar and *batea* are found everywhere, the spoons, forks, and plates are being replaced in areas where the population has access to and can afford metal or enamel counterparts. The tools of the carpenter are the ax and adz, and the machete is used when needed. Remarkably skillful work can be done with these three apparently crude implements.

Three wooden musical instruments are made by the countryman: a three stringed violin, called the *micho* in Ocú, and the *ravel* or *ravelito* in Soná; a guitar, called the *mejorana* or *mejoranera*; and drums. Basically there are two types of drums made, the two headed *caja*, and a single headed drum with slanting sides called the *tambor*. The *caja* is the type more generally used among the countrymen although in the Chorrera backland, the single headed type, there called the *tumba*, is used. Also in Chorrera they use the *bongó*, the double drums. In Palmas Bellas two single headed drums were distinguished, a larger one, the *tambor de cumbia*, and a smaller one the *tambor*. They evidently do not use the two headed *caja* in Palmas Bellas.

The *trapiche*, or sugar press, is to be found in most regions where sugar cane is still grown. There are at least two types, the most common of which is that moved by horses or oxen, and made of wood. This is found throughout Central America and is composed of vertical roll presses geared to each other. A hand powered type, also found elsewhere in Central America, is made of two horizontal parallel logs, which are turned and between which the cane is pushed. This is usually called the *revienta pecho*. The writer did not discover whether the single horizontal log lever type pictured by Stout[59] in use among the San Blas Cuna Indians is also to be found among the countrymen or not.

Work in gourds is ubiquitous. Half gourds are used in every household, town, and district, for handy containers of different sizes. They also serve as canteens for the countryman to carry drinking water to the fields. In Santo Domingo the half-gourd is called *chruca* and the gourd used for a water canteen is the *bangaña*.

---

[59] 1947, Plate 3B.

Two musical instruments are made from gourds, the rattle, *maraca*, and the *güiro*. To make the rattle, a hole is cut in on the gourd, stones are put inside, and a stick is placed in the hole as a handle. The *güiro* is a long gourd which has had ridges cut into one side. A stick is rubbed across this to produce sound for which the gourd acts as a sounding box. Hooper[60] reports that countrymen use gourd pieces as buttons. (See Appendix # 10)

Pottery vessels are of first importance in both the town and the country of Panama. They are almost always made by women. There are four major forms which are found over the entire Interior: the *olla* (cooking jar), the *cazuela*, *tinaja*, and *cántaro*. The *olla* is no fixed size, but two general types were distinguished by the informant in Soná: the regular size, 1½ feet in diameter, and the large *olla* used for making *chicha*, usually two to three feet in diameter. The *cazuela* has a round shallow bottom, and is used for cooking tortillas and other dry foods. It is deeper than the typical Mexican and Central American *comal*. The *tinajas* and *cántaros* are jars, the former being larger, up to two or three feet high, and used for storage, while the latter is smaller and used for carrying water.

Pottery making is usually the specialty of a few women. Sometimes each community has three or four who produce enough for the entire neighborhood. On the coast of the Azuero Peninsula, part of Veraguas, and in coastal Chiriquí, certain communities have specialized in pottery making and supply a local region. Where a community, either a town or *caserío*, specializes in the production, the women usually take their products to neighboring communities, and set up a shop in a small store or house. The townspeople and people from the surrounding countryside then come and make their purchases. The pottery is not sold from door to door. Most of the pottery in Panama is a dull finished, dark red ware. In Soná it was reported that they occasionally varnished the pottery. It was reported in Corozal, near Las Palmas, that almost all the women in the community could make pottery. (See Appendix, # 11)

Tile making, a specialty of men, is found over most of the more densely populated regions of the Interior and particularly in the larger towns. It is basically a town trait, however, and not characteristic of countrymen.

Leather is used by the countryman to make *zurrones*, large bags carried like kettle drums on horseback for transport. They are found most commonly in the Azuero Peninsula, Veraguas and Chiriquí. The seats of the *taburete*, and town and countryman's chair, is also of leather, and many make *cutarras*, the leather sandals used over much of the Interior.

Women in some parts of the Interior make cigars, usually of purchased tobacco, for their own smoking.

It was reported in Montijo that raw rubber is tapped from trees now in a semi-wild state; it is put on cloth to make rain capes and waterproof bags. The capes are of two kinds: the *roana*, for a person, and the *tapasilla*, used when riding horseback.

---

[60] 1945, pp. 196–198.

The writer failed to get information to the extent to which the processing of leather and tobacco is carried on in the countryman population.

Crude grinding stones are found over most of Panama's Interior, although they are gradually being replaced in some places by the commercial hand grinding machine. In El Espino, Sonadora, Margarita de Chepo, and Santo Domingo, it was reported that they were completely replaced by the hand grinder, while in Los Pozos, coastal Veraguas, and parts of Chiriquí, they were being rapidly displaced. The stronghold of the grinding stone is generally in the backlands. Where used, it is usually on a set of upright sticks in the ground or on a table. Only in Dolega, where the entire corn technology changes, it is used on the ground.

Hooper[61] reported certain other industries which are on the decline or practically extinct. The making of bows and arrows, of soap, of fuel oils from palm and fuel wax taken from wild beehives have been generally displaced respectively by the gun, commercially produced soap, and petroleum oil.

There is marked variation from one end of the area to the other in the division of labor in local industries. The following statements, with noted exceptions, may stand, however. Where still carried on, spinning and weaving of thread and cloth is woman's work. The professional making of clothing on order is also woman's work, but some men will make their own clothing. In heavier plant fibers, men make all baskets, and in the Azuero and Coclé-west Panama regions, women make all the hats. Beginning in Veraguas, men also make hats, and this situation is found also in Chiriquí. The production of wood products, whether done by specialists or not, is entirely in the hands of men. Pottery is made only by women, and tiles only by men. Leather products, the processing and fabrication, are both done by men, while women make cigars.

With respect to local specialization as opposed to general production, there is no rule. Depending upon the place, hats, clothing, pottery, canoes, etc., may be made by people in particular *caseríos*, a few individual specialists, or generally by anyone who needs the product. In general, home and local industries still supply the countryman, and to a lesser degree, the town dweller, with many of the necessities of daily life; particular local conditions and traditions have determined who makes the products.

7. TRAVEL, TRANSPORT, AND COMMERCE

The road system in Panama serves to connect only the principal towns of the Interior. In order for the countryman to use them, he must first get his produce to one of the towns. Consequently, the greater part of the countryman's travel is either by foot or horseback. Horses do not serve well to carry produce from the isolated fields to the home, so are usually used in taking produce from the home to the road-head or town where it is sold and transshipped by truck. Ox carts used to be much more common, but they have always been limited to the level and relatively unbroken country. With the opening of highway traffic,

---

[61] 1945, pp. 196–198.

ox carts have been replaced by trucks and now serve to transport goods from the bigger towns to those which are periodically isolated from truck travel through bad road conditions. The ox cart in Panama does not have the importance in the local economy which it does in all the other Central American countries; it is used principally on the Coclé and Azuero coast and to some degree on the Chiriquí coast. Carts have spoked wheels and are found both with a box type and open platform bodies.

As was mentioned earlier, the horse is the principal animal of burden. Mules are rare, although occasionally used. The western or Texas type of saddle is commonly used although they are usually extremely old and tied together with rope. In the course of this survey, the writer had saddles break and fall from the horse he was riding. Nevertheless, the use of saddles seems very common; one does not see as many people riding bareback as elsewhere in Central America. It is the custom in some parts of Panama for the men to ride and the women to walk. This was reported specifically in Ocú.

Transport of grain and other bulk products by horse ordinarily utilizes one of three containers: *jabas*, or large open-weave vine basket; *zurrones*, a pair of large leather sacks, or henequen bags. In the Coclé-west Panama region, the use of the *jaba* is predominant. In the Azuero Peninsula, the *zurrones* are also important, and in Veraguas, the henequen sacks are used more commonly. Varying from one local area to another, one may find the complete disuse of one or another of these three forms. In the Azuero area, there is an additional transport form used on horses. This is the *aguadero*, branches tied into a semicircular container in which are carried *tinajas* and milk cans. One is tied on either side of the horse in the same manner as the *zurrones* and *jabas* are. It was reported in Quérevalo, and is doubtless true in other places as well, that large rectangular lard cans were used to carry bulk products. A horse can carry up to six of these at a time.

While the horse is used to transport goods to the towns, from the field to the house the men and women themselves must carry the produce. There are also many people who do not have horses and are unable to rent one to carry their own products. The large carrying basket used by men, and in some regions by women also, is the same as that used in horse transport. It was reported, specifically in Ocú, that the term *jaba* was used for those baskets which were used on horseback, while the term *motete* referred to the same basket when carried by a man. The writer did not find this distinction in terminology to be the case everywhere. The two forms of *jaba* or *motete*, were described earlier. In carrying them, there are two shoulder straps, *manijas*, which go over the shoulder and under the arm. In the region adjacent to the Guaymí Indian area there is, in addition, a third *manija* which is used as a tumpline. This tumpline was found in San Francisco, Corozal (Las Palmas), Remedios, and Dolega. One informant said that it was only the countrymen who were *más cholo* (more Indian) who used it. In Dolega, some people use the Indian carrying bag, the *chácara*, to carry things on their back; the single carrying strap in this serves as a tumpline.

In San Francisco and the Cañazas region of Veraguas a flat set of poles or cane, called the *cañazo*, carried on the back with two shoulder straps and a tumpline, serves as a platform to which various goods are tied.

Wherever fairly good roads have been laid, truck travel and transport has immediately followed. The small passenger bus in Panama, called the *chiva*, plies these routes regularly.

The use of dugout canoes is to be found wherever streams and rivers are of sufficient size to make their use practical. In Palmas Bellas, it was remarked that the *cayuco* was as important to them as the horse was to the people of the Interior. Naturally, the use of waterways is most common along the coasts. On the Atlantic side this is particularly true since there are almost no roads whatsoever to carry traffic. The term *cayuco* is used for these dugouts over all the eastern part of the Interior and was found in use also in Querévalo, in Chiriquí; in Chepo, however, *piragua* is the general term. In Soná the term *bote* was used for the smaller dugouts, and *bongó* for the larger ones which were powered by oars instead of paddles. In San Francisco, they were referred to as *canoas*, and in Remedios, as *botes*. On the coast of Soná, sail dugouts are used; these tend to be wider and have flaring sides instead of the more common parallel sides.

Where the rivers go into the backlands it is not uncommon for a man to build a *balsa* raft, and float his goods down the river for sale. The raft is then dismantled and the wood also sold.

While the countryman lives basically in a subsistence economy, he is often intimately involved in the money economy of the country to gain many of the articles he uses daily. The channels of commerce usually run through the small country stores, or *abarroterías*, which are to be found in focal points in most *corregimientos*, and in general stores in every town. The people of Palmas Bellas and Chepo take most of their produce and do much of their buying in Colón and Panama, respectively, but as one moves out of the range of these cities, the town and country stores become the major foci of commerce.

There are very few markets in Panama of the type which are found in many other countries of Latin America. The standard Panamanian market is a place where meat is sold. Only in the cities and in the larger towns such as David and Santiago are the markets places of general sale. Even Chorrera, a town of over 8,000 people, does not have a general market. The sale of all products except meat is carried on individually with the storekeepers. The countryman will sell his produce to a store in the town, and the store in turn will resell it. These general stores are not infrequently run by people of oriental or near eastern extraction, and handle a wide range of products. Beside the local products which they buy from the countryman for resale, they handle cloth, clothing, commercially prepared foods, simple agricultural implements, basic necessities such as salt, sugar, soap, kerosene, lard and drugs. The *abarroterías* in the countryside, however, carry mainly articles of *"primera necesidad;"* this category includes such items as salt, sugar, cooking oil, soap, matches, and cigarettes. These stores will also handle locally made products such as baskets, and will buy small quantities of local agriculture produce.

When the countryman produces large quantities of cash crop, citrus fruits in the Chorrera region, for example, they usually take the produce directly to the larger towns and cities for sale. There is no sale, evidently, in Chorrera for oranges; they must be taken directly to Panama. Similarly, David serves as such a center in Chiriquí, Santiago in Veraguas, Chitré on the Azuero Peninsula, and Colón in the Atlantic coast area.

Some informants said that travelling vendors used to be much more common than now; whether this was the case the writer cannot say, but it is clear that such selling is of little importance now. The two specific cases of travelling selling which the writer encountered were the selling of net bags by the Guaymí Indians during the summer months, and the case of the women of La Peña who came to Montijo and would locate themselves in a house in town to sell their pottery.

Besides the general stores and *abarroterías*, the towns usually have a meat market and a few *cantinas*, drinking establishments. The meat markets are either municipally or privately owned, and usually consist of a small screened-in room set up in the plaza or along one street. The slaughterhouse facilities in general are not adequate, and where they exist, are limited for use in the slaughtering of cattle. The *cantinas* do a fairly good business, but in Montijo had to go out of business for lack of trade.

There is a certain amount of trade between the west coast of the Azuero Peninsula and the islands to the west with Puerto Mutis; the products of this trade, lumber, rice, cattle, pigs, and beans, go by truck to Santiago.

In Ocú, and less so in Penonomé, there is a small trade done through agents who buy the handicraft products of the countrymen and sell them to tourists. In Ocú is established the *Society of Typical Ocú Industries* which encourages the countrymen to produce their clothing, baskets, and so on, for sale.

8. THE DOMESTIC ESTABLISHMENT

As it is with rural people over most of the world, the home is the center of the countryman's life. He sleeps there, eats there, brings his produce for storage there from the fields, and raises his family there. While perhaps the most mundane of all aspects of daily life, the domestic scene is also one of the most critical. Most activities are channeled into or through the home. It is consequently of extreme importance to have an understanding of some of the mechanics of living which go on in the home. It should be remembered, however, that while the home is thus of critical importance, it is also merely the scene of such activities and does not determine all the activities which take place in it.

Every countryman's house has a yard. This is equally true whether he lives in a small nuclear town or in a dispersed *corregimiento*. If houses are crowded together in a town, then the yard is usually at the back of the house, away from the street and the daily activities of the home are carried out there. If the house is in the countryside, then the yard surrounds the house, and the activities may be carried out in whatever part of the clearing is favored by the individuals.

Depending upon the importance of cattle and in the region, there may or may not be a fence which encloses the entire yard area. If the cattle must be brought home at night, the countryman will frequently have a fence and the yard will serve as a corral. The yard is usually a dirt area with patches of grass and a few, often scrawny, trees. It is sometimes swept by the woman of the house, but this depends upon the person. It is not uncommon to find a roofed structure with no walls set to one side of the house. This may be used for storage and for cooking. It is not uncommon for the daytime living of the inhabitants to center in the open structure rather than in the house itself. The yard is the scene of many activities. Chickens, turkeys, ducks, and pigs wander in it, the men repair their saddles and baskets, make their new baskets, *bateas*, and other smaller wooden items. The children play there, the dogs sleep there, and the women carry on the multitude of daily chores there.

The countryman's house is basically a series of poles on which is set a roof. Binding is done with vines. Between the roof and the ground, a wall surface of palm fronds, cane, poles, or occasionally boards, will be placed. If the surface is cane or poles, a coating of mud (*embarrada*) may be put over the wall surface. This is called *quincha*. The roof is usually of palm fronds or grass. With the exception to be noted, the countryman's home is almost always rectangular, rarely square. In the Azuero region, the basic house changes from a rectangular to an apsidal floor plan, parallel sides with rounded ends. The only other regions in which houses of this form are to be found is occasionally in the Guaymí area, and a few around Chepo. While the writer is not certain, he suspects that the latter houses are built by people who immigrated from the Azuero region.

In many places, especially in the larger towns and along the highway, the use of tile roofs is very common. Tile, however, is basically not the countryman's but is the town dweller's material. The typical town house in the Azuero region is a rectangular house with a two-shed roof of tile (to be referred to hereafter as the Chitré-type house). There is usually in front a *corredor* (porch) and the back section of the house has the kitchen. This house, which is to be seen lining the streets of the towns in this region, is spreading to the country and replacing the basic countryman's house. Around Chitré itself, the walls of this type of house are sometimes built of cement blocks. This, however, is still limited to the fairly wealthy people. (See Appendix, ✻12)

The roof of the countryman's house is usually a four-shed variety, with the front and rear shed long, and the end sheds coming to a point at the top. Whether palm or grass is used on the roof depends almost entirely on the availability of the materials locally. The use of these two materials tends to give the roof a different appearance, however. The grass roof appears to be smooth, and the corners are rounded. The palm roof is rough, and the front and back sheds overlap the two end sheds, giving the appearance of the end sheds being under the front and back ones. These differences, however, should not be interpreted as being different roof types, but results of the different materials used. Occasionally when a sheet of galvanized iron is available, it will be put on the roof ridge to prevent rain from leaking through.

The wall surfaces of the houses depend to some degree upon the caprice of the owner. Since the wall is dependent upon the existence of the poles which support the roof, a wall can be placed between any two poles. Because of this, houses are seen which have three quarters of the floor surface walled in, and the remaining quarter as a porch. The roofed structure mentioned earlier as a storage and kitchen place is nothing more than a basic house with no walls at all.

In Palmas Bellas there is a house type fundamentally different from that just described. While the structure is the same, the house tends to be square, set up off the ground, and to be entirely of wood except for the roof which is usually of galvanized iron. Chiriquí also presents greater variation in house types than are generally to be found in the rest of the Interior. There, more tile is used on roofs, and one finds boards being used more often for walls. Around Chorrera there is a common additional variation to be seen on the basic rectangular type. This involves the addition of a porch on the front, and sheds extending out from each side. The extension provided by these sheds gives additional interior floor space.

It is quite common to find that the inside of the countryman's house has been divided into two sections with a wall-high partition dividing one from another. The two sections are usually a general "living room" (*sala*) and a bedroom (*dormitorio*). Such internal divisions are more commonly found in town houses and houses located nearer the highways and towns. The floor of the countryman's house is usually earth. Only in the towns are floors of wood, cement, or tile to be found.

Construction of the countryman's house is done in a number of ways. The future owner has a number of alternatives, depending upon the region in which he lives. Usually, together with a few friends, one of whom has some experience in carpentry, the countryman will put up his home himself. In some cases in the country, and more commonly in the towns, contractors will be called in and direct the work, perhaps doing it all with paid labor. In the Azuero region, Veraguas, Coclé, and parts of Chiriquí, it is quite common to hold a *junta*. In the Azuero region, and the colony Margarita de Chepo, the *junta* is used for putting the mud coating on the walls. In Montijo, Corozal (Las Palmas), and Remedios, it was reported that the *junta* was specifically for putting on the roof. In Los Pozos it is customary to have a *víspera de junta*, a large party the night before the work is to be done. The following day the owner supplies food and drink during the work and the occasion is generally festive. The owner pays all expenses and it usually turns out to be more expensive than to employ labor to do the work. This *junta*, however, is not considered to be an exchange labor situation; the owner is not obligated to go and work on *juntas* which others give. In Chorrera it was reported that it took about 12 *jornales* (man-days) to make the frame of a house, 12 more to make the roof, and 10 to put mud on the walls. The mud preparation would take longer if the source were distant.

The countryman has a variety of furniture in his home, most of it simple. There are benches, stools, leather seated chairs (*taburetes*), and various kinds of sleeping surfaces. The benches are usually a crude board with four legs. If the legs are stuck in the ground, they are called *barbacoas*. The stools are of three main types; the *tuco*, a solid log section, usually with cuts for handles; the small, three legged stool; and a low stool made of one or two boards, either with a flat surface or V-shaped, and board sides. Another kind of bench is a plain log with the upper side shaved flat. The *taburete* is generally a leather seated chair, although the term is occasionally used to refer to stools. It is the standard chair for both town and country, but since it requires some carpentry, it is not found in all homes.

The countryman's bed is usually made of sticks stuck in the ground with a framework and poles laid across the frame for the surface. Over this may be put a blanket, hide, piece of cloth, or *petate*. This has been partially replaced in many places by the canvas cot, similar in style to the commercial camper's cot, but larger and made of heavier wood. It is called *tijera*. The framework beds usually stand two or three feet off the ground. While hammocks are found in many homes, they are rarely used for sleeping. Children occasionally sleep in them, but there is usually only one in a house and it is used for daytime lounging. Most countrymen houses have a part of the ceiling covered over with cane or poles, sort of a half-attic, called the *jorón*. The *jorón* is also used for sleeping, most commonly in the uplands. Sleeping on the floor was reported only from El Espino and said not to be extremely common there. To reach the *jorón*, for climbing trees, or wherever needed, the *guarúm*, a single log with notch-steps cut in it, is used everywhere.

It is standard practice over all of Panama to have a kitchen in a separate room of the house, or more commonly, under a separate shelter. Where the houses are small, it is usually the practice to build two houses immediately next to one another, using two roofs, and having a common wall between them. The center of the kitchen activity is at the fire. In the backlands and *corregimientos*, the fire is usually on the floor between 3 stones, but it is also sometimes on a raised platform covered with earth. This platform is usually waist high, of poles set in the ground, and with stones stuck in the clay or earth surface. The cooking pots are placed on these stones. Even where the raised platform for the fire is used for cooking, it is not uncommon to find another fire burning on the floor for making *chicha*.

Grains are frequently stored in the *jorón*, especially items like rice which may be kept either on the stalk or in sacks. The *jorón* provides a limited space, however, and since it is sometimes used for sleeping, grains must often be kept elsewhere. It is the custom in many places, especially Coclé, the Azuero Peninsula, and Veraguas, to make small storage shelters (*trojes*) in the fields, and to leave the grain there until one is ready to bring it home. Such *trojes* are also built next to the house in some places. The usefulness of the field *troje* depends upon respect for another's property among the countrymen; in only one place was concern expressed that it was not safe to leave the produce out where it could be so easily stolen. In the Soná area beans are often stored in a *tanque*, a stiff fiber woven storage bin set off the ground and covered with large leaves and ashes to keep out insects.

Water is usually stored in the kitchen in a pottery *cántaro* which is commonly kept on a stand of sticks off the floor. It may be carried in pottery jars, large gourds called *tules*, tin cans, or coconuts. Salt is kept either in the *jorón*, over the fire if possible, or hangs in a dish over the fire. This serves to keep it dry. Kitchen equipment usually includes various pottery containers of the types described earlier, plates, eating utensils, pots and pans, and gourds. These are kept on board shelves which are hung from the wall, or in boxes set up on legs against the wall. The grinding stone is usually set on two forked sticks, called the *orqueta*. The degree to which homemade products outnumber industrially produced goods was mentioned earlier. *Bateas* are used for preparing food, for washing, and any kind of activity for which they will serve. Unless the kitchen is a separate open structure, the wooden mortar is usually kept outside.

While it was not possible to collect extensive data on food preparation and diet, a few notes were systematically kept with respect to the use of certain items and techniques. The most common preparation of corn is to remove the grain from the cob, and break it down in the wooden mortar, cook it, and grind it finer on the stone or metal hand grinder. The use of the large wooden mortar for smashing corn is being replaced in some of the larger towns by commercial power grinding machines. This was reported in both the Azuero Peninsula and in Chiriquí. It was said in El Espino and San Francisco that it was a practice to mix the ground corn with coconut milk for moistness in making the *masa*. This technique of corn preparation is significantly different from that used in the rest of Central America and Mexico; the latter requires the breakdown of the grain shell by soaking in water with lime or ashes. The only place where this method was encountered in Panama was in Dolega, where ashes were used. Since it is traditional that Dolega was formed originally by a distinct Indian group, the Dorasque, it may be that this region of Chiriquí is the southernmost extension of the area of the Meso-American corn preparation technology.

In Dolega also is found the use of a large grinding stone which was worked on the floor, again different from the rest of Panama. The grinding motion used in Dolega differed in that a large stone is rocked over the corn grains rather than being rubbed across it. The grinding stone with a concave grinding surface is called the *tumba*. This rocking motion for grinding corn is found commonly in South America, while the scraping motion is typical of Meso-America. The combination in Dolega of the use of ashes to break down the corn, a Meso-American trait, and the rocking grinding motion, a South American trait, is an example of the transitional nature of the earlier Indian cultures in the area. Today in Dolega, as elsewhere, the other grinding stones are also being used and are being replaced by the hand grinder.

Scattered over most of the Interior some houses were found to have the dome-shaped clay ovens set up on a stand. The women who have these usually specialize in the production of bread for the community and sell their product. It is a specialty and not a custom practised by everyone.

The production of fermented drinks is found throughout the countryside of Panama. The most common drink is corn *chicha*. The older method of starting the fermentation process by chewing the corn has been replaced in most of the eastern section of the Interior by the use of *raspadura*, boiled sugar-cane juice. In Veraguas and Chiriquí, however, the use of *raspadura* has not entirely supplanted the chewing method. This reflects in part the same retention of customs of Indian origin which is found in other aspects of life in the area adjacent to the Guaymí. It was reported from Montijo, and may well be true in other places that sugar cane is grown, that simple fermented sugar-cane juice in water, *guarapo*, is a very popular drink. It was said to be more common than corn *chicha* because it was easier to produce. (See Appendix, ⋕ 13)

Also found in the Azuero Peninsula, Veraguas, and Chiriquí, is the production of palm wine. This is made by cutting down a palm, usually the *corozo* or *palma real*, and cutting out the center of the stump. The sap seeps into the cavity, and is left for a few days to ferment. There was no evidence that fruit wines of any kind were produced. Pineapple, papaya, and some other fruits are prepared into sweet drinks but usually were not fermented.

The preparation of corn in different ways is highly elaborated among the countrymen. The following is a list of some of the dishes which are prepared in various places: *tortillas, bollos* (balls of *masa* cooked in a soup), *tamales, empanada* (like *tamales*, but fried), cornbread, *arepas* (mixed with sugar or cheese), *atól* (a sweet corn drink), *cocidillo* (*chicha* made from green corn), *chiricano* (like *bollos*, but cooked in the oven), *chicheme* (corn, rice and sugar), *harinita* (toasted with sugar added) and a coffee-like drink of toasted corn. Among other dishes eaten by the countryman are: beans and rice, *guacho de frijoles* (a solid mixture of meat, beans, rice, yams, yuca and a few other things), rice and coconut, *cocada* (sugar and coconut milk), and a coffee-like drink made of okra. Milk is very rarely drunk, being made into cheese or given to the animals. Eggs are usually sold, and meat is eaten rarely since it is expensive. As was mentioned earlier, products of hunting and fishing are in many areas more important than domesticated animals. Bananas, plantains, the fruits of various palms, particularly the pejibaye and *corozo*, and coconut are also of major importance in some regions. In general, however, corn, rice, yams, yuca, and yautia, form the basis of the daily diet. (See Appendix, ⋕ 14)

Over most of the Interior the clothing of the countryman is simple. The dresses of the women are plain homemade affairs, sometimes extraordinarily shabby in the back country, and the men wear industrially produced trousers and shirts. Shoes are worn almost entirely by those who live in or near the towns, and the sandals, *cutarras*, are found in scattered use everywhere. As a general rule, the countrypeople go barefoot. The only section of the country where a characteristic costume has been retained is that centering on Ocú. There the men wear white, sometimes embroidered, shirts, called *cotona*, and trousers, called *chingo*. The women wear a full skirt, the *pollera*, and an embroidered blouse, the *corpiño*. The entire costume is referred to as the *montuna*, and includes the hat type described earlier. This costume, usually without the embroidery, is found as far as the Azuero east coast, west to Montijo, and north to the main highway. The costume is thus well localized, and claims that it is the typical dress of the countryman in general are false.

9. FAMILY AND *COMPADRE* SYSTEM

The family of the countryman is basically a nuclear, neo-local, bilateral family. This means that the people who usually compose the domestic unit are the parents and unmarried children, and do not regularly include either paternal or maternal relatives. Also, it means that a child recognizes descent coming through both parents, and all four grandparents. Depending upon the economic status of the individuals concerned, however, it is not uncommon to find one or more relatives living with the nuclear family. There is a tendency in some localized areas, such as in part of the backlands of Chorrera, Sonadora, and Querévalo, for the family to assume a patrilocal form, i.e., for a son to bring his wife to live at the home of his parents. Such cases seem, however, to be the exception and not the rule.

There is a very curious situation to be found in the Panamanian country domestic unit. It will be remembered that in rural Panama there are about 91 women for every 100 men. This means that the woman should be fairly secure in the domestic unit, were it simply a case of men needing women. From the material collected during the survey, however, this does not seem to be the case. There were a number of reports, particularly from Veraguas, of numerous cases of houses in which a woman and her offsprings lived but in which there was no husband. It is impossible to make entire sense out of this situation without more intensive field studies into the nature of the countryman family and factors involved in separations. However, there are three factors which may clarify certain aspects of the issue.

First, common-law marriages are almost twice as common as are formal marriages in the rural areas (see Table 15). This situation in itself would not be significant were it not for the fact that Panama is predominantly a Roman Catholic country, the clergy is interested in having people married, and the clergy is not markedly undermanned.

Second, the economic division of labor between the sexes varies in such a way that there seems to be a tendency to find a balanced domestic unit where women either do not participate in the subsistence agricultural field labor, or in some situations where they work constantly in such labor. In agriculture, there are four main ways in which women may participate: they may work fairly full time with the men; they may work full time because the men are occupied more in hunting or fishing; they may work only in certain specialties, such as in rice agriculture; or they may work occasionally as auxiliaries whenever and wherever they are needed. Most unbalanced families seem to be found where the women work regularly *with* the men, and where they work in a specialty or as auxiliaries. Where they do no field labor, the family tends to be balanced; and where they do field labor because the men hunt or fish, the family also tends to be balanced. It should be noted that this does not seem to hold true for other specialized woman's industries, such as pottery making, baking, or hat making. Whether these specialties are present or not does not seem to affect the balance of the family in the country as a whole.

The third factor which seems to be of importance becomes clear when one compares the Ocú region with the rest of the Interior. In Ocú, it was reported that the family is generally balanced, that separations are infrequent, and that there are relatively few cases of women with offspring living without men. Ocú, too, is the only place where one finds a culture which is markedly conservative, retentative of old traits in costume, handicrafts, and customs. While it cannot be confirmed without further research, it seems likely that the balanced families of Ocú also stem in part from their traditional conservatism.[62]

While none of these factors, the number of formal marriages, the degree of cultural conservatism, and the division of agricultural labor, explains entirely the presence of unbalanced families, it is the writer's opinion that the last is of the greatest importance. Where the woman's economic role is well defined in terms of her own activities, whether it be a role which excludes agricultural work, or one in which she bears the burden of the work because the men are acceptably occupied in hunting or fishing, there can be a recognized division of labor between a husband and wife. Where the role of the woman is not so clearly defined, where she may or may not work in agriculture depending upon the momentary economic condition of her husband, then she may prefer to leave her husband. Similarly, where a husband is dependent upon his wife, entirely for agricultural work, as he would be if he were hunting or fishing, he would be less likely to leave her. The economic condition of the husband plays a large part in whether women will work, since he can employ labor if he has the money.

Once given the fact that unbalanced families are not infrequent, it is easier to understand the radical difference between the proportion between the sexes in the rural and urban environments. It will be remembered that in 1950 there were about 107 women for ever 100 men in the urban situation, while there were about 91 women for every 100 men in the rural areas. If a woman is living without a husband, and has children to support, she has fewer alternative ways of earning a living in a rural area than she does in the urban area. In a town or city she can take in washing, iron, sew or do a variety of domestic work. In the country, these opportunities are limited since no one has servants, and everyone does their own washing, ironing, sewing, and so on. The urban alternative for some women seems to be more desirable.

The preceding discussion should not be misinterpreted as saying that the majority of the countrymen unions are unstable. Such is patently not the case. It is not too uncommon for a couple to break up early, if they find themselves to be incompatible, but once they have lived together for some time, they tend to remain so. The manner of obtaining a wife doubtless plays some role in this situation. There are two general ways, the formalized, in which the boy asks the parents of the girl, and then the parents discuss the affair and make the arrangements; and the informal, whereby the man simply takes the girl, or she leaves to go and live with the man.

---

[62] Hernán Porras (in correspondence) has suggested a further possible factor: there may be a relationship between land ownership and marriage. Unfortunately, the material from the survey does not provide data on this.

It was the present writer's impression that where formal marriage was undertaken, it reflected a greater adherence to a recognized form, and consequently, was more likely to hold. Where it was not done, it reflected to some degree a veering from the recognized form, and was less likely to hold. While the clergy is not extremely numerous in Panama, most of the main towns of the Interior have a priest. The present writer suspects that it may not be so much a case of the clergy being weak in numbers which has produced so many common-law unions, as it is that they have not made great efforts to reach the countrypeople. Hooper[63] points out that the countryman who has little cash cannot afford a wedding.

In the few residential genealogies, which the writer recorded, there were a number of cases of domestic units which were made up of a man, a woman, their children, and the children of the woman by another man. It was not ascertained whether the father of these other children retained responsibility for their welfare or not.

When separations do take place, if the couple has been living together for some time, the goods are usually divided between them. Usually the woman can keep the house if she wants, but if she is responsible for the break up she will leave. The woman takes the children. The goods of a deceased person are divided equally among the heirs.

Incest restrictions usually prohibit marriage between first cousins, but permit it between persons who are second cousins or more distantly related.

The artificial kinship bond of the *compadrazgo* is of considerable importance over most of the Interior. In seeking a *compadre*, the countryman generally looks for a friend or relative. However, it is also common to seek out someone in a town, usually the owner of a store or someone whom the countryman feels can help him in time of need. Which is preferable seems to be a matter of local variation. Only in Chepo and San Francisco it was reported that one ordinarily tried to get a person who would be in a position to help; in Sonadora, Santo Domingo, Los Pozos and Corozal (Las Palmas), it was reported that the ordinary pattern was to get a friend or relative.

Compadres are generally sought for baptism, confirmation, and marriage if there is one. Different persons are asked for baptism and confirmation almost everywhere, but it was not uncommon for the *padrino* of baptism to be called again for a marriage. In Querévalo it was reported that for a baptism it was customary not only to have a *padrino* and *madrina*, but also a *contra madrina* who held the child during the ceremony. The *contra madrina* was not as important as the others later.

In certain places it was reported that the bond of *compadre* was considered to be so critical that incest restrictions extended to prohibit intermarriage (formal or common-law) of children of *compadres*. This was reported from Palmas Bellas, El Espino, and Los Pozos. In a number of other towns, informants were uncertain as to whether it was the practice to follow this prohibition or not.

---

[63] 1954, pp. 242–243.

In general, one is not impressed that distant kinship, whether consanguinal or affinal, plays an overbearing role in the life of the countryman. As was mentioned earlier concerning the agricultural work patterns, relatives will often be included in a *peonada* or *junta*, but this is more a function of the fact of proximity than it is of kinship. That someone is a relative means that you can live with him if you are in difficulties, you can ask him for help, you must observe incest restrictions if they prohibit union with the person. But in the daily activities the nuclear family is of principal importance and more distant relatives do not seem to play such an important role. *Compadres* are generally important. Almost everywhere the writer went he was told that "great respect" existed between *compadres*. Only in occasional instances, however, was this underscored by ritual observances between a godfather and his godchild, or between *compadres* themselves. It was frequently specified that one held his *compadre* in greater respect than he did his own brother. It seems that the artificial kinship bond has to some degree replaced the actual kinship bond in importance. A person can fight bitterly with his relative, but he cannot do this with his *compadre*.

10. NOTES ON THE LIFE CYCLE

Childbirth usually takes place in the home. The usual practice is to call a midwife (*partera*); in some places where there are no practicing midwives, they must go to the nearest town to have one come over. To baptize the child, the parents must travel to the nearest parish center. Baptism (and possibly also confirmation) is the only church-centered event which all countrymen observe, and the fact that they will make the effort to have a baptism done makes it clear that they can reach a church if the motivation is strong enough. In some places, and depending upon whether the countryman has money, there may be a small fiesta after the baptism ceremony. (See Appendix, #15)

The childhood of the countryman consists in playing about the house and yard until he or she is old enough to participate in the daily routine of the adults. A child of school age will go immediately to the fields to work when he returns from school. The countrymen children are limited in the number of other children with whom they may associate outside of school; their friends of comparable ages must live nearby or be brought over on the occasion of a prayer session or *junta*. The schools, in some regions, are trying to form clubs and promote other activities for the children, but these do not alter the fact that an able son or daughter is an economic asset to the parents.

Many children are taken to church for confirmation. As in baptism, the father looks for *compadres* on this occasion. Puberty is not ritually observed, and adolescence and early adulthood of the countryman involves a gradual shift from less responsible to more responsible activities. While disapproved of by the parents, sexual activities may begin during adolescence and a girl may have one or two pregnancies before she settles down with a man.

Courtship is either thoroughly informal, in general, or involves the steps described earlier. Marriage, when done formally, may involve a small fiesta, depending upon whether the families can afford it. The customs described in Ocú probably represent the most elaborate pattern to be found in the countryside. According to the informant there, "couples do not live together prior to marriage. The boy will indicate his desire to marry by throwing bits of dirt or something at the girl, and if she is interested, she will throw something back. The boy's father asks the father of the girl unless there is some hostility between the families, in which case an intermediary is sought. If a fiesta is going on, the boy, girl, and her parents will share a *copita* of *guaro*. (See also Appendix, # 4 and 7)

"After the church ceremony, the new pair mount the same horse and the party goes to the girl's house. On the way, one of the fathers brings out a bottle, and everyone is expected to drink from it. Then later, on the road, there is a person who plays the guitar. When they arrive at the house, there is a large fiesta called *boa*. Frequently, then, the girl will remain in her own house and the boy will return home for up to a week. Then he will come and get her. In a few rare cases, if the two cannot cohabit on the first night they are together, through timidity or for some other reason, they separate for good immediately. Men usually want a virgin; if after the marriage the husband finds the girl is not virgin, then they frequently fight and the man leaves." (See Appendix, # 16)

As was mentioned before, a new couple almost always takes up residence in a new home. This may be built by the man, or with a *junta*, or the new house may be rented until such time as the man can afford to build his own house. The tendency is to build in the same general neighborhood as the parents, with a slight tendency to remain closer to the boy's home than to the girl's. However, there is no rule about this and particular circumstances determine the case.

Adulthood for the countryman involves the many activities which are described elsewhere in this report. In general, the round of work is interlaced with *juntas* and prayer sessions upon the death of some friend, relative, or neighbor. Baptisms, marriages, and birthdays serve as occasions for fiestas, and in some places, a person will throw a party in order to make a little money. There are usually rare trips to the towns for matters of commerce or religion. As old age overtakes the countryman, if alone, he may move in with some brother or other relative, and help in whatever way he can in return for his upkeep. Old men can usually make baskets and carry some of the lighter field work, and old women can cook and keep house for a younger man who has no woman.

Death provides an occasion for considerable social intercourse in the life of the countryman. In some cases, if a church is nearby, a Mass will be held, but the usual pattern is for a novena to be held beginning on the night of the death. It is not uncommon for people to come from some distance to these novenas, and the family sponsoring the prayers will provide coffee, drinks, cigarettes, and sometimes food. In some places, the visitors will bring food and other items to help defray the cost of these novenas. The general pattern following this is to have a *rosario* prayer session at the end of a month, and for each succeeding month up to a year, and annually thereafter. There are variations on this, however. Sometimes a *rosario* is held two weeks after the death, or after six months. Much of this depends upon the local tradition and the ability of the family to bear the expenses of these sessions. In Remedios and San Francisco it was reported that at the time of the death, eight nights of prayer, an *octava*, was held instead of a novena, and in both places the *rosarios* were held only after a month and at the end of a year, and not repeated again.

The learning of prayers is a specialty of certain men and women, and they are called in at the time of death to lead the prayer sessions. They may charge for this, but it is frequently done for nothing. These specialists are simply referred to as *maestros* in Sonadora. While it is more common for these *maestros* to be women, in the backlands they are frequently men.

In the countryside, the older method of burial was to place the corpse on a *barbacoa*, a platform of sticks, throw a cloth over it, and bury it. This is replaced in most places now with coffins made by local woodworkers. In Soná and Ocú it was reported that among the poorer people the burial was still done on a *barbacoa*. Burial is usually done within twenty-four hours since there is no method of preserving the corpse and the climate produces early decay. Also in Soná it was reported that everything connected with the death, the bed, clothing, etc., was destroyed and a candle was kept burning for a month at the place the person died.

Another old custom, which has died out in many places, was reported to still be carried on in Ocú and the backlands of Sonadora. This is the holding of a fiesta instead of a novena, when a child dies. It was variously reported to be practiced with children under one year of age and those under five years of age. The rationale behind this was that since the child was very young, he cannot have suffered, that he was going to heaven and everyone should be happy about the fact that he is safe. In Sonadora it was reported that one dance, the *curacha*, in which couples danced apart, was used during this fiesta. Music was provided by the countryman's instruments, the violin, guitar, and drum. The reason given in Soná that this custom was disappearing was that in the second decade of the century a law was passed which forbade dances at funerals.

If the home is near enough to a town with a cemetery, the body will be carried there for burial. However, in many cases this is not practical, and local small cemeteries are used. Where a town has a cemetery, it is cleaned once a year or so by a *faena*, or work group called together by the *alcalde*. This is sometimes done specifically on the Day of the Dead in November, just prior to the national fiesta on the third of that month.

In some of the towns around David, Chiriquí, there is a custom which the writer did not encounter anywhere else in the countryside of Panama. There are organized in Las Lomas and Querévalo a number of funerary societies. "In Las Lomas," according to the informant, "there are five *Centros Funerarios*, one in each of the *barrios* and *caseríos* except one. Each one has a house. Almost everyone in the area belongs to one or another of these centers. They meet every Sunday for organizational business. The members pay 10¢ a month. The money is then used to make coffins and defray funeral expenses when a member dies. There is no local cemetery in Las Lomas, and all burials are made in David. The members of the *centro* either make the coffin or employ a carpenter to do so. The family has to pay for nothing. The members then go in the funeral procession."

In Querévalo, there is one *Centro Funerario* to which about 120 people, one third of the population, belong. The *centro* is about 18 years old. There is a directing council composed of seven important people, a president, vice-president, secretary, treasurer, and three other persons. The members meet once a month. Each person pays 10¢ per month, and an additional 15¢ every time a member dies. The *centro* takes care of all funeral expenses and gives $5.00 to the family. Expenses include the coffin, paying the priest, and the expenses of the first *rosario* prayer session. Subsequent prayer sessions are paid for by the family.

The writer had the impression that funerals and attendant prayer sessions were important social occasions for the countrymen. It might develop upon more intensive study that more revolves about the death customs than were apparent during the course of the survey.

11. SOCIAL STRUCTURE OF TOWN AND COUNTRY

There is a basic distinction in the social structure of the Panamanian countryside between two types of populations, the town dwellers and the country dwellers. The distinction involves differences in economic orientation, usually in wealth, in living materials, religious participation, political participation, and general value orientation.

Angel Rubio[64] recognizes this distinction by calling the town deweller *lugareño*: "While the countryman population relies upon a weak, self-sufficient, agricultural subsistence economy, and is almost totally marginal to the money economy, the ... *lugareña* population moves within the money economy, is more commercial, and probably, with more dependence on cattle and a pastoral economy. In the first—the countryman population—there appears to be a greater survival of Indian economic and cultural practices (the culturally disorganized Indian and the mestizo or *cholo* of the uplands); in the second—the *lugareña* population—we believe there is a greater participation of Spanish culture elements, as much as in the human type (creole or mestizo) and in preference for a pastoral economy. It should not be forgotten that the Spanish colonization moved into the lowlands in the region of the Pacific savannas (where the *lugareña* population is found) and that the economy of the Spanish colonizer in the 16th and 17th Centuries in the Peninsula was fundamentally pastoral and cattle raising. ..."

A further distinction which should be made, however, is that there are some towns which participate predominantly in the countryman kind of economy in which agriculture is still of primary importance. Palmas Bellas, Santo Domingo and Querévalo are cases in point. All three are nucleated, and Santo Domingo is quite large; but all are inhabited principally by town-dwelling countrymen. They are quite distinct from the usual town-dwelling population which is to be found in Chepo, Ocú, Montijo, San Francisco, Chorrera, or even Alanje. The Palmas Bellas, Querévalo, and Santo Domingo populations are in an intermediate position between the predominantly self-sufficient countryman and the town dweller oriented to the commercial economy and town-living pattern. In the discussion which follows, we will discuss differences and relationships be-

[64] 1950b, pp. 79–80.

tween the town dweller and countryman. Of the localities visited during the survey, Margarita de Chepo, the communities of the Chorrera backlands, El Espino, Sonadora, Corozal, and Las Lomas were predominantly countryman communities; Chepo, Montijo, San Francisco, Soná, Remedios, Alanje and Dolega were towns in the sense of which Rubio speaks.

In general the town dweller depends upon a business or agriculture and livestock with employed labor; the country dweller is basically a subsistence agriculturalist. The town dweller will usually be a landowner, even if it involves no more than the site of his home or his business; the country dweller will usually be a *usufructario* (using land as he needs it, but not having title to it) or a renter. His own home he will consider as being on land which belongs to him, but he actually rarely has title to it. The town dweller, usually being a trader of sorts, has more money than the countryman; the countryman lives more directly from the goods he produces, and usually has fewer commercial products in his home. The town dweller will usually have better looking clothing, his house is usually more substantial, and his furniture will often be made by a carpenter. With the priest residing in the town and the church located there, the town dwellers participate much more frequently in formal religious activities than do the country dwellers. Even when a rural settlement has a chapel the priest comes very seldom. The urban women are much more active in lay religious associations. Only the townspeople hold administrative offices in the municipal organization; and the political leaders, sometimes referred to as *caciques*,[65] live in the towns. They correspond in many of their functions to that of a ward boss in the United States. Because it is they who provide for many of the immediate needs of the country people, they retain considerable control of the vote. The town politician, being frequently also a storekeeper, may withhold credit should a countryman fail to vote properly. In general, the value orientation of the townspeople is towards accumulation of wealth, a certain amount of conspicuous consumption, and retention of symbols of cultural and social differences which distinguish them from the countryfolk. The country people, on the other hand, are oriented much more towards gaining the immediate necessities of life. Only in certain regions is an effort made to perpetuate symbolic differences to distinguish them from the townspeople. This is, for example, found in the dress of the country people in the uplands of the Azuero Peninsula. The town dwellers are more interested in events in the outside world, in the politics of Panama as a nation, in the status of trade and national economy as reflected in local business; they are better travelled, usually having been to Panama City, the Canal Zone, and occasionally to other countries. The country dweller's orientation of interest is usually towards his own life; politics are important to him specifically in terms of the local political boss, not in terms of the national political figures who are represented locally.

Depending upon the particular community there are frequently found to be subdivisions within these two main classes. Among the town dwellers in some of

---

[65] Hooper, 1945, pp. 240–241.

the long established towns, there is often found an "upper crust," referred to locally as the "aristocracy" or *primeros* (first class people). This "aristocracy" is usually somewhat endogamous, retains a certain amount of wealth, and holds the reins of political power in the immediate region. They are sometimes referred to as *blancos* (a term also used for the town dwellers in general at times). This group is usually quite class conscious and counts some professionals among its number.

Below the "aristocracy" may be found the rest of the town dwellers, persons of middle or lower wealth status, people who have been successful in commerce, employees, or distant relatives of the "aristocracy." Included too in this group are the business men of foreign extraction, such as the *"chinos"* and *"arabes,"* terms used for persons of oriental and near eastern origin. In some places, this town population is referred to as the *segundos* (second class). The countryman or woman who comes to live in town usually moves into the lower fringes of this level. There are usually many more social relations between the *segundos* and the countryfolk than between the latter and the *primeros*. The *segundos* are frequently more apt in exploiting the class differences than are the *primeros*. They can ally themselves together with the countrymen in disputes against the "aristocracy," and frequently have many fast friends among the countrypeople.

Within the countryman population, there is an almost universal recognition of a distinction between those who are *más acomodados* (better off) and those who are *más pobres* (poorer). This distinction, however, is not one which a person is necessarily born to, as is the distinction between the *primeros* and *segundos* in the towns. Within a person's lifetime he may move from a poor status to a better off status, or the reverse. The distinction is one primarily of wealth and use of wealth. It is not really a class distinction at all.

A further distinction to be found among the countrypeople reflects territorial proximity to the towns and major routes of transport and commerce. The people who live nearer the town are thought to be *más relacionada, más avanzada,* or to have *más organización de la vida*. All these expressions mean that they have more in common with the town dwellers, they use more commercial products, use better clothes, know a little more of ways of the town or possibly even the cities. The people who live in the backlands, in the mountains and semi-isolated from the towns and commerce routes are said to be *más tímidos*. They are more difficult to deal with, more afraid of the outsiders, more dependent upon material traits which they make themselves, and in general have less contact with the town people.

It should be remembered that the entirety of the system we are describing here exists only in some places. The country dwellers themselves are concerned with the entire system only when they come to the town or when a town person comes to the country. There are many towns, further, where the distinction between the *primeros* and *segundos* does not exist or now survives only in a most tenuous form. In the towns where there has been a large recent increase in population, such as in Santiago, Atalaya, La Chorrera, and David, various other elements and factors have entered the picture to produce a considerable alteration in the social structure.

The countryman is usually conscious particularly of his own rural community, his friends and relatives in neighboring communities and towns, and only slightly of the entire structure within which he lives. In one region, that of the mountains and backlands of Azuero Peninsula, the countrymen are more conscious of their differences from the townspeople. They are said to greet each other with the expression, "*cómo están los manos*", and call each other, among themselves, "*manos*" or "*manitos*."[66] Hooper reports that this term comes from *hermano*, brother, and in this way the countrypeople of this region express the fact that they consider themselves brothers. The writer has received information from diverse sources, both in the field and from outsiders who have worked in this region, that the term *manos* refers to "hands," and stems from the fact that they are supposed to shake hands upon meeting.

The social relations and attitudes which exist between the town and country dwellers varies from one of excessive class consciousness, such as exists between the city-bred urbanite and the Indian, to one of close personal friendship, tied with bonds of economic interdependence and artificial or actual kinship bonds. Many of the countrypeople are dependent upon the towns for their supplies. The degree of this dependence varies with the proximity of the countryman to a town and transportation routes. The town dweller, in turn, is dependent upon the countryman for various foodstuffs and certain articles of handicraft, such as pottery and baskets. Also, many of the town businessmen require the countryman's trade to keep in business. As Hooper has noted, there is usually considerable cordiality between the town and countrypeople; this is probably more true of *segundos* than *primeros*. There are frequently actual kinship bonds between the two, usually through a countrywoman who has married or lives as the common-law wife of a town dweller. In addition to this, there are many countrypeople who seek out townspeople as *compadres* since the townspeople can help them if they are in need. The town people usually are glad to accept these requests since the more *compadres* one has, the more trade it means for one's store, the more political influence one can wield, and the more places there are where one can expect hospitality when travelling in the country.

Besides the towns such as Palmas Bellas, Santo Domingo, and Querévalo, which are composed of individuals who live on subsistence agriculture, every town has a small population of subsistence agriculturalists. In populations such as these the distinction between the town and country dweller shifts and is not merely based on economic or occupational differences but also to local residential difference. These people are farmers and yet live on the fringe of or in an urban settlement pattern. They have many of the characteristics of the town dwellers, and also retain many countryman characteristics. They tend to make a distinction between the agriculturalists who live as they do and those who live back in the hills in more rural establishments.

---

[66] Hooper, 1945, pp. 237–38.

The terminology applied by the town dwellers to those in the countryside is usually *campesino* (countryman) or *cholo*. The latter term refers to the racial mixture of white and Indian which is seen in many of the country dwellers. Since the same mixture is to be seen in the towns, the term also has a cultural connotation, referring to the "more Indian" way of life carried on in the country. The countrypeople call the townpeople *"los blancos," "gente del pueblo," "enzapatados,"* etc. The people of Palmas Bellas refer to the countrypeople who live in the region around Gatún Lake as *"naturales,"* a term which usually means "Indian." This terminology reflects the fact that the Palmas Bellas population is primarily of negro extraction and has an Antillean as well as Spanish heritage, while those living around Gatún Lake have a culture more closely related to the earlier Indian cultures.

In general the class structure one encounters in the towns and countryside of Panama reflects different ways of life, different occupations, and different educational opportunities. It is mainly in the larger towns that one finds the caste-like retention of an "aristocracy," but this seems to be weakening and disappearing in the towns which are seeing commercial growth with a more wealth-based system; elsewhere, in the towns where the population is not noticeably increasing and no new commerce has entered, there may be some retention of this upper class, but one also finds that members of this class have left to go elsewhere. The town and country population share many folk beliefs in common, although the town people seem to feel that "education" can push aside the superstitions which they think are characteristic only of the countryfolk.

12. POLITICAL STRUCTURE

The political structure of all Latin American countries is established by law. The fact that the lower levels of administration are directly concerned and in contact with the governed, however, frequently bring about variations from the official national pattern. In the brief description to follow, we will take up the lower echelon political structure as it was observed and explained during the survey. Unfortunately, the brevity of the survey permitted only glimpses of the functioning of this structure.

Panama is divided into nine provinces and one *comarca*. The comarca of San Blas is an Indian reservation area controlled by the San Blas Indians and its internal structure does not follow that of the rest of the country. The nine provinces are divided into a total of sixty-four districts, and these in turn are subdivided into some 335 *corregimientos*.[67] The standard district organization includes a mayor and municipal council elected by the people of the district. Housed in the municipal building are a judge, appointed from the provincial capital, and a *personero*, also appointed from the provincial capital. The *personero* acts to check the competence of the elected municipal officials, and as an investigator into civil and criminal cases. There will usually be a national police post

---

[67] Census 1950a, p. 11.

in the district capital as well. The district center is always a town and the district officials are always townsmen.

The mayor appoints a *corregidor* from each of the *corregimientos* to be the chief official of those areas. (There may be some variation from this in the urban *corregimientos* of Panama and Colón; here we are concerned only with the rural structure as observed during the survey.) The *corregidor* is the principal rural official. He seldom has any office aside from his home, and his functions consist in settling local disputes, keeping track of the allotment and requests for usufruct of government lands, and giving permission for minor fiestas; he also refers anything beyond his jurisdiction to the mayor in the district capital and acts as his agent in the countryside. He is responsible for keeping the roads and bridges in his *corregimiento* in order, and the cemetery, if there is one, clean; for this he calls a *faena* (sometimes pronounced *fajina*), a work session of the able-bodied men of the area. Sometimes these are voluntary and sometimes mandatory. To work effectively in the *corregimiento*, the *corregidor* cannot be excessively strict about demanding that people participate in the *faenas*, so they are usually considered as being voluntary.

The national political organization also recognizes a further subdivision within the *corregimiento*, the *caserío*. The 1950 Census lists 6,638 *caseríos* in the republic. The *caserío*, however, is not, strictly speaking, a territorial unit in the same sense that the *corregimiento* is. While the *corregimiento* is an area with generally agreed upon boundaries, the *caserío* is a focus of population with a name. When one refers to a *corregimiento*, he is referring to a specific land area; when he refers to a *caserío*, he refers to a grouping of houses. However, since a *caserío* is always named, there is a tendency to assign territorial limits. These may vary from time to time with the particular land being worked by the people who live in the *caserío*.

Under the *corregidor*, *regidores* are named in each of the principal *caseríos*; their immediate area of jurisdiction may be one or more *caseríos*. Generally the *corregidor* will name the *regidores*, but their appointment must be approved by the district mayor. There is frequently another official whose place in the structure varies somewhat from one area to the next. He is the *comisario*. In some places, *comisarios* are appointed directly by the mayor to act as his immediate executives; elsewhere, they may be subordinate to the *regidores*, or there may be a switch in terminology, and the *comisario* will be in charge of principal *caseríos* and the *regidores* will have smaller centers under their jurisdiction.

The net result of this political structure is that the administration of districts is entirely under the jurisdiction of townsmen; the *corregidores*, *regidores* and *comisarios* are named by the district mayor or must have his approval. The functions of rural officers subordinate to the mayor are slight. Since the countrymen frequently have little direct contact with the district officers, their knowledge of the political system focuses on the *regidores* and *corregidores*; since they have relatively little authority, the political structure does not play a very large role in the countryman's life. Only in specific issues, such as obtaining license for using land, is the official of great importance.

Distinct from, but frequently being incorporated in, the national political structure is the pattern of informal authority and leadership to be found in the rural communities. The settlement pattern of the countryside, small groups of houses and many isolated homes, tends to make certain neighborhoods recognized. A person will tend to have more intercourse with certain of his neighbors than others. The particular limits of a given neighborhood will usually be determined by the nature of the terrain which encourages or discourages travel and contact. Within such neighborhoods are formed the *juntas* and *peonadas*, and people of the neighborhood join together more often in dances, novenas, and other social activities. Within a neighborhood there tend to be one or a few people who through ambition, ability, intelligence, or for some other reason, are looked upon as being outstanding. This should not be interpreted as meaning that the countryman is a slavish follower; such is not the case. The countryman is as individualistic as any of his Central American rural counterparts; but on the occasions when issues arise, there are some who tend to take the lead and others who retire. Frequently these local leaders are named as *corregidores* or *regidores*, and their leadership is utilized; in other cases, they have no official position, but are simply the people who "know more," or "whom you should see."

The writer encountered some evidence that the various neighborhood alliances are shifting, and it is quite probable that the importance of a particular leader will vary from time to time. The people named as *corregidores* and *regidores* are not necessarily middle-aged or elderly people who are considered to be competent and experienced. Since these posts are filled completely by appointment, and the control is held by a townsman, the people whom he likes or trusts are appointed. This means that it is often a relatively young person who will have official jurisdiction over a segment of the rural population. The countrymen are often quite satisfied to have young people in such positions, since it usually means that they will not be too demanding of their elders in matters of control.

13. NOTES ON RELIGION

The town and country dwellers of Panama are predominantly Catholic. The particular fiestas sponsored, how they are fomented, and some of the customs connected with them are considered later under the discussion of each of the towns. In general, the countryman's religious activity consists in attending a few of the annual fiestas in the nearest town; going occasionally to Sunday Mass if he lives near enough; attending local fiestas in the places where a *caserío* has a patron saint or baptising and confirming his children in the faith; an annual fiesta; attending the novenas held upon the death of a neighbor; sometimes celebrating the day of the saint which is kept in the home; and holding a *rogativa* when in need of rain. Rarely does the countryman participate in the religious brotherhoods and societies which exist predominantly among the women of the towns; such societies require a church, a saint, and enough people to participate. As between townsmen and countrymen, however, the latter are, generally, more devoted than the former.

Protestant missionary activity thus far has been felt in the zone nearest the Canal, the Colón-Chepo and the Chorrera-Coclé regions, and in Chiriquí. Where the Protestants are to be found, it usually is a particular *caserío* or a particular *barrio* which is involved. Through the major part of the Azuero and Veraguas areas the people are strongly Catholic; in some places they are clearly hostile to Protestants. It was mentioned in both Ocú and Soná that the townspeople in particular were so strongly Catholic that they would not permit Protestants to come in. In the *barrio* of La Pita of Alanje, the Protestants are referred to as *cuadrados*, evidently taken from the "Four Square Gospel." (See Appendix, # 17)

It was noticed in a number of the towns visited that there were half finished new churches. It was explained in each case that these were the results of political promises made before one of the elections. "We will have to wait until next election time before we can get some more money to have more work done," was the dejected comment heard in one town. In general, each district has a priest, but in some cases there are not enough priests to go around. There were relatively few instances, however, of the priests making much effort to visit the countryside. They remained, for the most part, in the towns and administered to the needs of the townspeople. This has doubtless played a great part in the nature of the contemporary participation in religious activities on the part of the countryman.

14. IDEAS OF SICKNESS AND PRACTICES OF CURING

In general, the countrymen have as much access to western medical facilities as they do to other aspects of urbanized western culture. The further one lives away from the principal towns, the less he can use the medical facilities. Proximity to medical facilities, however, has not succeeded in completely displacing many of the concepts of illness which have grown up in traditions of the countrypeople, nor of replacing the local *curandero*, or curer, in handling many of these illnesses. To have an understanding of the folk medicine of a people, one must realize that different symptoms are classified in a different manner than among people more familiar with western medical ideas; and that this different form of classifying calls in different kinds of cures and different curers. While some of the ideas and practices to be described below are found principally in the countryside, many of them are common among the townspeople as well.

One informant distinguished three kinds of people: (1) those who simply do not believe in hospitals and doctors, have little faith in them, and always go to a *curandero*; (2) those who, if possible, will go first to a doctor or the hospital, and if they fail to be properly cured, will then go to a *curandero*; (3) those who will always seek a medically prescribed or patent remedy. Most townspeople fall into one of the latter two categories, while most countrymen fall into one of the first two. In view of the acceptance which medical services have been given when they have gone into the backlands, it seems clear that among the countrymen there would be fewer in the first category if there were better medical facilities available.

In the discussion to follow, we will take up first some of the more commonly recognized illnesses which imply a classification of symptoms different from those of modern medicine, including some of the difficulties attributed to human molestation; and second take up a few of the curing techniques and kinds of specialists involved in the folk medicine.

Pujo.—This term generally refers to dysentery. It is usually described as wanting to defecate but being unable to. In some places a bloody stool is considered as merely one symptom of *pujo*, in others *pujo con sangre* is distinguished from ordinary *pujo*; in Sonadora, *corredera* or *viajedera* refers to mild dysentery, *pujo* refers to bloody stool. *Pujo* is sometimes attributed to drinking too much *aguardiente*, also said to come on when one is working; lemonade was stated to be one cure.

Empacho.—This term is not used everywhere but the condition is recognized; it is indigestion, "full stomach," or "dirty stomach." The standard cure is some sort of purgative. In Sonadora, *barriga mala* is the term used for the same condition.

Pasmo, Viento, Aire.—These three terms cover a group of ills; they are sometimes used together, or one will be used instead of the other. In general, *pasmo* is an ache or pain almost any part of the body. In the Azuero region and Veraguas it refers to an inflamed cut, sometimes said to be due to the sun's rays entering the cut, other times said to be due to getting the cut damp or soaked; in Los Pozos one gets *pasmo* if his body is too hot and he becomes damp; in Ocú, *frusión* is a pain in the joints, while *frusión con pasmo* is an inflamed cut. *Pasmo* can also occur to a menstruating woman. When one has *pasmo*, it is said that "he has been hit by the cold" (*le ha caído frío*) in Soná; in Sonadora, *dolor de ijá* is a liver trouble which "comes like a wind," *viento*; in El Espino *pasmo* was stated to be the same as *aire*, any kind of ache; in Santo Domingo it was a swelling produced by a blow, cut, or bite, and *viento* pains are said to come when one has strained himself.

There are some herbal remedies to cure *pasmo*: *hierba de pasmo* (El Espino), and depending upon the kind of *pasmo*, there are *pasmos de sol, pasmos de agua,* and *paico of hediondo* plants used in Soná; also in Soná anything "cold" (*frío*) was said to be good for all *pasmos*. In El Espino, a herb called *mastranto* is taken as a tea for *aire* and stomach ache; the herb rue is rolled into small rolls and placed in the ear for earaches; in the backland behind Sonadora, an herb, *salbia*, is used to remove *aire* when manifested in headaches, and the fat of chickens and tortoises are used for the same purpose; also in Sonadora, a substance called *tracomaca de aire* is bought in drugstores and placed on the head to take out the *aire*; in Los Pozos and Montijo one will say that "I have *aire*" when he has a pain resulting from a strain or other cause; in Ocú, *viento subido*, a pain in the stomach, causes people to vomit; in Montijo *viento* may be cured by massages and also with *santiguar* (making the sign of the cross and praying). (See Appendix, ※ 18)

In general, one may fall ill of *viento*, *aire* or *pasmo* if overheated, and becoming damp or chilled, having a cut which is allowed to get wet or into which the sun's rays fall, by straining oneself, or if in a weakened condition such as menstruating or having just had a child. It may be cured with special herbs, certain kinds of lards, and certain treatments such as massages and the *santiguadera*. It can affect almost any part of the body but it is most common as headaches, stomach-aches, back-aches, pains in the joints, or where a blow, cut, or bite, has become inflamed.

Mal de Ojo or to be *Ojeado*.—This is basically the same "evil eye" or "strong look" which is found elsewhere in Latin America. In El Espino, it may be caused by a pregnant woman or a person who is in a bad temper, "who has not slept well." It will cause a child to fall ill of a fever or a headache; it can be cured, if a woman caused it, by wrapping the child in the undercloths of the woman; if a man caused it, he must strike the child. In Ocú, it was said that the sick child must put on the shirt, turned inside-out, of the person who has the strong look; also, the child could be cured by being bathed in the urine of the person who caused the sickness. In Montijo, it was said that sometimes the *"vista fuerte"* was intentional but more often it was not. Either the person who did it must cure it, or a *curandero* must be called in. The cure involved giving the child a bath on Tuesdays and Fridays at midnight and using *santiguar*. A pregnant woman, it was said, had a glance so strong that she could not only *ojear* a child, but make a snake stop moving by staring at it. In Soná too, it was said that the child ill of *mal de ojo* must wear the clothes of the person who did it and bath in his urine; also, that the person with the strong look can affect animals.

Witchcraft.—There seem to be two or possibly three different kinds of grades of witchcraft. *Brujería*, or witchcraft as such, consists in making people deathly ill, in turning oneself into an animal, flying, making a person lose his way on the road, or putting frogs, lizards or snakes in someone's stomach. This kind of witchcraft seems strongest in the Azuero and Veraguas regions, and possibly in the backlands of Coclé and Panama; no material on *brujería* of this kind was collected in Chiriquí. A milder form of witchcraft is called "doing *daños*," or damaging a person. This kind of damage consists in headaches, or other mild infirmities, and any competent *curandero* can do them and cure them. It was said in Montijo that most of the common ailments were attributed to such *daños*. In some places the workers of these milder troubles are called *hechiceros*, sorcerers, and their works, *hechizos*; this distinction does not seem to be consistently employed everywhere, however.

Curers and Curing Methods.—There are generally two types of *curanderos*: those who utilize pharmaceutical remedies, herbs, and other non-occult remedies, and those who practice semi-secret or secret remedies. It is this latter class which is sometimes thought also to practice *hechizos*. While the term *curandero* is standard over most of Panama, in Palmas Bellas the term *cuyoso* was used for this status. The curer who practices *daños* is often accused of making someone sick while in the pay of one person, and then being called in by the patient and being paid again for curing him. Curers are generally men, but witches may be either men or women. In Sonadora it was reported that curers tended to specialize somewhat; some knew more about snake bites, others about hemorrhages, still others know about broken bones. The writer encountered few cases of *curanderos* living in the towns; they are generally agriculturalists who practice their specialty on the side.

One of the most common methods of diagnosis of the *curanderos* is to take urine from the patient and hold it in a bottle against the sun so that its shadow falls on a white handkerchief; by observing the shadow, the curer can determine what the cause of the ailment is and prescribe treatment for it. Curing frequently involves one or more of the many herbs which are to be found in the countryside. The writer was given the local names of a number of such herbs and vegetable cures: *caraña* and *chutra* are saps used for pains; *hierba buena*, for pains, fever, and stomach-aches and malaria; *toronjil* and *paico* for *lombrices* (worms); *salbia* to remove *aire*; *hierba malaba* for *pujo*; *ruda* for earaches; and the various *hierbas de pasmo*. One of the most common curing devices is that called *santiguar*. The *santiguadera* consists in saying a prayer and making various ritualistic movements, such as the sign of the cross, over the sick person. It is used particularly in serious cases and in cases of *ojeado* and *hechizos*.

Among the other specialists to be found in the countryside are the *comadronas* (midwives) and the *padroneras* or *sobadoras*. The midwives are ubiquitous; there are few if any communities which do not have a woman somewhere nearby to help in the delivery of a child. The *padroneras* or *sobadoras* are a type of *curandera* who specialize in massaging; they were reported specifically in western Veraguas and eastern Chiriquí, but may exist elsewhere also, although the informant in Dolega said she was not familiar with the term. The particular technique of the *sobadora* seems to involve giving a special prayer, making a *santiguadera*, massaging the stomach to bring the gas (*viento*) to the abdomen, and then placing a patch with the black *caraña* sap on the navel. This is particularly important after childbirth, but it is done in other cases as well.

The concepts of "hot" and "cold" which play such an important part in disease etiology and curing in certain other parts of Latin America do not seem to be so strong in Panama. In most places visited it was acknowledged that some distinction was made between some foods and substances which were considered to be "cold" or "fresh," and others which were thought to be "hot". The concept of "cold" in connection with *aire* and *viento* was mentioned earlier. In Montijo it was stated that when a woman was menstruating, she should not eat cold things. Among the foods thus classified were pineapple, watermelon, oranges, and papayas. In Ocú two statements were made which suggest that the idea is not entirely absent. One was in connection with the mixed sowing in agriculture; it was said that beans were sown alone, and not with corn because the corn "is somewhat hot and does damage to the beans." The other was a comment made by the townsman informant from the upper class, who thought that women who did ironing with the charcoal iron were prone to die from tuberculosis. This last comment would make sense if based on the concept of a person being overheated, then chilled and contracting a resultant respiratory infection. (See Appendix, ⁑ 19)

While, as is noted shortly, there is some credence given to the existence of certain spirits, the writer found no real evidence that *susto* or *espanto*, common in both Peru and Central America as an illness, was present in Panama. One informant said that if a person was frightened enough, he would get sick, and another said that the soul left one when it fainted, but returned when he came to. Neither of these seemed to imply any complex syndrome or ailment. The term *bilis*, also somewhat common elsewhere, was mentioned by only one informant; he said that it was a dizziness one has if he gets sick.

15. NOTES ON THE SPIRIT WORLD

It was neither intended nor possible to gather much data on the spirits which may live among the countrymen, but a few notes were taken which will be recorded here for the record.

We have elsewhere mentioned the witches, *brujas*, who are said to be able to fly, lead men astray on the road, make people sick and turn themselves into animals. The witches are real people who have these powers. The spirits to be mentioned now are not known people but remain as spirits.

The *tulivieja* is a woman who is said to have lost her child and comes around the houses crying *"tulivuí, tulivuí;"* since she is looking for another child, the people keep their doors closed. (See Appendix, ⁑ 20)

The *duende*, or fairy, was described in Soná as being a devil in the form of a boy with white hair. In Montijo *duendes* were said to be small people who wore large hats and that they would call to children they would show them games. If the child went with them, he never returned.

The *silampa* was a white spirit which, when one first saw it, was only a few inches high. It would suddenly start to grow, however, until it reached the clouds. When the writer asked what the *silampa* did, the reply was that no one has ever stayed around long enough to discover whether he could hurt a person or not!

Two other spirits are the *chivato*, the "goat that is a devil," and the man without a head. It was said in San Francisco that on the Day of the Dead in November the dead have a procession in the cemetery. A spirit of a dead person will always return to his old haunts such as his house.

The *tulivieja* is similar to the *llorona* found further north in Central America, except that in Panama it has evidently been combined with the child-stealing theme which is also found elsewhere. The *duendes*, described in Panama as being little men with large hats, are essentially similar to some of the *duende* characters of Guatemala, such as the *sombrerón*. Again the child-stealing theme is combined.

16. RECREATION AND DIVERSION

The patterns of recreation and diversion are quite different in the town and the countryside. For the countryman, diversions consist principally of activities which also have some other function: work *juntas* and *peonadas* provide a chance for social intercourse and pleasure; the religious fiestas held occasionally in the countryside or attended at certain times in the town provide both entertainment and observance of religious observations; the novenas held at the time of death, while not precisely entertaining, provide an important diversion from the daily round of field work; a baptism, marriage, or birthday may be the occasion for having a dance, or someone may sponsor a dance simply in order to make a little money. Civil or secular fiestas, such as the national fiesta on the 3rd of November, or Carnival, may be observed in the countryside, but they are much more important in the towns. When a countryman actually has leisure, such as while waiting for his dinner to be prepared in the evening, or after dinner if there is no novena or other activity, he finds his pleasure in sitting in his or a neighbor's yard, telling jokes, discussing local events, playing with the children, mending a basket, sharpening his machete, or some other activity which may be carried on while resting.

In Panama the humor, stories, and dances of the country are becoming recognized as a real national folklore. Musical instruments are made almost everywhere in the countryside, principally the guitar, three stringed violins, and drum; more rarely are found the gourd rattle, simple flute, and *güiro*, the grooved gourd which is scraped. All countryman fiestas and dances have small groups playing these instruments. Even in town fiestas, when the countrymen attend, they bring their instruments; dances of countrymen are usually held apart from those of the townspeople. The writer did not have the occasion to observe any of the countryman dances, but many were counted as being distinct by his informants: the *cumbia, tamborito, curacha, mejorana, zapatero, socomón, llanero, taboña, el punto* and various others were named as always using the countryman's music. Sometimes, if available, an accordion will join the group, but in many places it is preferred to use only the local instruments. Although inquiries were made, the use of masked dances was nowhere reported to the writer during the survey, except during holy week in San Francisco. (See Appendix, #21)

Sports, as organized efforts, are limited to townsmen, mainly because they require more people than the young countrymen can get together at one time, and the countrymen have never found much time for such activities. The young men, who would participate in games, must work along with their elders in subsistence activities. Occasionally a *fútbol* (soccer ball) will find its way from a school into use among the local young men who live in the vicinity, but this seldom involves more than half a dozen boys kicking the ball back and forth. Baseball, which is popular in the towns which have teams, is limited principally to the townsmen.

The towns provide *cantinas* and sometimes billiard halls for entertainment and relaxation, but again it is usually the townsmen who patronize them. The countrymen are not often in town at night unless for some occasion such as a fiesta, religious observance, or on business. As elsewhere in Central and South America, there are various urbanities and townspeople who have complained about the amount of drinking which may accompany a countryman celebration. During the course of the survey, no fiestas were seen, nor were there any drunken countrymen.

III. COMMUNITIES INCLUDED IN THE SURVEY

It was hoped in the course of the survey that it would be possible to delineate cultural regions within the general countryman culture area of Panama. It was felt that such a delineation, predominantly impressionistic, but checked against systematically gathered comparative materials, would be useful in con-

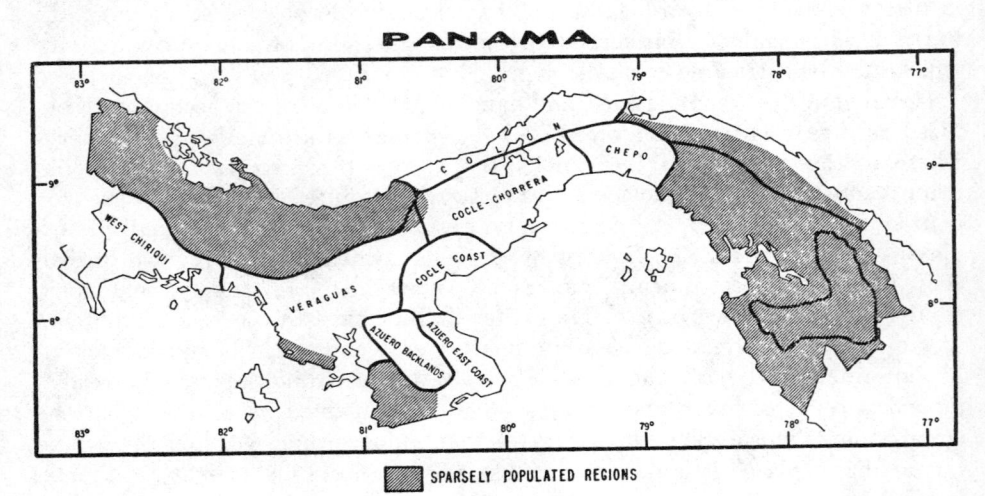

PANAMA

SPARSELY POPULATED REGIONS

ceptualizing the countryman culture. Unfortunately, while the data gathered in the survey provided considerable evidence of differences between communities and some evidence of regional differences, it did not provide sufficient data on regional differences to adequately confirm or deny the impressions which the writer received.

The present section of the report is intended to provide some specific information on the communities visited and a brief discussion of the regions of the countryman culture based upon the writer's impressions. The descriptions include, particularly, data on the religious organization of the communities; this varies so much from one town to another that it was felt that it would be more appropriate to include it here than in the earlier general sections.

The countryman culture area of Panama has experienced varying histories, has had varying contacts and felt varying influences. There have developed, because of these differing histories, certain foci of regional variation. One region which stands out as being fairly distinct from the rest of Panama is the Colón coast. Here, the people consider themselves to be distinct from the *"naturales"* who live further inland, and the economy is more dependent upon bananas, plantains, and coconuts than elsewhere. Racially, the people are more predominantly negroid.

The Chepo region, also with a heavy negroid racial component, has been in the past more dependent upon forest products. Today, however, Chepo is the scene of immigration from some of the more heavily populated regions of the Interior and it may be that in the future it will come to be more similar to the regions to the west. The districts of Colón, Chagres, Arraiján, Panama, and to a lesser extent Chorrera, have felt the immediate impact of the canal and the Antillean cultures.

Beginning in Chorrera, and continuing through the districts of the Province of Panama west of the Canal, the upland districts of Coclé (the northern part of Penonomé, La Pintada, and Olá, the backlands of Natá and Aguadulce), the Province of Veraguas and extending into parts of central Chiriquí, exists what we may call the Basic Countryman Culture. The major characteristics of this culture are described in Part II of this report. Unfortunately, the survey did not include any communities in this broad region between Sonadora in Coclé and San Francisco in Veraguas. There were suggestions, on the basis of cultural similarities, that there might be a distinction or regional division to be found between west Panama and the Coclé uplands on the one hand, and Veraguas and parts of Chiriquí on the other.

Coastal Coclé, due to a fairly heavy concentration of *haciendas*, tends to fall into a separate region. Coastal Herrera and Los Santos also form another subdivision on the basis of certain cultural differences, and more important, due to the heavy concentration of population and an incidence of nucleated settlements of countrymen. This area is characteristic of more intensive economic exploitation. The uplands of Herrera and Los Santos form yet another regional division due to the outstanding cultural elaboration and conservatism to be found centering around Ocú. This region, it should be noted, has not conserved merely Indian traits, but has rather manifested an elaboration on the countryman culture in terms of certain habits of interpersonal relations and some material items such as clothing. Both coastal and uplands here are predominantly white racially, although there are enclaves of mestizo and negroid groups.

The basic countryman culture to be found in Veraguas impressed the writer as being the most homogeneous of any studied on the survey. The material gathered in Montijo, San Francisco, Soná, Corozal, and Remedios was extremely similar. The differences seem to rest mainly on local social organization, the strength of the class system, and local voluntary groupings.

Chiriquí offers the most difficult to characterize of all the Panamanian provinces. Its eastern coastal section and parts of the central uplands seem essentially part of the basic countryman culture. However, coastal Chiriquí is also an area of *hacienda* exploitation, and many parts of the uplands have seen recent development in a diversification of crops which is to be found nowhere else in the country. Aside from the Canal Zone itself, Chiriquí has probably been subjected to a greater variety of influences than any other part of the country. Costa Ricans have moved in and out of the area, Americans from the Canal Zone have settled there, it was an early center of Indian conversion, and the adjacent Guaymí area itself plays a significant role in the borderline between the Panamanians and Guaymí. The Barú coast has been the center of United Fruit Company exploitations, and the Barú-Costa Rica border has Indian groups as well as mestizo scattered across the countryside.

The map shows the approximate extensions of these regions. The reader should recognize that they are impressionistic and should not rely too heavily upon the delineation made. The brief notes to follow, concerning the various towns surveyed, take up the communities in order running from east to west.

1. CHEPO AND LA MARGARITA DE CHEPO

The Chepo region to the east of Panama City is Pacific coastal plain. It is generally rolling, low hills, broken by many small rivers. The landscape varies between open savanna grass land on which is grazed cattle by the owners of plantations, and densely wooden secondary growth into which are cut the agricultural plots of the countrymen. In June, when the survey was made, the area was very green, but the forest appeared to have little of the more tropical foliage—no air plants, for example. Sauer[68] calls it "scrub palm savanna." There is a good deal of surface water, occasional swamps, and evidently (since there are some artesian wells) some subterranean water as well. Our informants said that the soil in general was good, but there were areas, such as were visible around Chepo, where there were quantities of inhospitable red clay. To the north, running almost parallel to the coast, the mountains rise sharply.

Most of the land to the west of Chepo is owned by large *haciendas*, while to the east, along the rivers, live groups of Cuna Indians. The population of Chepo appears to have a negroid component, but there are many who appear predominantly white or mestizo. The population of La Margarita, on the other hand, is predominantly white with a touch of Indian mixture.

La Margarita is a recent colony, started about eight years ago by people from the Las Tablas region of the Azuero Peninsula. As a result, there is considerable divergency between the culture of the La Margarita population and that of the general Chepo population. Culturally, the La Margarita people still have the way of life of the Azuero region.

Chepo is close to the terminal point of the main automobile road running east from Panama, and La Margarita is about a twenty minute walk to the north of Chepo. Formerly, there were some five or ten families from Chepo living in what is now La Margarita, but most of them moved out some fifteen years ago and now there are only two of the forty odd families who came originally from the Chepo area.

Chepo itself gives the impression of being crowded with wooden houses. For the most part the houses are built very close together, some with tile roofs and some with metal. On the outskirts of the town are a number of poorer houses

---

[68] 1950a, map.

of cane, wood, and palm with palm roofs. At a glance, they are similar to those of La Margarita, but they are generally smaller. While Chepo is a nucleated settlement, La Margarita is a dispersed countryman settlement with houses scattered over the broken savanna land. The houses are all of palm, pole, or *embarrada* walls, with palm roofs. There is no order or streets, and most are between 50 and 100 meters from the next one. They are usually located near a few trees.

In Chepo is a district mayor's building, with a police station, telegraph and telephone. There is neither service to La Margarita; a runner employed by the municipality carries messages to the surrounding *corregimientos*. There is a central plaza with a church and a priest who says Mass every day. He is also responsible for teaching doctrine. The countrymen of La Margarita are at present building a chapel of *embarrada* walls in their community. While the patron saint of Chepo and the surrounding region is *San Cristóbal*, the La Margarita people have brought *la Señora de las Mercedes* from Las Tablas and have her for their patron saint.

The mayor in Chepo names a *regidor* from La Margarita to act as the local official there and also as the agent of the municipality. The *regidor* keeps his position until the mayor names someone else to replace him. He is always a local person and receives no salary.

While there are no public health facilities in La Margarita, there is a sanitary unit located on the west edge of Chepo in which is stationed a nurse. In La Margarita there is a private house with *embarrada* walls which has been rented as a school building. It is, like the rest of the buildings in the *caserío*, a Las Tablas type construction. There is a single woman teacher, a native of Chepo, who walks over each day. The school has a total of 32 students, of both sexes, divided into three grades. If they want further schooling, which few do, they go to Chepo. The teacher said that many children did not go to the school because their parents were too poor to give them sufficient clothing, notebooks, pencils, and so on. Since the government has not provided these necessities, they work with a few old school books, and little more. In the yard around the school is the only latrine in the *caserío*. During the period of our visit, eight children asked permission to relieve themselves, but only one of the eight used the latrine; the rest went to the back of the school building.

The teacher said that no extension activities had been carried out here. She thought when we arrived that we were a mission from "Point IV" which had been promised her. She was looking forward to receiving materials for the school, especially things to read. She said the school had a Parents Club (*Club de Padres de Familia*) but that it never met. In Chepo there was such a club which did meet and discuss the problems of the school. Two years ago, she said, the government sent milk for school lunches, and each child would bring a little corn and rice and ½ *real* (2½¢); but because the school is small, they stopped the milk after one year.

In Chepo, two major fiestas are observed, that of the patron saint, *San Cristóbal*, on the 25th of July, and Holy Week. A novena is started on the night of the

16th of July, and the fiesta itself lasts from the 25th until the 30th. They hold social dances, have bullfights, and a long procession lasting from about four p.m. until midnight on the 25th. While there are no local customs which distinguish this fiesta now, they used to have dances called the *Gran Diablo* and *Montazuma*, in which masks were used. There was also a dance, *el Congo*, for which people painted their faces. The *el Congo* dance was held during Carnival time and the *Gran Diablo* was held during the fiesta of *Corpus Cristi*. Both these stopped some decades ago, however. To sponsor the fiesta of *San Cristóbal*, there is a *Junta Católica* which yearly names *mayordomos*, about ten from the town of Chepo, and one from each *caserío* like La Margarita. In addition, some are named in Panama City. The function of the *mayordomos* is to collect money for the fiesta. They go from house to house and collect anything they can, usually between 25¢ and $5. While the priest helps in the planning of the fiesta, he charges the usual fees for the religious phases of the celebration.

While La Margarita is a community of countrymen, Chepo is a town of minor commercial importance. It is the roadhead for the forest products traffic coming down the Bayano River. According to Carles,[69] Chepo was founded in the 16th Century, and was described by Raquejo y Salcedo in 1607 as a town which has "... its Indian governor with an *alguacil* and two *mandadores*; every year they have a sowing of corn in common and harvest about 200 *fanegas* and store them in a public house. This they pay the priest for doctrine and cover the other expenses of the church, and if there is some left over, it is distributed among the poor and old by the *mandadores* whose responsibilities are public things." During the 16th Century, the Chepo region was the scene of flights of negro slave groups from the transit zone, the most famous of which was under the negro leader, Bayano. These refugee groups probably account in some degree for the negro racial component which is to be found in the contemporary population. In recent years, however, Antillean negroes have also moved into this region.

La Margarita represents a new phase of social and cultural history in the Chepo region. The countryman, whose culture saw its more characteristic development in the Interior, is now moving into this region, and as the rural population grows, this movement may be expected to increase. Chepo may gradually become one with the culture which is more characteristic of the provinces of Panama, Coclé, and the Azuero Peninsula.

2. PALMAS BELLAS

Palmas Bellas, formerly called Lagarto, is a nucleated settlement set on the west bank of the Lagarto River and the shore of the Atlantic Ocean. The coastal area in which the town is located is of fairly uneven surface with year-around rainfall and tropical forest. Constant cutting in the immediate region has left much of the area in dense shrub growth with high palms. Drinking water is taken from the streams which are abundant in the area.

---

[69] 1950, p. 129.

While the people of Palmas Bellas are predominantly negroid, there are some with a strong Indian component. According to the 1950 Census, 529 people lived in Palmas Bellas itself, while another 444 lived scattered out in the *corregimiento*. The houses in the town are fairly close together, arranged in rows, with areas of green grass between them. There is only one road in the town, the main highway which runs from Colón to Salud, a town six kilometers to the west of Palmas Bellas. Along the river going inland and around the perimeter of the town are a number of palm houses, but most of the houses in the town itself are of wood with metal roofs. The people who live outside the town limits in the *corregimiento* are located along the banks of the river. The rivers in this region provide the main highways for travel and transport.

Palmas Bellas is a *corregimiento* of the district of Chagres, the capital of which lies just to the east of the Lagarto River. The mayor of Chagres names the *corregidor* of Palmas Bellas. This functionary, in turn, names two *comisionados* who aid him in the town administration, and one *regidor* along each of the principal rivers of the *corregimiento*. There is one national policeman in Chagres and one in Palmas Bellas. The fact that Chagres is the district capital is a sore point with the people of Palmas Bellas. They feel that since their town is more than twice as big as Chagres, and that "the people of Palmas Bellas are harder working and more progressive," Palmas Bellas should be the capital. They also point out that Palmas Bellas has a full six grade school, while just prior to the time the survey was made Chagres closed up its school entirely and sent the children to the Palmas Bellas school. Palmas Bellas also has a diesel light plant, and Chagres has no source of power. The informant felt that the situation would not change, however, since Chagres has traditionally been the district capital.

The town itself is divided into two parts: the North Barrio, which lies between the highway and the ocean, and the South Barrio which lies on the other side of the road. Formerly the North Barrio was known as *Guachapalí*, which the informant said meant "Barrio of the Jamaicans," while the South Barrio was called *Hoyo de Sapo*. According to the informant, the original inhabitants of the town settled in the area which is now the South Barrio; later, "Jamaicans" moved into what is now the North Barrio area. This group formerly spoke English, but all these people are dead now. There is evidently no particular antagonism between the two *barrios*; that expressed towards Chagres being a sufficient outlet. The names of the *barrios* were changed about 15 years ago, at the same time that the town changed its name from Lagarto to Palmas Bellas.

Most of the population in the *corregimiento* is similar to that found in the town, but the informant said that there were three *caseríos* in the backland which were composed of *"naturales."* The Palmas Bellas people tend to think of themselves as being quite distinct from the Interior population of an Indian background.

The town has a wooden *corregiduría* building with a telephone, but it only calls to Chagres, a quarter of a kilometer away. There used to be a line to Colón, but it was stolen sometime ago and has not been replaced. Mail leaves and is brought in from Colón by *chiva* once a week on Wednesday or Thursday. The *chivas* run daily between Colón and Salud.

Palmas Bellas has no public health facilities, but as was mentioned, the school is fairly large. There are no schools in the backland of the *corregimiento*. There is a Parents' Club, but its main concern is with the state of the school building. The *corregidor* expressed some concern over the quantity of mosquitoes in this area and hoped that the government would soon send them some DDT.

The town has a set of concrete pillars standing for a new church. A presidential candidate had promised them a new church if he were elected, so the villagers went ahead and put up the posts on their own. Then the candidate, having won, built the new church in Chagres. At present, there is a *Junta Católica* responsible for this, but nothing is being done. For the sponsoring of the fiesta of the patron saint, *San Juan Bautista*, there is a group called the *Avanzada Juvenil de Palmas Bellas*, made up of young people. They give dances and take the responsibility for naming the *mayordomos* of the fiesta. There are usually between 70 and 100 *mayordomos* who are named in the town, the *caseríos*, and in Panama. Usually the ministers and president of the country are among those named as *mayordomos*. *Mayordomos* are expected to give a fixed amount, $3.00 for boys and $2.00 for girls. The fiesta lasts 2 days and is always held over a week-end even though the proper day may fall during the week. On Saturday there are dances, and a Mass and procession are held on Sunday. This is the only fiesta held here, and it is the only time during the year when the priest comes to the town. For Holy Week, the people go to Chagres. The priest comes from Colón every week to Chagres to hold Mass. Besides the social dances, there are cockfights during the fiesta. There is no bullfighting.

The writer was able to get very little history concerning Palmas Bellas. An old woman was consulted, and she claimed to be over 70 years of age; she had come there as a child and the town existed at that time. To what degree the population is descended from colonial negro groups and to what degree Antilleans have added to the population in recent times is difficult to estimate.

3. THE CHORRERA BACKLANDS: COROZALES AFUERA, COROZALES ADENTRO, YAYAS ADENTRO AND ZANGÜENGA

The town of Chorrera lies on the main highway, forty or fifty minutes west of Panama City. Since 1930 it has grown from a town of a little over 2,000 to one of over 8,500. One would expect from this that the entire region around Chorrera would reflect something of this expansion and even actively participate in the growth. However, there are no all season automobile roads leading out of Chorrera to the country inland and only an hour or two by horseback brings one into the midst of the countryman population, *caseríos* scattered over the broken, hilly, and wooded landscape. The people in this region think of themselves as living either *más adentro* or *más afuera*, that is, as "further in," or "further out." The road leading into this area leaves from the town of El

Coco, a few kilometers down the road from Chorrera. It winds over small hills, a wide road which serves well the horseback travel for which it is utilized. The growth is heavy secondary brush and forest; while there are many high trees, there are none of any impressive diameter. On both sides of the road are scattered cleared areas, pastures, coffee groves, orange orchards, and cultivation plots. In the morning and evening one sees tree sloths perched high in the trees. Like most of the interior, there is still to be found deer, peccary, rabbits, and a variety of snakes and lizards.

During the survey, four *caseríos* were visited, but data was collected in only three of them. Racially, the people seemed to vary from one to another of the three major stocks to be found in Panama: Indian, negro, and white. All were mestizo. The writer was told after his visit that there has been a strong Antillean increment in this backland population coming in from Gatún Lake and the Canal Zone. The writer did not notice that the population he visited was any more specifically negro than were other groups down the west Panama and Coclé coast.

The first *caserío* visited was Corozales Afuera. There was a Y in the road, and one could see three sets of houses and the school building. As elsewhere, the other homes were scattered about in clearings in the forest. While the people prefer to have their homes near a stream, the population is not everywhere spread out along water courses. There are a number of wells, and drinking water for the most part comes from these. One well will usually serve two or three houses. The wells are generally shallow, and must be cleaned out each morning in order to get clear water. Near to or surrounding each house is an orange grove with grass underneath. These spaces serve also as pasturage. The fields are fenced in, since there are enough cattle around to damage the crops if they stray through them.

The *caseríos* visited belong to one of two *corregimientos* of the district of Chorrera: Hurtado and Herrera. Each has a *corregidor*, named by the mayor in Chorrera, who is the principal administrative officer in the neighborhood. He is in charge of issuing permits to use lands, to know who is using which land and thereby avoid disputes between the various farmers, and sets fines on those who use land without permission; if there is a fight, he acts as a judge, may fine offenders, or send them to Chorrera; he issues permission to hold dances or sends the people to the mayor in Chorrera to get permission for other activities; and he calls the countrymen to work on the *fajina*, or work project, in fixing the roads and repairing bridges.

To help him, the *corregidor* names *regidores* in some of the more distant *caseríos* and *comisarios* to aid him generally. A *regidor* may be sent to attend dances to make sure there are no fights, or to help a traveller, or to act as foreman at a *fajina*. The *regidor* in Corozales Afuera lived across the road from the school. He said that he had held three *fajinas* during the seven months he had been serving in that capacity. Two were in October, one each day, to fix roads, and one in November to fix a bridge.

The local officers have no public building. They serve as long as they are appointed, and their office is in their home. There are no communication facilities in the *corregimientos* except for a runner or horseback rider.

The *corregimientos* have neither church nor chapel. Those who want to will go to Chorrera for Sunday Mass, and most people will go in for the Fiesta of San Francisco, and on either Thursday or Friday of Holy Week. The only local religious observances are the novenas and *rosarios* held at the time of death. These are well attended.

Quite a few of the *caseríos* have single room houses used as schools. Some have wooden buildings with metal roofs, the only such buildings in the region, while others have houses similar to those used as homes. The opinion of the countrymen vary concerning their teachers. Most want the teachers to be there, and are offended when the teacher may absent himself for periods of time. In Corozales Adentro a Parents' Club has been started; they meet the first Sunday of each month or when the teacher asks them to. Besides the fathers of the families, there are also other men, called *cooperadores*, who are not yet fathers but who help with the activities of the club. The men clean the school garden, and collect money to build a new school.

4. EL ESPINO

The *corregimiento* of El Espino is located just to the north and west of the main highway. It is spread out on the rolling and broken coastal plain. As in most of the rural settlements, there is no real center. Along the road going up to El Valle is a handsome new cement school building and a little further on is the home of the *corregidor*. In general, however, the houses are scattered back from the road and only a very few of them are in sight. The general architecture is slightly different from that to be found in the Chorrera areas. The house roofs are not so steep, and straw roofs are more common than palm. The people get their water from the streams, rivers, or shallow wells; the only deep well in the *corregimiento* is that at the school. Within the *corregimiento* the houses are occasionally grouped into sets of three, four or five, a small group thus forming a *caserío*. The *más acomodados* tend to live along the road, and have windows in their homes. But there are relatively few of these.

There is no mail, telephone nor telegraph service. All are found in San Carlos, the town center. There are *chivas* which run up the road to El Valle, so people may use them if they desire, or send down messages by them. There are five or six *regidores* in the *corregimiento*, and the *corregidor* has one *comisionado*. However, work sessions are not called usually; once in a great while the mayor in San Carlos will call for some men to do some work, but this happens very rarely.

There is no church, but one fiesta a year is celebrated. At present, it is held in the school building, but the informant thought that previously it was held in the house of the man who lived across the road. This man is called the *dueño de la fiesta* and is responsible for sponsoring the fiesta. Others will come and contribute money to help with the expenses, but he makes the arrangements.

The priest then comes from San Carlos and brings the saint, *San Juan Bautista*, with him. He holds a Mass and a short procession. There is no Catholic committee or other organization which is involved in sponsoring religious activities. The only other time the priest will come is if they request him to come and hold a *rogativa* for rain.

The school in El Espino has six grades and over 100 students. Some of them come from other *corregimientos*. It is a new building, and the teachers, under the stimulation of an extension group, have started a Parents' Club. This club collects funds for the school to make a dining room and supplies food for the school lunches. The school served as the center of the extension work which was carried on in the district for a year. The informant felt that the agricultural work of this project did not have much influence on the countryman. Efforts were made in introducing home gardens, and planting tomatoes, large peppers, lettuce, cabbage, hot peppers, and onions. Very few of the new items were taken into the general agriculture or diet of the countrymen. The school teachers felt that Parents' Club was not entirely a success as it was necessary to tell them what to do and frequently there was little response. In observing briefly a meeting of this club the survey team heard the teacher in charge telling the parents what to do.

El Espino is a town very much oriented towards fishing. Most of the men spend a good deal of their time at the ocean catching fish and other sea foods. The women, consequently, probably carry relatively more of the agricultural activity than is the case in other countrymen communities. This type of division of labor is similar to that which was found in this area at the time of the conquest. The informant claimed that much more fish than domestic meat goes into the diet. El Espino is a town which, while located near the junction of two paved highways, still retains the essential way of life of the countryman.

5. SONADORA

Sonadora lies northeast of the provincial capital of Penonomé in the valley of the Zarati River. The general landscape is similar to that of Chorrera, being broken savanna land, covered with various stages of second growth. As in the Chorrera backlands and El Espino, the houses are dispersed over the countryside and aside from the school building, there is no real center of the *corregimiento*. In general, the population tends to live near the rivers but this is mainly because the rivers serve as sources of water; they are generally too small for travel.

Sonadora is a *reguduría* of the *corregimiento* of Pajonal. The *regidor* carries on his business from his home. The functions of the *regidor* are similar to those of the *regidores* in El Espino and the Chorrera backlands.

There are no religious activities sponsored by the countrymen aside from the praying done at the time of death and familiar observances of house saints. As elsewhere, these provide an occasion for social intercourse. The school has been sponsoring Masses recently, but the people themselves never call the priest. Sonadora has no patron saint. *San Juan Bautista* is the patron of Penonomé, but this day is not observed in Sonadora. There is a small chapel in the cemetery, but it is not used for holding Mass. The people go to Penonomé for religious activities when they want to.

Until a year prior to the survey, the school in Sonadora was a *quincha* building but then a new one, similar to that in El Espino, was built and now has six grades. Not all the children in the *regiduría* attend this school as it is more convenient to go to schools in other administrative divisions which are nearer their homes. The school is sponsoring four clubs. The Parents' Club is supposed to provide help for the teachers and the school. The Agriculture Club was formed a few months ago by the teachers for the men of the area. The Youth's Club, formed about the same time as the Agriculture Club, is made up of young men, those who are not yet married. The 4-S Club, equivalent to the 4-H Clubs of the United States, is made up of school children. Since all the clubs are relatively new, it is not possible to say what effect or success they may have. There are two people from the agricultural extension service who are working with the teachers at present. While there are no permanent public health facilities in the *regiduría*, the doctor from the clinic in Penonomé comes to Sonadora once every two weeks, and spends the day at the school seeing any patients who come. He was there the day of the survey visit and there was a good sized crowd of countrypeople waiting to see him. As was mentioned above, the school is also sponsoring Catholic Masses now.

6. SANTO DOMINGO

Santo Domingo is one of the three largest towns in the Province of Los Santos. It is a nucleated settlement of about 300 houses. The houses are mainly the Chitré type with tile roofs, but set against one another to give the impression of a solid wall along the street. A number of the streets in the town are paved, and there is a large dirt area which comprises the plaza. A small white church stands opposite one corner of the plaza and the other sides are lined with houses. While the streets of the town are generally straight, they do not all run at right angles to one another.

Although Santo Domingo is a town, as opposed to the dispersed rural *caseríos*, it is nonetheless largely composed of countrymen who go out to their fields. It is a pattern of living which is quite different from that to be found over much of the Interior. As in the rural *caseríos*, however, the *corregidor* here has no special building; he carries on his official business in his home. The town receives electric power from the light plant in Las Tablas. There is a public telephone, but no telegraph. Mail comes in twice a week by automobile, but newspapers come in daily.

The landscape around the town is similar to that found over most of the east coast region of the Azuero Peninsula. It is generally flat with occasional rolling areas. Much of the land is in pasturage.

The town has a large well and a pipe line which carries the water to various public outlets. There are in addition a number of artesian wells. There are a few people who are employed to keep the water system in order.

The population in this area is predominantly white. There is relatively little negro and Indian mixture except in certain localized populations.

While Santo Domingo has a church, the priest comes from Las Tablas to officiate. He comes once a year and there is no one in charge to keep the church in order. The titular fiesta, Santo Domingo, usually lasts five days, but there is no *Junta Católica* or local group responsible for it. The money to pay for the Mass is collected in various ways; one year, the school teachers took over the responsibility. There is no system of *mayordomos* for making this collection. In general, it may be said that the fiesta is more sponsored by the owners of *cantinas*. Until two years ago there was a *Sociedad de Damas Dominicanas* (Society of Dominican Dames) which worked sporadically for the church, but the club dissolved due to personal friction within the organization. During the titular fiesta, they have bullfights, dances and fireworks.

The town has a school with six grades which serves the entire *corregimiento* and some adjacent regions as well. There is a Parents' Club which was said to be very active. Meetings are held when there is some reason to have one. Last year they were responsible for having a tank for the town water system installed. There is a sanitary unit building here, and the medical team comes over from Las Tablas every two weeks. Usually a doctor, dentist, and nurse come and stay until all the patients are taken care of. Recently an agricultural agent came to test herbicides and insecticides. As yet he has not done much work directly with the people, but he only began a short time ago.

According to the informant, Santo Domingo was founded something over a century ago in a nearby area called Rincón Grande. Tradition has it that due to scarcity of water there it was later moved to its present location and called La Teta. It is said that the first families came from Antón, and the informant said that this may be true as there are a number of family names common to the two places. There has been a gradual increment to the population from neighboring areas since. During this period of its history, the town was informally divided into *Teta Arriba* and *Teta Abajo*; they were not *barrios* in any very active sense. In 1917 the priest in Las Tablas had them build a church, and brought the image of *Santo Domingo* to be their patron saint. Since this time, the name of the town has been Santo Domingo. The old terminology of referring to *arriba* and *abajo* still remain, however.

There is at present one section of the town, Miraflores, which is referred to as being a *barrio*. This is a section of dispersed homes on the north side of the town.

There is in the town a *Sociedad Santo Domingo Progreso* made up principally of young men and women. They hold dances to collect money in order to build a new sanitary unit. The club has about 36 members now, although it was formed only a year ago with ten founders. They have a meeting every two weeks. In Panama City there is another club of young people called *Santo Domingo Unido*. They hold lotteries, dances, and pay personal quotas in order to collect money for the club in Santo Domingo. They also plan to send actual materials, such as cement, for the new sanitary unit. The town also has a baseball team which has games with teams from surrounding towns.

The fact that Santo Domingo shows many characteristics of a countryman community in its general organization reflects the fact that it is composed mainly of farmers and is not basically a commercial town. During the short visit of the survey, there was no evidence of the clear-cut class system which is to be found in other towns where landholders and shopkeepers have long since divided themselves from the countryman population. Class distinction, such as described in general terms earlier, may exist, but they were not in evidence during our visit.

7. LOS POZOS

Los Pozos is the only town included in the survey which was not visited. The better part of one day was spent in trying to get there, but the jeep in which we were travelling at that time got stuck in the mud and the party spent three hours before it was freed.

Los Pozos is set almost in the middle of the Azuero Peninsula in the low mountains which form the backbone of the area. The land is rough, broken and hilly. The soil was said to be humid with a good deal of clay. The town itself includes a nucleus of about 60 or 70 houses; immediately next to the town are three *barrios* of dispersed houses: Calle Arriba, Calle Abajo and El Chorro. The majority of the houses are the rectangular type with tile roofs to be found elsewhere in the peninsula. During part of the year one may reach Los Pozos by automobile; otherwise it is about a three hour trip by horseback from Pesé.

Los Pozos is a district capital. The district offices are in a rented building. There is a telephone in this building, but the town has no telegraph service. Mail arrives twice a week by horseback or by foot carrier. About five people in the town receive newspapers and there are some ten radios. There is a diesel generator which provides electric current from six in the evening until midnight. The rivers in the region are generally too small for river travel. In Las Minas, two hours away by horseback, is a small airfield to which light planes from Santiago go when hired to do so. The upkeep of the various horseback roads is generally the responsibility of the owners of the land along the way. The mayor may call people to clean up a section where no one claims land, but this is voluntary. He will also call a work *junta* when the town cemetery needs cleaning.

While the census lists five *corregimientos*, besides the area surrounding the district center, our informant listed nine *corregimientos* in the district and said that each had a *corregidor*. In the district capital itself, the municipal officers include the mayor, who is elected; a municipal judge, named in Panama; a *personero*, named in the provincial capital of Chitré; a secretary to the judge; a municipal council, elected in the district; various *comisarios*, named by the mayor; a garbage collector; and a slaughterhouse keeper. The informant stated, however, that the slaughterhouse had not been used for some two years.

A sanitary unit was established in Los Pozos about two years ago in a building bought by the government. The doctor from Pesé used to go there every two weeks but due to failure to receive allowances, has not gone recently. The sanitary inspector of Pesé, under the direction of the inspector in Chitré, has visited there about eight times a year since 1947. There is a school of six grades, and there are other schools scattered in the *corregimientos*. In Los Pozos there is a Parents' Club, but it is not very active.

The town has a stone church, but the priest resides in Pesé. The major fiestas of the town are *San Roque*, the patron saint, Holy Week, and the celebration of All Saints Day and the Day of the Dead. In addition, the secular celebration of Carnival is observed. The fiesta of the patron saint lasts three or four days and includes besides the Mass and procession, bullfights, cockfights, and social dances. During Holy Week, a purely religious celebration, two Masses are held. There is a *Junta Católica* in Los Pozos which is responsible for the upkeep of the church and church equipment. For the celebration of Carnival, the town is divided in to eastern and western, *arriba* and *abajo* segments; each segment tries to out-do the other in the celebration and giving of dances.

8. OCÚ

Like Los Pozos, Ocú is located in the uplands of the Azuero Peninsula. It is best known in Panama as the region where the *montuna* and *pollera*, the so-called "typical" countryman costumes, are still used. Ocú is, however, in fact the center of conservatism in the Interior. The town itself does not differ much from other upland towns of a similar size in the Interior; the climate is less tropical, but the town has the characteristic grassy spaces which typify many Interior towns. The town houses vary from the Chitré type, typical of the Azuero area, to a more typical house of this region, one with four corridors around it, and to various more elaborate and "modern" homes of the wealthier people. Outside the town, the homes are dispersed in very much the same way as is characteristic of the rest of the Interior, but there are also nucleated *caseríos*. The countryman's homes are made of poles or cane, and have roofs of straw, palm, or sugar-cane leaves. While the town has a deep well and water main system, the countrypeople get most of their water from shallow wells, springs, and streams.

Ocú has a fairly large district capital building, set on a small plaza. There is both telephone and telegraph service in the town and telephone wires go to one *corregimiento*. Mail comes in three times a week from the town of Divisa by car, but newspapers come in daily. The informant said that about 60 newspapers come into town daily. A private enterprise runs a diesel power plant which provides electricity for the town.

The municipal officials include the mayor and a council of seven, together with two complete sets of council alternates; all these are elected. The district has four *corregimientos*, aside from the area surrounding the town, and a *corregidor* in each.

A block up the street from the plaza on which is located the district building is another plaza on which faces the church. The townspeople of Ocú, and to a lesser degree the countrypeople, are very religious. There is a *Junta Católica* in Ocú which carries the responsibility for the church. In the town there are at least four sodalities: the *Hijas de María*, made up of unmarried women, who celebrate Mass, confess, and sing on the first Sunday of each month; the *Archicofradía del Corazón de María*, composed of both men and women, who celebrate the first Saturday of each month; the *Corazón de Jesús*, a group of women who, in addition to celebrating the day of June 12 with a procession, fiesta, etc., celebrate the first Friday of each month; and the *Congregación del Carmen*, which celebrates the day of their saint. The informant listed some twelve fiestas aside from Christmas, Holy Week and the titular fiesta, which are celebrated[70] with a novena and Mass. Some of these involve a single person sponsoring the fiesta, others involve sodalities. The patron saint, *San Sebastián*, is celebrated from the 19th to the 24th of January. A *junta* is named each year. For the last three years there have been two of them, one named by the priest to collect money for the religious phase of the celebration, the other named by the alcalde or by a vote of the town. The fiesta is preceded by a novena, and during the days of the fiesta itself there are fireworks, cockfights, bullfights, and various other activities. On the final day the custom of *gallota* is observed, during which everyone serves drinks and people visit from one place to another.

The countrypeople participate primarily in the Christmas fiesta, Holy Week, and the fiesta of *San Isidro*. For the Christmas fiesta, the priest annually places the responsibility of providing nine nights of fireworks on the countrypeople. He usually names certain *corregimientos* each year to do this. There is considerable rivalry to see which group puts on the best display; some $60 to $70 go up in smoke nightly. San Isidro, May 15th, is usually celebrated with a *rogativa*. A few countrywomen belong to the *Hijas de María* and come in for the monthly celebration. Otherwise, it is only the countrypeople who live near the town who attend the various fiestas and the Sunday Masses. Various communities in the countryside have patron saints and chapels. Where these are present, the priest goes to say Mass for the celebration. The countrymen usually have a Judas figure during the Holy Week.

While the great emphasis on religious activity is more marked among the town dwellers than among the countrypeople, the latter show considerably more activity in this respect than is found in many other places in the Interior. Another important factor is that the priest, who came to the town about four years ago, has been very active in fomenting more Catholic celebrations. One informant made the comment that Ocú had so many saints that it was necessary to periodically replace them in the church since there was not enough room to hold all of them at once.

The town, like Los Pozos, is divided into two subsections, *Calle Arriba* and *Calle Abajo*, for the celebration of the fiesta of Carnival. On the outskirts of

---

[70] (*Santa Rosa de Lima, Nuestra Señora del Perpetuo Socorro, Corazón de Jesús, Corazón de María, Carmen, Cristo Rey, San Isidro Labrador, María Auxiliadora, La Purísima Concepción, La Milagrosa, San Antonio de Padua,* and *San Rafael.*)

town are four *barrios* composed of poorer people: El Palito, Llano del Cementerio, El Mamey, and La Punta.

Ocú has a number of secular associations. The upper class, businessmen, and professionals maintain a Lions Club. The teachers of the Ocú region have a *Centro de Colaboración*. The director of the public library sponsors a *Club Juvenil de Lectores* which is composed of students in the fourth, fifth, and sixth grades. A Club 4-S was started this year in the town, and they plan to start others. There is a one year old Sports Club which is made up of young men; their main sport is baseball, but they are making a volley ball court. Another association of young people, *Unión y Progreso*, promotes the celebration of Carnival and sponsors dances. In 1946 a *Comité Pro-Hospital*, with a directive council of upper class men, was started. There are two organizations concerned with promoting tourism in Ocú. The *Centro Social de Ocú* is a club composed of many of the townspeople, but the directing council is composed of professionals, many of whom live in Panama City. The *Sociedad de Industrias Típicas Ocueñe* was formed by a group of townspeople to promote the local production of typical handicrafts. They try to get the countrypeople to produce more of the products which the society then buys and sells to tourists.

Ocú has a large school, and there are a number of them in the *corregimientos*. There is also a sanitary unit in the town.

The Ocú region is certainly one of the most fascinating of the Panamanian Interior. The number of customs which have been preserved or which noticeably differ from the general countryman culture to be found in Panama, Coclé, and Veraguas is marked. When making the survey in Montijo, the informant there was careful to point out that the eastern part of the district of Montijo had a different sort of population, the *manitos*, who were actually part of the Ocú population. They were distinct, in his opinion, in many ways from the rest of the Montijo countryman population. This latter group were more like the rest of the Veraguas population. Why Ocú differs so much from the rest of the countryside of Panama is a question which can only be answered with recourse to history. In common with the major part of the population of the Peninsula, they are racially whiter than most of the Interior population of Panama. It is not that they have preserved old Indian traditions to a greater degree than the other regions since many of the characteristics of their culture are not Indian. Instead, it is a local development of a distinctive local culture, produced by people of predominantly European stock, and including many economic traits taken over from the Indians.

Ocú today gives evidence of having one of the strongest class systems to be found in the Panamanian countryside. The distinction between the town-dwelling upper class and the countrypeople is stronger and more obvious than anywhere else the writer visited in the course of the survey. The cultural differences which the countrypeople retain are as significant in the maintenance of this class system as are the attitudes and behaviors of the town dwellers.

9. MONTIJO

The town of Montijo is set a few kilometers back from the Gulf of Montijo. The countryside around the town is similar to that around Chorrera, many small, rough hills and occasional level areas. As was mentioned in connection with Ocú, the population racially varies somewhat. In the eastern part of the district, the people tend to be whiter, while in the center and to the west, there is more evidence of Indian and some negro mixture. The town itself is nucleated, generally running north and south. In the countryside, the people tend to live in *caseríos* of houses fairly near to one another. The main exception to this is to the south on the eastern coast of the Azuero Peninsula where the houses tend to be fairly isolated from one another. The town itself is composed of three parallel streets, the center one being the "highway" which runs from Puerto Mutis on the Gulf of Santiago. This highway is occasionally impassable during the rainy season. Some of the houses in the town are generally similar in plan to those of the Chitré area, but are made of wood rather than of poles and mud. There are also a number of smaller pole and cane houses with straw or palm roofs. These are mainly rectangular; there are fewer of the apsidal type to be found this far west. It was reported that it was common here to mix cow dung with the mud which is occasionally used to plaster on the inside and outside of the walls of these houses. Water in the town comes from five deep wells, but in the countryside it is taken principally from superficial wells and streams.

The district government personnel are housed in a small wooden building with a metal roof. The officers are the mayor and the municipal council of six, all elected; a judge, named by the judge in Santiago; a *personero*, named by the *fiscal* in Santiago; an agricultural agent; and a secretary and janitor named by the mayor. The function of the *personero* is to investigate crimes in the district, analyze the problems, and give his findings to the judge.

There are five *corregimientos* in the district. Two of these are islands in the Gulf of Montijo, Gobernadora and Leones. According to the local informant, one *corregimiento* listed in the census, La Garceana, does not ordinarily have a *corregidor*. In the larger *caseríos* there are *comisarios*, and in the smaller are *regidores*. All these officials, the *corregidores*, *comisarios*, and *regidores*, are named by the mayor. The mayor calls occasional *faenas* to help clean up the town or the cemetery, but they are voluntary; the Department of Public Works is responsible for the condition of the road.

Montijo has a telephone, but no telegraph service. The mail comes in twice a week by car, when the road is passable, and otherwise by horseback. No newspapers are sent in, although some who go to Santiago bring them back with them.

At the time of the survey visit, the Montijo church was still under construction. The outside was finished, but the inside was not. There is no resident priest; the parish headquarters are in the town of Atalaya, and the priest comes to Montijo six or seven times a year. There are no local religious sodalities, but a *rosario* is said every night in the church. According to the informant,

Montijo is in the peculiar situation of having two patron saints. The biggest celebration is for *Candelaria* on the second of February. This fiesta usually lasts three days and begins on the 31st of January in Puerto Real, a port above Puerto Mutis on the Gulf. This tradition stems from the old days when trade from the islands was more important than now, and the island people would arrive a few days before the fiesta, bringing their produce for sale. They would sell this in Puerto Real, and instead of waiting for the fiesta to start in Montijo, they would begin in the port. This became known as the *Feria de Puerto Real* and has traditionally been the start of the Montijo fiesta. In Montijo, the fiesta includes, besides the Mass and procession, bullfights, fireworks, popular dances, and social dances (*bailes "de gala"*). They used to have cock fights but this sport has died out.

The other patron saint, *San José*, is celebrated in a much smaller fiesta. Besides these two celebrations, Holy Week and Christmas are celebrated, and *El Carmen* is celebrated on the 16th of July in a purely religious fiesta.

There used to be several civic societies in Montijo, and a sports club, but all have broken up. One of the societies put the fence around the cemetery, and another started the new church. There is a *Junta Católica* which has been irregularly active; it is responsible for promoting the patron saint fiesta and in getting funds for furnishing the church. The *Junta* is named by the priest, and at times by the archbishop. But most of the other associations have evidently broken up due to individual disputes between the members.

Montijo has a school with six grades, and there are schools in seven of the *caseríos*. While the town school roof is in bad condition, the building itself is one of the largest which the writer saw in the course of his visit. The school director has a Parents' Club, but it is fairly inactive. The parents do not take much interest in the affairs of the school, especially "when there is something to be done." An attempt to get each man in the town to give one day of work for two new school rooms did not bring much response. The informant said that the people prefer to help indirectly, if they must, but not directly.

There are no public health facilities in the town. For a period of about three years, until four years ago, a private doctor came in once a month by plane with a nurse and dentist. This was called the "caravan," and the doctor did it to provide an example to the government. He finally had to give it up, however, because it cost him too much. The drugstores in Panama helped him by providing drugs, and the Canal Zone provided the dentist now and then. Now, however, no public health personnel visits the town.

An agricultural agent was first named here four years ago. He left, and was replaced by another two years ago. The work of the present one consists principally in vaccinating animals. He pays no attention to the agricultural work, and very few people consult him about any problems which they might have.

The town has no particular *barrio* division, but formerly the town was divided for the purpose of celebrating the Carnival fiesta. The two sides, *tuna de abajo* and *tuna de arriba*, each used to have a drum and they would bring the drums to the center and meet. Now, however, there is just one drum for the entire town and few people participate in the fiesta.

Carles[71] says that Montijo was founded in 1591 by Pedro Fernández Cortéz. Well into the 17th Century, Montijo and Santa Fe formed the two principal cities of what is now the Province of Veraguas. The Gulf of Montijo was for many years a relatively important port. Until the commercial expansion of Santiago, which benefited from the fact of being both on the principal national highway and being the provincial capital, Montijo was a more important town. The town today gives the impression of being very much slowed down. Between census of 1930 and 1950, the population of Montijo changed from 769 to 768; this, if nothing else, points to stagnation. It is the only district capital in Veraguas which has lost population or remained the same during this period; all others have increased even though it has been only slightly in some cases.

During the course of gathering data in Montijo, there were numerous questions which were answered as, "it used to be that way," or "we used to do that, but not any more." The writer had the feeling that Montijo was settling back, waiting for some new movement which might bring the town back to a place of some importance.

10. SAN FRANCISCO

San Francisco is located in central Veraguas savanna country. The town itself is not dissimilar in outward appearance to the other towns in the general area; trees are scattered through it, there are a few well-defined streets and it is a commercial center for the surrounding countryside. It has seen a slight increase in population between 1930 and 1950, from 706 to 814. The population is predominantly mestizo, with very little evidence of negro ancestry.

The town itself has one deep well and a pipeline which supplies water for most of the inhabitants. Those of the town who do not have access to the main water source use surface wells. In the countryside water comes from such superficial wells and from the rivers and streams. The countrypeople in general live fairly isolated from one another but there are small groupings of houses in some of the *corregimientos*. Almost all country houses are rectangular and made of poles, cane or *embarrada* with straw or palm roofs.

In the town the municipal governmental officers include the mayor and treasurer, a judge, and a *personero*. There are also two policemen and a national tax collector. In the district there are four *corregimientos* in addition to the areas surrounding the town. Within each *corregimiento* there is a *corregidor*, and a *regidor* for each four or five *caseríos*; in each *caserío* there is a *comisario*. All these officers are named by the mayor. In the countryside the *corregidores* call *faenas* for road repair work, but the main road from San Francisco to Santiago is under the Department of Public Works. In town the cemetery is cleaned when the mayor or the teachers call a work session.

The town has a telephone, and there is also one in the *corregimiento* of San

---

[71] 1950, pp. 130, 132–133.

Juan, but there is no telegraph service. The mail comes in every Wednesday and Saturday and a number of people receive newspapers daily. There is daily bus service to Santiago over the road which terminates to the north in Santa Fe.

San Francisco has a church and a priest. While there is no regular *Junta Católica*, the mayor and priest annually name a *junta de festejo* (fiesta committee) which is responsible for sponsoring the major fiesta. The *junta* names *mayordomos* both among themselves and from the town in general. While San Francisco (in October) is the patron saint of the town, it is observed with a one day religious celebration. The main fiesta is that of *San Roque*, held on the 16th of August. For this there are the usual religious observances as well as bullfights, cockfights, and dances. The fiesta usually lasts three or four days.

In the town there is a sisterhood of the *Hijas de María* which celebrates the first Friday of each month, and a group which sponsors the religious fiesta of *Sagrado Corazón*. During Holy Week the Judas figure is used, and in addition some men dress up as women, putting the *chácara* over their heads, follow the Judas about weeping; they are called the *lloronas*. In the procession there is a *centurión penitente* who, dressed in black with a black face piece and carrying a bell, takes two steps backwards for each three forward. Christmas is also celebrated.

In the countryside, at least two of the *caseríos* have patron saints. In Corral Falso, where there is also a chapel, *La Cruz* is celebrated on the 3rd of May, and in *San Juan* the patron is celebrated on the 24th of June. The countrypeople who live near the town come in on Sundays for Mass.

The town of San Francisco has a very large new school which was being finished at the time of the survey. It was one of the most impressive school structures which the writer saw outside the principal cities. It has eight grades and one teacher specializing in agriculture and two in domestic economy. They are just forming a Parents' Club now. There is no agricultural agent in the town, but there is a sanitary unit which is visited by the medical team once every two weeks.

There is a sports club which plays baseball, and a group called the *Fuerza Cívica* also made up of young people. The informant said that the function of this latter club was "to protect the countryman and to produce public works, such as the new school which was started through their efforts." Just what was meant by "protect the countryman" was not made clear.

There is evidently no division in the town for the celebration of Carnival, although they do hold a fiesta at that time.

11. SONA

Soná and Santiago are the two largest towns of Veraguas. Soná has not seen the phenomenal growth over the past twenty years that has taken place in the provincial capital, but it has considerable commercial importance for the surrounding region. From the coast to some 30 kilometers north of Soná the landscape is the broken savanna land which is typical of many of the towns thus far described. Between this point and the cordillera, however, there is a belt of plains, rolling and flat grasslands broken only by streams. Until 50 years ago, the greater part of the district of Soná was still virgin forest, but the growing population, burning and cutting its way towards the coast, has left only the section on the south still in a virgin state. Over the greater part of the district are to be found the individual houses of the countryman; in a few places, up to twenty-five will be built closer together, forming a *caserío*, but the majority of the inhabitants live a kilometer or so from their nearest neighbor.

The town of Soná is a nucleated settlement on the highway between David and the capital. It is the district center, has a hospital, and a large school which sponsors a Parents' Club. The writer had the feeling that Soná was a town in which most interests were pointed to the outside. Commercially important for all of western Veraguas, there was little in the town itself which drew one's attention. It offered none of the exciting activity of Chitré, none of the picturesque conservatism of Ocú nor the genial decadence of Montijo; it was a town growing along with the rest of Panama, playing its economic role, but with little of an outstanding individualistic character to be found in some other towns. On the other hand, from the information gathered, Soná suggested a town in stage of convergence of the upper classes; there used to be a *"primera,"* and *"segunda,"* but this distinction was no longer of any great importance; one had the feeling that the townspeople of Soná were becoming one and that the greatest remaining distinction lay between them and the countrypeople to whom they referred as *"cholos."*

Soná has a church and a resident priest who serves the entire surrounding region. Some of the *corregimientos* have chapels which he visits annually. Two fiestas are celebrated commonly in the countryside. *San Juan Bautista* and *Santiago*, as well as the patron of a particular locale. In the town, the fiesta of *San Isidro*, the patron saint of the town, *San José*, Holy Week, and Christmas are celebrated by both townspeople and countrymen. Few countrypeople attend the townsmen's celebration of such days as *Corazón de María* and the *Virgen de Fátima*, or the secular fiesta of Carnival. Countrypeople will observe some holy days by not working, and others will have fiestas in their homes to celebrate the day of a particular saint.

There are no religious brotherhoods among the countrypeople, the priest being responsible for organizing the few larger fiestas which are held outside of the town. In town, however, there are some societies which take the responsibility for sponsoring the observances of certain saints' days. *Carmen*, *Fátima*, *Corazón de María*, and *Corazón de Jesús* are a few of these. These are mainly participated in by women; the men are not very active in such observances. One informant made the comment that the town "was very Catholic, to the point of being fanatical." Not long ago the discovery that a former priest had not decomposed after being buried led the people to believe that a miracle had taken place in their midst; the priest's body is now on display in a sanctuary at the back of the church.

12. COROZAL

Corozal is a *caserío*, center of a *corregiduría* in the district of Las Palmas. It is illustrative of the rural settlements in which countrymen of Veraguas live and very similar to the rural region surrounding Soná. Corozal itself has a number of houses stretched out along the road between the highway and Las Palmas, but such a concentration is not generally typical of the isolated homesteads which are more commonly found. Corozal, like the Corozales in the Chorrera backlands, has no telephone, telegraph, or formal mail communication services. The *corregidor* lives in his home in the *caserío*, and a little way down the road from his home is the school building. For the first time this year the school has six grades and a Parents' Club, but the latter is not very active.

The people of Corozal go to Las Palmas for Holy Week celebrations, but observe the fiesta of *San Juan* here in the *caserío*. Some also celebrate the fiesta of *la Purísima* with dances, but aside from this, Christmas is the only general religious celebration. There are a few men who go to Las Palmas on the first Friday of every month to pray with the society of *Corazón de Jesús* which the priest sponsors there.

Aside from the school sponsored Parents' Club, there are no civil or religious sodalities maintained by the countrymen of Corozal. There is no agricultural agent that they know of who is supposed to be active in the region, nor are there any immediate public health facilities available.

Corozal is a settlement of countrymen; distant from neighbors, a few families live in the immediate vicinity, and are principally oriented towards the business of living and the occasional celebrations of saints' days or novenas.

13. REMEDIOS

Remedios, founded at the end of the 16th Century, was long an important colonial town and is the largest town in eastern Chiriquí. It was a center for conversions of the Indians in the 17th Century, but today is very close to the Guaymí Indian area. Of the four *corregimientos* outside the surroundings of the town, which is the district center, three are entirely Indian and one has a mixed Indian and countryman population. The area of the district of Remedios which is not predominantly inhabited by Indians is occupied by large *haciendas*. Cattle is one of the main products of the Remedios area, and it is produced principally on the large landholdings. The countrymen who do not work on the *haciendas* may seek some of the limited government land available, may take over land in the Indian region, or may rent land from the *haciendas*. When the last of these is done, it is usually with the understanding that the land will be left in pasturage for the *hacienda* owner. This leaves little for the few countrymen of the district.

The countrymen settlements in this area are usually *caseríos* of a few houses, a different pattern from that reported for the Indians; in the latter case, the houses are isolated one from another. The town of Remedios is nucleated, spreading generally along the main highway. The general appearance of the town gives little suggestion of its long history. Due to the fact that almost 45 % of the district population is Indian, the district mayor does not have immediate control over the entire population in his area. The Indians are directly under their own governors and do not feel responsible to the district mayor.

The church and priest in Remedios serve the entire district. The mayor names a *Junta Católica* which arranges the principal fiesta of the town, the Day of the Kings, in January. Holy Week, the Day of All Saints, and *San Juan* are also celebrated. The principal fiesta is generally similar to those held in other centers with dances, cockfights and bullfights. There is one religious society, the *Hijas de María*.

The upper class men of the town have a Lions Club, and the writer was told of one other civic group which is present. The school in Remedios has six grades and sponsors a Parents' Club. There is no agricultural agent here, although there is one in the neighboring district of Las Lajas, a fast growing center to the west of Remedios. Remedios has an active sanitary unit. There is telephone and telegraph service in the town, and a telephone line to the *corregimiento* of Nancito.

14. ALANJE AND QUERÉVALO

Alanje, once an important colonial town, and Querévalo, a nearby semi-rural settlement, are located on the coastal plain to the west of the provincial capital of David. In March, when the survey visited these towns, the countryside was incredibly dry, an impression enhanced by the land-burning under way and the dust from the roads. Alanje, the district capital, is only slightly larger in population than Querévalo, the former having 544 and the latter 467 inhabitants in 1950. Alanje, however, has a ratio between the sexes which is characteristic of urban Panama, having 118 women for every 100 men, while Querévalo has a ratio which is characteristic of rural Panama, having 82 women for every 100 men. Alanje is a nucleated town, but spread out along the cross streets which compose the town. Querévalo has a nucleated settlement, but people also live out from the settlement. Alanje has a definite townsman class, together with old settlers who differ in their orientation from the general countryman. Querévalo, on the other hand, is made up primarily of countrymen, although some of them live in the nucleated settlement.

Transportation to Alanje is most satisfactory over the diesel *"motor"* car which runs between David and Puerto Armuelles. The line does not touch Alanje directly, but is about a twenty minute walk from the town. There is a road to David, but it is barely passable. The inhabitants of Querévalo, who live an hour by horseback from Alanje, do not utilize the *motor* to go to David, preferring to go by horseback. Both towns have electricity, and there is telephone, telegraph, and mail service in Alanje. There are people in both towns who have radios.

The only district officials in Alanje are the mayor and secretary, both of whom receive salaries. The mayor names the *corregidores* in the four *barrios*; there is only one officially recognized *corregimiento* aside from Alanje itself, but due to the size of the area involved and the large population of the district (over 6,000 in 1950), *corregidores* are named to the locally recognized *barrio* divisions. These *corregidores* name *regidores* to act as agents under their jurisdiction.

A priest arrived to take over the parish of Alanje about a month before the time of the survey. Prior to his coming, fiestas were arranged by a few local faithful people. There was a *Junta Católica*, but it functioned irregularly. While the complete name of the town is Santiago de Alanje, and *Santiago* is supposed to be the patron saint, by far the most important religious celebration is during Holy Week, and the most important image is *Cristo*. The story goes that when the town was originally founded by the Spanish, it was located at a place now called Pueblo Viejo on the road to the town of Guarumal. At that time, the cemetery was on the location of the present church, a fact which the informant felt was attested to by the discovery of many bones when the excavations for the present church were made. Due to banditry, however, the town suffered badly. Then an old man came along and told them that the bad luck of the town was due to the fact that they had no *Cristo*. To get one, he told them to find him a large log and provide him with a house and food. They did this and he shut himself in the house. Food was handed to him through the window and for a few days the people heard nothing. So they opened the door and there, in a clean house, with no wood chips or any other evidence of wood working, they found a *Cristo*; the old man had disappeared.

Other stories are connected to this one. In locating a tree trunk for the old man, one woman refused to let them have one of her orange trees. Later her tree dried up, while the stump of the tree from which the log had been taken grew up again and gave good oranges. Later in the history, they tried to take the *Cristo* to David, but when they got out on the road, a terrible storm broke and they had to return. As soon as they made the church, the storm cleared. Because of the miraculous history of the *Cristo*, the Alanje people consider Holy Week to be the most important fiesta of the year.

Beginning on the Friday prior to Palm Sunday, there is a procession; other processions are held on Palm Sunday, Monday, Tuesday, Wednesday, and the major procession comes on Good Friday. This is followed by further processions on Saturday and Sunday. All the processions except that on Palm Sunday, which is early in the morning, are held at night. There is also a Mass said every day during the week. The Good Friday procession lasts from about 8 in the evening until about 4:30 in the morning, although the priest in charge will sometimes end it earlier. There are also stories connected with the processions, such as the *Cristo* not wishing to leave the church, or the image growing very heavy.

In Querévalo the principal fiesta is *San Juan Bautista*; it lasts two days and includes dancing and horse racing. There are no religious sodalities now although there was one a few years ago.

15. LAS LOMAS

Las Lomas is a *corregimiento* in the district of David. It lies to the east of the provincial capital, bisected by the main highway running to Panama. As in Alanje, the rural territorial subdivisions of the *corregimiento* are known as *barrios*. The three principal *barrios* of Las Lomas are Llano del Medio, which had a population of 865 inhabitants in 1950, the largest of the various *barrios*, Llano Grande, in which is located the *corregiduría* building, and Llano Vichal. There are in addition three other population centers, Hato Viejo, Mata de Nance, and Quiteño, which are referred to as *caseríos*. There is one *corregidor* and six *regidores*, one in each of the *barrios* and *caseríos*. There is a considerable amount of municipal land in the *corregimiento*; when a man wants to build a house, he asks permission and the municipality gives the land use for it. This land is not given for cultivation, only for houses. It remains with the family as long as they need it, but since most sons build new houses, the old ones are usually abandoned upon the death of the old people. The land then reverts to the municipality and is turned over to someone else if requested.

Las Lomas has no patron saint, but the inhabitants are in the process at present of building a church. For the last three years (at the time of survey) there has existed a *Sociedad Pro-Iglesia* which consisted of a directing council of five important people and seven other members. But everyone in the community has cooperated in both money and work towards the completion of the new church. The principal fiesta which has been held in the past is Christmas, on the 24th of December. The priest comes from David, holds Mass and baptizes and confirms people. Most people take their children to David for baptism, however. Otherwise, the principal religious activities consist in the novenas held upon the death of a family member, for saints, and the *rogativa* held in April if the rains are late in coming. Many people will attend the fiesta of *San José* in David. Las Lomas was the only place where it was reported that saints kept in the home tended to be inherited through the family.

Each of the *barrios* and *caseríos* in Las Lomas, except Vichal, has a *Centro Funerario*. Almost everyone in the area belongs to one or another of them. At the time of the survey, the informant said that an effort was being made to get the people of the three *barrios* and of the *caserío* Mata de Nance to build a single large *Centro Funerario* to serve the populations of the four areas. Four men who have been leaders in the *barrios* have formed a directing council for the new venture. They plan, among other things, to build a house for a widow who has none. The sanitary inspectors who have worked in Las Lomas have planned to take advantage of the funerary societies in order to foment public health education.

Las Lomas has some 16 schools scattered through the *corregimiento*. It was reported that there were football, baseball, and basketball teams, composed of young men. The football team plays against teams from other towns. Formerly there was a baseball club, but the adults made it break up because of damage being done to homes in the area. The members still get together occasionally.

16. DOLEGA

Dolega is located in the foothills above David to one side of the paved road which runs to Boquete. The railroad from David also runs through the town, and there are both telephone and telegraph services available. Electric power is supplied from David. Dolega, a district capital, is the traditional home of the Dorasque Indians. Although there is little to remind one today of this history, the town cannot be said to be any more "typical" of the western Chiriquí area than are either of the others included in the survey. It is, however, a community located in the mountains rather than on the coast itself and differs from the latter region in that most of the countrymen are either landowners or have enough land available that they are able to rent to carry on their own subsistence agriculture. The district itself has some 65 hectares of land which it rents out.

While the town is nucleated, the houses are not set very close to one another except along the principal streets. The houses in the *corregimientos* are generally scattered with a few small concentrations. The most common source of water is from wells; peculiar to this area is the use of a square well structure, sometimes of cement, sometimes of cane. Water is seldom taken from streams. The population here, as in Veraguas, is generally mestizo, mixed Indian and white, with little evidence of negro admixture.

The district offices are located in a building on the principal street of the town, facing the plaza, and there is a church, although they have not had a priest for two years now. The priest from Boquete comes down every Sunday to say Mass. A *Junta Católica* helps the priest when he is in town, but in general the religious societies which have existed in the past have been fairly weak. The fiesta of the patron saint, *San Francisco de Asís*, is held on October 4th; it is principally a religious celebration although there are some dances and the *cantinas* do a bit of business. Holy Week is celebrated, with the Judas figure, but there are no other special customs connected with it.

There have been various civic associations but they have not had any more success in staying active than the religious societies have. There is one at present working on a library.

IV. A COMMENTARY ON THE ECONOMY AND CULTURE OF THE COUNTRYMAN

The data provided on the preceding pages has been collected and ordered to give a background for people who are going to have to work in the countryside of Panama. Except occasionally, we have not been too concerned with the historical antecedents of the situations we have described; our purpose, rather, is to delineate the general cultural picture which the practical worker will encounter when he goes into the field. This should be immediately utilizable in two ways: (1) The worker will have some general knowledge of the cultural and social situation he may encounter in the region chosen for work; and (2) if he encounters a problem which seems to have its origin in the social or cultural situation, he will be more able to study the problem through various ideas provided in the description. It is to be emphasized here, and not forgotten by the worker, that the present description cannot substitute for adequate study of the local scene. Every town, community, and settlement is different in the particular social processes under way at any one time, and the direction that changes may take are determined by the situation present at the time. The present study, then, should be regarded as something in the nature of a general "anatomy" of the culture and society of the countryside of Panama; the person who is going to work in the field can use this anatomy to help orient himself, but the understanding of the local "physiology" can stem only for more intensive study on the local scene.

By way of a summary concerning some of the phases of the culture which have been discussed, this section will take up some of the specific problems which are faced by the countryman in certain parts of his country. Each of these problems, taken in conjunction with the nature of his culture and society, demand solution. The critical fact to remember is that if the solutions to these problems are not reached with some view to the future ramifications of the actions involved, then they may in the long run produce even greater problems through local solutions reached by the population. The persons in charge of programs in agriculture, livestock, public health, public works, and so on, should never lose sight of the fact that the solution of any problem in the lives of a people must be done in terms of understandings which those people have, and yet must be so adjusted as to avoid catastrophic results from inept planning.

Most, but not all, problems faced by the countryman can be traced to three general phases of his culture and society; a growing population; an agricultural technology of low efficiency; and an economic and social organization which at present does not tend to either control population size or improve productive techniques. Panama as a country does not have at present the population problem which is faced in many other parts of the world. However, the population is growing in the rural areas to the degree that within the next few decades a real problem will appear if steps are not taken to avoid it. The provinces of Herrera and Los Santos and the coastal area of Chiriquí may be taken as previews of what will happen in the future. In Coclé, the situation is still not quite as critical, and in Veraguas, there is considerable land left for exploitation. The population expansion of Herrera, Los Santos, and Chiriquí, has brought certain movement in recent years: the regions to the east and west of the Canal Zone, the west half of the Azuero Peninsula, and western Chiriquí have been seeing new colonists. However, the new colonists, and those who have remained in the overpopulated areas, are all using precisely the same techniques of exploitation which was a contributing factor to the pressure in the first place.

The technology of the countryman, described earlier, needs a fairly large amount of land for a single family, exhausts the fertility of that land rapidly, and never produces a very high yield. There is little question that serious extension work directed at the benefit of the countryman could increase the yield and ease what will be in the future a serious population problem, not to speak of the problem of erosion and land loss which will result from not taking steps in time.

The third factor mentioned above, the economic and social organization of the countryman, is in fact not a single factor but a series of interwoven factors, the precise nature of which varies from one part of the area to the next. Neither of the two principal units of the countryman social organization, the nuclear family and the neighborhood, are highly structured in most of the area. It is likely that in certain places, such as the Ocú region, the family is stronger than elsewhere. But in general, to base any long term, serious solution to the agrarian and population problem on a misconception of either of these units will be a mistake. The family, as was pointed out, is frequently unbalanced; that is, the man or woman may leave his or her spouse. The neighborhood is evidently a more stable unit than the nuclear family, but frequently its territorial organization makes it very difficult to work with. Nevertheless, it may be a most important local social unit to be utilized in the planning of local programs.

The functioning of the neighborhood today reflects a certain amount of local sympathy and cooperation between its members. *Juntas, peonadas*, prayer sessions, and local dances are held by neighborhood groups. The neighborhood group, however, is also one of the main socialization mechanisms in the countryside culture. The current agricultural techniques are passed down from generations not merely from father to son, but also by periodic contact with others working in the same manner in *juntas* and *peonadas*. The group from which a person learns techniques, then, is generally larger than the immediate family. Hence, while the neighborhood is an important part of the learning situation of the countryman, it is also a mechanism which may make changing the techniques a difficult process.

The countryman really has no other important social groupings outside of the nuclear family and neighborhood. The societies and associations which are found in one form or another in most of the towns are not specifically a part of the countryman culture. If they did exist, they would probably, through demands of territorial access, be based on the neighborhoods. The school, which is a favorite channel for rural organization by many governments, did not impress the writer as being an adequate substitute for the neighborhood group. The school is usually a center for a number of neighborhood areas, and usually is not entirely aware of the role which it may play in the mind of the countryman. In most cases there is no recognized unit which is specifically a neighborhood; the school area, the *corregimiento*, and the area under a *regidor* are all established on other considerations.

Another phase of the economic organization of the countryman which will be critical in the promotion of increased production is the distinction between subsistence crops and cash crops. Whenever possible, the countryman grows as much as he can in order to eat some and have an excess to sell for cash; this in turn permits him to buy some of the commercially distributed necessities. The importance of this varies, since in the backlands the necessity for cash is less, while near the towns and main roads it is greater. Nevertheless, any improvement of the countryman's economy will be dependent on the possibility that some of his produce will be salable. If he has a bad year, what he does produce can be consumed; if he has a good year, then the excess can be sold. This means in principle that the countryman must spend his time in producing a crop which is both saleable and edible; his produce must be able to function as either a cash or subsistence crop. The countrymen in some parts of the country have suffered badly when they put considerable work into sugar-cane production and then found that they could not sell it. The consequence of this situation is that the countryman in general must specialize in crops which he can eat and which other people will want to buy to eat. This means that crops which are going to be difficult to get into the diet of the population should not be heavily promoted.

The agricultural economy of the countryman, as it stands, is also hindered through the fact that the cash production is always low, seldom providing any capital for expansion or investment in more productive and more expensive methods. The countryman traditionally works with a machete, *coa*, and ax, but even if he were to become convinced that other tools were better, he could not afford them. The countryman has land, but he has little credit. There is no need to go into this problem extensively; agronomists and field researchers have reported it from many countries.

The territorial organization of the countryman is based in part on the nature of landholdings which exist. The shifting agriculture demands land, and under the system of getting permission to use land for a year or two only, the shifting agriculture is promoted. Ofelia Hooper commented to the writer that the land laws of Panama are excellent; the only problem is getting them into action. In this, she hit on one of the points which the writer found to be quite serious in parts of the countryside. In various places the countrymen with whom the writer talked were not aware of the fact that they could own land; they believed that the land which belonged to the government would always be available for the shifting cultivation. This reflects the urgency of dissemination of information of the nature of the land laws of the country so that the countryman will have the opportunity to take intelligent advantage of them.

This, however, brings us to another aspect of the social and economic organization which tends to inhibit development of the countryman economy. As was described in the section on town and country social structure, there is a vast difference between the classes to be found between these two areas. In some cases it is not to the advantage of the townsman, who himself is an exploiter of land, to promote intelligence concerning the possibilities of land exploitation among countrymen. A person who needs additional cattle land in a densely populated area will not promote the division of land into familial agriculture plots. As Miss Hooper has also pointed out, this should not be the case; there is only 18% of the land in use in Panama now in private hands, and under 16% of the total area is in use. The large landholders should not be disturbed by the small cultivator, but instead should encourage him to be aware of the fact that there are still vast areas of the country where land may be had for cultivation.

Related to the promotion of adequate knowledge concerning the land laws is the necessity of surveying the areas of possible population expansion, and adequately publicizing the true nature of the thinly populated areas. Internal colonization is going to be the answer to the countryman's problem for many years to come; preliminary studies can do much to promote intelligent movement and to avoid problems of a population arriving and suffering through inadequate preparation. This does not mean that great schemes of controlled colonization are necessary, but certain minimum precautions such as testing soils, locating water supplies, and providing for at least minimum transportation access. One of the problems of which the countryman himself is most aware is the inadequacy of existing road and transport facilities. As Miss Hooper has pointed out, where there is good land, there are no roads, and where there are roads, there is no good land left.

With respect to the three main phases of the countryman's problem in Panama today, we have thus far emphasized the issues connected with land and economy. Of equal importance with this is the fact that the nature of the territorial social organization does not permit at present any control over population size. This problem exists in many places in the world and seldom have adequate answers to it been found. Nevertheless, it would be well to recognize the fact that the increase in population, if it continues, must eventually bring about striking changes in social organization and possibly override many of the efforts which may be undertaken in the realm of agricultural improvements. Under the present social organizational forms, i.e., the family and neighborhood organization as it exists in the countryside, there is no method which will be effective in the near future to control population growth. A dispersed population, in which common-law marriage and permissible alternative role for spouses is recognized, is not going to permit of much control.

The status of the countryman culture today is the result of an original blend of Spanish and Indian traits, with some influence of traits which stem from Africa, the Antilles, and more recent Western European culture. Of great importance, however, is that this blend has perhaps seen more loss than retention of original traits from both Spanish and native sources. The Spanish conquest served to destroy much of the Indian culture, as can be seen by the deculturated status of the contemporary Guaymí and Cuna. The Indian environment, however, into which the Spanish culture was introduced, also broke down much of the Spanish pattern. The emergent social organization which was based on a population of mestizo peasants saw little eleboration or extreme local growth except in certain limited regions such as Herrera and Los Santos where admixture with the Indian population was relatively small. We might say that where either an Indian pattern (such as among the Guaymí or Cuna) or a Spanish pattern (such as Ocú) has predominated, there is a more elaborate culture than where the two have been well mixed (the basic countryman culture). The countryman culture is a blend which seems to have chopped off the more elaborate traits of each of the basic parent cultures. This, it must be remembered, is in some part due to the fact of social stratification in which the countryman culture is characteristic of the population furthest removed from national development and lowest in the Panamanian social order.

REFERENCES

HSAI Handbook of South American Indians, Bureau of American Ethnology, Bulletin 143, Ed. by Julian H. Steward. Washington, D. C.

Biesanz, John. 1949. "Cultural and Economic Factors in Panamanian Race Relations," *American Sociological Review*, 14: 772–79.

———, 1950a. "Race Relations in the Canal Zone," *Phylon*, 11: 23–30, First Quarter.

———, 1950b. "Social Forces Retarding Development of Panama's Agricultural Resources," *Rural Sociology*, 15: 148–55, June.

Biesanz, John and Smith, Luke M. 1951. "Race Relations in Panama and the Canal Zone: A Comparative Analysis," *American Journal of Sociology*, LVII: 7–14, July.

Biesanz, John and Biesanz, Mavis. n. d. *People of Panama and the Canal Zone*. Columbia University Press. (In press.)

Census, 1940. *Censo de Población de Panamá, 1940, Vol. 10, Compendio General*. Contraloría General de la República. Panamá.

———, 1950a. *Boletín Informativo, No. 3*. Dirección de Estadística y Censo. Panamá, August.

———, 1950b. (Various mimeographed tabulations of the agriculture and livestock census) Dirección de Estadística y Censo. Panama. Issued 9 and 10 March.

———, 1950c. *Boletín Informativo No. 2*. Dirección de Estadística y Censo. Panamá. February.

———, 1950d. *Primer Censo Nacional Agropecuario; Resultados Generales*. Dirección de Estadística y Censo. Panamá. September.

Gilmore, Raymond M. 1950. "Fauna and ethnozoology of South America." *HSAI*, Vol. 6, pp. 345–464.

Hooper, Ofelia. 1945. "Aspectos de la Vida Social Rural de Panamá," *Boletín del Instituto de Investigaciones Sociales y Económicas*, Vol. II, No. 3, pp. 67–315. Panamá. February.

———, 1952. "Algo de Nuestro Rico Folklore Indio." Manuscript.

———, n.d. "Las Fronteras Interiores de Panamá y sus Conquistadores." Manuscript.

INCAP, 1951. Nombres de Alimentos en Centro América y Panamá. Preparado por Susana Judith Icaza. Instituto de Nutrición de Centro América y Panamá. Guatemala. Dittoed.

James, Preston. 1942. *Latin America*, New York.

Johnson, Frederick. 1948a "The post-Conquest Ethnology of Central America: An Introduction." *HSAI*, Vol. 4, pp. 195–198.

———, 1948b. "The Caribbean Lowland Tribes: The Talamanca Division." *HSAI*, Vol. 4, pp. 231–252.

McBryde, Felix Webster. 1953. "America Central; Vegetación Natural (generalizada)." a map in *Atlas Estadístico de Costa Rica*, Ministerio de Economía y Hacienda, Dirección General de Estadística y Censos, San José.

Lehmann, Walter. 1920. *Zentral-Amerika*, Part I. "Die Sprachen Zentral-Amerikas." Berlin.

Mason, J. Alden. 1950. "The Languages of South American Indians." *HSAI*, Vol. 6, pp. 157–317.

Platt, Robert S. 1938. "Items in the Regional Geography of Panama." *Annals of the Association of American Geographers*, Vol. 28, pp. 13–36.
Rubio, Angel. 1950a. *Pequeño Atlas Geográfico de Panamá.* Panamá.
―――― 1950b, "La Vivienda Rural Panameña." *Banco de Urbanización y Rehabilitación*, Panamá. *Publicación No. 18.*
Sauer, Carl O. 1950a. "Geography of South America." *HSAI*, Vol. 6, pp. 319–344.
――――, 1950b. "Cultivated plants of South and Central America." *HSAI*, Vol. 6, pp. 487–544.
Stout, D. B. 1947. "San Blas Cuna Acculturation: An Introduction." *Viking Fund Publications in Anthropology, Number Nine.* New York.
――――, 1948a. "The Cuna." *HSAI*, Vol. 4, pp. 257–268.
――――, 1948b. "The Choco." *HSAI*, Vol. 4, pp. 269–276.
――――, 1952. "Persistent Elements in the San Blas Cuna Social Organization." *Indian Tribes of Aboriginal America*, Ed. by Sol Tax, pp. 262–265, Chicago.
Wassén, S. Henry. 1952. "Some Remarks on the Divisions of the Guaymí Indians." *Indian Tribes of Aboriginal America*, Ed. by Sol Tax, pp. 271–279. Chicago.

APPENDIX

Notes by Ofelia Hooper

The following notes were written in essentially the form given below by Miss Ofelia Hooper after reading the first draft of the preceding manuscript. Some of the notes amplify the material provided in the text; some indicate a slightly different point of view with respect to the same material; others provide data which is somewhat at variance with the text material. Since it was not possible for either Miss Hooper or the writer to initiate further studies to resolve the differences in observation, it was felt that the reader should be allowed the benefit of both until such time as further studies may be made. The writer wishes again to express his indebtedness to Miss Hooper for permitting the incorporation of these notes and for the great help she provided during the survey. There are few people writing today who know the Panamanian countryman as well as she.

The following notes are divided into sections; for each the page on which the subject is discussed in the text is given.

1. (page 38) It would be of interest to investigate the influence of three factors in the localization by district of the Indians: (1) Many of the districts have no clearly defined limits. (2) The limits and territory of districts have often been changed through laws, but there is no geodetic map of Panama on which to establish such changes. (3) There are indications of nomadism among the Indians. In the census form used for Indian families it was asked where the persons were born. It was surprising to see the far away places from which they came. These immigration currents, the improvement in the production showed by the immigrant Indians over those who remained stationary, and the customs of having two home locales (one for agriculture and one for livestock) will all influence both the long range and immediate picture of Indian distribution.

2. (page 63). It should be noted that while sometimes it is private land which

is rented, it is also often the case that the so-called owner of the land has no more right to the rented land or to collect rent in services than does the countryman who transforms it into pasture ground. Most of the time the only right the so-called owner has is that he fenced the land in with wire. Legally it still belongs to the state.

3. (page 66). *Foods of Second Importance.* Cocoa, *mamey*, *guaba* (not what is called in English guava or in Spanish *guayaba*, but *guaba*, a leguminous plant producing a large unedible bean enveloped in an edible, sweet, white cotton), and *chayote* should be added. More scarce, but present on many farms for familiar use are peanuts and *Sesamum orientale*.

4. (page 68). *Rastrojo*, in familiar terminology, refers to the stubble growing up in a field which has been burned over, subjected to the *roza*. The other growth constitutes the *monte* which is cut down and burnt; the cultivation carried on after the cutting of the *monte* is the *roza* and that after the *monte* again begins to grow, the *rastrojo*. *Rastrojo* also, for many Panamanians, refers to the wild vegetation which grows up among the cultivated plants before it grows so big that it can be considered in the category of *monte*, *rastrojo grueso*, or *monte grueso*. The agriculturalist who cuts only *rastrojo* because of lack of land, lack of strength for cutting *monte*, lack of help of neighbors, or lack of will, is considered to be inferior. The women always note whether a man cuts *monte* or *rastrojo*. In both the *monte* and *rastrojo* one cuts and burns, and may take out two or three harvests. All this does not mean that there are not other terminologies, but this is the terminology used in Las Minas (Province of Herrera) where I come from.

5. (page 69). In the terminology which I hear most frequently the *chuzo* is a piece of hard wood with a sharp edge. The *coa* is called *chuza* in some places, but the *chuzo* is used as much as the *coa* by those unable to purchase the latter. The difference between the *coa* and *chuzo* is that the *coa* has a metal point while the *chuzo* is merely a wooden stick with the end cut in a point, like on a pencil, or sliced with a transversal cut leaving one side sharp. This *chuzo* is used when there is no money to buy a *coa*.

6. (page 70). Apparently the differences between the *junta* and *peonada* are: (1) the party: the *peonada* which has a fiesta passes into the category of *junta* or *juntica* to distinguish it from a *junta* as a social event. The *juntica* is intermediate, a *junta* of the poor people. (2) Those participating in a *junta* do not receive a salary; those in a *peonada* are paid with money or by *peon por peon*. (3) The number of people participating. (4) The participation of women apart from those of the family. Where the women do not work in agriculture they attend the *juntas* but not the *peonadas*, except when they are held for their own benefit or the benefit of those near the family. Women accept invitations for *juntas*, *embarras* (putting mud on a house wall), and *piladeras* (to pound rice or coffee in the large wooden mortar); but they do not accept invitations to *peonadas* without special reason. (5) At *juntas* anyone who attends is treated like a guest; at the *peonadas* this is not so since only enough food is cooked for the people expected. (6) For *juntas* the authorities must be advised; for *peonadas* this is not necessary. The *juntas* are less frequent each year, but they are still not uncommon; just since

reading your book I have been told of two, one in Guararé, and by a friend of mine who travelled in the mountains on the Atlantic coast who said he solved the problem of lunch by encountering a *junta*. There used to be another kind of group exercise called the *cargaderas de rancho*. They would uproot an entire *rancho* (pole frame house), insert supporting beams, and carry it to another lot where excavations had been prepared for the supporting posts. I have not heard of the *cargaderas de rancho* for many years now.

7. (page 71). The women work in the *juntas* to pound rice or coffee. These *piladeras* are usually done on moonlight nights. They are very popular among the younger people since a young man and woman may do the work together; generally sweethearts or those falling in love do this. Many who sponsor *piladeras*, however, to insure that the work actually gets done, will place people in groups of three around the mortars; this way doesn't attract people so much, however.

8. (page 74). Dynamite not elaborated in the home but bought or obtained—which makes it doubly illegal—from public works is used. The practice of making gunpowder in the home has not come to my attention. Dynamite is also taken to the country by those who go from the city; it is usually the city people who use it, since the countrypeople find it hard to obtain.

9. (page 76). *Bijao* is an herbaceous plant with no trunk, and with leaves similar to those of the banana, but very narrow and small; the back side is covered with white dust. There are many varieties, such as Paradise Bird, Lobster, *Chichica, Zapatillas de la Virgen*, and others. The San Blas Indians probably use strips of the *bijao* in making some of their baskets.

10. (page 78). The gourds, or *tulas*, are used very much as you indicate. Also the *totumas de calabazo*, of small size, constitute the glasses and cups of most of the rural homes. They are used as glasses by both town and countrymen, but cups only in the countryside. The large ones serve as receptacles for washing rice or vegetables, for bathing in the river, to carry liquids or grains from one vessel to another, to take along as a container when one purchases sugar-cane juice, milk, *guarapo*, corn, coffee, salt, etc. They also serve as measurers. *Totuma* is a half-gourd. *Coco de calabazo* (which have nothing to do with coco as in coconut) is the long gourd which is cut and often wrapped with vine for greater stability. In some country homes they have *el coco de la miel, el coco de la sal, el coco de ordeñar* (the *coco* for honey, for salt, or for milking). In a culture where paper and containers are missing, the *bijao* as paper and the gourds as containers play an important role. If you ask a countryman to show you the property title to his land, should he have one, or the birth certificate of his son, or any other document, it would most probably come out of a *coco*. In La Enea, Guararé, they use the *coco de camaronear*, a *coco* with the cover attached by rubber, into which shrimp are placed immediately after removing them from the net. *La cuchara de olla* is the *coco* type gourd, but cut lengthwise so as to form two spoons without handles. The buttons covered with yarn on the *montuna* shirts are made of gourds. The *bangañas*, or water carrying gourds, are also used for carrying honey, liquor, *guarapo*, or *chicha*.

11. (page 79). The oven and potter's wheel are not used in Panama. Diana

Chiari de Gurber, who is reviving the native industries, is introducing it for the first time in the culture of Panama.

12. (page 84). Cement block houses are the exception but they exist not only in the outskirts of Chitré, but in many other places in Panama. There are small molds to make blocks which the families rent or borrow, and all the family makes the blocks for the house. In Chicá, in the highlands of Campana, I saw a dwelling where the family, without destroying the old house, was surrounding this with walls of blocks made by themselves. They planned to tear down the old walls as soon as the new were finished. Since they could not afford to buy much cement at a time, they made this house in this way. This practice is found scattered in many places but is not very common.

13. (page 88). The list of drinks used by the countrymen is extensive:

Not Fermented:

(1) *Chichas*: (a) fruits used include oranges, pineapple, papaya, *nance, guanábana*, watermelon, *tamarindo, corozos*, and in general, any fruit. The difference between fruit *chicha* and fruit juice is that no water or sugar is added to the juice; the *chicha* is a combination of the juice, sugar-cane syrup or boiled sugar, or white sugar, and water. (b) Cereals used for *chichas* include not only corn, but rice, oats, barley. Boiled whole kernel or ground grain is used, mixed with water, sweetened, and sometimes flavoring of cinnamon, ginger, vanilla, etc., and milk. (c) Sweet corn *chichas* are of various types: (i) toasted corn, ground, boiled, sweetened, and flavored as are the other cereal *chichas*; (ii) sprouting corn *chicha*: the corn is placed to germinate, wrapped in *bijao* or banana leaves, in a container with a little water; the water is changed to avoid getting a bad odor; after the corn begins to germinate, it is boiled and ground. (iii) boiled corn: full kernels are boiled, ground, strained, and sweetening is added. (iv) *Pujillo*: new hard grains of corn are hulled until they are broken open, then boiled and strained. (d) *Chichas* of the *corozo* palm fruit: the red *corozos* which give the black or white fat are hulled, peeled, and boiled, strained, and sweetened. The black fat results from toasting before grinding, and the white fat comes from not toasting the nut; this is much used for medicines and for the hair. They also make *chicha* of the *caña brava corozos*.

(2) Other Sweet Drinks: (a) Sweet *guarapos*: (i) sugar-cane juice, freshly extracted. It is common to go to the milling places to drink this *guarapo*. (ii) *Guarapo* of the boiled sugar-cane juice (*raspadura*). This is hot water sweetened with the boiled sugar-cane juice or with the blocks resulting of crude sugar (*panela*). Many drink this instead of coffee. Even in the homes of people who are better off the *tacho de guarapo* (pottery jar of this type of *guarapo*) is always on the fire. In a culture where confections, ice cream, sodas, chocolates, jams, jellies, and other such sweets are not available, this type of *guarapo* satisfies the desire for sweets. (b) Fresh or sweet palm wine: this is made of the sap of the royal palm, the same tree from which the heart of palm (*palmito*) is taken. The sap seeps into the hole cut in the fallen palm, and is drunk directly. (c) Tea made of ginger, cinammon,

limón herb, lemon, leaves or bark of the orange tree, seeds of *malagueta*, or nutmeg; the tea is made out of any one of these things, not all mixed, and sweetened. (d) Coffee, sweetened with *panela* or *raspadura*; the coffee is boiled with water, then a little cold water is added to settle the grounds. In many homes coffee is always ready for whoever wants it. Besides coffee there are other coffee-like drinks, but made from cashew nuts, peanuts, okra, and cacao.

Fermented Drinks:

(1) Corn *Chichas*. *Chichas* are sweet when drunk the same day they are made. Some, in fact quite a few people, do not consume it in this way but let it ferment until it has varying degrees of alcohol in it. There are families who keep gourds in which fermented, or *chicha agria* (bitter chicha) has been kept; they say the gourds do not become slimy. It is pitiful to see peons in Veraguas who go to work with their only lunch a gourd of bitter *chicha* and a few *mangos* and *guayabas*. This practice also exists in the central provinces, but there it is the exception while in Veraguas it is the rule, particularly in the district of Santiago. The men of San Blas also carry with them gourds of *chicha* when they go fishing on the sea or for agricultural work on the main land; but among them I have never seen bitter *chicha* used; they usually carry sweet *chicha*. Carrying *chicha, guarapo*, tea or coffee has the advantage that it is boiled and the men do not have to drink impure water elsewhere. Chewed *chicha*, if it exists, is extremely rare. In the communities I know there are always jokes about chewed *chicha*, but I do not know a single person who has really seen or consumed chewed *chicha*. This does not mean that the practice does not exist, but I have not observed it, nor do I know of any who really has. The use of *raspadura* has probably made the chewing unnecessary to obtain faster fermentation.

(2) Strong *Guarapo*. As with corn *chicha, guarapo* is also allowed to ferment until it has varying degrees of alcoholic content.

(3) Strong Palm Wine. As in the other cases, this is allowed to ferment; just after the fermentation begins, it tastes a little like champagne or some soft drinks. Later it becomes more alcoholic. The *guarapos* and palm wines turn into vinegar of good quality if they do not spoil after fermenting.

14. (page 88). There are many other foods as well as those mentioned. Among these are: *guisados*, a stew made of soft rice or rice soup to which is added green plums (*micoyas*, or *jobitos* in Chiriquí), ripe plantain, squash (*zapallo*), green papaya, yautia, yams, yuca, etc. It is different from *sancocho* (a thin stew of boiled yuca, meat, etc.) in that it is heavier. Some put sugar in the *guisado* of green papaya. Another similar food is the *gaucho* which has more rice, and usually is specifically a bean *gaucho*, a dove *gaucho*, or a chicken *gaucho*. The *gaucho* has rice, beans or meat, and the other things as an exception, and is heavier than the *guisados*. Another food is *cabanga*, made of grated green papaya, from which liquid is extracted and boiled with honey. It is very popular. Wrapped in strips of banana stalk it is a substitute for chocolates. A desert is made of orange peel which is left in water until it loses its bitterness, then is boiled with honey.

15. (page 92). Children are usually born in the dwellings, but if it should happen that the mother is not in the house, she will have the child wherever she is.

I agree with you that the scarcity of clergymen is not the main cause for the couples not to legalize their matrimony. It can be, and I think is one of the many factors, but as you observe, they could look for a priest should they really want one as they do for baptism. Baptism is more important to them; if a child is not baptized, if he is still a *moro* (that is, not yet christianized, a moor), then the elfs, witches, or the devil can take him. But couples who are not married by the clergy do not suffer any such threats by *duendes, ojeo, brujas, tuliviejas, silampas*, etc.

16. (page 93). For the weddings of those who can afford it, they eat *lechona*, suckling pig, and *tortillas* made for the occasion. These *tortillas* are small with a delicate edge. The bride dresses in white, with gown, veil, and crown like the townspeople. This is becoming more common while the *pollera, tembleque* (hair ornament), and *pañolón blanco* (large square shawl) are becoming more infrequent. In Las Minas I felt sorry to see that when choosing the dress to buy, everyone talked, everyone chose, except the bride. She had very little to say. I also felt sorry to see how they walked with high-heeled shoes, which they wore for that single occasion, spoiling their natural grace and suffering with shoes which made them uncomfortable. This is all changing. The bridegroom takes the bride on his horse, or each goes on his own if the bride's family owns a horse, or they walk; but the bride wears her entire wedding outfit with veil and gown. The accompanying parties walk or ride horses with them, playing the *mejorana*, singing and drinking liquor. When we lived at Las Minas, we always knew when there was a wedding because the guitar playing would go on all night. Since many of the guests would have no place to sleep, they would remain awake all night playing the guitar.

17. (page 102). The *Evangelio Cuadrado*, as it is explained in Panama, comes from "square deal," or something like that. The people have confused the Point IV program with those of the *Evangelio Cuadrado*; and the *Misión Agrícola de Arkansas* (the Agricultural Mission of the University of Arkansas) with the protestant missions. The error has not been serious, because it has not spread, but it has damaged the work in two towns in the Las Tablas district (Province of Los Santos) and in Chicá (district of Capira, Province of Panama). The people can be convinced, but since there is so much need for the work and so few resources we have had to postpone the work in some of these places. Elsewhere, they think that such confusion is a great joke.

18. (page 103). Egg omelets (*tortas de huevo*) fried with *mastranto*, wrapped in cloth, wet ashes, hot, fried tallow, in a cloth bag, is used in Las Minas as a medicine for external application; a *mastranto* plaster is used for abdominal pains and one of ashes is used for a twisted ankle.

19. (page 105). A plaster of *caraña* (a kind of resinous gum) is placed on the navel, and used as a medicine for styes. Also some rub the finger in the palm of the hand until it is hot, then place it on the stye and then point out a person with the finger; this person will have a stye. For *mollera* they also use *caraña*, but this practice is rare nowadays. For *mal de vista*, rose leaves left in water which was exposed to the night air or dew, dew picked from yautia leaves or from something

less poetic, or water in which a coin was left overnight, all are used. *Nubes* (clouds) in the eyes are said to be cleaned by putting sugar in the eye. For pimples (*granos*) water of the road picked up when it rains and dew plays an important part in the medicine of the countryman. Various things left in the dew are used: pineapple, cypress, nut, oranges, and leaves of various plants, the *higo matapalo*, *hierba de pasmo*. For serious burns, they wrap the patient in banana leaves. Kitchen soot, cobwebs, and pit-holding rags are used on wounds. Greases used for massages play an important role; they are not only lubricants for the skin but are believed to have medicinal qualities. They use fats of snake, monkey, wild hog, armadillo, alligator, turtle, etc. Unscrupulous merchants put lard in different bottles and sell all 'fats" requested. Fox is used for asthma; I believe it must be well broiled or roasted. For erysipelas, the affected part is rubbed with a live frog; if the frog dies, it means that the disease has been passed on to the animal. For pneumonia a cock pigeon is cut in two and placed, while warm, on the chest. The *balsamina* (balsam apple) is boiled in water for liver trouble.

The countrywomen believe that they must not eat fruits during menstruation and during the days following childbirth. Bathing, crossing a river, exposure to rain or getting wet in any form is believed to be harmful. Women who are expecting to become mothers "have cravings" which are irrational desires to eat something that is not within their reach. The cravings must be satisfied, otherwise children will not be able to close their mouths and will be called *"boquiabiertos."* The hot and cold things have a great importance as a cause of sicknesses and as medicine. Some women say, of sickness in others, that it was caused because the person did many foolish things.

In most communities that I know there are a series of stories which exist: the story of the *chivato* which always begins, *"hasta que se me espeluca el cuerpo;"* the one of the man who shot a doe and found the bullets of his gun in the body of a beautiful neighbor, with blood scattered from the spot where he shot the deer to the house of the neighbor; that the neighbor was a witch, and had been the person that he had heard whistling at midnight; the story of the patron saint of a place which had been found there, which could not be moved from the spot and therefore had determined that the town be built there; the story of the saint which escapes from the altar at night to help somebody who is in danger and calls for him; the tale that if a witch whistles at you, you must tell her to come look for salt; then the first woman who comes to ask for salt, a thing very common in a country where there are no stores, is a witch.

20. (page 106). The *Tulivieja* or *Tepesa*, with the hair disheveled, with the feet backwards, is supposed to be a woman who had to give birth to a child during a dance; she killed the child in order to be able to return to the dance which had been interrupted by the childbirth. Afterwards, without children, she was burdened by her crime, wished to undo it since she could not enter heaven; but her feet were turned backwards, taking her always back to the place of the crime, and she is asked: "Does it weigh on you?" (¿*te pesa?*). As a result, she goes about wishing to take children from other people.

21. (page 107). There are two types of situations in which masks are (were)

used: (1) Those of Carnival. They do not follow traditional patterns, and wear costumes for fun. There are the *culecos* (evidently from the term for brooding hen, *clueca*) from whom you have to run as they throw water or water mixed with indigo at anyone they can. Some *culecos* used to dress with dry banana leaves and were called *congos*. I do not believe that you see these masked people nowadays. (2) The *diablicos*, dirty or clean ones, with masks of animals, devils, or angels, who make noises with inflated pig bladders.

Part Three

NICARAGUA

WITH APPENDIX BY DORIS STONE

1954

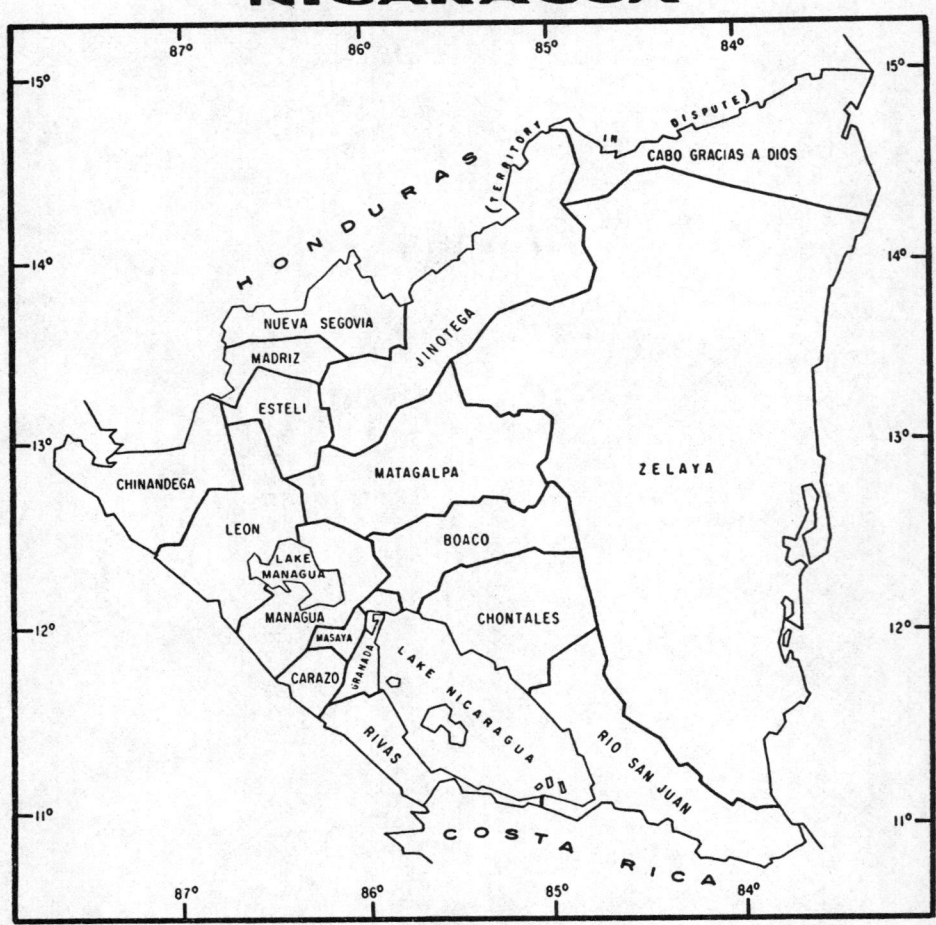

Departments

INTRODUCTION

This report is the second in a series which is intended to provide a picture of the territorial delineation of contemporary cultures of Central America and a preliminary description of the Spanish-speaking rural societies of the various countries. The general nature of the surveys on which these reports are based is described elsewhere. The survey in Nicaragua took place from the 1st to the 30th of August, 1953, and was preceded by a week of preliminary investigation in Managua earlier in the year. The general route followed in the survey is indicated on the map which accompanies this report.

The writer was accompanied during the survey in the highlands by Dr. Lyle Saunders of the University of Colorado, and on a major part of the entire survey by Mrs. Adams. Dr. Leonardo Somarriba, Minister of Public Health of Nicaragua, and Dr. Rodrigo Quesada, Chief of Section VI of the Ministry, were very helpful in providing the writer with initial information and letters of introduction to aid in his work. Miss Estella Herrera, Health Education Supervisor of the Ministry accompanied the writer on the investigation in the community of La Orilla, and Mr. László Pataky joined him in the trip to Monimbó. Mr. Pataky also provided the writer with information on certain areas he was unable to visit. Sr. Sofonías Salvatierra provided background information and copies of his publications on Nicaragua and Central America. The *Oficina Central de los Censos*, and its Chief, Dr. Adolfo Lola Blen, provided copies of all the census materials published to date concerning the 1950 Census and certain publications on earlier studies. Miss Emma Reh, FAO Nutritionist, made available data which she collected during a visit to Monimbó. The writer received invaluable help from public health officials, teachers, civil, judicial, and military officials in the various departments where the survey was made. Mr. and Mrs. Harold Mahlmann of the Institute of Inter-American Affairs provided helpful data and facilities for a much needed rest during the course of the survey. Mr. and Mrs. Herbert Sapper offered the hospitality of the Ingenio San Antonio during the work in the Department of León. The persons who served as informants during the survey, of course, provided the greatest help and must remain nameless; it is the policy of the survey to allow informants anonymity to protect them from criticism should the results of the survey displease.

The manuscript was read by Doris Stone. A few years ago Mrs. Stone made a trip into Matagalpa Indian region and made a series of notes concerning an area which is much less Hispanicized than the *municipio* of San Ramón which was visited during the present survey. Mrs. Stone was kind enough to consent to write up a brief description of this region in order to provide the reader with an idea of the less Hispanicized Matagalpa Indians. This is a valuable contribution to our knowledge of this region and the writer is deeply indebted to Mrs. Stone for making her material available. It appears as an appendix to the present report.

To all the people who have helped in providing material and collaborated in the preparation of this manuscript, the writer wishes to express his thanks; he accepts all responsibility for the form and the content of the report.

March, 1954.   R. N. A.
Guatemala.

TABLE OF CONTENTS

	Page
Introduction	149
I. The Culture Types of Nicaragua	153
II. The Atlantic Littoral	153
III. The Population and Its Distribution	158
IV. The Culture of the Ladino Town and Country Dweller	165
1. Introductory Note	165
2. Land and Labor	165
3. Agriculture	169
4. Other Exploitations and Local Products	175
5. Travel, Transport, and Commerce	179
6. The Domestic Scene	183
7. The Family and *Compadre* System	189
8. The Social Structure of Town and Country	195
9. Political Structure	199
10. Religious Activities	204
11. Ideas and Practices of Sickness and Curing	211
12. Notes on Recreation and Diversions	216
V. Communities Visited on the Survey	216
1. Ocotal and Segovia	217
2. Chirincocal and Pueblo Nuevo	219
3. San Pedro	220
4. San Rafael del Norte	220
5. San Ramón	221
6. Santo Tomás	222
7. Teustepe	222
8. El Sauce	223
9. Tipitapa	225
10. Telica	226
11. Nagarote	227
12. La Orilla	228
13. Rivas	228
VI. The Spanish-Speaking Indians of Nicaragua	229
1. The Background of Contemporary Indian Groups	229
2. The Matagalpa Indian Group	232
3. The Pacific Belt Indians: Subtiaba and Monimbó	238
A. Subtiaba	238
B. Monimbó	241
VII. Concluding Notes	245
1. The Central Highlands and Pacific Belt Regions of Ladino Culture	245
2. The Mestizoisation of Nicaragua	249
3. The Population, Social Structure, and Economy	250
4. Implications for Action Programs	252
References	255
Appendix. Brief Notes on the Matagalpa Indians of Nicaragua, by Doris Stone	256

I. THE CULTURE TYPES OF NICARAGUA

Nicaragua cannot be divided into completely homogeneous culture areas. The original Indian cultures present in the country at the time of the Spanish Conquest differed markedly from one region to another, and since the conquest different regions of the country have seen violently different cultural and social influences. Nevertheless, by taking into account some of the more gross variables in the original Indian picture and in subsequent influences, it is possible to distinguish general areas of different culture, and to some degree within these, subareas or regions of cultural variation. An analysis of the numerous factors which have played a role in steering the development of different regions and communities in different paths must be taken up on another place. The purpose of the present paper is to describe briefly the general outlines of these differences as they appear on the contemporary scene.

Nicaragua today may be divided into two major socio-cultural areas: the Atlantic littoral, a region of heavy tropical rains, of coastal savannah and mountain forests, diverse languages, and thin population; and the highlands and Pacific coast, a region of relatively dense Spanish-speaking population, distinct rainy and dry seasons, of mountainous and level areas. Of these two areas, the survey was concerned only with the second. There was not sufficient time to give attention to the Atlantic departments, and so they are treated briefly herein and the major part of the work is concerned with the highland and Pacific belt regions.

Neither of these regions are homogenous within themselves. The Atlantic littoral is composed of peoples of extremely diverse cultural and social, as well as racial, origins. In the highland and Pacific regions are to be found communities with varying cultures resulting from the differential retention of earlier Indian traits, differing colonial treatment, and different contemporary economic emphasis. The principal cultures of Nicaragua today include the Atlantic coast hunting, fishing, and forest exploitation cultures of the Ulva and Miskito Indians, the agricultural Indians of the Matagalpa region, the few semi-urban but agricultural Indians of the Pacific belt region, the agricultural Ladinos of the towns and countryside, and the urbanites of the major cities. In the sections to follow, most of these cultures will be taken up in more or less detail. Where no actual field work was done, a brief sketch is given of data which is available; where field surveys were carried on, a more extensive account is given. In all cases, however, the treatment is of necessity superficial and rapid. Our concentration is on the town and country Spanish-speaking populations since it is they who form the greatest majority of Nicaraguans and it is among them that Nicaragua must look for its development.

II. THE ATLANTIC LITTORAL

The Atlantic littoral of Nicaragua includes only seven percent of the population of the country, but encompasses over fifty percent of the land area. It is a region of a long and somewhat swampy coastline, backed by a broken savannah country which extends into heavy forests reaching into the mountain slopes. Politically it includes the entire Department of Zelaya, the comarca of Cabo Gracias a Dios, large sections of the departments of Río San Juan and Jinotega,

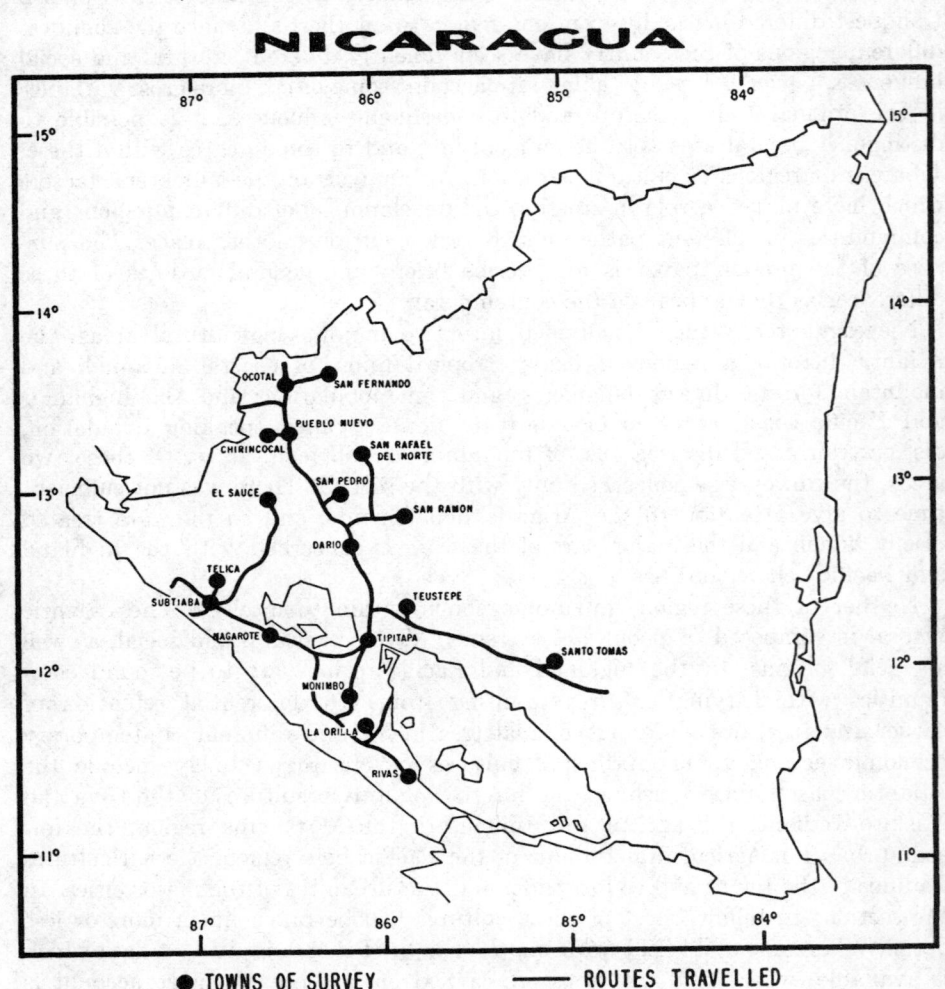

NICARAGUA

● TOWNS OF SURVEY   —— ROUTES TRAVELLED

and the eastern skirts of the departments of Matagalpa, Boaco, and Chontales. The culture of the inhabitants of this region is somewhat known, but most of our sources date from over twenty years ago, and there is reason to think that the region has witnessed changes during the intervening period. The rise of banana production, then its sudden stoppage due to disease, the World War, the growing mining centers, and most important, the gradually increasing interest in the region by the Nicaraguans, have doubtless brought in their train many alterations in the general picture which we have available at present.

For information on this region, the general history is provided in a number of sources: Squier[1] summarizes the general picture until that date; Salvatierra[2] provides a longer account of early history, and good general summary is to be found in Conzemius.[3] We have no specific social anthropological studies, but Conzemius[4] provides a good general ethnography, but is very weak on social organization; Pijoan[5] adds further specific data. For a general background picture of the Atlantic coastal area, Conzemius is probably the most handy. The data given by Pijoan is taken in great part from that source, and unfortunately gives the impression at times that the same situation existed in 1946 as was reported in 1932. In addition, Pijoan is a little careless, and adds a few errors (such as identifying the Paya as an "eastern Nicaragua" group, when they are in fact located in northern Honduras). Practically no intensive archaeology has been done in this region. Pijoan's account of the health and related customs of the Miskito of the Coco basin is a valuable study and should be more widely known in Nicaragua. Kirchhoff[6] gives a general summary of the customs of the entire Atlantic coastal region of both Nicaragua and Honduras, but adds nothing to the work of Conzemius with respect to Nicaragua. Another general description with odds and ends of information is Jose Vitta's 1894 report which was published in 1946. Unfortunately, there is no information in the article as to how this information was collected, and whether Vitta actually did much field research. He gives population figures for that period, but there is no way of judging their reliability at present.[7]

Johnson's 1948 map of the contemporary location of Indian groups on the Atlantic coast[8] places the Miskito along the entire east coastal region, and the various groups of Sumus in the Coco, Banbanbana, Prinzapolka, and lower Tuma Rivers; the Ulva are located in the basins of the tributaries of the Río Escondido, and the upper reaches of the Tuma River. The Rama he has located at three points along the coast from San Juan del Norte to Rama Cay (*"Ramaque"*), although data at present available tends to restrict them to the last of these locations. Johnson's distribution for these groups is dependent principally upon the description given by Conzemius in 1932. There may be an important inland concentration of Miskito to be found along the Coco in the region studied by Pijoan, from Bilwaskarma to San Carlos; however, Pijoan does not make clear whether the people with whom he treats in this region are Mosquitos, Sumus, both, or a partial blend. Conzemius does identify groups living up the Coco as being Mosquito.

While the term *Miskito*[9] can still be used to refer to an identifiable Indian population on the Atlantic coast, racially a large percentage have long been mixed with Negroes. Conzemius, however, has pointed out that "The Miskito readily intermarry with foreigners. They assimilate all races; the children always

---

[1] 1855. [2] 1939. [3] 1932. [4] 1932. [5] 1946. [6] 1948.

[7] László Pataky's *Nicaragua Desconocida*, which is in preparation, promises to provide considerably more information on the Atlantic region.

[8] HSAI, Vol. 4, Map 5.

[9] Both *Mosquito* and *Miskito* are found generally in the literature; the writer prefers *Miskito*.

speak the language of the mother and grow up as Miskito, whether the father be 'Creole,' 'Ladino,' Carib, Negro, Sumu, Rama, Paya, North American, European, Syrian, or Chinaman."[10] Conzemius holds that due to this characteristic the population of the Miskitos was increasing and their culture was being retained in spite of extensive contact over many years with various outsiders. In 1932 he estimated the population of the Miskitos to be 15,000, and Pijoan in 1946 gave an estimate of 20,000. If these figures are anywhere near the truth, they indicate a significant increase in population. Conzemius also states that the total number of Miskitos exceeds the combined number of all the other Indians on the Miskito coast (which includes part of Honduras as well as Nicaragua);

Table 1.—Population speaking an Indian language in the home
(*Dirección General de Estadística*, 1954)

Language spoken	Total number	Department of Jinotega	Department of Zelaya	Comarca del Cabo Gracias a Dios
Sumu only	387	26	361	—
Sumu and Spanish	360	212	148	—
Miskito only	15,539	292	5,156	10,091
Miskito and Spanish	5,184	227	2,709	2,248
Other languages	5	—	5	—
Other languages and Spanish	21	—	21	—
Total Indian language speakers	21,496	757	8,400	12,339
Total speaking only an Indian language	15,931	318	5,522	10,091
Total bilingual	5,565	439	2,878	2,248

if this is still true today, the total Miskito coast population of peoples with an Indian way of life is probably between 30,000 to 45,000. On purely territorial grounds we may guess that two-thirds or three-quarters of these are in Nicaragua, which would give us a figure between 20,000 and 34,000. We may assume in gross terms that these people are rural. The 1950 Census gives a figure of approximately 55,000 as the rural population of the Atlantic littoral; we may then estimate that perhaps one half of this population are Indians and the majority of that group are composed of Miskito Indians who live in the coastal region and along the Coco River.

Although the figures are very probably deficient, due to the problems involved in census taking in the Atlantic region, the 1950 Census does provide some data on the degree to which Indian languages are spoken in that area.

[10] Conzemius, 1932, p. 13.

This information clearly indicates that the Indian language speaking Miskito is generally concentrated in the northern portion, in the region adjacent to and extending into Honduras. The Sumu, however, much fewer in number, are found both further inland and further south.

The rest of this population is composed racially of Negroes, whites, zambos, mulattoes, Black Caribs, or other ethnic groups. Conzemius identifies as specific population groups the following:

(1) *Creoles*, around Bluefields, Pearl Lagoon, San Juan del Norte, and the Corn Islands. "These are descendants of the Negroes and mulattoes brought as slaves from Jamaica by the English settlers during the eighteenth century. They intermarried with Miskito and Rama Indians and speak the English language. The Creoles practically all belong to the Moravian Church . . ."

(2) *Negroes* and *Mulattoes*, scattered in the countryside. "They are chiefly of English speech and have arrived lately from Jamaica, the Cayman Islands, the Bay Islands, and British Honduras. There may be found also a few "Patois," that is French-speaking Negroes from Haiti, Martinique, Guadeloupe, Santa Lucía, and Dominica, besides some Spanish-speaking Negroes from the interior of Central America or from the coasts of Colombia."

(3) *Ladinos*: "Locally they are generally called 'Spaniards,' but they are largely of Indian extraction with only a very slight admixture of Spanish blood. They arrived chiefly as rubber bleeders and gold seekers, and lately as Government officials. Since the incorporation of the Mosquito reservation into the Republic of Nicaragua (1894) their number has rapidly increased; they are particularly numerous at Bluefields and the Pispis mining district, but may be found scattered throughout the country."[11] Concerning the group of government officials, Pijoan has some interesting comments: "The governments of the two republics, Honduras and Nicaragua, have territorial representatives known as *comandantes* and these are Ladinos. The commandant may have other Ladinos on his staff or as is often the case works in close collaboration with the traders. In the upper Coco River the commandant is stationed at San Carlos. He patrols the area, listens to complaints and his decisions are autocratic. He is in military uniform and his status is one of army discipline. The various companies, i.e., fruit enterprises, rubber development agencies, etc., have many Ladino foremen who work in close harmony with the *comandante*. From the Indian point of view considerable friction exists between himself and the government representative."[12]

(4) *Black Carib* or *Garif*: Most of this group is to be found on the north Honduras and British Honduras coasts, but according to Conzemius, "They have also formed several small settlements at Pearl Lagoon." The Black Caribs are descendents of a mixture of Carib Indians and Negroes which took place in the 18th Century in the Leeward Islands, and were then moved to the mainland.[13]

(5) *Miscellaneous Foreigners*: North Americans, Chinese, and Syrians are also to be found along the coast. The first group are principally connected with

---

[11] 1932, p. 7. [12] Pijoan, 1946, p. 16. [13] Conzemius, 1932, pp. 6–7.

the various fruit, mining, rubber or other exploitative enterprises in the area. The Chinese and Syrians evidently are active in local trade.

Evidence that the Altantic coast is of increasing interest to Nicaraguans may be seen in the fact that the town of Bluefields is the seventh largest town in the republic, and except for Matagalpa, is larger than any town outside the Pacific belt region. There is regular airline service in six towns in the Atlantic area, more than to any towns in the Pacific belt and highlands regions combined; and the highway to Rama, which will provide a shipping port on the Atlantic, is being worked on at present. Even in view of its possible value, however, the long projected interoceanic canal from San Juan del Norte to the Pacific seems remote, although there is a sturdy population of oldtimers in San Juan who are awaiting the day that the town will once again become of international importance.

III. THE POPULATION AND ITS DISTRIBUTION

From the point of view of differing social and cultural characteristics of the population, Nicaragua can be divided into three parts: The Pacific coastal belt, the central highlands, and the Atlantic littoral. The reason for making this division is provided from time to time in the report. For the discussion of population we will divide the country by departments as follows: The Atlantic littoral includes the Department of Zelaya, the comarca de Gracias a Dios, and the municipio of Río San Juan in the Department of San Juan. In some figures, as will be apparent from the tables, the census reports do not provide data to distinguish the information on the municipio of Río San Juan; where this is the case, the Department of Río San Juan is given as a total. The central highlands includes the departments of Boaco, Chontales, Estelí, Jinotega, Madriz, Matagalpa, Nueva Segovia, and the municipios of Morrito and San Miguelito of the Department of Río San Juan. Topographically, the central highlands actually stop within the departments of Chontales and Boaco, and within the municipios of Morrito and San Miguelito, and extend into the Pacific departments of Managua, León, and Chinandega. The overlap is slight, however, and the change in social and cultural characteristics is gradual enough that the departmental lines serve as satisfactory gross divisions. The Pacific coastal belt includes the departments of Carazo, Chinandega, Granada, León, Managua, Masaya, Rivas, and the municipio of San Carlos of the Department of Río San Juan. The assignment of this last *municipio* to the Pacific coastal belt instead of to the central highlands is arbitrary, based only on impressions gained by the writer from photographs of the town of San Carlos that it more aptly could be placed in the Pacific zone than in the highlands. Since no survey was made there, whether this assignment is valid or not must remain a question for the present.

The Pacific belt has three kinds of topography. The central highlands stop short of the east side of the great lakes, so it may be said that these lakes lie entirely within the Pacific belt. On the southwest side of the lakes is a short

NICARAGUA

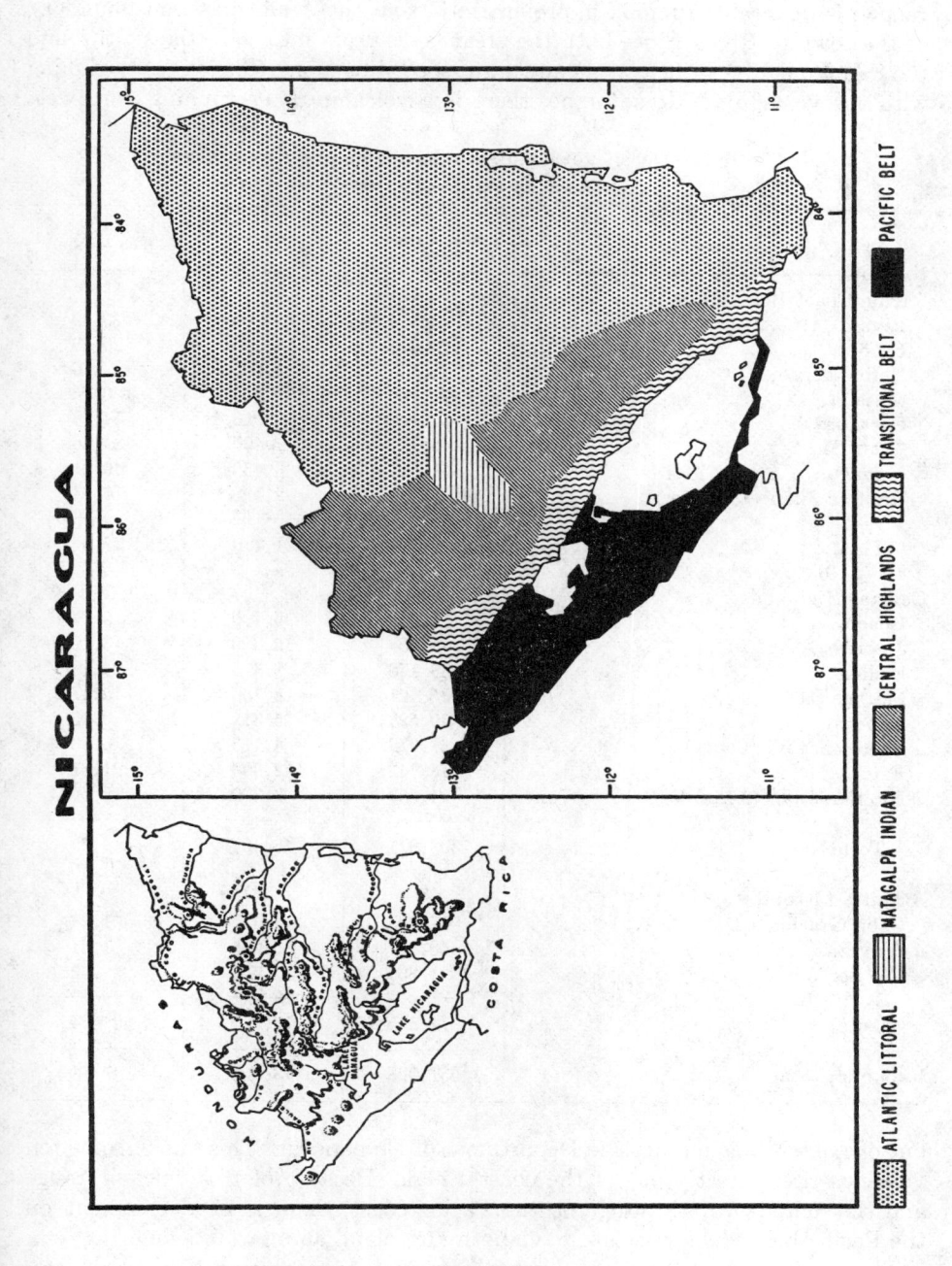

range of mountains running approximately from the Managua-León boundary to the town of Rivas. Since both the great lakes drain into the Atlantic through the San Juan River, the continental watershed runs along this range. Beginning with the volcano of Momotombo, there is a volcanic range running northwest

Table 2.—Density of population by region and department
(*Calculated from Census*, 1950a)

	Population	Area	Density (Pop./sq.Km.)
Pacific Coast Belt			
Rivas	43,314	2,200	20.29
León	123,614	6,100	20.26
Chinandega	81,836	4,600	17.70
Masaya	72,446	600	120.74
Carazo	52,138	950	54,88
Granada	48,732	1,400	34.80
Managua	161,513	3,450	46.81
Río San Juan (1 Munic.)	3,684	2,190	16.81
Total	589,277	21,490	27.4
Central Highlands			
Boaco	50,039	5,400	9.27
Jinotega	48,554	15,200	3.19
Madriz	33,178	1,375	24.12
Matagalpa	135,401	8,750	15.47
Chontales	50,529	5,311	9.15
Nueva Segovia	27,078	4,125	6.56
Estelí	43,742	2,000	21.87
Río San Juan (2 Munic.)	4,550	3,300	13.79
Total	393,071	45,461	8.7
Atlantic Littoral			
Cabo Gracias a Dios	17,323	14,300	1.24
Zelaya	56,497	55,985	1.01
Río San Juan (1 Munic.)	855	1,765	.48
Total	74,675	72,050	1.04
Republic: total	1,057,023	148,000	7.14

out of Lake Managua into the Department of Chinandega. This line of some ten volcanos rises directly out of the coastal plain. Because of this volcanic range and the more southerly range on the Pacific coast, there is no department on the Pacific belt which does not have both an upland and lowland zone.

The population of Nicaragua has its greatest concentration in the departments of Carazo, Granada, and Masaya, in the small range lying to the south of Lake Managua and the west of Lake Nicaragua. While it is easy to think of this as a coastal population, it should be kept in mind that the concentration is actually in an upland area. By department, it will be seen on Table 2 that while all the Pacific belt departments have a density of approximately 17 per km² or over, only two of the seven central highland departments have a density over this figure and the Atlantic littoral is under 2 inhabitants per km². The density of population for the Pacific belt as a whole is over three times as high as that for the highland area as a whole and, of course, considerably above that of the Atlantic littoral. This concentration of population in the Pacific coastal belt is not due merely to the greater urban concentrations there. Calculating approximate density of the rural population on the basis of the area of the entire regions, the central highlands has a density of rural population of 7.23 per sq. km, while the Pacific belt has a concentration of almost twice as much, 14.18 per sq. km.

Table 3.—Rural and urban populations by cultural regions (*From Census*, 1950a)

	Total	%	Rural	%	Urban	%
Pacific coastal belt	589,277 100%	55.7	304,780 51.7%	44.4	284,497 48.3%	77.1
Central highlands	393,071 100%	37.2	328,146 83.6%	47.7	64,925 16.4%	17.5
Atlantic littoral	74,675 100%	7.1	54,848 73.5%	7.9	19,827 26.5%	5.4
Total	1,057,023	100	687,774	100	369,249	100

Of course the Pacific belt also has the greatest urban concentrations. While there are five cities of over 10,000 people on the coast (Managua, 109,352; León, 30,544; Granada, 21,035; Masaya, 16,743; and Chinandega, 13,146); only Matagalpa in the central highlands reaches the population of 10,323.[14]

Table 3 shows the percentages of rural and urban inhabitants in the central highland and Pacific zones. While the two areas just about share the number of rural inhabitants, 83.6% of the total highland population is rural, while only 51.7% of the Pacific population is rural. Table 4 provides the relative percentages of rural and urban for the various departments. Here it will be seen that not only are the highlands as a whole more rural than the Pacific belt, but every individual department of the highlands has a higher rural percentage than does any Pacific department. The highest percentage of rural highland inhabitants by department fall into the adjacent departments of Boaco, Matagalpa, Jinotega, and Madriz.

Unfortunately, the figures for the 1940 Census as a whole are not reliable.

[14] All figures for 1950.

The census bureau reports that the actual count in that year was 835,686, but that this was increased to 983,160 to "cover possible omissions." They note, however, that this increase was probably larger than necessary. Consequently, we cannot rely heavily on the figures provided. Table 5 gives the figures as provided for 1906, 1920, 1940, and 1950. Between 1920 and 1940 there is a recorded rise of 60.4% in the population, but the relative percentage of rural

Table 4. Relative rural and urban populations by department and major regions of the country (*Census* 1950a; *percentages calculated*)

	% Rural	% Urban
Pacific Coastal Belt		
Rivas	69.3	30.7
León	65.3	34.7
Chinandega	60.9	39.1
Masaya	58.6	41.4
Carazo	58.2	41.8
Granada	40.7	59.3
Managua	28.2	71.8
Río San Juan (1 Munic.)	66.4	33.6
Central Highlands		
Boaco	87.6	12.4
Jinotega	87.6	12.4
Madriz	86.4	13.6
Matagalpa	85.3	14.7
Chontales	79.7	20.3
Nueva Segovia	78.6	21.4
Estelí	77.7	22.3
Río San Juan (2 Munic.)	77.7	22.3
Atlantic Littoral		
Cabo Gracias a Dios	93.7	6.3
Zelaya	67.1	32.9
Río San Juan (1 Munic.)	64.1	35.9
(Río San Juan entire Dept.)	64.3	35.7
Republic: total	65.1	84.9

and urban changes only 0.6%. Since the 1940 figures are unreliable, there is no way of telling whether this proportion has remained the same over the years, or whether there has been an interim change.

Nicaragua as a whole has a slight preponderance of women over men (see Table 6). In the highlands the numbers are almost equal, while in the Pacific belt departments there is a more marked number of women, 107 per 100 men. The proportion between the sexes is about the same for urban populations in both the central highlands and the Pacific belt, about 127 women per 100 men. In the rural populations, however, the Pacific belt has a lower proportion of women to men than does the central highlands.

Table 5.—Relative change in rural and urban populations, 1940–1950

	Total	Rural	Urban	Source
1906	600,000	402,000	198,000	Census 1950b
%	100%	67%	33%	
1920	638,119	419,945	218,174	Census 1950b
%	100%	65.7%	34.3%	
1940	(983,160)*	(617,896)	(365,264)	Census 1950b
%	100%	62.8%	37.2%	
1950	1,057,023	687,774	369,249	Census 1950a
	100%	65.1%	34.9%	

* The actual count in 1940 was 835,686, but this was increased "to cover possible omissions" to 983,160. The Census notes that this increase was larger than necessary.

Table 6.—Proportion of women to men in total, urban, and rural populations—1950 (*Census* 1950a)

	Total	Rural	Urban
	Women p/100 men	Women p/100 men	Women p/100 men
Pacific Coastal Belt			
Rivas	109.1	101.2	131.0
León	101.9	90.1	128.9
Chinandega	95.2	80.6	123.2
Masaya	104.5	95.0	120.0
Carazo	107.7	95.5	127.4
Granada	114.9	92.6	133.8
Managua	115.9	90.4	128.6
Total	107.0	91.0	127.3
Central Highlands			
Estelí	105.9	99.1	132.8
Boaco	99.7	95.7	132.2
Jinotega	97.7	93.6	133.0
Madriz	101.8	98.3	127.1
Matagalpa	96.0	92.1	122.4
Chontales	105.9	93.0	126.9
Nueva Segovia	100.3	93.7	129.3
Total	99.0	94.3	127.6
Atlantic Littoral			
Cabo Gracias a Dios	117.2	118.2	102.0
Zelaya	90.8	82.7	48.4
Río San Juan	85.8	76.6	114.9
Nicaragua: total	103.2	92.5	126.6

The male birth rate in Nicaragua is regularly higher than the female rate, and in the rural population this preponderance is maintained. The predominance in the number of women over men in the urban population, however, begins to occur in the 1 to 5 year old age group.[15] In all ages of 6 years and above, there is a preponderance of women over men in the urban population. This obviously cannot be explained solely in terms of selective migration of women to the urban centers. The vital statistics for the country (1945) show that through most of the early years there is a higher mortality rate of males than females. While this possibly accounts for the early predominance of females over males in the urban population, it does not tell us why the males of early age groups have a heavier death rate.

In the rural populations, the lowest relative number of women are found in the three adjacent Pacific departments of Managua, León, and Chinandega, and in Zelaya and Río San Juan in the Atlantic littoral. The Pacific department of Rivas, and the highland departments of Madriz and Estelí have nearest equal proportions; the remaining Pacific coastal and highland departments vary between 92 and 96 women per 100 men.

In general, there may be said to be significant demographic differences between the Pacific coastal belt and the central highlands. Taken together, the Pacific belt departments contain the greater percentage of the population and the greater concentration of the population. The highlands, on the other hand, have not only a slightly larger rural population, but that population comprises almost 84% of the total highland population, while on the coast the rural population is only about one half of the total population. As would be expected, then, the greater part of urban population, 77.1% is found in the coastal departments, and most of the larger towns are found there. The rural population of the highland departments varies between 77 and 88% of the total population of the departments concerned, while on the coast the rural population is between 28 and 70% of the population.

There is no evidence that there has been any great change over the past thirty years in the proportion of rural to urban population for the country as a whole; it was about the same in 1920 as it was in 1950. In general, there are more women than men in the urban areas, and more men than women in rural areas.

The census figures provide no information on the racial composition of the population. In general, the population of the Pacific coast and the highlands is mestizo, but there are certain regions where a white population or Indian population predominates. For example, in León and Granada, and certain towns in Nueva Segovia, populations with a high white component are found. The Atlantic littoral varies tremendously from populations which are predominantly Negro, to mixed Negro-Indian, to a now increasing mestizo population, and scattered populations of still fairly pure Indians.

---

[15] Census 1950a, Table 6.

IV. THE CULTURE OF THE LADINO TOWN AND COUNTRY DWELLER

1. INTRODUCTORY NOTE

In the central highlands and on the Pacific coastal belt live the greater majority and greater concentrations of Nicaraguans. Approximately 65% of these people are considered as rural. They live in small communities or in scattered isolated homes. Others live in small towns which are considered as urban; they are centers of commerce for the rural regions and contain many people who are not directly dependent upon agricultural activities for their livelihood. It is with the culture of these people that the following section is concerned. Following this there is a brief description of the various communities which were included in the survey and on which the descriptions are based. In the course of the description of the culture, as was the case in the discussion on population which appeared earlier, a distinction is made from time to time between traits which seem more common to the central highlands or more common to the Pacific coastal belt. Further distinction is made between the generally Ladino, or town and countryman populations, and three groups which are considered by the Nicaraguans to be *Indian*: the Matagalpa Indians of the San Ramón area, and the residents of Subtiaba and Monimbó. The so-called Indian groups are taken up in a separate section, and the distinction between the highlands and the Pacific belt is further elaborated.

2. LAND AND LABOR

Nicaragua, like most of Central America, is basically an agricultural country. According to the 1950 Census, two thirds of the total population of 14 years and older were occupied in the cultivation of crops, the care of cattle, and related activities.

From Table 7 it is clear that the central highland population is relatively more occupied in agricultural pursuits than is that of the Pacific coast belt. Whereas 78% or more of the highland departmental populations are so engaged, 74% or less of the Pacific coast population are classified in this general category. This group may be classified into four general types of relationships with respect to the land and other agriculturalists:

(1) The *hacendado*, or large landowner, who employs labor which ordinarily lives on the *hacienda* if it is a cattle or coffee *hacienda*, but may live in a separate settlement if it is an agricultural *hacienda* devoted to other crops. The *hacendado* himself usually does not spend all his time on the farm, having also a house in one of the major cities of the republic. In general, the Pacific belt farms are devoted to agriculture, usually rice, corn, cotton, coffee, sugar, or sesame seed, while the highland *haciendas* are devoted to cattle or coffee.

(2) The *finquero*, who owns a small farm on which he lives and which produces enough to support him, his family, and to employ one or a few laborers

either full or part time. *Fincas* are usually planted in diverse crops and will also have some cattle.

(3) The small landowner, a subsistence farmer, who has one or a few plots of land which he tends full or part time. The remainder of his time he works as a laborer on a *finca* or *hacienda*.

Table 7.—Percentage, by department, of economically active population (i.e., that which is 14 years and older) which is engaged in agricultural and related persuits (*Dirección General de Estadística*, 1954)

Department	Percentage of the economically active departmental population engaged in agriculture, fishing, hunting, lumbering, and related labors
Pacific Coast Belt	
Rivas	70.84%
León	66.02
Chinandega	72.71
Masaya	73.09
Carazo	70.78
Granada	50.55
Managua	30.36
Central Highlands	
Boaco	84.06
Jinotega	84.81
Madriz	81.43
Matagalpa	83.57
Chontales	78.96
Nueva Segovia	83.04
Estelí	84.06
Atlantic Littoral	
Cabo Gracias a Dios	91.21
Zelaya	66.80
Río San Juan	76.99
Republic: total	67.68%

(4) The laborer or *mozo* who owns no land and works full time on *fincas* and *haciendas*, or, depending upon the region, in some of the specialized exploitations such as lumbering, mining, etc.

Table 8 gives the approximate number of persons in these categories as reported by the 1950 Census. The category of "employers" includes both the *hacendado* and *finquero* defined here, but as will be noted some distinction is possible.

Except for the departments of León and Boaco, the departments of the Pacific belt and the central highlands are again distinct on the matter of salaried labor as opposed to employers and independent agriculturalists. The Pacific pattern is fairly steady: in all departments except León there are a high percentage of salaried labor, a low percentage of independent agriculturalists, and a very low percentage of "employers." This, I believe, can correctly be interpreted as meaning that the coastal population is predominantly a laboring population, that there are few *finqueros* and few independent agriculturalists. The central highlands, however, provides two different patterns, both distinct

Table 8.—Percentage by department of economically active population of 14 years and older according to employment status
(*Dirección General de Estadística*, 1954)

Department	Salaried labor	Non-salaried persons			Total
		Total	Employers	Work for self or family	
Pacific Coast Belt					
Rivas	71.79%	28.21%	8.77%	19.44%	100.00
León	53.13	46.87	11.08	35.79	100.00
Chinandega	65.06	34.94	7.80	27.14	100.00
Masaya	64.96	35.04	11.26	23.78	100.00
Carazo	69.81	30.19	9.95	20.24	100.00
Granada	65.96	34.04	11.72	22.32	100.00
Managua	71.54	28.46	5.96	22.50	100.00
Central Highlands					
Boaco	50.81	49.19	26.23	22.96	100.00
Jinotega	41.67	58.33	17.98	40.35	100.00
Madriz	32.03	67.97	16.43	51.54	100.00
Matagalpa	43.11	56.89	22.21	34.68	100.00
Chontales	41.92	58.08	8.69	49.39	100.00
Nueva Segovia	34.79	65.21	25.68	39.53	100.00
Estelí	35.19	64.81	33.68	31.13	100.00
Atlantic Littoral					
Cabo Gracias a Dios	17.58	81.42	1.58	80.84	100.00
Zelaya	49.50	50.50	9.15	41.35	100.00
Río San Juan	45.93	54.07	28.55	25.52	100.00
Republic: total	55.04	44.96	13.52	31.44	100.00

from that of the Pacific belt. All central highland departments have a relatively low percentage of salaried labor; except for Boaco, which has 50.81%, all the others have between 34 and 42%. However, the non-salaried population tends to fall into two general types, those in which the percentages of employers is relatively high, and those in which it is relatively low. The difference in these patterns probably reflects a relative difference in the importance of *finqueros* as opposed to independent agriculturalists. According to the figures, the *finqueros* would be of relatively greater importance in Estelí, Boaco, Nueva Segovia, and Matagalpa, while the subsistence farmers are of greater importance in Madriz

Chontales, and Jinotega. This difference is probably more pronounced as one examines local regions within the highlands rather than in terms of gross departments.

In general, the *hacienda-mozo* pattern predominates in the Pacific belt. There are a number of small landowners scattered through the coastal region, but in many places, such as Tipitapa, most such lands are being or have been bought up by the *hacendados*. The *finca* pattern is relatively more common in the highlands and is found in some coastal environment towns such as El Sauce, Telica, and Nagarote. Also in the highlands, around Matagalpa for example, are to be found large coffee farms. This tends to be fairly localized, however, for as one moves away from Matagalpa, there are more and more *fincas* and fewer large farms.

Since the cattle and coffee *haciendas* usually need a constant labor force, there are usually resident *mozos*. During the coffee harvest many small landholders and renters will come to participate in the harvest. Not only do the people of the highlands participate in this, but many coastal people who prefer the coffee work to sugar-cane harvesting will go to the highlands. In Nagarote it was said that the local people preferred the coffee work to the sugar work. There is a different labor pattern involved in this, since coffee harvest utilizes a whole family, men, women and children, while sugar harvest involves the men only.

The *hacienda* involved in sugar and general agriculture usually has a fairly small permanent labor force and employs many people during times of heavy work. Many of the people around Telica will spend the months of June to January or February working on the *haciendas* and *fincas* of general agricultural production, then the men will go to the sugar plantation from January to June to participate in the sugar harvest.

There are two land rental patterns to be found in Nicaragua. One, which is found predominantly in some coastal areas, is the rental of land in large quantities for one or a few years in order to plant cotton, sesame seed, or whatever other crop the planter feels will have a good market at the time of harvest. For this, land may be rented from *finqueros* or *hacendados*. This type of rental is restricted to those who have the capital to make such investments and is usually done by city businessmen, speculators, and *hacendados*.

The second type of renting is done by the subsistence agriculturalists and *mozos* who live in rural communities but have little or no lands of their own. They will rent small parcels from the *fincas* and *haciendas* for their annual subsistence cultivations. There is no recognized rental rate for these lands and the cost varies from place to place. The rent can often be paid in produce as well as in cash. It was reported in Telica and Tipitapa that one *fanega* (roughly between 300 and 330 lbs.) of corn grain was the payment expected for the rental of one *manzana* (10,000 square varas) of land sown in corn. In Tipitapa it was said that the same land could be rented for cash for between C$ 70 and 100. In La Orilla, C$ 100 was the reported rate. In San Ramón and Santo Tomás, the usual rate was 600 lbs of corn on the ear, considered as 1 *carga*, for a *manzana* of land.

It was reported in Rivas that *haciendas* would rent out lands with the stipulation that the renter should leave the land sown in pasturage grass when he finished.

The expression *medio-en-medio* in Nicaragua refers to the type of usufruct wherein a landowner supplies a piece of land, a poor agriculturalist works the land, and the produce is split fifty-fifty between them. In San Pedro this is a fairly common method of working the land. There, the *hacienda* supplies the land, the seed, the oxen, and the cart to carry in the produce; the worker supplies his labor. The same pattern was reported from nearby San Rafael del Norte, but it was there specified that the owner also supplied some labor to aid in the harvest. In San Rafael this type of usufruct was called *siembra en medio*. Almost all types of annual crops are sown in this way: wheat, potatoes, corn, beans, and sorghum.

While in most parts of the republic landownership is an individual matter, there still survive a number of *ejidal* lands. Theoretically, the entire municipality of Santo Tomás is *ejidal* or municipally owned land. A *canon*, a minimum amount of money, is paid annually for the right to the land by the persons who use it. While the municipality thus owns the land, it evidently does not have the right to take the land away from the usufructuary. So what the *canon* boils down to is a municipal land tax rather than a rental payment. In Santo Tomás it was said, by way of example, that a man might have 100 *manzanas* in this way, and since the local agriculture is primarily shifting, he would move around within his land from year to year.

The same situation was reported to be the case in Telica; all the lands were supposed to be *ejidal*, every one paid a *canon*, but the municipality did not have the right to take the lands away from the usufructuaries. In Darío the informant said that all the land within a radius of one half league of the town were supposed to be *ejidal*, but the municipality did not collect a *canon*. In Nagarote and Tipitapa it was reported that much of the land had formally been *ejidal*, but that the titles had been lost and no one had made any effort to retain them. In Nagarote it was said that the *ejidal* lands used include all those within a radius of a league of the town. The writer received no report of *ejidal* lands in any of the highland towns except Santo Tomás.

3. AGRICULTURE

There are three different complexes of agricultural technology to be found in Spanish-speaking Nicaragua: mechanized, ox-plow, and dibble. The mechanized agriculture is limited to those who have *haciendas* or who rent large areas of land for cultivation. It is most common in the coastal area and in intermountain valleys of the highlands. In general, its distribution is the same as that of the *haciendas*. Nicaragua has seen considerable development in mechanized agriculture in recent years.

The agricultural complexes which are most common in terms of the number of people employing them, however, are the ox-plow and the digging stick. In certain places, such as Monimbó, it was reported that the dibble was the preferred form until recent years, and that now the ox-plow has superseded it. It is not possible to state on the basis of the survey what the precise history of the introduction of the wooden plow has been in Nicaragua, but its present distribution seems to depend upon certain functional problems and to be complementary to that of the digging stick complex.

Where the land is level and has already been cleared, the wooden plow is usually used. If the land is too rough, or needs cleaning for the first time, then digging stick agriculture is used. The difference between these kinds of land are recognized by the use of such terms as *montaña* or *serranía* to refer to lands which are too rough for the plow, *monte* for lands which need cleaning for the first time, and *valle* and "level lands" for those lands where the terrain permits the use of the plow.

These two different forms of agriculture are known in some places by different names. In San Rafael del Norte and San Fernando the digging stick agriculture was called *milpa*, the Meso-American term for corn field. In San Fernando, this was in contrast to *labranza* which referred to the plow agriculture work. In some places, it was specifically mentioned that one form of agriculture was utilized by one portion of the population, while the other was used by another. People who own or have the good fortune to have, rent, or work *en medio* on level lands use only the plough agriculture, except if they have to clear new land. This group includes the vast majority of the *finqueros*, some of the small landholders, and many of the people such as were found in San Pedro who own no land themselves. In Monimbó and Subtiaba it was specified that almost everyone now uses the plow where the terrain permits, and that since few own the oxen and equipment, they hire out someone to do the work for them.

The digging stick agriculture may be carried on by some *finqueros*, but it is mainly used by the subsistence farmers and people who rent uncleaned land to cultivate. It was reported that the great majority of agriculturalists in Teustepe, Santo Tomás, the eastern or *montaña* part of El Sauce, and about half the population in San Rafael del Norte use the dibble agriculture. On the coast, it was specified that the digging stick was used only in *monte* lands and in some of the more difficult areas around La Orilla, around the volcanos, and other similar regions.

From this, it is clear that there is no gross regional distribution of one type of cultivation as opposed to the other. Most municipalities have both types of land, although in some, such as Tipitapa, Rivas and other generally level regions the digging stick work is done mainly in lands which need clearing.

Land usage falls into a different pattern depending upon the type of cultivation. Plowed lands are used regularly year after year. They usually receive no fertilizer except that corn stalks may be plowed in and a series of cross plowings made to turn up the soil thoroughly and very rarely are they irrigated. The land which is being cleaned for the first time by axe, machete, and digging stick to be converted to plow land will usually be worked for two or three years in this manner until all the trees have been cleared out, then it will be turned over to plow work. Most digging stick agriculture, however, is shifting; a piece of land is cleared, the *roza*, early in the first year, then later burned just prior to the rains, and planted. It will be used for two or three years, then left to rest an equal length of time. It will then be cleared again for a few years, and again left to rest. In Santo Tomás it was reported that the land was left fallow for up to six years.

The digging stick complex is clearly derived from the native culture of the region, while the plow and oxen are equally clearly Spanish introduction. The only region in which the digging stick complex is generally common is the Matagalpa Indian area. As was mentioned earlier, however, the two forms of cultivation have today become complementary to handle different types of problems. There is evidence that there is still a change under way in some places from one form to the other; the report from Monimbó indicated that the use of the plow was a fairly recent innovation there.

The implements used in plow work consist of the wooden plow which is basically the same as was brought from Spain and is found today in Mexico and Peru. The *chusa* a long pole with a metal point is used in some parts of Nicaragua to prod the oxen, but the writer was told that it had been outlawed as being too harsh on the oxen and consequently was falling into disuse. The plow is used to break up the soil for planting and, as mentioned before, for turning in corn stalks. Its use as an implement of cultivation varies, however. In the northwest coastal area, specifically in El Sauce, Telica, and Nagarote, a heavy wooden *descultivadora*, a large inverted U-shaped, wooden implement with metal blades, is dragged down the rows by oxen. This serves as the principal cultivation implement. In Nagarote it was also reported that cultivation was done with the plow itself. The most common cultivation implement used in the plough agriculture, however, is the *macana*, a long handled implement which is a cross between a flat shovel and a hoe, the head of which is smaller than either.

Digging stick agricultural implements consist principally of the digging stick. The main type is that called the *espece*, a long stick with a flat, square-bottomed metal blade. The *espece* is found in this form in both the highlands and the coast, mainly in a belt running down the center of the country north and south (in San Rafael del Norte, Darío, Teustepe, Santo Tomás, Monimbó, La Orilla, Tipitapa and Rivas). To the west, various other terms and forms of the implement are used. In Ocotal, a pointed digging stick called the *pujaguante* is used, while the square-ended implement is called the *coba*[16] and is used for digging post holes. In Chirincocal, the digging stick is called *estaca*. In El Sauce and Telica the implement is usually a piece of old machete tied on a stick, and is called respectively *tunco* and *cobín*. In Nagarote it is called the *coba*. In the Matagalpa Indian area *coba* is the general term used.

In some places where the digging stick is called *espece* there is also used a wider implement which is called *coba*. This latter implement is about the same size as a *macana*, but is straight, not bent as is the *macana*. Over most of the coast this

---

[16] *Coba* is the pronunciation used over most of Nicaragua for the *coa*.

coba is used mainly for digging holes, not for planting. In general there seems to be little regional reason behind the varying terminology used for these implements.

In cleaning land the ax and machete are standard implements. The machete is also used for *limpia* or cleaning, during the cultivation, especially in bean patches. In Chirincocal it was reported that a special curved tipped machete was used in cleaning; it was called the *machete de taco* and said to come from Honduras. Also in El Sauce a curved machete was reported, there called the *cuma*. The use of the *azadón*, or hoe, is scattered over most of the country with no evident reason behind its present distribution. Another implement found fairly commonly (seen on the coast) is the *horquilla*, a forked stick used as a rake in gathering cut weeds for burning.

The major crops raised by the Nicaraguan farmer are listed below. Those rated as being of "first importance" were said to be cultivated in almost every community visited and, with the exception of millet which was said to be used for fodder by *finqueros*, was important in the diet; or, are very commonly found. Those of "second importance" have a more limited usage. Some of the crops are more generally grown on the large *haciendas*: cotton, sesame seed, sugar cane,

List of crops of contemporary importance in countryman agriculture, according to source of origin

	Present in the new world at the time of conquest	Not present in the new world at the time of conquest
First importance	corn (*maíz*) beans (*frijoles*) ayote (*pipián, ayote*) *quiquisque* *yuca* *papaya* tomato (*tomate*) *guayaba* *achiote* avocado (*aguacate*) cotton (*algodón*)	sorghum (*maicillo*) rice (*arroz*) sugar cane (*caña de azúcar*) citrus fruits *mangos* sesame (*ajonjolí*) plantains (*plátanos*) bananas (*guineos, bananos*)
Second importance	*chile* sapote (*zapote*) gourds (*jícaros*) soursop (*guanábana*) pineapple (*piña*) sweet potato (*camote*) *maguey* *pejibaye* *cacao*	bread fruit (*fruta pan*) coffee (*café*) ginger (*gengibre*) yams (*ñame*) wheat (*trigo*) apple (*manzana*)
Not encountered	broad beans (*habas*)	yautia (*otóes*)

List taken from writer's survey; identification from INCAP, 1951; sources from Sauer, 1950b; terms in italics are those used in Nicaragua.

and coffee (also an important *finquero* crop in highlands). There are also certain crops which are generally restricted to either the highlands or the lowlands. Coffee, potatoes, and wheat are commonly found in the highlands (both in Pacific belt and central highlands), while bread fruit, soursop, mamay, cotton, coconut, zapote, papaya, and sesame are generally lowland crops.

The planting of corn, sorghum, and rice is usually done immediately after the first rains in May. The time of harvest varies somewhat from place to place and of course with the crop involved. Corn matures in August and in some places is harvested at that time. A trait common over much of Nicaragua is using the very young ears of corn from the base of the stalk as food. In many places, especially on the coast, it is common to *doblar*, or bend over the corn on the stalk after it ripens, and leave it on the stalk until October or December, at which time it is harvested. Another use of corn is as a fodder crop. *Guate*, as it is called, is corn in the flowering stage which is harvested and used as animal feed. For some of the poorer people, this is a useful cash crop as it may be grown in a short time. Rice is frequently not planted until June. The sowing of two crops is fairly common over most of Nicaragua, both in the highlands and on the coast. In San Rafael del Norte, the *primera* is sown in May, the second, or *postrera*, in September or October. Corn, beans, wheat, and potatoes are all sown in the *postrera* in San Rafael. The most common *postrera* crop everywhere is beans. In some places beans are not sown with the first crop at all. In Santo Tomás it was reported that the first bean crop was sown in July. Yuca was reported to be only a *postrera* crop in El Sauce.

There are, of course, a number of crops which last for more than a year: plantains; bananas (called *chahuite* in Santo Tomás), especially the *banano cuadrado*; and coconuts. The practice of sowing mixed crops seems to be limited to those who have very little land. The informant in San Pedro said that beans were frequently planted in rows between rows of mixed corn and beans; he said that they felt that sorghum did not do well when done in mixed plantings with corn.

The division of labor in agriculture shows a marked variation between the highland and Pacific belt region. It was reported in all coastal towns that women worked in the fields, in the thinning of cotton, the harvest of corn, beans, cotton, sesame, and rice, and in some places the cleaning of land. Women generally work where there are *haciendas* and one reason for the use of women may lay in the fact that they receive a lower wage than do the men. In general, women do not work in the fields in the highlands. The major exceptions to this encountered on the survey were in Ocotal, where there are some *haciendas* and *fincas* which produce lowland crops such as cotton and sesame, in San Pedro where most of the population is composed of *mozos*, and in the Matagalpa Indian area. Also, during the coffee harvest, whole families, women, children, and men participate, but this is a limited seasonal work. It was reported in San Rafael del Norte that it used to be the custom for the women to do the planting, following the plough, but that this custom has died out. On the other hand, in Monimbó, it was reported that only recently women began to participate in the field work, dating specifically from the time of mechanization in the area. In the region between the highlands and the coastal belt, it was reported that women did not do field work in Santo Tomás and Teustepe, that they did in some parts of Darío, and that they did work in El Sauce.

Where women do work, it seems to be mainly in the *mozo* population, which is, of course, part of the *hacienda* pattern, and among the coastal small landowners and possibly also *finqueros*. In the highlands, it is evidently only among the landless that the women work, except in the case of the Matagalpa Indian group which is a distinct problem. The specific types of labor, in which women do not participate are in the actual plowing and in the *hacienda* harvests of sugar cane. For the sugar cane harvest, men from the coastal and piedmont region migrate to the larger *haciendas* and spend the five or six months of harvest there. It is not the custom to take a family along for this harvest since the sugar cane *haciendas* do not have living facilities to take care of the women and families. As a result, the women stay at home and continue to carry on the work in *haciendas* and *fincas* nearby.

Among those working for themselves, the usual custom is for a man to work by himself or with members of his family. The *finqueros*, *hacendados*, and occasionally small landowners, will employ *mozos*. Exchange labor, called *mano vuelta*, however, seems to be principally a highland trait. It was reported to be present in Tipitapa and all highland towns, but not in Teustepe or El Sauce. Besides Tipitapa, the only coastal community for which exchange labor was reported was Nagarote in which it was specified to be relatively uncommon. In Monimbó it was said that they used to have exchange labor many years ago, but that the custom was no longer observed. Where used, *mano vuelta* usually does not involve over three or four persons. It was nowhere reported that labor *juntas*, such as are found in Panama, were used.

The use of *rogaciones*, prayers and religious processions for rain, were reported from every survey site except Tipitapa. There it was said that they practically never have them. This may be due in part to the fact that almost the entire surrounding region is in large *haciendas*. In San Pedro, it was said that they were held in the nearby departmental capital of Estelí; the county people around San Rafael del Norte go to San Rafael to have them. Similarly, the people of Chirincocal usually go to Pueblo Nuevo for a *rogación*. Only in Teustepe was it specifically stated that the *rogaciones* were only held out in the *caseríos* and not in the town. In Chirincocal the *Virgen de Fátima* was the saint always carried in the *rogación*, but this may be due in part to the fact that this *virgen* is the most important saint in that region.

An important aspect of the agricultural technology is the threshing of wheat, sorghum, rice, and beans. For this the Nicaraguans use a square platform made of a series of small sticks set one next to the other. This platform type has the general name of *tapesco*, and the term is also used for the attic portion of a house similarly made. There are two general types of threshing stands, one set about a meter off the ground, and one set on a high platform, two or three meters off the ground. Three sides of the threshing platform are enclosed by stick and brush walls to prevent the grain from falling out the sides. The high threshing stands are preferred for the threshing of wheat and sorghum, the low for rice, and both are used for beans. The high stands permit the chaff from the wheat to be blown away while the grain falls to the ground on a skin below. While beans and wheat are flayed, the rice is beaten against the platform. The threshing platform goes under a number of different names. The term *tapesco* is used generally through the coastal regions and in Ocotal. In the highlands, the term varies: in San Pedro, San Rafael, and San Ramón, and in the coastal town of Tipitapa, *toldo* is used, while in Teustepe and Santo Tomás, *torril* is used. The threshing stand is fairly standard equipment in most Nicaraguan countryman yards.

One of the principal problems which faces the farmer, whether they are large landholders or subsistence agriculturalists, is that of credit financing of their cultivations. There are in most departmental capitals branch offices of the National Bank. These offices are authorized to give loans, usually in installments, for agricultural work, but they are given only under extreme care and with inspection by the bank of the properties to be used. In this way loans are practically unobtainable by subsistence agriculturalists since they are considered to be very bad risks. The people who cannot be financed in this manner by the bank must rely on loans from private individuals; this frequently results in an entire crop being sold prior to the harvest on a credit basis and at a sum very much below the market value of the crop at the time of harvest.

4. OTHER EXPLOITATIONS AND LOCAL PRODUCTS

The importance of hunting varies considerably. In general, there is little hunting done today in the more highly populated highland region and in the region to the south of Managua. It is of considerable importance as one moves into the eastern highlands, towards the Atlantic coast, and it is still of some importance in León and probably Chinandega.

The principal animals hunted are the deer, rabbit, peccary (*saino*), armadillo (*usuco* in San Rafael del Norte, *cusuco*, in El Sauce and Subtiaba), the *guarda tinaja*, (the agouti), and the *jabalí*, or white lipped peccary; of more limited importance is the *tigre*, *león*, *tigrillo*, *coyote*, *pizote*, monkeys, *iguanas*, alligators, and raccoons. Many of this second group are killed for their skins or to eliminate them as pests and are not important as food. In general, the coastal hunting is not of extreme importance for food, while in some of the highland backlands it does comprise a relatively important part of the diet.

The standard implements used by the Nicaraguans are the shotgun and the .22 rifle. Some people still have old muzzle loaders, and some also use pistols. Except for the Matagalpa Indian area, the use of the lance in hunting was reported only from San Rafael del Norte. Its use there is probably influenced by the proximity of the Indian region. On the coast firearms are the only weapons used. The only use of traps reported, aside from the San Ramón region, was in catching pigeons in Telica. There the boxfall-trap, called *tureca*, is used.

Depending upon resources, fishing is of considerable importance to some of the countrymen. Fishing in the highland is generally unimportant except in the eastern region adjacent to the Indian area. The use of vegetable poisons is known through most of this area but its use is somewhat restricted. Some of the poisons will also kill domesticated animals who drink from the poisoned streams and it was consequently reported in San Rafael del Norte that such poisons are very little used. In the backlands of Chontales, however, poisons seem commonly used as they are in the Matagalpa Indian area. The vine called *barbasco* and certain tree barks were the poisons reported in use in this highland area. Nagarote was the only coast town in which the use of fish poisons was reported. The *simarra*, a vegetable poison, was said to be used. This poison is sometimes thrown at low tide at the fish weirs built to catch the fish which have become trapped during high tide.

The use of gunpowder in fishing is fairly widespread in both the highlands and coastal region. The use of nets is important where fishing is carried on extensively. The *chinchorro*, described from El Sauce and Tipitapa, is a long net between 15 and 30 yards long, by 1 to 2 yards deep. It is dropped into the river or lake, and swung around in a wide circle and closed. The fish thus trapped are either removed by men who enter the water, or the net is swung up on the shore. The *atarraya* is a round throwing net about two yards in diameter with weights on the outer edges, also reported from El Sauce and Tipitapa. The *enredador*, reported from Tipitapa, is a long net, up to 60 yards in length, and about a yard and a half deep, which is spread out along the shore of a river or lake. Men then beat along the shore scaring the fish out. The net is so made that when fish swim into it, they become entangled and cannot escape. The fish are then lifted out of the net by the men. In Telica, a throwing net called the *sacamate* was reported; whether this is the same or a variant of the *atarraya* the writer does not know. Where used, nets are usually made locally by the men out of commercially purchased manila. Fishing with hook and line is also fairly common; in Tipitapa it was reported that a man will set up five or six simple poles and keep watch on them. In general, fishing is done by men, but in Tipitapa it was said that women also participated in the work. This is probably an exception to the general rule, as Tipitapa has a number of families dependent upon fishing for a source of income.

In Nagarote and Subtiaba also it was reported that some people make a living out of fishing. The most common method employed in the sea is to use an *estero* or well near the shore; at high tide these fill up, and at low tide fish are trapped in them. Gunpowder or fish poisons may be thrown in to kill the fish and make them more easy to remove. Weirs of branches are also made which work on the same principle.

Domesticated animals are of importance in the life of the Nicaraguan, but the major production is limited to large *haciendas*. Most *finqueros* have one or a few cattle, many will have a team of oxen, and most countrymen, both *finqueros* and poorer, have corral fowls, chickens, turkeys, and ducks; pigs are generally kept whenever they can be afforded. The poorer people will frequently have a cow or two, but in the highland valleys there is often not enough land available for even small herds. In the highlands those who have larger herds usually keep them up on the mountain sides, or else have *haciendas* devoted specifically to cattle.

For beasts of burden, the horse, donkey, and mule are all used in different areas. Donkeys are used in certain regions, reported mainly from Ocotal, as beasts of burden, and in the valleys and on the coast the ox cart is a standard form of transport. Oxen are also important wherever the plough is used, this being principally in the level valley lands and on the coast. For coastal work the oxen are being replaced on the large *haciendas* through the mechanization of the agriculture, but among many of the *finqueros* and all the small landowners and renters oxen are still the principal source of field power.

Sheep are kept occasionally in the highlands; the only specifically reported case was from San Rafael del Norte. While goats are kept over most of the country, they tend to be found more often in coastal communities than in the highlands. The keeping of pigeons and parrots is much more common on the coast than in the highlands. Over most of the country the countrymen bring in tree trunks which contain hives of stingless bees and hang them on the outside wall of the house or, if in town, in a patio.

The production of material items for use in the home and field is found both at the domestic level and by community specialization. In the home men usually make *bateas*, the large open dishes of wood, which are used for a variety of purposes. In the northern departments of the central highlands the *bateas* are usually long, with rounded ends; in Chontales the characteristic *batea* is round; in the Pacific belt both round and long *bateas* are made. Men also make their own plows and the handles for their other tools. The usual tools for wood working are the adz and machete. The construction of carts, dugout canoes, and sugar presses is usually done by specialists. Carts are generally made in the larger towns. Some of the best are said to come from León where *guanacaste* wood is used for the wheels exclusively. The León carts are exported as far as Ocotal to the north. The typical Nicaraguan cart has the solid wooden wheel; it is the same type which is to be found from Guanacaste in Costa Rica along the entire Pacific belt to the Lempa River in El Salvador. In El Sauce and some other centers, sides are provided by hanging palm leaves from a pole and hanging the frame on supports about two feet above the floor level of the cart. The sides made in this way are called *toldo* or *caniza*, and the front and back sections referred to as the *pechera*. The construction of dugout boats is, of course, limited to those areas where they can be used. Along the shores of both lakes and some of the larger rivers they are used by fishermen. They are generally built by specialists and made between two and five yards long in the Pacific region, but up to 12 yards long is common in the Atlantic slope rivers. They are termed variously *botes*, *cayucos*, and *piraguas*. The most common type of *trapiche*, or sugar press, is the standard geared vertical roller type, moved by ox power or by motor. Meshing sections may be made either of wood or metal, depending upon the wealth of individual. The two-man, parallel horizontal roller type *trapiche* is called the *sangarro* (*singarro* in Santo Tomás) and while still widespread, is less used than the animal powered type. In Telica it was said that a small metal *trapiche* moved by men was to be found. The pole-in-hole type of press, called the *muela*, was reported from San Rafael del Norte and among the Matagalpa Indians.

The production of basketry and other stiff fiber products tends to be somewhat specialized regionally. The town of Totogalpa makes *petates* which are sold over much of the highland area. The women of San Rafael del Norte make *alforjas* and rope. It was reported in Tipitapa that both men and women make baskets, palm hats, *alforjas* (twin fiber bags hung over a horse or mule), *petates*, and *mecate* (string and rope). Masaya is probably the principal center in the Pacific departments for the production of all kinds of fiber products. In the *barrio* of Monimbó the entire population, men, women, and children, are adept at weaving baskets and other palm products. The *barrio* of San Juan was reported to specialize in the making of string. The town of Trinidad, in the edge of the highlands in the Department of Matagalpa, was said to specialize in the production of hats. Women in the countryside around El Sauce make hats with a tall crown and wide brim, in a highly ornate style, and *alforjas*. Rope probably has a more generalized production than other fiber products.

Pottery production in the highlands is more generalized than in the Pacific departments. In the highlands women in most of the *caseríos* make what pottery they need, and frequently a few women will specialize in its production for the local area. In the Pacific belt, however, the towns of Tolapa and La Paz Centro and a few other centers each supply a fairly large region. La Paz Centro produces highly painted polychrome figurines and models, similar to, but cruder than the Antigua Guatemalan pottery, and a red domestic ware with floral designs in white. The latter is reminiscent of the Guatemalan Chinautla ware. The standard domestic ware includes *ollas, comales, cazuelas, cántaros*, and plates. In the comarca of Barro, near Malpaisillo, four different sized ollas are made and sold as a set, one inside the other. The largest is nearly a yard high. Black pottery is made in the Matagalpa-Jinotega region and was also reported (but not seen) from the *barrio* of El Calvario in Masaya. Making pottery is everywhere a woman's specialty.

There are various other local specializations found in Nicaragua. The production of horsehair trappings, bridles, etc., are elaborately made in the Matagalpa-Jinotega area. The weaving of such horsehair products is found elsewhere, but the work in this region has developed into an elaborate craft and the products are sold over a good part of the republic. The *zurrones*, called *árganas* in Ocotal, the twin leather bags used to carry produce by horse or mule back, are usually made locally by the people who use them. They were seen most commonly in the highlands, in the departments of Matagalpa, Jinotega, Estelí, Madriz and Nueva Segovia. Since mules and horses in this region are among the principal forms of transport, the *zurrones* are of great importance.

Trinidad was mentioned as one of the principal centers for the production of grinding stones. While no data was gathered on other possible centers there are doubtless a number of them. The making of tiles is of considerable importance, but there seemed to be no particular pattern of production organization. In some places such as Teustepe they were produced only during the summer months; in La Paz Centro and the adjacent southwest coast they are produced in some quantity. In the Pacific belt the poorer people do not use roof tiles, while in the highlands they are seen commonly both in the countryside and towns. In El Sauce and San Rafael del Norte it was specified that tiles were made in the countryside as well as in the towns.

The use of gourds for transport is very common although it was seen more in the central highlands than on the coast. The large *jícaro* is used in some places instead of baskets. For carrying water to the fields the general type is the hourglass shaped gourd; south of Darío and to the east, however, round gourds are used for this purpose.

Seamstresses operate in almost all the towns, making clothes principally for women. In Santo Tomás it was reported that the women still made soap, *jabón del país*, of pig and cow fat. To what extent the countryman population in general is still dependent upon locally made soap was not determined. Raincapes of raw rubber cloth are made in Masaya and sold over most of the republic. There are women in most towns who make bread which is sold by children on the streets.

Very common throughout the countryside is the local production of musical instruments. While unfortunately no data was gathered in the highlands on this subject, there seemed to be two different patterns on the coast. In Tipitapa, Teustepe, El Sauce, and in the highland town of Santo Tomás, the making of guitars and violins was fairly standard. In El Sauce and Tipitapa they also made *mandolinas*, the mandolin. In El Sauce, in addition, they made the *bandoleón*, a mandolin with a leather topped sounding box. The other pattern consisted of the construction and use of drums. In Subtiaba and Telica two-headed drums are made, and in Telica a flute is made of *carrizo*. It was specifically stated in La Orilla, Tipitapa and El Sauce that drums were not made, and in Telica that neither the guitar nor violin was made. In Monimbó the Indian *alcalde* has a drum which is used to call meetings with, and in Subtiaba it was reported that a drum was used during *faenas*.

5. TRAVEL, TRANSPORT, AND COMMERCE

In recent years the government of Nicaragua has been extending a string of highways through the Pacific and central highland regions of the country. While at the time of the survey it was still not possible to reach the country's second largest city, León, by automobile, the highway system will soon permit the traveller to reach most of the major cities and towns of the republic with ease. As elsewhere in Central America, the establishment of such a highway system has a tremendous effect on modes of transport in those areas accessible by road. At present this effect is being felt the most strongly in the Pacific region where heretofore most of the heavy transport of goods has been by ox cart. Wherever possible truck transport is replacing the ox cart. For the great number of rural dwellers, however, this means only that it is easier to get from one large town to another. Within the rural regions the horse, mule, cargo ox, and ox cart still remain the most important means of transportation. Travellers use the horse and mule and in many cases go on foot.

While both the horse and mule are used over most of the Pacific and central highland regions, the horse tends to be the preferred animal for coastal travel and the mule is preferred in highlands. While donkeys are seen here and there over much of the country, the donkey itself is usually kept for breeding mules or for specific tasks, such as carrying water to the towns. The writer was impressed that the proportion of travellers one saw using horses and mules was higher than that to be seen in Panama, El Salvador, or eastern Guatemala. Both women and men in the country travel in this manner. The older style of woman's travel was side saddle, and one still sees women riding this way quite frequently and side saddles are to be purchased in many of the larger towns in the country. The mode is changing, however, and it is also very common to see women riding astride. Quite frequently trousers will be worn under or instead of a dress when women ride astride.

The ox cart was discussed in an earlier section. Oxen are also important beasts of burden in the more rugged and thinly inhabited sections of the central highlands. They were seen or reported as being in use in Paredes on the Nueva Segovia northeast border, San Rafael del Norte, Jinotega, the area to the east of Matagalpa, and Santo Tomás. In the latter place it was said that the pack oxen were also very useful in swampy areas where their strength permitted them to drag themselves along where mules and horses could not go.

For transporting goods on horses and mules, the twin leather sack or *zurrones* are used throughout most of the central highland region. In many places henequin bags are also used, and along the Pacific coast they are preferred. In a few towns, noted specifically in Ocotal, and Teustepe, donkeys are used to carry water up from the river or wells to the houses. This is a regular trade, for the men responsible charge a price for the service. The containers used, called *cojinillos* in Ocotal, are boxes with two sides of wood and the top, bottom, and other two sides of sheet metal. A donkey will carry two of these containers and each container about 10 gallons of water. In some places horses and mules are used in this trade. In Juigalpa and Santo Tomás the more common form of bringing up water was in large drums called *pipas*, carried on an ox cart frame and drawn by oxen. These huge drums were filled at the source, then the water was distributed to houses. For the distribution metal *cántaros* were used. The use of metal *cántaros* seemed to be limited to these professional water vendors and was not common in the population in general as is the case in parts of El Salvador. The writer was told that they were originally imported from Germany before the Second World War, and that their use was restricted pretty much to the coastal zone. It is certain that they have not replaced the use of pottery *cántaros*.

It is the custom over most of Spanish-speaking Nicaragua for women to carry burdens on their heads. There are some specific exceptions to this, however. In San Rafael del Norte it was reported that the women did not follow this practice, but carried on the hip; in San Ramón and Darío it was said that they carried both on the head and on the hip. In San Ramón it was specified that loads such as firewood and baskets of bulk were carried on the head, while *cántaros* were carried on the hip. In general the practice seems to be for the men to be responsible for bringing in the firewood; the use of women in this work seems to be limited to the Matagalpa Indian area. When men carry things it is usually on the shoulder, in *alforjas* (attached pairs of fiber bags), or in some places such as Totogalpa, they will employ a strap across the chest. The use of the tumpline, *bombador* (or *bambador*), was reported from the Matagalpa Indian area and from Tipitapa. In Tipitapa it was said that both men and women carried loads with the tumpline. In Santo Tomás and Monimbó it was reported that they used to use this method but that they did so no longer.[17] In Tipitapa the term *mecapal* is used for the tumpline; since this term was originally Mexican it suggests that the trait is a survival from the *Nahua* speaking groups formerly in this area. In Monimbó it was said that both men and women carried things on their hands; the writer did not observe this practice on the part of the men, nor was it reported from any other town in the survey.

The transportation of products from the fields to the home is done either by ox cart, pack animal or by the men and women themselves. If the community has road or rail connections, further transport is usually done by truck or train, although if the roads are bad, ox carts are still preferred. If the community is somewhat isolated from such facilities, pack animals, and again where possible, ox carts are used to carry the produce for sale into the center.

The sale of products of the country as well as necessities provided from the centers is usually carried on in stores and occasionally by ambulant vendors. The town market is not found generally in Nicaragua. In some towns, such as in El Sauce and Telica, the municipality has a building in which meat is sold, and this is occasionally referred to as a market. Except in Monimbó and Subtiaba, the towns of Rivas and Ocotal were the only ones in which public markets were found on the survey. Such markets are more characteristic of the larger centers where there is a larger town population dependent upon country products. In Ocotal the market occupied a street corner. Two buildings facing each other were owned by the municipality, and the inside of one was the place where meat was sold; but the rest of the buildings were rented out to regular stores and the market itself consisted of vendors of greens, fruits and other country products, who sat on the sidewalk. In Rivas there were said to be two markets. One, the *mercado*, is used by the people in the adjacent rural region for selling their products. The other, the *mercado viejo*, is a privately owned establishment where vendors from more distant towns, such as Masaya, locate themselves to sell their goods. In Tipitapa it was said that before the war a group of Italian

---

[17] The survival of the tumpline in Tipitapa, reported in use from no other countryman centers except San Ramón, is a puzzle. The tumpline was reported by Conzemius (1932, p. 39) as being used only by the women among the Miskito and Sumu Indians and he considers the carrying on the head to be typical of the Spanish-speaking women only. Considering that it was reported to have been used previously in Monimbó it is likely that it was formerly a coastal Indian trait as well.

immigrants contracted for a large piece of municipal property to set up a market, but the Italians were removed during the war and nothing came of the project.

Both Monimbó and Subtiaba have markets in which the produce of the community members is sold. In both cases they are located on the borderline between the *barrio* and the city of which it is a part. In Monimbó this market is called the *tiangue* and in it are sold the variety of baskets and other fiber products produced by the inhabitants of the *barrio*. In Subtiaba the main products sold are fruits, greens, and meats; in addition, there are *chicherías* where refreshments are sold and small eating places.

In general, however, local commerce is carried on mainly through permanent stores. The stores are various types; the general store is usually run by a more wealthy townsman and carries a wide variety of products including hardware, drugs, imported food products, local foods, cloth, liquors, factory made clothing, and so on. It was pointed out in Ocotal that some of them are run by the *hacendados* and used to serve as commissaries for the plantations. The smaller store, or *pulpería*, is usually run by poorer people and deal especially in local food products, sometimes including meat. The number of *pulperías* in a town is usually two or three times the number of general stores. In Tipitapa the *pulpería* is called *caramanchel*. *Pulperías* are also found scattered throughout the rural areas which are more distant from the towns. Those rural dwellers living near the towns use the town commercial facilities, but in the more distant areas local people run *pulperías* to supply the local necessities. Also in the rural areas there are usually people who will keep a supply of salt, kerosine, a few patent medicines, and other articles which are sold in small amounts to the neighboring countrymen.

The sale of liquor is carried on in a number of different ways. General stores usually carry a bottle stock and most towns have a few *cantinas*, or bars, where drinks may be had. The production of *aguardiente*, the most common countryman drink, is a government monopoly and its sale is permitted under license to certain people in the towns. These locations are known as *estancos*. Usually the licensee will purchase the *aguardiente* by the barrel and sell it by the bottle; the consumer brings his own bottle.

As was suggested in the section on local products, there is a certain amount of regional trade in the countryside of Nicaragua. A few carts, some pottery, baskets, hats, and other woven fiber products, grinding stones, and a few other local products are sold in other communities. There is some regional trade in Nicaragua which covers fairly extensive area. Raincapes made around Masaya are for sale in stores in Ocotal, grinding stones from Trinidad are sold in Santo Tomás, *petates* from Totogalpa and other woven products from Monimbó are found in Estelí. In general, however, the regional trade seemed to be restricted to small areas, and where it was more extensive, depended upon middlemen and truck transport. An outstanding exception to this are the travelling vendors of *petates* from Totogalpa who were seen on the highway down to Estelí. Products from various of the departmental centers also find their way to the central market in Managua.

6. THE DOMESTIC SCENE

The Nicaraguan countryman usually builds his own home. In the towns it is much more the practice to contract a mason, a specialist, to do the work. In general, the town houses are of the patio type with a double shed roof and a roofed corridor facing the patio, away from the street. The more wealthy homes have a patio which is enclosed on two, three or all four sides by rooms and corridors. In a few of the towns there are to be seen the modern urban type house, but these are most common in the more heavily populated Pacific belt towns. In the countryside the homes of the *finqueros* and *hacendados* are usually square or rectangular with a corridor running around two, three or four sides. This style house is the country counterpart of the town patio house. The latter, so to speak, has its corridors and patio on the inside because of the limitations of space in the towns, while the former builds its corridors looking out on all sides and there is no patio.

Among the poorer town dwellers, the same general house form as that found for the wealthy is found in the highlands except that there is usually only the house and a single corridor at the back. The patio is not merely a flower garden, but is also a work area, and sometimes serves as a coffee drying patio. In the Pacific belt the same type of house is found for the medium wealthy town dwellers, but among the poorer the single rectangular type house with no patio is found. This home, to distinguish it from the patio type, we will call the *rancho* type.

The *rancho* is usually smaller, has walls of poles, cane, or mud covered poles, and in the lowland area has a straw roof. The straw roof is what gives the *rancho* its unique appearance, for the roof usually has four sheds instead of the two found on tile roofs. The *rancho* is the standard home of the poorer people of the Pacific coastal belt, and while seen more commonly in the countryside, it is also to be found in some numbers on the outskirts of the towns.

Quite typical of Nicaragua is an intermediate form of house between the patio type and the *rancho*. For the sake of making the distinction, we will call this the *cañol* house. The *cañol* house is a large rectangular home built on the general plan of the patio house, but without corridors or patio. It usually has a tile roof, and as a result has two-shed roof instead of the four sheds found on the *rancho*. It tends to be a longer rectangle, while the *ranchos* tend to be near to the shape of a square. The characteristic feature of the *cañol* house, however, is none of these features, but the fact that almost always attached to it are sheds at one or both of the short sides, and possible also at the back. These sheds, called *bajareque*, have a single shed roof which begins at the bottom line of the regular roof. Strictly speaking, the term *cañol* refers to the basic rectangular house in this construction, while the term *bajareque* is reserved for these side and back sheds.

The *cañol* house is the most typical country house of the poorer people of the highland region and is also found to some degree among the poorer coastal people. This latter group sometimes will add a *bajareque* to their *rancho*, thus combining the types. The *cañol* type is also to be found in some quantity among the poorer town people of the highland region. The *bajareque,* or shed addition, is usually closed in with a door leading to it from the main house. In this way it serves as an extra room in the house, to be used as a kitchen, bedroom, or storage room. In some cases, however, the *bajareque* is not closed in, but serves instead as an outside shed in which the farmer will keep his agricultural implements and odds and ends of boxes, boards, or other scrap materials which he may have need for later.

The *cañol* house usually has walls of poles or cane, although sometimes boards will be used. Among those who are a little wealthier, and particularly in the colder regions of the highlands, the pole or cane wall is covered with a layer of mud mixed with straw. This wall type is known in some places as the *vara-en-tierra* type. Distinct from the *vara-en-tierra* wall, although similar to it at first glance, is another type also commonly used in the *cañol* house and called the *taquesal*. The *taquesal* differs from the *vara-en-tierra* in that instead of having a single set of poles, there is a double framework of poles made between which and over which the mud is placed. The *taquesal* wall, then, is a framework filled with mud, while the *vara-en-tierra* is a framework covered with mud. Usually in filling the *taquesal* wall larger materials such as stones, old tiles, and anything solid and bulky will be used in addition to the mud. (Just to confuse matters, this type of construction is known as *bajareque* in El Salvador.) The *taquesal*, when new, is usually coated with a layer of mud, thus hiding the frame work, and making it indistinguishable at first glance from the mud covered *vara-en-tierra* type wall.

The use of *adobe*, or clay brick, for house walls in Nicaragua is evidently very much on the decline except in some of the coastal towns. In the highland towns the writer noticed a number of homes built of *adobes*, but on questioning the informants, was told that it was only in the older houses that *adobes* were used. In general where *adobe* was formerly used, the *taquesal* wall is now being used. *Taquesal* requires much less mud than do the *adobes*, and can use a great amount of very cheap scrap material such as broken tiles and stones in the fill. It is interesting to note that this shift from the *adobe* brick to the use of *taquesal* is a reversion to a different basic construction. The *adobe* construction consists of a heavy wall, on which is set a framework which supports the roof. The *taquesal*, on the other hand, as in a *rancho* wall, is built on poles which support the roof, and the wall is a fill which serves as a wind break and shelter, but does not serve as a roof support. In some of the coastal towns very large *adobes* are now being used in large houses and buildings, but these do not seem to be used much in the construction of the poorer homes. In Nagarote, large rectangular pumice blocks were being used in this way.

The *rancho* is perhaps the most common house type on the coast in total quantity, but due to the fact that most are found in semi-isolated villages and not so much in the larger towns one does not see too many in the ordinary course of travel. While *rancho* walls are usually of poles or cane, in some regions boards are used. The use of boards is generally irregular except that they are much more common in those towns near the Atlantic slopes. In Santo Tomás many houses are of boards, and in Villa Somoza the majority are of this material. Boards are often used interchangeably with poles, *vara-en-tierra*, or cane not only on *ranchos*, but also on the *cañol* type house. A term which is often applied to the *rancho* is *pajiza*. Here and there along the Pacific belt the *ranchos* consist of little more than two or three shed roofs. The lower sides of the roof touch the ground so that there is only a single wall in front, or on two-shed roofs, a wall in front and back.

In Subtiaba the typical house is the *cañol* home, but in Monimbó the *rancho* is standard. The Monimbó *rancho*, called a *posada*, is beautifully made, with the walls often of woven poles or cane. *Ranchos* usually have two rooms, a sleeping room called the *aposento* or *dormitorio*, and the *salita* or living room. In some, the kitchen is in the *salita*; in others, the kitchen will be under a separate shelter near the house or under a *bajareque* adjacent to the rancho. The kitchen is usually separate in those cases where there is only one room in the *rancho*. The *cañol* type house may be divided into two rooms or may be a single room with the *bajareque* additions forming the kitchen and bedrooms separately.

The furniture to be found in the Nicaraguan home varies greatly with the wealth of the inhabitants. In the poorer homes, usually the best piece of furniture is the leather seated and leather backed chair known as the *taburete*. *Taburetes* are evidently a very old style and while they may be found in the houses of the town dwellers, the more sophisticated do not use them extensively. Nevertheless, they are to be found in most parts of the country. Most common for sitting are the board or log benches with four legs. These are easily fashioned by the individual who needs one. Small low stools of three or sometimes four legs known as *patas de gallina* (chicken feet) are found mainly in the Pacific belt. Hammocks are used principally in the Pacific belt too, but they are not ordinarily used for sleeping. If a home is crowded for sleeping space, some of the children may be put in hammocks, but otherwise they are used for resting. Only in Nagarote was it reported that hammocks were used for sleeping. The wealthier town homes and *finca* houses have better made furniture; rocking chairs are particularly popular and even the poorer people will invest in them if they can afford to. It seems reasonable to suppose the popularity of the rocking chair for resting stems in part from the popularity of the hammock for the same purpose.

In general the poorer people have beds made of sticks set in the ground with a row of poles, or *tapesco*, laid across them. This is called the *cama de palos*, or *camastro* in El Sauce and *camarote* in Santo Tomás. The poor people in some places also sleep in the *tabanco*, the attic of poles laid across the beams at the top of the wall. This layer of poles is also called the *tapesco*. Large canvas or lighter cotton folding cots are used all over the highlands and the Pacific belt. Aside from string and spring beds to be found in the wealthier homes, they are used as extra beds and by many, particularly in the warmer regions, as regular beds in preference to more expensive beds. Since they are relatively cheap, they have replaced the *cama de palos* in many of the poorer homes. They are called *tijeras*.

It is common to use a *petate*, or woven grass mat, on the *cama de palos*. In some places they will use an old piece of cloth or burlap; in Santo Tomás it was reported that a *junco* or *tambor*, a large piece of tree bark, was used as a cover for these beds, and that some still used skins. From Teustepe and Subtiaba it was reported that leather beds were still used, but these seem to be very much in the minority. In Monimbó the *cama de palos* was used very much in preference to the *tijera*. In various instances boards will be laid on the *cama de palos* instead of poles.

It is common in most homes to have a small table on which is the picture of a saint with a few burnt candles and flowers set near by.

The entire furnishings of a countryman's house do not add up in quantity to the number of items which are to be found in his kitchen. The kitchen, which is almost always a separate room, apart in a corridor or in a separate shed or house, is usually littered with dishes, pottery, boxes, and a multitude of other things.

As standard equipment in almost every Nicaraguan country and town kitchen is a *molendero* and three legged grinding stone. The *molendero* is a long table, usually about six by two or three feet, which is set at a slight angle so that it may be easily drained into a barrel or pot set at the lower end. The *molendero* is about waist high and on the upper end is placed the grinding stone. Corn *masa* is ground on this and the water which drains out runs down the board and off into the waste container. Besides the *molendero*, many homes have a raised stove made of clay. The form of this stove varies, but unfortunately the writer was not able to determine if there was any regular distribution for the different types. One type consisted of a solid clay base, one to three feet high, on which were set stones or ridges of clay, and between these was placed the fire. Another type, which seemed to be characteristic more of the less well-to-do and perhaps of the Pacific coastal belt, was a wooden box, either set up on legs or sitting on the floor, which was filled with dirt and on which was built the fire.

The fact that many homes have a raised stove, or *fogón*, does not mean that they always use it. Many of the poorer homes have the fire on the floor, and even in the homes which have the raised stoves fires may be set on the floor if extra cooking must be done. The floor fires are usually set between three stones as are many of the *fogones* fires. A few houses in almost every town and rural area have an oven. The women who have them bake bread for sale around the town and make a small income in this way. The ovens themselves are of the types seen throughout Spanish America, the domed-shaped, brick or *adobe*, oven usually set on a strong stand off the ground. Sometimes the oven and the *fogón* will be on the same raised platform in the shed beside the house.

Water in the homes is stored in huge pottery *tinajas*. In many homes these are set in a wooden frame called a *tinajera*. Almost every town and country kitchen in Nicaragua, whether rich or poor, has at least a few *jícaros*, or dried gourd cups and bowls. The standard method of storing these when not in use is to hang them up side down on a stick. For this, many homes have hanging from the rafters a forked stick, or a small piece of wood with sticks stuck in it. This is called the *garabita* or *garabatero*. Sometimes these sticks would be set in a board on a shelf, but more commonly they hung. Also very common, particularly in the homes where there was no *tapesco* over the fire, was a round, flat, string or bark basket hung from three or four strings from the rafters. These were usually made of a wooden loop with a string net tied across it. This is called *matayapal* in Chirincocal and *escusa* in Nagarote. Salt, chili, and various kitchen items were kept in this. Most of the kitchens had a table or two, and a variety of hanging shelves, boxes, and boards which are used to store foods, enamel cooking equipment, pottery, glasses, dishes, and cutlery. Set just outside of most kitchens is the large wooden mortar, variously called *tarro* (Chirincocal), *pilador* (Santo Tomás), *cubo* (San Ramón), *pila de madero* (El Sauce), and *pilón* or *mortero* in most other places. The mortar is used principally for pounding rice, sorghum, and coffee. Nowhere was it reported to be used in the processing of corn. The shape of the mortar varies as well as its name. In Chirincocal it was straight sided, and curved in towards the base, then flared out again to the same diameter as the top. In San Fernando it was straight sided. In San Ramón and the adjacent Matagalpa Indian area it was shaped like a deep bowl on the outside.

In many houses, and particularly in the *cañol* and *rancho* types, a *tabanco* or *tapesco*,[18] or frame of poles, is set on the rafters over the corner in which the fire burns. On this are put the cheeses, salt, and sometimes grains, to keep them dry and to keep insects and rodents out of them. The *tapesco* is also used as a regular storage place for some of the grains, particularly sorghum and rice. This seems to be more common in the Pacific belt than in the highlands where ceilings tend to be higher and *tabancos* are not so common. The storage of corn, sorghum, and beans is often in a large board box, called a *bunque*, or in a separate little rancho building, the *troja*. The use of the *bunque* was observed more in the highlands. In El Sauce it was specified that the *trojas* were always in the house since if they were outside, the grain might be stolen. However, elsewhere it was reported that it was common to have the *trojas* outside and apart from the house, and in some cases they were set up in the fields. The storage of *guate*, the half mature corn used as fodder, is usually on a *ramada*, or high frame work of sticks outdoors to keep it out of the way of the animals. *Finqueros* in both the highlands and on the Pacific belt will often dig a silo to ferment grain to make a more nutritious food for the animals. A hole is dug in the earth, perhaps four meters across and six meters deep; this may be lined with brick. Into it are put layers of sorghum, corn, or sugar cane, interspersed with sugar cane sap. The sugar foments a fermentation of the grains and produces a highly nutritious fodder for the animals.

The processing of corn in the Nicaraguan homes is fairly simple. In many places the hand grinding machine has eased the work of corn grinding, but in general it has not entirely replaced the grinding stone. Even in the many towns where it is common, the corn is still ground a second time on the stone to make

---

[18] *Tapesco* is a generic term for a mat of woven sticks; *tabanco* refers specifically to the partial ceiling.

it finer. The corn is soaked in water with either lime or ashes prior to the grinding to break down the outer shell. Whether ash or lime is used seems to depend upon local or personal preference, and cost. Lime is generally more expensive since it must be purchased. Many people expressed a preference for ashes, however, particularly if they were "good" ashes such as burnt banana peels. Pine ashes were not thought to be very effective. In the Chontales mining area it was said that some people used the commercially sold carbide which was sold for the miner's lamps. It was said in Monimbó by one informant that she preferred to use lime when making *masa* for *tortillas*, but to use ashes for *tamales* because it made a smoother *masa*. In the Pacific belt the *masa* goes under the name of *nesquisal*, or *nesquisado*, or in Teustepe, *nesquiso*, *nixtallo*, or *nixtamal*.

In Santo Tomás it was said that *nesquisado* was used specifically for *masa* fixed with ashes. Unfortunately, no data was collected in the highlands on the name used for the *masa*, so it is not possible to say at present whether there is a regional variation in this or not.

In Ocotal, it was said that in former years women used to wash corn in the river by placing it in a basket, then submerging the basket in the water and stamping on it with their feet. This manner of washing the corn has been reported from neighboring Honduras, but the writer did not encounter it elsewhere in Nicaragua. It may be used however. The preparation of corn, as was mentioned before, does not involve the use of the mortar. It is everywhere soaked in ashes or lime, and then ground on the stone, or by machinery (either the home machine by hand, or in the larger towns in a motor commercial grinder) and then by stone. The mortar is, instead, specifically associated with crops of foreign origin, rice, coffee, and sorghum.

Corn is prepared in various ways. It is eaten green, both as the tiny *chilotes* and as the larger green *elotes*. When harvested thoroughly mature and dry it is prepared as *tortillas*, to be found at most meals in every country household. In the highlands the *tortillas* tend to be small and thin, but on the coast they frequently are up to 8" across and of varying thickness. The *masa* is also prepared into *tamales* and *nacatamales*. The *tamal* and *nacatamal* are basically the same, but the latter is a highly elaborated form. While the *tamal* may have nothing but the corn *masa* and perhaps a little piece of meat, the *nacatamal* will be decked out with tomatoes, potatoes, rice, yuca, chili, and some kind of meat or fowl. In San Pedro it was said that corn was also ground with meat to make *albondigas*, dumplings. There are a number of drinks made with corn. *Atol* is made from the *masa* of green corn, and *atolillo* of dry corn. *Pinol* is made of toasted corn, and *pinolillo* of toasted corn and cacao. *Pozol* is ground after cooking, sweetening added, and drunk. *Tiste* is evidently a term used in some of the coastal towns (Subtiaba, La Orilla, and Monimbó) for the *pinol* and *pinolillo* drinks. There is also a dish called *rosquillas* prepared from corn and cheese. *Chicha*, fermented with the aid of crude sugar, is a fairly common drink; perhaps equally common is *cususa*, the distilled *aguardiente* made from *chicha*. The *cususa* is made by the countryman in clandestine stills over most of the countryside. Corn bread is made in various forms, sometimes mixed with other flour or other ingredients such as cheese.

The principal ingredients in the countryman's diet are corn, beans, coffee, rice, squash, and a little meat. Reported to be of some importance from almost all towns surveyed was white cheese. Plantains and the *guineo cuadrado* were also important. *Chicha*, as a fermented drink, was made not only of corn, but frequently of corn and sorghum mixed, and of pineapple. Other foods are mentioned in the section on agriculture. Whether or not palm wine, *chicha de coyol*, is made seems to depend largely upon the local abundance of the coyol palm. It was reported as being made in Ocotal, Tipitapa, and Subtiaba, but not in Chirincocal, El Sauce, and Santo Tomás.

The clothing of the countryman in Nicaragua is generally plain. In the towns and among the wealthier countrymen, clothes are bought in the towns. Many of the women sew their own, but no cases were reported of men making their own clothes. In general, men wear straw hats and many women, particularly those who work in the fields, also will wear them. The poorer generally go barefoot or have sandals, frequently made of rubber tires. Occasionally men are seen with the old white peon's clothing of the high necked, long-sleeved shirt hanging outside the trousers, but blue working clothes have for the most part replaced this. Rubber *capotes*, raincapes, are worn by many during the rainy season. The poorer women will wear their hair in braids, while the wealthier town women wear it shorter and have an annual permanent wave from a travelling specialist. The straw hat with a tall pointed crown and wide brim seemed of somewhat restricted distribution; it was seen principally in the northwestern Pacific belt region and in the adjacent highlands of Estelí.

The washing of clothes is done by the women in the local stream or river where one is present. If there is a scarcity of water, well water will be used. It is common for a home to have a large flat stone in the back yard or patio on which the washing is done if there is no running water nearby. In El Sauce and some other Pacific belt towns a large flat area of stones is sometimes prepared in the back yard; it is usually circular and up to fifteen or twenty feet in diameter. It is used for laying out clothing for bleaching and is also used to dry the wash.

7. THE FAMILY AND *COMPADRE* SYSTEM

In a sense, the nuclear family, composed of a man, his wife, and unmarried children, may be said to be the basic social unit of the Nicaraguan countryside. There are a number of factors, however, which modify the form of the family unit.

Until a few years ago the law of Nicaragua required that marriage be performed as a civil act before it could be carried out in a religious ceremony. This law was changed, however, so that now people may be married in the townhall or in the church, depending upon their preference. Table 9 gives the figures on the number of people living in a state of marriage and free union, and the number of the married persons who have chosen only the civil or religious ceremonies. It is of considerable interest to note that while the total of civil and religious ceremonies is fairly close in the Pacific belt departments, there are over three times as many persons married only by the church as only in civil ceremonies in the highlands. In both areas, however, the combined cere-

Table 9.—Number of persons who are married (total, civil alone, religious alone) and who live in free unions (*Dirección General de Estadística*, 1954)

Department	Marriages			Free union
	Total	Civil only	Religious only	
Pacific Coastal Belt				
Rivas	6,458	824	856	4,715
León	18,046	2,614	3,193	15,249
Chinandega	10,677	2,019	2,063	13,483
Masaya	10,587	1,564	1,348	9,315
Carazo	7,294	1,369	1,448	7,280
Granada	8,065	861	1,588	5,768
Managua	26,816	5,528	1,910	21,872
Total	87,943	14,779	12,406	77,682
Central Highlands				
Estelí	8,404	967	2,450	3,124
Boaco	8,571	731	4,474	4,883
Jinotega	9,746	464	3,751	4,124
Madriz	5,081	844	1,574	4,125
Matagalpa	26,692	3,425	9,771	13,513
Chontales	7,718	1,261	1,771	6,563
Nueva Segovia	4,391	543	1,424	2,937
Total	70,603	8,235	25,215	39,269
Atlantic Littoral				
Cabo Gracias a Dios	3,178	1,245	874	2,544
Zelaya	10,885	2,984	2,146	7,705
Río San Juan	1,264	246	239	971
Total	15,327	4,475	3,259	11,220
Republic: total	173,873	27,489	40,880	128,351

monies vastly outnumber either one or the other, but this cannot be interpreted as indicating a preference since many of these doubtless come from the time that the civil was a legal prerequisite for the religious ceremony.

There are various factors which can play a role in the differential in the relative number of civil and religious marriages in a given region, and it is not possible here to determine for any specific locality what the specific local reasons may be. Priests may be more active, for example, in the highlands than on the Pacific side. Nevertheless, the consistency from department to department within the general zones in this matter suggests that the importance of marriage in the church has been retained as a much stronger tradition in the highlands than it has on the coast. This is especially impressive when one compares the total number of persons in religious marriage to the number in free unions: in the highlands there are some 62,000 persons married in the church as compared with 39,000 living in free union; in the Pacific belt, however, there are

Table 10.—Number of persons married and in free unions in rural and urban areas (*Dirección General de Estadística*, 1954)

Department	Urban Married	Urban Free unions	Rural Married	Rural Free unions
Pacific Coast Belt				
Rivas	2,282	960	4,176	3,755
León	7,149	4,135	10,897	11,294
Chinandega	5,053	4,274	5,624	9,209
Masaya	4,935	3,431	5,652	5,884
Carazo	3,954	1,989	3,340	5,291
Granada	5,482	2,437	2,583	3,331
Managua	22,007	13,483	4,809	8,389
Total	50,862	30,709	37,081	47,153
Central Highlands				
Estelí	1,970	629	6,434	2,495
Boaco	1,190	416	7,381	4,467
Jinotega	1,277	191	8,469	3,933
Madriz	797	373	4,284	3,752
Matagalpa	4,082	1,472	22,610	12,041
Chontales	1,963	1,194	5,755	5,369
Nueva Segovia	992	427	3,399	2,510
Total	12,271	4,702	58,332	34,567
Atlantic Littoral				
Cabo Gracias a Dios	237	103	2,941	2,441
Zelaya	3,918	1,804	6,967	5,901
Río San Juan	427	191	836	780
Total	4,582	2,098	10,744	9,122
Republic: total	67,716	37,509	106,157	90,842

73,200 in religious marriages as compared with 77,700 in free unions. Marriage, as a religious sacrament, is taken much more seriously in the highlands than in the Pacific region.

The situation given by the figures with respect to free unions was strongly supported by data collected in the survey. It was reported in four highland towns (Ocotal, Chirincocal, San Rafael del Norte, San Ramón Indians), two towns on the edge of the highlands (El Sauce and Teustepe) and only one Pacific belt town (Nagarote) that the number of marriages were generally greater than the number of free unions. In five Pacific belt towns, however, (Rivas, La Orilla, Tipitapa, Subtiaba, and Telica) and one town at the edge of the highlands (Darío) that the number of persons in free union exceeded the number formally married.

Table 10 shows that, in general, marriages are less common in the Pacific belt rural areas than in all other regions. There, and only there in departmental terms, are there more free unions than marriages. It is of interest to note that

Table 11.—Percentage of households with female heads, by department (*Dirección General de Estadística*, 1950)

Department	Number of families	Number with women household heads	Percentage
Pacific Coast Belt			
Rivas	7,173	2,410	36.6%
León	19,179	5,710	29.8
Chinandega	13,571	3,634	26.8
Masaya	12,063	3,513	29.3
Carazo	8,961	2,520	28.1
Granada	8,290	2,870	34.7
Managua	26,675	8,100	30.4
Central Highlands			
Estelí	7,237	1,792	21.2%
Boaco	8,201	1,878	23.0
Jinotega	8,328	1,400	16.8
Madriz	5,579	1,191	21.2
Matagalpa	22,217	3,675	16.6
Chontales	8,243	1,745	21.2
Nueva Segovia	4,317	925	21.4
Atlantic Littoral			
Cabo Gracias a Dios	3,360	1,901	56.6%
Zelaya	10,774	2,084	19.4
Río San Juan	1,294	314	24.2
Republic: total	175,462	45,662	26.0%

while in the rural areas there are almost the same number of women reportedly in free unions as men (46,422 to 44,420), in the urban areas the number of women in free unions is considerably higher than the number of men (21,638 to 15,871). Free unions, as they appear in rural areas, then are evidently reflective of a fairly common situation which both men and women regard as pretty much the same; in the urban zones, and this includes all municipal capitals it must be remembered, there are a good number of women who consider themselves living in free union but who evidently are not so regarded by the men upon whom they depend. Whether this reflects an unstable free union situation, concubinage, poligamy, or a combination of these cannot be stated upon the basis of present evidence.

The stability of families in general may be suggested by the data on the number of families which were reported to have female heads of household.

As was the case with proportions of free unions, so here there is a regular distinction between the highland departments and those of the Pacific belt. In the former the percentage of homes with women chiefs of family is between 16 and 23%, while in the latter, it varies between 26 and 37%. The data from the survey was in accord with these figures. It was my impression that, with the exception of the town of Monimbó, separations were more frequent in the Pacific belt than in the central highlands. It was reported that they were common also in the highland communities of Chirincocal and San Pedro. In Santo Tomás separations were said to be common, but much less so among formal marriages than in cases of free unions. The Matagalpa Indians of the San Ramón area and the countrypeople of the Ocotal area were said to form fairly stable unions. In El Sauce, also, people in free union, called *mancebo*, were said to separate with much greater frequency than those who were formally married. There is little doubt but that there is correlation between the departments in which there are free unions and indicated instability through a high percentage of women chiefs of families; however, although it is common to associate these two facts, it may well be that they are both better related to a third set of circumstances in view of the fact that there are so many ways in which these two regions differ.

It seems not unlikely that the relatively higher percentage of free unions and cases of women chiefs of family in the Pacific belt are derived in some part from the fact that the *hacienda* economy, and, consequently, the *mozo*, is much more common in the Pacific belt than in the highlands. It will be remembered from Table 8 that the highland region has a much higher percentage of independent farmers, both *finqueros* and subsistence farmers, than is found in the Pacific belt. On the Pacific side salaried labor accounts for between two-thirds and three-quarters of the entire economically active population, whereas it includes only between one-third and one-half of the comparable highland population. The division of labor between men and women in the Pacific belt is such as to not only permit but to encourage free unions and frequent separations. Many women regularly work in certain of the harvests (for example in cotton) with children, while men regularly work in others (as, for example, sugar) without women. The nature of the *hacienda* economy of the Pacific belt produces a mobile population, and a mobile population usually does not lead to extremely stable family unions.

The limitation of choice of marriage partners by incest prohibitions seems to vary somewhat with class membership. There is a much greater tendency for members of the upper class in the towns to marry among themselves than there is among the rural people. The class situation in many towns is such that town endogamy has been going on for so long that marriage between first cousins is sometimes not only a preferable marriage, but occasionally the only possible marriage at a given time for the upper class people within the town. Such community endogamy was also reported for the uniformly lower class town of

Monimbó. Marriage between first cousins is equally permitted among the rural people, but is evidently a more random matter than it is in town. The rural people may actually have a wider possible selection of mates, both in the countryside and in neighboring towns; they are not so restricted by class barriers to marry within a small group. Marriage between persons who are first cousins is generally permitted, then, but marriage closer than this is generally prohibited.

The choice of residence upon the establishment of a union varies between formal marriages and free union, and between the town and country populations. In general, people undertaking a free union will take up a residence for themselves if one of the members does not already have a house. Neo-local residence of this nature is also the general tendency of the rural peoples. There are many factors which may enter the situation to indicate that the pair should take up residence in the households of one of the parents. Usually the lack of a house of their own or the fact that one of the parents has more room or more money and consequently provides a better chance for the young couple to earn a living will decide them to stay with the parents. Among the town-dwelling population, and particularly among the upper classes, there is a reported tendency toward initial matrilocal residence. Neo-local residence does not seem to be the initial rule but an alternative in this population. If the family is large, some of the children may take up a new home while others may stay with the family. It was reported in Ocotal, for example, that a newly married pair would quite frequently go to live in the home of the girl for a while. Only if the boy's parents were very wealthy would they take up residence there. The period of living at the girl's home was called the *internado*. This matrilocal tendency was also reported from the rural community of Chirincocal. The only area from which a patrilocal tendency was reported, and there too the neo-local alternative was said to be important, was the Matagalpa Indian area near San Ramón.

In the cases of separations it was generally reported that the house would stay with the woman; it was usually the man who left to live elsewhere. Thus even where matrilocality is not a tendency there may be a general tendency for a woman to remain with her house when once established in it.

The residential unit, then, may be composed of various related family members besides those in the immediate nuclear family. Besides this tendency, the informal adoption of young orphaned relatives, and the use in a servant capacity of poor godchildren is quite common. Also, odds and ends of brothers, sisters, aunts, and other relatives may take up residence with the countryman from one time to another. There seems to be no special rule, but rather a matter of practical convenience as to who may be added to the household and for how long.

The *compadre* system among the country and townspeople seemed to be quite strong. Everywhere it was reported that "great respect" existed between *compadres*. This seems particularly true in the central highland rural areas. From Chirincocal and San Pedro it was reported that the children of *compadres* were considered to be like siblings and consequently were not supposed to intermarry.

Whether *compadres* were chosen from among friends or from among a wealthier or higher class seemed to depend somewhat upon personal preference and somewhat upon class membership. Among the upper class, people of the same class were asked and selected from among friends. Among the poorer people, particularly in and near towns, there was a tendency to seek out a person in a better economic status. In the more rural areas, where wealth differences among the rural people tend to be smaller, personal respectability and friendship play a large role in whether a person is asked to be a *compadre* or not. The only place where the *compadre* system as such was reported to be not of great importance was among the Matagalpa Indians. There it was said that the parents will often wait until the moment of baptism and ask anyone who is handy to be the godfather of the child. Also in this group it is not the custom for an orphaned godchild to receive help from his godfather; they look rather to one's own relatives for this.

In some towns it was reported that there was a tendency to get the same godfather for siblings, but there was no evident consistency between one class or region and another in this. In general different godparents are sought for the rites of baptism and confirmation, but in a number of towns it was reported that not only were the same *compadres* obtained, but that it was preferred to have the same *compadre* for the different events.

8. THE SOCIAL STRUCTURE OF TOWN AND COUNTRY

The social classes in the towns and countryside of Nicaragua are generally quite distinct, but are territorially more dispersed than are the comparable classes of Panama. Basically, the population may be broken down into three social components, but the precise definition of each varies slightly from one place to another, and not all three are always present. The upper class, variously called the *primera, la sociedad, la aristocracia, sociales, gente decente, gente pudiente* (powerful people), and *ricos*, include the old established families of a town, the wealthy, the *hacendados*, the wealthier merchants, the more powerful political figures and military officers. The term *aristocracia* is sometimes reserved for members of the old families of León, Granada, Managua, and some of the older towns such as Ocotal, Masaya, etc. The middle class is composed of less well to do merchants, the small landowners, *finqueros*, and some artisans. They are referred to variously as the *segundos, los medio acomodados*; when there is no upper class present, they may also be be called *sociales* or *gente decente*. The precise definition of this class depends upon the absence or presence of a distinct upper class. In some places where the upper class is very weak, the middle and upper blend. In some towns it was specified, for example, that there was *"no aristocracia"* there, but that there were the *segundos* who composed the *sociedad*. In some places the group called *obreros*, or workers, specifically falls into this middle group and is distinguished from the *jornaleros*, or day laborers who form the main body of the lower class. Elsewhere, the term *obrero* is considered as being the same as *jornalero*, and refers only to the lower class.

The lower class itself is composed principally of landless people, day laborers, the countrypeople who have very little land of their own. They are called the *pobres, campesinos, proletariado* or *proletario, gente pequeña*, and are sometimes said to be *más indígena* (more Indian), as being uncultured or uncivilized, and sometimes referred to generally by the term *mozo* (servant), *jornalero* (day laborer) or *obreros*. Among the lower class, the people usually refer to themselves simply as *los pobres*.

Members of all three classes are to be found in both town and country, but if a country person is of the upper class, he is specifically an *hacendado* and not a *campesino*. If a townsman is of the upper class he is of the *aristocracia* or *sociedad* and not one of the *gente del pueblo*, a term of reference generally reserved for members of the middle and lower class. The countrypeople are generally all farmers, whether they be upper class *hacendados*, middle class *finqueros*, or lower class laborers; some of the townspeople will be farmers also, but others will be rich merchants, tradesmen and artisans of the middle class, or employees and laborers of the lower class. In other words, the country dwelling—town dwelling line cuts across the class lines.

It has already been mentioned that there is a tendency within some towns towards a town endogamy. This, of course, is not only town based but class based. The town of Nagarote, for example, was said to a large degree to be composed of members of seven large and interrelated sets of families. This is also true to some degree of some of the rural communities. The *cantón* of San Pedro has about twenty-six families; of these eight have the same surname, and four others share another. In other words, almost half the people come from one of two sets of related families.

In the towns there is frequently a residential difference if there are members of the upper class present. In Ocotal, most of upper class live in what is known as the *Barrio del Centro*, on the plaza and to the northwest of it; the middle class people live generally in the two *barrios*, Palermo and Las Brisas, to the south of the plaza, while the poorer people live in the *Barrio Coyolar* to the northeast of the plaza. El Sauce, in which there are generally recognized to be few if any members of the upper class, also has one section of the town in which it is said that generally poorer people live. Through the center of town runs a street called *Calle del Cuartel*; to the east of this street is the *Barrio del Calvario* and to the west is the *Barrio de la Parroquia*. This latter is also known as *Subtiaba*, and many of the people living there are said to be "simpler" and "more Indian" than those who live in the other *barrios*. In many towns, however, it was specified that there was no really significant class of wealth differences in the *barrios*. It seems likely, however, were careful studies to be made, that such residential groupings would probably occur more often than is thought. In the larger towns it is certain that some of the *barrios* are considered to be composed of simpler people. Two outstanding cases are the *barrios* of Subtiaba in León and Monimbó in Masaya. Subtiaba used to be a distinct Indian settlement outside the town limits of León. Over the years, however, it has become a *barrio* of the city but the city people regard the people of Subtiaba as Indians, and they, in turn, keep themselves apart from the rest of the Leonese population. In the case of Monimbó, the population has even retained certain features of its old political and social organization which derive from the colonial and early republican epochs. There is no doubt, however, that if there are no upper class people present, the residential differences between the middle and lower classes is not always distinct.

In San Rafael del Norte and in Chirincocal the writer also heard comments which suggested that the *campesinos* of the more heavily populated plains and valleys tend to regard themselves as slightly "more civilized" than those who occupy the rougher country, the *montaña*. One woman commented that a child she had adopted from the *montaña* when he was nine months old was turning out to be something of a savage due, she suggested, to the fact that he came from a *montaña* family. It is certainly true that the valley people are agriculturally better off than those in the *montaña*. It will be remembered that there are two recognizably distinct forms of tillage carried on in the level areas and in the *montaña*; the plow is used in the former, while the digging stick is the principal implement in the latter. Another distinction which the writer heard made between certain of the *campesinos*, is between the men who are cowboys, *vaqueros*, and live on the *haciendas*, and those who "work with their machetes," and are agricultural day laborers, living in their own houses. Whether there is felt to be some sort of class difference in these occupations was not clear, but in the case given the speaker implied that the *vaqueros* were perhaps "better people" than the field laborers.

The distinction between "Indian" and "non-Indian" is of importance in a number of places in Nicaragua. All Nicaraguans recognize a vast difference between themselves as bearers of Spanish heritage and the Atlantic coast Indians. One townsman near the Atlantic region explained seriously to me that of the Atlantic coast peoples, the Miskitos who are mixed with Germans or English were the finest type; the Sumu, or pure Indian was intermediate; and the zambo, the Indian mixed with negro, "is the most horrible; he can hardly talk; just a jumble of sounds!" No matter what the local belief pattern may be concerning the Atlantic coast population, the people of Boaco and Matagalpa recognize that there is clear distinction between the Atlantic coast Indian and the group which we have been calling in this paper the Matagalpa Indians. In San Ramón a constant distinction was being made in the course of the conversation between the customs held by the *campesinos* of San Ramón and the Indians of the same *municipio*. A similar distinction is made for the urban Indians of the Pacific belt, the people of Monimbó and Subtiaba. The basis for the distinction between these Indian groups and the *campesinos* and *gente del pueblo* is not that they speak a different language, for all speak Spanish; but rather it is partly based on the fact that the Indian groups retain slightly different customs, that they are thought to be racially more Indian and less white, and that they consistently form part of the lower class. Of these, customs, which include the place of residence, are perhaps the most important. A person can rise from the lower class, and there are many *mestizos* who racially look

Indian but are not considered to be such. But so long as a person retains his place of residence among a group which is considered to be Indian, he will be considered as one.

Of course, the differences recognized between the upper, middle, and lower classes within the national Nicaraguan groups are also dependent to a great degree upon differences in customs, but these customs in turn are more fundamentally dependent upon wealth differences and differences in antiquity of the family in Nicaragua.

In the countryside and towns alike there are certain important participational differences between the different class groups, but there is evidence that some of these are weakening. In the countryside many of the middle class farmers do not live in villages, but tend to live somewhat more isolated on their farms. The poorer lower class people tend to live in somewhat more clustered settlements. In many of the towns there are social clubs which are participated in by persons of principally one class. The situation in Ocotal provides a rather clear-cut club system. There are two clubs to which people of the upper class belong. The older, the *Club Social*, is located on the main plaza, and was until a year or two ago the only club of the upper class. To it belonged the principal *hacendado* families, the main political and military officers. Then a dispute occurred when a member of one of the families was prohibited admission to the club. In response, all the members of that family withdrew from the *Club Social* and formed a new upper class club, the *Casino Segovia*, which occupied a locale directly across the plaza from the old club. Today these two clubs are running and each sponsors a dance on a different night during the principal annual fiesta in the town. Many people, to avoid hurting feelings of the families involved, belong to both clubs. Besides these two clubs, there is a single club with a much larger membership, called the *Club Social de Artesanos*, referred to as a *club de obreros*. To this belong the members of the middle class. Some intermediate persons and some who want to retain friendships within both class groups will belong to one or both the upper class clubs as well as to the *Club de Obreros*. This also has a largo headquarters but is located a half block off the plaza. Besides these three clubs there are also smaller organizations, less formal and some without specific names, which are participated in by the members of the lower class. Ocotal is principally a town of upper and middle class people, however, so the majority belong to one or more of the three main clubs.

These social clubs are centers of recreation. They have one or more billiard and ping-pong tables, a room with easy chairs where the members may sit and talk, and regularly sponsor a large dance during the *Fiesta de la Asunción*. The existence of clubs and their importance varies, however, from one town to another. In some, such as in San Rafael del Norte, such clubs used to exist but have broken up. In Telica there is a *Sociedad Obrera*, but it does not have a building. In Nagarote there used to be both a *club social* and a *club obrero* but they broke up between 1945 and 1947 over political disputes. Rivas, a departmental capital like Ocotal, has such clubs.

The participation differences continue to be practiced, however, even if there are no formalized clubs to accentuate them. In Nagarote, for example, a group of men got together to help finance the construction of a new road which would give them year-around service to the capital. About the same time, two groups were established to promote the bettering of the park facilities in the town. As these groups formed, only the most wealthy, those who had a real vested interest in the road to get their products out went to work on the road group, while people of a slightly lower standing, but nevertheless public spirited, went to work on the park group. In Ocotal, there is a baseball team composed of "better" people who play in the town's regular sport field, *Campo Deportivo*. Poorer boys who want to play baseball usually get together in a plaza at the other end of town which is referred to simply as the *placita*.

The participational differences extend into the religious associations. In most of the towns a few of these associations will be composed principally of women of the upper class, or if there is no upper, of women of the middle class. The *Hijas de María* and the *Matronas* are frequently made up only of "better" women; women of "bad repute" are not allowed to participate. The *Acción Católica* of Ocotal is made up mainly of people of the upper class. The rather morbid extension of the class system into the cemeteries is mentioned in the next section. But as is the case with the social clubs in some towns, the cemeteries too seem to be giving up this formalized distinction in some places. It was said in San Rafael, however, that they were planning to build a *Salón*, another social club, which would be restricted in membership to the *gente decente*.

The class system in the towns and countryside of Nicaragua is a fairly strong and clearly recognized matter. Different wealth resources, different customs, different participation in social events, and different residence, all serve to distinguish members of one of the classes from those of another. While the lower class forms a large proportion of the total population, the middle class predominates in the towns.

9. POLITICAL STRUCTURE

As in the other papers in this series, we are concerned in this section with the structure and functioning of the political system in its lower echelons, and the nature of the national political organization is of interest to us specifically as it affects the people of the towns and countryside.

Nicaragua is divided into sixteen departments and the comarca of Gracias a Dios; the departments are divided into 122 *municipios*. The *municipios* in turn are divided into *comarcas* and then into *cantones*. In general the *cantón* is the smallest officially recognized territorial subdivision of the country.

In each departmental capital is located a civil administrative authority: the *jefe político;* the principal civil and/or criminal judges, the *jueces de distrito;* and the *comandancia* or military authority. At the municipal level in the *cabecera municipal* are an *alcalde* as civil chief, a *juez local*, and if a military post is present, a *comandante*. In the *comarca* there is usually a single official, the *juez de mesta*, and there may be a various number of *jueces de cantón* depending upon the area and size of the rural population. Such is the general hierarchy of officers to be found over most of the country. In practice, there are variations on this basic pattern.

The municipal capital is always a town, a nucleus of population which usually includes certain tradesmen, artisans and farmers. The municipal officers vary in number, but there are always an *alcalde* and a *síndico* named by the *Ministerio de Gobernación* in Managua. These officials are usually local men although they obtain their appointment from the national capital. There is frequently also an *alcalde suplente* who acts as an assistant to or substitute for the regular *alcalde* or *alcalde propietario*. The *síndico*, the second official in the *alcaldía* has various tasks. He is the local public prosecutor, may check local municipal funds, may have to sign divorces, land titles and various other civil documents, and may even be responsible for deciding where new streets will be laid. Most *municipios* also have a treasurer who is responsible for the public funds. The term *regidor* seems to be used rarely in Nicaragua, but was reported in Rivas, a departmental capital, there were three *regidores* under the *alcalde*, one of whom was the *síndico* and another the *tesorero*.

Varying with the town involved, there are a number of functions which the *alcaldía* performs and which may be handled by one of the officers already mentioned or for which there may be special municipal employees. There is a collector of municipal taxes, principally the monthly taxes on stores and other businesses; there may be a *fiel de rastro*, or public inspector of the slaughterhouse; a *panteonero* or person charged with keeping the cemetery in order; a secretary, and civil registrar. In Tipitapa there are actually only two municipal officials; the *alcalde propietario*, who also acts as the municipal treasurer and *registrador civil*, and the *alcalde suplente* who also acts as the *síndico* and secretary. In Nagarote there are an *alcalde*, *alcalde suplente*, and then one person who holds both the posts of *síndico* and secretary; in addition, there are a *fiel de rastro* and *cobrador municipal* (tax collector). In Telica are three officials, the *alcalde*, the secretary, and the *fiel de rastro*.

For the municipal judiciary the *juez de distrito* names one or more *jueces locales* in each town. There is a distinction made between the civil and criminal judge at this level, but in most cases a single judge acts in both capacities. In some towns there will be named a *juez local suplente* or substitute judge in addition to the regular *juez local*. In El Sauce, not only was there a separate *juez local civil* and *juez local criminal*, but each judge had a secretary and a *portero*, or general assistant.

In most municipal capitals there is a military post, often not consisting of more than a commandant and two soldiers. Except in the larger cities, there is no police force in Nicaragua distinct from the military. They act at one and the same time as the civil police and the army. The officers and men assigned to a town rarely are natives of the town.

In most of the medium sized and small towns which were municipal centers, there was no adequate municipal building. In some cases, there was a municipal structure which was being rented out as a store, being used as a school, too delapidated, or which had been taken over as the military post. In some cases, the *alcalde* held out in his own home, and in other a cheap one or two room structure had been set up in which there was a table and perhaps a cabinet for the municipal archives. In Tipitapa, San Rafael del Norte, and Santo Tomás a single room served as the municipal headquarters. In Telica and Pueblo Nuevo the *alcalde* used his own home. In some towns, the military post has not taken up the entire municipal building, and the *alcalde's* office, the *jueces locales*, and the military post are all housed in sections of the same building. Such is the case in San Ramón, El Sauce, Nagarote, and Teustepe. In the departmental capital of Ocotal, the town *alcalde* shares the second floor of a general governmental building with the *jefe político* of the department.

The writer had the definite impression during the survey that the *alcaldes* in general were not considered to be very important people by the urbanites in the capital. If one wanted an introduction to a local official, it was often assumed that it was an introduction to the local military commander and not to the *alcalde*, a civil official. If one wanted some service, it was again the military officer present to whom one was told to address himself, not to the civil officials. The *alcaldes* in general proved to be excellent informants for the survey, perhaps in part because they more often were local townspeople who did not have extensive political power and were consequently in a better position to see the life of both the wealthier and poorer people of the towns.

Government of the rural areas is comparatively simple. While in the towns which are municipal capitals there are judicial, civil, and military officers, there is only one officer in charge of a rural region, the *juez de mesta*. The *juez de mesta* is appointed by the municipal *alcalde* and is the principal official of the *comarca*, the next smaller territorial subdivision of the *municipio*. A *comarca* is very commonly referred to by both the town and countrypeople of Nicaragua as a *valle* (valley). Thus, in referring to a specific rural population, they will more often be referred to as the people of such and such a valley than as the people of that *comarca*.[19] The writer encountered no cases of a *juez de mesta* having a special building; generally he carries on his official duties from his home. He is always a local man, sometimes one of some prestige, but frequently merely a person whom the *alcalde* has found convenient to name as the local official. Sometimes two *jueces de mesta* will be named in each *comarca*, a *propietario* and a *suplente*. In San Ramón the *comarcas* are commonly called *cañadas*. In addition to the *juez de mesta* named in each *cañada*, the *alcalde* also names a *capitán de cañada* who is responsible for law and order within his area of jurisdiction.

Named by the *juez de mesta* within his *comarca* are a number of *jueces de cantón* who are responsible to him. In San Ramón, these men are called the *jefes de cantón*. The *juez de mesta* of the comarca of Chirincocal is responsible

---

[19] The writer cannot be sure at present, but it does not seem unlikely that the term *mesta* is related to this, since it refers to the confluence of rivers. Hence, a *juez de mesta* is the official who is in charge of a valley or a place where rivers meet.

for six *cantones* and has named a *juez de cantón* in each one. The appointment of the *juez de mesta* by the *alcalde* must be approved by the *jefe político*, and the naming of *jueces de cantones* by the *juez de mesta* must be approved by the *alcalde*. Even though the *juez de mesta* and the *juez de cantón* are called "judges," they are general civil officers, and under the general control and direction of the *alcalde* and not the judiciary authorities of the *municipio*. These officers may also be appointed in a town to aid the *alcalde* in local civil matters. Thus in Tipitapa there are three *jueces de mesta* and two *jueces de cantón* in the town. The Tipitapa officials with whom the writer spoke felt that this was a rather unusual situation; the former *alcalde* had named these *jueces* right at the edge of town.

Without doubt the most important authorities from the point of view of the rural people are the municipal civil officers and the *juez de mesta*. The *juez de cantón* is actually little more than the local representative of the *juez de mesta*. It is this latter official who acts as the *alcalde's* representative to most of the rural people.

While there is no longer a law in Nicaragua by which a person is required to provide a certain number of days a year in road work, the *día de vialidad* is still observed in some of the rural areas. These days of road repair usually fall in November or December, and to get the people together the *alcalde* tells the *juez de mesta* to name a certain number of people to do the work. Ordinarily, this work is limited to the particular *comarca* in which a person lives. The upkeep of the principal highways is in the hands of the national government and is no longer the responsibliity of the local officers. In one town the *alcalde* remarked that the rural people were "rebelling" against being called to road work, so the roads are not in as good condition as they should be.

Also frequently under the control of the civil officers is the local cemetery. As was mentioned earlier, there is sometimes a *panteonero* appointed to be responsible for the upkeep of the cemetery. There is also frequently an annual work session, or *fajina*, called of the community members to clean the cemetery. Some towns have a *Junta de Beneficencia*, or Welfare Group, or as in Ocotal, a *Junta Local de Asistencia Social* (Local Social Assistance Group) which takes over the responsibility for the cemetery. The Ocotal group is composed of seven members, four of whom are named by the Ministry of Government in Managua, and the remaining three are named by the municipality. In most of the towns of any size the cemeteries are divided into two, three, or four classes; first, second, third, and *de solemnidad*. The first class section is reserved for the best people of the town, economically those who can afford to put up a monument. The second class is usually reserved for the people of the middle class in the town, economically those who can afford to put up only a *lápida* or long cement slab over the tomb. When there is a third class section, it is the cheapest, and any sort of marker will do. The last section is for those who must be buried at the expense of the town, since they have no relatives or their families are too poor to be able to afford the third class section.

In some towns this class system in the cemetery is no longer observed; in some, however, two separate cemeteries have been kept, one for the wealthy upper class people, and the other for the poorer people. Besides the cemeteries near the towns, many of the *comarcas* also have their own cemeteries in which the local people are buried. In La Orilla, the *comarca* burial ground was divided into two general sections according to the wealth of the individual.

Most municipalities are theoretically responsible for the upkeep and use of a *rastro* or slaughterhouse. In fact, many towns do not have one, and in many of the towns which do, they are neither kept up nor used. Where they do exist, they are used principally for the slaughter of cattle, and pigs are usually killed in the private homes. A few towns control the sale of meat, even though some do not control slaughtering. These towns, such as El Sauce, have a special room in which beef must be sold. The right to sell the meat is charged a municipal tax. In the smaller towns beef is killed only once a week or so; in the larger towns it will be killed as often as every day. A very few of the larger towns have special slaughterhouses for pigs, but even some of the departmental capitals do not have these.

Most towns in the republic have government owned and operated telegraphic communication with other centers and to some there is telephone service. In general most of the power facilities in the small towns are in the hands of private individuals or companies that have generators which supply electricity during the evening hours. Unfortunately, the local power sources have not always proved to be very profitable ventures and as a result they are frequently inadequate. Few of the rural areas have any power facilities.

Aside from the nuclear town, which is ordinarily a municipal seat, the greater part of the countrypeople live in villages or in scattered villages (*caseríos*). A *cantón* is frequently also a *caserío*. Chirincocal and San Pedro are both *caseríos* which lay in the same *cantones* as other *caseríos*. The houses in both these *caseríos* are scattered across the countryside. In San Pedro they are in a more restricted area since there are a number of large *fincas* and *haciendas* nearby which occupy most of the land; in Chirincocal, most of the land is occupied by the *caserío* dwellers and the houses are at a greater distance from each other. The village of La Orilla between Nandaime and Granada is an example of a cluster of rural people who have been squeezed together almost completely by the presence of larger landholdings.

The villages and *caseríos*, which usually are politically *cantones* but in a few cases are *comarcas*, should be considered as the basic community unit of the Nicaraguan country dweller. It is within these groups that religious activities are carried on, that people work together, and that the most friends are known.

Before leaving the subject of political organization it should be mentioned that the *barrio* of Monimbó in Masaya has an organization which is quite divergent from that which has just been described. Since this is a special case, however, and has more historical and local interest than the general pattern found elsewhere, a description of the Monimbó system will be reserved for the general description of that *barrio*.

10. RELIGIOUS ACTIVITIES

Nicaragua is predominantly a Catholic country, but some areas have important Protestant groups.

These figures make it abundantly clear that Protestantism, as a common faith, is present only in the Atlantic littoral, and there specifically in the Department of Zelaya and the comarca del Cabo Gracias a Dios. As between the Pacific belt and the central highlands, Protestantism is considerably more common in the former; there are only 1,858 Protestants registered in the highland departments as opposed to 8,723 in the Pacific belt departments.

Within the large Catholic population there is diversity in observances due to various circumstances. While women are much more active than men in Catholic activities, both men and women are more active in the central highlands than in the Pacific belt. The people who act as prayer leaders in novenas and rosaries are almost always women. Only in the Matagalpa Indian area and in the town of Monimbó was it reported that men specialized in this.

Table 12.—Numbers of persons of various religious faiths, 1950
(*Dirección General de Estadística*, 1950)

Region	Total	Catholic	Protestant	Other
Department of Zelaya................	56,497	35,550	20,787	160
Comarca del Cabo Gracias a Dios....	17,232	6,282	11,010	31
Total Atlantic Littoral..............	82,818	50,715	31,997	197
Total Pacific Belt and Central Highlands.............................	974,205	962,700	10,581	843
Total republic......................	1,057,023	1,013,415	42,578	1,030

In Santo Tomás it was said that both men and women specialized in praying, but elsewhere, both in the towns and countryside, it seems to be a woman's specialty.

While women tend to specialize as rosary prayer leaders in both the towns and countryside, men more commonly participate in the prayers in the country than in the towns. In the towns the upper class women are frequently more active in church affairs than are those of the lower class. In the attendance of Mass the upper class townsman may be a fairly steady participant, but he does not frequently take part in the variety of other church activities and lay associations which occupy his female relatives.

Most of the towns of Nicaragua have a church, and some of the larger ones have more than one. Many of the churches date back to early in the republican epoch and there are a number which are of the colonial period. The older highland churches more commonly seem to be built with a single façade with no towers. The façade of these churches usually stands high above the roof of the church in the outline of an ornate inverted U. A bell is sometimes set in the center of the façade or may be in a separate bell tower structure. On the coast the churches much more commonly have two towers at the front. Small *hermitas* are to be found in various of the small rural communities, but in general the countryside does not have separate church buildings.

While there is usually a priest in each of the main towns of the republic, there are not enough to carry on activities intensively in both the towns and in the rural areas. As in other countries, the quality of the clergy varies, but the writer received the general impression that the priests in the towns he visited were fairly active. An informant in Telica, for example, commented that their priest, recently arrived from the far east, was very enthusiastic and was helping the community a great deal. In another case, the rural custom of a saint travelling from one home to another daily was stopped by the priest. In the town of San Ramón it was the custom until four years ago to have a bullfight during their fiesta, but the priest said he did not want them to have bullfights any more and threatened to refuse to say Mass for them if they continued. As a result they stopped. In general, a priest is most concerned with the church in the town where he lives. If he also has the responsibility of two or three other churches, even though they may be in populations equivalent or larger in size, his visits tend to be irregular.

Among both town and country dwellers certain religious observances are carried on in the home. Almost every home has a *cuadro*, a picture of a saint set in a corner, on a table, or shelf. Around it will be set a few candles, flowers, or other decorations, varying with the wealth of the family. The poorer people usually have only one or two *cuadros* while the higher class townspeople may have as many as five or ten. The number of *cuadros* which one has and whether their days are observed seems to indicate class in certain of the towns; the more one observes, the more time and money it involves; the wealthier women are more able to spend this time and money than are the poorer women. It is not uncommon to keep *cuadros* of some of the more important saints in the local church. The wealthier and more active women may even have one or two images of saints as well as *cuadros*.

The minimum respect shown towards the saint of a *cuadro* is to say a rosary on the eve of the saint's day. Much more common is to hold a novena for the nine nights prior to the day. The home *cuadros* are also used as the focus of the novenas held on the occasion of or in memory of the death of a family member. The particular saints kept in the homes vary from one house and one region to another, but among the more common are la *Virgen de Fátima, Corazón de Jesús, Virgen del Perpetuo Socorro*, and la *Purísima Concepción de María*.

In general, *rogativas*, more commonly called *rogaciones*, prayers for specific acts on the part of the saint or God, are held over most of the Spanish-speaking portion of the republic. Most *rogaciones* are held to ask for rain, and are consequently promoted by various of the community members. Some, however, are paid for by private individuals who want to be cured of some illness or wish that some other person be cured. *Rogaciones* are almost always held with a priest and involve both a special Mass and processions. In some places a particular saint is favored; in Chirincocal it was said that the *Virgen de Fátima* was always used in *rogaciones*. In some places the countrypeople come to the priest in the town church for a *rogación*; in others, the priest will go out to the *caseríos* and hold the *rogación* in the countryside. In some towns, mentioned specifically for Santo Tomás, *San Isidro* is celebrated annually to ask for a good harvest. This is not considered as a regular *rogación* since it is held regularly on the saint's day.

The church and religion enters the practical life of the individual in other ways besides helping to provide rain and cure illnesses. Baptisms are necessary for all children, marriages are frequently religious events, and death must be observed in a religious manner. Baptisms are frequently celebrated with familiar fiestas both in the towns and countryside. Wealth is the main limitation as to whether they are observed in this way or not. Among the poor they are not always celebrated. Marriage usually involves a familial fiesta. In some places a marriage fiesta will not be held if the family is still in mourning. It was specified in Santo Tomás and La Orilla that the marriage fiesta is held in the home of the boy's parents, while in Teustepe it was said that fiestas were held on the same day in the homes of both families. In Tipitapa it was said that the countrypeople will rent a house in the town for the celebration since they must go there anyway to have the marriage in the church. Elsewhere it was said that the fiestas for marriage would sometimes go on all night and not infrequently end up in machete fights between some of the participants.

When a member of the family dies it is the general custom to have a novena. The principal exception to this is in the case of the death of young children. It was reported that among the countrypeople in the regions around Ocotal, San Ramón, Darío, Tipitapa, to a lesser degree around Telica and La Orilla, and formerly around El Sauce, it was the custom upon the death of a child to hold a fiesta with drinks, food, music, and dancing. This custom has evidently disappeared in most of the towns, if indeed it was observed among the townsmen, and the evidence seems to point to a gradual decrease in its observance.

Over most of the republic it is customary to have a novena immediately following the death of an individual and one again at the end of the year. In some places, if possible, a Mass will be held shortly after the time of the death, while in others it will be held later, sometimes even at the time of the novena held at the year's end. As was mentioned before, it is usually women who lead the praying during these sessions. In San Rafael del Norte these women are called *beatas*. It is the general custom to serve food on the final night of a novena. It was reported as the custom in Nagarote that women did not attend funerals except in some cases where the deceased was a member of the same religious association. It was reported from Subtiaba that it is customary for a person who thinks he is going to die to decide which of his possessions, such as cows or pigs, will serve to pay for the Mass after his death. When the person dies the selected goods are used to pay for the Mass and a large dinner which frequently lasts all day and through the following night. During the funeral procession in Subtiaba a band plays; the informant felt that it was unique to the *barrio*.

Among the most active group of people in religious activities are townswomen.

In almost all the towns are to be found associations of women. The most common of these are the *Hijas de María* and the *Matronas*. The *Hijas de María*, synonymous in some towns with the *Sociedad de la Purísima Concepción*, is usually composed of upper and middle class single women. When a woman marries, she automatically ceases to be a member of the *Hijas* and may become a member of the *Matronas*. While the *Hijas* are to be found in almost every town and in many villages, the *Matronas* in general seem to be a less important association. In two towns it was reported that the *Matronas* no longer existed as a group, and in another, San Ramón, it was reported that they had become very much weakened through internal dissention. While the *Hijas de María* have a recognized time of celebration, the month of May, and in some cases the day of *la Purísima* in December as well, the *Matronas* may celebrate different days. In Santo Tomás, the *Virgen de Lourdes* is their special day; in San Rafael del Norte, the *Virgen de Guadalupe*; in Teustepe, they celebrate *la Purísima*; in Telica, the *Corazón de Jesús*. Where the *Matronas* exist they are usually more than merely a religious association devoted to a saint; they are also general helpers and organizers for some of the town's more important fiestas. In Teustepe, for example, the *Matronas* are responsible also for fixing the church for four of the major fiestas. In Santo Tomás, the *Matronas*, the *Hijas de María*, and another group of single women devoted to Santa Teresa, all help generally in the church.

Most of the towns have various other associations besides the *Matronas* and *Hijas de María*. In general each of the associations is responsible for a particular fiesta, sometimes more than one, and many help in the titular fiesta as well. While some are restricted to women in membership, there are many that have both women and men. Associations composed entirely of men are not so common. One example is the *Asociación de San José* in Santo Tomás. The better organized associations will name a president, treasurer, and secretary, and some a *capitán* who will be in charge of collecting funds for the association and its fiesta.

In many towns the main control of the sponsorship of the public fiestas is in the hands of the local priest. There are also a number of traditional ways in which the laity participates in sponsorship. Besides the associations, many towns have one or more *mayordomos* who are responsible for certain fiestas. The specific function of the *mayordomo* varies from one town to another. In some he is responsible for collecting money for a particular fiesta; in others, he may be the president of the association which sponsors a fiesta. His term of responsibility varies from a year to a lifetime, depending upon the local tradition. In Monimbó the *mayordomo* is personally responsible for paying for the celebration, but he has with him seven or eight *diputados* (deputies) who help him. Even where most of the religious activity is carried on by women the position of *mayordomo* will usually be held by a man. Among the principal exceptions to this were noted in Nagarote where the *Virgen de Fátima* and *Virgen Purísima* each have a *mayordoma*, and in Santo Tomás where the *Virgen de las Mercedes* has a *mayordoma*. In some towns, San Ramón, San Rafael del Norte, Monimbó, and Rivas, it was said that each saint and holy day had a *mayordomo*; in others, such as Teustepe, Subtiaba, Tipitapa, Pueblo Nuevo, Nagarote, and Santo Tomás, only some of the celebrations were in the hands of *mayordomos*.

Another method by which a fiesta is sponsored, and one which is found only rarely now, is the cultivation or rent of a piece of land belonging to the church. The term *cofradía* is used for this land. In Santo Tomás, the patron saint, which is *Santiago* and not *Santo Tomás*, has a piece of land. The priest, under the authority of the bishop, names a group of townspeople who are responsible for the land. Money from it is used to repair the church, the priest's residence, and to pay for the fiesta of Holy Week and part of the fiesta of the patron saint. This group is called the *Junta de Cofradía*. Its president is also the *mayordomo* for the fiesta of *Santiago*. The term *archicofradía* is used in Teustepe for an association of women who control the celebration of the *Santísimo*.

In some places the sponsorship or control of one or more of the fiestas has come into the hands of the civil authorities. In Teustepe the *alcalde* is responsible for annually naming a committee to collect money for the fiesta of the patron, *Candelaria*. In the rural settlement of Chirincocal, the *alcalde* of Pueblo Nuevo notifies the local *juez de mesta* who is then responsible for collecting money locally and giving it to the priest for the major fiesta.

Some towns have organizations which are not designed for the specific celebration of a saint or holy day, but rather as a general lay support for the church. In Telica there is a *Junta Católica* which, composed of both men and women, has taken the responsibility for the reconstruction of the church. Ocotal has an *Acción Católica*, composed principally of upper class men, who help the church financially. The members of this group also carry on a certain amount of social welfare work such as visiting and helping sick and poor people.

The participation in large fiestas by the countrymen is limited. It is the regular custom for the countrypeople to go to the nearest town to participate in the celebration of the major fiestas. Since few of the country communities have chapels or churches, aside from these trips to the nearby towns and occasional pilgrimages, their religious observances are limited generally to those which do not require a church. Among the most important of these non-church observances in the highlands is the visit of a saint to one of the homes in the community during one night every month or so. In Chirincocal, for example, the *Virgen de Fátima* spends one night or more in each house. During this night, the family of the house holds a prayer session and on the following day the saint is passed on the next house. The saint belongs to the church in the town of Pueblo Nuevo nearby and is returned there for her annual fiesta. For the rest of the year, however, she makes her daily visits. It is customary for the family which has the saint to give her a *limosna*, an offering of a few cents, while she is staying at their home. Over much of the highlands, except where it may have been stopped by a local priest as it was in San Rafael del Norte, almost every valley or rural community will have a saint which makes the rounds in this way. The countrypeople thus have a regular prayer session besides those which they may hold for the saints which they keep in their homes.

Some valleys will have more than one saint which makes the rounds in this way. In San Pedro it was reported that besides the *Virgen de Fátima*, there were also daily visits made by *Corazón de Jesús, la Purísima*, and the *Virgen del Carmen*. The saints which make the rounds within a certain valley or community are not supposed to leave the community. The path which they follow from one house to another is fixed so that a certain person will regularly receive the saint from the same family and in turn give it to a certain other family when ready. So far as the writer could determine, this custom is not very common in either the Pacific belt nor in the larger concentrations of population in the highlands.

In the celebration of fiestas there are some distinctive differences between highlands and the Pacific belt regions. Among the most outstanding of these is the custom to ask for a miracle which when fulfilled makes it incumbent on the petitioner to fulfill some promise. One of the commonest promises thus made is to wear a costume and dance in a fiesta. Throughout the Pacific belt region the local fiestas have large groups of people dancing masked and in costume. These dances are usually limited to one fiesta in each town during the year.[20] They are participated in by both town and country people. Since it is usually a different group of people who dance each year, there are usually no highly organized groups which continue from year to year. Rather, when the time for the fiesta draws near, the local priest will organize the people who have promised to dance into groups, usually in accordance with the costume they are to wear, and they will then practice their dance so that it can be done well at the fiesta. Dancing is not the only manner in which promises are fulfilled, but it is a traditional one in this region.

The costumes and masks include devils, masks portraying very ugly or very pretty people, animals, and Indians. There are some which represent Negroes and Mexicans. In Nagarote it was specified that very few women ever danced masked, but an exception was the dance of persons in cow costumes and masks; these were usually women. The only highland town in which the use of masks was reported was Boaco where the informants claimed that masks of mules, monkeys, horses, deer, dogs, tigers, bulls, and Indians were used. The informant, whom the writer did not trust extremely, said that the masks were used only by the *casta indígena*. On the basis of present data, the writer cannot be sure of the nature of the use of masks in this region, but it may represent quite a different pattern from the use of masks in the Pacific belt towns where people of all classes use them. It was also stated that people of both sexes, young and old, used masks in the Boaco region. An excellent collection of some of the older masks of the type used in the fiestas is to be seen in a private museum in the town of Nandaime.

What seems to be a significant exception to the general pattern of the Pacific Belt masked dance for a *promesa*, is the dance of *Moros* and *Cristianos* reported in Subtiaba. The Moors and Christians dance is to be seen in many Indian

---

[20] Doris Stone (in communication) says that some of these groups are organized for a period of three years.

fiestas of Guatemala today and is a historicodramatic dance done according to a set traditional form; it is not the means by which an individual shows thanks. Its specific form and function in Subtiaba was not ascertained.

Associated with the use of masked dances in the Pacific belt are the *gigantonas* or *gigantes*, huge figures of personalities which are carried in the processions. The "giants" are also to be found in Guatemala today as an important part of many of the local Indian fiestas.

Another fiesta custom, which insofar as the writer could find was more common on the coast than in the highlands, was the *gritería* at the *Fiesta de la Purísima* in December.[21] The *gritería* is related to the fact that in the towns where it is practiced many people keep *cuadros* or images of the *Virgen de la Purísima* in their homes. The custom involved the gathering together in the street of *pandillas* or groups of people who dance, sing, shout, and set off fireworks as they move about the town visiting in turn each of the homes in which the *Purísima* is kept. In the homes a small altar is built, or the regular home altar is highly decorated in readiness for the visits. As each group comes to a house, the home owners give them something to eat, sometimes merely fruit or candy, sometimes a much more elaborate selection of candy, drinks (usually nonalcoholic), fruits, toasted ears of green corn, *chicha de limón*, or *ayote en dulce* (squash sweetened). The more wealthy homes are supposed to provide more elaborate hand-outs. This *gritería* (which means literally a shouting or uproar) goes on all evening and quiets as midnight approaches. Then a Mass and procession is held, and all the people return home for a specially elaborate meal of which the principal dish is the *nacatamal*. Sometimes the fireworks and praying continue all night and the fiesta finally ends with further prayers on the following morning. The dance of *Moros y Cristianos* in Subtiaba is held on this day of *la Purísima*.

Aside from these possible differences, the major fiestas in the highlands and the coast are generally the same with local differences. Among the variety of recreational elements present are horse races, sometimes in the main street of the town; bull baiting in temporarily constructed bull rings; *carrera de cintas*; cockfights; gambling in the form of *loterías*, roulette wheels, or dice games; merry-go-rounds and ferris wheels; social dances, frequently separated for different social classes; and sports, principally baseball, between a home-town and neighboring team. There are almost always novenas held prior to the fiesta and one or more Masses and processions held during the fiesta.

The bull baiting which the writer attended in Granada in the Pacific belt consisted of a combination of bull baiting in which local young men take capes and bait the bull in the ring, and bull riding in which one of the men rides the bull during the process of baiting. The writer was told that this was generally typical of the bull baiting contests in Nicaraguan fiestas. The *carrera de cintas*

---

[21] The writer cannot be sure at the present time whether this custom is limited to the coast or not. Unfortunately, he first heard about it in the first coastal town visited, and consequently was able to check its presence in the coastal towns, but was not able to go back and check whether it was present in the highland towns which he had already visited.

is a contest on horseback whereby the contestants try to place a stick through a ring on the end of a hanging ribbon. It is found among mestizo populations in both Central and South America. The merry-go-round, ferris wheel, and gambling establishments are usually run by outsiders in the fiestas of smaller towns. Another trait which is common in Guatemalan Indian fiestas was also reported from Subtiaba; this is the *toro encohetado*, a framework built in the shape of a bull and on which a mass of fireworks are set. A man gets inside the framework and dances and runs around while the fireworks go off.

The variety of entertainment elements just described are not to be found in all the towns, nor are they by any means followed in all fiestas in any one town. The majority of fiestas held are more or less religious observances, usually limited to novenas, Masses and processions. It is only once or a few times a year in any one town that a major recreational fiesta will be held. Sometimes the major fiestas are held on the day of the patron saint of the town; in other cases, the day of the patron saint is a purely religious fiesta, and the heavy recreational element is held on some other day, such as on *la Purísima* or on the day of some other saint.

In the larger towns and in those in which there is a fairly distinct class system the social groupings at the fiestas tend to divide along the class lines. The social dances will be sponsored by one group or another and will be attended principally by the members of the class of the sponsors. This is also true in the holding of home novenas. In Teustepe it was reported that on the nights when important novenas are held, they will be held simultaneously in a number of homes. While theoretically a novena would be open to anyone who wishes to come, in most cases those sponsored by upper class people are attended only by friends, and the *gente del pueblo* will attend others.

The pilgrimage, or *romería*, pattern is quite extensive in the Pacific belt; the writer did not encounter it in the highlands to the same degree, except in the case to be noted. Some of the more important pilgrimages are to the various shrines of *el Señor de Esquipulas*. Among these shrines are those in the coastal towns of El Sauce, Telica, Tipitapa, and in the highland town of Esquipulas between Darío and Boaco. In each town a large annual fiesta is held on or about the 15th of January, the day of *Esquipulas*, and people from neighboring areas come to the center during the fiesta. It was said in one town that years ago people used to make the pilgrimage to the main shrine of Esquipulas in eastern Guatemala, but there were no reports that this had been done recently. The pilgrimage pattern has blended in many places with the general tendency to visit the big fiesta in a neighboring town. The main fiestas in most of the towns are visited by many outsiders, but frequently as much for the pleasure of the fiesta as to make a pilgrimage. The main centers for pilgrimages as such, however, seem to be located principally on the Pacific belt.

11. IDEAS AND PRACTICES OF SICKNESS AND CURING

While there are public health dispensaries and services in all the departmental capitals of the republic, and private physicians practicing in various of the towns, a great deal of curing goes on through home practices and remains in the hands of lay curers or *curanderos*. It is our purpose in this section to deal with some of the more frequently encountered concepts and practices with respect to sickness. A minimum of analysis will be attempted since the data is too scattered to warrant it.

Sicknesses are generally attributed to natural factors, such as foods, heat, cold, the physio-psychological attributes of an individual, or snake bites. Some are attributed to intentional sorcery of a witch or to certain spirits; and finally some are considered in the light of scientifically recognized specific diseases, such as whooping cough, measles, malaria, yellow fever, influenza, worms, etc.

Pujo.—In Ocotal, *pujo* is a constipation; it is said to have been caused by the child having been *asoleado*, having been too much in the sun's rays. It can also occur if an adult who is *asoleado* comes in and touches the child. If this has been the cause, it can be cured by having the person who caused it pick up the child, carry it around, and spit in its navel. In Tipitapa *pujo* is a kind of dysentery which is caused by drinking something which has the quality of being cold, such as lemon. It was said to be cured now by seeing a doctor and getting an injection of emetine. In Nagarote it was attributed to being *asoleado*, but could also be had from the strong glance of a woman. In general the term *pujo* refers to dysentery.

Empacho.—In Ocotal *empacho* was said to refer to tumors or inflamation in the joints; it was cured by massaging. In San Rafael del Norte and elsewhere, however, it usually referred to an intestinal or stomach trouble which occurred only in children and was generally attributed to eating the wrong food. The precise nature of the sickness was not more clearly described, but it was specified in a number of places that it could only be cured by a *curandero*. In Tipitapa it was said to occur in nursing children; if the father is playing with another woman and the mother becomes angry, then through the milk the child gets *empacho*.

Mal de Ojo, or Ojeado.—These two terms were used to refer to two somewhat different conditions. One, a conjunctivitis, was said in Ocotal to be caused by a child having been *asoleado*. The other, the common strong glance or evil eye is also related to someone looking at or touching a child when that person was overheated, had been bitten by a snake, or was a woman who had a naturally strong glance. In Tipitapa it is called *calor de ojo* and is related, as in some other locales, to the fact of overheating. The cures reported in Tipitapa and Santo Tomás were approximately the same, but the latter was fuller: if a person who has had a snake bite, or a woman who is *"muy caliente de la vista"* looks at a child, then the child will get *calor*. It is cured with a mixture of things such as *guaro* (*aguardiente*) and herbs. Rue and an herb called *hierba ajenjo* are important; they are put in a bottle with the *guaro*, then the bottle is placed in boiling water. When the *guaro* has turned green, the child is bathed in it and emerges *fresco* (cooled and refreshed). Another method which is also used is for the father to go out and work hard until he perspires, then to wrap his sweaty shirt around the child. The sweaty clothing of anyone would do almost as well.

In Nagarote the general symptoms and causes were called simply *sol*, while the term *mal de ojo* was used to refer to a different condition, an eye infection which came in June when a little animal which was found on the ears of corn was said to crawl into the eye of a person.

Pasmo.—The term *pasmo* is used to refer to various ailments. In Tipitapa it was said to be a kind of cough; in Santo Tomás it was said to be a kind of indigestion resulting from eating something which the person did not have the strength to digest; in Teustepe it was said to be a weakness or pain in the chest which made it very difficult for a person to work; in Nagarote it was said to be a skin infection which could be cured by doctors. The informants in Ocotal and La Orilla said they did not know of *pasmo* when questioned about it.

Dirt Eating.—Usually considered as a sickness, but sometimes not, is the extremely widespread custom found over most of Spanish-speaking Nicaragua of dirt eating. It is generally restricted to children, and the writer's informants frequently mentioned cases of children consuming so much dirt that they died of it. In some towns it was said that the parents had been making efforts to stop their children from eating dirt; but in more cases the informants said that they had eaten dirt as children and that it had not done them any great harm. Only in one town was it reported that it was also to be found among adults. The background and circumstances of the custom need considerable investigation, and the role it must play in programs of sanitation are only too obvious. It was evidently not related to ritual clay eating such as is found in the contemporary Esquipulas cult in Guatemala.

Calentura and Frío.—The characteristic of being too heated has already been mentioned in connection with other illnesses, but both *calentura* and *frío*, usually resulting from eating foods with the same characteristic, are also considered in themselves to be sicknesses. Catarrh is said to be the result of having been chilled, and if one has catarrh, he should not eat any of the foods which are considered to be *frío* or *fresco*. Among these foods are the citrus fruits (lemons, limes, oranges, bitter oranges), pineapple, tomatoes, watermelon, squash, chicken, rice, yuca, and drinks made of rice, oats, mango, sorghum or corn. In some towns the informants could name no foods which were specifically considered to be *caliente*. In Tipitapa, Santo Tomás, and San Rafael del Norte a few were named: beans, beef, corn, chili, and coffee. The concepts of hot and cold in relation to sickness, physical condition, and foods is clearly present in the Nicaraguan Spanish-speaking population, but the degree to which they are operative in diverse situations was not ascertained during the survey.

Susto.—In Teustepe and Monimbó it was said that people could become quite sick with *susto*, or at being frightened. In Teustepe it was claimed that it occurred mainly to pregnant women, but that it had caused another person to go crazy. One of the *curanderos* had said she needed a chicken and four *córdobas* to make the cure, but she did not succeed in the work. In Monimbó it was said that being *asustado* caused congestion in the stomach. It might be caused by a person or an animal, or anything which scared you. Sometimes it can be cured by a purgative, but sometimes it "goes to the brain," then it kills the person and there is nothing which a *curandero* can do to help. In Ocotal the informants were not sure that they had ever heard of *susto* as an illness.

Witchcraft.—Witchcraft was reported as being an important source of illness in every community except the more northerly highland areas visited. In Ocotal, San Rafael del Norte, and San Pedro it was said that witchcraft was known, but that it was very rare. The people were aware that it could be practised but since it occurred so infrequently they were not sure as to just what the consequences might be. In Ocotal it was said that it was much more common in the region around Masaya. The survey confirms the opinion that witchcraft is common in the Pacific belt, but evidently it is also quite common in the southern sections of the highlands and in the Matagalpa Indian area. In a number of the towns it was mentioned that the work of witches was generally more common in the *comarcas* than in the towns. The writer was impressed, however, that a number of cases were reported to him as occurring in the towns; the attribution by the townspeople that witchcraft was more common in the countryside may well have been protecting the in-group to some degree and perhaps trying to escape possible criticism for believing in witches too easily. The same was said, for example, in Monimbó, where the informant said that there was witchcraft in the *barrio*, but there was more of it in the "other" sections.

Informants generally said that they did not know precisely how the witches worked. They could be men or women, but in most of the cases cited, women were blamed. Most of the cases cited had to do with people who went crazy. It was also said that if a person was sick of anything which seemed to resist curative efforts that it would probably be attributed to witchcraft. In some cases it was said that the work of witches could be counteracted by hiring another witch. It was stated that some of the *curanderos* were also witches but they were generally considered to be distinct.

The Spirits.—In San Ramón, Teustepe, and Subtiaba mention was made of some local spirits which somehow cause a person to become sick. In San Ramón there were said to be three in particular, *La cegua*, a large, nude woman who would scare men; the *mico*, or monkey, which could transform itself into a human being or into another animal; and the *cadejo*, a dog like animal which scares people at night. In Subtiaba it was said that the *cegua* or *ceiga* was a woman who could transform herself into a monkey. Mention was made also of the *carreta nagua*,[22] an ox cart which goes at night but sounds as it if were not greased. It is a phantom, and the poles on the side of the cart are said to be little girls. In Teustepe an informant says that he believes he saw the *ceiga* when he was younger; she was very old and very ugly. Just what effect these and possibly other spirits had on man was not made clear to the writer. But it was evident that belief in them and in the work of witches was not restricted to members of the lower class or to country people. Middle class townspeople and some upper class persons also showed credence in them.

---

[22] Doris Stone (in communication) notes that this is probably the same as the *carreta sin bueyes* which is found in Costa Rican folklore.

Curing.—Besides the witches, there are many *curanderos* who resort to both secret techniques of curing and quite a few who work on a fairly open empirical basis. Some *curanderos* specialize in snake bites, and it was said in Rivas that most people prefer to go to a *curandero* with a snake bite than to a doctor. Another type of specialist is the *sobadora* or *componedora*, either men or women who give massages to pregnant women or to people who have broken bones or swellings. Most *curanderos* use both patent medicines and certain herbs in their work. It was also said in Teustepe that urine was occasionally used in the process of a diagnosis, although the informant did not know how. In Subtiaba and among the Matagalpa Indians it was said that the *santiguar*, or making the sign of the cross accompanied by certain prayers, was used in the course of some of the treatments.

There is evidently a considerable lore connected with pregnancy and childbirth, but very little material was gathered concerning it. Pregnant and menstruating women were said to avoid the look of a person who had been bitten by a snake since it could kill them. Midwives were reported to be present in all towns and country areas and evidently took care of the majority of the births.

In general, sanitary facilities in the towns were somewhat better than those in the countrysides. Informants claimed in some towns that the majority of the homes had latrines, but in general it was said in the *comarcas* that there were very few and usually none. In many places water was taken from wells, but it was more common to get it from nearby rivers. In some of the major towns it was said that the drinking water was taken from points in the river above the places where washing was done and fords were made, but the writer observed many times that the water was taken from whichever place was most convenient, and was often in the same area as the washing and fords. The inadequacy of the water supply was mentioned to the writer in a number of places. Where deep wells have been dug it is usually because there is no water any nearer the surface. Very commonly used for getting water from the wells are heavy curved logs, stuck in the ground, which curve up and over the edge of the well, and from which is hung a bucket. These are called *pescantes*. Another type which seemed restricted in use to certain parts of León, and possibly also Chinandega, is the *malacate* (name used in El Sauce), a wooden frame with vertical bars which are pushed around a vertical shaft in order to wind up the rope to which a bucket is attached. The *malacate* is more commonly seen in El Salvador. In Nagarote these were called *mecates* and it was said that they were used specifically in those wells which were very deep, and often horses or oxen were used to turn them. It is a very common practice for a man to dig a well and then to sell the water from it by the *cántaro* or bucket.

Doctors evidently were in demand wherever they were present. The writer encountered some specific evidences of resistance to the use of medical specialists, but was impressed that they would be used more if they were available. The only case of general resistance which was recounted to him concerned an effort to work in the center of the Matagalpa Indian region. The informant claimed that the doctor on this mission had found it very difficult to obtain the confidence of the people. Folk medicine beliefs are to be found in all social classes, however.

12. NOTES ON RECREATION AND DIVERSIONS

By far the most popular sport in Nicaragua is baseball. Unlike many other Spanish-American countries which have taken over soccer as almost the national sport, the various small and medium-sized towns of Nicaragua each have a *beisbol* team. Every town which the writer visited had either a team, a team organized as a sports club, or more than one team. The rural communities rarely have teams, but the young men from the rural areas will often go to the nearby towns in order to play. In some cases, as has already been mentioned, the sports club is composed along class lines.

Gambling games, especially dice throwing, are among the favorite Sunday pastimes in many of the towns, but it seemed more in evidence in the highlands than in the Pacific belt towns. The right to run a dice table is usually a concession let out by the local commandant. In San Rafael the dice were cubes with single red or black dots on the sides. They were rolled in pairs; a pair of blacks lost, a pair of reds won, and a red and black lost the throw. These games are usually permitted to open publicly only on Sunday and during fiestas.

Most towns have either social clubs with billiard halls or commercial halls. This game is a favorite occupation of the men and the halls will generally be crowded on Sundays, holidays, and in the evenings.

In the highlands cockfighting is a popular pastime, especially during the summer months. In some places, since it is a gambling game, it also is restricted to Sundays and the concession for it is let out.

In the countryside the principal recreation is had during the fiestas held for marriages, the novenas held for a saint or on the occasion of a death, and when visits are made to the towns. Most towns have a movie house which, depending upon the trade, may be open only once or twice a week, or more often. The countrypeople enjoy the movies as much as do the townspeople.

In San Rafael del Norte it was said that drunks were usually taken to jail on week days, but from 2:00 p.m. Saturday until 10:00 p.m. Sunday a person could get as drunk as he wanted and, unless he was causing a public disturbance, he would not be taken to jail. The sale of *aguardiente* in Nicaragua is also licensed by the Government, but there are stores in which beer may be bought and *cantinas* in which liquor is sold. In most places visited, the writer was told that clandestine *aguardiente* was made, usually of corn; since *chicha* too is a popular drink, there are a number of resources for the person who wishes to drink.

V. COMMUNITIES VISITED ON THE SURVEY

In this section we will provide brief descriptions of the principal towns visited on the survey. In addition to those treated here, the survey included Monimbó and Subtiaba which are treated in the subsequent section.

1. OCOTAL AND SEGOVIA

The region of Nicaragua known today as Nueva Segovia was one of the earliest settled regions in the country. An inscription on the cross in front of the church in Ocotal, capital of the department, notes the founding of the following towns: "first: 1524, Ciudad Vieja; second: 1611, Ciudad Antigua; third: 1654, reconstruction; fourth: 1690, reconstruction; fifth: El Ocotal—1803."

The site of Ciudad Antigua is still occupied, and is the center of a local pilgrimage pattern. The reconstructions which the monument faithfully records were necessitated principally by the raids up the Coco River by buccaneers. The final movement of the principal city to Ocotal was made in an attempt to move the population above the navigable portion of the Coco River, and thus provide better protection against raids.

Ocotal is still the last main town one passes through if he wishes to make a trip down the Coco River. The town is set just north of the wide shallow east-west arm of the river in a broad valley. The town is set well above the river and so is in no danger of being flooded during the rainy season. To the north of Ocotal rises the *Cordillera de Dipilto*, named after a small river which winds its way through the mountains, and across the valley. Ocotal is built on the edge of this river and it serves the inhabitants as a source of water for washing and drinking. The climate in Ocotal, during the visit in August, was pleasantly cool.

The town is laid out on the usual rectangular pattern with a main plaza in the center surrounded by the houses of the wealthier families, the military *cuartel*, the departmental and municipal administrations, the social clubs, and on one side, the church. The buildings are generally a single story, of *adobe* brick with very high ceilings and tile roofs. Besides the social clubs, Ocotal has two moving picture houses, a number of gas stations, a hospital and public health clinic.

There is very little rural population immediately around Ocotal. In the 1950 Census Ocotal was recorded as having an urban population of 2,672 and a rural population of only 117. This is because the *municipio* of Ocotal is fairly small; it is immediately surrounded on all sides by predominantly rural *municipios* so that the rural population of the entire department is 21,306 and the urban only 5,772. One informant told us that a large proportion of the population of the department were themselves, or were descended from people who originally moved in from Honduras; "they have many customs which are not to be found elsewhere in Nicaragua," he concluded.

Ocotal serves three main functions. First, it is the administrative center for the department; the *jefe político* and the military commandant are located there. Second, it is an important urban center for the many agriculturalists who live in the smaller communities or have farms in the department. It has stores, middle men, and a branch of the national bank where loans may be made. Finally, as it is close to the Honduran border, it is also a useful channel for the illicit traffic of goods from Honduras to Nicaragua and back. The importance of this trade varies with the relative price and availability of commodities in the two countries.

Most of the land in the immediate vicinity of Ocotal is in small and middle-sized *haciendas*. As one moves out to the smaller centers, however, the population becomes predominantly *finqueros*, small property holders, many of whom prefer to live in the towns rather than on their farms. One such town is San Fernando, located about an hour's drive northeast of Ocotal. The country through which one passes on this drive is somewhat eroded, and mainly in natural pasturage. San Fernando was originally a *caserio* of Ciudad Antigua, but years ago two families decided to move to the new site and the town was established in this way. People in Ocotal mentioned that there must have been an early blond component in the San Fernando population since today there are many blond, blue-eyed people. From the writer's observation, there were some blonds in the town, but the population now appears predominantly mestizo.

San Fernando itself is perched on a hilltop. The plaza is a wide open grass grazing area, with houses on all four sides but not built in a solid line. The people of the town are generally agriculturalists, as are their rural neighbors who live elsewhere in the *municipio*. They employ both the two forms of agriculture described earlier, the *milpa* system which is done with a digging stick and the *labranza*, done with the plow. Some years ago coffee was introduced as a productive crop into this region, and many of the small landowners cultivate coffee for export. The cultivation is generally careless, however, and since it is only part of a general subsistence agriculture it does not form a major proportion of the field labor.

The Spanish and mestizo settlement in this part of Nicaragua is generally limited to the west of the Coco River. From Ocotal, the river runs in a general easterly direction for a distance of about 80 kilometers. There it cuts north for about 50 kilometers, and then northeast down ultimately to the Atlantic plains. This line of 50 kilometers is the effective eastern barrier of mestizo settlement. Beyond this the population is extremely scattered and is predominantly Indian. While there has been a very slow immigration into the mestizo region, its boundaries are generally the same as they were a hundred or two hundred years ago. The writer was told that people from El Salvador had been coming up in recent years to look into the possibility of colonization in this region, but to what extent Salvadoreans have actually settled here the writer does not know.

The region immediately to the north of Ocotal, close to the Honduran border, is the scene today of a growing lumber enterprise. Concentrating mainly on the removal of large pines, the American company running this work is providing extensive employment to the people of the community of Dipilto and brings labor in daily from Ocotal itself.

In Ocotal there are three schools, two primary schools run by the government which go up to the sixth grade, and a private school for girls run by a group of nuns. There is also a night school in alphabetization for both adults and children. The rural school system is being expanded at present under a cooperative program between the Nicaraguan government and a Point IV agency. Until some years ago there was a high school, a *colegio*, but it stopped and all superior education is now received in Managua, León, or Granada. In talking with the people of Ocotal, the writer received the impression that a surprising large percentage of the upper and some middle class children continued their education through high school. There were also a number of cases of families which had sent their children to the United States, France and Spain for further education.

2. CHIRINCOCAL AND PUEBLO NUEVO

Pueblo Nuevo is another fairly old town in the highlands, but it presents an entirely different picture than does Ocotal. While the latter gives the impression of a neat, orderly community of white walls, red roofs, and general tidiness, Pueblo Nuevo gives the impression of a sadly ramshackle town, dusty, and generally unkempt. Part of the reason for this difference on first impression is that Pueblo Nuevo is constructed almost entirely of *taquesal*, mud on a wooden framework, while Ocotal is made of *adobe*. The *adobe* wall generally is longer lasting, and does not tend to flake off as does the *taquesal*; consequently, the latter, if not well cared for, soon gives the appearance that the wall of the building is crumbling. Pueblo Nuevo used to be on the principal road running south from Ocotal to the Pacific coast, but when the new highway was constructed a few years ago it was by-passed and is now definitely off the main line of traffic.

Whereas Ocotal derives most of its water supply from the river which flows by the town, Pueblo Nuevo depends largely upon wells. It was estimated that about one third of the homes in the town have wells.

The population of Pueblo Nuevo was a little under 1,000 in 1950, while the rural population in the *municipio* was over 6,000. One of the rural communities outside Pueblo Nuevo is Chirincocal. Chirincocal, to the west and slightly north of Pueblo Nuevo, is set in a broad valley, broken by ravines; the entire arable area is under cultivation. The land is so heavily used in this region that there has been considerable immigration of individuals to Segovia and the Pacific coast in recent years. Chirincocal is not untypical of many such rural communities in the highlands of Nicaragua. The population consists of subsistence farmers, most of whom own their own land. They vary in wealth from the *finquero* who raises some crops specifically for sale, and the *hacendado* who has a cattle farm or coffee plantation, to the small landowner and the *mozo*. Most of the larger landowners live either on their farms or in Pueblo Nuevo, but there are few, if any, owners who live outside the region. Transportation in the rural area is almost entirely by mule; some people have ox carts, but since the region to be traversed includes rough mountain land, mules are generally more satisfactory than are the carts.

The homes in Chirincocal are dispersed over the countryside. The people have intermarried and there has been no recent immigration into the area. Since the area is under heavy cultivation, there is a scarcity of wooded land except on the slopes of the hills. Some of the *cantones* nearby have schools to which the local children go. They receive a few years of primary education, but seldom more.

There is considerable intercourse between the countrypeople of Chirincocal and the surrounding *cantones*. The people go to town for the major fiestas, and the local circulation of the *Virgen de Fátima* is dependent upon the permission of the priest in town. Commerce, however, seems to be centering more on Estelí now since the road by-passes Pueblo Nuevo.

3. SAN PEDRO

Estelí is an active highland city of over 5,000 inhabitants; it is an agricultural center for the entire surrounding region, and is the second largest city in the highlands. Less than an hour by bad road to the east of Estelí is a small rural settlement called San Pedro. One can pass through it without knowing that he has gone through a place with a name. Its inhabitants are among Nicaragua's poorer rural dwellers, very few own any land, and most either work for neighboring *haciendas* or as sharecroppers. Like Chirincocal, there is no formal communication service for the people here, and the road is open only in the dry season.

The homes in San Pedro are scattered through a wooded and broken section of the countryside. One can seldom see more than two of the houses at one time. There are no roads properly speaking, but paths which run from one home to another. Most of the houses are in a section of the countryside which is of little use for agriculture since bedrock shows through in various places. The people are closely dependent upon nearby Estelí; some of them go to Sunday Mass there, and most of them make purchases there. The people of the community are bound together by the fact of kinship, proximity, and the regular movement of a group of saints from one home to another.

Basically the people are farmers. Whenever they can get land, they try to sow enough to live on, but it is seldom possible to get enough land to do this, and most of them must hire out at one time or another.

There is a local primary school which has about twenty students. The teacher lives in Estelí and travels daily to her work. They feel no need of any higher school since no one could afford the luxury of using it.

4. SAN RAFAEL DEL NORTE

San Rafael is northeast of Estelí; the road between the two is seldom passable, however, and it is easier to reach by following the highway south from Estelí, then east towards Matagalpa, and then north again through Jinotega. Between Jinotega and San Rafael the road passes through a long valley; San Rafael is located on the south slope of the *Cerros Pantasma;* this mountain range forms the westernmost branch of the long *Cordillera Isabella* which curves northeast out into the Atlantic plains. The land of the people of the *municipio* is divided into two classes, the *tierra fría*, or uplands in which the town itself is located, and the *tierra caliente*, the lower lands. The hillsides around the town used to be covered with pine, but through the years have been converted into pasturage lands. Through this region and elsewhere in the Department of Jinotega, there has been a gradual movement of population out into the *montaña*, towards the Atlantic coast. Water in the town comes from a small river called locally the *Río Viejo* or *Río San Rafael*. It is brought up to the homes in pottery *cántaros* by women.

Mail comes into the town twice a week, and there is a converted pick-up truck which serves as a daily bus between the town and Jinotega. The plaza is a huge grassy area which is used by the children of the town as a place to romp; animals are left there to graze, thereby keeping it well cropped. San Rafael, in comparison with other parts of Nicaragua, is cold. The roofs are high, as they are in other highland towns. A number of religious fiestas are celebrated in the town, but most are purely religious. The principal fiestas are in May and June (*Virgen de Fátima, San Antonio, and Corazón de Jesús*) and in December (*la Purísima* and *Guadalupe*). Aside from these, the titular fiesta, *San Rafael*, is held in October. There are two primary schools in the town, running through the first six grades. Each has a full complement of teachers and a director. There is no public health service except the vaccinator who has come through from time to time.

5. SAN RAMÓN

East of the major highland city of Matagalpa lies the town of San Ramón. The administrative center of the *municipio*, San Ramón has a slightly different problem to deal with than is found in the majority of the highland rural *municipios*; the great majority of the rural dwellers within its jurisdiction are highland Indians. While the town itself has a population of slightly under 600 (in 1950) the rural population is over 20,000, one of the largest municipal rural populations in the entire country; only the *municipios* of Managua, Matagalpa, and Jinotega have larger rural populations.

The town itself is roughly laid out in the rectangular cross pattern. The town dwellers are principally Spanish and mestizo, and a small part of the rural population are distinguished from the rest as being of the same stock. These *campesinos*, as they are called to distinguish them from the Indians, generally work on the *haciendas* or are *finqueros*. Formal communication facilities are available in the town in the form of telephone, telegraph, and mail which is brought in twice a week; there is no such service into the rural area.

San Ramón differs little on the surface from many other highland towns. There is no local priest, but there is a local woman who tends to lead in prayer sessions. The women are the principal participants in the religious activities of the town. There are two local schools, but they go only to the third grade. Parents who wish further education for their children send them to Matagalpa or to Managua.

6. SANTO TOMÁS

The Department of Chontales is felt by the local inhabitants as differing in many ways from the rest of Nicaragua. For one thing, it has long been a mining area, and some of the towns have so long been dedicated to this occupation that they differ considerably from other areas devoted exclusively to agriculture. From the point of view of its general culture, however, the department impressed the writer as being transitional between the highlands and the Pacific coastal belt. The town of Santo Tomás, which was included in the survey, seemed to be a highland town, but along the shores of Lake Nicaragua, the architecture belongs definitely to the Pacific belt.

The town of Santo Tomás is laid out in the rectangular pattern; many of its houses are of board, suggesting the proximity of the town to the mountain forest area which spreads into the Atlantic coastal region. Because of its location, the town receives more of the tropical trade winds which come in from the Caribbean, and consequently has a longer rainy season, from May until January or February, than do most of the highland towns. In the colonial period the town was located nearer to Lake Nicaragua, in the arid lake belt region. Through the *comarcas* mules and horses are the main forms of transportation, since much of the area is too wet during much of the year to use ox carts. Cargo oxen, however, are used by many of the countrypeople.

In the Mountains of Huapi to the north of Santo Tomás and the major mining towns of Santo Domingo and Libertad live Atlantic coastal Indians; the informant in Santo Tomás referred to them as *Sumus*. They seem to have little effect on the daily life of the people of Santo Tomás, however.

The patron saint of Santo Tomás is *Santiago*, who was patron of the old town before it was moved. *Santo Tomás* is not celebrated. The men seem to participate rather more in the religious activities than in other towns of a comparable size. They are completely in charge of one association which sponsors the fiesta of *San José* and there is a *Junta de Cofradía* which is in charge of taking care of a piece of land which is used to pay for the fiesta of *Santiago*. There are also a number of active women's groups. This was one of the few towns visited in the course of the survey in which *San Isidro* was celebrated annually and used as a means to ask for good crops. If a *rogación* was held, however, some other saint was used.

The school in Santo Tomás goes to the third grade. Recently a *Junta de Patronato Escolar* (Group of School Patrons) was formed with the *alcalde* as its head. The town is divided into two electoral *cantones* and everyone in the *comarcas* belongs to one or the other of the two subdivisions. These *cantones*, the *Oriental* and *Occidental*, seem to have no other special significance.

7. TEUSTEPE

Teustepe was the first town included on the survey which is located in what is geographically and climatically the Pacific coast belt. At an altitude of between 300 and 600 feet, it lies about 30 kilometers north of the northwest end of Lake Nicaragua. It is now separated from the main highway running out to the Atlantic coast by the Río Malacatoya which empties into Lake Nicaragua. In the dry season, the river remains fairly wide but can be forded by truck. Some years ago when the highway was in an earlier stage of planning, it was proposed to put the highway through Teustepe; towards this end a bridge was started. The bridge was never finished, however, as it was decided to put the highway on the other side of the river. The people of Teustepe today feel that the town is suffering commercially because of the decision to put the road on the other side; traffic now passes them up and it is only for some special reason that someone will ford the river to come to Teustepe.

The lowlands along the northeast side of Lake Nicaragua are very arid. Teustepe, as a town, looks arid itself; there are very few trees in the town, and the long empty plaza is brown. The river provides ample water for drinking, cooking and washing, but it is brought to town in tanks, *pipas*, or ox carts, or on the backs of *burros*. There are some wells, but in general they do not provide very good water. The land around the town is generally flat, but somewhat broken. The greater part of the population live out of the town on *finquitas*. The poorer people tend to live in *caseríos*. Agricultural products are brought into town by mule, and then transshipped by truck to Managua. The larger *haciendas* are devoted almost exclusively to cattle.

There is a priest in Teustepe, and there is a fairly active religious life among the townspeople. The pattern of celebrating saints in the home with rosaries and inviting people in to join in the praying seems particularly strong here. For the celebration of *Jueves de Corpus* in June four small altars are set up on the plaza and a procession is held which passes by them. These altars are not set up for any other fiesta.

There is one mixed school in the town with four teachers. The teachers usually only teach up through the fourth grade although they would give further classes if there was a demand for it.

In general, Teustepe has a transitional culture between that of the highlands and that of the Pacific belt. As is similar to the coast, exchange labor is not used, an *hacienda* economy predominates, the *coa* is used principally for hole digging and the *azadón* is used. In common with the highlands, women do not work in the fields generally, tile roofs predominate, and marriage seems to be more common than free unions. Although in climate and appearance the town reminds one of other towns of the Pacific belt, its cultural orientation seems to be partially towards the highlands.

8. EL SAUCE

The town of El Sauce, although located in the Department of León, lies at the foot of the highlands of the Department of Estelí. It is most easily accessible, however, by means of the branch of the railroad which cuts inland from León. Like Teustepe, El Sauce gives the impression of being a Pacific belt town, but culturally is transitional.

El Sauce is one of the towns in which the *Señor de Esquipulas* is the principal saint. The local legend concerning the arrival of the Black Christ in town is as follows. The present site of El Sauce used to be called *Los Llanos de Guayabal*. A man came one day from Guatemala, carrying on his back the figure of the Black Christ and asking alms for the *Cristo*. He stopped to rest under a *sauce* (willow) tree in front of the church. Then he continued and stopped for lunch up on the hill to the south of town. He found, when he stopped the second time, that the image of the Black Christ was not in the box in which it was being carried. Thinking he must have forgotten it, he returned and found it under the *sauce* tree. He picked it up and resumed his journey. When he next stopped to eat, he again found the box empty. Again he returned and found it in the same spot. So he decided to leave it there. Later a man was sent from Guatemala to bring the image back, and he died before arriving. This happened again later on. They built a shrine for the image, the town grew up around it, and they renamed it El Sauce for the tree. Such is the local legend of the miracle.

El Sauce itself is not a large town (population of 1,780 in 1950), but is of considerable importance as a rail station. El Sauce itself is not the railhead, strictly speaking, since the line goes on up to Río Grande. It is the principal station at that end of the line, however. Since there is practically no truck or automobile traffic into El Sauce, only *finca* owners have such transport means locally. The mule is the principal form of transport, and in the level areas, the ox cart is of considerable importance. The people of El Sauce recognize two distinct areas within the *municipio*: the western portion, which is located mainly on level land, on which the ox cart is an important form of transport, and the plow is used in cultivation; and the eastern part which is the western side of the mountains which compose the Department of Estelí, and in which the mule is the principal transport and most agriculture is done with digging stick.

The town is nuclear, and fairly well kept up although there are portions of it which are somewhat dilapidated. It is divided into two *barrios*, one of which is supposed to be somewhat poorer than the other, but there was some difference of opinion on this between informants. It is of interest that the supposedly poorer of the two *barrios*, called *La Parroquia*, is also known as *Subtiaba* and it is said that the people there are supposed to be more Indian.

While the patron saint of El Sauce is *el Señor de Esquipulas*, it is significant that there is not one Black Christ in the Church, but two. The major image, which stands over the main altar, is the image of the shrine and is the center of the local pilgrimages. The patron saint, however, is another smaller image which stands in a sanctuary at the back of the church; it is this image which makes the round in the processions. Besides the annual fiesta in January, a Mass is said for the Black Christ on the 15th of every month. Aside from the Esquipulas celebration, the most active fiesta held in the town is that of *la Purísima*.

The town has two schools, each going up to the third grade, and there are some eighteen schools of one grade each in the *comarcas*. The night school for alphabetization has started recently, but it was said that it was not well attended. There are also two private schools in the town, one run by the priest and one by a private individual. The first is for boys and has three or four grades, while the second has mixed classes and runs to the third grade.

Although there are a number of cattle *haciendas* in the *municipio*, the majority of the land is in smaller *fincas*. The writer received the impression that the general culture of the *municipio* was rather more like the highlands than the Pacific belt.

9. TIPITAPA

Teustepe, El Sauce, and Tipitapa are all in the general area of transitional culture between the central highlands and the Pacific coastal belt. While the first two tend to retain slightly more of a highland flavor, Tipitapa is slightly more coastal in its orientation. The casual visitor to Tipitapa can be easily misled by the fact that the principal highway runs through the town and has influenced the appearance of its main street. It is a popular stop for urban Nicaraguans for eating, since the fish from the lake provide an excellent meal.

Tipitapa is located on Río Tipitapa which is the channel flowing from Lake Managua into Lake Nicaragua. It is not more than three hundred feet above sea level, and is about halfway between the foothills of the central highlands and those of the Pacific coastal range. The area is predominantly an *hacienda* region and there is a growing problem of living space for the smaller agriculturalists. A great many of the homes of the *campesinos* are on *hacienda* lands and are periodically subject to moving when the land is placed under cultivation. The northern portion of the *municipio*, bordering on the departments of Matagalpa and Boaco, includes the foothills of the central highlands, and as is the case in Teustepe and El Sauce, presents a different picture in agriculture and transportation. The town of Tipitapa, of course, is well connected by transport facilities with Managua and most of the *haciendas* in the level area have roads; the uplands, as elsewhere, depend upon the mule. Tipitapa is the last *municipio* towards the Pacific coast where the writer encountered the use of the tumpline, called *mecapal* (from the Nahuatl, or Mexican, *mecapalli*). Everywhere else the writer encountered the use of the tumpline, it was known by the Spanish term *bombador*.

One of the most interesting social phenomena of Tipitapa is the presence of a *Sociedad Mutualista*, a mutual aid society, which was started about 1939. At present there are about 300 members, most of whom are townspeople but some of whom are from the countryside. Each member pays a monthly quota; the total is then divided into five separate funds. One is placed in a bank or loaned out to members at an interest; this is the *ahorro*, or savings fund, and is supposed to gradually increase the basic funds of the association. The second is used to help defray the expenses of the funeral when a member dies; in addition to this, when someone dies, all the members give an additional *córdoba* (approximately: ₡ 7.5 equal $1) which is given to the family of the deceased. The third fund is for *socorro*, aid to the sick members of the society. The last two funds are devoted respectively to administrative expenses and to a reserve fund. This local insurance association is the only one of its kind which the writer encountered during the course of the survey. It is similar in form to the funeral societies found around David in Panama, but is much broader in its functions. From the society a person receives not only help when he is sick or when a member of his family dies, but also loans should he need money for some other purpose. The very presence of the society suggests that Tipitapa, despite its location on the main highway and the destructive influence that situation might have on a communal cooperation, retains strong communal ties. Perhaps one of the factors which tends to promote this situation is that the proximity of Tipitapa to Managua leaves it with practically no local *aristocracia*. Almost all the townspeople are middle or lower class and can benefit from such a society. Such an organization would tend to be class bound in its membership and a strong component of the upper class would tend to deter its formation.

El Señor de Esquipulas is also the patron saint of Tipitapa, but the fiesta there is combined with Pacific belt fiesta traits such as masked dances. Until last year, there was only one school in the town, mixed; now there are two, each going to the second grade.

10. TELICA

Telica is located at the southwest base of the volcano of the same name. It is a thoroughly coastal belt town. The greater part of the land in the *municipio* is flat coastal land; there is some on the sides of the volcanos but it is little used. There are both *haciendas* and smaller *fincas* in its jurisdiction. While the town itself is a nuclear establishment, the countrypeople tend to live on their *fincas* or in *caseríos*. Within the town there are many unoccupied lots; yards tend to be large.

The road to Telica is passable during the dry season. The ox cart is the principal transport form but, according to the informant, this is gradually changing with the introduction of trucks. Mules are little used; horses are used by many for travel.

All the land in the *municipio* is *ejidal*, that is, it belongs to the *municipio*. Although the *municipio* has no right to remove the tenants, they pay the annual *canon* for the right of use. These funds remain in the *municipio* for local use.

The patron saint here also is *el Señor de Esquipulas*, and the fiesta, held in January, is also one of the major annual events. The writer was told in Telica that many people come from El Sauce for the Esquipulas fiesta here, and that many people from here went to El Sauce. It was denied in El Sauce, however, that many went to Telica. As in Tipitapa, it is only during the fiesta of *Esquipulas* that people will wear masks.

The two schools in the town each have two grades. Recently a *Junta Pro-Alfabetización* was formed locally to try to get people to learn to read and write. The *jueces de mesta* in the *comarcas* tried to promote the school in their areas. The schools are held in both the town and the *comarcas*, either during the day or night, depending upon when the people want them. The informant felt that they were having considerable success, with between twenty and thirty people attending at most of the schools.

11. NAGAROTE

Nagarote, with a population of over 3,000, was one of the largest towns included in the survey. It is located on the Pacific coastal flatlands, on the railway, about halfway between Managua and León. The local tradition says that Nagarote was originally an Indian settlement, but at the time that the town of León was moved from its old site to the present one, some of the refugees came and settled here rather than in the new location chosen for León.

Although Nagarote is accessible the year-round only by rail at present, a group of the *hacendados* of the town are collecting funds to build a highway to Managua. They have an agreement that when they have collected a certain amount, the government will supply the rest. The work on the road has already begun. Within the *municipio*, however, the ox cart is still the main form of transportation. Many of the *haciendas* are now using tractor-drawn wagons. To the south of the town begins the Pacific coastal range of mountains, and in this region the land is still opened with the digging stick. In general, however, the poorer people use the wooden plow, and the *haciendas* are rapidly becoming mechanized. The majority of the people in the *municipio* are *mozos* who either work on the larger *haciendas* or on the smaller *fincas*. Many of the *mozos* have small holdings themselves, or rent out a little bit of land annually. It is quite common for a man to work on a *finca* or *hacienda* during the morning from 4 to 11 a.m., then go to his own small cultivation during the afternoon.

The comarca of Tamarindo on the Pacific coast offers large salt flats. Many people, either as owners or workers, go from Nagarote during the months of November to May, the dry season, to gather salt. The majority of the owners are from Nagarote or from the neighboring municipio of La Paz. The workers who go there usually live in *ramadas*, branch and leaf shelters, and some take their families with them. Generally the women do not work in the collection of the salt. The informant expressed the opinion that while some of the people from the *municipio* went to the sugar harvest in the Pacific belt, they much preferred to go to the highlands to participate in the coffee harvests. When asked why, the informant said "They like the fiestas better there." Another reason is that some feel there is more chance of disease on the sugar plantations. The writer suspects, however, that one of the principal reasons may be social; he received the impression that in Nagarote families tended to be somewhat more stable than elsewhere on the Pacific belt region, and in the same manner that many will take their families to the salt flats, many preferred to go to the coffee harvest where they could take their families than to the sugar harvest where the men must go alone.

There were at the time of the survey two *Juntas Pro-Parque* in Nagarote. Each is concerned with the improvement of one of the two major parts in the town. They are composed principally of townspeople, but not the more wealthy *hacendados.* While the informant felt that the population of the town could be easily classified into social classes, he also said that the town was "practically made up of the members of seven large families."

The principal fiesta is that of *Santiago* in July. In it there were masked dances, and unlike the reports given in other coastal towns, it was said that many of the dancers were the same from year to year. While some of them dance because of having made a promise, others do it just for the fun of it or because they get handouts from the homes.

There are two government run schools in the town, each going through the fifth grade. In addition there are two private schools run by private individuals which give the entire primary education. Each of the *comarcas* also has a school of one grade.

12. LA ORILLA

La Orilla is a small *caserío* of countrypeople located on the road between Nandaime and Granada. Composed almost entirely of *ranchos*, it has a group of houses along the side of the road, and a few other scattered out elsewhere. Almost all the people of La Orilla are *mozos*. Many also rent a little land from one of the *haciendas* to plant on. The rent is sometimes paid as a given sum, and sometimes in terms of the value of the harvest. A great many of the men of the community go annually from January to May to cut sugar at the sugar plantations. The women also work regularly in the nearby *haciendas*.

Even though La Orilla is a poor community, the local cemetery is divided into two sections; those who can afford it are buried in a lined pit in the section *"más arriba,"* while the others are buried *"más abajo."* There are a few *finqueros* in the town and some who are better off from other means. In general, however, the population is poor.

Since it is close to Nandaime, and both the municipal and parish headquarters are there, much of the ceremonial and official life of the community is oriented towards the larger center. *Santa Ana*, the patron of Nandaime, comes to La Orilla for a Mass and procession just prior to the major fiesta in Nandaime. Some of the local people participate in the masked dances in the town. The community has a small chapel, but it has no saint as yet. Some of the people attend the fiesta of *Esquipulas* in the town of La Conquista. When someone dies, it is the local custom for the women to participate in the novena, and the men to attend the funeral. It was reported that there is no local *curandero* in the village and that most of the people went to see a doctor in Nandaime when they were ill. There are three schools of one grade each in the community.

La Orilla is one of the numerous small rural communities which make up the *mozo* population of the Pacific belt region. These communities are culturally more or less dependent upon larger municipal centers depending upon their proximity.

13. RIVAS

Rivas is the capital of the department of the same name. It is located on the relatively level coastal area near the Lake of Nicaragua. It was possible to spend a very short time in Rivas during the survey, and it turned out to be quite difficult to get an adequate informant in the time allowed. Consequently, relatively little was learned concerning the countrypeople living nearby. The informant claimed that the rural population was strongly "Indian," and that there were some Negroes who had come over from the Atlantic coast. The beginning of a negroid component in the otherwise mestizo population is significant, since the Costa Rican Province of Guanacaste which borders Nicaragua to the south of Rivas has a noticeable negroid component in the rural population. This suggests that the movement of the Negro population has been, at one time or another, up the San Juan River, into Rivas and south into northwestern Costa Rica.[23]

The town of Rivas itself had a population of just under 5,000 in 1950, and an even larger rural population. It is dominated by the administrative centers of the civil, judicial, and military. While there is a paved road all the way to Managua, transport in the countryside is still predominantly by ox cart, mule and horse. Carriages ply a taxi trade in the town as they do in some of the other larger Pacific belt towns. The majority of the rural people are *mozos* and own or rent a small parcel of land for their own cultivation. It was said to be a custom for a man to rent out a piece of land which needed clearing, to cultivate it, and then sow it in pasturage and return it to the owner.

The town has a number of schools, both public and private, two of which provide education for a few years above the primary level. In the *comarcas* the schools are usually of one grade each. There is a public health unit in the town and an office of agricultural extension. The town has an active religious life, but they no longer hold masked dances. These are still to be found in some of the *comarcas*, however.

VI. THE SPANISH-SPEAKING INDIAN OF NICARAGUA

1. THE BACKGROUND OF CONTEMPORARY INDIAN GROUPS

It is not the purpose of the present paper to review the general history, insofar as it is known, of the Indian cultures of Nicaragua. In order to have some understanding of the contemporary Indian survivals in the country, however, it will be necessary to provide a brief and very generalized picture of this history.

At the time of the conquest, there were at least two, and possibly three general culture types in Nicaragua. The first of these, which we will call the Meso-American, was found in a group of tribes which inhabited the Pacific belt region from the Bay of Fonseca to the Gulf of Nicoya. In what is today Nicaragua, they included the groups which were called the Nahuatlato, Subtiaba, Nagrandan, Mangue, Nicarao, and the Orosi. These tribes spoke different languages, but in all cases, it is believed that the languages which they spoke

---

[23] Doris Stone (in communication) feels that this negroid component derives from the slaves formerly used on large *haciendas*. The Guanacastecan, she notes, has often gone to Puerto Limón to work and has not objected to interbreeding with Negroes there.

were affiliated with language stocks which were to be found further to the north. They were related to the general stocks to which Mexican languages belonged. With the exception of a few isolates further south, they were the southern most extension of the Meso-American languages. The tribes which spoke these languages seem in general to have had certain other aspects of their cultures in common with the more northerly Meso-American groups.

The second group includes the peoples who lived in the Atlantic coastal areas and the center of the country. The main groups here were the Miskitoan peoples, who lived on the east coast itself, the Suman who lived in the uplands, and the Matagalpan, who lived in the central highlands region. Each of these terms refers to what is supposed to have been a distinct, but related linguistic group, and all three are generally considered to be affiliated with the general Chibchan languages found further south in Central America and in northwestern South America. Not only were these groups related linguistically to the Costa Rican, Panamanian, and Colombian peoples, but they also shared numerous other culture traits with those peoples.

Basically, then, we may say that the Nicaraguan population at the time of the conquest was divided into two quite different kinds of Indians; one, those living on the Pacific belt, were generally oriented culturally towards the north, and the other, living in the highlands and on the Atlantic coast, were oriented towards the south. However, there is a reasonable possibility that a third group should be distinguished in this picture. The Matagalpan group, from the evidence at hand, lived in the central highlands of Nicaragua. Johnson[24] distinguishes a "northern highland" group in Central America which includes this Matagalpan group and the Lenca who occupied a considerable territory in the highlands of neighboring Honduras and northern El Salvador. Unfortunately, we have almost no information on the Matagalpa culture at the time of the conquest. For the Lenca, both their present culture and archaeological remains have indicated, according to Doris Stone, that they had strongly felt the influence of the Mayan-Mexican groups which bordered them on the west and south. We have no evidence either one way or the other, at present, which clearly indicates that the Matagalpa group were similarly influenced as were the Lenca; Stone mentions that archaeological monochrome ceramic-stone complex, which characterizes the north coast of Honduras and the east coast of Nicaragua, is also found in the Matagalpa region; whereas remains in the Lenca area show definite Mexican-Mayan influences. From this we would tend to conclude that the Matagalpa group would be better classified with the other southern oriented groups, the Mosquitoan and Suman, rather than being set aside as a distinct group with the Lenca. However, in view of the fact that they were territorially closer to the groups of Meso-American affinity, and that they were a highland group as were the Lenca and many of the Mayan and Mexican groups, they too *may* have received considerable influence from the north.

When the Spanish came into Nicaragua, the first permanent settlements

[24] 1948a, p. 61.

were made by people who came up the southwest coast from Panama. There was some conflict overland in Honduras between different conquerors, but the principal Spanish settlements were made in the Pacific belt and then in the highland region. The Spanish, after the first blush of exploration, did not like the Atlantic coastal plain and for practical purposes did not settle it. This Atlantic coastal area early received other influences, first at the hands of the buccaneers, most of whom were not Spanish, and later with the informal consent of English authority, through the attempt by the English to establish an independent but English dominated region. Added to this was the fact of the immigration of many English-speaking Negroes into the Atlantic area at a more recent date, and we have a general picture of the Pacific belt and highlands under the cultural domination of the Spanish, and the Atlantic coastal area under the cultural domination of the English. Culturally the English had much less influence on the Atlantic coastal Indians than the Spanish had on the Indians in their area of influence.

A gross picture of the acculturation situation is as follows:

Geographical territory	Indigenous culture orientation	Post-conquest influences
Atlantic Coastal	South American	English and Anglo-Antillean
Central Highland	South American (*possible* Meso-American influences)	Spanish Colonial
Pacific Belt	Meso-American	Spanish Colonial

From this it is apparent that each of the geographical territories has seen a different combination of culture-contact circumstances. The Atlantic coastal region, originally South American oriented, was subjected to non-Spanish cultural influenced; the central highlands, also oriented to South America, was under the Spanish colonial control; and the Pacific belt, which was oriented towards Meso-America, came under Spanish control.

In the communities surveyed in this study, we are concentrating on populations which have been dominantly Spanish in their cultural origin, and are not dealing with the Atlantic coastal area except summarily. In the highlands and Pacific belt, however, we are concerned with three populations which reflect the fact of this early indigenous difference in cultural orientation. The Indians in the San Ramón area of Matagalpa are among those which were originally South American oriented, but came under Spanish domination, and the communities of Subtiaba and Monimbó on the Pacific coastal belt are groups which were originally oriented culturally towards Meso-America, and then under the Spanish domination. If the picture were as simple as this, we would not expect to find Meso-American traits surviving in the Matagalpa groups. However, as has already been mentioned, it is likely that not only prior to the conquest, but probably also afterwards, these highland groups did receive influences from their Meso-American neighbors. A further influence of critical importance is in the manner of Spanish colonization in these regions. It was weaker in the regions bordering on the Atlantic coast, and since the contemporary Matagalpa group is in this region, it is likely that they were never subjected to as intensive acculturative influences as were the peoples on the Pacific belt. It is not possible to say on the basis of present research whether the fact of an indigenous culture difference or the fact of differential Spanish influence has had a greater importance, and in which particular aspects of the culture one or the other has been the most important.

In the sections to follow immediately, we are going to give brief descriptions of the culture of the San Ramón Matagalpa Indians and the peoples of Monimbó and Subtiaba. In thinking about these groups, we should keep in mind these background differentials which we have just discussed.

2. THE MATAGALPA INDIAN GROUP

The *municipio* of San Ramón lies an hour to the east of the departmental capital and principal highland city of Matagalpa. The population of the *municipio* in 1950 was recorded as 20,748, of which only 578 were town dwellers, and the remaining 20,170 were recorded as being rural inhabitants. Prior to about 1905, the town was a *barrio* of the *municipio* of Matagalpa, but at that time it was formed as a separate *municipio*. The informant, a mestizo resident of the town, estimated that perhaps 80% of the rural population of the *municipio* was what he termed *"indio"* and the remainder were mestizo *campesinos*.

The Indians, he said, all spoke Spanish, but pronounced it with an accent; they spoke what could be called a dialect of Spanish. The Indians are distinct, so far as this informant was concerned, from both the *campesino* population and the Indians of the Atlantic coast. The principal factors in the distinction were that they practice quite different customs and that they "looked" more Indian. The general area occupied by these Indians, as outlined on the writer's map by the informants, was bordered on the north by the Río Tuma; the line to the west ran from the settlement of Tuma in a line southwest approximately to San Ramón, then cut more south and included the settlement of San Dionisio, then went east to the Río Grande de Matagalpa, and followed the river, then in a line northeast to Muy Muy Viejo, and then north again to the Río Tuma. An informant from Boaco, interviewed in Teustepe, said that this Indian population was also to be found in the entire region to the north of Boaco, including the region around Muy Muy. This involves a region which almost doubles the size of the area outlined by the San Ramón informants. However, the Indians who were said to live in the region north of Boaco were not the sole occupants of the area; there is a mixed population of Indians and *"españoles."*

Discussions with other persons in Nicaragua left no doubt in the writer's mind that in the San Ramón region is to be found a large population of Hispanicized Indians which may be considered to be distinct from the Miskito and Sumo of the Atlantic coast. The Indians described as living north of Boaco are probably of this same group, but the section further east may consist more of the Atlantic coast population of Ulvas. In all likelihood, this group of Indians may be considered to be descendents of a Nicaraguan highland Indian group. While our data on the ethnic history of this area is very scanty, it seems reasonable to call these people *Matagalpa Indians*.

Matagalpa is a term which has been used by anthropologists to designate a language spoken in portions of Nicaragua, Honduras, and northern El Salvador at the time of or shortly after the conquest. Johnson, relying on other sources, summarizes as follows: "Information concerning the *Matagalpa* is limited. They spoke a language related to *Ulva* and *Sumo*. At the present time knowledge of them is confined almost exclusively to their language. The early information indicates that the language was spoken in northwestern Nicaragua and in southwestern Honduras. An enclave speaking a language related to *Matagalpa*, usually called *Cacaopera*, was identified soon after the conquest in northeastern El Salvador. Remnants, strongly Hispanicized, have been reported near Cacaopera in eastern El Salvador. Other groups have been located along the Nicaraguan-Honduran frontier, around the Pantasma Valley, near Estelí in Nicaragua,[25] and at Lislique. Another group has been located near the town of Matagalpa."[26]

Aside from the linguistic identification, of more importance for our understanding of the place of this contemporary group, is its possible cultural affiliations. In what is today Nicaragua, Doris Stone believes there were two basically Central American and distinct culture types to be found prior to the conquest. "The first is most clearly seen on the Caribbean coast, extending from the *Paya* area of Honduras through the Costa Rican mainland and into South America, and south through the *Ulva-Matagalpa* of southeastern El Salvador and southern Honduras and Nicaragua to the *Corobici* of the Nicoya Peninsula. The second is that of highland peoples such as the *Lenca* tribes of Honduras and El Salvador. The first is characterized by the monochrome ceramic-stone complex, referred to above, while the second shows evidence of subsequent influence from the Maya and the Mexican peoples."[27] Stone, then, tends to align the Matagalpa Indians not so much with the Lenca, archaeologically, as with the Caribbean coastal peoples, specifically the *Ulva*.

On the map prepared for the Handbook of South American Indians,[28] Johnson has placed contemporary *Matagalpa* groups in five specific regions: between the towns of Matagalpa and Jinotega; along the Río Estelí, just north of the town of Estelí; along the Río Pantasma; on the Nicaraguan-Honduran border between the Río Coco and the Río Choluteca; and in northeastern El Salvador. We will concern ourselves only with the Nicaraguan groups here. Although the writer made numerous inquiries, he received no report on Indians today living in the Estelí region. In San Rafael del Norte, which is the center surveyed nearest to the Pantasma River, similarly no reports were given concerning such Indian groups.[28a] In both places distinctions were made between countrypeople who lived in the valleys and those who lived in the *montaña*, and between the two

---

[25] Stone, correspondence. [26] Johnson, 1948a, p. 61. [27] Stone, 1948a, p. 187. [28] HSAI, Vol. 4, Map 5.

[28a] László Pataky reports that a population a few miles north of San Rafael is called "Indian" locally.

different forms of agriculture described earlier. The only population group which the writer visited, which might be considered Indian today although no one so referred to it, are the people living in the town and vicinity of Totogalpa, just south of Ocotal.

Thomas Belt, an English civil engineer who lived in Chontales for the four years prior to 1872, made a trip from Chontales up through Estelí, Totogalpa, and Ocotal to Dipilto in search of mine labor, and commented both for the Estelí region and the town of Totogalpa, that there were numerous Indians. Except for Totogalpa, however, the area in which these Indians which he mentioned lived seemed to be occupied also by a mestizo population.[29]

On the basis of this information, the writer would at present make the following guess as to the present status of the Matagalpa Indians. Through most of the central highland region, the people who some years ago might have been considered to be Indian have blended with the mestizo country population to such a degree that there is now recognized more to be a class than an ethnic difference. A person may be referred to as "looking" Indian, the use of certain traits, such as the tumpline, may be traditionally remembered to have been of Indian origin, and the dibble stick agriculture may be thought of as being of Indian origin as opposed to the Spanish origin plow agriculture; but such traits are not automatically classified in this way. The country population of most of this region is thought of as being more or less "cultured," or being richer or poorer, but not so much of being "Indian" and "non-Indian."

However, in the San Ramón area there is a marked contrast to this; there, a large population group is singled out as being specifically "Indian" even though they do not speak a distinct language. Although it is not possible on the basis of present knowledge to identify this group linguistically with that known as *Matagalpa*, it seems reasonable to assume that they are at least the descendents of some highland group which lived in this general region. Since the only highland group which has regularly been identified with this area is the *Matagalpa*, we may conclude that the San Ramón Indians are Matagalpa Indians, and for the sake of convenience, we will refer to them as such since San Ramón itself is a mestizo-Spanish town.

Before turning to the culture of the contemporary Matagalpa group, a word more about the Totogalpa population. The writer is not convinced that this group of people which Belt described in the last century should be considered as a Matagalpa group. It is his feeling, the reasons for which must be provided in another place, that this group may well be the descendents of the *Maribichicoa*, a group which Johnson says split off from the *Maribio* or Subtiaba people of the Pacific belt, prior to the conquest. Whether this can be demonstrated or not must await further investigation.

The description of the culture of the contemporary Matagalpa Indians to be given in the following pages is doubly deficient. During the course of the survey, which was devoted principally to mestizo populations, there was no time to make the trip which would have been necessary in order to spend time in some

---

[29] Belt, 1888.

of the Indian settlements. Consequently, the information gathered was second hand, from two informants in San Ramón, and both informants, although lifelong local residents, were mestizos and not Indians themselves. Fortunately, Mrs. Doris Stone made notes during a visit she made into the interior of this region and these she has written up as an appendix to this report. By utilizing both the data in this section and that provided by Mrs. Stone, the reader will be able to have some idea of the nature of the process of ladinoization which is taking place among the contemporary Matagalpa Indians.

The local settlements of the rural people of San Ramón are known as *cañadas*, not as *comarcas* as is customary in the rest of the republic. *Cañada* means literally a ravine, and so falls into the general pattern of referring to the settlements as valleys. In general the settlement pattern is highly dispersed. There are some cases where the houses are grouped in small *caseríos*, but generally most of the Indians live on their own *finquitas*, on their own land. Except to San Ramón itself and to some of the surrounding *haciendas* and *fincas* owned by mestizos and Spanish, there are no automobile roads through the *municipio*. Ox carts are not used by the Indians; the roads are usually too rough and do not permit. Transport of goods is done on mule back and more commonly by the men and women themselves. The informant made the distinction that "only *inditos* carry things; *campesinos* do not." Both men and women use the tumpline for carrying things, although it is more commonly the men who do this. Sacks are generally used when the tumpline is employed. If a mule is used, then the Spanish type *zurrones*, or leather sacks, will often be used. Women also carry things on their head and on their hip. Firewood, which is evidently the woman's task to gather, is usually carried on the head, as are baskets; *cántaros*, pottery water jugs, and children are carried on the hip. Animals are not used to carry water; this is a woman's task. Some Indians have oxen which they use to run their sugar presses and as pack animals. It was also specified that Indian women never rode horseback; this custom was limited to the *campesinos*.

The Indians subsist on both agriculture and hunting. The latter is not only important as a source of food, but also because the skins may be sold to the Nicaraguans. Although it was said that a few had plows, by far the greater number use the *macana*, *coba*, ax, and machete. The ax and machete are used for clearing the land, the *coba* for planting, and the *macana* for cultivating grains. The metal parts of the *coba* and *macana* are made by blacksmiths in San Ramón, but the axes and machetes are imported. The agricultural work is done equally by men and women; the informant thought that there was no distinction made in the types of field work done between the sexes. The family unit in this work consisted principally of the domestic unit, however, and did not include married children who lived in other houses. Exchange labor between two people is fairly common, but it seldom involves more than two. For threshing grains the low *toldo* is used. Stingless and stinging bees are kept for their honey and the fruit of the pejibaye palm is collected, although it was said that it was not usually specifically cultivated.

The main animals hunted are the deer, *saíno* and *guarda tinaja*. Shotguns, bows and arrows, and a lance with a metal point called the *fisgas* are used in hunting. The bow is a little over a meter long and uses a string of manila fiber. The arrow is about as long as the bow and has a metal point. The informant said that no blowgun was used. A basket-like, trapizoidal, fall-trap called the *tureca* is used to catch birds; grain is used as bait. Fishing is done principally with a harpoon, the bow and arrow, and vegetable poisons. A vine, *pate*, and the bark of a tree called *cuaginiquil* are sources of poisons. The Indians do not, said the informants, use gunpowder in fishing.

During the coffee harvest in the Matagalpa region a great many of the Indians come into the *haciendas* to pick coffee. The *haciendas* have large dormitories which house them during this period. The steady workers on the *haciendas* are not Indians but mestizos; the informants said they generally lived "better" than the Indians. The Indians do no spinning or weaving; the men usually buy their clothes ready-made, and the women buy the cloth and make their own. Very few wear shoes. The women generally wear their hair in two braids. Many of the women make pottery and use it not only themselves, but sell it to mestizos and town dwellers in the region. Both men and women make baskets.

The Indian homes are almost all of grass or straw; clay walls and tile roofs are limited almost entirely to the mestizo population. Unlike the nearby *campesinos*, the Indians keep their fire on the floor between stones and do not use the raised *fogón*. The beds are the *camas de varas*, beds made up of poles laid across branches. On top of this skins, *petates*, or sacks are placed. Food is stored in the house in the *tapesco*, the attic, which is reached by a log ladder. Some also sleep in the *tapesco*. Household equipment includes short sections of tree trunks as stools, called *tacos*. No stools with legs are used, but benches of boards or logs with legs are found. Very few use tables. Pottery, *bateas* made by the men, *jícaros* or gourds of various types are used. There is often a *troja* or extra grain storage room set next to the house. The mortar, called *cubo*, is used for coffee, sorghum, and rice, but not for corn. It is of a shape which differs from those generally found elsewhere in Nicaragua. While round, the top has a diameter considerably larger than the bottom and the sides are straight from top to bottom. The standard grinding stone is used, and generally ashes rather than lime are used in the making of the corn *masa*. The homes are usually rectangular, but with a single room which includes the kitchen, and a single door. There will frequently be a fence of sticks or occasionally barbed-wire surrounding a small *sitio* in which the house is located. Each person builds his own house.

The Indians nearer the town make purchases there, but those who live further away use small stores which are scattered in the rural areas. There is no Indian market, and all trade is carried on between individuals or with stores. The lack of an Indian market contrasts with the Pacific belt Indian groups which generally have markets.

The informants could tell of no political organization among the Indians which differentiated them in any way from the general rural dwellers. This type of organization is described in the section on political structure. The main difference between this and other areas is the presence of a *capitán de cañada*, a position which was not reported from any other center. Whether this is a special post set up because of the fact that the population is Indian, or simply because such a large proportion of the population is rural the writer cannot say. Each *cañada* has its own cemetery which is under the local authorities.

Family units are evidently quite stable among the Indians. A couple very rarely separates after settling down together. Formal marriage is quite common according to the informants, because at periodic intervals missions of priests go out into the *cañadas* and marry the people. Residence is generally neo-local, but with a strong patrilocal tendency. A new house is always built, if possible, on the land of the parents of the man. Marriage between cousins was said to be very rare; a couple will usually be unrelated. The *compadre* system is evidently not extremely strong, but *compadres* are sought for baptism, marriage and confirmation. All *cañadas*, except three, have a school with one teacher and a single class of boys and girls.

Unlike the *campesinos*, the men predominate in the religious activities of the Indians. Many of the *cañadas* have chapels and, where established, there are local Catholic associations which are responsible for them. These groups are composed entirely of men. It is customary to have a single *mayordomo*, a man, for a saint or holy day, and the man will hold the post until he wants to get rid of it or until the priest wants it changed. The *mayordomo* is responsible for collecting money for the fiesta of the saint or holy day. The saints celebrated are generally the same as those celebrated among the *campesinos*. The informant from Boaco said that the Indians attended the fiesta of *Santiago*, the titular fiesta of Boaco, every year and had masked dances. The informants in San Ramón said they did not use masks. Each family has its own image or *cuadro*, and celebrates it with a novena and fiesta. They get permission of the local authorities to have the fiesta. Novenas are also held when an adult dies and another is held at the end of the year. There is a fiesta at the end of the novena at the end of the year. In all these prayer sessions it is the men who "know how to pray," and not the women as among the *campesinos*. When a child dies, a fiesta and dance is held rather than the novena.

There are both men and women *curanderos* among the Indians; they use mainly herbs, patent medicines, and rituals in their healing. There are also numerous midwives.

The fiestas of the Indians are held with the music of the guitar and violin. They have "regular social dances," said the informants, but did not play any of the sports. They make *chicha* and clandestine *aguardiente* and both are used during the fiestas.

This general picture given of the life of the Matagalpa Indians in the municipio of San Ramón differs principally in details from the general life which could be described for some of the poorer *campesinos*. Many of these details are significant, however, and it is the writer's impression that further differences would be found were a field study to be made among this population group. Nevertheless, it serves to emphasize the fact that the *campesinos* today are a slightly different cultural blend of Indian with Spanish but that in some ways both the *campesino* and Matagalpa Indian population may be said to be a continuous population with difference in degree rather than in the kind of culture.

3. THE PACIFIC BELT INDIANS: SUBTIABA AND MONIMBO

All through the colonial and republican periods the wealthier Nicaraguans preferred to live in the Pacific belt. The major colonial cities of León, Granada, Managua, Masaya, and other concentrations of population were all on the Pacific belt. Early attempts were made at converting the Indians beginning with the famous peaceful conversion by Gil González Dávila. Reports from travellers at the end of the 16th and early 17th Centuries indicate that the Indians in some parts of the coast were making serious attempts to become acculturated to Spanish ways. Ponce [30] reported that the Indians of El Viejo, outside Chinandega, prided themselves on wearing Spanish clothes and of speaking Spanish even though they spoke very little of it. Vásquez de Espinosa[31] reported that all the Indians of this town were *Ladinos*, since they went about dressed as Spaniards. Nevertheless, in various places along the Pacific belt, there have remained isolates of Indian groups which have resisted total assimilation. Two such towns, or in fact *barrios*, were included on the survey; Monimbó, a *barrio* of Masaya, and Subtiaba, a *barrio* of León. The two are extremely different in many ways, and provide divergent illustrations of the course which acculturation over the centuries has taken.

A. Subtiaba

León is the second largest city of Nicaragua, and has been an important Spanish center since early in the colonial epoch. Up until the time of the survey the city could not be reached by automobile in the rainy season, although a highway from the national capital is under construction. For many centuries the town of Subtiaba was a separate *municipio* which lay just outside of León. Subtiaba was always thought of as being an Indian town, although for many years now the people have spoken Spanish and taken over Spanish customs. As León grew the outskirts of the city gradually reached Subtiaba, and the smaller town was incorporated as a *barrio* of the city. Today it borders on the section of the city known as La Ronda. In many ways, however, it has remained a distinct town. The city has not extended to it all its municipal services. Although a substation for telegraph has been established on the very border of the *barrio*, Subtiaba has no mail service and does not share in the León city water system. Water in Subtiaba must be taken from private wells.

It is hard to say whether the people of Subtiaba should be called "urbanites" or not; they live in the town area of León, their clothing is hardly distinguishable from that of the other poorer urbanites; they speak Spanish, and in most ways act just like other mestizos. On the other hand, there are some overt characteristics which stamp them as rural people. They generally go barefooted; the women carry things on their head; and their principal occupation is agriculture.

---

[30] Ponce, 1873.
[31] Vásquez de Espinosa, 1948.

Most travel to and from work is done on foot. Quite a few men have ox carts, made by carpenters locally. Some also have horses or mules, although donkeys are not common. Men generally do not carry things themselves. Quite a few of the men are fishermen; for this they build themselves *cayucos*, dugout canoes, usually about two and a half yards long.

Most men are occupied in agriculture. They own relatively little land themselves, so most must rent it. In addition to this a great many work on the *haciendas*. In their own work they use the wooden plow, the *macana*, and the machete. Those who do not have plows or oxen themselves will rent them. Many of the women work in both the *hacienda* labor and along with their husbands in the subsistence agriculture. Most men will go to one of the sugar *haciendas* during the harvest season. Since there is no established credit system by which the small farmer can obtain advances on his crops at a reasonable rate of interest, many of the farmers must borrow money on their crop at a low value from the *tierra tenientes*, the landowners. This frequently results, through repeated borrowing during the cultivation period, in the entire crop having been sold at a low price before it is harvested.

Some of the men hunt the animals in the region: rabbits, the *garrobo* or male iguana, deer, the armadillo (*cusucu* is the local name), the *guarda tinaja*, pigeons, *saino*, and so on. Alligators and *tigres* are hunted for their skins which can be sold. A number of the men spend most of their time fishing in the sea, using either hook and line or *esteros*. A number of the women get clay from a place between León and El Sauce and make pottery. These women usually do not participate in field labor since they can earn money with their handicraft. Some women will sew their own clothing, others will buy it ready-made. There is practically no industry in spinning, weaving or fiberwork. The men occasionally make a drum which is used during their social activities, or when they are engaged on some *fajina* work for the church or in cleaning the cemetery. Between themselves they rarely use exchange labor, preferring to work individually. The informant said that they did not trust each other very much for this kind of work. There is a market on the boundary line with León where the people of Subtiaba sell their produce of fruits, vegetables and some meat. There are small eating places and *chicherías*.

The homes in Subtiaba are almost all the *cañol* variety, with walls of corn or sorghum stalks and roofs of tile. Some few have walls of boards and some have straw roofs. The *bajareque* addition may be seen on some of the houses, but the general pattern seems to be the single rectangular building with a two-shed roof. The houses are generally set in *sitios*. Kitchens are generally in separate rooms or separate from the rest of the house. Grinding is done on a stone on the *molendero*. Some have the fire on the floor, others have a raised box of earth in which three stones are placed, and still others little kerosine stoves. Ashes are usually used in the *nesquisado*. The general kitchen equipment of pottery vessels, gourds, and a few enamel pieces are found almost everywhere. Some homes have ovens outside. Most houses have *tapescos* above the fire for storing cheese. The people sleep on cots or leather beds. According to the informant, they do not make much corn *chicha*, but do make *chicha de coyol*, or "palm wine" whenever possible. They also eat *palmito*, the heart of the palm.

According to the informant the community has no political organization outside of that of being a *barrio* of León. They have four cemeteries for the members of the *barrio* in which burial is free, and hold occasional work sessions to clean them. It was said that relatively few of the people were formally married and that separations were quite frequent. The women were the fixed feature of the homes, and there was a tendency for men to move about. Although it was said that in the middle and upper classes of León a temporary matrilocal residence is not uncommon, no such tendency was reported in Subtiaba. Although considerable respect is shown between *compadres*, there is no feeling against the children of *compadres* marrying. Different *compadres* are preferred for different siblings and for different occasions. In general, *compadres* were chosen more from among friends in the *barrio* than from among people in higher classes. The population of Subtiaba itself includes none of the upper class to be found in León. The people are generally of the same lower class and all are occupied in more or less the same pursuits. Those who wish to move up in the class system usually leave Subtiaba and take up residence in León or elsewhere. To the people of León, the people of Subtiaba are *"los Indios;"* they are set aside as not merely poorer people or lower class people, but are still thought to be ethnically different.

In religion, the women are generally more active than the men. There is an association of *Hijas de María*, but the other three religious associations, *Virgen del Carmen*, *Corazón de Jesús*, and *Santísimo*, (the last of which is also called *cofradía*) have both men and women members. One informant said that the men of Subtiaba were generally not as active as the men from the higher classes in León. The celebrations of *Corazón de Jesús* and *Santísimo*, as well as of *San Cristóbal*, *San Roque*, and the patron saint, *Santa Lucía*, are the responsibilities of *mayordomos* who may be either men or women. Two of the principal fiestas are *Santa Lucía*, in which there are *gigantonas* (called *el Pepe* and *el Enano*), dances, and rhymes are made up about people in the town, and the fiesta of *la Purísima*, which has the *gritería* and the dance of the Christians and Moors. The informant said that the *Corazón de Jesús* travels from house to house in much the same way as it does in highland communities. The church in Subtiaba is an old colonial structure, one of the tourist sights of Nicaragua. There is also a congregation of Baptists in the *barrio*; they have a small church of their own.

The informant felt that one of the traits which distinguished the Subtiaba culture from that of the neighboring mestizo population was the fact that the funeral procession always employed a band to play. In addition to this, a Mass, novena, and all night dinner is held which is attended by both sexes, with all women wearing black. No fiesta is held at the death of a child, however. There is a considerable belief in spirits to be found in the *barrio*, and many of the illnesses are attributed to witchcraft. There are *curanderos* who tend to specialize in various kinds of sicknesses and cures. There are also a number of empirical midwives, but some of the women are attended now by trained midwives.

There are four schools in the *barrio*, each of which has mixed classes and goes up to the third grade. All of the schools are in rented houses. There is also a night school now for reading and writing as part of the current national alphabetization program, and according to the informant, it was fairly well attended, principally by younger people who were not able to go to school during the day. The young men of the town play baseball as a sport, and while some are members of teams with headquarters in other parts of León, there is also a local club.

In the general overview, there is very little to distinguish the culture of Subtiaba, insofar as the information gathered during the survey permits, from the general small town and rural culture to be found elsewhere in the more densely populated region of Nicaragua. The fact that they are called *"indios"* seems to the writer to be a case of the survival of a traditional term for the group, even though in most respects the group has at present lost almost all characteristics which would warrant the use of the term. It was said that the people of Subtiaba "looked" more Indian, and this may be the case; the writer did not see enough of them to judge one way or the other. From the point of view of the general social structure of the region, the Subtiaba population must be considered as a segment of the general lower class which has tended to be kept somewhat distinct in the minds of the Leonese through the use of the traditional term of *indio*.

B. Monimbó

Like Subtiaba, Monimbó is an old town, established at least by the end of 16th Century. Also like Subtiaba, it used to be a distinct settlement. Vásquez de Espinosa says that the town lay at a distance of a league from Masaya; today, Monimbó is a *barrio* of Masaya, with nothing more than a drainage ditch separating the one from the other. Again similar to Subtiaba, the people of Monimbó do not particularly benefit from the fact of being within the municipal jurisdiction of the larger town; they have no city water supply or other services which might be extended to them as townspeople.

For transportation the people of Monimbó generally carry their own goods. Only a few of the more wealthy have ox carts, and quite a few of them have mares which are used principally for travel. Women carry things on their heads, and the men carry in an *alforja* or in some cases will carry cargo in net bags on their heads. It was said that up until fairly recently, the tumpline used to be used but is no longer.

Today the plow and the *macana* are the principal cultivation implements. Years ago the *espece* was the main implement used and no one used plows. The main crops planted are corn and yuca; some rice, beans, *quiquisque*, and tobacco, are also cultivated. A small storage place is usually kept in the kitchen for the grains and tubers. Almost all the men in Monimbó are agriculturalists. They do not hunt or fish. While some have small pieces of land, the great majority of them work on *haciendas* or as *mozos* on *fincas*. Until about ten years ago the women did not work in the fields, but in recent years they have taken to working alongside the men in the *hacienda* labor. They usually work in certain types of activities, the harvest of cotton, sesame, and tobacco. Among themselves it is not the custom to work in exchange labor; they used to do it years ago but it is no longer practised. Most of the men return to their homes every night; very few go off to the plantations for the harvests or remain away for long periods of time.

While most of the people of Monimbó make their own furniture, cure hides as they need them, and some have ovens and bake bread, the principal craft of the *barrio* is work in fibers. The hats, bags, brooms, and *petates* made in Monimbó are sold eventually in many parts of the republic. Everyone, men, women, and children make hats; among the age and sex groups, however, it is probably the little girls who spend most of their time in this work. While pottery is made by some of the people who live in another *barrio* of Masaya, it is not a handicraft of Monimbó. On the border between Monimbó and the rest of Masaya is the *tiangue*, a type of market where the people of Monimbó sell their woven products.

Although the rest of Masaya is built in the general Spanish plan of rectangular blocks and *adobe* houses, the houses of Monimbó are scattered about the *barrio* in what initially appears to be no specific order at all. It is as if one walked from a forest into a wooded clearing and the houses were arranged rather at the will of the owners. The homes, which are called *posadas* by their owners, are generally made of poles or cane and have roofs of straw. There are frequently groups of two or three of them set close together. Each home is generally divided into two rooms, one being the *salita* and kitchen, the other being the sleeping room. Generally the fire is on the floor, but in some houses it is raised with the three stones set in a box of earth. There is a *molendero* for grinding corn, a great deal of pottery which comes from Diriá, Catarina, and other towns, miniature wooden chairs, the three legged stools called the *pata de gallina*, usually a small table on which is kept a *santo*, and the *cama de palos* with *petates* on them. Round wooden *bateas* are made by the men and used; the women often have a single metal *cántaro* which is used for carrying water to the house. On a tree near the house one may see the *wispal*, an ingenious device for collecting rain water. The *wispal* is simply a large multiple leaf palm branch which is tied to the main trunk of a tree with the leaves pointed up. The lower part of the branch hangs down away from the tree over a pottery jar. When it rains, the water which is collected by the branches and leaves of the tree runs down the trunk and much of it is drained down the leaves of the palm into the jar. Hammocks are rarely used by the people of Monimbó nor is it the custom to have a *tapesco* over the rafters. White corn is preferred for making tortillas and for this lime is used in the *masa*. For *tamales* it was said that ashes were preferred, since it removed the germ and made the *masa* smoother and whiter. As elsewhere in the countryside, *tortillas* are cooked on *comales* of pottery. For grinding corn most people in the town have the first grinding done by machine in the town, then do the final grinding by hand on the stone to make the *masa* finer. Both men and women smoke cigars which the women make of the tobacco grown by the men. The mortar does not seem to be very common in Monimbó; most people have their rice processed by machine in town.

For distances the writer was told that the people of Monimbó used a measure which consists of the distance between the fingers when one's arms are outstretched. This is called the *bordón*; it is somewhat standardized since a man may say that "his *bordón*" is actually a *bordón* plus two fingers.

Monimbó is a *barrio* of the town of Masaya, and as such is subject to the municipal officials of the larger town. However, Monimbó is also subdivided and has a series of local authorities. Within Monimbó there are two *barrios*, *Arriba* and *Abajo*. Each has an *alcalde* who is appointed every year. The people responsible for the appointment of these *alcaldes* are the *principales*, a group of older men who have been *alcaldes* before. At present, there are eight *principales*. Besides appointing the *alcaldes*, they also name *regidores* to assist the *alcaldes*. There are three *regidores abajo* and five *arriba*. The reason given for the difference is that the people *abajo* do not like to help the *alcalde* so much. Formerly there was another set of lower echelon officials called *mandones* who were general errand boys for the *alcalde*. These positions do not exist any more. The sign of the *alcalde*'s rank is his *vara*, a long, thin, polished pole with a small gilt cross on the top, and a large drum which is believed to be over 200 years old. The *vara* and drum are passed on to the new *alcalde* every twenty-fifth of December. At this time there is a prayer session in the old house before they are taken to the house of the new *alcalde*. The *alcalde* does not have a special building, but carries on whatever business he has from his home.

The functions of the *alcalde* today are limited. He calls the people together if the officials of Masaya or the national government wish to talk to them, and he is responsible for calling people out for the cleaning of the cemetery. Only the *alcalde* of *Abajo* is responsible for this last task. According to an informant from Masaya, the *alcalde de vara* from the *Barrio Abajo* of Monimbó also holds the position of *titante*, the official representative of the entire Indian community of Monimbó to the Nicaraguan officials. There seems to be some minor ill feeling between the two *barrios* of Monimbó, because an informant in one explained that the other had more "bad people" in it. According to a Masaya informant, Nicinomo is the only other town which has an *alcalde de vara* organization similar to that of Monimbó. The writer was unable to verify this.

Many of the couples in Monimbó are not married formally, but they tend nevertheless to maintain very stable unions. There is evidently very little tendency to break up a union once established. Residence is basically patrilocal; a woman will go to live in the home of her husband's parents until a new house can be built. The new home is usually built very close to the home of the parents of the boy. The building of the house is aided by people from all over the *barrio*. While there seems to be no tendency for endogamy within either of the *barrios* of Monimbó, there has been a tendency to marry within Monimbó itself. In recent years there have been more frequent marriages with people outside, but the tendency is still to marry within.

Compadres tend to be sought from among those who are somewhat better off economically. The children of *compadres* are not permitted to marry because they are thought of as siblings. The incest prohibition in Monimbó extends even up to cousins. A *compadre* may not come from one's own family.

There is evidently little tendency for specific families to retain leadership in the *barrio*. The *alcaldes* are chosen because of their ability and activity, not because they come from particular families. Aside from minor wealth differences, there is no recognized class system within Monimbó itself. The people of Monimbó, however, like the people of Subtiaba, are considered by the people of Masaya to be not only a much lower class, but Indians. There are recognized both ethnic and class differences.

The celebration of religious fiestas is in the hands of a series of *mayordomos*, men. Each *mayordomo*, who holds the post for a year, is responsible for the *cuadro* of the saint during the year and keeps it in his home. For each *cuadro*, in addition to the *mayordomo*, there is also a *patrona*, a *tenienta*, and an *alguacila mayor* who are all women. The *mayordomo* and the *patrona* each give the same amount of money for the fiesta, while the *tenienta* gives somewhat less. Also, the *mayordomo* names seven or eight men as *diputados* who are to help him. The *tenienta* is named by the *patrona*. Each year the *mayordomo* and the *patrona* name their successors for the coming year. Until 1910 or 1915, according to an informant in Masaya, the *mayordomos* of Monimbó used to have *cofradía* lands from which funds were taken for the sponsorship of fiestas, but at that time the *"políticos"* descended on the town and took the lands away.

Monimbó has no regular church of its own; most of the celebrations are held in the churches in Masaya. The writer was told that during the last century people of Monimbó still used occasionally to go to the shrine of Esquipulas in Guatemala and to have made the trip was considered a great distinction. No one has gone for many years now. There are still pilgrimages to *el Señor de Esquipulas* in the town of La Conquista nearby and to a shrine in the Department of Rivas. The *Barrio de Arriba* has a chapel or *hermita* to which some of the processions go from the main churches.

Prayers in the home are quite common. Most people hold a novena with singing for the saint which they keep in their home. For these and the novenas held on the occasions of death, a man who knows how to pray is asked to lead. There is one man who knows particularly well how to pray and he has trained various others to do it as well. Whether or not a novena is held depends upon whether the family can afford the expense or not.

Various ideas concerning sickness and curing were related to the writer in Monimbó, and some of these have already been described in an earlier section. Besides these, there were some which were not mentioned elsewhere in the survey. Small babies are said to fall ill of the *caída de mollera*; the fontanelle, is said to fall and choke the child. It is cured by women specialists who are midwives, masseuses and *curanderas*. These same women are called in on various childhood illnesses. It was said that malaria was thought by some in the *barrio* to be a type of *frío* which could be cured by some *curanderos* who used certain vegetables in the cure.

It was mentioned that during a girl's first pregnancy she was hidden. Unfortunately, no further or more specific information was gathered on this. An informant from Monimbó said that if anyone got sick, the people of the *barrio* were very friendly and helpful; they would come to sit up with the sick person, to help, and would stay over night if necessary.

There are a number of mixed schools of two grades in the *barrio*. For any further education, which most do not get, they go over to Masaya.

Monimbó strikes the writer as a town which has much more right to be called "Indian" than does Subtiaba. The preservation of various customs such as the colonially established *alcalde de vara* organization, certain disease concepts, the dominance of men in religious and praying activities, the stability of conjugal unions, the patrilocal residence, the scattered residence town plan, and some other customs which were said to have disappeared recently, such as women not working in the fields, the preferred use of the *espece* in agriculture, and the tumpline in transportation, are all suggestive of an Indian community rather than a Spanish or mestizo town. The political organization, although obviously of very limited function, is nonetheless in essence the same type of age-hierarchy structure which is still found today in the Mayan highland villages.

Of course, from the point of view of the resident of Masaya, the people of Monimbó are not only *"indios"* but are also of the lower class. In this, they have the variety of differing customs to point to as well as the fact that the Monimbó people are in fact for the most part agricultural *mozos*.

VII. CONCLUDING NOTES

As is the case with the other reports in this series, the data presented is directed principally at providing a general picture of the cultural situation in the country involved. Nevertheless, there are certain points of interest which can be derived from the information and a series of concluding notes is as good a place as any to give voice to them. While the following subjects are interrelated, as are the various phases of the culture and economy of the Nicaraguans, each is discussed as a theme in itself.

1. THE CENTRAL HIGHLANDS AND THE PACIFIC BELT REGIONS OF LADINO CULTURE

Mention has been made frequently of distinctions which were noted during the course of the survey between the communities of the central highlands and those of the Pacific belt. Such observed differences received further support from census taken in 1950 with respect to population density, rural-urban proportions, size of laboring population and landholding group, form of the family, and even in the relative predominance of the Protestant religion. There may be no single cultural trait which can be said to be exclusively characteristic of one of these two regions because there has been considerable movement over the centuries between them, and there is no geographical boundary which prohibits the diffusion of ideas or the movement of peoples; nevertheless, the regions are distinct and have been so through most of their history.

The main factors which have tended to shape the cultures of these regions occurred at at least three distinct historical levels. It will be remembered that in the discussion of the contemporary Indian groups of the Spanish-speaking region the fact of different aboriginal background was mentioned. The Pacific coastal belt was occupied by Meso-American peoples, while the highlands were occupied by a population which had a culture which was more closely related to the Indians to the south. The factor of the different aboriginal backgrounds is specifically evident in comparing the contemporary cultures of the Monimbó and the Matagalpa Indians. Until recently, women did not do agricultural work in Monimbó; women have done agricultural work regularly in the San Ramón area. Aboriginally, the tribes with Chibchan affinities and with a culture similar to those of the South American tropical forest usually were more dependent upon hunting and fishing; as a result, this more important work was handled by the men, and the women were frequently solely in charge of the agriculture. In the Meso-American groups, on the other hand, where the cultivation of corn and beans provided the subsistence staples, agriculture was predominantly in the hands of the men. From this background we have the situation today of the Matagalpa Indians, where women work in the fields, located in the highlands where Ladino women today usually do not work in the fields; and Monimbó, where only recently women started working in the fields, located in the coastal belt where Ladino women have worked in the fields for many years. The continued use by the people of San Ramón of straw or palm for roofing material is a retention of an Indian trait; the general Spanish trait in this region is to use tiles. The lack of any market center seems to be a holdover of the southern oriented culture; markets were fairly important in Meso-American societies, but not so in the Chibchan speaking tribes further south. The presence of a market in both Monimbó and Subtiaba probably reflects this old Meso-American pattern. The use of the bow and arrow among the San Ramón group is a southern trait, not a Meso-American trait.

In certain instances, then, we may distinguish certain trait differences which have been carried over from differences in the aboriginal societies. There is a second level, however, which derives from the colonial policy exercised by the Spanish towards the Indians. The fact that Monimbó and Subtiaba are nuclear towns and that the Matagalpa Indians live in a dispersed fashion are probably the result of the fact that the Spanish were much more concerned about reducing the population in the Pacific belt region where they (the Spanish) were settling and needing land than in the more distant highland region where they were not immediately interested. Colonial policy more often made for convergence of traits, however, than for differences. The importance of men in religious activities is clearly a trait which distinguishes the "Indian" societies today from the Ladino lower and middle class, but in some part it is due to the fact that the priests placed the running of the religion in the hands of the men. This in turn reflects a native pattern which was similar in both aboriginal regions; men were the religious leaders prior to the conquest.

Differences in patterns of colonial culture are probably of much greater importance than could be indicated by the survey. Two striking coastal traits, the *gritería* held for the fiesta of *la Purísima*, and the masked dances, seem definitely to have depended upon the nature of the religious customs fomented by the clergy. Without doubt the forms of the aboriginal culture played an important role in the early development here, but on the basis of the superficial research involved in the survey, it is impossible to analyze their relevance. Similarly, the fact that the façade of the highland churches generally differs from those of the Pacific belt indicates that possibly different religious orders were at work.

The third level, and by far the most important from the contemporary point of view, are the influences which have tended to produce differences in the Ladino society. Even with the fact that a great portion of the population of Nicaragua is in some degree of Indian descent, and that traits of an Indian origin may be distinguished, the Ladino culture of the country is predominantly Spanish in origin and variations in it seem to be predominantly due to variations in postconquest history. The two factors which impress the writer as having been most important in shaping the development of the modern Nicaraguan town and country culture besides the variations in the colonial culture patterns mentioned above, are environmental variables and variations in the basic economy and economic organization.

The environment has played a dominant role in the reinforcement or rejection of certain culture traits. The Spanish introduced the tile roof and the *adobe* wall. The environment decided whether there was to be adequate clay for the tile and whether it would be an easy adaptation for the Indian population. A population accustomed to living in the good ventilation of a cane house with a grass roof may not easily take to a damp, unventilated *adobe* building. Furthermore, tile introduced a new economic element, since someone had to make the tiles and they therefore were more costly than grass. The tile roof has taken over principally in the highlands and in the towns of the lowlands. The countryside of the Pacific belt has predominantly *ranchos* today. The environment played a role in the successful adaptation of the Spanish wooden plow. The plow and oxen could go where the land was level enough, but it was not adaptable to the rough land found in the highlands and in some of the coastal uplands, or even in the freshly cutover fields of the coast where stumps and roots still were plentiful. Consequently, environment helped in the retention of the digging stick agriculture of Indian origin so that the new and the old are found side by side today. In the same way that the environment affected the use of the oxen and plows, it restricted the useful range of ox carts; they too had to be used in relatively level land. In the rougher land man and woman continued to be important bearers of burdens, and the mule, the cargo ox, and to a lesser degree, the horse, were introduced as replacements where they could be afforded.

Probably of greatest importance for the general way of life of the people has been the nature of the economic organization. This is clearly apparent during the recent period. There are four traits which distinguish the highlands from the Pacific belt perhaps more clearly than any others. They are the predominance of an *hacienda* economy with the associated *patrón-mozo* relationship in the Pacific belt, and a predominantly small landowner economy in the highlands; the presence of exchange labor in the highlands, and not in the Pacific belt; the fact that it is common for women to work in the fields in the Pacific belt, but it is not common in the highlands; and the predominance of free unions on the coast and of marriage in the highlands.

These traits are interrelated, and if any one may be said to be critical, it is the presence or absence of the *hacienda* economy. With the dominance of the agricultural *hacienda*, and some of its specialized forms such as the sugar harvest, labor for women in the fields is at times an economic necessity for the *hacendado*. The presence of free unions in the Pacific belt is doubtless tied up with this fact as has already been mentioned in an earlier section. Exchange labor, too, is dependent upon the presence of a population in which each person has some work to do, but not an excessive amount; it is related to a subsistence agriculture economy, not to a cash agriculture economy. On the coastal belt where land is either cultivated in large quantities by paid labor, or in minute sections as a secondary subsistence means, there is no real place for exchange labor.

The differing nature of the economic exploitation in the highlands and on the coast is in itself derived from a variation in the colonial culture pattern, and there is evidence that today there is a gradual tendency for the highlands to develop an *hacienda* economy. This probably really began some years ago with the introduction of coffee as an important cash crop. Prior to this time the principal *haciendas* in the highlands were devoted to cattle; such exploitations did not require a large labor force and there was much land left for the small landowner and the *finquero*. Coffee, however, is a crop which necessitates a large labor force, and particularly so during the harvest season. Coincidently the harvest of coffee is a work in which an entire family can participate together. Coffee has not, as a result, had the effect of placing a strain on the solidarity of the nuclear family and of promoting free unions as is the case in some phases of the Pacific belt *hacienda* economy. Also, outside of harvest time, a labor force on a coffee plantation requires a steady force of men who will remain there for the harvest anyway. Again, this situation does place a strain on the family organization. The highlands, then, established with a general situation of family stability, formal marriage, and small landowners, is not converted to the coastal situation of unstable families and free unions by the mere presence of cattle and coffee *haciendas*. They, of course, have their effect on the landholding situation, and it is in this sphere mainly that they are being felt.

Another result of the presence of large *haciendas* which may be seen in some places, such as in a comparison of La Orilla on the coast with Chirincocal in the highlands, is that where there are small landowners, the rural population may be quite dispersed; where land is held principally by *haciendas*, the *mozos* usually are forced to live in a rather nucleated *caserío*. Because most of the land is owned by the *hacienda*, there is little land left for a dispersed settlement.

It may be seen that from the aboriginal times until the present, due in part to uncontrollable factors such as climate and terrain, and in part to historical variations such as differing colonial settlement and economic patterns, the central highlands have tended to retain traits which differentiate them from the Pacific belt. That the traits are interrelated is obvious; environment played a role in helping the Spanish to select the coast for large exploitations rather than the highlands; and the kind of exploitations they undertook had differing results in the social organization of the two regions. The differences in aboriginal cultures have now in great part been overshadowed by the vast ramifications of the economic system which has grown up during the colonial and republican history of the country.

2. THE MESTIZOISATION OF NICARAGUA

The population of the central highlands and Pacific belt of Nicaragua today is predominantly a mixture, racially, of Iberian whites and Central American Indians. There has been some intermixture of Negro in the southern portions, but this is evidently in a restricted zone and does not involve a very large part of the total population. The fact that the two main racial groups began with different cultures, that one was immediately socially subordinated to another, and that mixture was inevitable, has produced a fairly confused socio-cultural situation.

Why, for example, should the people of Subtiaba, who in almost every respect have a culture the same as that of the other rural coastal dwellers, be called "Indian"? They retain practically none of the traits developed in the colonial Indian society, such as the *alcalde de vara* which is retained in Monimbó, and there is no strictly aboriginal trait which they retain and other rural mestizos do not. The answer to the Subtiaba terminology issue is simply that for centuries Subtiaba was composed of a population which was racially Indian and which probably retained many aboriginal traits. Set so close to León, the cultural differences were clear. The terminology is then really a survival in itself, but instead of functioning to distinguish a variant cultural group, it is now used to distinguish a class group. The people of Subtiaba are no longer Indian in a cultural sense, but they may be called Indian, as the Nicaraguans evidently desire, as a means of distinguishing their lower social class.

The Subtiaba situation provides a key for understanding the pattern of mestizoisation which has taken place in Nicaragua. Let us state at the outset that we are not now concerned with race or race mixture; our subjects now are cultures and social classes. During the colonial period Indians who took on the dress and language of the Spanish were "Ladinos." These Ladinos were people who were no longer generally called Indians. People who were slower about making the changes continued to be called Indians. Since the Spanish of Nicaragua early established a class system with themselves in the superordinate position, as the Ladino class grew, it too gradually tried to establish itself in the class system. The only place it could take was above the Indian but below the Spanish. In this way, "Indian" became the term used to refer to a class of people who were below the Ladinos. In this way, too, it came to refer to any group of people, whether ladinoized or not, who were slower about changing their Indian traits. The Ladinos themselves probably played an important role in the retention of the label of Indian for a lower class.

The Indians of Monimbó, although more retentive of aboriginal and colonial traits than the people of Subtiaba, are Indians because they have been *relatively* more retentive than the other Ladino peoples of the area. Thus the use of the term Indian today is relative to a number of factors. The specific area is one; the specific time is another (if the Monimbó people dressed and acted as they do today one hundred years ago, they would have been called Ladinos); the relative clarification of the class system is another; the relative retention of aboriginal and colonial culture traits is yet another. The Subtiaba people generally use a plow in their agriculture, a Spanish trait; Ladino country people nearby may use the digging stick in *montaña* land, an Indian trait. But the Subtiaba people are called Indian because it has been so established in the social class system. The Matagalpa Indians are rural and are considered by the middle and upper classes to be socially equivalent to Ladino *campesinos*. But they are distinguished as Indian because they retain differing customs. Thus, relative to the time and place, the fact of different customs or the fact of a different place in the social class system may be the determining factor in whether a person is regarded as an Indian or not.

Over most of the Pacific belt and highlands today the population is culturally mixed; they have taken traits from both the aboriginal and the Spanish. The blending of traits has become such that in most places no further distinction is made between Indians and Ladinos except to indicate racial predominance. Thus Thomas Belt, in travelling from Chontales to Segovia in the 1870's, could say that here he met an Indian, there he met a Ladino, and clearly distinguish the one from the other, relative to the definition of that time. Today, for most of the heavily populated regions of Nicaragua, these distinctions have changed and one today can merely say that he met a poorer man or a richer man, a man of the lower rural class or a man of the middle rural class. In this case, there has been a change from the use of cultural criteria to relative standing in the social scale. The contemporary lower class in the rural areas have dropped off most of the aboriginal and colonial Indian traits which distinguished them as Indians 80 years ago; they have not had the opportunity to take over traits of the Ladino and upper class which required money and they have not had the social organization to develop a new series of traits. While they combine traits of Spanish and Indian origin, they have actually lost more of both. They are, like the *campesinos* of Panama, deculturated and the process of deculturation has left them as a part of the Nicaraguan social system, but in the lowest part of it.

3. THE POPULATION, SOCIAL STRUCTURE, AND THE ECONOMY

We have already reviewed the effects of the *hacienda* economy on the formation of family organization and marriage. In the earlier section on the social structure of the town and countryside, the obvious correlation between the sponsorship of the *hacienda* economy and the upper class was also mentioned. We now want to look briefly into the nature of the transition which the town and countryman of Nicaragua is witnessing today, and, if possible, to look slightly into the future.

The *hacienda* economy on the Pacific belt is old, but its expansion is new. What is today the largest sugar plantation in Central America, San Antonio, really got moving only at the end of the last century. The coffee industry of the highlands is only slightly older. Of even greater importance today is the introduction of mechanized agriculture. Nicaragua, perhaps more than any other Central American country, is seeing the mechanization of its plantations. This is occurring less rapidly in the highlands than in the Pacific belt where the level lands are more inviting to mechanization. The mechanization is a new factor in the general economic and social picture of Nicaragua.

Fifty years ago the wooden plow and the digging stick were still the symbols of the principal forms of agricultural exploitation. Also fifty years ago, the population of the country was only a little over half as large as it is now. During the intervening period, the population in the rural areas alone has risen from about 400,000 to almost 700,000. The rise in population meant that more land could be placed under cultivation by *haciendas* because more field hands were available. But the amount of land which could be cultivated did not increase in the same manner that it is now increasing with the introduction of mechanized agriculture.

While mechanized agriculture can take over some of the field work, the *hacienda* still needs a large labor force. Much planting and some cultivation can be done by machine; but some cultivation and most harvesting is still done by hand. So the rural laboring population is still needed on the *haciendas*, even if only in special seasons. Nevertheless, the specialization of the laboring force into certain types of *hacienda* work has already been felt. In Monimbó it was stated that the women began to work in the fields in numbers when the mechanized agriculture began. It is inevitable, however, that as mechanization increases, and as it becomes cheaper to do some tasks with imported machinery than with native labor, the rural *mozo* population is gradually going to be faced with a dilemma. Should they stay in the rural region and try to maintain themselves on a subsistence agriculture based on the wooden plow and digging stick, or should they move to the urban centers where they may work as laborers?

The economy of Nicaragua today spans the range from pre-conquest techniques to modern mechanization. Most of the population in the rural areas are limited to the less efficient of these, both through experience and lack of funds. If the mechanization proceeds and can produce foodstuffs at a low price, the people with the digging sticks will still have troubles making enough money to buy them. They are forced, for the time being, to continue a subsistence agriculture. While it was not possible to explore this phase of the situation in Nicaragua, the writer did not receive the impression that the urban expansion taking place reflected the expansion of an economically secure urban population. He did not receive the impression that there was so much industrialization in

Managua that hordes of rural laborers could come to the city to find work. There is at present a great deal of building and road construction, but this is likely to see its limit in the not too far distant future.

The future, as it appears to the writer, seems to indicate that for many years to come there will be a very large rural population which will be in part dependent upon available labor needs of the *haciendas* and on their own subsistence activities. As the large *haciendas* become more mechanized, the rural laborer will to some degree be thrown on the city, but many will also be thrown even more on their own subsistence activities. Unless a strong effort is made to familiarize them with more efficient techniques, and unless these techniques become financially available to them, the subsistence agriculture will continue with the wooden plow and the digging stick.

Nicaragua, like all Central American countries with the exception of El Salvador, has sufficient territory for the present. She should not be concerned that her population is expanding, if this were the only issue concerned. But taken together with the fact of traditional agricultural forms and the expansion of mechanized *hacienda* economy, an increase in population means that a large part of the rural population will gradually be unable to participate in the fruits of the economic expansion and unable to compete with it. This situation will in turn have its repercussions in the general social structure. The general class structure which is evident today, with the *mozo* and subsistence agriculturalist at the bottom, the *finquero* and town commercialist in the middle, and the *hacendado* and large business man at the top, will tend to be accentuated. Some of the middle group will participate more in the mechanized economy, others will either be reduced to the lower fringes of the middle group or move into some other occupation. The middle class farmer or *finquero* will have either to become mechanized or will be reduced to a subsistence level.

The upper class, which heretofore was based principally on the fact of traditional family position, is changing and will change further with the advance of the new rich, and the "upper brackets" will experience some violent changes.

It is not within the scope of the present series of reports to deal with the political implications of the social and economic situation discussed. Nevertheless it is worthy of mention that the accentuation of differences between a *mozo* and subsistence agricultural class on the one hand, and the middle and upper on the other, provides an extremely susceptible population group for the acquisition of radical ideologies.

The members of the *mozo* class will be facing increasingly difficult problems of economic survival; if satisfactory solutions are not provided within the framework of the present social and economic structure, they will very likely search for solutions outside this structure.

4. IMPLICATIONS FOR ACTION PROGRAMS

A. An obvious implication of what has gone before is the pressing nature of the improvement of agricultural techniques and credit facilities to subsistence agriculturalists. In the present trend, they are being left even further behind the national economic development than they were before. If they were a small element in the population, this might not have the national implications which in fact it does.

B. From the various data collected on cultural differences between country and town dwellers, and from impressions of middle and upper class urbanites, the writer was impressed that there is a greater cultural unity among the classes of Nicaragua than is to be found in certain of the other Central American countries. There is neither the strong cultural differentiation which exists between the Indians and Ladinos of Guatemala, nor even the rather wide gap which separates the Panamanian *campesino* from the urbanite. The Nicaraguan society has grown much more inward than has the Panamanian. With this, however, there has developed perhaps less sympathy between the various classes involved. Instead of saying that the rural subsistence agriculturalist is "low" because he has different customs, the tendency on the part of the upper class is to attribute his lowness to sheer stupidity and mental incapacity. The rural *mozo* instead of attributing the difference in his position and that of the upper class *hacendado* to wealth or political power, attributes it to a personal disinterest in anyone but himself. Even with many cultural similarities, there is a feeling of class stability reinforced by numerous attitudes which tend to personalize the attributes of the members of other classes.

This situation of cultural similarity could provide a background for people of one class to work within another. The welfare worker who comes from the middle class and attempts to carry on public health or agronomy activities in the lower class can depend upon a common bond of understanding about religion, can share in certain beliefs concerning local spirits, can both enjoy a baseball game, a social dance, and so on. The problems arise when one tries to carry on similar programs in two areas which differ in the fact that one has a *mozo* population while the other has a population of small landholders, where one has an unstable family organization and the other a fairly stable family unit, where one is dependent upon annual migrations to participate in certain harvests, and the other is more sedentary within their own locale.

The differences in the general social organization of the middle class group, both town dwellers and *finqueros*, and the lower class group, will present various problems. The *finquero* is, in a sense, a small *hacendado*; the subsistence agriculturalist is, in a sense, a *mozo* who is a little better off than most. Both live in the same region, in the same community or town. One considers himself "cultured," "educated," the other considers himself faced with practical realities. Whether in public health or agriculture, the approach to these people must be somewhat different, the manner of providing assistance must vary, and the kind of assistance given will of course be different.

C. At present the status of the Nicaraguan schools in the rural *cantones* does not suggest that they will be effective centers for the dissemination of teaching in agriculture or public health. The great majority of them have only one grade.

No particular rural inhabitant is concerned with the school long enough to consider it of very great importance. The school system itself is at present too occupied with improving its first task of providing a basic education in reading and writing to play a very effective role in other extension activities. Efforts are being made to improve the school system, but it would be unfair to ask them to dilute their effort at present with the addition of extension activities when the teachers themselves are in many cases only now becoming adequately prepared to do their traditional work.

The same is not true of the town schools. They too are weak, but most carry on at least three years of education. They perhaps offer a better chance for the incorporation of extension activities than do the rural schools, but one must also keep in mind that many of the students in the town schools are not being brought up to a life of agriculture.

D. There is a very important characteristic of Nicaraguan towns and rural communities which could be put to good use in the planning and development of local programs. This is the fact that for the most part, like Nicaragua itself, the community and town populations are ingrown. Few towns have seen extensive immigration of outsiders; most are composed of many interrelated families. This ingrowness permits of the existence of a communal interest which is not always present in Latin American Ladino or mestizo communities. The mutual aid society started in Tipitapa is based on this fact. The implication of this situation is that ventures in agricultural and public health promotion might well be carried on most effectively at the local level with a minimum of actual control and "running" from Managua. This does not mean that an outsider should rush in and start a school club or a parent-teachers' association. It does mean that the sensitive welfare worker can determine the nature of the local social relationships, discover what the local problems are, and build on these relationships from local resources. Financial help should not be withheld in a silly principle of depending completely on local resources, but with the provision that outside financing can be made on the condition that there is also local financing.

The fact (if it is a fact) that the ingrowness of many Nicaraguan communities could be utilized should not blind the worker to the fact that ingrowness is also a breeder of internal conflicts. The existence in a community of sharply defined classes, of competition for power in local activities within the classes, or of sharply divided feelings with respect to local leaders can have a detrimental effect on attempts to create locally sponsored programs. These situations sometimes can cause a local program to fail; in other cases they can be by-passed, and occasionally even used so long as the community is sufficiently ingrown to provide a situation of distinct social relationships.

E. There has been no attempt in the present paper to deal with the action implications of the cultural situation in the Atlantic littoral. The only paper on this subject, to the writer's knowledge, is that by Pijoan (1946). It is obvious from the literature available that the cultural differences between the Nicaraguan population of the highlands and the Pacific coastal belt on one hand, and the heterogeneous population of the Atlantic area do not allow of generalizations derived from one to be extended to the other. If and when the government or other agencies plan to do work in this zone, it can only be said that adequate preliminary study should be undertaken.

REFERENCES

HSAI Handbook of South American Indians, *Bureau of American Ethnology, Bulletin 143*, ed. by Julian H. Steward. Washington, D. C.

Belt, Thomas, 1888. The Naturalist in Nicaragua (2nd edition), London.

Conzemius, Eduard, 1932. Ethnographical Survey of the Miskito and Sumu Indians of Honduras and Nicaragua, *Bureau of American Ethnology, Bulletin 106*. Washington, D. C.

Dirección General de Estadística y Censos. 1945. *Anuario Estadístico de la República de Nicaragua*. Managua.

————, n.d. *Resultados del Censo Nacional de Población de 1950 (Avance de las Cifras Definitivas)*, Managua.

————, 1951. *Censo General de Población de la República de Nicaragua, 1950:* Vol. 1 *Boaco*, Managua.

————, 1952a. *Censo General de Población de la República de Nicaragua, 1950:* Vol. 2, *Carazo*. Managua.

————, 1952b. *Censo General de Población de la República de Nicaragua, 1950:* Vol. 3, *Chinandega*, Managua.

————, 1952c. *Censo General de Población de la República de Nicaragua, 1950:* Vol. 10, *Managua*. Managua.

————, 1954. *Censo General de Población de la República de Nicaragua, 1950:* Vol. 17, *Informe General y Cifras de la República de Nicaragua*. Managua.

Johnson, Frederick, 1948a. The Central American Cultures: An Introduction, in *HSAI*, Vol. 4, pp. 43–68.

————, 1948b. The Post-Conquest Ethnology of Central America; An Introduction, in *HSAI*, Vol. 4, pp. 195–198.

————, 1948c. The Meso-American Division, in *HSAI*, Vol. 4, pp. 199–204.

Pataky, László, Ms. *Nicaragua Desconocida*. In preparation.

Pijoan, Michel, 1946. *The Health and Customs of the Miskito Indians of Northern Nicaragua; Interrelationships in a Medical Program*. Ediciones del Instituto Indigenista Interamericano, Mexico, D. F.

[Ponce, Alonzo], 1873. *Relación breve y verdadera de Algunas Cosas de las muchas que Sucedieron al Padre Fray Alonso Ponce*. Madrid.

Salvatierra, Sonfonías, 1939. La Costa de los Mosquitos, in *Contribución a la Historia de Centroamérica*, Managua, pp. 397–545.

Squier, E. G., 1955. *Notes on Central America*, New York.

Stone, Doris, 1948. The Basic Cultures of Central America, *HSAI*, Vol. 4, pp. 169–194.

————, 1951. Una definición de dos culturas distintas vistas en la antropología de la América Central, in *Homenaje al Dr. Alfonso Caso*, Mexico, pp. 353–361.

Vasquez de Espinosa, Antonio, 1948. Compendio y Descripción de las Indias Occidentales. *Smithsonian Miscellaneous Collections*, Vol. 108. Washington.

Vitta, José, 1946. La Costa Atlántica, *Revista de la Academia de Geografía e Historia de Nicaragua*, Vol. VIII, No. 2, Managua, pp. 1–46.

APPENDIX

Brief Notes on the Matagalpa Indians of Nicaragua

By Doris Stone

The original extension of the indigenous group known as the Matagalpa included southeastern Honduras, part of eastern El Salvador, and the central section of Nicaragua, or better said, the departments of Matagalpa, Jinotega, and Estelí, with a tentative border at the northern margin of the fresh water lakes.[1] Today, however, they are reduced to the region of Cacaopera in El Salvador, and in Nicaragua, in the vicinity of the town of Matagalpa and the upper reaches of the Tuma River.

Their language seems to have disappeared, only a few words remaining; but from existent vocabularies collected in the nineteenth century and the beginning of the twentieth, a connection between the Matagalpan speech and the Chibchan dialects has been noted.[2] This suggests a relationship to the peoples of eastern Central America and Panama. Curiously enough, little or nothing has been reported on the life of the Matagalpa, possibly the most important paper, a treatise by the Franciscan fray Rodrigo de Jesús Betancur, was lost before it could be of use to science.[3] A brief comment concerning this group, however, has been preserved in an account of the accomplishments of Fray Margil de Jesús which was published in Mexico in 1763. The following excerpt presents unique ethnological data which even though possibly influenced by other cultures, nevertheless contains material which can be considered essentially connected with the Matagalpa.

1 ... "The people of Matagalpa, Solingalpa, Molaguina, Xinotega, and Muimui, all belonging to the same district, beheaded each week eight adults and children, and sacrificed their blood to the devil, misrepresented by their idols, in a cave which was the picture of hell itself; keeping the flesh for the horrible nourishment of their cruel brutality. They had skins of diverse animals, in order to transform themselves into them, through the strength of [the] diabolical pact; and they mixed stupidly with the demons, which appeared to them in representation of brutes. He gave them malignant powders, stones, and roots to kill, torture, hunt, and for harmful love affairs. He appeared to them in the form of a coiled serpent, and they gave him sacrilegious adorations. ..."[4]

The notes presented at this moment were made in 1950 on an exploratory trip in a vain effort to gather linguistic data, and are far from being sufficient. Among the groups visited were some at the *hacienda* La Algovia and others between the Yasica and Guasaca Rivers, tributaries of the Tuma River.

Communities.—The indigenous settlements of the Department of Matagalpa are known as *comunidades* or *cañadas*. The word *cañada* signifies a ravine, and with a creek or water-hole. In itself, the application of such a term to these com-

---

[1] See e.g., Lehmann, 1920, b. 1, p. 479; pp. 481–482.

[2] Lehmann, 1920, b. 1, pp. 479–482; Mason, 1940, pp. 75–76, 86–87; Johnson, 1940, pp. 112–113.

[3] Lehmann, 1920, b. 1, p. 480. [4] de Vilaplana, 1763 p. 116.

munities is interesting as it denotes to what extent the Indian has been pushed from the fertile arable land of his forebears. The exact data of the founding of the *cañadas* is not known. They have been important as reductions in the religious sense, as a source of supply for men in civil wars, and to a certain extent as a means of controlling workers for the large coffee *haciendas*.

The principle *comunidades* of the Matagalpa are El Horno, Sabana Grande, San Marco, Ilapa, El Jocote, and Iquililay. All are managed from above by the *jefe político* of Matagalpa, even though they are independent as respects the details of their internal organization. The *jefe político* names the *juez de mesta*, or as the Indians call him, *juez de la mesta*, or judge of the union, and the *capitanes de cañada*. The *alcalde* or mayor of Matagalpa names the *juez* or judge of the *cantón*. Both of these officials have a staff with colored ribbons or pieces of cloth on top as an insignia of their position. The *juez de la mesta* is in direct control of the *alguaciles* or police officers, while the *juez de cantón* serves as a councilman.

Each *cañada* names its individual president. The people who compose the population are known as *comuneros*. The land belongs to the community as a whole and cannot be sold. An individual is alloted from 10 to 50 *manzanas*.

Farming.—As a rule, there are from two to five heads of cattle per family. Farming is not done in a large scale, and is typical slash-burn agriculture. A digging stick is used for making holes when planting, and an armadillo shell or gourd is tied around the waist for carrying the seeds. The excuse for the scant cultivation is fear of taxes. Food grown for personal living includes corn, beans, rice, sorghum, and some ayotes (*Cucurbita peop* L. Sp.), varied types of bananas including the red, and plantains. Gourds of all sizes are grown for use in the household as cups, plates, and cut in pieces for spoons, etc.

Cotton, both white and brown, sugar cane, and tobacco are grown in the patio of the houses in very small amounts and only for personal use because of tax fears. Crude wooden sugar presses run by men or by oxen are occasionally seen. Chiote (*Bixa Orellana* L. Sp.) is also grown at the house sites. The pejibaye palm (*Guilielma utilis* Oerst.) is not cultivated today but was planted by aboriginal tribes in pre-Columbian times.

Foods.—The common meat proteins are chicken (*boluka*), wild pig (*singkol*), and eggs (*manjaré*). Vitamins are derived from *achiote* and flowers such as the *izote* (*Yucca elephantipes* Regal), and the inflorescence of palms. Chicha also serves as an important foodstuff despite the fact that it is a drink. Its principal base is corn but the Matagalpa add crude brown sugar to quicken the fermentation. Little coffee is used, the common substitute being *pico de pajaro* (*Cassia* Sp.). The dough for *tortillas* is prepared with ashes. *Tamales* are wrapped by preference in black *bijagua* leaves (*Calathea* spp.) called *guaylé*. They are said to give a better flavor and keep the *tamal* drier. One of the principal plates is *posol*, a corn gruel, which is prepared by grinding and boiling.

Food Storage.—Corn and rice are kept off the ground in shelters made of poles and roofed with grass, plantain, or banana leaves. The floor of the storage platform is generally of *capulín* bark. *Majagua* fiber is used in place of nails. One end is left open. At times, *tabancos* in the main house are used for this purpose.

Houses and Furnishings.—The typical house is rectangular in shape and made of wood with pole braces tied with *majagua* (*Hibiscus tiliaceus* L. Sp.) fiber. Grass or the leaf of a palm are the most common roof material. There is only one door, but often a partition of planks separates the sleeping quarters from the rest of the house.

Furnishings are simple. A *tapesco* or kind of storage shelf, sometimes used as a bed, is made of poles and hangs from the roof. Beds are made of wooden planks resting or nailed on to four legs which raises them off the ground. Skins, *petates*, or old sacks are put on top. Occasionally, hammocks are used. Low wooden stools called *machos*, with four feet and at times decorated with a protruding head and tail are customary. They are similar to those found among the Boruca and the Talamanca tribes of Costa Rica.[5] Baskets for storage purposes or for hens to lay eggs, dried animal skins, feathers, moss, medicines in bottles or in gourds hang from the house walls. At times a cheap print of a saint or even a small image is an added adornment. Stone *metates* are used for grinding corn, and a straight-sided wooden mortar serves for other grains. Salt is always kept in a gourd or wrapped in leaves above the fire to protect it from moisture. Ladders made from a single notched log are used to reach the *tapesco*. The hearth varies. The older method consisted of three logs in the center of the dirt floor. Today, however, stones and even built up hearths of wood and earth are common.

Hunting.—Whenever possible the Indian has an outdated shotgun or rifle, but the most common arm is the bow and arrow. The bow is made of wood called *guata* or *parrá*. Pita (*Aechmea magdalenae* André) fiber is used for the string. The arrows are similar to those of the Talamancan tribes of Costa Rica. The delicate part of wild cane (the *verolis*) is attached to the tip with wax and pita thread. Generally a knife blade forms the head, but for fishing barbed black palm or pejibaye is used. The bow is held almost horizontally with the arrow passing under the index finger. Lances with knife blades as points are also used for hunting. Traps made of cane are used for birds with grain for bait. They are similar to those seen today among the Lenca of Honduras.[6]

Fishing.—Fishing is done with the bow and arrow, a kind of harpoon made with a long nail attached to a wooden stick which in turn is tied to a cane, and with vines. These last are *guaslala*, a three-sided but rounded vine, which dyes the water a light iodine color, and the more common *paté* which is also three-sided but triangular. There are two kinds of *paté*; one which dyes the water green, and the other light red. Pregnant women are not allowed on fishing trips when vines are used. The husband washes his mouth out with the contaminated water before gathering the fish. Non-pregnant women stay on the river bank and make the fire with which to cook the catch. The vine is mashed fine before it is put in the water and the creek or river is dammed.

Dress.—The Matagalpa wear the same cheap cotton clothing as the ordinary laborer. Little trace of their ancient weaving remains. However, occasionally one sees a crude imitation of a spinning wheel with the wheel itself of cedar. This is more like an apparatus for making rope and undoubtedly is the result of

---

[5] Stone, 1949, fig. 7c 6. [6] Stone, 1948, p. 206.

Spanish colonial influence. For the most part the spun thread is utilized for household sewing, although a type of loom made with nails and no back strap is sometimes used for making cloth. Hide sandals are worn, the strap going between the big toe and behind the heel.

Handicraft.—Baskets of varied shapes and sizes are woven by men and women from a wild bamboo known as *carrizo*, which yields both green and brown canes. The bamboo is stripped and woven.

The region of Matagalpa has long been famous for its pottery, in particular a black ware. There are three common forms in the indigenous communities; flat dishes, rounded vessels with indented and rolled rims, and water jugs, both with and without a spout.

Carrying Devices.—The most common method of carrying is the tumpline, called *bambador*. Saddle bags or *surtunes* are bought or interchanged in the neighboring department of Chontales. On the whole, they are infrequently used.

Musical Instruments.—Drums are made of cedar and the hide of a calf's stomach. Sticks are used to beat them. The *nambiro*, a gourd covered with hide and a waxed stick in the center to be pulled in and out, is also used. In addition, there are the *caraca*, a stick with notches which is rubbed by another stick, and the *quijongo*, a long bow made of wild cane and a piece of wire or taut string with a small gourd fastened to it. This last is used to keep the rhythm and emits a weird noise when the gourd is covered and uncovered. Violins and guitars are also used.

Dances.—Certain *cañadas* have chapels and in these cases the principal task of the *mayordomo* is to collect funds to be used in celebration of the local patron saint's day. In some communities, mask dances are performed by the men on these occasions. These are Spanish colonial in character, in particular the dance of the *diablos* which is carried out on the day of *San Francisco*.

Birth.—At childbirth the mother stoops on the dirt floor of the house. The umbilical cord is cut with a knife made from wild cane. It is buried under the hearth and a fire is made on top. This assures that the mother will not have pains as she is warm.

Marriage.—Marriage takes place at an early age. When the girl is around eleven or twelve an arrangement is made by the boy's father or at times by the boy himself, with the father of the girl (or the mother if there is no father). The girl moves to the boy's house. This is done with the idea that the young people "grow up together" and that "the boy will not leave home." When the priest periodically vists the *cañadas*, he often performs a religious ceremony.

Death.—The godparent or nearest personal friend of a dying person is called to stay with him. The last bit of the dead man's food is kept for nine days in the house so his spirit will be able to eat. It is said that formerly this food was put into the grave with the body.

A cross is wrapped in black and called "in mourning." At the end of nine days there is a feast. At the end of the year, the godfather or the friend who assisted the dying man undrapes the cross. He and the neighbors often take this cloth to Mass at Matagalpa on the New Year and the closest relative of the deceased kneels on the step in front of the central altar with the material. This person says "Se deja el luto" (mourning is over). Then all return to the *cañada* and a feast is held in the house of the dead man.

When a child dies, there is a feast or dance but no nine day period of waiting or novena.

REFERENCES

de Vilaplana, Padre Fray Hermenegildo, 1763. Vida Portentosa del Americano Septentrional Apóstol el V.P. Fr. Antonio Margil de Jesús. Relación Histórica de sus nuevas y antiguas maravillas.

Johnson, Frederick, 1940. The Linguistic Map of Mexico and Central America. In *The Maya and their Neighbors*, pp. 88–114. New York.

Lehmann, Walter, 1920. *Zentral Amerika*. 2 vols. Berlin.

Mason, J. Alden, 1940. The Native Languages of Middle America. In *The Maya and their Neighbors*, pp. 52–87, New York.

Stone, Doris, 1948. The Northern Highland Tribes: The Lenca. In *Handbook of South American Indians*. B.A.E. vol. 4. Bulletin 143. pp. 205–217. Washington.

————, 1949. The Boruca of Costa Rica. *Papers of the Peabody Museum of American Archaeology and Ethnology*, Harvard University, vol. XXVI, No. 2. Cambridge

Part Four

GUATEMALA

1955

GUATEMALA

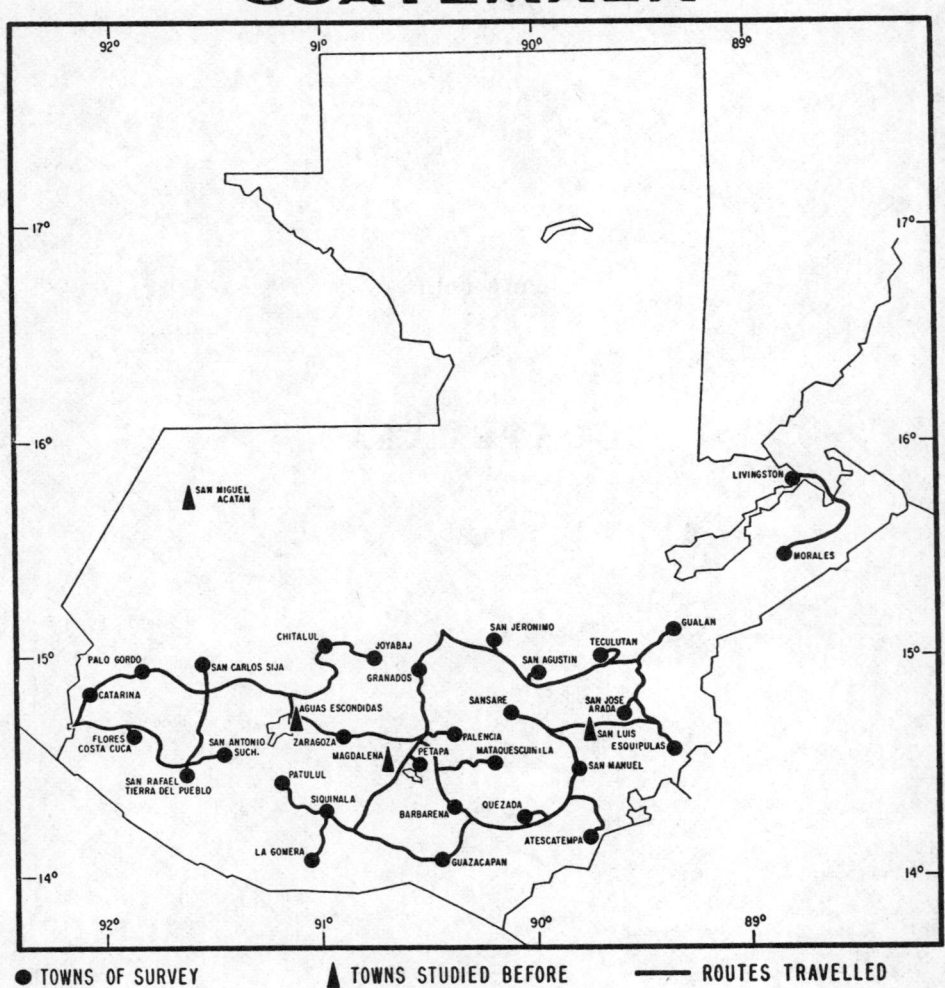

INTRODUCTION

This report is the third in a series which is intended to provide a picture of the territorial delineation of the contemporary culture areas of Central America and a preliminary description of the Spanish-speaking rural cultures of the various countries. The general method followed in the field survey and analysis was the same here as in previous studies in the series. The major exception is that part of the information on the towns in the center and eastern part of the republic were collected by Mr. Norman Craig, who accompanied the writer on the surveys. By doubling up on the work, it was possible to finish the field surveys in a shorter time than had been the case in previous surveys.

In the analysis and description which follows, certain data have been omitted, not because they are unimportant, but because the unusual length of the paper required that a line be drawn somewhere, and the writer felt that the data left out either would be the least significant in terms of the long range cultural picture or were available in some form elsewhere. The particular points omitted in the description are: schools and education; recreational customs (outside the fiestas); and extension activities in agriculture and public health.

An important factor enters in the present study which does not play a role in the others in this series. This is that the writer has been living in Guatemala since late 1950, and as a result, is much more familiar with the local scene than with the other countries. While this made him none the less a learner during the survey, it was possible for him to make interpolations in his material from Guatemala which he would have hesitated to make for countries where his own background did not permit.

As has been the policy in other reports, the cultural descriptions provided in the present report concern the Spanish-speaking population of the country. In Guatemala this means that about half the population is excluded from systematic consideration. The writer feels that this is fair because of all the populations of Central America, the Guatemalan Indian has received the most extensive study to date. Because of this the gap in our knowledge concerning the Guatemalan Ladino is particularly noticeable. For those readers who are not familiar with the literature on the Indian, a separate selective bibliography is appended so that they may be directed to some of the works available. It should be mentioned that there have been two studies of communities in which Ladinos were an important element, that of San Luis Jilotepeque (by Gillin, Tumin, and others) and Aguas Escondidas (by Redfield). Both studies provide extensive descriptions of many phases of the lives of the Ladinos, but as has become clear from the survey, there is regional variation in many aspects of the Ladino culture. Because of this, the reader is referred to these works for more intensive probing into types of Ladino culture which are described only briefly in the survey here presented.

The field work was facilitated by letters of introduction provided by the former Director General de Sanidad, Dr. J. Antonio Mendizabal; the writer was accompanied by and utilized notes taken by Mr. and Mrs. Manning Nash and Mrs. Adams on the western portion of the trip; Mr. Norman Craig on the center and eastern portions; and Mr. Joaquín Noval, in Mataquescuintla. The extensive knowledge of Mr. Walter Hannstein of the eastern piedmont and coast and the western part of the country has been a constant source of correction for the writer's ideas.

The Dirección General de Estadística was helpful in providing certain information which was not published in final form, and Dr. Ruth Puffer, statistician, aided the writer in the interpretation of certain data. The first draft of the present manuscript was read by Drs. John Gillin, Allan Holmberg, Robert Redfield, Sol Tax, and Nathan Whetten. To all these people, and especially to the last for his critical comments, the writer owes a debt of gratitude. To the numerous informants who provided the basic information upon which the descriptive information in this report depends, the writer wishes to express his special thanks, and regrets that the policy of the series prevents revealing their names in the publication. The writer accepts, of course, all responsibility for the form and content of the present report.

Due to recent political changes in Guatemala, certain changes have occurred concerning some of the descriptive material in this report between the termination of the survey (March, 1954), the first draft (October, 1954) and this final draft (May, 1955). Such changes are mentioned in the text, but no attempt at a resurvey has been attempted.

May, 1955 R. N. A.
Guatemala, C. A.

TABLE OF CONTENTS

	Page
Introduction	263
I. LADINOS AND INDIANS	267
1. Definition of the Ladino	267
2. Variations in Indian Culture	270
3. Some Demographic Differences	274
4. The Distribution of the Ladino Population	283
5. The Processes of Ladinoization	288
II. THE CULTURE OF THE LADINO TOWN AND COUNTRY DWELLER	293
1. Land and Agriculture	293
2. Other Economic Activities	313
3. Travel, Transport, and Commerce	318
4. The Domestic Establishment	323
5. Family and *Compadre* System	327
6. General Social Structure	332
7. Political Organization	342
8. Religious Activities	349
9. Sickness and the Spirit World	362
III. LIVINGSTON AND THE BLACK CARIB CULTURE	371
IV. COMMUNITIES VISITED ON THE SURVEY	383
1. Three Ladino Towns of the Western Highlands: Zaragoza, San Carlos Sija, and Esquipulas Palo Gordo	384
2. A Ladino *Aldea* in the Western Highlands: Chitatul	385
3. The Ladinos of a Western Highland Indian *Municipio*: Joyabáj	387
4. The Ladinos of the Upper Motagua: Granados, Palencia, and Sansare	388
5. The Ladinos of the Middle Motagua: San Agustín Acasaguastlán, Teculután, Gualán, and San Jerónimo	391
6. The Lower Motagua: Morales	393
7. The Ladinos of the Eastern Highlands: San José la Arada, Esquipulas, San Manuel Chaparrón, and Mataquescuintla	394
8. The Ladinos of the Southeastern Highlands: Atescatempa, Quesada, Barberena, and Petapa	397
9. The Southeast Coast: Guazacapán and the Barrio San Sebastián	399
10. The Central South Coast: Siquinalá and La Gomera	400
11. The Modified Indian Communities of the Southwest Coast: Patulul, San Antonio Suchitepéquez, and San Rafael Tierra del Pueblo	401
12. A Southwest Ladino Piedmont Community: Flores Costa Cuca	402
13. A Mixed Town of the Coastal Border Area: Catarina	403
V. DISCUSSION	404
References	409
Selected Bibliography of Studies of Guatemala Indian Communities	411

I. LADINOS AND INDIANS

1. DEFINITION OF THE LADINO

In visiting Guatemala anyone can recognize that there exists a wide variety of people; the members of the population obviously vary in skin color and physiognomy, and even more obviously in costumes, language, and customs. For general purposes the Guatemalans tend to divide all these people, whether they are black, coffee-colored, brown, or white, and whether they wear any one of the multitude of different forms of dress available, into two major types: Ladinos and Indians. The 1950 Census recorded the population as divided into 1,296,397 Ladinos, and 1,491,725 Indians; the Indians accounted for 53.5% of the total population.

The greater part of the present study is concerned with the Ladinos. The reason for this is that the Guatemalan Indians have been fairly intensively studied in many of their aspects, and while much work yet needs to be done, the interested person does have some basic sources to which to turn.[1] We know very little systematically, however, concerning the Ladino.

How to determine whether a person is to be classed as an Indian or Ladino is really quite easy. In perhaps 90 to 95% of the cases, one need only ask him. His answer will be in accord with what everyone else considers the person to be. Such a degree of accord means that there is a great deal of common understanding with respect to the characteristics which mark a person as being Indian or Ladino. The distinction of people into one of these two general groups is no mere academic question, but an important practical problem for anyone working in Guatemala. If you meet a man on the street dressed in old clothes, overalls perhaps, wearing no shoes, and displaying a swarthy complexion and possibly certain facial features which you may believe are characteristic of the Indian population, it might be unwise to ask him whether he is an Indian or Ladino; if you err, he might be somewhat insulted. And yet simply by his appearance, you cannot tell. In fact, unless you do ask him or someone who knows him, there may be no way you can be absolutely sure whether he is one or the other. The terms Indian and Ladino, as they are used today in Guatemala, do not primarily denote racial groups. They represent what we can best call socio-cultural groups which have some historical racial parallels. Basically, the distinctions between the groups are social and cultural; there may be, but not necessarily, certain racial differences as well.

The Indians are people who manifest a certain series of customs and the Ladinos are those who manifest a generally different set of customs. The difference between Indians and Ladinos had its origin, of course, with the conquest in which the Spanish, a distinctive racial population which carried one set of customs, came into contact with and started to mix with the Indians, a different racial population with a different set of customs. At first the term Ladino was used to

---

[1] See *infra*, Selected Bibliography on Guatemalan Indian Studies.

refer to Indians or other groups that had taken over the Spanish language and other Spanish customs.[2]

In Guatemala, and adjacent parts of Central America and Mexico, however, the term Ladino gradually became extended to refer to anyone who did not have

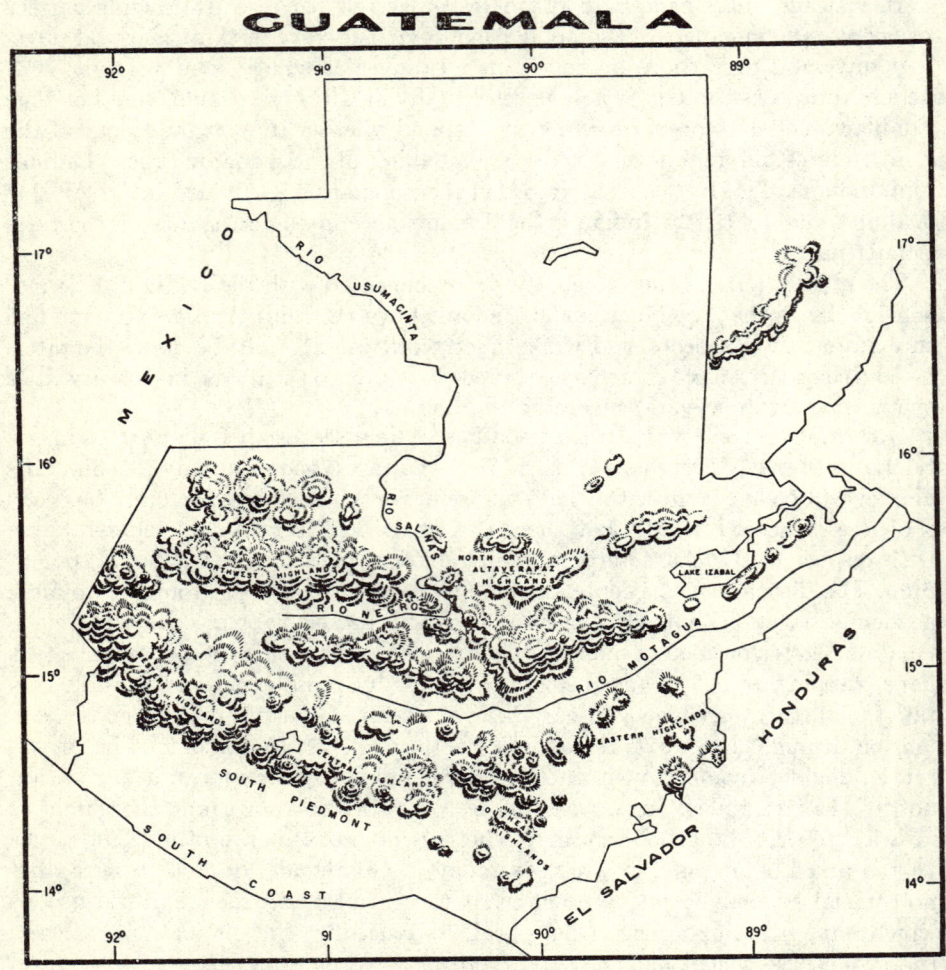

GUATEMALA

Schematic Topography

or retain Indian customs; it came to include people who never had, nor whose ancestors had, Indian customs. Thus the term Ladino gradually incorporated people who used customs which were not Indian customs; race did not necessarily have to have anything to do with it. Of course, people who retained Indian customs tended, racially, to retain Indian physical features because they tended to intermarry within their own ethnic group. People who were called Ladino, on

[2] McBryde, 1945, pp. 12–13.

the other hand, might include anyone from a "pure-blood" Indian to a person of strict Spanish descent; constant remarriage within either racial population is obviously likely to perpetuate features and customs of that population. There is, therefore, a strong correlation between Indian race and Indian culture, and non-Indian race and non-Indian culture. However, this does not mean that a person who appears to be of a particular racial group is always going to be classified in the corresponding ethnic group.

Consequently, the term Ladino should not be confused with either the terms *white* or *mestizo* which are used elsewhere in Latin America.[3] The Ladino may be either white or mestizo, or even Indian, racially. Or he can even, as is the case in the town of Livingston, be a mixture of Negro and Indian. The term Indian then refers to a socio-cultural group, and the term Ladino has come, in general, to refer to any person who is not a member of the Indian group.

With this as a general picture, we may approach some of the variations in usage, variations which are also of great importance. Thus far we have spoken of the terms, Indians and Ladinos, as if they were determined only by the characteristics of the person to whom they are being applied. In fact, when a person uses the term Ladino, he is expressing a relationship between himself and the person to whom he is referring; and whether he uses Ladino or some other word will depend in some part upon his own characteristics. Let us take some examples: (1) An upper class Guatemalan of Spanish biological descent and Spanish cultural heritage disclaims being a Ladino; to him, Ladino is the same as mestizo. Thus, while other Ladinos and Indians would consider him to be Ladino, he would not so consider himself. (2) The Indians of the San Marcos piedmont may make a distinction between the town-dwelling Ladinos, and a local *finca* owner of German descent; to them, there is a difference. To an Indian from some other part of the country the San Marcos Ladinos would be Ladinos, whether of German descent or not. In both these cases, something in the past cultural experience of the individual leads him to make a distinction which is not generally made by the rest of his countrymen.

Another variation is the degree to which the concept of race or racial superiority enters the picture in a given community in the definition of either ethnic group. This too will be discussed later, but it should be mentioned here. In the Atlantic coast town of Livingston, there are at least five distinct ethnic groups which are recognized by all the inhabitants; racially, all have clearly different features. Yet, four of the five are classified as Ladino: the Chinese, the Black Carib (African Negro and Island Carib mixture), the European white, and the east (India) Indian; only one group is classified as "Indian", and this is the Maya Indian group. This does not mean that the members of these groups are thought

---

[3] Anthropologist Morris Siegel (1941), after studying at San Miguel Acatán, used the term *white* to refer to the Ladinos and the expressions "white racial superiority" and "racial dichotomy" to characterize their relationships with Indians. Whether Siegel would intend this to mean that movement from one group to the other is prohibited because of this "dichotomy" is not clear, and whether his ideas would run counter to those expressed here would depend upon the role he assigns to race.

to be alike racially; it is simply that the racial difference between them is not considered as significant as the cultural difference between the entire aggregate of them and the one Maya Indian group. Within the Ladino group, distinctions are clearly made and differential endogamy generally practised. The other extreme from this is where the concept of race has been utilized to bolster a caste-like distinction. Such is evidently the case to some degree in San Luis Jilotepeque; it was suggested by the writer's informant in Atescatempa; and was claimed by Siegel[4] to be the case in San Miguel Acatán.

In summary then, the terms Indian and Ladino may be considered to refer to members of distinct socio-cultural groups, with the proviso that the term Ladino refers to various socio-cultural groups, the most common of which is that with a Spanish-oriented cultural heritage. Variation in the use of the term will arise from variations in the characteristics of the person involved, variations in the particular social position of the speaker, and variations in the degree to which the concept of race has become integrated with the picture.

2. VARIATIONS IN INDIAN CULTURE

Occasionally persons familiar with Guatemala have tried to define a series of characteristics which would once and for all bring out the distinctive differences between Indians and Ladinos. As is clear from the preceding discussion, this is not made easier by the fact that the term Ladino may cover a number of different ethnic groups even though it is more specifically applied to the Spanish-American culture bearer. Nor is it easy in the view of the nature of the variations to be found among Indian communities. The present section will take up in brief a method for classifying Indian communities.

There are two important ways in which no two Indian communities may be said to be alike. The first of these is the fact that ". . . the people of each *municipio* constitute a unique group, united by blood and tradition and differing from all others in history, language, and culture."[5] Thus it is possible to identify the persons of many communities simply by the clothing they may be wearing; we can identify a man from Sololá, a woman from Chichicastenango, or a man from Todos Santos, because each of the persons is wearing a costume which is quite unique to their *municipio* or a restricted region. The costume is only one of the many customs in which the people of different Indian towns vary. These differences, it should be noted, almost all fall within a general pattern and theoretically it should be possible to write up an ethnography of the Guatemalan Mayan Indian which would indicate certain of the norms and the variations to them. These *municipio* differences are basically differences in *kind*, not of degree.

The second important way in which the *municipios* differ is the degree to which they have adopted contemporary Ladino traits and the degree to which they have given up traits which would otherwise distinguish them as being Indian and not Ladino. This may be thought of, in part, as the degree to which the members of a given Indian community have been ladinoized. It is important to note

---

[4] 1941. [5] Tax, 1937, p. 433.

that we are speaking of the degree to which *contemporary* Ladino traits have been taken on; for much of the so-called Indian culture is of Spanish origin and was taken over during the colonial, and even in the republican periods. Thus to speak merely of the degree to which a community shows traits of European origin would be quite misleading.

The writer has found it convenient to think in terms of a general continuum from the contemporarily least Ladino-like Indian to those which are most ladinoized. Along this continuum, exclusive of the Ladinos themselves, three points may be chosen around which cluster most Indian towns. The first of these would be that which we would think of in a common-sense way as being the "most" Indian, or the "pure" Indian of today. These societies are found principally in the western and northwestern (and possibly the Verapaz) highlands, and include the community one usually has in mind when thinking of "Guatemalan Indians." These communities have retained to some degree a distinct socio-political-religious organization, both men and women have some distinctive features of clothing, most of the women and some of the men are still monolingual (speaking only an Indian language), and the use of Indian surnames is still very common. With further empirical analysis, other traits can probably be distinguished for the Indian communities clustering around this point of the continuum, such as the use of the *temascal* (sweat bath), the retention, although perhaps in an attenuated form, of the Maya calendar, the use of a highly developed system of diviners and curers, etc. This type of Indian culture and community we refer to as *Traditional Indian*.[6]

If the Traditional Indian may be considered to stand close to one end of the continuum, then the next, or middle stage, involves the loss of a number of these traits and the crystallization of "Indianism" around another group of traits. Among those which disappear or remain in a weak form are the political-religious organization and the distinctive dress of the men (possibly retaining only a red cloth sash). All the men and many of the women become bilingual, but the Indian language is still retained as the mother tongue. Also, women generally retain distinctive clothing, although it may not always be possible to identify one's village by the nature of the costume. Although not necessarily always the case, the use of the *temascal* often disappears, the Maya calendar is usually no longer functional, and the curers and diviners find considerable competition from Ladino spiritualists and other lay curers. The Indian communities and cultures which cluster around this point of the continuum we call *Modified Indian*. The Modified Indian still has many traits which set him aside as clearly being Indian: the woman's distinctive costume, the leadership of men in religious activities (although most of the activities themselves are of Catholic origin), the cooking still done between three stones on the floor (except in the Verapaz and Huehuetenango), the men still use the head tumpline for carrying goods, and the community still retains its integrity as an Indian community. The people still manifest resistance to one of their members becoming a Ladino through the

[6] Term suggested by Whetten.

adoption of Ladino customs. The Modified Indian is to be found in the piedmont and upper coast region[7] of the southwest from Mexico through Suchitepéquez. It then cuts up into the highlands in the departments of Chimaltenango, Sacatepéquez, Guatemala, and probably into the Baja Verapaz. Scattered communities in the midwestern highlands may be considered as Modified, as possibly some in Totonicapán, and the Indian communities in the east, the Pocoman and Chortí speaking groups. The Chortí perhaps lie somewhere between the Modified and Traditional.

Moving along the continuum towards Ladinoism, we come to the third cluster point, that which we call the *Ladinoized Indian*. In Ladinoized Indian cultures and communities most of the traits which one can observe with the eye as being distinctively Indian have disappeared. Neither sex retains any distinctive dress, almost all the people are monolingual again, but this time speaking only Spanish, the use of Indian surnames has just about disappeared, and the head tumpline somewhat replaced by carrying on the shoulder or with pack animals. Nevertheless, at this stage there are still a few traits which distinguish the group as being Indian and not Ladino: the men still tend to take the lead in the religious rituals; cooking is still done by preference on the floor; and most important, the group is still territorially distinct, whether it is as a separate community (as in some of the Jutiapa communities), as a separate *barrio* (as in Guazacapán and Chiquimulilla), or as a less well defined fringe group around a Ladino community (such as in San Agustín Acasaguastlán). The Ladinos generally refer to the Ladinoized Indian group as "Indian," but depending upon their locality unity, there is sometimes some question as to the degree of whether they should be considered as Indians or just poor people (for poverty also frequently characterizes them). The members of the Ladinoized Indian group usually consider themselves to be Indian, again except possibly if they form merely the fringe population of a Ladino community. The Ladinoized Indian is still Indian in that most people, both within and without the group, consider them as Indians, but it is highly ladinoized in that much of the content of the culture is Ladino. Actually, of course, some of the traits which they share with the poor Ladinos are of Indian origin, but in terms of contemporary social distinctions, this is irrelevant. Planting corn with a digging stick can no more be considered an Indian trait today than can Catholicism be considered a non-Indian trait. Both are completely integrated into the ways of life of both ethnic groups. The Ladinoized Indian today is found principally in the eastern and southeastern parts of the country: coastal Santa Rosa, central Jutiapa, western Chiquimula, and scattered in the middle Motagua Valley. The writer knows of no Ladinoized Indians in the western part of the country.

Both theoretically and practically, when one moves further along the continuum, he enters the Ladino category; the final loss of Indian traits, by definition, means that there is no longer any Indian.

---

[7] McBryde sets the 200 meter, or approximately 650 feet altitude, as about the lower limit of the Indian; this would apply to what we call the Modified Indian, as there are no Traditional Indians living in this region. McBryde, 1945, p. 13.

These categories or points on a continuum refer specifically to groups of people, to communities, no matter what their relationship to a group of Ladinos may be. While it may be a convenience to call an individual "traditional," "modified," or "ladinoized," it may lead to some confusion if the terms are used carelessly. The terms apply specifically to groups and members of groups which hold certain social norms (distinctive culture traits) and retain a specifically distinctive social organization, even if it be no more than as a separate social group. The terms may be applied to individuals insofar as they are functioning members of such communities. The individual who abandons his Indian community, goes to live in Ladino environment, but is unable to shed the personal habits which are derived from his old culture, obviously retains certain Indian characteristics. These characteristics, however, are personal habits; while historically related to the customs of his old community, they are not being transmitted to his children nor are they shared with the other members of his present community. Nathan Whetten brings up this question from another theoretical point of view:

"Actually, I would think that the classification could apply to either individuals or groups. Does your discussion imply that there is likely to be more uniformity in a given community than actually exists? Is it not likely that in any Modified Indian community you will also find Ladinoized Indians, possibly a few Traditional Indians, and even a few Ladinos? If this is the case would not your terms apply individually as well as collectively? In other words, isn't the community category deduced pretty largely from the sum total or the average of the individual categories?"[8]

By taking up various of these points, the nature of the concepts should become clearer:

(1) The categorization does not imply that perfect uniformity actually exists in any community. Within any of them, there are individuals whose personal habits vary from the norms, whether they be towards ladinoization or psychopathological. But a member of a Modified community generally participates in the socio-cultural organization of that community, his habits are shared with other members. In the Modified town of Magdalena, for example, there are a few people who practically never use the Indian language and dress like Ladinos, but they participate in the Indian religious organization and marry women of Indian families. If they were to leave the community, and go and live in Guatemala City, and deny being Indian, they might well be considered as Ladinos. But as community members, they clearly share important distinctive traits with the rest of the members of the community, even though they vary from the norm in personal habits.

(2) Whether or not Ladinos live in an administrative unit or not does not alter the categorization of the Indian community present. The examples of Joyabáj and Guazacapán described later in this essay provide examples of extremes in terms of the continuum, but in both cases, Ladinos are an important part of the town population.

(3) The community category is often suggested by the presence of such traits as the sweat bath, the use of the *mecapal*, the fire between three stones on the floor, but it is not deduced from the presence of these traits, nor is the categorization based on them. An Indian community, whether Traditional or Ladinoized, is identified basically on two

---

[8] Nathan Whetten (in correspondence).

points :(a) the application of the term "Indian" by the members and non-members of the community, by both Indians and Ladinos, to the community and members thereof; and (b) the presence of some distinctive social organizational characteristics (distinct from those of the Ladinos) in which the members participate and in which the Ladino non-members do not participate. Now, in terms of individuals, we may say that the presence of the Indian community is defined by the fact of collective participation; but from the socio-cultural point of view, we may also say that there exists an organization which is distinct from the organization of the Ladino population, and the people who participate in this organization are called Indians. Thus the term Modified or Ladinoized can apply to an Indian who participates in this organization, but does not necessarily apply if he leaves and refuses to participate in it.

3. SOME DEMOGRAPHIC DIFFERENCES

For a discussion of the population of Guatemala, there are unfortunately available no comparative figures of Indians and Ladinos on anything except

Table 1.—Number of *municipios* by the percentage of Indian population present
(*Taken from Census*, 1950)

Percentage of municipal population recorded as Indian	Number of *municipios*	Percentage of *municipios*
0 – 10.0	61	19.3%
10.1– 20.0	22	7.0
20.1– 30.0	10	3.2
30.1– 40.0	7	2.2
40.1– 50.0	18	5.7
50.1– 60.0	16	5.1
60.1– 70.0	23	7.3
70.1– 80.0	33	10.5
80.1– 90.0	41	13.0
90.1–100.0	84	26.7
Total	315	100.0%

gross municipal population and some data on vital statistics for the year 1952. Both populations, however, have fairly distinct distributions, and there is a tendency for a given municipal unit to be either predominantly Indian, or predominantly Ladino, but not mixed. Table 1 provides the figures on the number of *municipios* which have varying percentages of Indians and Ladinos.

If we make a threefold classification of Indian, Mixed, and Ladino, with Indian being any population unit which has 70% or more Indians, Ladino being any such unit with 30% or less Indian, and Mixed being any such unit which has between 30% and 70% of these two ethnic groups, then we may say that in Guatemala as a whole only 65 or 20.6% of the *municipios* are mixed; 158 (50.2%) are Indian, and 92 (29.2%) are Ladino. The importance of these figures should not be underestimated; it means that about 80% of the *municipios* contain populations which are predominantly Indian or predominantly Ladino.

This tendency for a given population unit to be predominantly Indian or Ladino, but not mixed, holds for the municipal units, but not for the departmental units. For the country as a whole in 1950 there were 8 departments which were Ladino, 7 which were Mixed, and 7 which were Indian. The difference between this distribution and that for the *municipios* is based on the fact that while there are certain departments which are predominantly Ladino, this population is also to be found in considerable numbers through most of the republic. Thus

GUATEMALA

Indian and Ladino percentages by *municipio*

Huehuetenango, San Marcos, Quezaltenango, Suchitepéquez, Chiquimula, and Baja Verapaz, which are often thought of as being Indian departments, actually have a rather high percentage of Ladinos.

For gross comparisons we will distinguish between three groups of departments: the eight Ladino departments (El Progreso, Santa Rosa, Izabal, Escuintla, Guatemala, Zacapa, Jutiapa, and El Petén), the seven Mixed departments (Jalapa, Sacatepéquez, Retalhuleu, Baja Verapaz, Chiquimula, Suchitepéquez, and Quezaltenango), and the seven Indian departments (San Marcos,

Huehuetenango, Chimaltenango, El Quiché, Alta Verapaz, Sololá, and Totonicapán). While using these departments as blocks cannot provide an entirely accurate picture of Ladino — Indian differences, it is a satisfactory method of sug-

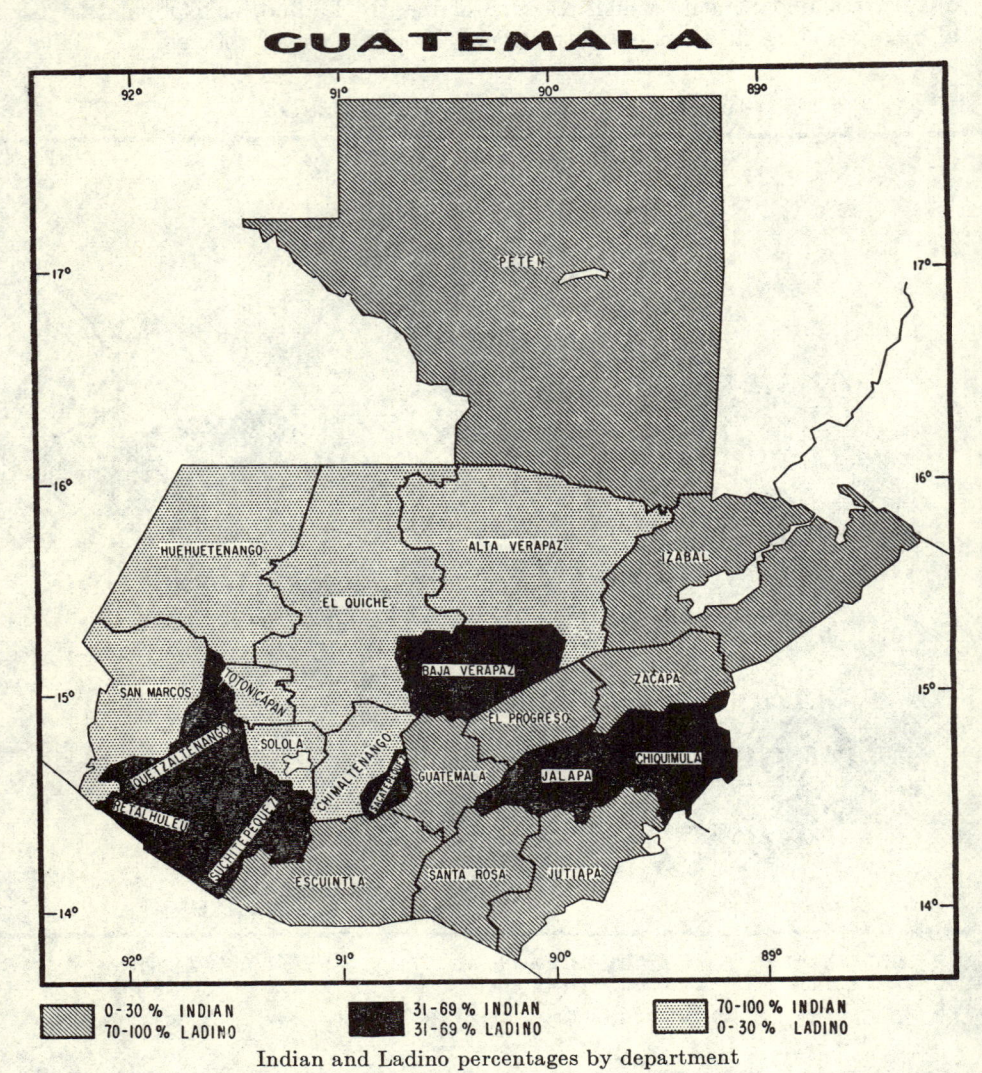

GUATEMALA

Indian and Ladino percentages by department

gesting some gross differences between the two groups. Table 2 provides some of the basic characteristics of these three groups of departments. It will be noted in the Ladino departments as a whole that 16.7% of the population was Indian, and in the Indian departments, 17.6% of the population is Ladino. Consequently, in all figures for the Ladino and Indian departments as blocks it should not be forgotten that in each there is a small but significant percentage of members of the other ethnic group.

The Guatemalan Census of 1950 makes the urban-rural distinction in terms of the population living inside or outside of the municipal capitals. It must be recognized that the greater part of the population living in these capitals is agricultural and that many of the municipal populations are very small[9] and consequently would be regarded as being rural were a census to be made on a classically sociological basis.

The figures on the respective percentages of Indians and Ladinos living in municipal capitals (Table 2) make it abundantly clear that there is a greater tendency for Ladinos to live in capitals than for Indians. Only in Santa Rosa and Sacatepéquez is the percentage of the total Indian population resident in capitals larger than the percentage of Ladinos resident in these towns.[10] There is evidently a distinction to be seen, however, as between those Ladinos resident in Indian departments and those in Ladino departments. If we exclude from the discussion for the moment the Department of Guatemala in which the national capital provides a unique and extreme Ladino urban aggregate, and compare the remaining departments, we find that in only two of the seven Ladino departments is more than 30% of the Ladino population resident in the municipal capitals; in comparison, in all but two of the Indian departments, more than 30% of the Ladino population so resides. In Totonicapán and Sololá, over 75% of the Ladinos are town dwellers. This fact concerning Ladinos in the Indian regions was pointed out years ago by workers in that area,[11] but it has generally been ignored that the reverse is true in the Ladino areas.

With respect to population density a different alignment arises as between these departmental groups. In considering the issue, a better idea of the general situation of the country is obtained if the departments of Guatemala and El Petén are excluded from the general calculations. Guatemala, containing the national capital, has a density of 207.5 per km^2, vastly greater than any other department in the country; El Petén, on the other hand, has a figure of only 0.4 per km^2, much below any of the figures for the rest of the country. Since the present study is trying to describe certain of the characteristics of the town and country-dwelling population of the country, both Guatemala and the Petén tend to greatly influence the figures, one with the unique national capital, and the other by including a huge area which is hardly populated or used.

If these two departments are arbitrarily excluded from consideration, the figures given in Table 3 are the densities of each of the groups of the departments.

In general, the areas of Ladino population are less densely populated than either Indian or Mixed areas. Of particular note, however, is the fact that both the Ladino and Indian departments fall far below the density of the Mixed departments. The Mixed departments have a density which is more than twice as great as the Ladino departments and almost half again as large as the Indian

---

[9] Page 204 of the 1950 Census provides the following figures: 45.1% of the 315 *municipio* capitals are under 1,000 population; 72.4% of them are under 2,000. Only 9, or 2.9%, are over 8,000 population.

[10] This point was called to the writer's attention by Nathan Whetten.

[11] Tax, 1937, p. 432.

Table 2.—Selected population data on Guatemala. All data, except as noted, are taken from 1950 Census, or by comparison of 1893 and 1950 censuses

Departments	Total 1950 population	Ladino percentage 1950	Increase in Ladino percentage 1893–1950	Density per Km²	% of total population	% of total Indian population	% of total Ladino population
Eight Ladino Depts..........	1,001,773	83.3					
El Progreso................	47,678	90.9	(2)	24.8	26.3	13.5	27.6
Santa Rosa................	109,812	90.5	11.7	37.2	21.2	38.1	19.4
Izabal.....................	55,191	85.3	15.4	6.1	38.2	10.2	43.0
Escuintla..................	123,809	84.1	13.4	28.2	24.4	18.2	25.6
Guatemala.................	441,085	81.7	14.9	207.5	73.4	42.7	80.3
Zacapa....................	69,533	81.1	25.9 (2)	25.8	25.4	11.6	28.6
Jutiapa....................	138,768	80.8	6.5	43.1	19.7	9.3	22.2
El Petén...................	15,897	71.9	5.0	0.4	46.8	19.4	57.5
Seven Mixed Depts..........	689,185	39.0					
Jalapa.....................	75,091	49.5	1.1	36.4	25.2	17.1	33.4
Sacatepéquez..............	59,975	48.8	11.6	129.0	72.8	77.4	68.0
Retalhuleu.................	66,066	48.5	8.4	35.6	26.9	17.5	36.9
Baja Verapaz..............	66,432	41.4	8.1	21.3	14.7	11.5	19.2
Chiquimula................	112,837	37.9	4.0	47.5	17.3	8.6	31.6
Suchitepéquez.............	125,196	32.6	2.6	49.9	24.7	16.6	41.4
Quezaltenango.............	183,588	32.0	2.0	94.1	33.5	24.8	52.3
Seven Indian Depts.........	1,097,164	17.6					
San Marcos................	230,039	27.9	−2.0	60.7	12.1	6.1	27.6
Huehuetenango............	198,872	26.5	8.6	26.9	16.3	12.2	27.7
Chimaltenango.............	122,310	22.5	−1.6	61.8	37.3	32.0	56.2
El Quiché.................	174,882	16.3	−0.3	20.9	13.1	8.9	34.3
Alta Verapaz..............	188,758	6.6	1.6	21.7	10.4	6.9	59.7
Sololá.....................	82,869	6.2	−1.9	78.1	33.2	30.4	75.6
Totonicapán...............	99,434	3.4	0.2	93.7	20.0	17.6	88.0
Total republic.............	2,788,122	46.5%	10.9%	25.6	22.9	16.3	32.9

(1) Material on the percentage of Indians and percentage of Ladinos who live in capitals was suggested by Nathan Whetten.
(2) Zacapa and Progreso formed a single department in 1893.

departments. To understand this we must explore the situation in various of the departments. In the Indian departments, El Quiché and Alta Verapaz, both have large northern regions which are very lightly populated; in both, the population is concentrated in the southern portions. In the Ladino departments, Izabal may be conveniently divided into two sections, the southeastern and more populated section, and the northwestern and unpopulated section, a geographical extension of the region of low population density of Alta Verapaz. If these gross areas of underpopulation could be removed from consideration, the density for Indian occupied areas would be even greater than the Ladino.

The net result of these comparisons of density indicates, however, that while the Indian departments are more densely inhabited than are the Ladino departments, the Mixed departments are the most densely populated of all.

It might be noted that the Ladino department with the highest density, aside

Table 3.—Comparative Regional Densities

	Density of population inhabitants per km^2
Six Ladino departments	22.5
Seven Mixed departments	48.0
Seven Indian departments	33.9
Total republic	25.6
Total republic (minus Guatemala and Petén)	32.9

Table 4.—Population growth, 1778–1950. (*Taken in part from Orellana, 1950*)

Year	Total population	Ladinos	Indians	% Indian	Density
1778	392,272	80,485	311,797	78.4%	3.6
1837	(1)	179,047	(1)	(1)	(1)
1880	1,224,602	379,828	844,744	68.9	11.3
1893	1,364,678	481,954	882,733	64.6	12.5
1921	2,004,900	704,973	1,299,927	64.8	18.4
1950	2,788,122	1,296,397	1,491,725	53.5	25.6

(1) Data on Indians and total population in this census was very defective.

from Guatemala, is Jutiapa, adjacent to El Salvador. Moving from Escuintla towards El Salvador, there is an increasing density of population by department: Escuintla, 28.2; Santa Rosa, 37.2; Jutiapa, 43.1; Ahuachapán, 73.9; and Santa Ana, 110.7.

This suggests that the higher density of Jutiapa is related to the fact of the high Salvadorean density; whatever factors have been at work in producing the high Salvadorean density may also have been at work in attenuated form in Jutiapa.

Turning now to the problem of growth, it is possible to trace the Ladino population size since the census of 1778. There is some reason not to rely heavily on the earlier figures, and data on Indians at the same time were not always available, so these figures are presented principally as general background material.

Table 4 indicates that while the Indian population increased approximately 4.8 times between 1778 and 1950, the Ladino increased 16.1 times, or over three

Table 5.—Birth and death rate and natural increase of population in Indian and Ladino departments, 1952. (*Taken from Maldonado Juárez, n.d.*)

	Number of births/1000	Number of deaths/1000	Net increase of population
Ladinos in:			
Ladino Departments:			
El Progreso	60.3	20.3	40.0
Santa Rosa	53.4	18.9	34.5
Izabal	56.0	16.9	39.2
Escuintla	59.0	29.9	29.4
Guatemala	48.3	19.3	29.0
Zacapa	54.6	19.2	35.4
Jutiapa	49.9	18.2	31.7
El Petén	49.7	10.6	39.1
Indian Departments:			
San Marcos	37.6	16.0	21.6
Huehuetenango	45.2	14.8	30.4
Chimaltenango	36.7	14.6	22.1
El Quiché	40.9	14.0	26.9
Alta Verapaz	41.9	14.4	27.5
Sololá	38.3	10.8	27.5
Totonicapán	37.4	17.6	19.8
Total Ladinos in republic	48.3	18.5	29.8
Indians in:			
Ladino Departments:			
El Progreso	47.5	29.6	17.9
Santa Rosa	45.7	19.6	26.1
Izabal	46.9	30.4	16.5
Escuintla	36.3	32.4	3.9
Guatemala	44.6	25.0	19.6
Zacapa	30.6	11.9	18.7
Jutiapa	76.5	35.8	40.7
El Petén	70.9	35.1	35.8
Indian Departments:			
San Marcos	51.4	26.2	25.2
Huehuetenango	56.2	24.9	31.3
Chimaltenango	52.4	37.3	15.1
El Quiché	59.4	25.8	33.6
Alta Verapaz	54.0	24.6	29.4
Sololá	49.2	31.1	18.1
Totonicapán	53.0	41.0	12.0
Total Indians in republic	53.2	29.1	24.1
Total republic	51.0	24.2	26.8

times as fast as the Indian population. The percentages for Indian population given for 1880, 1893, and 1921 may not be highly reliable, but there is little doubt that the change between 1778 and 1950 is fairly representative of the actual relative decline in Indian population.

The growth of the Ladino population may generally be attributed to any or all of three operative factors. (1) There has been a constant process of ladinoization going on so that in each generation there are doubtless some Indians who move out of the orbit of Indian culture and attach themselves to the Ladino society; while they may not be considered as Ladinos (although they often are), their children are usually so considered. (2) Where immigration has occurred, it has increased the Ladino population, not the Indian population. (3) The natural increase of the Ladinos is larger than that of the Indians. The first of these processes will be examined in the next section, but in any case, we have no fig-

Table 6.—Birth and death rates and natural increase of population in Indian and Ladino departments: Summary. (*Taken from Maldonado Juárez, n.d.*)

	Ladinos			Indians		
	Population 1 July, 1952	Births 1952	Deaths 1952	Population 1 July 1952	Births 1952	Deaths 1952
8 Ladino Departments	890,150	45,754	17,811	173,763	8,600	4,713
7 Indian Departments	206,892	8,304	3,095	971,858	52,563	27,806
	Number of births per 1000	Number of deaths per 1000	Natural increase	Number of births per 1000	Number of deaths per 1000	Natural increase
8 Ladino Departments	51.4	20.0	31.4	49.5	27.2	22.3
7 Indian Departments	40.1	15.0	25.1	54.1	28.6	25.3

ures on it; concerning immigration there is no data immediately available to provide us with figures on growth; but on vegetative growth there is some relevant information.

Maldonado Juárez[12] has made available departmental figures on the births and deaths (excluding born dead) for the year 1952 including the population estimate for the Ladino and Indian populations. As will be evident from some of the figures, there is reason to doubt the accuracy of some of these figures, but in their totality they probably do suggest the general differences in the groups involved. Table 5 gives the data by departments, while Table 6 provides a summary by socio-cultural group per departmental type.

Referring first to Table 6, the summary of the data, the following conclusions seem warranted for the year 1952: (1) In Ladino departments the Indian and Ladino birth rates are practically the same, but due to a lower Ladino death rate, the Ladino natural increase is 1.4 times as large as the Indian. (2) In Indian departments, both the birth and death rates of the Ladinos are lower than

[12] Maldonado Juárez, n.d.

those of the Indians, but the natural increases of the two is the same. (3) Comparing Indians in the two types of departments, the birth rate is slightly higher in the Indian departments, while the death rates are more or less the same; this has resulted in a slightly higher natural increase of the Indian population in Indian departments as over that in Ladino departments. (4) Comparing Ladinos in the two types of departments, both the birth and death rates are lower in the Indian departments, but the differential is such that the natural increase in Ladino departments is 1.25 times that in the Indian departments.

These conclusions are open to various interpretations, and since they are for only one year and based on questionable records, it is perhaps unwise to explore them too extensively. However, the differential between the Ladino and Indian populations in the Ladino departments as compared with the Indian departments is supported by the comparative 1893–1950 growth given in Table 2; the Ladino population has been growing more rapidly in Ladino departments, while it is just about holding its own in the Indian departments. In view of this, it is reasonable to conclude that the differential growth of the Ladino populations due to natural increase differences under these two sets of conditions (i.e., in Ladino as opposed to Indian regions) is probably a fact.

The differences may probably be explained in part by the fact that much of the Ladino population in Indian departments compose an elite: they live under conditions more conducive to a lower death rate. Why the Ladino birth rate should be lower in Indian departments, the writer frankly does not know.

In the comparative Indian figures, there is a slightly lower natural increase among Indians in Ladino departments than in Indian departments. This is due not so much to a differential in death but in birth rate. As in comparative Ladino figures, the key to much of our understanding of these differences depends upon factors in fertility, and for this part of the world we have no studies whatsoever on this subject. In view of the high Indian birth rate, however, it is clear that a reduction in death rate of 10 per 1000 would result in a relative increase in the Indian population over the Ladino population.

Turning for a moment to Table 5, there are a few points of interest. Ladino figures, both in Ladino and Indian departments, show much greater consistency as between departments than do the Indian figures. This is doubtless in great part due to more adequate reporting. This is related to greater municipal control by Ladino authorities and probably a more widespread understanding of the requirements for registry of vital statistics. The Ladino departments are among the more highly literate, while the Indian departments are among the highly illiterate.[13] However, the Indian birth rates recorded in the various Indian departments are fairly consistent, the death rates somewhat less so. The most divergent figures are those of Indians in Ladino departments. The birth rates are recorded as ranging from 30 to 71 per thousand, while the death rates vary from 11 to 36.

---

[13] See Census, 1950, p. 120. Of the five most literate departments, four are Ladino, one Mixed; of the five least literate departments, all five are Indian.

4. THE DISTRIBUTION OF THE LADINO POPULATION

On the map the general region of Ladino population is indicated in terms of Indian, Mixed, and Ladino *municipios*. Without considerably more historical research than is available at present, it is not possible to delineate the fundamental reasons why the Ladinos have their present distribution. It is possible to outline some of the factors which probably account for this distribution, however, and for the present the reader will have to draw his own conclusions.

Climate and Altitude

The Ladinos are found in warm and generally not high regions. The eastern highlands of Guatemala are lower than the western highlands. The Ladinos are mainly found in the subhumid Motagua Valley, east highlands, and in the warm piedmont of the southeast. As exceptions to this there are Ladino pockets located high in the western highlands, and there are various tropical and warm arid areas which are not occupied by Ladinos. The main possible exception to this general picture is the Ladino population to be found in the Department of Guatemala. This department is higher than many parts of the eastern highlands and the Ladino population here must be explained in terms of colonial history and as the meeting area of the southeastern Ladino region and the Motagua Valley region. The eastern highlands themselves provide an interesting confirmation of the correlation between Ladinos and lower regions. In the center of the eastern part of the country are two large enclaves of Indians, the Pocoman in Jalapa, and the Chortí in Chiquimula and Zacapa. Between these two groups there is a Ladino corridor running south from Zacapa through the western part of the department of Chiquimula, and into Jutiapa. This corridor corresponds in fact to one of the principal lowland corridors which cut across Central America from one ocean to the other. To the west the land becomes rugged in Jalapa, and in the east rise gradually the Honduran Cordillera del Merendón and further north the Montañas del Gallinero.

There are two important tropical regions which are occupied by Ladinos and not by Indians, but which are not densely populated. These are the Atlantic rain forest region of Izabal and the low Pacific coast. It has only been in recent years that Izabal has seen any extensive growth, and it seems principally due to immigration from neighboring Honduras and from the interior of Guatemala. The Atlantic coast region is one of heavy rainfall throughout most of the year and it never appealed to the Spanish as a zone of a settlement (as it also never appealed to them to establish settlements over most of the Central American north coast). The Pacific coast of Guatemala is a region of distinct dry and rainy seasons. This coast may conveniently be thought of in two parts, the high coast and the low. The low coast is that which extends from the littoral to an altitude of five or six hundred feet; the high coast extends from that point to the base of the piedmont at an altitude of between 1000 and 1200 feet. The Spanish settled through much of the high coast region, especially that of the southeast. Their settlements in the southwest, however, were not so important. They were not particularly drawn to the low coast; it is an area of fairly heavy forest growth and as one approaches the littoral there ensues a region of bayous and swamps which make travel and agriculture fairly difficult. As a result, the principal Spanish coast towns were built as ports. The Ladino has gradually moved into this region to occupy it but it is still thinly populated.[14]

There is another important division of the southern coast called to the writer's attention by Lawrence Stuart. From Escuintla to the west is an area of much higher coastal rain fall than is the area to the east. The western coast then provides more tropical conditions than does that of the east. Spanish settlement evidently went into the southeast coast to a much greater degree than in the southwest coast, and it seems not unlikely that this variation in environmental conditions was in great part responsible for the differential settlement.

Travel Routes

There is some correlation of Ladino population distribution with travel routes, but there is not as much as would be expected. The outstanding instance has been the line more recently followed by the railroad in the eastern part of the country. If the line of the railroad were superimposed on the map of Ladino distribution, it would be seen that the entire line from Puerto Barrios to Escuintla, and from Zacapa to El Salvador goes through Ladino *municipios* with only one exception. The only Mixed *municipio* through which the line runs is that of Chiquimula (54.2% Indian). Otherwise it runs through Ladino portions of Izabal, Zacapa, Progreso, Guatemala, Escuintla, Chiquimula, and Jutiapa. This rail line, of course, follows an even older trade route through these regions. The railroad itself is clearly not responsible for the Ladino distribution since the oldest rail lines are those which run through the southwestern part of the country, a region which is predominantly Mixed or Indian today. With a few exceptions these southwestern lines were opened for traffic before the turn of the century. The eastern lines, however, did not open until later: Puerto Barrios to Guatemala in 1908, and Zacapa to the El Salvador border in 1929.

The effect of the establishment of the railroads was evidently not to carry Ladinos heavily into regions where they were not already fairly well established; it may have, however, served to further ladinoize the regions where they were already established. The departments of Zacapa and El Progreso saw a tremendous increase in Ladino percentage between 1921 and 1950: from 57.4% to 81.1%.

Neither roads nor railroads, in themselves, can be said to have been extremely powerful factors in the ladinoization of Guatemala, except insofar as they represent the crystallization of other factors (such as lowlands for the railway) or as they combine with some factor already present (such as the fact of a region already being highly ladinoized). Perhaps the most telling element in the relative importance of transportation routes is the fact that mere contact with another culture is not notorious for making great changes in the way of life of the Guate-

---

[14] See McBryde, 1945, pp. 14–15 for a description of the southwest settlement pattern.

malan Indian. Anthropologists have been reporting this situation for two decades and the writer has seen nothing to give strong indications that it is still not a valid observation. The Guatemalan Indians have been travelling over their own country for years and there is probably not an adult Indian alive who has not had some contact with Ladinos; hence the introduction of better means of transportation does not mean that the Indian will automatically become ladinoized. It does mean, however, that it is easier for the Ladino to penetrate in larger numbers. Tumin relates how during his 1942 residence in San Luis Jilotepeque that in order to reach Guatemala it was necessary to go east (instead of west) to the railroad station at Ipala, then north by train to Zacapa, and finally southwest towards Guatemala; a trip of two days to cover a straight-line distance of 90 miles.

Another case of Ladino distribution evidently being related to a travel route is to be found in southern Quiché. This will be described later in the paper with respect to the community of Joyabáj.

In general it may be said that travel routes have opened the regions traversed to settlement by Ladinos, but whether or not they choose to settle them beyond the mere point of route-supporting communities depends on other factors. One of the major old travel routes in Guatemala, that of the Río Dulce, Lake Izabal, and then from the town of Izabal to the Motagua Valley has left no significant Ladino population. On the other hand, the southwest coast region is a travel route to nowhere, and it has become quite ladinoized.

Possible Indigenous Regional Differences in the Colonial Period

Anthropologists have often had reason to note that the Indian cultures as highly distinctive entities had long disappeared from the Motagua corridor and the southeastern region. Otto Stoll, writing in 1883, noted, with respect to the Xinca language spoken in Santa Rosa, that "It is urgent to have a new study of this language before it disappears completely..."[15] Archaeologists have sorrowfully noted that no groups of Pipiles have been identified in Guatemala to provide them with some ethnographic background for their archeological problems. It seems that it must be more than a mere coincidence that the specific regions of Guatemala in which the Spanish established their culture, and in so doing displaced the indigenous cultures, are specifically regions where non-Mayan speaking groups lived. If one compares the present day distribution of Ladino *municipios* with the map made by Stoll on the earlier distribution of the various indigenous language groups, there is a remarkable correlation. There were in eastern Guatemala five principal languages spoken: the Mayan languages of Chol, roughly from Zacapa north; Chortí, in more or less the same area in which it is found today, but extending east to Zacapa; and Pocomam, extending from Mixco in the west, in a wide belt east through Jalapa to the present Salvadorean border. The Mexican affiliate language, Pipil, was found in regions along the Motagua Valley from Zacapa running west and then

[15] Stoll, 1938.

northwest to Salamá; near the south coast in the region including the towns of Esquintla and Cuilapa; and then along the present Salvadorean border south of the Lake of Güija. These two last groups were split by the Xinca speaking region which included coastal Santa Rosa and ran up to Jutiapa. In addition to these five groups, the Chol, Chortí, Pocomam, Pipil, and Xinca, there was a group called Pupuluca between the Xinca and the Salvadorean border, and a language called Alagüilac spoken in San Cristobal Acasaguastlán. The Xinca language has not been clearly related to any major linguistic stock.

At the time of the arrival of the Spanish the Chol region was relatively unoccupied. So of the remaining groups we are particularly concerned with the Mayan groups of the Chortí and Pocomam, the Pipil, Xinca, and the Pupuluca. Of these, the only two which have retained any cultural integrity are the two Mayan groups, the Pocomam, now much reduced within the Department of Jalapa and scattered in the center of the country, and the Chortí, who evidently occupy pretty much the same region as they did previously. The Pipil as a socio-cultural group have evidently disappeared from Guatemala although Mexican language Indians are still to be found in El Salvador. The Xinca remain only in a highly ladinoized form in the towns of Guazacapán, Chiquimulilla, and Taxisco in coastal Santa Rosa. Besides these groups, there is an Indian population to be found in four contignous *municipios* in central Jutiapa. The writer has been unable to visit this group, but it was reported to him in Atescatempa that there is no Indian language now spoken among them. While this group probably represents the survivors of the so-called Pupuluca, it may well include as well descendants of the Xinca and Pipil who lived nearby. The Jutiapa Indians may retain some distinctive customs which warrant their retaining the designation Indian, but they probably are as highly ladinoized as are the surviving Santa Rosa Xinca groups.

The fact that the Ladinos have penetrated specifically into the regions of non-Mayan speaking groups, and that the Ladinoization of the Indians has been specifically evident in these regions, presses on one the possibility that the culture of these groups provided some means by which they were more easily assimilated by the Spanish culture than was the case in the Mayan speaking groups. Since we have no adequate accounts of these groups, nor has research been done in the colonial history of this region, we can only conjecture at present that the remarkable correlation in alignment of these regions with the contemporary Ladino region must have some meaning. As in the case of the contemporary population density of Jutiapa, it is not unlikely that further light can be thrown on this problem when it is studied in conjunction with the situation to be found in El Salvador. It is not strictly a Guatemalan problem.

The Plantation Economy

It has repeatedly been said that the alteration of the basic economy and established residence pattern of a population will bring in its wake profound change in other phases of the culture of that population. An example frequently used in Guatemala is the effects of the introduction of large scale coffee production in the latter part of the 19th Century. The introduction of an element such as this must be considered carefully, and on the basis of the distribution of the Indian population today, we can draw some conclusions concerning the importance of coffee and other cultivations in the expansion of the Ladino population in Guatemala.

In the first place, the development of coffee as a crop did not serve to bring Ladinos in great numbers into regions where they had not been before. Coffee was developed principally in the western piedmont and highlands and the Verapaz highlands, both predominantly Indian regions. The western piedmont, however, was in great part not heavily occupied at the time that coffee *fincas* began to be established. This resulted in the situation wherein coffee farmers, few in number, initiated the system of bringing Indians down from the more northern highlands to work the piedmont farms. This served specifically to bring Indians, and not Ladinos, into the western piedmont. In the northern region, specifically the Alta Verapaz, there were evidently enough Indians within the area to suffice for the necessities of the work. So while the first step in the coffee development did bring some Ladinos into new regions, it actually served in a greater degree to expand the effective area of Indian occupation.

The second stage in this picture concerns what happened to the culture of these Indians after they became *colonos* on the coffee *fincas*. There is little doubt that the establishment of the coffee *finca* life was very destructive to much of the older culture; they could not retain any politico-religious organization, they did considerably less *milpa* farming, they came to a new region which was not inhabited by the old territorial spirits, and their settlement pattern was established for them by the formation of the *casco* of the *finca*; in these and many other ways, the *finca* Indians lost a telling amount of their old culture. But, this did not make them into Ladinos. The principal coffee regions of today are not considered as Ladino regions by either Ladinos or Indians; the southwestern piedmont and Alta Verapaz are predominantly Indian, and San Marcos, Quezaltenango, Suchitepéquez, Chimaltenango, and Sacatepéquez are all Mixed or Indian departments. So while we can say with some assurance that the creation of *finca* Indian populations is destructive to Indian culture, we cannot say that it is consequently creative of a Ladino society. This distinction will be taken up in detail shortly.

Another plantation type introduced into Guatemala, that of banana production, has played quite a different role in the Ladino expansion. There have been two principal types of banana production in the country: that done in conjunction with the coffee *fincas* where the banana plants served as shade for the coffee trees, and that done on plantations created specifically for banana production. In the first case it was common for the same labor force which worked on the *finca* to take care of the banana harvest. In the second, however, a different situation resulted. The two main banana production centers were established in the southwestern part of the Department of Escuintla and in the Department of Izabal. This section of Izabal was already a Ladino region at the time the banana production began, but was relatively unoccupied. The

Tiquisate section of the Escuintla coast was also unoccupied. In both cases the plantations were located in hot coastal regions. It was not easy to convince highland Indians to come to these coastal regions as they had been brought to the piedmont and highland coffee farms; they were frankly frightened of the coast and its attendant diseases. The main population which could be drawn on to these farms were people who did not object to the climate, and this meant mainly a population of Ladinos. In Tiquisate there was introduced a predominantly Ladino population into a region which had been relatively unpopulated previously. In this way, the Tiquisate plantation served to extend the Ladino region along the Escuintla coast. Izabal was Ladino anyway, but it was strengthened by the new Ladino population.

In general, it cannot be said, then, that the creation of the banana plantations had a very great ladinoizing influence on the Indians; it did, both in Escuintla and Izabal, extend the effective area of Ladino occupation.

5. THE PROCESSES OF LADINOIZATION

Heretofore the term "ladinoization" has been used as if it referred to a single sequence or combination of processes. In fact, the term covers two quite distinct and separate phenomena, the ladinoization of an individual and the ladinoization of an entire community or group.

Individual ladinoization involves the social process of social mobility and the learning of new personal habits by the individual involved. It means that an individual has moved out of one social caste or class, and through a change of habits and associates, has moved into another. *Group ladinoization,* in which an entire community gradually sheds Indian custom, does not involve social mobility, but is essentially an acculturative process whereby a social group gradually become more Ladino-like and less Indian-like; it is a process whereby the social norms and social organization of the group changes.

The process of group ladinoization, which we may also call acculturation, is a slow process. It is the process involved in the change of an Indian community from the Traditional to Modified, Modified to Ladinoized, and Ladinoized to Ladino status. Within the group itself, the changes in individual habits often occur between generations; the older generation clings to the older habits which are more characteristically Indian, the younger generation has shed some of these and adopted corresponding Ladino habits. The process of group ladinoization does not necessarily make Ladinos out of the members of the group. If Traditional in nature, it makes them more Modified; if Modified, it makes them Ladinoized; and only if already at the threshold of Ladinoism, does the group ladinoizing process change Indians into Ladinos.

The individual in the group ladinoization process is not a single deviate from his society; he is one of an entire segment of the society involved in establishing new norms. The change is one of altering the internal customs of the group, not one of raising the social level of the group. The Ladinoized community in which the last vestiges of Indian organization and custom are disintegrating does not move into a higher social class position; it is still at the bottom of the local social scale.

The factors which induce group ladinoization are various, but usually come from outside of the society itself. These factors bring stress into the society, and a shift towards Ladino culture brings some relief from the stress. Such factors may originate in a change in the environment, alterations in the basic economy, the entrance of an overwhelming Ladino population, a change in national laws and political policies, etc.

An illustration of the last mentioned is to be seen in the ladinoization of many Traditional Indian communities in recent years, where an important initial stage in the process has been the destruction of the religious-political organization of the community.[16]

The introduction of the political party system (1945 to 1954) has been one factor. Since the older politico-religious system is founded on an age-hierarchy system, and its leaders are older people who usually remain in the community and retain their position of power because they have demonstrated ability through years of activity in the religious and political system of the community, these leaders rarely participated in the formation of local political parties. The parties have meant nothing to them and superficially have had no effect on their ruling position. This permitted the parties to be formed entirely by younger men in the communities, usually by the Ladinos with the support of dissatisfied Indian elements. Since the older leaders saw little threat in the formation of the parties, they usually did little to resist their foundation. A crisis arose in the communities, however, when the time for an election came and the political parties insisted that a candidate of their choice be selected. The candidate of the parties was almost never a person who would have taken the position in terms of the older age-hierarchy system. Since the parties had the support of the national government, the departmental government, and the police, it usually meant that a party candidate took the position of mayor, thus thrusting a damaging wedge into the age-hierarchy system. Since this mayor had power, *de facto*, the age-hierarchy lost the ability to function, and waged a loosing battle against the newer system. The loss of the age-hierarchy system has been an important step in the modification of Indian communities.

Another circumstance which has produced a change from the Traditional to Modified Indian communities is that of the wholesale removal of a population from its old geographical setting and its transplanting either in chunks or individually to a plantation. Most of the Indians of the coffee regions of San Marcos, Quezaltenango, Retalhuleu, Suchitepéquez, and Escuintla may be considered Modified Indian, and have become so through the destruction of their old social organizational patterns and attendant value structure. This destruction occurred through their transplantation into a new economic and

---

[16] There is in preparation at present a symposium covering some ten case histories of such change. The material described in the present report was available to the writer prior to the symposium.

environmental situation. It should be noted, however, that this removal and the consequent change does not convert the Traditional Indian to being a Ladino or even generally to the stage of Ladinoized Indian.

We have not had enough studies on Modified and Ladinoized Indian groups in Guatemala to have a clear picture as to what types of circumstances bring the shift from one to the other. The particular Ladinoized Indian societies with which the writer is familiar generally have one characteristic (aside from their cultural characteristics) in common: they form minority groups in regions which are predominantly Ladino. Such is the case with the Indians of San Agustín Acasaguastlán, of southern Santa Rosa and central Jutiapa. While it is not possible to demonstrate it at present, the writer suspects that the change from Modified Indian to Ladinoized Indian may, in general, be a long term process. It is doubtless affected by an increased tendency for individual ladinoization, but it is also affected by the tendency for such groups to be relegated to the bottom of what may (depending upon the population) be a fairly complex Ladino class structure. The change from Traditional Indian to Modified Indian is, from the Ladino point of view, merely a breakdown in the Indian society. The Modified Indian is still looked upon as a distinct ethnic group, and there are various customs which set it aside from the Ladino culture and society. The change from Modified Indian to Ladinoized Indian, however, brings the Indian much closer culturally to the Ladino, and often begins the integration of the Indian social group in the Ladino class structure. Stoll mentioned in 1883 that the Xinca were probably going to lose their language and in the 1940's it was possible to still get a word list. While it is impossible to say whether the 1880 Xinca would fall into the category of Modified Indian, it is unlikely that they could have been classified as Traditional. This means that a considerable period of time has elapsed in the process in this group.

There is a social factor which may arise in the change from Modified Indian to Ladinoized Indian and to Ladino. As a given Indian group grows more like the Ladinos in customs, there may frequently be a tendency on the part of the Ladino group to crystallize the groups into a caste structure. The Indian of San Luis Jilotepeque would be considered as Modified on the basis of our categorization, and in San Luis, Tumin[17] has described in detail what he calls a caste structure. Roberts[18] has pointed out how much more strict the distinctions between the groups are in San Luis than in Aguas Escondidas where the surrounding Indians would be classed as Traditional. This tendency to crystallize into caste situation differences which had at one time been generally considered as ethnic differences probably occurs specifically in those situations in which the Indians and Ladinos are living in some numbers in the same physical community. If a community is almost entirely Indian, the Ladinos have nothing to gain by making much of a caste system since they must, in practice, live with their neighbors, but the same general restrictions as to intermarriage hold. An example of the latter would be the town of Magdalena Milpas Altas. So long as a group remains in the category of Traditional Indian, the customs of the Indians and

---

[17] 1952. [18] 1948.

Ladinos are so distinct that there is little problem of much passing from one group to another. The very nature of the ethnic differences prohibits rapid group ladinoization and individual ladinoization through marginal contact simply does not occur with any great frequency. But when an Indian group has become Modified, and even more so when it passes on towards being Ladinoized Indian, then it must be fitted anew into the Ladino society and in this process, it seems likely that a caste situation is likely to develop.

With respect to this development, it may be noted that it is probably in this same situation that the social importance of race is brought up as being of importance. As customs cease to aid in the identification of the Indian group, the Ladinos must resort to some other characteristic. This introduces the occasionally ludicrous situation in which a Ladino, who racially appears to be mestizo, puts social distance between himself and an Indian who is also racially mestizo, because of presumed racial differences.

With respect to Traditional Indian societies, race is of minor importance; when it does become an issue, it does not manifest the characteristics of racial prejudice as are found in some other parts of the world, but is included as one of a number of social distinctions in the delineation of an Indian class or caste group.

The change from Ladinoized Indian to Ladino, presumably the last possible stage in the process of ladinoization, is difficult to identify since once the term Ladino is applied to a group, it is not easy to discover which elements may once have been Indian. One such group may be that in the municipio of San José la Arada. In this *municipio* an older Ladino inhabitant confided that most of the population was Indian because they had Indian antecedents. The people to whom he referred as Indians, however, claimed to be Ladinos and from the point of view of their society and culture, it would be difficult for an outsider to classify them otherwise. The most likely reason that it is difficult to identify the situation in which Ladinoized Indians are changing into Ladinos is that the process necessarily involves the dissolution of the Indian society; thus in the change from Traditional to Modified or Modified to Ladinoized we are still dealing with Indian societies, but in that from the last of these to Ladino, we are dealing with the disappearance of a social entity.

Individual ladinoization, as was mentioned before, is quite a distinct process from group ladinoization. It involves a person moving out of one socio-cultural group and into another. This social mobility may be basically classed into two types: (1) movement horizontally from any one of the Indian categories to that of New Ladino, or the limbo and disconnected status wherein the person lives among Ladinos as a Ladino, but because of the retention of personal habits of Indian origin (speaking dialectic Spanish, for example), is often thought of as an Indian;[19] and (2) upward mobility from one of the Indian group categories into the middle class of the Ladino population. Of the two, the former is much the most common, but the latter, because of the tremendous personal adjustments and perseverance involved, is more spectacular. Both types of movement

---

[19] The Totonicapán Indian described by Behrendt (1949) is one such person.

involve basic habit changes and a relinquishing of participation in Indian social organization. But the former occurs more commonly in a slow, unconscious or semi-conscious manner, while the latter usually involves some positive motivation on the part of the individual concerned to "better himself." A case of horizontal movement is of an Indian who leaves his home community in Baja Verapaz to seek work on the Pacific coast. While at first he makes regular trips to his old home, these gradually become more infrequent, more and more his habits become adjusted to the Ladino coastal milieu and less and less can he fit into his old Indian society. A case of vertical mobility is that of an Indian who takes up some Ladino skill such as truck driving or school teaching, leaves his own community, and because of his occupational specialization enters not the laboring Ladino class, but some bracket of the middle urban class in some other community.

It will be noted that in both cases cited, the movement out of the Indian socio-cultural context and into the Ladino was accomplished through separation from the group. This, perhaps, is not an absolute necessity for such movement, but it makes it much easier. Mobility within one's own community is difficult, since everyone always knows one's antecedents. King reports from his work in the Alta Verapaz that "Among the Ladinos an ideal picture of social mobility for the Indian is painted, in which the assumption of certain patterns of behavior makes ladinoization possible. But when questioned about well educated Indians who obviously have all the stated prerequisites, the Ladino generally assesses the Indian in these terms: 'He is almost Ladino, but not quite'."[20] The writer found the same situation to hold in the Modified Indian community of Magdalena. There, a man who had taken over most of the Ladino traits, and occasionally referred to himself as a Ladino, was almost universally considered by both Ladinos and Indians of the community as *"algo Ladino,"* i.e., almost Ladino, but not quite.

Communities vary in the degree to which they allow social mobility within the bounds of the local society. Tumin describes the situation in San Luis Jilotepeque as one in which social mobility, for practical purposes, does not exist, and he indicates this by referring to it as a caste system.[21] The development of a caste-like situation is doubtless related to the length of time that Ladinos have been resident in the community and its apparentness depends upon the degree of ladinoization of the Indian community involved. In Traditional Indian communities where there are resident Ladinos it may be said without any question that two castes do exist, but the relationship between the castes is often superficially cordial, and lack of mixture is a matter of mutual desire. The very fact of such extreme custom differences between the two groups almost precludes intermixture. But as we move into Modified and Ladinoized Indian communities, it becomes easier for the Indian to alter his customs, Ladino goals become more attractive, and as a result it may become necessary

---

[20] King, 1952, p. 142.
[21] Tumin, 1952. See also Roberts, 1948, for a comparison of two communities.

for the Ladinos to strengthen their superior position by attempting to crystallize the caste situation.

The solution to all these situations is for the individual Indian to change his place of residence. If he moves to another town or the city, adopts Ladino customs and divests himself of Indian behavioral characteristics, there is little interest to inquire whether he was born Indian or Ladino. The separation serves to remove him from the restraints placed on his mobility by both his old Ladino neighbors and his Indian family and associates. It does occasionally occur that the individual changes from Indian to Ladino within his own community, but these may probably be considered to be extraordinary cases. There are various cases of people who through personal maladjustment to the Indian culture and society take over Ladino customs, but they are usually regarded like those cited in Magdalena and by King in the Alta Verapaz. If they do make this change, it is possible frequently for their children to achieve a firmer hold on the Ladino status.

In general, a complete change from Indian to Ladino within one generation is a difficult thing; over two generations, however, it is not only much easier but doubtless occurs with some frequency. And if this is combined with separation from the natal community, then acceptance is practically assured.

There is little doubt that through much of its recent history the growth of the Ladino population has been due in some measure to the ladinoization of portions of the Indian population. On the basis of present evidence, however, it is impossible to estimate the relative importance of these increments in comparison with the evidently greater natural increase to be found among the Ladinos. It seems certain that ladinoization, both individual and group, goes in spurts. A changing economic or political situation may set up stresses in which communities become more ladinoized and in which individuals find themselves personally forced to give up the Indian way of life. This is a subject which needs a great deal more study. To date, most investigations of Ladinos and Indians have been on inter-ethnic relations, and we have little intensive work on which to base conclusions concerning the inner workings and importance of the ladinoization process as such.

II. THE CULTURE OF THE GUATEMALAN TOWN AND COUNTRY LADINO

1. LAND AND AGRICULTURE

In this and the following sections on the culture and society of the Guatemalan Ladino it is necessary to realize that we are principally concerned with a group which comprises less than half the total population of the country. Many of the figures which are available from the population and agricultural censuses are given for departmental units and do not provide data on the distinct sociocultural groups. Therefore, it is necessary at times to continue to talk in terms of the Ladino, Mixed, and Indian departments which were delineated earlier.

Also, some material refers to the country as a whole and, of course, includes the Indian as well as the Ladino departments. In other words, while we want to speak of the Ladinos of Guatemala, it is necessary at times to speak of all of Guatemala.

For the total land area of the republic, the *agropecuario* census of 1950 provides the breakdown shown in Table 7.

Table 7 indicates that there is a relatively high percentage of land under cultivation in Guatemala, in view of the mountainous terrain of the country. As a matter of comparison, for example, the amount of land under cultivation in Panama is only about 3.3% of the total land area of the country as opposed to the 18.6% in Guatemala. In general, 30.7% of the land of the country, excluding the Petén, is cultivatable and now in *fincas*; of the remainder, 29% is

Table 7.—Distribution of land surface in Guatemala, 1950. (*Estadística, Mensaje Quincenal*, No. 38, 15 *Junio*, 1952. *Guatemala*. p. 2)

	Kilometers^2	Percent
Total land area of the Republic (excluding Belice)	108,889.0	100.0%
Not exploited, and occupied by populated areas, roads, rivers, lakes, etc.	40,631.0	37.3%
Occupied by forests, savannahs, and national lands of the Petén	31,611.0	29.0%
Occupied by *fincas*	36,647.5	33.7%
1) In agricultural exploitations	20,222.5	18.6%
2) In land which is usable, but not used in agriculture at the time of the census	13,171.5	12.1%
3) Not usable for agriculture	3,253.0	3.0

in the Petén and 37.3% is either not exploited or otherwise occupied in the rest of the country.

There is no precise correlation between the percentage of land in *fincas* and those occupied by the different ethnic groups. It develops that the distinctly Ladino departments fall into two extremes on this point (see Table 8, column H); Izabal, Zacapa, and El Progreso have under 50% of their total area in *fincas*; Escuintla, Santa Rosa, and Guatemala have over 75% of their lands so occupied. Jutiapa has about 63% in *fincas*. This difference, observed here in terms of amount of land occupied in *fincas*, between those Ladino departments of the Motagua corridor and those of the south coast will be seen to have correlates in many of the phases of agriculture and culture of Ladino Guatemala. Since it will crop up from time to time, it is well at the outset to think in terms of at least two foci of Ladino culture: the Motagua corridor and the south coast.

Of the remaining departments of the republic, all the Mixed departments have between 25% and 75% of their lands in *fincas*, while the Indian departments show considerable variation in the matter. Totonicapán has only 18.8% of its land in *fincas* while Chimaltenango has 62.5% privately held.

While *finca* size varies considerably over the republic, by far the greater

Table 8.—1950 Agricultural economy: Land
Sources: Col. A–H—EMQ, various issues; Col. I—El Espectador, 1954. Ratios calculated from EMQ data

Department	A Total No. of *fincas*	B Area of *fincas* in *manzanas*	C No. *manzanas* per *finca*	D No. irrigated *manzanas*	E No. *manzanas* irrigated per 1000 *manzanas*	F No. irrigated *fincas*	G No. irrigated *fincas* per 1000 *fincas*	H % of Land in *fincas*	I *Manzanas* expropriated 1/53–5/54 Agrarian reform
El Progreso	5,619	125,304	22.3	1,465	11.7	245	43.6	45.6	14,995
Santa Rosa	15,321	375,141	24.2	5,513	14.7	235	15.3	88.9	38,953
Izabal	4,739	290,052	61.2	—	—	—	—	22.5	118,097
Escuintla	10,648	649,361	60.9	9,708	14.9	52	4.9	100.0	209,330
Guatemala	18,331	252,297	13.7	1,930	7.6	1,298	59.2	83.3	33,213
Zacapa	5,973	164,153	27.6	3,093	18.6	1,086	181.5	42.8	2,759
Jutiapa	21,464	289,113	13.5	1,089	3.8	91	4.2	62.9	17,353
El Petén	2,162	20,532	9.5	—	—	—	—	<1%	—
Total Ladino Dept.	84,257	2,165,905	25.6/17.8*	22,798	12.3	3,007	35.6	57.1	434,700
Jalapa	11,807	162,624	13.7	422	2.6	67	5.7	55.2	4,509
Sacatepéquez	9,024	51,178	5.7	411	8.1	76	8.4	77.0	6,227
Retalhuleu	8,542	192,473	22.6	909	4.7	16	1.9	72.6	18,336
Baja Verapaz	11,761	222,541	19.2	865	3.9	313	26.6	49.9	23,355
Chiquimula	15,008	121,174	8.1	842	6.9	427	28.5	39.1	1,047
Suchitepéquez	12,420	236,938	19.0	9,384	39.5	40	3.2	66.2	43,301
Quezaltenango	19,540	179,691	9.2	613	3.4	123	6.3	64.4	7,125
Total Mixed Dept.	88,102	1,166,619	13.1	13,446	11.5	1,062	12.2	51.9	103,900
San Marcos	33,724	316,237	9.4	6,872	21.7	606	18.0	58.4	13,669
Huehuetenango	32,025	342,722	10.7	1,082	3.2	875	27.4	32.5	48,048
Chimaltenango	18,054	176,800	9.8	611	3.6	128	7.1	62.5	30,376
El Quiché	25,642	279,914	10.9	516	1.9	151	5.9	23.4	73,764
Alta Verapaz	28,187	702,352	24.9	148	.2	10	.4	57.3	128,563
Sololá	13,559	56,248	4.2	186	3.4	290	21.3	37.1	2,063
Totonicapán	17,620	28,513	1.6	18	.6	20	1.1	18.8	—
Total Indian Dept.	168,811	1,902,786	11.3	9,433	5.0	2,080	10.2	41.2	296,483
Total	341,188	5,235,358		45,677		6,149	18.0		

* Calculation minus Depts. of Escuintla and Izabal.

number of holdings are small. Preliminary data from the *Agropecuario* Census of 1950 shows the results for the country as a whole (Table 9).

The bulletin from which the data appearing in Table 9 was taken noted that the mode of between 2 to 5 *manzanas* held good for the entire republic except in certain parts of the west where "small landholdings are very numerous." It will be seen, however, that almost half the *fincas* are under 2 *man-*

zanas (about 3½ acres) in size, while over 75% of them are under 5 *manzanas* (about 8⅔ acres) *manzana* is equal to 1.736 acres.)

The relative amount of land in *fincas* changed somewhat after these data were collected. During the years following the 1945 revolution, the Guatemalan Government promulgated a number of acts which affected the nature of the economic relationships, landholdings and land usufruct. The principal acts were the Agrarian Reform, the Law of Forced Rental, and the establishment of a labor code and agricultural labor unions.

The Agrarian Reform has resulted in the splitting up of many *fincas* into small landholdings. Escuintla and Izabal, the two departments with the highest number of *manzanas* per *finca* in 1950 are among the three most affected by this (see Table 8). By May of 1954, 209,330 *manzanas* (approximately 1,465 km²) or slightly under one third of the total *finca* area of Escuintla and 118,097

Table 9. Number of *fincas* by size for the republic. A 10% sample from *Censo Agropecuario*, 1950 (*From Estadística, Mensaje Quincenal*, No. 16, *June* 15, 1951, p. 8)

Size in *manzanas*	Number of *fincas*	Percentage Each	Percentage Sum
Less than 1	6,990	21.0%	21.0%
1 to less than 2	8,795	26.5	47.5
2 to less than 5	9,544	28.7	76.2
5 to less than 10	4,055	12.2	88.4
10 to less than 32	2,579	7.7	96.1
32 and over	1,278	3.9	100.0
Total of 10% sample	33,241	100.0%	

manzanas of Izabal, or slightly over 40% of the *finca* land had been repartitioned. While data on the number of new *fincas* and their relative size was not available at the time of writing, it is clear that this will have a tremendous effect on the relative size of landholdings in these departments and in other sections of the country where the Agrarian Reform has been particularly pressed. According to data provided before the revolution of June, 1954, the four departments which had been most affected by the repartitioning of lands were (in descending order) Escuintla, Alta Verapaz (128,563 *manzanas*, or 41% of *finca* land of the department), Izabal and El Quiché (73,764 *manzanas*, or 26% of *finca* land of the department). In all, 20% of the *finca* area of Ladino departments was expropriated, 15.5% of the *finca* area of Indian departments, and 8.9% of that of the Mixed departments. However, the Agrarian Reform was a political move as well as an economic measure, and the degree to which any given department was hit was determined as much by political motives as by economic fact. As a result, outside of Escuintla, Alta Verapaz and Izabal, the remaining departments in which a great deal of land was repartitioned had little to do with the relative size of the *fincas* present in the departments; in

Zacapa, for example, which had the third highest departmental *manzana* per *finca* rate (27.6) in the country, only 2,759 *manzanas*, or less than 1.7% of the *finca* lands, were repartitioned.

The Agrarian Reform was designed to break up large landholdings which were not actually under cultivation. It had little effect on smaller landholdings which fell into this category or which might be regularly rented out. Large *finca* holders in Guatemala comprised a relatively small percent of the entire population. Owners of smaller holdings, of course, included many more. The Law of Forced Rental was designed to bring small landholdings, which had previously been rented, under control and on a regulated rental basis. By this law lands which had been rented out or which were not being used by a landholder would be subject to forced rental at what would amount to a payment of 5% of the value of the crop annually. In many parts of Guatemala where large *fincas* were not common this law was felt much more heavily than was the Agrarian Reform, but it did not receive the publicity and political propaganda which the latter received. Also of importance was that the Law of Forced Rental hit many of the middle landholders, persons who were often of a local upper class. This law, administered by the municipalities, was an attempt to weaken the power of the small property holders as the Agrarian Reform attempted to weaken that of the large landholders.

From the point of view of the local Ladino culture in Guatemala, the Law of Forced Rental had a social effect which was different, but culturally more immediately felt than the effect of the Agrarian Reform. While the Reform redivided the land, the main body of customs at which it struck were those of the *finca* owner group and of the *patrón-mozo* relationship. The people who received the land began to work on a new economic base, for themselves if the land was *milpa* land, or for a government controlled cooperative if the land was in cane or coffee; but generally the same work went on as before. The Law of Forced Rental struck rather at the body of customs involved in the relations between established social classes within a locality and the pattern of labor related to these classes. Previously in Guatemala (and in fact it continues in many parts today) sharecropping had been much more common, and rental for a whole variety of locally established rates was standard. The Law of Forced Rental succeeded in destroying various of these older customs and, in so doing, destroying certain of the established relationships which existed between the upper and lower local classes.

The establishment of agricultural labor unions on the large *fincas* was one of the first of the government efforts to reduce the strength of the large landholder and provided the agricultural laborer with a tool by which he could fight the *finquero*. There is little doubt that there was abuse of labor during the period previous to the 1945 revolution; the establishment of labor unions, combined with setting up labor judges who were instructed to favor the laborers, succeeded in destroying the entire paternalistic basis upon which the majority of the larger *fincas* had previously been administrated. The establishment of a labor law by which high indemnities were to be paid for laborers who were fired, and labor unions which prevented the firing of anyone they wished to retain, made a large labor force a liability from the *finquero's* point of view and destroyed the social relationships which had theretofore existed between the *patrón* and the *mozo*. The unionization of labor and the accompanying labor code did not have an immediate effect on the land situation.

Thus three major pieces of legislation were directed at attempting to destroy certain existing socio-economic relationships, and each was aimed at a crucial point in these relationships. The unionization and labor code tried to establish the laborer with certain rights as against the *finquero*; the Agrarian Reform was directed at setting up many of the laborers as small landholders, although they would still be dependent upon the government for their holdings and in so doing shift their dependence from the *finquero* to the government; and the Law of Forced Rental was designed to destroy the existent socio-economic relationships between the renter and the holder of medium and small parcels of land.

At the time of writing the government which established these various reform measures has been overthrown and replaced by another which was against the abuses and probably more extreme phases of the previous government's policy. The Law of Forced Rentals has been abolished, and the Agrarian Reform is under revision. The future effect of these acts will depend, obviously, on the policies and activities of the new government. There is little doubt but that the social relationships at which the older measures were aimed will not easily be reinstituted to their former full strength.

On the basis of the contemporary landholding situation that exists in the country it is possible to distinguish economic strata within the Ladino agricultural group. While the great majority of Ladinos are agriculturalists, it is not possible to provide precise figures, since the census figures for 1950 on this subject were not available at the time of writing. A reasonable guess is that about 65% of the Ladino population is so engaged. These agriculturalists may be classified into five major economic types: the *finquero*, large landowner who may or may not reside on his land; the *medium holder*, or person who has medium sized holdings, usually lives on the land or more commonly in a municipal capital near the holdings; the *small holder*, the person who owns more or less enough to live off of, and usually lives on his holding or in a community nearby; the *renter*, who will rent enough to live off of; and the *laborer*, who works as either permanent or day labor. In fact, within the bottom three brackets there is much overlapping; a small holder may rent extra land if he needs it; both the small holder and the renter may work part time as labor, and in some regions, will commonly participate in the coffee harvests. Within the group here classed as laborer there are two groups which should be distinguished: the *colono* or farm laborer who is resident on the farm where he works and who usually receives free from the farm some land on which to plant his own *milpa*; and *jornalero* or the day laborer, who lives in his own house either in an *aldea* or town, and who works by the day. It is the *jornalero* who may also rent some land; the *colono* rarely, if ever does.

Socially, the *finquero* is usually a member of the class we later will characterize as being cosmopolitan upper. These large landholders usually have closer social ties with other *finqueros* and urbanites than with local people. They therefore live either on their farms or in the nearest large center, a departmental or the national capital. It is generally on the farms of the *finqueros* that one finds *colonos*, and the old *patrón-mozo* relationship is basically one between the large landowner and his resident labor. The medium landholder is usually a member of a local upper class, and may work with day laborers and renters. He may have some *colonos* on his farm but there are usually not very many. His own residence is usually kept either on the farm or in the nearest local center, be it a municipal or departmental capital. As will be indicated in Section IV of the present paper, the medium landholder often composes what might be called an "irrigation aristocracy" within some of the departmental communities; where there is irrigation water available, it is usually the owners of the irrigable land who form the local upper class. The particular combination of the various economic groups to be found regionally is described in Section IV.

For Guatemala as a whole, there may be said to be three major socio-economic patterns: (1) the *finquero-colono* pattern; (2) the medium holder-*jornalero* pattern; (3) the independent subsistence farmer pattern. These patterns, of course. are related to the size and productivity of the landholdings. The independent subsistence farmer may be said to be found in some quantity over the entire country with the exception of certain zones which are under intensive plantation production, such as portions of the southwest piedmont, the major banana plantations, and parts of the central and southwestern coast. The medium holder-*jornalero* pattern is to be found mainly in the Ladino regions of the Motagua Valley, the eastern highlands, southeastern highlands and southeastern coast. There are areas of the southeast piedmont which have the *finca-colono* pattern.

The establishment of the Agrarian Reform obviously must have an effect on the size of the area and population involved in the *finquero-colono* pattern; the law of forced rentals has had its effect on the medium landholder-*jornalero* pattern. Both have tried to convert the subordinate members of the pattern into individual subsistence farmers.

Turning now from the general social organization related to the landholding system, let us take up some of the specific relationships which exist in certain types of land usufruct. In the rental of land, there have been three ways in which one pays for the privilege of usufruct over someone else's land: payment in cash or in crop value of cash; payment in labor; and sharecropping. Payment in cash or crop value of cash is to be found throughout the Ladino region. This type of payment is simply straight rental of a piece of land for cash or for a set quantity of crop. The amount of crop which one may pay will usually have nothing to do with the excellence of the crop, but will be related to the amount of cash which one would pay if he had it to pay. The payment of crops in this situation is a substitute for payment in cash. The amount paid varies from region to region. In the southwest piedmont, between 125 and 200 *mazorcas*, or ears of corn, is the rent due on one *cuerda* of land. In San José la Arada,

800 *mazorcas* would be paid for half a *manzana*. While this type of rental is cash based, account is usually taken of the quality of the land and the excellence of the year's harvest, and payment may not be pressed heavily if a crop turns out to be very bad.

Payment in labor is most commonly found in one of two ways: as a variation of sharecropping, and as a means of guaranteeing a labor force for a given *finca*. It is customary over most of Guatemala for the large *fincas* to provide land on which the laborers may plant their own *milpa*. Actually, nothing is paid for this land; it is provided that the laborers will be able to grow some of their own food and so that they will not have to go far away to get land to do this. In some cases, this land is provided for people who may come annually to work on a coffee *finca* distant from their homes, in which case the land is near the laborer's home and not on the *finca* itself. Ladinos from Zaragoza go to the Escuintla region to work in this manner; they harvest coffee and are given land on which to plant.

The land guarantee for labor exists as a portion of the relationship between the *finquero* and *colono*, and sometimes between medium holder and *jornalero*.

Sharecropping is a basis of payment which is fundamentally different from cash payment or labor payment. Sharecropping is based on the idea that a person works the land of another, and the two split the gains in accordance with the amount harvested. There is a great deal of variation in sharecropping methods in Guatemala, and on the basis of the survey it is not possible to distinguish regions of distinct usage. Sharecropping as such, however, seems to be most common in those regions in the east and Motagua Valley. Furthermore, there seems to be a definite trend towards a decreasing use of sharecropping, a situation which has been encouraged by the Law of Forced Rental. In Gualán, Teculután, and Atescatempa, the most liberal sharecropping system the writer has encountered anywhere in Central America was reported. In these communities it was said that the owner and sharecropper each provided one half of all the supplies needed, and they both also supplied one half the labor; the crop was then divided. In Mataquescuintla a unique form of sharecropping was reported. There the sharecropper would work ten *cuerdas*[22] of forty *varas* each, and the harvest of one of these *cuerdas* would go to the owner of the land. A variation on this was for the sharecropper to have ten *cuerdas* of 25 *varas* for himself and one of 40 for the owner. The custom in both these cases was for the sharecropper to do the cleaning of the land, the sowing, and the cultivation; the owner would then harvest his portion and the sharecropper his. The Mataquescuintla sharecropping is limited to *milpa*, i.e., corn, or corn and beans. Land for all other crops is paid for.

A type of sharecropping (common elsewhere in Latin America) is that called *al partir* in Chitatul. The landowner provides the land and the seed, the sharecropper provides all the work, and the produce is divided half and half between

---

[22] The *cuerda* in Guatemala varies in size from 25 to 40 *varas*, or Spanish yards. It is usually specified which is used, and sometimes both extremes will be found in use in the same community, as is the case in Mataquescuintla.

the two. In Zaragoza yet another form is found: there a man who gets ten *cuerdas* for himself is expected to prepare ten more *cuerdas* for the owner. He does all the work on his own, and does the first cleaning and first cultivation on the land for the owner. The owner does his own planting and harvesting on his own land. It was said in Zaragoza that most people were quite pleased with this form of rental and had not switched to the legal 5% payment decreed by the Law of Forced Rental. The harshest sharecropping system reported was that said to exist prior to the Law of Forced Rental in Guazacapán. The informant providing the information was rather emotionally in favor of the government measures, and claimed that Guazacapán had had the hardest sharecropping system with which he was familiar in the entire country. It consisted in the sharecropper not only doing all the work on the land, and then splitting the crop with the owner, but giving three additional days of labor to the owner.

Sharecropping is essentially a relationship which exists between the medium holder and the individual subsistence farmer or laborer. The *finquero* rarely bothers with sharecropping. Consequently, there is reason to see some correlation between the distribution of sharecropping as reported on the survey and the distribution of the medium holder population. The fact that sharecropping is disappearing today makes it difficult to confirm this correlation; it is in general being replaced by straight cash based land rental. Sharecropping, when it involves the mutual labor of both the owner and renter, is not likely to be done when there exists a great social class gap between the two individuals concerned. Thus it does not seem to be very common for sharecropping to exist in areas where there are significant Indian groups since the caste barrier makes the persons concerned reluctant to work together. Nowhere in the Indian area was such labor reported. Similarly, sharecropping does not occur between a *finquero* and a laborer. Consequently, it is not found in those regions where the land is primarily in the hands of large *fincas*, such as Escuintla was prior to the Agrarian Reform. It seems likely, however, that sharecropping must also be correlated with an old Spanish pattern, and not only with the sociological structure which has survived and supported it in certain regions. That it is found principally where medium holders are found provides us with an understanding of its sociological support and also a suggestion that it came in with this older structure. We naturally ask ourselves the question if, with the creation of numerous new landholders of the medium and small category, a sharecropping pattern will emerge in those areas where the Agrarian Reform has been most active. The writer suspects that the answer is no. There is no inherent relation between sharecropping and medium and small holders. The two were and are related historically in certain parts of Guatemala, but this does not mean that such a relationship need be re-established as new medium holders are developed in regions where sharecropping was never intensively practised before. Considering the trend away from sharecropping in those very regions where it is still based on the old social structure, there is little reason to think that it will re-establish itself elsewhere in the country.

Communal landownership is fairly rare in Ladino Guatemala. The *ejidal* lands which were established during the colonial period were almost all broken up during Barrios' regime in the last century. The writer encountered only two cases of communally owned property in the course of the survey and in one the land had been established after Barrios' time as private property held in common by a series of co-owners. It was not communal in the sense of belonging to a community as such, but belonged to a specific series of families which had purchased it. In Quesada, the only community in which data was collected on the matter, a large *finca* was purchased about 1890 by a group of families living in what was then the *aldea* of Quesada. The level lands of the *finca* were divided up among the various families involved, and the uplands were set up as communal property of the co-owners. Control of these lands is in the hands of a *Junta Directiva de Terrenos Comunales* (Directing Council of Communal Lands) which is elected every two years by the co-owners. All the co-owners, being the heirs of the original co-owners, have the right to use the communal land for cultivation, subject to the approval of the Council. The Council is concerned that a certain portion of the land be retained for pasturage grounds and that there is adequate forest land preserved. They must approve the burning over of the ground for cultivation and see that the weeds have grown high enough before permitting it to be used again. The fact that most of the land of Quesada is in the hands of heirs of the original purchasers of the land from the *finca* or in communal land resulting from the same purchase has meant that neither the Agrarian Reform nor the Law of Forced Rental had much effect in the community. The only other community in which it was reported that communal lands were held by co-owners was an *aldea*, El Terrero, in the *municipio* of La Gomera. No specific data was gathered on the situation there.

Municipal ownership of lands was still fairly common in Guatemala, but was being affected by the Agrarian Reform. The amount of land held by a *municipio* varies greatly; in the Indian *municipio* of Totonicapán most of the *municipio* is in municipally-held lands. This, however, is an exaggerated case. The town of San Rafael Tierra del Pueblo takes its name from the fact that the land, prior to the Agrarian Reform, belonged to the *municipio* of Mazatenango. It was rented by the residents at a rate of 25¢ per *cuerda*, usually in lots of 50 or 100 *cuerdas* each. The right to rent a given parcel of land was inherited within a family. Municipal lands were among the first affected by the Agrarian Reform. In the town of Petapa bad feeling developed on the part of the inhabitants who had previously rented this land; in the process of the Agrarian Reform, many outsiders came in to claim the land and when it was divided up the inhabitants of Petapa who had previously worked the land lost it to these outsiders. In many cases the *municipalidades* formerly charged a minimum of rent or no rent at all for use of the municipal lands. At the time of writing the status of these municipal lands is uncertain.

While a great deal of work is done on rented land or through sharecropping, there are also many Ladino subsistence landholders who work their own lands. The agricultural work on one's own land is accomplished principally by one's own labor, the help of the family, by employing laborers, and through exchange labor. It is almost unheard of for a *finquero* to do his own field labor, but among the medium holders it is not uncommon for the landowner to participate in the field labor as a director of his hired laborers. Among the small holders and renters, of course, the man does almost all his own work. According to the data collected on the survey, the participation of women in agricultural work occurs

Table 10.—1950 Agricultural economy: People
Source: EMQ, various issues. Ratios calculated from EMQ data

Department	A No. *fincas* giving information	B No. of people occupied	C No. people per *finca*	D No. people under 14 years old	E Number of men	F Number of women	G No. women per man	H No. children per man
El Progreso	4,379	16,411	3.8	4,887	7,963	3,561	.45	.61
Santa Rosa	12,934	49,433	3.8	10,998	29,413	9,022	.31	.37
Izabal	3,316	12,664	3.8	2,876	7,233	2,555	.35	.40
Escuintla	6,693	37,701	5.6	4,131	29,033	4,537	.16	.14
Guatemala	13,595	51,421	3.8	11,625	29,470	10,326	.35	.39
Zacapa	4,230	18,970	4.5	4,992	9,313	4,665	.50	.54
Jutiapa	19,139	62,494	3.3	15,009	33,734	13,751	.41	.45
El Petén	1,177	6,343	5.4	1,328	3,287	1,728	.53	.39
Total Ladino Dept	65,463	255,437	3.9	55,846	149,446	50,145	.34	.37
Jalapa	9,311	46,541	5.0	10,312	21,118	15,111	.72	.48
Sacatepéquez	6,687	17,182	2.6	2,341	11,897	2,944	.24	.20
Retalhuleu	7,246	27,398	3.8	4,216	18,318	4,864	.27	.23
Baja Verapaz	9,987	34,626	3.5	7,461	19,598	7,567	.39	.38
Chiquimula	11,528	46,328	4.0	11,921	22,975	11,432	.50	.52
Suchitepéquez	7,951	43,703	5.5	7,102	28,907	7,694	.27	.25
Quezaltenango	15,597	65,956	4.2	13,122	38,064	14,770	.40	.35
Total Mixed Dept	68,307	281,734	4.1	56,475	160,877	64,382	.40	.35
San Marcos	29,565	106,426	3.6	20,587	65,756	20,084	.30	.31
Huehuetenango	28,315	98,213	3.5	20,103	60,242	17,868	.30	.33
Chimaltenango	14,802	46,595	3.1	7,247	32,906	6,442	.20	.22
El Quiché	18,614	70,556	3.8	16,529	38,768	15,259	.39	.43
Alta Verapaz	24,534	104,065	4.2	21,853	57,165	25,047	.44	.38
Sololá	12,374	39,852	3.2	7,673	23,139	9,040	.39	.33
Totonicapán	14,069	49,916	3.5	12,786	22,934	14,196	.62	.56
Total Indian Dept	142,273	515,623	3.6	106,778	300,910	107,936	.36	.36
Total	276,043	1,052,794	3.8	219,099	611,233	222,463	.36	.36

among Ladinos only in certain specialized activities on *fincas*, and hence only within the renter and laborer groups. With the single and outstanding exception of the Carib population of Livingston it may be said that Ladino women generally do no subsistence agriculture. The main agricultural activity in which women regularly work is in the harvesting of coffee on *fincas*, and it is again only the women of the lower economic levels who do this. This data collected from the survey seems to be in violent disagreement with statistics published by the Guatemalan government on the basis of their *agropecuario* census of 1950. According to the data provided by the census (see Table 10, column G) for the country as a whole, the ratio of women to men working in agriculture is .36; the range is from a low of .16 for the Department of Escuintla to a high of .72 in the Department of Jalapa. Among departments with a high ratio are the two Ladino departments on the Motagua, Zacapa (.50) and El Progreso (.45). According to the census data the Motagua region is very different from the Escuintla region in this matter, the former having a rather high ratio while the latter has a very low ratio. The writer is frankly at a loss to explain this discrepancy between the data gathered on the survey and that provided by the census. The census data do not seem to conform to the obvious facts of woman labor in such matters as coffee harvest; the Department of Suchitepéquez, for example, is given a ratio of only .24 and yet it is well known in Guatemala that the women in the coffee region of this department participate in the coffee harvest there. It may be of significance that the census gives approximately the same distribution for a high child-man ratio in agricultural work. The lowest departments in both child-man and woman-man ratios are Retalhuleu, Suchitepéquez, Escuintla, Chimaltenango, and Sacatepéquez; the departments with the highest ratios are Zacapa, El Progreso, Jalapa, Chiquimula and Totonicapán. It is clear that whatever it is that the census may have been measuring in this matter showed a marked variation between the south coast and the Motagua corridor.

The practice of hiring workers is found throughout Ladino Guatemala and among almost all the economic strata. It is often thought that it is only the *finqueros* and medium holders who have occasion to hire peons; this is definitely not the case. Anyone who may have some land to work, who needs help, and who has the money to pay for it, may hire a man for a few days. Among the renters and small landholders a man may act one day as the employer and the next as an employee. It is not uncommon for a man to employ help during the periods of heavy work in his own fields, and then go out to seek work himself during the off season. Thus the employer-employee distinction is almost socially meaningless within the lower economic strata. The social importance of the relationship develops when the employer is of a higher socio-economic strata.

Exchange labor, like sharecropping, is evidently on the decline in the Ladino population. Except for Livingston where a unique situation exists, exchange labor was reported from only seven towns and in most of those was said to be fairly rare. In Morales and Gualán it was called *cambio de mano* and *cambio mano*; in San Jerónimo and Granados in Baja Verapaz it went under the Quiché term, *cuchubal*; and in Palo Gordo it was called *mano por mano*. The only strictly Ladino community on the south coast in which it was reported was La Gomera, and there it was said to be very rare; there are very few small landholders there. In Tierra del Pueblo, where the population is principally Modified Indian, exchange labor was of some importance. Outside of Gualán and Morales, the only town surveyed in eastern Guatemala in which exchange labor was used was Quesada, and it occurred specifically with respect to the use of oxen; even there, however, it was said to be rare since most people had their own oxen. Exchange labor is similar to sharecropping in that both involve people on the lower economic levels. It occurs between persons in subsistence agricultural and laboring groups.

Annual migrations for economic purposes are very common in Guatemala. They are principally of three types: migration during the agricultural off season in the area of residence to the banana plantations at Tiquisate or Bananera; migrations during the coffee harvest to pick coffee on the *fincas;* and migrations to rent land on the coast for cultivation.[23] People from almost all the highland communities in which there are no large *fincas* participate in the labor migrations; migrations for the purposes of cultivation on the coast seem to be more a matter of community tradition. In some cases, the migrants will rent land from coffee *finqueros* and in return participate in the coffee harvest. The town of Palo Gordo presented the most extreme type of migratory planting pattern. In the *aldeas,* which are partially composed of Indians, it is common for people to go down to the piedmont and coast for the coffee harvest. Many of the townspeople themselves, however, go to the coastal plain around Ayutla for planting. After preparing and planting the fields around the town in the highlands, they go to the coast in April or May to make a first planting there; they then return to the highlands to carry on the cultivation. In August they go again to the coast for the first harvest and the second planting. Many will then remain on the coast and work in the coffee harvests, but by November all have returned again to Palo Gordo for the highland harvest. Again in January they return to the coast to take up the second harvest there, and come back again to the highlands to prepare the land for the next year's crop. Almost all this travel is done by bus at the cost of a dollar a trip. Usually the woman will go with the man to the coast, but some member of the family will remain to keep watch over the highland crop while the rest are working on the coast. While on the coast they rent land and make a temporary *ranchito* in which to live. It was reported in Palencia that some of the local people there followed a pattern similar to that of Palo Gordo, taking up two coastal harvests as well as the single highland harvest.

The lines of migration for renting and cultivating coast lands tend to run directly south and north. People from Palencia and Zaragoza go to Escuintla, people from Esquipulas Palo Gordo go to Ayutla. Migrations for planting on the coast are less common in the eastern part of the country than in the west. In part this is due to the fact that there are more local small *fincas* on which work may be had in the *oriente,* and the country itself is lower and does not have such a long growing season as is the case in the western highlands, and the southeast coast is narrower. It is quite common for people in towns near the Salvadorean border, Atescatempa and San Manuel Chaparrón for example, to go to the coffee harvests in El Salvador rather than in Guatemala. There is in the east, however, a greater tendency for people to go to the banana plantations in search of labor than is the case in the west.

---

[23] There is also migrant labor for the sugar cane harvest on some parts of the central Pacific coast, but the writer has no estimate of the relative number of people involved. It is fairly certain that it does not involve the migration of the whole family, as is the case usually for coffee harvests, since only men work in sugar cane harvesting.

The actual non-mechanized agricultural work carried on by the Ladinos of Guatemala is little different from that found in the Indian areas. There are regional variations, but these are not based so much on the fact of ethnic differences as on areas of colonial influence and geography. The implements used by the agriculturalists consist of items passed down from both Spanish and Indian traditions. From the Indian cultivations have come the digging stick and from the Spanish the hoe, plow, and machete. The machete is the only agricultural implement found universally in Ladino Guatemala. The hoe has a very wide distribution, the digging stick somewhat more restricted, and the plow is restricted to certain specific regions. The distribution of implements of Spanish origin must be seen in the light of their total contemporary distribution and not merely that within the Ladino regions.

There are two basically different types of machetes to be found in Guatemala: the straight and the hooked. There are variations on each, in some cases due to differences in manufacturer's designs and in some due to modifications made on the implements by the agriculturalists. The most common machete is the straight blade; depending upon local preferences or different use the specific form of the blade varies. These machetes go under various names; the most common are *collins, acapulco, calancheño, viscaíno* (also *viscaña, viscallo*), *colima*, and *corvo*. The other machete is hooked form which goes under the general name of *calabozo* (or *calabaza*).[24] While the straight machete is usually about 2½ feet long, the blade of the hooked machete is usually only a little over a foot or a foot and a half long. The principal variation on the hooked machete is made in some regions by bending the blade so that it may be used for cutting weeds more easily; this bent form goes under various names (*panda* in Esquipulas, *espano* in San Manuel Chaparrón, *cuma* in Atescatempa). While the straight machete is found in all parts of the country (although in Chitatul it was specifically said that it was not used for agriculture) the *calabozo* has a limited distribution. The *calabozo* is found in the east and north (Jutiapa, adjacent Santa Rosa, Jalapa, Chiquimula El Progreso, Zacapa and Baja Verapaz) and is reported by Goubaud, Rosales and Tax as being common in Huehuetenango.[25] This machete, also found elsewhere in Central America, has more or less the same distribution in Guatemala as does the wooden plow. The curved *calabozo* was said in some places to be specifically for the cleaning of the fields prior to the planting, and in others for cleaning during the cultivation. As is the case elsewhere in Central America, the machete is an implement of many uses; not only does it serve to cut down bush, but may be used as an implement of cultivation, for chopping wood, for wood working, and a variety of other purposes.

The hoe, presumably of Spanish derivation, is found almost everywhere in Guatemala. In some places, particularly in the midwestern highlands, it is the only implement of cultivation aside from the machete. The hoe varies in size depending upon the preferences from one region to another. It is used not

---

[24] Gillin, 1951, pp. 13–14, evidently confused the two terms for he has *corvo* applied to the hooked machete and *calabozo* applied to the straight.
[25] Goubaud, Rosales, and Tax, 1944, Map 3.

only as is the North American hoe, but also serves as a shovel and to chop brush. Aside from Livingston, the only region of Ladino population surveyed in which the hoe was not used was the coastal and piedmont region of Quezaltenango and San Marcos; there the machete and digging stick were the principal implements of cultivation.[26]

The digging stick, the principal implement of Indian origin which is used over much of Guatemala in agriculture, is used throughout the Ladino region. Oddly enough the only region in which it is absent in Guatemala is in the highland belt running from the Department of Guatemala to the Mexican border, an area which is overwhelmingly Indian. The digging stick is nowhere used alone; it is always supplemented by the machete, frequently by the *azadón* and sometimes by the plow. The term used for the digging stick varies somewhat and the writer could not determine any distributional pattern with respect to the Spanish terms. *Macana* seems to be the most common term, but *estaca, cubo, pujaguante, chuso, barretón,* and *huisute* are also found. Only the last, *huisute*, coming from the Pocomam Indian word *wisuk'ta*[27] has a specific distribution and that is the Pocomam region.

The use of the wooden plow in Guatemala, like the hooked machete, has a limited distribution but includes portions of both the Ladino and Indian regions. The data provided by the *agropecuario* census confirms the findings of the survey in this (see Table 11, Column B). There are three principal foci of wooden plows, Zacapa (500 per 1000 *fincas*), Huehuetenango (345 per 1000 *fincas*), and Jutiapa (226 per 1000 *fincas*). The other departments which form the belt from the east to the northwest all have over 81 wooden plows per 1000 *fincas*, Chiquimula (82 per 1000 *fincas*), Jalapa (116 per 1000 *fincas*), El Progreso (138 per 1000), Baja Verapaz (129 per 1000), and El Quiché (102 per 1000). In addition, the Department of San Marcos is recorded as having 127 plows per 1000 *fincas*. The use of the plow is determined by two factors: tradition and terrain. Within the area where tradition has dictated its use, it is limited by the actual terrain available. In all the departments concerned there is a great deal of broken and hilly land on which it is either impractical or impossible to use a plow. The wooden plow is always drawn by oxen and always requires that the land be reasonably level. It is of interest that the use of the wooden plow has recently extended. In Chiquimula, where there has been introduced a locally fabricated metal plow, it is being replaced by the new implement; but in the lower Motagua Valley (Morales) it was reported that the wooden plow was only introduced about 20 years ago and at present its use is on the increase. There was no evidence either from the survey or from the *agropecuario* census that the wooden plow is used in the Escuintla region; it was reported on the survey to be used very slightly in Suchitepéquez and further to the southwest

---

[26] Walter Hannstein suggests that the reason for the absence of the hoe in this southwestern region is that the German coffee farmers prohibited its use in the area under their control. It was the implement which was most responsible, in their estimation, for causing the situation which permitted erosion (conversation).

[27] Gillin, 1951, p. 14.

but the census data indicates that there were very few such plows in this region in 1950. The recent introduction of the plow into southeast Izabal reflects the recent spread of independent agriculturalist Ladinos into this region.

The present distribution of the plow in the Ladino region strongly suggests a correlation between the local medium holder social element and this colonially

Table 11.—1950 Agricultural economy: Implements
Source: EMQ, various issues. Ratios calculated from EMQ data

Department	A No. of wooden plows	B No. of wooden plows per 1000 *fincas*	C No. metal plows	D No. metal plows per 1000 *fincas*	E No. of tractors	F No. *carretas* and *carretones*	G No. of *trapiches*
El Progreso	774	137.6	75	13.3	4	162	118
Santa Rosa	257	16.8	543	35.4	14	382	260
Izabal	81	17.1	19	4.1	21	32	5
Escuintla	90	8.5	917	86.1	386	2,058	90
Guatemala	112	6.1	672	36.6	81	899	59
Zacapa	2,991	500.0	46	7.7	2	259	155
Jutiapa	4,861	226.5	520	24.2	12	278	102
El Petén	—	—	6	3.8	7	11	42
Total Ladino Dept.	9,166	108.9	2,798	33.2	527	4,081	831
Jalapa	1,365	115.6	107	9.1	13	176	54
Sacatepéquez	100	11.1	177	19.6	6	216	8
Retalhuleu	31	3.6	101	11.8	43	343	55
Baja Verapaz	1,516	128.9	141	12.0	4	106	115
Chiquimula	1,226	81.7	328	21.7	—	47	238
Suchitepéquez	30	2.4	192	15.5	57	603	43
Quezaltenango	232	11.9	259	13.2	37	330	47
Total Mixed Dept.	4,500	51.1	1,305	14.8	160	1,821	560
San Marcos	4,263	126.3	163	4.8	21	91	116
Huehuetenango	11,059	345.0	362	11.3	9	17	230
Chimaltenango	68	3.8	499	27.6	18	349	51
El Quiché	2,611	102.0	81	3.6	4	16	153
Alta Verapaz	32	1.1	36	1.3	8	54	99
Sololá	4	.3	39	2.9	2	47	5
Totonicapán	6	.3	28	1.6	1	6	—
Total Indian Dept.	18,043	107.0	1,208	7.2	63	580	654
Total	31,709		5,311		750	6,482	2,045

introduced implement. It cannot be mere chance that one of the strongest regions of medium holders has the most intense use of plows, whereas other regions, particularly the central south coast, have so few plows in use. It is probably significant also that the distribution of *trapiches* (sugar presses) as recorded in the census is essentially the same as that of the wooden plow. Both implements are colonial introductions; both are limited through factors of terrain or climate or both; and both are generally less common in the regions in which the New Ladino predominates. The *trapiche*, however, has of course followed the spread of sugar-cane production, whereas the plow is not restricted to the cultivation of a single crop.

Since the evidence points to the fact that the hooked machete has approximately the same distribution as does the plow and *trapiche*, it is suggested that its spread may have occurred about the same time as that of the other two implements.

Mechanized agriculture in Guatemala as of the time of the *Agropecuario* Census of 1950 and the time of the survey in 1954 had not developed as extensively as it had in certain other Central American countries. The great increase in mechanization in Central American agriculture has been a post-World War II phenomenon, but in Guatemala it was very much slowed by fear on the part of the wealthier farmers that the government sponsored labor unions, Agrarian Reform, and Law of Forced Rental, would reduce both their land and capital. Since it is not the purpose of this paper to explore the entire agricultural economy of rural Guatemala, we will take two implements, the tractor and the metal plow, for discussion as indications of the area most involved in mechanization (see Table 11). Of the tractors recorded in 1950, 386, or 48% of the total of 750 counted, were in the Department of Escuintla, and there is little doubt that the great majority of these were owned and operated by the United Fruit Company in the Tiquisate plantation. Even aside from this intense concentration, however, the distribution of the remaining tractors has been, in the main, complementary to that of the wooden plow. Thus the departments in which there were the most tractors were Escuintla (386), Guatemala (81), Suchitepéquez (57), Retalhuleu (43), and Quezaltenango (37). The region of the Old Ladino medium holders had among the fewest tractors per department: Zacapa (2), El Progreso (4), Baja Verapaz (4), Chiquimula (0), Jalapa (13), Jutiapa (12), and Santa Rosa (14). As has been the case of other distributions, there is a distinct difference between the Motagua corridor and the Escuintla region with respect to tractors. The type of terrain in the Motagua Valley itself does not militate against the use of tractors; indeed, the valley lands in El Progreso and Zacapa are flat and would be well suited to mechanized cultivation. This distribution seems to indicate that the medium holders in the Motagua corridor have been conservative with respect to the adoption of mechanization.

The distribution of metal plows is influenced by two factors: the introduction of mechanization, and the presence of wooden plows. While the census data on the number of metal plows counted makes no distinction between plows drawn by a tractor and those drawn by oxen, it is possible to make this distinction here. The highest number of metal plows per 1000 *fincas* is in the Department of Escuintla where there were 917, a rate of 86 per 1000 *fincas*. The departments with the next highest metal plow per 1000 *fincas* fall into two blocks: Guatemala (37), Sacatepéquez (20), and Chimaltenango (28); and Santa Rosa (35), Jutiapa (24), and Chiquimula (22). In the Department of Guatemala it is not possible to say how many of the metal plows are drawn by tractors, but the fact that there are 672 plows and only 81 tractors suggests that most of them are drawn by oxen; however, in the course of the survey of the towns of Petapa and Palencia, there was little evident use of metal plows at all. Those in Sacatepéquez and Chimaltenango must, in the main, be drawn principally by oxen.

The eastern block of three departments in which metal plows are relatively numerous are without doubt areas in which the metal plow is used with oxen. None of the three departments had over 14 tractors in 1950, and one, Chiquimula, had none; but in 1950 there were recorded a total of 1391 metal plows for this region. Mention has already been made of the local fabrication of metal plows in Chiquimula; in the survey it was not discovered whether there were other centers of manufacture of these implements, but in view of their distribution it seems likely that there may be.

As was the case with the tractor distribution, there is very little use of metal plows in the Motagua Valley. Izabal had 19 or 4 per 1000 *fincas*, Zacapa had 46 or 8 per 1000 *fincas*, El Progreso had 75 or 13 per 1000 *fincas*. Baja Verapaz had 141 metal plows, but only 12 per 1000 *fincas* and Jalapa had 107, but only 9 per 1000 *fincas*. In this, this region is again distinct from the southern coastal region. The fact of an eastern center of production, however, has placed the metal plow in a part of the Ladino region in which it is not correlated with the tractor. While the use of the tractor is almost wholly restricted to the wealthier economic class, the metal plow (where used with oxen) has been adopted by both the medium holder and small holder groups. The metal plow and oxen is evidently following the distribution of the wooden plows.

Although each of the implements here discussed shows certain regional distribution, there are other factors which limit the specific use made locally of a given implement. The most important of these, already mentioned in connection with plows, is the terrain. Over most of Guatemala the land within a given *municipio* can be divided into the highlands and the lowlands. These sections go under different names locally; some distinguish between *tierra fría* and *tierra caliente*; in many regions the highland sections are referred to simply as the *montaña* or *altos*, while the level lands are called *planos*. Sometimes, as is the case in the middle and lower Motagua Valley, the lowlands are called valley lands and their cultivation is restricted to the irrigated portions along the river. The possession of one as opposed to the other of these types of land usually reflects a wealth difference and a social difference. The lowlands are almost always more productive, sometimes giving two or even three crops a year instead of one; the lowland areas where irrigated, and in some places simply because they are more level, provide better land for crop diversification. As a result, the lower lands for one reason or another usually are more productive and in the hands of the wealthier members of the local society. In some places, the distinction also has an ethnic significance, such as is the case in Joyabáj, where the Ladinos tend more to occupy the *tierra caliente* while the Indians occupy more of the *tierra fría*. These two types of land bring about different cultivation forms. The higher lands are usually rough, often stony and somewhat eroded; they cannot be worked effectively with a plow and in some cases even offer problems for the hoe. As a result, the *montaña* lands are always worked with a digging stick, or in some cases, with a hoe. A man who works a piece of lowland with the plow may also have occasion to work some higher lands with the digging stick. The use of one implement, then, cannot be said inevitably to characterize a given economic strata of the community, although the fact of being an owner of lower lands is indicative of a higher economic status.

The practice of agriculture in Guatemala, as elsewhere, depends upon much more than mere implements. Techniques for increasing the crop yield are utilized in varying degrees over most of the republic. Canal irrigation, limited also by available water supply, is found principally in Ladino departments. The data from the census and that gathered in the survey were somewhat in conflict over the amount of irrigation to be found in the various regions of Ladino occupancy. The data from the survey is in agreement with the census in that perhaps the most intensive irrigation is to be found in the middle Motagua corridor, particularly the Department of Zacapa, and to a lesser degree El Progreso and the departments of Guatemala, Chiquimula, and Baja Verapaz. Also, there is agreement that some irrigation is to be found in Escuintla and Santa Rosa. However, the census reports the departments of Suchitepéquez and San Marcos as having the greatest number of *manzanas* per 1000 under irrigation and the data from the survey did not confirm this.

The use of irrigation varies from one community to the next and depends on the amount of water available. There are three main patterns of using irrigation water: one is to use it to squeeze in an extra *milpa* or corn crop annually; another is to use it specifically to grow vegetables and other horticultural crops; and the third is to use it for special large scale cash crops such as sugar cane or fruit trees. The irrigated portions of Petapa, Palencia, San Manuel Chaparrón, Mataquescuintla, and Atescatempa are generally used for horticulture and sometimes a little *milpa*. In Teculután, San José la Arada, Esquipulas, San Sebastián (Guazacapán) and Siquinalá the irrigation water tends more to be used to produce an extra *milpa* crop. In San Agustín Acasaguastlán and some other towns of the Motagua Valley the valley bottom is irrigated and used to produce large crops of sugar and fruits. In the east of Guatemala the term *"apante"* is used to refer to a crop which is produced with irrigation water.

Fertilizer is used very little among the Ladinos of Guatemala. Those who have cattle may turn them loose in a corn field after harvest, providing the animals with fodder and the field with some fertilizer. This, however, is neither constantly nor intensively practised. Chemical fertilizer is rarely used, although it was reported as being used by some in Petapa. The fertilizers which are used consist of three main types: animal manure; burnt weeds and *milpa*; and unburnt weeds and *milpa*. Of these, the first and the last are the best from the point of view of the soil, but do not have regular distribution. The burnt *milpa* and weeds custom is fairly common over much of the eastern part of the country. The placing of weeds and old *milpa* in the ground to rot is more common among

Ladinos who live in the Mixed and Indian regions. The writer cannot say, however, whether this custom is more common among Indians than Ladinos or not.

Whether or not land is allowed to rest and for how long depends upon various factors. In general, land will be used until it becomes evident that it is not producing well. As a result, irrigated lands are used year after year with no rest at all, and hill lands are seldom used for more than three consecutive years. How long a piece of land is left to rest usually depends upon how long it requires for the weeds to grow high again. High weeds indicate that the land is again ready to be planted in *milpa*. The only exception to this general picture is in areas of very great rain fall, such as the lower Motagua, where the weeds grow so fast that it is more profitable to clean off a piece of new land than it is to remove the weeds from a piece recently under cultivation.

The only case of crop rotation the writer encountered in the course of the entire survey was in the town of Quesada. There it was reported that land was used annually and there was a great shortage of water and consequently no irrigation. The custom was to alternate tobacco, the local cash crop, with *milpa*. In addition, animal fertilizer was used.

In general, care of the land among the Ladinos of Guatemala may be said to depend in great part on the economic status of the individual. The major *finqueros* take fairly good care of their land and usually operate the farms on some general sort of plan which involves care to avoid erosion and to keep the land producing. As one moves down the economic scale, however, it becomes evident that the urgency to use the land available, no matter how productive, perpetuates numerous practices which are generally not very profitable from a long range point of view. The poor man must use his land as long as it will produce. As a result, we find hilly regions constantly being opened to erosion and planting being done on land which at first glance would be considered useless even for second or third rate grazing ground. Similarly, the poor are the least able to provide fertilizer for their lands, and it is their lands which need it the most. There is some indication from the survey that inadequate agricultural techniques are not correlated with the fact of a population being either Ladino or Indian, but rather that there is such regional variation within the Ladino population that in some cases the practices are superior to those employed by Indians and in others they are much worse; there is, in addition, considerable variation within the Indian population so that no simple comparison is possible.

The number of harvests produced annually depends upon the crops involved and the local climate and irrigation possibilities. In general, *milpa* gives one harvest a year in the highlands and two on the coast. In the few two-harvest regions where it is also grown under irrigation, it produces three crops a year. It is not at all uncommon for the *montaña* of a given *municipio* to produce a single crop while the lowlands of the same jurisdiction produces two crops. The fact that two crops are possible on the Pacific coast has already been mentioned with respect to the migrations from the highlands for coastal planting.

There is a certain amount of crop specialization among Ladino communities.

The specialized irrigated production of sugar cane and fruits in San Agustín Acasaguastlán, has already been mentioned. The town of Palencia produces a great quantity of *güisquil* and some *güicoy*; Sansare has almost half its cultivated land sown in *yuca*; many towns in the east and on the south piedmont specialize in coffee as a cash crop; and some of the higher towns such as San Carlos Sija, produce wheat in considerable quantity. Quesada, as was mentioned, produces tobacco, and the Carib town of Livingston produces the special subsistence crop peculiar to the Carib culture, cassava. Some towns find it easier to produce certain crops because of the nature of the terrain or the fact that the normal subsistence crops do not yield locally. In this way Granados produces *maicillo* as its principal staple instead of corn. Almost all towns, however, plant *milpa* in great quantity and it is the *milpa* produce which provides the major part of the rural Ladinos' subsistence. The Ladinos who sow on the Pacific coast often will plant rice as a part of their subsistence crop instead of corn. As was the case with agricultural techniques, there is no outstanding difference between the Ladino and Indian practices; the Indians have long since adopted many of the Ladino crops, and the Ladinos have long since become dependent upon the basic *milpa* crop for subsistence. This is less true among the Ladinos of the Motagua Valley where they have specialized production of certain crops. But even some of these crops (*yuca* in Sansare, *güisquil* in Palencia) are of New World origin. As is true throughout much of Central America, however, corn is the staple of local production.

The development of Ladino (and for that matter Indian) agriculture in Guatemala has been singularly unaffected by extension activities. This is not because either population is particularly resistant to the introduction of change, but because extension activities have been very weak. The principal positive effect of extension activities reported on the survey was from the town of Esquipulas Palo Gordo where metal plows, cultivators, and new techniques had been introduced and taken over with considerable enthusiasm. In Chitatul, however, it was reported that the extension agent who had worked for years in a nearby town had had almost 100% failure in trying to introduce new methods among the Ladinos of the *aldea*. The Indians of this region, it was reported, were much more receptive to the adoption of new techniques than were the Ladinos. The particular reasons for the rejection or acceptance of new techniques is probably to be found within the particular economic and socio-psychological structure of a given community rather than in gross statements about Indians and Ladinos. The municipal secretary in the town of Morales assured the writer that the local *regidor de agricultura* (the municipal alderman in charge of agricultural matters), who had lived in Morales all his life, was just as competent to advise on agricultural techniques as was any expert in agriculture since the former had worked in agriculture all his life.

2. OTHER ECONOMIC ACTIVITIES

The dependence of the Guatemalan Ladino on products derived from hunting and fishing is limited almost entirely to a very few restricted regions. In general, the specific regions in which either hunting or fishing are of any importance are: (1) the Atlantic coastal forest area in the Department of Izabal; (2) specific lakes such as Atescatempa, Amatitlán, or Izabal; and (3) the Pacific coastal zone. In the highlands there is very little hunting except for sport or as a means to kill plant pests.

The principal weapons used in hunting are shotguns, both modern breech loaders and old muzzle loading cap guns, and .22 caliber rifles. The main animals hunted are deer, rabbits, *iguana*, armadillo, wild pigs, pigeons, wild turkeys, alligators, and the *tepescuintle*. The only hunting traps reported in use were a clumsy stone-fall described from Granados, and the *cacaxte*, a box fall-trap for birds and a large one for coyotes and wolves reported from Esquipulas Palo Gordo. In Palo Gordo it was also said that almost no one hunted in order to sell the meat, but only to kill animals which are endangering the crops; to sell meat, it was said, would make a hunter lose his luck in hunting.

Fishing was more common than hunting. The fishing implements used seem to be fairly standard over much of the republic. The *atarraya*, or circular throwing net, was reported in use on both the Atlantic and Pacific coasts and on Lake Atescatempa. Similarly, the *trasmayo*, the long sweep net handled by two or three men, was also reported from both coasts. The most intensive fishing community visited on the survey was the Carib town of Livingston; the fishing techniques there will be described in Section III. Along the Motagua River, all the way from Granados to the sea, it is common to find the *tapescos*, fish weirs of poles, set up across stream, which funnel the fish down into a basket in the center. The hook and line is used almost everywhere that fishing is carried on. The use of fish poisons seems to be fairly rare now, but it was reported from both the Motagua corridor and the Pacific coast. In both places the poison was referred to as *barbasco*, the term used for certain kinds of fish poisons over all of Central America and parts of South America. In Morales it was said to be of two different types, one of which was a bark of a vine that was thrown into the water to stun the fish; in Guazacapán the local *barbasco* was reported to be taken from the fruit of a tree called *palo de sacramento*. Both in the lower Motagua corridor and along the entire Pacific littoral fish provide an important part of the diet. Inland along the Pacific coast its importance varies with relation to the proximity of rivers, and as one moves into the highlands, the streams provide very little profit for the fisherman. Shrimp are caught in the Pacific coast rivers in cone-shaped baskets set up with the open end up stream, but this seems to be more an Indian than Ladino practice.

Lake fishing by Ladinos varies considerably from one lake to another. In Izabal, the Golfito, and along the Río Dulce fishing is usually done from dugout canoes, but the same general implements are used as were mentioned earlier. In Lake Amatitlán fishing is most commonly done with hook and line, sometimes from rowboats, but more often from the shore. In Lake Atescatempa *balsa* rafts are used as platforms from which fishing is done. Fishing in Atescatempa is a seasonal affair. Between January and April people from various parts of the *municipio* and some from outside go down to the lake and build temporary houses of grass. They remain in these during the fishing season. During this season one sees many nets hung out to dry and the *balsas* lined up along the shore. Between May and August the fish are breeding and fishing is not carried on. For the rest of the year the few families who live around the lake fish occasionally but no real catches are expected until the season begins the following January. Most of the fish are sold right at the lake as people from other nearby towns come down there to make their purchases. In Lake Atitlán the fishing is carried on by Indians or by Ladino sportsmen; there is no real Ladino fishing industry there.

Commercially the most important fishing areas in the country are the two coasts and the coastal rivers; the inland lakes provide very little fish for the country as a whole.[28] The fishing practices used along the coasts show little that is specifically Indian; the types of nets and other implements used are to be found throughout Central America. Only the *balsa* rafts of Atescatempa and the dugout canoes of the two coasts may be said to have been originally Indian. Socially, fishing on the lakes is more often an individual affair; along the rivers, where the *trasmayo* net is used, groups of men will work together in the collection of the catch.

In all, neither hunting nor fishing plays a dominant part in the life of the Ladino of Guatemala; he is specifically, both in Spanish and Indian heritage, an agriculturalist and it is only along the Pacific and Atlantic coasts that there exist populations wholly dependent upon fishing for a livelihood.

Like the Indian, the Guatemalan rural and small town Ladino is quite dependent upon local products and a regional trade. This is perhaps more true of the Guatemalan Ladino than it is of the Ladino of Nicaragua or Panama. The regional trade which is so characteristic of the Indian of Guatemala[29] is also important to the Ladino, but is considerably modified by certain Spanish patterns which have taken over in certain spheres of production. In general, the Ladino system of production is considerably less specialized regionally than is that of the Indians. Whereas Indian towns will tend to specialize in the production of certain goods for distribution over an entire region, Ladinos will tend much more to depend on a few local producers. Regional trade is more important to the Ladinos for those commodities which have their origin in the Indian culture. The making of pottery and string and fiber goods is more involved in regional trade than is the production of Ladino clothing or other products which stem from the Spanish culture: metal goods, shoes, straw hats, and tailored clothing. To take extreme examples, there are many Indian towns in the western part of the country which do not make a woman's skirt; most of this skirt material is produced in a limited area around Totonicapán and Quezaltenango and is exported by ambulatory vendors to the numerous towns where the Indians purchase it and make their own skirts. In Ladino communities, however, either a woman will sew her own dress or take the materials to a local

---

[28] International Bank, 1951, pp. 104–105, notes that Guatemala as a country has the lowest per capita fish consumption of any country in Latin America.

[29] Tax, 1952; McBryde, 1945.

seamstress and have the dress made for her. When a vendor does appear with ready made articles, they have usually been produced in a factory in the national or in one of the departmental capitals. In general, however, the Ladino is dependent upon individual local specialists for such products, while the Indian is dependent upon community specialization and regional trade.

One item which reflects differences between the Indian and Ladino patterns is to be seen in the manufacture and distribution of pottery. Pottery is today produced within a number of different economic systems in Guatemala. There are Indian communities, such as Chinautla, Rabinal, San Luis Jilotepeque, and Comitancillo, in which women produce hand-made pottery of various types and send it out over a region for sale. This is the scheme of production which supplies the greater part of the western and central part of the country. Within the region in which this Indian communal specialization exists and operates, there are a number of centers of Ladino "factory" production of pottery, such as the towns of Totonicapán and Antigua, in which wheel made pottery is produced in great quantity by men and sent out over the entire region for sale. In addition to these two types of production there is a third, that is found in scattered *aldeas* in which a few women (but not the entire community) make a few pottery products for local consumption or on local order. Little if any of this last type of product is sent out over a region for sale.

In the major regions of Ladino occupation, a number of things have occurred to alter this pattern somewhat. In the Motagua Valley and the departments of Jalapa and Chiquimula there have remained certain Indian centers of production, one of the principal of which is San Luis Jilotepeque. In addition to this, there are numerous *aldeas* of both Indians and Ladinos in which minor production goes on to supply the demand of a more limited region. In the southeast (Jutiapa and Santa Rosa) there are no major centers of production, but the minor *aldeas* and small municipal centers have grown in importance so that in Jutiapa, for example, there are various *municipios* such as Zapotitlán, Pipiltepeque, and El Barreal which make pottery for distribution over the general region of Jutiapa. Similarly, the town of Ixhuatán in central Santa Rosa produces pottery for a limited regional distribution. In the south and southwest coast region, there is practically no pottery production, probably due in some part to the lack of proper clays. All the pottery used in this region is shipped down from the centers of production in the adjacent highland region; the Ladinos are thus dependent upon both the Indian and Ladino production centers for these wares.[30]

Where large centers of pottery distribution still exist, they are of two types: Ladino production centers (Totonicapán, Antigua) or Indian hand production centers. If the Indian centers have become less important through the gradual disappearance of an Indian culture in a region, what usually remains are minor centers in which a few women still produce a moderate amount for the demands of the local community or for distribution within a local region.

The other principal products which are at least partially of Indian origin and are of importance in the Ladino production scene are fiber products (baskets,

---

[30] See McBryde, 1945, pp. 54–55, and Map 15.

mats, string, rope, net, fire fans)[31] wooden bowls, dugout canoes, and various domestic items such as starch, candy, etc. Most of the other types of home production, whether specialized or not, are of Spanish origin: carpentry, shoemaking, making of western men's clothing and women's clothing, tile making, masonry, weaving (on vertical looms by men), tanning, iron work, crude sugar production, fat making, candlemaking, baking, tin working, firework production, and saddlemaking. The degree to which any of these specialties are to be found in a given town or community depends considerably on the size of the community.

There are a few extraction industries which are carried on by Ladinos, but again it is those which are of specifically Indian origin which involve some regional distribution of the product. There are numerous places in the highlands where deposits of limestone permit the exploitation of lime; these, for the most part, are exploited on a small scale and have a limited regional distribution. The exploitation of wood, on the other hand, is usually a local matter except when there is enough capital available to export it to the departmental and national capitals.

There is a distinct difference to be found in local and home productions between the Ladinos who live in the predominantly Indian area of the western highlands and those who live within the Ladino region. In the former, there are fewer hand industries practised among the Ladinos than in the latter, probably due to the fact that the specialization of the Indians in many lines of production makes it unnecessary for the Ladinos to take up such specialization. However, there may also be other factors operating. For example, in the *aldea* of Chitatul it was reported that none of the Ladinos had taken up the trade of tailor, but that some Indians had learned it and supplied the needs of the Ladinos. Tailoring of western clothing is hardly of Indian origin, and this switch in ethnic specialization is quite peculiar. Furthermore, we find that not only does this lack of numerous hand industries in any one locale characterize the Ladinos in the west, but it also characterizes many of the Indians. So from the Indian populations of Patulul, San Antonio Suchitepéquez, and Tierra del Pueblo there were reported to exist almost no local industries among either Indians or Ladinos, except those individual specialties of Spanish origin. Where there was specialization among Ladinos in the west, it seemed to follow the Indian pattern of community specialization, and in the few cases known, climate played a strong role. Thus Palo Gordo and to a greater degree San Carlos Sija specialized in the production of wheat, a production permitted by their altitude. It appears that in the Indian regions Ladino specialization has conformed to the general Indian pattern except for the addition of certain individual specialists who provide for needs not provided for by the Indian economy. In Ladino regions, the Indian economic pattern has hung on only with respect to certain articles which were

---

[31] Ladinos were reported to make rope products in Sansare and Chitatul; baskets in Palencia, Morales, and Mataquescuintla; fire fans in Petapa and Sansare; fish nets in Siquinalá, Atescatempa, and Morales. Only in Barrio San Sebastián of Guazacapán, an Indian community, did it take on the aspects of a community specialization in *petates*, fire fans, nets, net bags, hats, etc.; elsewhere, only a few people, but of both sexes, specialize in the production. Fishing nets were usually made by the men who were to use them.

of Indian origin and are still to some degree produced by Indians. But again, there are Ladinos who have moved into the production of many of these items (especially in fiber and pottery work) and in so doing adopted certain Indian patterns.

The degree of dependence on hand produced goods among rural Ladinos is in the main determined by two factors: the degree to which the given individual or family is of an Indian background, and their economic status. People of Indian descent, to be found in some numbers along the south coast, still utilize many products which they make for themselves. This is much less true of the Ladinos of the Motagua corridor. The wealth of the individual is also of great importance in this. As a Ladino can afford to purchase things which are made by local specialists or things which are imported from the national capital, he will usually do it. The use of china instead of pottery and gourds, of metal bowls instead of pottery and wood, are both indications of wealth and of prestige. Similarly, a dress produced by a seamstress is better than one produced at home, and one purchased in the city is better than either. The products of the home industries, as the list given earlier indicates, enter into almost every phase of living: kitchen articles, furniture, equipment for transport (horse trappings, carts, etc.), clothing, farm implements (local blacksmiths will often produce some of these tools), rockets and *bombas* for the celebration of religious events, food stuffs and condiments, etc.

3. TRAVEL, TRANSPORT, AND COMMERCE

The transportation of goods and people among the Ladinos of Guatemala covers a broad range of cultural development. Human transport is still of great importance in bringing crop produce and forest products into the home or to a road head; horses and mules are used almost everywhere; ox carts are used in certain regions, but are now being replaced by the truck and train.

Human transport comes to the contemporary Ladino through both the Spanish and Indian traditions. The Spanish tradition is simply carrying a burden on one's back; the Indian tradition is to carry it by *mecapal* or head tumpline. There are in fact, among the Ladinos, two different forms of *mecapal* in use: one, the head tumpline is certainly of Indian origin; the other, the chest line in which the carrying strap passes across the chest instead of the forehead, is of problematic origin. While the Ladino refers to both these as *mecapal*, we will distinguish them here by the terms tumpline and chest strap. The tumpline is used by Ladinos in two major regions: among those who live in the central, western, and northwestern Indian highlands; and along the south coast. The use of the tumpline in the latter region has decreased considerably as the ox cart, mule, and horse, have become the more standard means of transport. It is still used by New Ladinos, however, and Indians who have come down from the highlands. The tumpline is almost unknown among the Ladinos of the eastern highlands and the Motagua corridor; only in Gualán was it reported that it was used by Ladinos, and it was said that the shoulder strap was also used. Elsewhere, such as in Esquipulas, it was stated that only Indians used the tumpline.

The use of the chest strap was found scattered in the eastern highlands and Motagua corridor (Palencia, Granados, San Jerónimo, Gualán, Mataquescuintla, and Barberena), but nowhere else. The use of the string or net carrying bag, sometimes made in pairs like saddlebags, is found over most of the southeastern highlands and the south coast. They were not observed to be in particular use in the northeast highlands or Motagua corridor, but the writer's observation may have been faulty in this. Among the poor Ladinos, where it is customary to use neither the tumpline nor chest strap, transport is effected simply by putting the burden on the back or on the shoulder. In some places the use of the tumpline has developed into a symbol of Indianism; as was described before, this is by no means the case in the western highlands where Ladinos in many towns (Zaragoza, Joyabáj, Chitatul, Palo Gordo) use it regularly. In the east, however, and along the southeast coast, where the Ladionoized Indian tends to be of a lower social class within the Ladino class system, the use of the tumpline often indicates that the wearer is of the low and poor Indian class.

Transport by Ladino women is limited principally to carrying pottery *tinajas* of water from the local source of supply to the home. Ladino women do not generally, as is the custom among Indian women in many parts of the country, bring in the firewood. With the exception of the eastern highlands, the water jar is almost inevitably carried on the head in the same manner as it is carried by Indians. In the east, however, there is an interesting exception to this practice among both Indians and Ladinos. There, in some towns, it was reported that the *tinaja* was carried only on the hip (Esquipulas, Quesada, Barberena, and in Barrio San Sebastián of Guazacapán) while in other towns it was reported that *tinajas* were carried, sometimes two at a time, on both the head and hip (Sansare, San Manuel, and Atescatempa). Among the Indians of San Luis Jilotepeque the most common method of carrying the *tinaja* is on the hip. In view of the regional difference noted in this, it seems not unlikely that the practice of carrying the water jug on the hip in the eastern part of the country may have been an early regional Indian trait.

The use of horses and mules, both as means of transport and for travel, has been and still is a typical Ladino trait. In fact, given an area in which these animals are used, it is frequently a matter of wealth whether they are used or not. Thus in the western highlands it is not uncommon to witness mules and horses being used as pack animals by Indians, and as has already been mentioned, poorer Ladinos will frequently have to carry burdens themselves. Wherever there are Ladinos, however, these animals will be found in some quantity. The use of donkeys has never become popular as transport among the Ladinos of Guatemala. With few exceptions, the only donkeys kept are those used for the breeding of mules. In the entire survey, the only place that reported them used as beast of burden was Atescatempa.

The ox cart, as a trait of obvious Spanish origin, has a very peculiar distribution in Guatemala. It is most in evidence in the central part of the south coast and in certain highland valleys (around the national capital they are much used). They were not much in evidence nor were they reported to be much used in either the Motagua corridor nor in the major portion of the highland region, except along the main road to the east of the capital (in Barberena, Quesada, and Atescatempa). Many excuses are given locally as to why carts are or are not used. In two towns within an identical environmental region the terrain will be given as the reason for their use or disuse.

The writer has not been able to decide on any particular set of factors which can explain the current distribution of the use of ox carts. The only differences noted in the carts themselves were that the cart used in the Baja Verapaz area (around San Jerónimo) had smaller wheels than those found in the central highlands and south coast. It was reported that most of those used in San Jerónimo were produced in the national capital, however, so this difference is one of local preference and tradition and not merely one of local construction tradition. There is little doubt that the use of ox carts is gradually being pushed to one side through the extension of passable truck roads. Already the long ox trains of the early part of the present century have disappeared and been replaced by trucks. The retention of the ox cart today where roads are good is due usually to the fact that they come from some place where the roads are bad; as such, however, they are most commonly used for carrying non-spoilable products to the national capital or other centers (such as firewood and charcoal). Ox carts, of course, never have been of much use in very hilly country. For this reason, mules and horses have generally been more popular forms of transport in Guatemala than have the carts.

Travel today over great distances is done almost entirely by bus. Horses and mules are still necessary for travel within the countryside if one is not to go on foot, and the roads are still generally limited enough so that the breeding of mules and horses is still an important business. The practice of women riding side saddle is still to be seen now and then in the eastern part of the country; in San José la Arada women riding both side saddle and astride were seen.

Communication between the various towns of Guatemala is gradually improving, but it is still at best a slow matter. Most Ladino municipal capitals have either a telephone or telegraph now, but mail still may take up to five days or a week to go a distance requiring a four-hour automobile ride over a relatively good road. The fact that the country has air service to many of its departmental capitals hastens the arrival of mail to these locales, but may leave another place, equally distant, with service taking three or four days. It is easy to go by bus almost anywhere where there is a road in Guatemala. Over the more travelled routes, particularly in the west, there is constant and regular traffic. The Indians are generally great travellers and many of them now prefer to go by bus than walk. In the east, however, except to such centers as Esquipulas and the departmental capitals, it is not always easy to get transportation when one wants it. The railroad provides regular service to the towns along the line, but one may often have to wait many hours or even a day or more to continue one's trip from the station. There seems to be little doubt that the Ladino, unless he is wealthy enough to own his own vehicle, is frequently little better off than the Indian when it comes to transport.

The distribution of goods among the Ladino communities of Guatemala is similar to that of Indian communities. In both cases, the Ladinos are generally in charge of stores of any size, while Indians are generally occupied more in the sale of products by ambulatory vendors who, depending upon the situation, will sell from house to house or in the local markets.[32] Stores run by Indians are usually limited to small single rooms or merely an open door with a shelf behind it and the merchandise consists of a very few items which are of daily use (candles, salt, *panela*, matches, cigarettes, soda pop, beer, coffee). All Ladino towns have a few stores of some size and everywhere there are some few Ladinos who make the sale of products their main occupation.

One of the most outstanding differences between the Ladinos of the western, Indian, area of the country and those of the more ladinoized regions is their role in store keeping. Throughout most of the Indian towns, the Ladino has notoriously played the role of the main entrepreneur in commerce and mechanical devices. As Tax[33] has noted, stores are almost always run by Ladinos. This role of the Ladino in the Indian region has led one anthropologist, in some disgust over their parasitic activities, to refer to the town-dwelling Ladinos of one western highland community as " ... these wholly lazy, dishonest, weak Ladinos ... " Whether this is an accurate characterization or not would depend upon one's experience, but it is only fair to point out that while the Ladinos may live off the Indians, the Indians very much need the products the Ladinos provide and, without the stores, would have no other means of procuring them. Such a characterization of the Ladino, however, must be restricted to those who live in the Indian communities; for as will be pointed out here, and later in Section IV, there are Ladino communities in the western highlands, as well as all the Ladino communities elsewhere, in which the Ladinos live off field labor just as much as do the Indians.

There does exist a basic and important difference, however, between the general trade of the Ladino region in comparison with that of the Indian. This may be summed up in Tax's remark to the effect that the market is today as clearly an Indian institution as the store is a Ladino institution.[34] The market is an essential part of Indian life; a great deal of the distribution of goods is dependent upon it, a great deal of time is spent in activities related to marketing, and market days are arranged so that they play an important role in the weekly activities of the persons living in the region. In Ladino areas the market day plays no such role; in many Ladino towns there is no market; in some there is a daily,

---

[32] Tax, 1952, p. 52, says that house-to-house peddling is characteristic only of Ladinos or Ladinoized Indians. This may well be true in the western highlands, but after some four years of living in Guatemala City, the writer is sure that the vast majority of peddlers who have come to his house have been Indians, most presumably from either Modified or Ladinoized communities, but probably the former.

[33] *Ibid.* [34] Tax, *Ibid.*, and McBryde, 1945, pp. 81–85.

permanent, market; in yet others, both a daily market and a weekly market; and in a very few, a weekly market only. In those towns in which weekly markets are held, there is a further important distinction between the Indian and Ladino patterns. In the Indian area, towns within a region tend to hold their markets on different days so that vendors and buyers may go from one market to another. In the Ladino regions, both in the east and on the south coast, weekly markets are held almost unfailingly on Sundays and secondary markets, where held, are on Thursday. Of all the towns surveyed, only three held special markets on any days besides Sunday and Thursday: in Barberena it was reported markets were held on both Saturday and Sunday, while in Flores Costa Cuca, there was a market on Monday. In the latter case it was explained that because of the Sunday market in nearby Coatepeque, most people went there on Sunday. In this case the Indian pattern has taken over in a Ladino town. In the *aldea* of El Sitio, in the *municipio* of Catarina, a market is held on Thursday and Friday. Of the rest of the towns, 13 had no market at all, two had only a daily market with special Sunday market, three had daily markets and special markets on Thursday and Sunday, and three with markets on Thursday and Sunday only.

This is obviously different from the Indian pattern. While Indians will attend markets in various towns within a given commercial region, Ladinos tend much more to restrict their marketing activities to the nearest local market. Consequently, there is usually no reason for markets in neighboring *municipios* to be held on different days; individuals can go to the commercial center nearest their homes and obtain the products they need. The marketing pattern is not, as it is among the Indians, a common and essential part of the regional distribution pattern. This difference means that in the Ladino areas, regional trade is not as important as it is in Indian regions. While the Indians have a series of equally important market centers, the Ladinos tend to look up a ladder of progressively more important market centers. For the Ladino of any given community, the most convenient purchase point may be either stores or market within his own community or the nearest *municipio* capital. The next most important center will be the nearest departmental capital or similarly large commercial center; and the final center, the national capital. The Indian will move about among numerous centers which are more or less equally important.

The influence of the Ladino system in the process of ladinoization may be seen by comparing the market systems of the southwest coast, where the majority of the Indian population may be classified as Modified, with that of the western highlands, where the population is partially Modified Indian but more commonly of the Traditional Indian. The market which uses various days of the week is to be found principally in the western highlands; but on the south coast, as McBryde noted, ". . . the chief day for all markets is Sunday, when laborers, who are by far the most numerous element of the population, are free to attend... The secondary day, where there is one, is Thursday, and the big towns, such as Mazatenango, have daily markets."[35] The survival of the Indian system is to be found in the fact of having a special day for the mar-

---

[35] McBryde, 1945, p. 83.

ket at all. As one moves down Central America, away from the area of former Mexican and Mayan culture, one finds in contemporary life little evidence of the "market day." Markets, further south, exist either as small daily affairs under the control of the town government, they do not exist at all, or are to be found as isolated survivals in towns of Meso-American culture, e.g. Monimbó in Nicaragua.[36]

4. THE DOMESTIC ESTABLISHMENT

As is the case with other Central American Ladinos, the domestic practices and equipment of the Guatemalan varies tremendously with social class differences. Our concern here is specifically with the rural dweller who does not share regularly in the upper and middle urban culture of the country. Among this population group it is possible to distinguish certain areas of differences in domestic characteristics.

The nature of the materials used in Ladino house construction is determined principally by tradition, wealth, and environment. The standard Ladino town house in a highland town is made of *adobe* walls and tile roof; among the poorer Ladinos of the same town, the people living around the outskirts of town, the New Ladinos and Ladinoized Indians, *ranchos* of pole or cane walls and straw or palm leaf roofs are used. The wall of *bajareque*, a wooden frame filled with clay, used to be a poor man's wall in some towns, but due to its earthquake resistant qualities, it is becoming more popular for the homes of the more well to do. *Bajareque*, however, also has a fairly well defined regional distribution: it is found particularly in the eastern highlands and coast (San José la Arada, Esquipulas, San Manuel, Mataquescuintla, Atescatempa, and Barrio San Sebastián of Guazacapán); elsewhere, if used, it forms a minor part of the wall forms in use. The other main wall type found in use is that of wooden boards; this wall is found in two particular types of environments, the very hot coasts of the Atlantic and Pacific, and in certain places in the plateaus of the highlands. The board houses of the coastal areas usually have roofs of corrugated metal or palm, depending upon the wealth of the owner. Occasionally a board house with a tile roof will be seen. In the highlands, a few towns in areas of forest exploitation are found in which boards are the most common wall type. Many Palo Gordo homes are made of boards as are the homes in some Indian communities in this region.

In general the Ladino home is made up of few rooms; if nothing else, the kitchen is separate or outside. In addition to this, however, a bedroom is often kept distinct from the general room of the house. In towns, it is not uncommon, of course, to find homes of many rooms among the wealthier people. Among the poorer, those who live in *ranchos*, there is usually only one room. The *ranchos* on the coast, which are often built as an adjustment to the hot climate and not because of economic necessity, may have two or three separate rooms. The usual highland *adobe* house of the poorer person consists of two rooms facing on a *corredor*, porch, which runs the length of the building. This porch

[36] See Doris Stone's comments in HOC, p. 67.

usually faces away from the street except in the case of isolated houses in the countryside. The town houses, in this way, form a blank wall with one or two windows facing the street. The logical extension of this type of house is, of course, the patio type home which is to be found among the wealthier people of the towns and cities. The *ranchos* are not usually built on this old Spanish pattern; instead of sitting on the street with a wall to the public, they are usually set in the middle of a lot away from the street and surrounded by a yard. In the highlands such houses may be surrounded by *adobe* walls, but on the coast it is not the custom to use walls for this purpose. In the coastal towns it is customary to build the houses along the main street in the Spanish fashion, wall to wall, but as one moves away from the center of town the houses will be set in yards and separated one from the other.

There are few outbuildings used by the Ladinos. In some towns, where local municipal control has been particularly strong, many of the homes have latrines; latrines are very uncommon in the countryside. There are usually no particular animal shelters; chickens commonly roost in trees. The principal structure outside the house to be found in many towns is some sort of granary or storage bin, a *troja*. The storage of corn (and wheat in the upper western highlands) is accomplished in various ways, and so far as the writer could determine, there was little if any regional significance in the methods used. The poorer people generally store the corn on the cob, stacked in a corner of the house set aside for the purpose. If there is the desire, an outside shed may be placed against one of the walls of the house to accomplish the same purpose. Among the very poorest and in homes which still have them, corn may be stored in the *tabanco*, the ceiling surface set at roof level in a *rancho*. In the eastern part of the country the use of cylindrical metal silos which fit in the corridor of the home is becoming increasingly popular and provides much better protection than do the older methods. Among the older structures which are being replaced by these silos are the outdoor elevated platform of poles on which corn cobs would be stacked; the indoor chest in which corn grains are placed, mixed with sand, in order to discourage pests; and the types already mentioned above.

The furniture used by the Ladino reflects, in perhaps more than any other way, his economic status and the degree to which his background may be Indian. For sleep, the poorest will use a woven palm mat (*petate*) on the ground; the next better off use a *tapesco* or board bed (a *tapesco* is a surface of poles). From this one moves on to the frame beds strung with rope, leather, or cloth surfaces; on all these it is common for a person to place a *petate* on the surface prior to sleeping. Finally, mattresses may be placed on these beds. In the coastal areas canvas cots are quite commonly used by those who can afford them. Over much of the east and the two coastal regions the hammock is commonly used for daytime resting.

Furniture for sitting varies from sawed off logs, to the almost ubiquitous low bench of four legs, to chairs made by carpenters. The *butaca*, an angular leather covered chair of some antiquity, is still found in some use over much of the republic, except in the southeast. Scattered through the center and western part of the republic the use of small, low benches cut in the form of animals is still to be found. They are used principally by Indians, but they are also to be found in Ladino homes. The common small bench used in Guatemala among the eastern and south coastal Ladinos is called *taburete*, a term which elsewhere in Central America refers to a specific type of leather covered chair.

Poor Ladinos, like the Indians, often use *cofres*, wooden chests, to store their clothing and other items. Also, it is common to have a small altar, or at least a picture of a saint somewhere in the house. It is customary among both Indians and Ladinos of the towns and countryside to use the home for business when necessary. Consequently, many homes have a room on the street or road which is used as a store.

One of the principal domestic distinctions to be found in the normal life of the Ladinos and Indians of Guatemala is that the Ladinos separate kitchen facilities from the rest of the house whenever possible. If the climate is warm and the family poor, the cooking will be done on the corridor or merely under a palm shelter; but unless the family is of Indian background, it is most uncommon to find a Ladino family which uses the same room for cooking and sleeping. Among Indians, however, this is relatively common.

The Ladino kitchen and its equipment offer a number of features which provide regional distinctions. While the grinding stone may be said to be found everywhere, the manner in which it is used varies. Among the Ladino people of the far eastern departments, specifically Chiquimula, Jalapa, Jutiapa, and part of Santa Rosa, it is customary to support the stone waist high on two or three sticks set in the ground. This method is also to be found in use across most of El Salvador, and oddly enough, among the Indians of the Alta Verapaz in Guatemala. Elsewhere, the Ladinos almost all use a table called the *molendero*; the stone is placed on one end of this table (sometimes part of the stone is supported by a stick) and the corn is ground directly on to the board surface. The board is usually tilted and has a rim around the edge to direct the water flowing down it, out a hole at the lower end and into a bowl. The *molendero* is also in use further south in Central America.

Another feature in which there is regional difference in the country is in the type of stove used. The standard Indian method of cooking is on a floor hearth set in three stones. The standard Ladino method is on a raised *poyo* or *fogón*. There are basically two different types of *poyo*; one is a real stove in which the fire is lower than the top of the stove itself; the other is what amounts to being a raised ground surface on which a fire is built. The second of these is by far the most common type of *poyo*; the first is used by the more wealthy.

The *poyo* of the second type is made in three different ways: one is simply the construction of a block of *adobe* or some other material on which a fire is built; a second is the construction of a large low box which is filled with earth, and on which a fire is built; and the third is the use of a raised board platform (a box with no sides, if you like) on which is dried mud and which serves as the fire platform. The principal regional variation to be found in these *poyos* is not in the way in which the platform is made so much as in the way the surface is used. In the towns of the eastern departments (Chiquimula, Jalapa, Jutiapa, and parts of Zacapa, El Progreso, and Santa Rosa) a horseshoe shaped clay ridge is set on the dirt platform, and the fire is built inside this. This raised ridge serves to hold the pots, *comales*, and other cooking utensiles. This ridge, called *hornilla* (literally, a "little oven"), is found in use down through El Salvador. To the west of this area, the same three stones used by the Indians on the floor are to be found set on the surface of the raised *poyo*. This type of cooking apparatus is clearly a direct shift from the Indian use of three stones on the floor. The raised platform with three stones is generally found among the poorer Ladinos in this region, while the solid *poyo* with the fire set below the surface is used by the wealthier. Over most of the country the poorest Ladinos, mainly New Ladinos, frequently retain a fire on the floor either instead of using a raised surface or in addition to the raised surface. In some places anyone who retains a fire on the floor, however, is considered to be an Indian.

Ovens are found over all of Ladino Guatemala, but in most cases they are used particularly by those women who bake bread for sale or only during special seasons of the year, such as for Holy Week. The only towns visited on the survey in which it was reported that ovens were definitely not used (aside from Livingston) were towns which had a population which was predominantly Indian (Barrio San Sebastián of Guazacapán, Patulul, and Tierra del Pueblo).

There is a great deal of kitchen equipment which is to be found in almost every home. The fire fan was reported to be used in most of the towns in the republic; pottery vessels for cooking, and among the poor for eating, are used in all homes although they are being replaced among the wealthier with iron and other metal products. The large wooden mortar, used for coffee, rice, and *maicillo*, is found particularly in the east and on the south coast. It is absent from the Ladino towns of the western highlands (except in the case of Palo Gordo where many of the people spend part of their time on the coast) and in the middle Motagua Valley (Sansare, San Agustín, Teculután, and also in San Jerónimo). Elsewhere, depending upon the presence of the produce for which it may be effectively used, it is very common and is found in various forms. The writer could discern no particular significance to the distribution of the straight sided mortar as opposed to the cone shaped type. The mortar is nowhere part of the corn technology in Guatemala.

In the preparation of *nixtamal*, lime is used almost universally by the Guatemalan Ladino. The use of wood ash was reported only for particularly poor families in Zaragoza and San Manuel, and for the elaboration of special *tamales* for Holy Week in Siquinalá.

There is much in the kitchen of the Ladino which has been borrowed or derived from the Indian cultures of Guatemala. Many of the common and favorite foods, the techniques of preparation of corn and beans, are taken directly from the aboriginal cultures. Since there are studies of the Indian culture available in which many of these traits are described, and since the Institute of Nutrition of Central America and Panama has been carrying out studies on foods and food preparation, it was not felt to be necessary to go into this subject in the present survey.[37]

5. FAMILY AND *COMPADRE* SYSTEMS

The family among Guatemalan Ladinos, as among Ladinos elsewhere, forms the basic unit of the social organization. The Ladino family, however, differs in many ways from the Indian family, and plays a somewhat different role in the total life of a community. Also, among the Ladinos, there is considerable variation in the nature and functioning of the family from one social class to another.

Basically, the Ladino family is neo-local and bilateral; this means that a man and woman, when they live together, go to a new place of residence, and recognize descent from both sides of their respective families. There is a tendency in certain parts of Guatemala, however, for the new couple to live for some time at the home of the boy's family before they move into a residence apart; this temporary patrilocal residence is particularly characteristic of the Ladino communities of the central and western highlands, and was also reported from Sansare, Mataquescuintla, and San José la Arada in the eastern highlands. It was said not to be the practice in either the Motagua Valley nor on the south coast towns surveyed (except in Flores Costa Cuca, and in San Sebastián, the Ladinoized Indian *barrio* of Guazacapán).

The establishment of a home among Ladinos does not differ much from the methods reported elsewhere in Central America. A man and a woman usually decide for themselves if they wish to live together or marry; if the families involved are fairly well established (not necessarily financially, but in point of time) in a community, a formal request may be made through an intermediary to the girl's parents. If not, or if it is felt that the parents will offer some resistance, then the pair may simply elope and set up housekeeping.

Restrictions on whom one may marry vary from one part of the Ladino region to another. In general, first cousins may not marry one another nor live together. However, it was consistently reported in all but one of the eastern highland towns that either such alliances were tacitly permitted or that they were known to occur and no particular social control was brought to bear to avoid them. The only exception to this was in the town of Quesada. Towns along the south coast (in Siquinalá, La Gomera, Patulul, and Catarina) reported that while cousins were not supposed to marry, nevertheless they sometimes did live together. No restriction against cousin marriage was reported in Morales and in Gualán it was said that cousin alliances did take place in the face of a general feeling against them. In the middle Motagua Valley and the central and western highlands, however, the prescription of cousin marriages was evidently observed with greater care. There is a generally good correlation between the presence of the tendency towards temporary patrilocality and the observance of the prohibition of first cousin marriage. The weak observ-

---

[37] A representative collection of the publications as of 1953 is to be found in INCAP, 1953.

ance of the cousin restriction is also fairly well correlated with a relatively high degree of common-law marriages.

The data in Tables 12 and 13 indicate that there is some relationship between the fact of a reported high degree of common-law marriage and a lack of tendency towards temporary patrilocality on the one hand, and permissive alliances between first cousins on the other. These traits, furthermore, are specifically typical of the eastern and south coastal regions, not of the Motagua Valley or of the central or western highland Ladino communities. It will be pointed out

Table 12.—Correlation of traits: Permitted first cousin alliances and tendency towards temporary patrilocality (*Chi Square equals* 5.711, *significant at the 95% level of probability*)

	Towns showing tendency towards temporary patrilocality	Towns not showing tendency towards temporary patrilocality	Total
Alliances between first cousins permitted.	2	10	12
Alliances between first cousins not permitted.	9	5	14
Total of towns on which there was data.	11	15	26

Table 13.—Correlation of traits: Amount of common-law marriage and alliances between first cousins (*Chi Square equals* 9.644, *significant at the 99% level of probability*)

	Reported high amount of common-law marriage	Reported low amount of common-law marriage	Total
Alliances between first cousins permitted.	9	4	13
Alliances between first cousins not permitted.	2	13	15
Total of towns on which there was data.	11	17	28

in the next part of this paper that the middle Motagua and the central and western highlands are the locale of the Old Ladinos, while the south coast is a zone of Ladinos who are either of fairly recent Indian descent or who are fairly mobile; it seems clear that the tendencies towards common-law marriages and towards weak incest restrictions, are to be found among the new and mobile Ladinos, while the tendency towards temporary patrilocality is not characteristic of that group. It should be noted, however, that the tendency towards patrilocality is reported nowhere in the Motagua Valley except in the upper reaches and tributaries, in the towns of Sansare and Granados, and Joyabáj. Temporary patrilocality, then, cannot necessarily be interpreted as being a survival of a recently weakened Ladino trait, but must be related to some other factors. The main region in which it was reported was in the Ladino communities which are enclaves in the Indian highland region; it may well be that temporary patrilocality has been used by the Ladinos because of their position within the Indian region. Whether this is diffusion from the Indian practices, a survival of a much older Ladino custom, or due to some functional relationship which exists in the Indian areas (such as possibly restricted land of Ladinos), is not clear.

Common-law alliances are generally found, as might be expected, among poorer and lower class Ladinos; the common-law relationship, however, is fairly well recognized among all classes, and illegitimacy in Guatemala, as elsewhere in Central America, carries relatively little stigma. Unfortunately, the data from the 1950 Census on civil status (including the numbers of common-law unions) were not available at the time the study was made.

Under Guatemalan law marriage may be a religious affair, but it must be a civil affair. Which type is used is not merely a matter of choice if one wishes to marry; he must be married in the municipal headquarters, and then if he so desires, by a priest as well. This means there is a double expense in connection with a wedding if one wishes religious sanction for it. Furthermore, there have been relatively few priests in Guatemala since the time of Barrios. Holleran[38] reports that there were 119 priests in 1872 and 120 at the time of her study in 1946; this indicates that not only have there not been very many priests in recent decades, but that the number has not increased with the population. The church, then, even though it may wish to promote religious sanction for unions, has not had the personnel to carry out its desire. The Guatemalan law does not say that people living together must marry, but says that if they marry, they must be married legally before they may be married by the church. Interest in civil marriage requires at least a minimum amount of legal sophistication, since the significance of the civil ceremony is that it provides for the legal recognition of the union. Divorce, and until recently inheritance, could legally follow only a legal civil marriage in the eyes of the law. The net result is that among the poorer and less sophisticated people, civil marriage is rather meaningless except as a preliminary for the church marriage, and priests are so scarce that religious sanction often is felt to be of little importance.

It seems clear that common-law unions are relatively more characteristic of Mobile and New Ladinos. More strict observance of marriage formalities are found in the Ladino enclaves in the central and western highlands and along the Motagua Valley. In general, the Ladino communities on the south coast were not reported as being very observant of marriage formalities, and in the eastern highlands the degree to which marriages were carried on varied. The term used for the common-law relationship through most of Ladino Guatemala is *amancebado*. The importance of formal marriage in the Guatemalan countryside is in part dependent upon class and in part dependent upon the degree to which family lineages are considered to be of importance. Importance of family lineages, in turn, is more or less related to the middle and upper class. Among

---

[38] Holleran, 1949, pp. 235–236.

Old Ladinos and upper class Ladinos, then, formal marriage is assumed to be necessary; as one moves down the social scale and out into the countryside, marriage becomes less important.

The Ladino family tends to be smaller than does the Indian family. Table 14 gives data concerning the average size families for each of the departments of the country, together with the average size for the departments of each type. The reason behind this difference between the ethnic groups is probably due to the difference in residence pattern noted above. Indians tend more commonly to observe a temporary, and sometimes permanent patrilocality, while the Ladinos do not oberserve this custom so much. As a result, an Indian home may have more relatives living in it than is the case in Ladino homes. It will be noted from the table, for example, that the two Ladino departments which

Table 14.—Number of persons per family by department, 1950. (*Census*, 1950)

Ladino departments	No. persons per famliy	Mixed departments	No. persons per family	Indian departments	No. persons per family		No. persons per family
El Progreso	4.8	Jalapa	4.8	San Marcos	5.2		
Sta. Rosa	5.0	Sacatepéquez	5.0	Huehuetenango	5.7		
Izabal	3.7	Retalhuleu	4.5	Chimaltenango	4.7		
Escuintla	4.0	Baja Verapaz	4.7	El Quiché	6.0		
Guatemala	4.9	Chiquimula	4.9	Alta Verapaz	5.5		
Zacapa	4.8	Suchitepéquez	4.5	Sololá	5.6		
Jutiapa	5.1	Quezaltenango	5.0	Totonicapán	5.4		
El Petén	4.8						
Total Ladino departments	4.7	Total Mixed departments	4.8	Total Indian departments	5.4	Total Republic	5.0

have a predominant number of mobile Ladinos (Escuintla and Izabal) also have the lowest number of people per family.

Another possible reason for the greater number of people per family among the Indians could be that the Indian birth rate is slightly higher (see Tables 5 and 6); however, the net increase in Indian population is smaller than the increase in Ladino population, since the death rate in the former is much higher.

Stability in the Ladino family is a subject which could be discussed at great length, but is also a subject on which we have really too little systematic information to draw any reliable conclusions. We have already discussed certain factors which obviously are related to stability of a given domestic unit: value placed on family lineage (i.e. Old Ladinos as opposed to New and Mobile Ladinos); tendency toward temporary patrilocality as opposed to straight neolocality; formal marriage as opposed to common-law union; and strictly observed cousin marriage prohibition as opposed to permissive cousin marriage. In addition to these there are economic factors which are probably more important than any of these already listed. Private landholding as opposed to labor (either permanent or temporary) on a plantation doubtless plays a strong part in the stability of a unit. Extreme degrees of instability are to be observed in some

Ladino situations. In one cattle farm in the piedmont of Santa Rosa, the switching of partners is evidently the rule instead of the exception, and even open polygamy is practiced by some.

In general, it is quite clear that both the principal ethnic groups of Guatemala tend to be endogamous; Ladinos marry Ladinos and Indians marry Indians. The region in which this seems to be less observed is among the New Ladinos and among some of the Ladinoized Indians. In this population the line between Indian and Ladino is frequently thinly drawn and often not observed when it comes to marriage.

The *compadre* system is of recognized importance over almost all Ladino Guatemala, but there seems to be no particular regional significance to the variations in its observance. *Compadres* are generally sought among the more wealthy and Old Ladino people in those communities in which such families form a significant portion of the population. As often as not, however, the wealth differences are not terribly great, and as such, do not play much of a role in the selection of *compadres*. Of critical importance is that a man must have "respect" for his *compadre*; thus the choice may be of a wealthy person for whom one has respect, or it may be for a person of the same general economic status. It is not uncommon for Indians who live in a state of dependence upon Ladinos to ask the latter to act as godfathers for their children.

Compadres are commonly sought for baptism, confirmation, and marriage, but as has already been noted marriage is not always observed, and bishops are frequently not around to carry on confirmation, so the baptism *compadre* is the most important. Most country Ladinos will not go out of their way to have their children confirmed, but they will make the effort to have them baptized. While the writer would hesitate to make any broad generalizations with respect to the functioning of the *compadre* system, it has been observed in some situations of extreme family instability that the *compadres* are accorded particular respect; in such situations, the artificial kinship system has actually to some degree taken over certain of the functions of the real kin system.

There is some tendency for the same godfather to be sought for each of the siblings in a family, but the practice is by no means universal; it was reported in twelve towns. In only three towns was it reported that different *compadres* were usually sought; elsewhere it was said that it made no particular difference.

The prohibition of marriage between the children of *compadres*, as an extension of the incest regulations of the regular kinship system, was reported in 18 towns; in nine towns it was said that such unions were permitted, while in the remaining three it was said that children of *compadres* were not supposed to marry, but cases did occur. Permissiveness in this respect was most common in certain towns of the eastern region, particularly the Old Ladino towns of the Motagua Valley and in the eastern highlands. The fact that such unions were reported to be prohibited in the region populated principally by New and Mobile Ladinos adds some support to the idea that the *compadre* system may be replacing the regular kin system in certain of its functions.

6. GENERAL SOCIAL STRUCTURE

The social structure of the Guatemalan Ladinos involves a number of different types of relationships and the classification of various situations. The present discussion will be broken up to separate considerations of various phases of the structure as follows: (1) Indian-Ladino Ethnic Group Relations; (2) Ladino Social Types; (3) Ladino Class System; and (4) Divergent Ladino Population Elements.

(1) *Indian-Ladino Ethnic Group Relations.*—The one fact, above all others, which differentiates the Ladino social organization of Guatemala from those to be found in the other countries of Central America is the presence of the large Indian population. As has been noted elsewhere, the Indians of Guatemala outnumber the Ladinos in the total population and there are few areas of the country where Indians do not appear at least as traders. Since the Indian is all pervading, it is well at the outset to examine the nature of the relationships which exist between Ladinos (in this case an "ethnic minority") and the Indians.

The writer has not been able to delineate to his own satisfaction any series of specific factors which may be said to account for the nature of the Indian-Ladino relationships as they are to be found in the various corners of Guatemala. The history of each community has provided certain events peculiar to that locale and directed development of the relationships. There are some general factors which, as they differ, have had differential effects on these relationships; they are: the degree of ladinoization of the Indian population involved; the general pattern of socio-economic relationships; and the settlement and residence patterns of the two groups.

The "degree of ladinoization," of course, includes a wide variety of elements, both social and cultural. In terms of the three types of Indian culture delineated earlier, the Traditional, Modified, and Ladinoized, relationships are affected by the presence of obvious differences in Traditional Indians as opposed to more subtle differences in Ladinoized Indians. Similarity in culture which exists between Ladinoized Indians and lower class Ladinos permits greater contact, communication, and consequently, intimacy. The fact of this similarity works in a different way between Ladinoized Indians and higher class Ladinos; in these situations, the Ladinos often find it necessary to make a special effort to guard the integrity of their social class from the movement of the Indians. In order to retain their superordinate position, they find it necessary to invent or call to the fore obscure differences between the two groups. It is in this type of situation that one usually finds race being used as a criterion to differentiate the groups.

Where a Traditional Indian group is in contact with Ladinos, the differences in custom and language are so obvious that it is quite unnecessary to invent extra differentiating criteria. Thus the relationships usually develop in certain channels due to other factors. Many of the differences observed by Roberts[39]

---
[39] 1948.

might be attributed to the difference in the two situations he examined. The Indians of San Luis Jilotepeque, who lived in something of a caste system, can be considered as falling in the Modified category; those of San Antonio Palopó are Traditional. In the latter situation, the people of San Antonio were not socially so strongly differentiated from the Ladinos of Aguas Escondidas. The reason for this, in part, is probably that the culture of the two is so divergent that widespread intimate social interaction is made almost impossible and so need not be guarded against. The situation reported in the survey in San José la Arada and in Atescatempa both reflect situations in which the Indians have become so like the Ladinos culturally that the latter have found it necessary to resort to matters of feeling and obscure criteria to differentiate the two. In Atescatempa the Ladino informant's description of the differences between Yupiltepeque Indians and Ladinos consisted in holding his hands far apart, and saying, "There are Indians, and there are Ladinos." In brief, then, where the cultural differences between the two groups are great, the relationships which spring up between them are generally due to other considerations (most likely those discussed below); but where these cultural distinctions are not marked, then the Ladinos frequently find it necessary to resort to a crystallization of a class or caste system with attendant attitudes to retain themselves in a superordinate position.

The general pattern of the economy in a given region will play a determining role in the nature of the social relationships which exist between the Ladinos and Indians of a community within the region. In rural areas, the pattern of land exploitation and attendant labor relations set the picture for many Indian-Ladino relationships. In areas where there are both Indians and large agricultural enterprises it is almost inevitable that the landowner will be Ladino and the laborer Indian. The relationship inherent in such a situation is, of course, the *finquero-colono* (paternalistic employer-employee) pattern. While the paternalistic character of this relationship was considerably reduced in the years 1945–1954 under the development of agrarian unions and the reduction of the legal recourses of the landowners, the specific quality of the paternalistic relationship depended in great part on the personality of the landowner, but in general it stemmed from the almost complete dependence of the Indian on his employer. Much of his food was provided in rations by the employer, all medical attention available was dispensed by the employer, money for sponsoring fiestas was donated by the employer, repair of the *colono* home was provided from the same source; the laborer even turned often to his *patrón* to be godfather of his children. Numerous factors tempered this set of relations; the socio-cultural origin of the employer, his wealth, whether he lived on his land or not, the size of the Indian population, and so on. Paternalism also existed in Ladino regions, of course, but to the writer's knowledge it seldom was as strong as between Ladino and Indian.

The *finquero-colono* relationship is only one of the types of relationships which has sprung up between Indians and Ladinos because of the economic system. Another is to be seen in the Indian areas where smaller landholdings are prevalent. In many of these regions Ladinos have established themselves in small numbers; they carry much of the local commerce, buy local products, lend money on future crops, run travel and transport facilities, and (as has been reported from one Indian town) even control the saints which the Indians must pay to pray to. The status of such Ladinos may be said to be something between symbiotic and parasitic. Again, the degree to which they exploit the Indian depends greatly on the particular Ladinos and Indians involved. In some cases the Ladinos are little more than honest businessmen and cannot be considered as being either parasitic or exploitative.

The importance of economic superiority in determining the relationships between the two ethnic groups is nowhere better illustrated than in Chitatul. Chitatul is a community of Ladinos in a heavy Indian region; the Ladinos are economically no better off (and in some cases are worse) than many of their Indian neighbors. While the Ladinos used to employ Indians as day laborers, in recent years the Indians have either been too busy working their own lands or have gone to seek better paid jobs elsewhere; as a result, sons of Ladino families now work locally for hire. Also in recent years, the Indians have been buying up land in the Ladino community. The Indians have even taken over certain statuses which in many communities are principally Ladino: political agents and tailors. The Ladinos have been reluctant to act as *alcaldes auxiliares* in the community, so the Indians occupy these jobs, and as such, are politically superordinate to the Ladinos within the Ladino administrative structure. The tailors in the region are Indians and the Ladino men have their suits made by Indians. With respect to economic interdependence, the Indians and Ladinos work almost as equals, and as a result, they have tended to become equals in many other phases of their living. The Ladinos have even learned the Indian language. It should be noted, however, that the two groups have remained socially distinct; there is no intermarriage, and dances and general entertainment are carried on separately. Although there are two soccer teams, one Indian and one Ladino, they rarely play one another. They each play outside teams of the same socio-cultural group as themselves. In some respects, the Indians are considered to be superior to the Ladinos; principally among these are in matters of midwifery and curing. The Ladino will usually go to an Indian specialist in matters of childbirth and illness.

The case of Chitatul is described not because it is typical, for it is definitely not; but rather because it illustrates the extremes to which Indian-Ladino relations may develop. It is an example of the turn relationships can take if Indians are able to achieve economic equality or superiority.

The third factor which usually plays a role in the type of relationship which may exist between Ladinos and Indians is the settlement and residence pattern. It is in fact not entirely clear whether a settlement pattern is more the determinant of relationships, or the reverse. Where the relative number of Indians or Ladinos is very small, there tends to be no very great significance attached to the relative location of the two groups. Where there are relatively large numbers of each, however, there is a strong tendency for each to live in fairly well defined areas, sometimes in separate *barrios* of a town (such as is the case in Joyabáj and Guazacapán) or in separate communities. The old Spanish colonial pattern was, of course, for the Spanish to live in the center of town and the Indians on the outskirts. This pattern is still retained in many communities.

Once a settlement pattern is established, however, for whatever reason, it tends to crystallize certain relationships. Proximity brings contact, contact involves communication and association, and these latter two demand regulation. The regulation means a crystallization of relationships. Again, the differences observed by Roberts[40] in his comparison of Aguas Escondidas with San Luis Jilotepeque may in some part be due to the differing settlement pattern involved. Where there is close physical proximity between the two groups they tend to be much more interdependent economically and for services; where they are separated into distinct communities, each community must supply certain of the services.

(2) *Ladino Social Types.*—For lack of a more suitable term, the expression "social type" is here being used for a cross classification of Ladinos on the basis of two sets of criteria: (a) the length of time which they have been Ladinos; and (b) the length of time their ancestors and themselves have been residents in a given locale.

(a) The expression "Old Ladino" refers to Ladinos who have been so categorized all their lives and the main portion of whose ancestors have been so classified. An Old Ladino is one who (correctly or not) claims considerable white ancestry and usually Spanish cultural tradition, and whose claims are generally honored by his neighbors. The expression "New Ladino" is applied to those people who are recently, perhaps within one or two generations, derived from the Indian socio-cultural group, and who make no such claims of Ladino ancestry.

(b) Ladinos are also classifiable in terms of the degree to which they and their ancestors have retained residence in a specific locale. People who, for example, now live in the same community in which they were born and in which their parents were born may be considered as "non-mobile" Ladinos, or Ladinos of long residential continutiy. People at the opposite extreme, whose parents came from one community, who were born in another community, and perhaps now live in yet a third community, are "mobile" Ladinos, of short residential continuity. It should be noted that this concept of residential continuity refers not merely to the individual himself, but also includes his immediate ancestors.

Theoretically, these two classifications produce four possible subtypes:

	Mobile	Non-Mobile
New Ladino	New—Mobile	Old Non-Mobile
Old Ladino	Old—Mobile	New Non-Mobile

---

[40] 1948.

The significance of these four subtypes, that is, whether they exist as functionally distinct entities, or whether they are merely theoretical possibilities, can only be determined by further study. In the course of the present survey, three of the subtypes were of evident importance: the Old, Non-Mobile Ladino; the New, Mobile Ladino; and the New, Non-Mobile Ladino. In the present essay, these three are referred to as Old, Mobile, and New, respectively, unless otherwise specified.

In terms of culture, we find that Old Ladinos tend to have retained more of the culture traits which stem from the Spanish colonial period than have New Ladinos, and to have more readily adopted newer traits. New Ladinos, whether mobile or not, have made the final move to being Ladino so recently that they have never taken on traits which came in during the earlier historical periods unless their ancestors took them on as Indians. In terms of the communities surveyed, Old Ladinos appear as the upper class in the towns of the middle Motagua Valley, the upper classes to be found in many of the towns of Jalapa and Chiquimula, the Ladino populations of Ladino towns in the western Indian region (such as San Carlos Sija, Palo Gordo, and the Ladino population of Joyabáj) and possibly the upper class in such towns as Palencia, Zaragoza, and Flores Costa Cuca (although there are indications that the last of these should not be included on the list).

New Ladinos are to be found in greatest predominance along the south coast and scattered through the eastern highlands. The New Ladinos are found as lower class members in the eastern highlands, along the Motagua, and whole communities so composed may be found in Jutiapa and Santa Rosa; they also form a great part of the population in the southwestern departments. The Mobile Ladinos are to be found in the greatest number in the central region of the South Coast (Escuintla and adjacent Suchitepéquez and Santa Rosa) and in the southeastern half of the Department of Izabal (to the east of Lake Izabal). As is to be expected, Mobile Ladinos are most common in those regions which until recently were unpopulated. On the other hand, regions which are gradually seeing over-population, such as the rural central highlands, permit no room for newcomers. In most communities where Old Ladinos are to be found, however, there is usually a lower class which is composed of New Ladinos or Indians. In the Motagua Valley and the eastern highlands the lower class is generally Ladinoized Indians or New Ladinos, except in specifically Indian areas (such as the community of San Luis Jilotepeque and the Chortí towns) in which a lower caste tends to consist of Modified Indians. In the central and western highlands, the lower class is usually Modified or Traditional Indians in those communities in which Ladinos are to be found.

The importance of the distinction between these different types of Ladinos is to be seen in various aspects of the Ladino social system. For example, intermarriage between New Ladinos and Ladinoized and even Modified Indians does occur, whereas between Old Ladinos and any Indians it is almost unheard of. In the development in recent years of communist activities in rural areas, it has been specifically the Mobile, then the New and last the Old Ladinos who have manifested interest in such activities.[41] In terms of adjustability and receptivity to new traits, it is the writer's impression that Old Ladinos must be dealt with in a different manner than that used with New and Mobile Ladinos.

(3) *Ladino Class System.*—The class system of a Ladino community, while in many ways correlated with the social types described above, is not identical with it. There is in a community of Ladinos usually one of the following situations: (a) no clear cut social classes; (b) two social classes; or (c) three social classes. Each of these refers only to the Ladinos (or at best including the Ladinoized Indians of a community) and not the Indian population which may live near by. In some places, a rationale for distinguishing four social classes could be made if owners of large plantations were included in the system.

The only place visited on the survey where it was evident that no social classes existed was that within the Ladino community of Chitatul. There a very few Ladinos lived in a region which was predominantly Indian. Two thirds of the towns visited evidently had a two class system among the Ladinos, and this seems to be the most common for the countryside as a whole. Two towns (San Agustín and Teculután) evidently had an emergent middle class of small merchants, chauffeurs, clerks, and artisans, while three reported this class to be fairly well developed (San Jerónimo, Esquipulas, and Guazacapán). A three class system was also reported from La Gomera and Gualán, but in these cases the third class consisted of the superimposed upper cosmopolitan class of wealthy urbanites who owned plantations within the jurisdiction of the *municipio*.

Not counting the role which may be played by the Indians, then, there are four classes which may be found in a Ladino community: a low class of laboring people and small landholders, generally poor; a local upper class, wealthier, landholders and businessmen; a "middle class" of small merchants, artisans, clerks, etc., between these two; and a cosmopolitan upper class of plantation owners who may not actually be resident in the community much of the time. The lower class is usually referred to by such terms as *los pobres, gente del pueblo, gente humilde,* or *gente sencilla;* if they are countrypeople and the speaker is a townsman, they may be called *tímido.* Tumin[42] reports the term *populacho* to be used in San Luis Jilotepeque for this group. If this population is very recently New Ladino, or mixed with a Ladinoized Indian population, some of them may be included under the term *"los indios."* The wealthier group in a community also goes under a number of different designations: *ricos, de más educación, de más conversación, gente de más respeto, acomodado, aproporcionado, privilegiado, la sociedad.*

The middle class group which was found developing in some towns did not go under any very regular term; *medio ricos* was sometimes applied to them, but it was also occasionally used for the "wealthier" group in a community with two classes. The plantation owner, the fourth class mentioned above, is of course limited in number and regionally restricted to those areas in which large *haciendas* and *fincas* are to be found. In fact, these plantation owners

---

[41] Newbold, 1954.   [42] 1952, p. 213.

frequently play a very small part in local social life unless they are landowners and more cosmopolitan than anyone else in the region.

There is a general correlation between these classes, the social types mentioned earlier, and the socio-economic groups delineated in the section on land and agriculture:

Social Class	Social Type	Socio-Economic Group
Cosmopolitan Upper	(Urban)	*Finqueros*
Upper Class	Old Ladinos; possibly a few wealthy New Landinos	Medium holders; the "irrigation aristocracy"; wealthy commercialists
Middle Class	Old Ladinos, a few Mobile and New	Medium and small landholders; small commercialists; artisans and specialists
Lower Class	Mobile and New Ladinos and Ladinoized Indians, if present	Small landholders and other subsistence agriculturalists; land renters; *colonos*; *jornaleros*

There are some communities in which New Ladinos have not entered in any significant numbers and which have not been particularly receptive to Mobile Ladinos. Quesada was evidently an example of this. In a sense, all the co-owners of the communal land in Quesada are Old Ladinos.

While the above outline is probably satisfactory theoretically for a gross picture, in fact there are many communities that have Indian residents as well as Ladino. Where this is the case, the Indian can usually be located in the structure on a par with the lower class Ladino but always as a separate sociocultural group. Although there may be Indians who are accorded considerable respect in the community, it is unlikely that the Indians as such will be graded any higher than the general Ladino lower class. Under some circumstances, particularly when the Indian group in question is Ladinoized Indian, they may be placed below the Ladino lower class.

With respect to the local upper class, which in many circumstances is composed of Old Ladinos, Tumin has provided us with a series of characteristics from his study in San Luis Jilotepeque. The characteristics he describes probably will stand for the Old Ladino upper class almost anywhere in the eastern region of the country: ". . . they are among the wealthiest people in town; . . . they give the biggest and most admired parties; . . . they own the most land; . . . they are the elite among whom political power circulates, each caucus or party taking its turn, depending only on the regime in power at the moment; . . . their children get the most formal education; their wives are the best-dressed; their houses the most sumptuous; their claims to reputable family lines the best-established; their intimations of important connections with social life in Guatemala City the most frequently heard and widely accepted; and each tends to control, singly or in collaboration with others of their friends, the respect, admiration, and political subservience of estimable blocks of Indians and lesser-ranked Ladinos." "At any given moment, however, two criteria above all tend to predominate, in the sense that they are considered by others as the most important single items and that objectively they are matrix criteria from which the others tend to diffuse. These are (a) family name or reputation, and (b) economic position." As Tumin points out, these kinds of things can "be considered as both criteria of ranking and the consequences of being ranked highly."[43]

The relation between many of the other characteristics listed by Tumin and establishment of lineage is close. A family will tend to remain in a given locale if it is being economically successful there. There is then a very close correspondence between the two characteristics which Tumin considered to be the most critical in San Luis, and which the present writer also found to be constantly the most important through the various towns he surveyed. Wealth, of course, brings in its chain other characteristics in the Ladino system: education, bigger parties, political power, better clothes, etc.

In terms of social class there are certain areas in which the population which we have called Mobile Ladinos have taken an upper position in the total local social system. Where Ladinos have entered a region which is inhabited entirely by Indians, or where Indians have entered one inhabited by Mobile Ladinos, the Ladinos take a superordinate position with respect to the Indian. If there are no Old Ladino families present, the Mobile Ladinos are numerous, then class distinctions tend to develop.

This class system among the Ladinos, however, is one which is based almost entirely on wealth, and as such does not have many of the characteristics of the social classes based on the Old-New distinction. While it is not possible to be certain without more intensive study, the writer suspects that the town of Catarina has a Ladino class structure basically similar to this. In a situation of this type, the longer the Ladino population remains fixed, the more some families tend to take the ascendency; some families remain, become established, and become "old" families; others break up, disperse, and through poverty or lack of acuity join the lower class of Ladinos. Thus the crystallization of a class system among Ladinos in a specific region or community in Guatemala depends upon the existence or gradual creation of an Old Ladino group.

(4) *Divergent Ladino Population Elements.*—The populations and relationships which have been described so far deal generally with peoples who are generally of Spanish and/or Indian origin. Besides these, there are other Ladinos in Guatemala who should be considered at least briefly because they play some role on the local scene. Among these are the Ladinos who are of recent, foreign origin. From the point of view of contemporary distinctions, the most important of these peoples started coming into Guatemala during the last century, the Germans and a few other European nationalities, and later the North Americans. The Germans came to Guatemala most specifically because of the coffee production which became intensified in the second half of the last century. This population, in general, tended to retain close ties with their home country even into World War II when there were established German Bund groups in support

---
[43] Tumin, 1952, pp. 210–211.

of Hitler. Basically, the German group resisted being changed into "Guatemalan Ladinos." They frequently had children by Ladino or Indian women, and not infrequently recognized these children; but more often than not their formal families were established by marriage with other Germans in Guatemala, other parts of Middle America, or with persons they brought over from Germany. As a result, in those regions where they became firmly established, principally in the Alta Verapaz and the piedmont and coast of San Marcos, there was created a foreign upper class as a part of or superimposed on whatever the existing social structure may have been. There was a period in the first three decades of the present century when the foreigner who came to live with this society in San Marcos learned German rather than Spanish, as it was the language of trade and significant portion of *finca* society. The Second World War brought about government intervention on most of the German owned *fincas* and the internment of a great number of the Germans in Guatemala; the fact that the Germans had retained themselves as such a distinct extra-national entity served to subject many of them to this even though they, and in some cases their parents, had been born in Guatemala. The net result of the removal of Germans and later the nationalization of the *fincas* served effectively to destroy this German society. Many never returned after the war, and those who did often had no lands to which to return. The vestige of this German society today is to be seen in two phases of the population. There were some Germans who did separate themselves from their motherland, and retained their lands through right of being Guatemalan citizens. These families have tended to intermarry among upper and middle class *finca* and urban Ladinos and with foreigners of other nationalities. The other vestigial group is composed of craftsmen and mechanics who came into Guatemala during the period of the existence of the German society; they sometimes arrived as flotsam, sometimes were brought over by the German *finqueros*, and sometimes came as entrepreneurs to take advantage of the need for skilled trades as an adjunct to the *finca* work. While many of this skilled group were also removed during the war, many returned. Unlike the German *finqueros*, they carried their skills with them, and upon their return needed only capital to start to work again: they were not heavily affected by the loss of land as was the deposed *finquero* group. Today this German group no longer stands distinct as it did prior to the war; it has tended to blend with other foreign groups and the upper and middle class Ladino groups in the country.

The social class history of the other foreign groups in Guatemala has varied somewhat from that of the Germans; there were some English and North Americans who, of course, were not dispossessed during the war. The principal American economic holdings in Guatemala were those of the United Fruit Company. Large land losses were suffered in the early 1950's through the promulgation of the Agrarian Reform Act. At the time of writing, the effect of these losses cannot be adequately estimated. From the point of view of the foreigners in general, however, the Agrarian Reform and the government which sponsored it were antagonistic to North Americans. Following the war, some Americans came to Guatemala, but by 1950 the leftist tendency of the government had become so pronounced that Americans did not feel encouraged to initiate new enterprises in the country, and some of the older ones were selling out. Socially, most Americans have followed the same general conduct as did the Germans, although their society is more based in commerce than in agriculture. They tend to form an extra-national group within the country, blending with various of the other European nationalities on the one side, and with the Guatemalan middle and upper class on the other. Their language remains American English and their social contacts and culture are both in general and in detail as North American as they can make them.

Another group, limited regionally to the short Atlantic coast, which stands apart from the rest of the Ladinos of the country, is the Black Carib Indian or *Moreno* population. In general terms, such as for purposes of the census, this population is considered Ladino, i.e., non-Indian. Racially and culturally, however, they are very distinct from the rest of the Ladinos and Indians of Guatemala. Racially the Black Carib are predominantly Negro. Culturally, they retain the language and much of the culture of the Antillean Indians with which their ancestors intermarried. They neither look nor act very much like any of the Ladinos under discussion in the present paper. The culture of the Carib will be dealt with in Section III; our particular concern here is his place in the social structure of Guatemala.

The town of Livingston, the principal Carib center in Guatemala, is a complex combination of ethnic groups which will require considerable study before it is well defined. While the principal population is Carib, or *Moreno* as they are called locally, there are in addition the following distinct groups: Ladinos (of Spanish descent), Ladinos (of other than Spanish extraction), Indians (of the same general culture as the Alta Verapaz Indians of the Cobán region) and East Indians (originally of India, but who arrived in Livingston by way of the West Indies). In terms of general stratification, the *Moreno* is considered to be above the Guatemalan Indian but below the rest of the Ladino population; in fact, however, their ethnic differences makes simple stratification an over-simplification of the social structure which exists. To the Ladino (Spanish origin), the *Moreno* is a very peculiar person; he is very happy, talks a great deal, simply does not like to get involved in physical fights, retains queer customs which are referred to as being primitive and barbaric, is frequently trilingual (speaking Carib and Spanish from early childhood, and learning English through contact with the Carib of British Honduras), is not terribly interested in accumulation of wealth, etc. There is no doubt but that there is a fairly strong feeling from the point of view of both *Morenos* and Ladinos that intermarriage is out of the question. The *Moreno*, culturally, has taken over a good deal of the Ladino culture of Spanish origin, and a few traits from the Guatemalan Indians.

Yet another group which comes under the general heading of Ladino, but which is somewhat distinct, is the Chinese. The eastern and coastal towns of Guatemala have quite a few persons of Chinese extraction who are almost always businessmen. Socially, this population element is considered in some degree as a part of the general Ladino society; they have taken over many of the customs of the Ladinos.

7. POLITICAL ORGANIZATION

Between the time of the field work on which the present report is based and the time of analysis of the data a revolution occurred which may affect the official structure of the political system. Nevertheless, the nature of the political structure at the time the field work was done reveals a good deal about the general situation of political control. In the description to follow, the structure as it existed at the time of the study will be presented; this picture, in view of the immediate uncertainty of the future, will provide as good a guide to the nature of Ladino political organization as the writer can prepare at present.

At the time of the Census of 1950, Guatemala was divided into 22 departments and 315 *municipios*.[44] The government of a department was in the hands of a governor appointed by the president; the government of a *municipio* was officially elected by the population of the *municipio*. The *municipio* in Guatemala is the minimal territorial unit which manifests any local autonomy. Below the *municipio* are units of population and territory which are under the control of persons appointed from the *municipio*. The importance of the *municipio* as an Indian socio-cultural unit was first pointed out by Tax and has been thoroughly recognized by succeeding students.[45] The relative socio-cultural distinctiveness of the *municipio* decreases, however, as one moves into Ladino population areas. Since Ladino culture tends not to be confined to municipal bondaries, the significance of the *municipio* among Ladinos rests on somewhat different grounds.

The Ladino *municipio* is socially meaningful in terms of the town which is the municipal capital. To the Ladino living in the countryside, the importance of his living in one *municipio* instead of a neighboring one is that he must go to the municipal capital for certain things: all orders from the central government are channelled through the municipal capital; the police and political control stem from the municipal capital, and that center will probably be the principal center for marketing goods and buying supplies. The Ladino will, of course, be tied, and very likely sentimentally attached to land which he may own in a particular locale, but it is often of no great importance to him whether the name of the *municipio* in which the land is located is one thing or another.

The territory of a *municipio* is usually divided into smaller divisions. These are ordinarily *cantones* and *fincas*. *Cantones* are distinct territorial subdivisions of *municipio*; they are not aggregates of population. *Fincas* are large private landholdings which are of some size and which would probably be considered as *cantones* were they to be divided up into small holdings. The population aggregates which live outside of a municipal capital but within the territorial limits of the *municipio* are usually referred to as *aldeas* and *caseríos*; the *aldea* is larger, the *caserío* smaller. A *finca*, of course, usually involves a population aggregate also, and is thus both a territorial unit and a population group. The terms used

---

[44] There were 322 *municipios* at the time of writing. [45] Tax, 1937.

for these units are not universal for all of Guatemala. There are some regions which do not use the term *cantón* for a territorial unit, and in these *municipios* the *aldeas* and *caseríos* are often felt to have certain rural territorial extension. As is the case in most Latin countries, each population aggregate of any size is officially classified in terms of a country-wide system; thus a given community will be classified officially as a *ciudad, villa, pueblo, aldea,* or *caserío,* more or less on the basis of its size and importance. One hears the term *villa* very little used in practice, however, and similarly the term *ciudad* is usually reserved for large departmental capitals and the national capital.

Towns are often subdivided territorially into *barrios* or *cantones*. This use of the term *cantón*, should be noted, is different from that already mentioned. The *barrio* or *cantón* urban subdivision is usually a clearly delineated territorial subdivision of the community. Sometimes the term *barrio* will be used rather indefinitely to divide a town into two parts, an upper and a lower, and usually certain streets or landmarks are recognized as the dividing line between one *barrio* and another. So far as the writer could tell, the use of the term *cantón* for the urban subdivisions is more common in the central and western part of the country, while the term *barrio* was more common in the east; there are exceptions to this, however, particularly as the term *barrio* is also found in quite common use in Indian towns of the west.

Basically, like almost all Central American countries, the local governments in Guatemala are strongly controlled by the central government. Centralized control was a hall mark of Spanish colonialism and has continued to be characteristic of the republican governments. During the decades prior to the revolution of 1945, all officials at the departmental, municipal and lower levels were appointed. With the establishment of the constitution the new system provided for the election of the local municipal mayor (*alcalde*), the aldermen (*regidores*) and the legal representative (*síndico*); they in turn appointed various paid employees and the auxiliary personnel in the smaller towns and rural areas. However, in various instances, particularly in Indian towns, the municipal secretary was not appointed by the elected officials but by the departmental government.

Centralized control was maintained over the municipal governments in various ways. In those areas where the secretary was appointed from the departmental government, his influence was strong and followed the directions of his departmental chiefs, not necessarily the desires of the local municipal body. Furthermore, in each departmental capital there was an Electoral Board (*Junta Electoral Departamental*) which could and wherever necessary did declare municipal elections null and void and install municipal officials who had followed the political policies of the departmental leaders. Finally, municipal governments have always had and continue to have very restricted sources of income; as a result, most are heavily dependent upon the national government for financial aid in any community public works or betterment project. Such aid is withheld, of course, if the minicipal leaders do not behave in accord with the political policies of the departmental leaders. It has often mistakenly been thought that the mere fact of elections gives local autonomy; the spectacle of Guatemala during the years between 1950 and 1954 is not the only case history of how a central government can maintain centralized control over local municipal governments in spite of an active elective system.[46]

The particular hierarchy of local officials which was to be found in most Ladino communities was established in a general way by the municipal code, a national law. In practice it worked out something as follows. There were three classes of officers: elected municipal officers; appointed minicipal employees; and appointed auxiliary officers. The elected officers included the *alcalde, regidores, and síndicos*. There was usually one *síndico* although four towns in the survey had two, and one had three. The number of *regidores* varied: 13 towns had four, 9 had five, 4 had six, and one had eight. This group of elected officials was known as the municipal council, and was theoretically the governing body of the *municipio*. Most of the municipal councils met about every two weeks. In an earlier period it was often customary for the *regidores* to serve turns, each staying in the *juzgado* or *municipalidad* (as the municipal building is called) during the daytime hours. In a community in which there were four *regidores*, each would then serve one week in four. With the advent of the new constitution in 1945 this system was put aside and officially it was decided that the *regidores*, since they were not paid, did not have to serve these turns. Nevertheless, some towns have retained this *turno* system (Grandos, San Jerónimo, San Agustín, and Palo Gordo). It is quite common for the *turno* system to be retained in Indian towns, but it evidently was quickly put aside by most of the Ladinos.

The new constitution provided for certain responsibilities to be assigned to each of the elected officials. These were set up in the form of inspectorships of education, of culture, of public health, of agriculture, of supplies, of municipal funds and property, of roads, water, public works, drainage, sports, police, and various other items added on by the specific *municipios*. In principle each *síndico* and *regidor* was supposed to hold one or more of these inspectorships. In fact, at the time that the survey was made, the inspectorships were little more than formalities. In seven of the towns complete ignorance was manifested by municipal officials as to what the inspectorships were, who held them, and what they did. In one case when the usual practice of turning to the published municipal code proved futile because it could not be located, the mayor said that the use of such inspectorships were relics of a by-gone age anyway, and the only reason anyone paid any attention to them was that it was decreed that one must. It was perfectly clear that in fact the inspectorships meant little; where they were actually put in action, they were often interpreted entirely differently from one *municipio* to the next. The inspectorship of public health, for example, was said variously to include the following functions: inspect cattle prior to slaughter; look after the water system; inspect markets; check to see that vendors had licenses; and to make sure the streets were clean. The inspectorship of agricul-

---

[46] More detail on cases of the exercise of such centralized control in local political matters will be found in a forthcoming symposium on political change in Guatemalan Indian communities, under the editorship of the present writer.

ture involved the following possibilities: look into boundary disputes; act as a fire watch; make sure people were obeying the forestry laws; and act as technical advisor in agronomy to farmers. One municipal secretary insisted that the local *regidor* assigned the agriculture inspectorship told his fellows how to plant and that he knew more than any graduate of an agricultural school because he was a farmer. For some of these inspectorships no explanation was given; what the *regidor* in charge of "culture" may have been supposed to do evidently escaped most of the municipal officials as much as it did the surveyors.

The appointed municipal employees included usually at least a secretary and a treasurer (sometimes held by a single man), and a *guardia municipal* (sort of a general messenger and sometimes janitor). Then, depending upon the size of the *municipio* and its wealth, one or more of the following might be included: first official, second official, and third official (men who acted as assistants to the secretary), one or two scribes (typists), assistants for the *guardia municipal*, a gardner, a man in charge of the water system, a man in charge of the municipal electric light plant (usually a diesel plant), an inspector of the public market, an inspector of the public slaughterhouse, a guardian of the cemetery, and a municipal nurse. It is probably safe to say that there is no municipal capital in Guatemala (except possibly for the towns which are also departmental capitals) which employ all these people, but some will be found in most towns. It was specified in most towns surveyed that the municipal *alcalde* made all appointments of employees except those of the secretary and treasurer, and for these the municipal council had to give approval. It can be seen that the functions of some of these employees duplicate possible functions of the inspectorships which might be assigned to the *regidores*.

The final group of governmental persons are the appointed auxiliary officials. These are usually of two types, although as will be noted the two occasionally overlap: those who are appointed from the municipal capital to act as ancillary personnel in the town, and those appointed from the smaller towns and rural areas to act as agents of the *alcade* in those regions. The general term for these persons is *alcalde auxiliar*; if he was provided with helpers and persons who could act as substitutes for him, as was usually the case, they were called merely "helpers." The most common system followed in naming these persons was to name one *alcalde auxiliar* and some helpers from each *aldea* and larger *caserío*. If the rural region was divided into *cantones*, then one might be named from each *cantón*.

The terms used for this personnel also are gradually changing. With the revolution of 1945 it was decided that the older term *alguacil* carried a bad connotation and should be replaced with the simple term *ayudante* (helper). The *alguacil* formerly had the duties of both messenger and policeman. In some regions another old term, *ministril*, was formerly used. In the course of the survey, the survival of these old terms was reported only from towns in or adjacent to the western Indian region or in communities in which populations of Ladinoized Indians still lived. *Alguacil* was reported in Tierra del Pueblo, Guazacapán and San Jerónimo, while *ministril* was used in four towns of the south coast, Siquinalá, La Gomera, Patulul, and Catarina. Another term, *regidor auxiliar*, has also survived in Tierra del Pueblo and Palencia.

The general functions of these rural auxiliary personnel is to report disturbances of the peace, to act as police if none be present in cases of intense disturbance, and to carry orders from the *municipalidad* to the rural people. For this last function, it is the custom in many *municipios* for the rural *alcaldes auxiliares* to come to the municipal capital every Saturday morning to meet with the municipal *alcalde*. In many *municipios* it is not uncommon to find *juzgados auxiliares* located in the larger *aldeas* and *fincas*, buildings in which the *alcaldes auxiliares* hold forth. While the appointment of the auxiliary personnel is under the jurisdiction of the municipal *alcalde*, it is an old custom which was still in force in 1954 for the owners of a *finca* to give his approval or suggest the name of the *alcalde auxiliar* of the *finca*.

The other type of auxiliary personnel, that named within the municipal capital, was reported from six towns. In general, it consisted of a system basically similar to that set up for the rural regions, only in this case each *barrio* of the town was considered in the same light as was a rural *aldea* or *caserío*; thus from each *barrio* or *cantón* of the town an *alcalde auxiliar* and his helpers would be named. From each of the two *cantones* of Petapa, an *alcalde auxiliar* and two *ministriles* were named; an *alcalde auxiliar* and four *alguaciles* were named from the *cantones* of Palencia, and two or three *alguaciles municipales* served turns in Granados. The other towns in which such a system was reported were Mataquescuintla, Morales and Palo Gordo.

In Palo Gordo and San Carlos Sija a system which combines the town and rural auxiliary personnel has developed. In the former place there are five *ministriles auxiliares* named from the town, and each serves a turn of working one week in five. In each of the aldeas there is also named an *alcalde auxiliar* and five *ministriles*; each week the five *aldeas* which are nearest the town send one *ministril* each to serve the week in the town *municipalidad*; in this way, there are a total of six *ministriles* present at all times in the town (one from the town and five from *aldeas*). In the San Carlos Sija the system is somewhat different, since there are no auxiliary personnel appointed in the town. There the various *aldeas* are classified into two categories, those which have *juzgado* buildings and those which do not. In all *aldeas* an *alcalde auxiliar* and seven *regidores auxiliares* are named. In those *aldeas* which have *juzgados* this personnel remain in the *aldea*; the seven *aldeas* which have no *juzgado*, however, each sends six *auxiliares* to the town to serve there for a period of a week. Thus each of these *aldeas* sends its personnel in one week out of seven for duty in the town.

The use of auxiliary personnel serving in turns is a survival of an older form of municipal service which still is retained in many Traditional and Modified Indian communities. Such Indian organizations have been described elsewhere,[47] but it probably is worth mentioning one case for those who may not be too

---

[47] The reader is referred to the monographs describing Indian communities (for example, Wagley, 1949, Bunzel, 1952, and Cámera, 1952) for descriptions of the older Indian political organization.

familiar with the literature on the Guatemalan Indian. In the town of Joyabáj there is a regular municipal organization with *alcalde, regidores,* and so on. All these people, however, are Ladinos, and almost 75 % of the people of Joyabáj may be classified as Traditional Indians. There is in addition to this Ladino municipal structure, an Indian organization. This organization, presumably recognized officially at one time, was at the time of the survey a voluntary organization run by the Indian elders to act as a sort of liaison between the Ladinos and the Indians. It was composed of two *alcaldes,* one of whom takes the turn on alternate weeks; four *regidores,* each of whom takes turns, one week in four; and three *mayores* with five *alguaciles* each, each group of which takes the turn of one week out of three. In Joyabáj the municipal offices are on the second floor of the municipal building; these Indian personnel (one *alcalde,* one *regidor,* one *mayor* and five *alguaciles* at a time) sit on benches at the bottom of the steps leading up to the Ladino offices. Within the Ladino political structure these Indians have officially no place; in fact they do serve a purpose to relate the Indians to the Ladino organization, but represent a late stage of disintegration of the Indian political organization.

A municipal organization may be said to have functions which are oriented in two different directions. On the one hand, it is the lowest important element in the national administrative structure; it is the hand of the national government. In this position it acts merely as the orderly of the political and administrative leaders in the national and departmental capitals. On the other hand, the municipal organization also faces towards the population of the towns and countryside within its jurisdiction. It is responsible for the public order, and as governmental activities extend themselves, for an increasing amount of activity in various phases of the lives of the community and its inhabitants. Among the activities which the community may oversee are the establishment and care of a market place, a slaughterhouse, the cementery, control of irrigation water, rental of municipal lands, provision of electric power, overseeing of the school, care of bridges and roads in its jurisdiction, and establishment of a municipal dispensary.

A third of the towns visited had no slaughterhouse, but the rest did and they were under municipal control. In at least three of the towns a *fiel de rastro* or inspector of the slaughterhouse, was employed; elsewhere, the control of the slaughterhouse was under the supervision of the *regidor* responsible for public health or one of the *guardias municipales.* Nowhere was there evidence that the personnel responsible for inspecting meat was particularly qualified to do so.

The establishment and care of the cemetery has been a long standing function of the municipality. The tradition is still strong in the towns and countryside of Guatemala for each family to clean the burial plots of their dead just prior to the Day of All Saints in November. In almost all towns visited on the survey it was reported that the people would all go out annually to do this work; in some places it was said that no "order" from the *alcalde* was necessary since it was so much a matter of tradition; elsewhere, the municipal *alcalde* would send out the order via the *regidores* in town and via the *alcaldes auxiliares* in the countryside. In some towns a municipal employee, a custodian of the cemetery or a gardner, gives the cemetery a second annual cleaning in May or June, while in a few towns it was reported that the population is called out a second time for this.

Seven of the towns visited reported having fairly large holdings in municipal lands; one, Tierra del Pueblo, was an *aldea* located wholly on municipally-owned lands. Under the Agrarian Reform Law of 1952, all the municipal lands were to be repartitioned and at the time the survey was made this was still in process. With the revolution of 1954, however, one of the early policies of the new government was to return all municipal lands to the *municipios*. As a result, the status of these lands is somewhat uncertain at the time of writing.

The public school system, as elsewhere in Central America, is run directly from the Ministry of Education in the national capital. Nevertheless, as has already been noted, there is supposed to be a *regidor* assigned in each *municipio* to oversee the educational activities. The principal interpretation put on the duties of this post by informants was to see that the teachers showed up when they were supposed to, since this was, apparently, the principal complaint. However, sometime before the survey was made, a new law became operative by which each *municipio* was supposed to establish a *Junta Local de Educación*, or Local Board of Education. The general composition of the Board was to include one representative of the municipality (usually interpreted locally as being the *regidor* assigned to the inspectorship of education), two teachers and two community members. In some towns there were three of each of the teachers and community members, and in one place three teachers and five parents. While the actual establishment of this *Junta* was not really an accomplished fact in most of the towns visited (it was always about to be done, or they were just in the process of doing it, or it had just been founded but it had not done anything yet), the proposed range of its activities was quite surprising. Not only was the *Junta* supposed to check on the activities of the teachers and the attendance of children, but it was to have the right to alter the school curriculum if it felt it to be necessary. This was quite a broad innovation to bring into a society which was used to centralized control in most of its affairs. Whether this ruling will continue in effect or not cannot be said at present, of course, but it seems evident that it will take a good deal more than legislation to introduce many of the townspeople and countrymen into the idea of having a responsibility for the excellence of the school.

Of course, local political organization involves more than the structure and functioning of the municipal and sub-municipal system. Politics in its broader meaning of the control of power in the human community also has many other phases. During the ten years from 1944 to 1954 there developed in Guatemala the political party system. This system was encouraged by the government, first as a means of achieving a liberal and democratic political system, and later as a means of retaining the incumbent politicians in power. At the time of writing, however, all these parties had been outlawed and had ceased to function, at least publicly. There is little doubt that in the course of their development they served in many cases to split communities, and to underline differences which may have existed previously. There were many towns visited in which the mayor was a very young man. In some places this was commented upon, sometimes with satisfaction, sometimes with dissatisfaction, but there is no question that an older political power system in which the older men of the community were somewhat looked to for leadership was undergoing a severe test. In some cases it was quite evident that the young *alcalde* acted as little more than a figurehead for the activities of the municipal secretary who had been appointed to his job.

In most *municipios* there are also agents of the national government, men not responsible to the *municipio* officials for the exercise of their authority. Outside of towns which are also departmental capitals, however, these agents are usually one of two types: national police officers and *comisionados militares*. In some of the municipal centers there is a small post of the national *Guardia Civil*; these posts rarely have more than two or three individuals, and they are not found everywhere. Their assignment depends upon the size of the community, its importance commercially and politically, and its reputations as a locale of conflict. Theoretically, there is named in each *municipio* a *comisionado militar*, a man responsible for recruitment. The *comisionado* is allowed to name assistants in the larger *aldeas*. These men are responsible to the nearest military authority.

8. RELIGIOUS ACTIVITIES

The religion of the Guatemalan Indians of the western highlands has attracted the attention of social scientists and tourists alike because of its remarkable fusion of traits of Catholic and indigenous origin. Among the Indians, not only is the form of the religious practices of interest, but the resultant religion plays a large role in the life of the individuals concerned. The religiousness of the Indian contrasts sharply with that of the Ladino. It is likely that the Guatemalan Ladino is about as religious as Ladinos of other Central American countries; in comparison with the Indian of his own country, however, his religious activities seem drab and uninspired.[48] Nevertheless, religion enters the life of the Ladino at baptism, and depending upon his sex, social position, and community, plays a more or less important role until his soul is prayed for anywhere up to seven years or more after his death.

In most Ladino communities baptism is looked upon as a necessary rite for the child; since there is frequently no local priest, however, it is necessary to carry the child to the center where the priest holds Sunday Mass or to wait until he comes to the community for a fiesta. Both were reported as ways of solving the problem. In a very few places it was reported that the community members did not much care whether the child was baptized or not. Celebration of a baptism by a familial fiesta seemed to depend not only on the relative wealth

---

[48] Holleran, 1949, has published a good account of the history of the Catholic Church in Guatemala with respect to its relations to the state and national history. The reader is referred to that source for an historical picture of the formal church.

of the family involved, but also on various local preferences in the matter. In six of the towns it was simply said that the baptisms were not celebrated; in six others it depended upon the financial ability of the people involved as to whether a fiesta was given or not.

Confirmations are carried out wherever possible; if and when a bishop happens to be available, confirmations are in order. In the course of his visits around Guatemala, the writer has often had the impression that bishops must do little else than confirm. The writer encountered no regular custom of holding a fiesta in the home when a child was confirmed. Marriage, however, evidently is celebrated whenever the families involved have enough money. The custom among Ladinos is for the fiesta to be held in the home of the boy's parents; in only one community (of the ten in which information was collected on the subject) was it said that the fiesta was held in the home of whichever family was more wealthy.

The ceremonies of death in the town and countryside of Guatemala are highly important for the Ladinos. Since death comes at unpredictable times, there have long been acceptable ways of dealing with it without dependence on the clergy. Where a priest is available and where the families involved can afford it, it is customary to hold a Mass and start a novena on the first night following death. Among people who adhere to Catholic customs more strongly, this Mass may be repeated on the anniversaries of the death for a number of years thereafter. In 26 towns it was specifically stated that besides the novena held at the time of death, another was held at the end of the first year; in four of these towns it was said that yet another was held at the end of the seventh year following the death, while in two others it was said that a final novena was held at the end of the second year. These novenas are times of family visiting and fairly intense interaction. However, they are usually attended more by women than by men. With very few exceptions the prayer leaders were specified to be women. Of all the Ladino populations visited, only in La Gomera and Zaragoza was it reported that sometimes a man would lead these prayers. This is a point of significant difference from some Indian communities. In Modified and Ladinoized communities, where the novenas also play an important role in the lives of the community members, it is more common for the men to lead these sessions. Thus in the Modified community of Magdalena Milpas Altas, and in the Ladinoized Indian groups in Barrio San Sebastián of Guazacapán, San José la Arada, and Catarina, men lead the novenas. Some of the Indians of the southwest piedmont, however, do not seem to conform to this general picture. In both Patulul and Tierra del Pueblo it was reported that it was the women, among Indians, who lead the novenas and not the men. The writer is not prepared to say why this variation in the general picture should occur.

The relative importance of women in religion among Ladinos, however, is further attested in four western Ladino towns located within a fairly heavy Indian region (Flores Costa Cuca, Palo Gordo, San Carlos Sija, and Chitatul; also in Quesada). In these five towns it was reported that only women participated in novenas at all; men had nothing to do with the activities. The great importance of women in novenas among Ladinos is only one example of their relatively greater importance in religious affairs in general; as a general rule (as has been noted by various observers) the change from Indian to Ladino means a change from man-dominated religious activities to women-dominated activities.

A custom which is evidently of Spanish origin but which has very little survival today is that of giving a fiesta and dance when an infant dies. This custom, which also survives elsewhere in Central America, was found only in the eastern and southeastern towns of Guatemala. In three towns (San José la Arada, Barberena, and Esquipulas) it was reported that the custom was still observed in the more rural regions, but that it was not practiced by the townspeople. In three other towns it was said to have been practiced by the Ladinos within the memory of the present generation but not to be practised now (Guazacapán, Siquinalá, and La Gomera). In only one Ladino community was the custom said to still form an active part of the death observances, and this was the community of Quesada. It was reported by Ladino informants in Atescatempa that the Ladinoized Indians of Yupiltepeque observed the custom. There is no evidence which could point to this being a trait of Indian origin, nor even one which the Indians took over with any great enthusiasm in the colonial period. It was reported nowhere from the western and northern Indian regions. The only reference the writer has been able to locate on the possible Indian use of this custom is a curiously worded statement to the effect that the rituals for a child have "a formal cheerful character consistent with the idea of baptized infant blessedness."[49] Today it is still not the general custom to hold a novena for the death of a child; a one-night wake is held instead. In the town of Zaragoza it was reported that special singing was carried out in the home and then in the church on the death of a child.

Novenas are almost always held in front of the altar in the home. It was reported in most all sites surveyed that it was characteristic of homes, both rich and poor, to have such altars. Among the rich it was more customary to have small images, while among the poor, pictures sufficed. The degree to which the saints were celebrated varied greatly. In twelve of the towns visited (with no particular regional distribution pattern) it was said that it was something of a custom to celebrate the principal saint in the house with a *novena de santo* on or near his day. The most extreme form of this celebration was reported from Zaragoza where the writer received the impression that such novena singing was one of the principal pastimes. In nine of the towns it was stated that it was not a local custom to hold such novenas; the towns so reporting were mainly from the southwest coast (Catarina, Flores Costa Cuca, Tierra del Pueblo, San Antonio, Patulul, and Siquinalá; also San José la Arada, Teculután, and Sansare). There is little doubt that among Ladinos in general the celebration of a *novena de santos*, where held, is principally the work of women; Zaragoza would be the only possible exception among the towns surveyed.

Every community visited except the *aldea* of Chitatul had a Catholic Church

---

[49] This comment is repeated by Tax and Redfield (p. 35) and by Benjamin and Lois Paul (p. 192) in their respective articles in HOC.

building (in two communities they were in the process of being constructed) and at least 18 of the 30 communities had one or more Protestant chapels. The poorest church was that of Granados which consisted only of walls and roof; it had absolutely no interior furnishings, neither altar, benches, nor saints; it was, however, in the gradual process of construction and from the comments made by informants, the survey team was given the impression that even this was a great improvement over the past. While the Catholic temple in a municipal capital is usually referred to as an *iglesia*, *oratorio* is the term applied to those in the *aldeas*. Most *aldeas*, of course, do not have *oratorios*, but 13 of the *municipios* visited had at least one *aldea* with such a place of worship.

The manner of maintaining a church building in good repair varies over the country as a whole, but within the eastern region there seem to be two fairly common systems. One of these may be called the *hermandad* system, since the organization involved usually goes under this name. The *hermandad* was reported from five towns (Teculután, Gualán, Esquipulas, San Manuel, and Quesada); it consists of a group of women, usually from among the better class, headed by one who is called the *capitana*. From the cases reported, the *hermandad* is evidently a fairly permanent body; it reflects again the relatively important part played by women in Catholic affairs. The other method found in the east is the *comité* system, a temporary group, usually composed of both men and women, which is created when the church is in need of funds for some specific purpose. In Granados and Petapa, for example, where the churches were under construction, there were *Comités Pro-Construcción de la Iglesia*; in San Agustín there was a *Comité Pro-Reparación*; elsewhere there was a *Comité de la Iglesia* (Sansare), *Comité Pro-Iglesia* (Barberena), and a *Comité Católico* (Morales). As one moves west, the method of sustaining the physical facilities of the church become more varied. In Siquinalá there is a *cofradía* group which has taken over the function of collecting funds for the church as well as sponsoring the fiesta of its saint. In Zaragoza it was said that all the town's people were so strongly Catholic that they all pitched in to help whenever the church needed it; there was no special organization to handle the collection of funds. In Joyabáj, a community with a large Traditional Indian population in the *municipio*, the wives of the Indian *cofradía* leaders kept the church clean; in Palo Gordo there was a permanent church committee (members of both sexes) and three *sacristanes* (sextons) appointed by the municipal *alcalde*. In Catarina a group called the *Agrupación Sabatina* had been formed; it was evidently essentially similar to the *hermandades* to be found in the east in that it was composed entirely of women and was a permanent group. However, this group also had taken on the additional responsibility of teaching the town children Catholic doctrine.

It is not unlikely that the variation found in the western towns is due at least in part to the fact of the Indian population and its customs with respect to religion. Where present, the Indian population is usually much more active religiously than are the Ladinos; as a result, they often take over a great part of the activity in such things as church maintenance, as has apparently been the case in Joyabáj. Of the two principal types of church support found in the east, the permanent *hermandad* of women and the usually mixed, temporary committee, the writer suspects that the former is probably the older, or better said the more traditional. Committees may, obviously, come and go, but the permanent women's groups indicate some degree of tradition.

The relative scarcity of priests in Guatemala during its recent history has already been mentioned. Of the towns visited, nine had resident priests, eight had visiting priests from one of the departmental capitals, while 12 relied on priests from other *municipio* capitals. Of the twenty which did not have priests, only five were visited every Sunday. For the most part, the remainder had a priest a few times a year, usually for the principal fiestas or when one was brought over for a special Mass. The Guatemalan Ladinos, like their Indian neighbors, have long become accustomed to carry on many of their religious activity without the help of a priest. However, among the Ladinos this had doubtless led to a reduction of religious activity, while among the Indians it has usually led to merely a reformation of activities on a non-priest-dependent basis. The only *aldeas* which ordinarily have the services of a priest are those which are in a *municipio* in which a priest is resident. Thus a given priest will usually carry the responsibility for his own church, the *aldeas* within the immediate *municipio* and the churches of certain adjacent municipal capitals. As has been the case elsewhere in Latin America, the priests in Guatemala have achieved a mixed reputation. In Joyabáj, for example, the informants were full of praises for the resident priest; he had achieved numerous changes in the condition of the church and, from the Ladino informant's point of view, had improved the entire church situation by prohibiting the Indians from burning candles on the floor of the church and from burning the indigenous incense, *pom*, which makes quite a heavy smoke. On the other hand, the informant in one community in the east said that it was better for the priest not to come out, for every time he did he got into trouble with one of the local girls. In recent years the priests in Guatemala have been under considerable stress from politically based anticlericalism. The priest's retort, under the past government, has often been to fight politics with politics; one such case was reported from an eastern town in which the informant said that the priest had refused to come to the town unless called by an anticommunist. There is little doubt that the relative importance of the priest depends to some degree upon the religious activity present in the community, and recently, the degree to which the church has been the political opponent of the government. Following the revolution of 1954, there was an upswing in clerical influence.

With respect to the number of Protestants in the towns and countryside of Guatemala, unfortunately the results of the 1950 Census are not yet available, and the figures from the 1940 Census are unreliable. From the data gathered on the survey, the writer would guess that 2% to 4% of the Guatemalan population is Protestant. The Protestants are of a number of different sects but are generally referred to simply as "evangelicals." Nowhere in the survey was there reported to be any real conflict between the Catholics and Protestants. Indeed, it was more often reported that greater ill feeling existed between diverse Protestant sects than between the Catholics and any particular Protestant group. Most Protestant communities are the result of missionary work. The quality of this work has evidently varied considerably. In San Agustín, informants noted that a medical missionary had made an extremely good impression on the town and had been responsible for many conversions. On the other hand, in most communities visited the number of Protestants reported usually did not number over 40 or 50 people; this does not indicate that missionary work on the whole has had extensive success. While the writer cannot be sure of these facts, nor of his interpretation of them, it is his impression that the relative lack of success among Ladinos may in part be due to the general lack of religious enthusiasm characteristic of many Ladino men. Ladino men do not participate extensively in the Catholic religious activities and it seems unlikely that they would find stricter Protestantism any more attractive.

Ladino Protestants have developed a number of customs which differentiate them from their Catholic neighbors. In one eastern community it was reported that they do not get godfathers at all, while in Barrio San Sebastián of Guazacapán it was said that they looked for *compadres* only among themselves. Protestants cannot, of course, participate in many of the customs of Catholic significance which form an important part of the Ladino cultural landscape. They are excluded from the common religious exercises (baptisms, confirmation, religious fiestas, lay religious groups, dances, etc.) which form an important part of Ladino life; furthermore, the teachings of the Protestant sects usually frown heavily on the use of liquours and cigarettes; the former of these are important parts of most Ladino celebrations.

The social organization of religious activities among Catholic Ladinos is found functioning not only at the family level and among friends, as is manifested in the novenas for the dead and for the house saints, but of course it is also of great importance at the community level and among volunteer groups within the community. Perhaps the major social organization form at the community level in religious affairs is that set up to handle the financing and arrangements for the annual major fiesta. In most cases (as will be noted below) this fiesta is the *fiesta titular*, that is, the fiesta held in honor of the saint for whom the town is named. Throughout the various communities surveyed, the mode of sponsoring this fiesta fell into one of two general patterns. The first and most common of these, the dual pattern, found throughout the region of Ladino dominance (i.e. the Motagua Valley, the east, southeast, and into the center south coast) consists in the existence of two distinct groups in the community, one usually named by the municipality and responsible for the arrangement of all non-religious aspects of the fiesta; and the other responsible for the collection of funds and sponsoring the religious portion of the celebration. The other pattern, which may be distinguished as the single pattern, involves only one group or aggregate of individuals working in some sort of coordination; this group is responsible for both lay and religious aspects of the fiesta. The single pattern is found principally in the central and western highland and piedmont communities.

In the dual system, the municipality annually names a group of men to form a *Comité Pro-Feria* (or *Comité Pro-Fiesta, Comité Pro-Fiesta Titular,* or *Comité Católico*). This group exists only during the period prior to the fiesta and is responsible for collecting funds for civil aspects of the fiesta and promoting the non-religious customs associated with the celebration. At the same time, there exists another group, which may be organized in various ways, which undertakes the responsibility for the religious phases of the celebration. They put the church in order, collect funds to pay for the religious aspect, arrange for the priest to come (if he is to come). Among the various towns surveyed the mode of sponsoring the civic aspect showed considerable consistency; such was not the case among the groups which sponsored the religious aspects. Before going into these differences, however, it would be worthwhile to describe the mode of sponsoring the fiestas in the western region.

In the regions in which Indians form the predominant part of the general population, *cofradías* exist for the care of the saint and the sponsorship of the fiesta. In Catarina, the *Cofradía de Santa Catarina* consists of an irregular number of *alcaldes de cohetes* (literally, mayors of the fireworks) and *alcaldes de cera* (mayors of the wax candles) who volunteer every year to handle the expenses of these items for the next year. At the same time community members get together and make contributions to pay the priest. In San Antonio Suchitepéquez a somewhat unique *cofradía* was reported; it was said that the *cofradía* was generally in the hands of the poor people of town, that they were responsible for collecting money for the fiesta, etc. However, among these people the women took the responsibility every other year while the men took it on alternate years. Of greater curiosity, however, is that it was reported that it was not these people, the poorer men and women who took care of the image of San Antonio; instead, this was kept in the home of the wealthy people of the town and passed among them. Anyone could come to pray wherever it happened to be located at the moment and give a contribution.

In San Antonio it was said that the image stayed a month at a time in each of the homes it visited. The same general system was reported from Patulul, but the length of time spent in each residence was not definite. The whole system differed in Patulul, however, because there the Ladinos and the Indians each sponsored different fiestas. In Joyabáj the Indians and Ladinos also formed distinct *cofradía* groups. In the two Ladino *cofradías* (*Concepción* and the *Virgen del Rosario*) a *mayordomo* kept the saint for the entire year; he was aided at the time of the fiesta by a number of auxiliary *mayordomos* (who were numbered first, second, third, etc.) who provided money and other aid for the sponsorship of the fiesta. Among the women there were *capitanas* who play a role similar to that of the *mayordomos*.

In the *aldea* of Chitatul, there is a single *cofradía* which consists in little more than in caring for the saint during the year in one of the homes. In San Carlos Sija the *cofradía* has taken another curious form. There the principal man in the *cofradía*, the *cofrade*, takes responsibility for the *Virgen de la Concepción* but may keep it anywhere he chooses. Evidently for the past few years he has kept it in Guatemala City, since he spends much of his time there. He brings it back during the fiesta and for a month or so at a time if the townspeople so request. For sponsoring the fiesta he pays much of the cost, but is helped by auxiliary *cofrades* who may take over certain expenses such as was reported from Catarina. There is a *cofrade de bombas*, one for candles, and there is a *presidente de las cintas* who is elected after the *carrera de cintas* (see below) each year, and who pays for the major dance during the fiesta for the next year.

The town of Palo Gordo provides the principal exception to the general western pattern of a single group handling the sponsorship of the fiesta. There exists both *cofradías*, one in particular for the patron saint of Esquipulas, and a *Comité de Festejo* made up of men and women who collect money for the main fiesta. Unfortunately, we failed to find out whether this committee was appointed by the *municipalidad* or not. Each of the *cofradías* in Palo Gordo have four *cofrades* who are replaced annually. The privilege of being a *cofrade* is evidently important, as people compete for the position. No two *cofrades* in a *cofradía* may come from the same family, nor may they be succeeded by a family member. The *cofrades* get *mayordomos* to help them; a *mayordomo* of candles, one of the altar, one of fireworks, one of the novenas, etc. Just as the *cofrades* may not be family members, so it is forbidden that the *mayordomos* appointed be members of the same family as the *cofrades* of the *cofradía*. Both men and women may be *cofrades*.

The custom of Ladinos and Indians to have separate *cofradías* and separate fiestas is to be found in almost all communities in which there are considerable numbers of each. Thus in Joyabáj the Ladinos have two *cofradías* celebrating two fiestas, while the Indians have seven, celebrating as many fiestas. As is usually the case, the Indians have the responsibility for the titular fiesta. In Joyabáj this is the *Virgen del Tránsito*, celebrated in August. Ladino informants consistently reaffirmed that where both Indian and Ladino religious organization existed, the Indians were more active and "took their religion more seriously." Thus in Joyabáj each of the Ladino *cofradías* has a *mayordomo* who keeps the image of the saint during the year, and he has various (an irregular number) other male *mayordomos* and female *capitanas* who help with expenses when it comes time for the fiesta. In the Indian *cofradías* there are a fixed number of *cofrades* (five *mayordomos* and five *capitanes*). Since many of the Indians live in the rural *cantones* and not in the town itself, it is customary for the main *mayordomo*, who is responsible for the saint for the year, to rent a house in town if he does not own one. Either he or his wife must live at the house as long as they have the saint. As is the case elsewhere in many Traditional Indian communities, these positions of *mayordomo* are part of the total Indian religious-political structure; thus here it is necessary for a man to have been a *mayordomo* before he can hold one of the posts of *regidor* or *alcalde* described earlier in the section on political organization.

It can be seen that the main pattern of fiesta sponsorship in the west is the *cofradía* consisting of a various number of *cofrades*, or *mayordomos* and *capitanas*; these officials usually change annually, although the principal *cofrade* or *mayordomo*, who keeps the image of the saint, may keep it for a number of years under some circumstances. This system also carries into the east in some towns, but generally becomes weaker as one moves away from the western area. In Mataquescuintla there is a large *cofradía* of *Santiago*, the patron saint, which is composed of five groups of five *mayordomos* each and five groups of four *capitanes* each. These people carry the entire responsibility of the religious portion of the fiesta. While the principal image remains in the church, the *cofradía* has a smaller image which is kept in a permanent house belonging to the *cofradía*. Anyone may borrow it to take home to pray to for anything up to nine nights (a novena). This fairly large *cofradía* organization in Mataquescuintla forms part of a generally large Ladino religious organization which was reported for the town. Besides the *cofradía* for the patron saint, there are at least eight other *cofradías*, one of which was reported as having as many as 32 *mayordomos* and 27 *capitanes* with memberships which change annually (except in the case of two where it changed every two years). All have images in the church as well as smaller images in the houses owned by the *cofradías*. Besides the *cofradías* there are also two organizations with permanent memberships; these are called *sociedades* (also referred to by one informant as *hermandades*, but the term should not be confused with that used for the church upkeep groups) and may have as many as 190 members. The difference between the *sociedad* and *cofradía*, as noted, is that the former has a permanent membership and is sort of a club, whereas the latter is composed of changing membership. Two of the *cofradías* in Mataquescuintla were said to be composed of poorer people, while that of the patron saint was reported to be held mainly by the wealthier.

In other towns in the east the *cofradía* is used as a means of sponsoring the religious portions of the fiesta (such is the case in Granados, with five to seven *cofrades*), but in some cases it is not a *cofradía* in the sense just described. In San José la Arada, Esquipulas, and Atescatempa for example, the so-called *cofradía* consists of a small group of women headed by a *capitana*. Elsewhere, the form differs. In San Agustín a group of representatives from each of the *barrios* of the town join with the municipally named committee to plan the fiesta; in Teculután a second committee of two men handle the religious portion of the fiesta. In Siquinalá the priest names a *Comité Católico* in the same way that the municipality names a committee for the non-religious aspects of the fiesta. Essentially the same system is used in La Gomera, except that it was reported there that the community members name this religious committee and the list is sent to the priest for his approval.

As is the case in other parts of Latin America, the fiestas celebrated by the Ladinos of Guatemala may be classified into one of two types: public and private. The main public fiestas are Holy Week, Christmas Eve, and the local *fiesta titular*. Some towns celebrate a few additional public fiestas such as *Corpus Cristi*, and in almost all *Todos los Santos* is observed with special visits to the cemetery and is prepared for by the annual cemetery cleaning. Christmas Eve, or *Noche Buena*, is usually celebrated with a minimum of nine nights of the custom known as the *posada*, in which the images of Joseph and Mary are carried from one house to another in search of a lodging place. The *posada* is a strong Guatemalan Ladino custom. In a few towns there is a special *cofradía* for the two saints which sponsors the *posada*. Also in some towns there are a number of pairs of images which make the rounds. While nine is the most common number of nights for the pair of images to seek lodging (remaining in a different house each night), there is some variation. In Petapa and San Manuel it was said that the *posada* began about a month before Christmas Eve; in Palencia two weeks, in Atescatempa twelve days, and in Sansare only six days. In San Rafael Tierra del Pueblo, Christmas Eve is the principal fiesta of the year, more important than the patron saint, *San Rafael*. There it is attended by certain of the customs which elsewhere are usually only associated with the titular fiesta, the bullfight and masked dances.

The principal fiesta of the year in most towns is the titular fiesta celebrating the day of the patron saint of the town. However, in a number of towns Ladinos have taken another day as their principal fiesta. In some cases, the reason for this change in fiesta days is not clear. Such is the case in Barberena, where the patron is *San José*, but the *Virgen de la Merced* is the principal fiesta; in Petapa, *San Miguel* is the patron, but *la Virgen del Rosario* is the principal day celebrated; in San Carlos Sija, the *Virgen de la Concepción* is the principal saint celebrated, not *San Carlos*. In all these towns the day of the titular patron saint is still celebrated, but only religiously, with a Mass and procession; there is no entertainment associated with it.

The probable reason for the cases just cited is suggested by certain of the remaining cases. In Patulul, Flores Costa Cuca, and Joyabáj, the titular fiestas for the patron saints are the responsibility of the Indians. Thus, in Joyabáj an Indian *cofradía* sponsors the fiesta of the *Virgen del Tránsito;* in Patulul, *la Magdalena* is the patron saint, and is celebrated in a fiesta sponsored by a *cofradía* of Indians; and in Flores Costa Cuca, the Indians are responsible for the celebration of *Candelaria*, while the Ladinos celebrate *San Antonio*; which of the two was the actual patron of the *pueblo* could not be determined by asking informants. In both Joyabáj and Patulul it is of significance that the principal Ladino fiesta was the celebration of the *Virgen de la Concepción*. It seems that in a good many towns where the Indians are in charge of the patron saint, the Ladinos have taken over this fiesta as their main celebration. In Guazacapán this process may have evidently gone the whole way so that now *Concepción* is considered to be the titular fiesta, but it is not celebrated by any of the Indians of the Barrio of San Sebastián. It seems not unlikely that where a saint which is not the titular saint of the town is celebrated as the principal fiesta, it may be that at an earlier point in time the Indian population was responsible for the titular saint, so the Ladinos took over another as theirs. Such may well have been the case in San Carlos Sija where *Concepción* is the principal contemporary fiesta and *San Carlos* is celebrated only with a Mass and procession. Whether Guazacapán in bygone years had some other patron saint, perhaps recognizable today as one of the six saints celebrated by Indian *cofradías* of the Barrio San Sebastián, is difficult to say; it does, however, seem likely.[50]

---

[50] The *Cofradía del Niño Dios* of San Sebastián celebrates six saints or holy days; for each of these there is a *mayordomo* and a *capitán*, a man and a woman, but the latter does not

Before continuing with a description of the public fiestas, it would be well to mention briefly the private fiestas. The distinction between these two types of celebrations is that in the former the entire community, or a significantly large segment thereof, participates in the celebration; in the latter, a limited clique, family, or organization sponsor the fiesta for its own private satisfaction. The socially most important types of private fiestas celebrated are those sponsored by associations. Such associations are not extremely common in Ladino Guatemala; it was mentioned that two were reported in Mataquescuintla. The *Hijas de María* was reported to exist in San Jerónimo and San Carlos Sija, but in the former the membership included both married and single women, whereas in the latter only single women (the more correct in terms of usual Catholic practice) were members. In Palo Gordo it was said that this organization used to exist, but died out. The *Hijas* customarily pray every night of the month of May and then celebrate a Mass at the end of the month. The principal remaining type of private fiesta is little more than an elaboration of the celebration of a novena for the house saint. The most intensive elaboration of this was reported from Zaragoza. It was reported that during the nine days of the novena for San Antonio that many people in the town prayed most of the day. They would go from one home to the next, praying an hour before the saint in each residence. However, this was done only on invitation indicating that it was done principally between groups of friends. A *sociedad* was also reported in Zaragoza, that of *Sagrado Corazón de Jesús*; the members of this organization include both men and women, and in being members, they are supposed to take communion on the first Friday of every month. If the priest does not come to town on that day, then they must go to a neighboring town to fulfill the promise.

To return to the public fiestas, each community usually has one fiesta (usually aside from Holy Week and Christmas Eve) which is the principal celebration of the year. As was mentioned, in most cases this is the titular fiesta; in some cases there are two such fiestas, one celebrated by the Indians and one by the Ladinos. In the brief notes to follow, the phases of the fiesta to be described are specifically of the Ladino fiestas; they will also be found in many of the Indian fiestas, but the latter should be considered apart, a task which is not a part of the present study.

Each fiesta has its religious and its non-religious phases. The religious aspects usually includes specifically a Mass on the day of the saint and a procession in which the saint, and perhaps some other saints as well, are taken on a journey around the village. In many cases some of the townspeople will hold a novena on the days prior to the day of the fiesta. Accompanying this will be a good quan-

---

have to be the wife of the former. Each *mayordomo* keeps the image for which he is responsible in his own home and takes it to the church for the day of its fiesta; a *mayordomo* holds his position for two or three years. The six *mayordomos*, each responsible for their own saint, are collectively responsible for the image of the *Niño Dios* which is kept in the *cofradía* house. The six holy days for which they are responsible are: *Niño Dios* (24 December), *Sangre de Cristo* (12 January), *Dulce Nombre de Jesús* (12 January), *Santa Cruz de Mayo* (3 May), *Cristo del Dolor* (Friday and Passion Week), *San Nicolás* (10 September), and *San Pedro Mártir* (29 April).

tity of fireworks, usually *cohetes* (exploding rockets), *bombas* (bombs shot in the air to explode), and fire-crackers. Fireworks are also used with respect to the lay portions of the fiesta.

The lay aspects of the fiesta are either commercially or communally sponsored. Among the commercial items are the *sarabandas*, or five-cents-a-dance pavilions; in the *sarabanda* you bring your own girl or buy your way in and dance with someone else's. The *chinamas* are the temporary stalls which are set up by both travelling vendors and local people to take advantage of the increased trade which takes place during the fiesta. The importance of a regional fiesta may be measured by the number of *chinamas* which are set up for it. The *lotería*, or bingo-type gambling game, is to be found in almost all fiestas, whether big or small. They may be run by either local people or outsiders. Cockfights are also a means of gambling which are very popular in nine of the towns included in the survey (no discernible pattern of distribution), and bull baiting in which the bull is played with but not killed was still an important part of the fiesta in seven of the towns (four scattered along the south coast, two in the east, and San Jerónimo).

Aspects of the fiestas which are generally sponsored by some segment of the community but are not commercially oriented include races and sports: horse races, bicycle races, running races, the *carrera de cintas* (in which ribbons with rings are hung up and men on horses or bicycles ride under them trying to spear the ring and tear down the ribbons), the greased pole (on top of which is a prize and up which the men try to climb to win it), *futbol* (soccer) and basketball, the *toro de fuego* (a framework in the shape of a bull's body and to which are attached a great variety of fireworks which go off as a man runs about carrying the framework), *loas* (which are stands set up at points around the town and from which theatrical, often comic, performances are given) and dances. The dances sponsored by the community are usually of two types, those to which one goes by "invitation" and those which are free. The free dances, usually sponsored by the *municipalidad*, are not extremely common; typical are the *bailes sociales* in which "invitations" may be purchased for 50 cents or a dollar. Such dances usually are restricted to the local upper and middle class people, since it is only they who can afford to "buy an invitation." In addition to these dances there are the *bailes típicos*, the so-called typical dances. These are costumed dances danced only by masked men and for the most part are restricted to Indian communities and Indian fiestas. However, the dancing of *bailes típicos* were reported as being done by Ladinos as part of their fiesta in Petapa, Sansare, and San Carlos Sija. In addition, they were said to be danced in the fiestas in the *aldeas* in the *municipios* of La Gomera, Siquinalá, and San Agustín. The Indians of some of the Ladino communities danced them (Esquipulas, Flores Costa Cuca, and until fairly recently in Barrio San Sebastián of Guazacapán). The principal masked dances are the Dance of the Moors and the Dance of the Conquest. In the town of Flores Costa Cuca it was reported that the *bailes típicos* had only begun during the year of the survey; an Indian from the highlands had convinced some of the Indians of the *municipio* to undertake the dance, and he taught them for over a month how to do it. As is the case in Indian communities, the masks and the costumes come from a limited number of highland centers, the principal of which are San Cristóbal and Chichicastenango. They are rented and not purchased.

Aside from the aspects already described, the survey touched on two other phases of religious activity, *rogaciones* and *romerías*. The *rogación*, or *rogativa*, is the prayer for rain. Common over most of Central America, it was reported as taking place in 21 of the towns visited. In only five was it specifically said that they were not used. Of these five, Gualán and particularly Morales are near the Atlantic coast where there is usually ample rain and no need of prayers. The writer is not sure that the information from the other three towns (San Rafael Tierra del Pueblo, Esquipulas, and San Manuel) denying the use of *rogaciones* is correct. In general, *rogaciones* are carried on by the people who want to make the prayers; they may be townspeople or countrypeople; if the latter, they may have a procession with a saint from their *oratorio* or from one of their homes, or they may come to the nearest town and take the saint from the church for the purpose. Most commonly, the patron saint is taken out for the *rogación*. The ritual consists principally in taking the saint out in a procession in the middle of the day when the sun is at its hottest and permitting the saint to see how arid and dry the landscape is, to allow him to perspire a little to feel how much rain is needed, and then return him to the shelter of his church. In one *rogación* observed on the main road in the eastern part of the country (between Jutiapa and El Progreso) there were between 30 and 40 men, women, and children; six of the men wore colored paper and cloth costumes and rode on mule or horseback. The women wore black on their heads and a few of them kept up a low chant. The saint taken out in this *rogación* was San Isidro.

Romerías are the pilgrimages which many Catholics, both Indian and Ladino, make periodically to the shrines and scenes of miracles. From the reports given in the various towns, some thirteen places were named as being centers of pilgrimages. Of course, the most important was that of Esquipulas, located in Guatemala close to the Honduran border. Second most common was Antigua, particularly the shrine of *Jesús Sepultado* in San Felipe; and third in importance was Sonsonate, the Salvadorean pilgrimage center. While the shrine of Esquipulas is by far the most important shrine in Guatemala, all three of these may be considered to be shrines of first importance. The principal difference is that Esquipulas is visited by people from all over Guatemala and from other countries of Central America as well, while Antigua is more of regional importance within Guatemala. On the basis of the present data, the relative importance of Sonsonate cannot be estimated. There were three centers which may be considered to be of secondary importance, Ayutla (the *Señor de las Tres Caídas*), Chiantla (*Virgen de Candelaria*) and Chajul (Christ of Golgotha). Ayutla evidently draws Guatemalans only from the southwestern part of the country, Patulul and San Carlos Sija having been the most distant towns which reported people going there; in a visit to the shrine shortly before the principal day of the pilgrimage, an Indian woman from Tehuantepec, in México, was there. Both Chiantla and Chajul are evidently more important as places of Indian pilgrimage than as

Ladino centers, and both evidently draw principally on the northwestern highland population.

There are in addition various tertiary pilgrimage centers to which people in neighboring departments may go. Those reported in the survey include: Amatitlán, Río Hondo (Department of Zacapa), Taxisco (Santa Rosa), Mulúa (Retalhuleu), Masagua (Escuintla), Tactíc (Alta Verapaz), and Jumaitepeque (Santa Rosa). For the Ladino of eastern Guatemala, there is little doubt that Esquipulas and Sonsonate are the most important pilgrimage centers. Nine towns (including Esquipulas) reported that local people went to Sonsonate. The area drawn upon by Antigua, however, extended from the Salvadorean border (Atescatempa) on the east, to Joyabàj and Patulul; its importance to the north, east and west does not seem so great.

It need not be mentioned that *romerías* are responsible for a constant movement of Ladinos. Esquipulas, for example, has two main periods of worship; in mid-January and during Holy Week. In fact, the entire period between late December and the weeks following Easter is one constant movement to and from that center. During the principal times of worship, it is necessary to bring in extra police from as far as Zacapa to handle the crowds. While the pilgrimage is often thought to be more an Indian trait than Ladino, in fact the reverse may be truer.

From this brief survey, it can be seen that religion enters numerous facets of the life of the Guatemalan Ladino, and while he may not be as intense about his worship and religious activities as is his Indian neighbor, a considerable amount of time of the Ladino woman is spent in novenas, preparing for a fiesta, collecting money for the church, and together with her husband or man, in making a pilgrimage (by bus wherever possible) or in holding a procession to ask for rain in the depth of the dry season. And even the Ladino who will pay attention to religion in no other way will frequently take advantage of a religious fiesta to have a few drinks.

9. SICKNESS AND THE SPIRIT WORLD

The subject of this section is not illness as it is diagnosed by scientific medcine, but the concepts of illness which are found with some prevalence among the Ladinos. Where these concepts coincide even crudely with scientific concepts, no comment is necessary. There is a wide range of ideas and practices, however, which vary from the concepts of western science, and for the most part, these are parts of the cultural tradition of the Ladinos. As will be only too apparent, much, if not all, of these traditional forms of conceptualizing illness and the accompanying cures are shared with the Indians; in some cases, the Indians themselves form an essential part of the Ladino's curative social system. In the survey, inquiries were made about a limited number of traditional illnesses which were known through previous studies to form some element in the way of life of the countryman of Central America. In the course of the survey, no unreported "folk illnesses" were uncovered, but most of the questioning on the subject was directed towards clarifying the status of those already known, and no time was spent in exploring for new forms. The description which follows, then, is an attempt to point out the importance of traditional illness and curing concepts and practices among the Ladino population; not to give a comprehensive picture of those practices. The description will be divided into three main parts: illnesses; types of curers; and spirit activities.

There are three illnesses which have to do with food, the stomach, indigestion, and bowel trouble: *empacho*, *pasmo*, and *pujo*. With certain minor variations, the concepts surrounding these three illnesses retained a remarkable consistency from one Ladino town to another over the entire republic. *Empacho* almost everywhere referred to indigestion from overeating or waiting too long to eat. Waiting too long to eat occurs when, for example, a man is working out in the fields and in order to get a piece of work done, must stay out late and so gets back too late to have his meal at the usual time. There are other possible causes and processes involved in *empacho* also. In Granados it was said that something is formed in the stomach which makes it impossible to pass food; in Catarina it was said that food will stick to the intestines and thus cause indigestion; in Palo Gordo it was said that it came specifically from eating things which were too dry (such as dry bread) or too "cold" (such as cold *tortillas*). Cures for *empacho* consist most commonly in patent medicine purges, massages (usually with pig fat), and some herb tea.

Pasmo refers to a more specific stomach trouble, one which involves nausea and vomiting and which is commonly thought to be derived from eating "bad food." "Bad food," however, refers not only to spoiled or rotten food, but also to certain foods which under certain conditions may be considered to be improper. Mentioned a number of times in this respect were unripe fruit, fish, in one community chicken was mentioned, and fresh fruits. A clearer glance may be had at the general nature of *pasmo* when it is noted that not only eating certain kinds of food will produce it, but that the qualities which these foods usually have is that they are too "hot" or too "cold." Furthermore, it may be contracted by getting one's hands hot, as from ironing, and then getting them wet in cold water (Flores Costa Cuca), or from going in bathing in the river after having eaten something "hot" (Tierra del Pueblo), or from bathing after one has been working and sweating (Palo Gordo), or that it may come simply from eating something which is "hot" (Sansare), or something "cold" (La Gomera). *Pasmo* would seem to refer to illnesses derived not merely from foods which are spoiled, but from eating foods which are too "hot" or too "cold" or indeed, from being in the wrong state of hotness or coldness. This type of disease etiology is very common among the Indians[51] and among Latin Americans in many other countries.[52] The specific relation of hot and cold food-produced troubles to *pasmo* seems to be the connection which is more peculiar to Guatemala; in Panama, for example, *pasmo* is related to hot and cold, but in terms of air,[53] and not of food. Among the Ladinos the principal cures for *pasmo* are patent medicines and various herb drinks. In general, herb preparations are more popular

---
[51] See Adams, 1952. [52] See Foster, 1951 for example, and 1953.
[53] See survey on Panama, Part Two, this volume.

for the cure of *pasmo* than for the cure of *empacho*. Whereas the cures for *empacho* placed emphasis on the use of drugs, the cures for *pasmo* place them second to home remedies.

Pujo, the third gastro-intestinal trouble in local medicine, was reported from almost all towns; the principal exceptions were three towns in the very center of the country, Petapa, Palencia, and Granados. *Pujo* generally[54] is taken to mean either dysentery and diarrhea or the straining to defecate which may accompany dysentery. In some instances it was said to refer specifically to such difficulties in children, and in two cases (Gualán and San José la Arada) was said to be only a disease of corral fowls. Scattered in four communities from one end of Guatemala to the other (Morales, Teculután, Guazacapán, and Catarina) *pujo* was said to be caused by the force of a person who was particularly "strong," a person who was sweating or pregnant. As will be noted shortly, such is the standard cause for the disease known as *ojo*. Where *pujo* is so interpreted, its cure is similar to that recommended for *ojo*; the person who was responsible for causing the condition should pick up the child and caress it. In two towns (Mataquescuintla and Siquinalá) it was reported that *pujo* was related to the concepts of hot and cold. In the latter place if a person who just finished bathing caressed a child, the child might get *pujo*; the cure again was to caress the child, but this time not immediately after bathing. In Siquinalá, however, *pujo* was not said to be strictly a form of dysentery but merely a weakness in the child. Cures for the more common variety of *pujo*, dysentery, included various home remedies and some patent medicines. Lemonade and lemon juice in water were both recommended, as was chili pepper, a drink of honey, purgatives, and pig's blood cooked in an intestine. A different *pujo* cure was reported from San Carlos Sija, there it was said that a child with *pujo* was wrapped in a sheet, and swung back and forth by two other children; a real cure was most likely to be effected if the sick child could be swung in a complete circle.

Ojo, to which the etiology of *pujo* was similar in three towns, may probably be regarded as being ubiquitous in Ladino Guatemala. The only town in which the informants denied knowing of the ailment was Atescatempa. *Ojo* is commonly translated in English as "evil eye," but actually may not have anything to do with either evil or the eye. It is generally represented as being an invisible force which emanates from certain people who are particularly "strong." Such people characteristically include women who are pregnant or who are menstruating, or a man who has been perspiring or who is drunk. This quality of strength is variously referred to as being "strong blood," "heavy blood," "bad blood," "violent blood," "*humor fuerte*" or "*humor muy fuerte*." The process by which this force affects a child is simply that the person who has it passes close to the child. It can be prevented in a number of ways, the principal of which is the use of a charm, usually a red ribbon, red beads or a small cross, tied somewhere on the child (and on small animals too, for they also are subject to the force); in Teculután it was said that a bracelet containing a lizard's nail, or braiding the feather of a certain bird in the child's hair could prevent it. In

---

[54] *Pujo* in Appleton's Dictionary is translated as tenesmus.

only one community was it mentioned that pretty children were supposed to be particularly susceptible to the effects of such force (San Agustín), an idea which receives much credence in some Indian communities. An interesting divergence from the usual cause of *ojo* with which the writer is familiar was reported in Catarina: there it was said that it could occur to any bad child who had been so much as looked at; this definitely moved the culpability away from a person with strength to the child who is made sick.

The form the illness itself takes may involve fever, convulsions, skin eruptions, or probably a variety of other manifestations. The cure for *ojo* usually requires that someone (in many places, the person who was responsible for the illness) pass an egg over the body of the child, usually in the form of a cross. At times it is specified that the person should also make a small cross of rue and hold this with the egg while it is passed. The egg is then broken in a bowl of cold water and from the appearance of the interior of the egg it is decided if the illness was *ojo* or not and the *ojo* itself is cured; diagnosis and cure are a single process. It was also reported from a number of towns that it may be cured if the person who was responsible for it picks up the child and caresses it. There were various other locally recommended remedies, one of which included urine, another powdered cigars, another donkey excrement, etc. Quite a few recommended that the person responsible, or someone who knew how, should take certain things in their mouth (such as *aguardiente*) and spray it on the child. Many also recommended the preparation of an herb tea. It was repeated by a number of informants that *ojo* was a very serious ailment, and if measures were not taken to prevent it and to cure it if contracted, it was almost certain that the afflicted child would die. The cases of small animals were very tragic because the only way one knew that they had become sick was when they died; if a small animal had *ojo*, there was no remedy. Such was the power of some "strong" people that they had merely to look at turkeys or chickens and the fowls would instantly drop dead. In Guazacapán the interesting comment was made that the only animals which died were those which belonged to poor people; to what degree this was said ironically and to what degree with credence is difficult to know.

In one community it was reported that it was possible to get *ojo* without having been affected by another person; beside the type of *ojo* resulting from a "strong" person, there was also *ojo de luna* and *ojo de sol*; in these cases a person could get *ojo* by being exposed overlong to the moon or the sun. These types of *ojo* were cured in the same way as was the other. In Guazacapán it was said that one type of person who can cause *ojo* is one with a *"lunar negro en el ojo,"* that is, a person with a black spot or blemish in his eye.

Children are in general more subject to such illnesses than are adults. *Caída de mollera*, falling of the fontanelle in infants, is not caused by force or strength in someone, but through mishandling; if an infant is treated roughly, set down suddenly, or moved about violently, his fontanelle will fall down in his throat and choke him. It can usually be corrected by the mother, and if not, the person usually regarded as being expert in its cure is the midwife. The usual cure involves turning the child upside down so that the fontanelle will fall back into place. It also helps to suck on the top of the head and to place the finger on the roof of the child's mouth and push. *Caída de mollera* was reported from all parts of the Ladino region.

Perhaps one of the most terrifying ailments to which both child and adult alike may be subject is *susto* (or *espanto* in parts of the eastern highlands). Briefly, *susto* consists in a person being suddenly shocked or frightened by something. The classical reasons for receiving such shocks are falling in water or suddenly becoming afraid that you will drown if in the water; suddenly seeing an animal or reptile; or seeing a spirit or ghost. What happens after this may vary. In four towns, there was little more involved; the person would simply become sick from the shock, would be taken to church, be prayed for, and presumably get well. In twelve other towns, however, the act of being frightened involved shaking the soul loose from the body and leaving it in the place where one received the fright. The cure then involved in gaining the soul again and restoring it to the body. The general distribution of soul loss being associated with *susto* seems to involve the area of Old Ladinos and the western highland and piedmont region. Six towns reported that no *susto* existed at all (Petapa, Palencia, Granados, Atescatempa, Quesada, and Chitatul); these, taken with the four in which soul loss was said not to be related to susto (La Gomera, Guazacapán, Barberena, Sansare) make what appears to be a belt separating a southwestern zone of soul-loss-*susto* combination from a zone with the same combination in the northeast. Aside from the fact that certain of the towns (San Manuel, Esquipulas, Mataquescuintla) of the east used the term *espanto*[55] instead of *susto*, neither from the data gathered on the survey nor from other available information was it possible to delineate any certain differences between *susto* and soul loss as it appeared in these two zones.

Where related to soul loss, the cure for *susto* may involve not only going to the priest and requesting him to pray, but also calling upon a *curandero* or someone who knows how, to go to the place where the soul was lost and to ask it to come back. This type of praying, from the data gathered, is a simplified form of that which has been described elsewhere.[56] Nowhere among the various Ladino towns visited was it reported that the soul, once lost, was kidnapped by some spirit as has been reported from some Modified Indian communities.[57] The kidnapping seems to be a trait which has developed in the gradual acculturation of Indians, and does not seem to be a part of Ladino culture.

Another type of ailment which shows a split east-west distribution is that known as *hijillo*. Depending upon the region in which one finds himself, *hijillo* may be one of three somewhat different ailments or conditions. In the far eastern highlands, specifically in the region of the Pocomam and Chortí Indians[58] and spreading up into the Motagua Valley, it is a bad air which emanates from a corpse, and which may do harm to anyone who may be in a slightly weakened condition. It will enter any wound and cause it to become infected. Through

---

[55] Gillin, 1948. [56] Gillin, 1948; Adams, 1952. [57] *Ibid*.
[58] Wisdom, 1940; Gillin, 1951 and reported from Esquipulas and San José la Arada.

the center part of the country and in most of the middle Motagua Valley (in Gualán, Teculután, Sansare, Palencia, Mataquescuintla, Petapa, Barberena, Guazacapán) *hijillo* has nothing to do with bad air from corpses at all, but is a tumor or boil which grows up in the crotch of the leg or the armpit. As such, it is variously interpreted as being a condition due to "bad blood" or "weak blood" in the individual, or to a blow received on the afflicted part of the body. As we move farther west, however, *hijillo* again becomes associated with the air of the dead, but this time not merely of human corpses, but of dead meat of any kind. In Flores Costa Cuca, Catarina, Palo Gordo, and possibly San Carlos Sija, the concept of *hijillo* is that the air carried by the dead meat will enter the wound which one may have and infect it and make it worse. Unless you actually touch the meat or have a wound, or are in some way sick, the *hijillo* is not supposed to be very harmful. There is a combination of the eastern type and the central type in the communities of San Manuel and San Agustín, by which the *hijillo* of the human corpse will specifically enter a boil and inflame it. The informant in Siquinalá was not sure, but thought there was something of this order involved there. In Morales, the types found in the far western towns were reported. From other towns in the south and center, it was said that *hijillo* was unknown (Atescatempa, Quesada La Gomera, Patulul, Tierra del Pueblo, Chitatul, Granados, San Jerónimo; in the last named place the word was known, but was said to refer to the protective ferocity of a bitch caring for her litter of puppies).

The variations in the concepts attached to *hijillo*, to *susto*, and even to *pujo*, should be sufficient warning to the unwary not to assume that a given illness is interpreted the same over all of Ladino Guatemala. In the course of the survey a number of illnesses were described which were not consistently checked through most of the towns surveyed. It is worthwhile to mention some of these to give an idea of something of the breadth of the Ladinos' ideas of sickness and practices of curing. *Disipela* (correctly erisipela), a bad swelling on the lower leg, was said in Palencia to be cured with *"agua de monte"* and by passing a frog across the leg; in Mataquescuintla it was cured by drawing three live frogs, one at a time, over the leg and then throwing them to the right or to the south. Chills, coughs, and other maladies are caused by *aire* or *viento*; a draft, such as these, may enter one's body and cause an ache almost anywhere (San Agustín); a *viento* from the north can cause people to go insane. Being overheated and suddenly becoming cold may not only bring about *pasmo*, but also other conditions, such as simple chills. For cures, it was reported in Chitatul that the Ladinos of that community will often use an Indian sweat bath as a curative measure; in Petapa, the small blessed clay bricks sold from Esquipulas were said to help in stopping female hemorrhages. Rue and another herb were recommended in Zaragoza for heart attacks; mother's milk placed in a hole cut in an onion, and heated, is said to be excellent for stopping an ear ache if poured in the ear.

Before turning to illnesses related to spirits and other spirit activities, there is another kind of condition which has received various kinds of interpretation: earth eating. Earth eating, principally among children, but also in some places among adults, was reported from all Pacific coast and piedmont towns (except

San Antonio from which there was no data) and most eastern towns. In the highlands, where data was collected on the subject, it was reported as being present but very rare in Zaragoza and San Carlos Sija, and absent from Petapa, Palencia, and Sansare. In Quesada, San José la Arada, and Guazacapán it was said that people especially looked for a soft black earth (called *talpús* in Quesada). Reasons given for eating earth varied as follows: in San Jerónimo, Guazacapán, and Patulul it was said that people eat dirt because the worms in their system demanded it; in Quesada it was thought to be a custom because it was a way of strengthening the blood, so it is a type of remedy; in Esquipulas it was said that it was believed to be a craving of the pregnant women who in turn passed it on to the embryo and which manifests itself when the child got big enough. It was also mentioned in Esquipulas that if a woman let her child go hungry, he would seek out dirt to eat. The earth eating complex mentioned here should not be confused with the eating of the clay tablets purchased at Esquipulas; the latter is blessed clay (or said to be) and is often taken as a remedy.

It was mentioned in connection with *susto* that it was possible to be suddenly frightened by a spirit and thus fall into a state of *susto*. The spirits play a relatively important role in the lives of Guatemalan Ladinos. Three principal kinds are distinguishable: traditional spirits, such as the *cadejo*, *llorona*, etc.; witches, usually people who are alive and practice black magic; and the spirits of the dead who are called upon in seance. Concerning the first, relatively little information was collected during the course of the survey. The type of interview on which the survey depended was not designed to gain the confidence of informants to the degree that open discussion of such spirits would be easily forthcoming. Futhermore, in the municipal capitals, where most of the interviewing was done, there was evinced some concern that the interviewers might be laughing at the "country yokels" for believing in such "superstitions." In general, on the basis of other experience as much as on the data gathered in the survey, it may be said that the traditional spirits which are most commonly recognized among the Ladinos are: the *cadejo*, the *siguanava*, the *llorona*, the *duendes* (fairies), and the *sombrerón*. Some of these do little harm; the *cadejo*, a spirit dog, is even considered to be the protector of drunks at night. The *llorona* and *siguanava*, however, if one sees them at night, may cause *susto*. In Morales it was said that people had become ill because of seeing spirits, but no mention was made of specific spirits.

The place of witches in Ladino society varies; in some towns (San José la Arada, San Manuel, Petapa, Patulul, San Antonio, Palo Gordo, Zaragoza and San Carlos Sija) it was specifically said that witches were known quantities, but that they existed only in the Indian population. In five towns (San Agustín, San Jerónimo, Joyabáj, Chitatul, and Catarina) it was said that there were Ladino witches too, but in some of these cases it was specified that there was no one in the town who fitted the description. In one town, Flores Costa Cuca, it was said that in Ubico's day, some twenty years ago, all the witches were tossed into jail and had their beans (divining devices) taken away from them. As a result, there have been no witches in the town since. In Guazacapán and

San Jerónimo a number of cases of witchcraft were cited to the interviewers, and in one instance one of the victims was brought in to relate his own experiences. With respect to illnesses, the usual trouble attributed to witchcraft involves such things as having one's stomach full of rocks or some animal which has been placed there by a witch; it is usually possible to go to a *curandero* to get cured of such troubles, but such *curanderos* are usually considered to be witches themselves.

The spirits of human beings are usually considered in the light of lay Catholic thought; they are ghosts which must be properly laid to rest and for that end novenas are held and proper attention is paid to the day of All Souls in early November. Through spiritualists, usually in seances, it is possible for a person to achieve communication with these spirits to get their advice or help in something. Spiritualists are almost always Ladinos, but Modified and Ladinoized Indians will also resort to them. Unfortunately, no data was collected from most of the eastern towns as to whether spiritualists were present in the communities or not. In general, of the remaining towns, eight said there were spiritualists present and eight said there were not; of the latter, however, it was specified that many people went to see spiritualists in certain neighboring centers. In the east and center regions spiritualists were reported in Teculután, Sansare, and Zaragoza, while the people of Petapa were said to go over to nearby Villa Canales when they wanted one. The remaining towns of this region reported not having any locally (San Agustín, San Jerónimo, Granados, Palencia, Barberena, Siquinalá). In the west, spiritualists were reported as being active in San Carlos Sija, Palo Gordo, Catarina, Flores Costa Cuca, and Patulul; people from Siquinalá visit spiritualists in Mazatenango.

The principal activities of the spiritualists (most of whom are women) is divination and curing. One of the most common ways in which they were used as curers was for the spiritualist to call on the spirit of some doctor and to ask his advice on how to cure so-and-so's ailment. The doctor would then provide some sort of cure. In some cases, the spiritualist herself would do the cure. In Flores Costa Cuca the informant explained how he preferred to patronize a spiritualist in Mexico to whom he wrote. On two occasions he had written to Mexico concerning conditions which troubled his wife (the first time she had three stomach tumors, the second time she was weeping tears of blood) and achieved very satisfactory results. The thing he liked best about these cures was that they came invisibly from Mexico, and he had to send only *un peso de quetzal* (one dollar) for each cure. The appeal of spiritualism is evidently strong to many Guatemalan Ladinos. Only in Palo Gordo was it reported that both men and women practice it. The writer knows of other cases of travelling spiritualists and spiritualists in the capital city who were men, but in the towns it evidently has not fallen to the men to practice it.

Spiritualists are only one of numerous sources to which the Guatemalan Ladino may turn in case he or his family become ill. The mothers themselves are usually brought up to be familiar with various home remedies, including ingredients which come from both the pharmacies and the herb garden. If children and infants are ill, the midwives, who are to be found in both town and country (variously called *comadronas* and *parteras*), may be called in to cure such things as *ojo*, *susto*, *caída de mollera*, or other infant ailments. Perhaps the most popular town curing agent is one who is never paid directly, the village pharmacist. These men sometimes have a year or two of medical education, and sometimes are merely practical curers. But it is most common for both town and countrypeople to seek their advice as to what to buy for a given ailment.

Many communities, particularly those which have Indian populations living nearby, have *curanderos*. These men (for they are usually men) may be practical curers, such as the pharmacists, or may have some traditional lore for the cure of special troubles such as *susto*, *pujo*, *hijillo*, etc. In Palo Gordo four such specialists, besides the Indian witches, were distinguished: the *curandero empírico* who owned a small drug store; the *curandero* who fixed broken bones; the woman herb curers; and those who specialized in such things as *susto*. Only in San Carlos Sija was it said that women specialized in the last type of curing. Besides these professional or semi-professional *curanderos* (only four towns reported that there were none), most towns have people who "know how" to do certain cures, or people who are simply known to have a good touch in curing. Such people are not professionals, they do not charge any fee, and give help merely as a favor. Finally, besides all these, there are the doctors who are available in a few towns. In Zaragoza, for example, a doctor from the city has purchased a house and usually spends the week-ends there, practising on Saturdays in the locality. A Protestant missionary doctor spent about three years in San Agustín, leaving behind a very good reputation. Those who live near enough to a departmental capital and can afford it can visit doctors there. In general, however, there are too few doctors and the service too scarce for people to get much medical attention. For people who work on *fincas* and *haciendas*, there has usually been in the past (although there has tended to be some change in this) a person on the *finca* who undertook the medical care of the laborers. Sometimes this individual was the owner, sometimes the administrator, or someone else. This person would dispense medicines as needed, give worm cures, and shots of penicillin whenever it was thought to be necessary. These may be classed with the curers who "know how" but practise in the capacity of being responsible for the health of the laborers in his care.

The final type of curer is the priest. Whereas the Indian may take cases of *susto* immediately to a *curandero*, the Ladino is more likely to take it to the priest. The priest may also be called in on dangerous cases of *ojo*, or possibly on other cases where the difficulty is clearly beyond the ability of medicines and herbs to effect a cure. Resorting to religion is not limited to calling the priest, of course, as charms consisting of a cross of resinous pine are used to protect children against *ojo*, and prayers are part of many cures.

The Ladino of Guatemala is in many ways similar to the Indian with respect to his ideas of sickness and practices of curing. The Indians have a slightly different system, some elements are present which are absent from the Ladino's curing system; but the same thing is true in reverse. Whereas some Indians have a spirit who may steal a man's soul in *susto*, the Ladinos can communicate with the souls of dead people. As was suggested earlier, there is much of the Ladino system, especially in the western and northwestern areas, which is dependent upon the Indian. The Indian curer and curing methods are all important to the Ladinos of Chitatul. While further study would be necessary to confirm this, it seems that the curing trade is to some degree lacking in prestige; old women spiritualists or midwives may do curing, or Indian *curanderos*; it does not begin to acquire prestige until it enters the more urban context of the pharmacy and the trained medical doctor. And these two men do not have cures for many of the ailments which can attack the human body and soul.

III. LIVINGSTON AND THE BLACK CARIB CULTURE[59]

On Guatemala's brief Atlantic coast at the mouth of the Río Dulce lies the town of Livingston, formerly an important gate to Guatemala. Today no automobile or truck road reaches Livingston, and to visit the town one must go by launch from Puerto Barrios. While Livingston no longer provides the main route for sea-borne travellers into Guatemala, it is still a town of some commercial importance for the traffic coming via railway and river from the Alta Verapaz region. For the social scientist, however, Livingston is unique, not because of its general history but because it is the principal urban settlement of that unique combination of racial and cultural characteristics, the Black Caribs. In the present section we will describe something of the culture of the Caribs and the community in which they live.

Livingston is located on the west bluff of land overlooking the mouth of the Río Dulce. It is composed principally of wooden board buildings with corrugated metal roofs and, among the poorer homes, wooden houses with palm roofs. The houses are generally a few feet off the ground as the Atlantic coast sees much rain in the course of the year. The main street of the town, which is an extension of the semi-paved road which leads up from the wharf which serves the settlement, is lined with buildings in the Spanish style, with two or three large doors opening into the single front room or shop. The major public buildings are located off the main street, mainly near the bluff overlooking the ocean.

The dry season in Livingston lasts only about two months, April and May; some years will ignore the dry season, however, making it difficult to plant new crops. Formerly, and still today in many of the houses, the major water supply comes directly from the rains. The water falling on the roofs is collected in huge wooden drums of some 15 to 20 feet high and 10 to 15 feet in diameter; by means of a spigot at the bottom of the barrel, the water can then be tapped as desired. There is today a municipal water system, but the town authorities felt that it was inadequate and that a good water supply was one of the town's problems.

---

[59] For the reader interested specifically in the Ladino culture of Spanish derivation and its regional variation, it is suggested that the present section on the Black Carib be skipped, and that he turn to Section IV.

The town of Livingston is divided into eight *barrios*, five of which lie along the Atlantic coast, two along the Río Dulce, and one in the interior corner between the rest. The general population distribution within the *barrio* system represents the principal ethnic and socio-cultural groupings in the town. From the point of land forming the bluff at the mouth of the river, and moving up the sea coast, the five *barrios* (Barique, San José, Pueblo Nuevo, París, and San Francisco or Nébago) overlooking the ocean are inhabited principally by the Black Caribs, or *Morenos*. Back of these five *barrios* lie two more, El Centro (which includes the principal stores and the wharf) and Minerva (inland from El Centro), which are inhabited principally by Ladinos, or "Spaniards," as they are called by the Black Caribs, of European or mixed descent who share the general culture of the Ladinos of whom we have been speaking in the previous sections of the present paper. Up the Río Dulce, and adjacent to the El Centro Barrio, is the Barrio Bacadillo, the region of the town in which a few "Spaniards live," but more particularly a third ethnic group, descendents of people who have migrated from India to the West Indies, and finally to Livingston. These people are known by the *Morenos* as the *kuli* people. Like the *Morenos* they are Ladinoized in many of their customs, but they have retained certain differences in their way of living which distinguish them, if ever so slightly, from the Ladinos of European descent. Besides these three general residential areas, there are also among the "Spaniards" a few Chinese businessmen. On the outskirts of the inland side, there are to be found some families of Mayan Indians of the general culture of those who inhabit the Alta Verapaz region. There are distinguishable in Livingston, then, perhaps five groups of diverse racial and cultural ancestry. Racially, we may distinguish the Black Carib (predominantly negroid in appearance, but combined with American Antillean Indian), the mestizo-white (to be found in the Ladinos of Spanish and other diverse European origin), the Indian of India, the American Mayan Indian, and finally the Chinese. Culturally, there are Black Carib Indians, Mayan Indians, possibly traits stemming to the African ancestors of the *Morenos*, the Indians of India culture, a few distinguishable effects of the culture of the Chinese, and the Spanish-American culture of the Ladino.

Our concern here is going to be principally with the culture of the *Moreno*; a few notes will be made concerning the *kuli* people in order that the reader may see what are some of the ways in which they remain distinct from the other groups. The remaining groups will only be mentioned insofar as they play a role in the relationships and way of life of the *Moreno*, or as they contrast strongly with that group.

All *Morenos* are considered officially to be Ladinos, and in numerous ways they have the same habits and traits of the other Ladinos. They all have Spanish names, for example. They speak a language (or at least a variety thereof) which came to them as part of their inheritance from the Indians of the West Indies of whom they are descended.[60] In addition to this, all adults and most

---

[60] Taylor, 1951, p. 138, summarizes his findings with respect to the nature of the British Honduras Black Carib language as follows: "The Black Carib speak a language whose mor-

of the children speak Spanish, learned early in life as a second language (and now taught in the schools). Many adult Caribs are, however, trilingual and speak English as well. English is the second language of the Carib population living in Belice or British Honduras, and there is a constant and fairly heavy traffic of visitors between Livingston and Belice. While the use of English is retained principally because of these contacts, it is also a tradition from an earlier period in Central American history when English influence was strong on the north coast and the English language was the most important European language in use in the region.

The Black Carib population, of which the Livingston *Morenos* form a part, is found scattered along the north coast of Central America from British Honduras to Nicaragua. Taylor[61] has given an account of their early history and something of the contemporary distribution. That interrelationships between the Black Caribs of the entire length of the coast are still of importance was illustrated in the case of one of the writer's informants. Born in 1887, his mother came from Livingston, but he had French speaking Black Carib relatives in Honduras, and grew up in San Juan del Norte in Nicaragua, close to the Costa Rican border, with relatives who spoke principally English. He went to school in Trujillo on the north coast of Honduras, and now lives in Guatemala, but makes occasional trips to Stann Creek and other towns in British Honduras.

This personal history illustrates another characteristic of the Black Carib population; they are a coastal people. In Guatemala they live only along the Atlantic coast and not even any distance up the Río Dulce. A very few have gone up to Guatemala City or inland to work on plantations, but in most cases they return. This propensity to remain on the coast effectively restricts the places where they may hire out to the port operations at Puerto Barrios. The consequences of this will be noted shortly. This coastal orientation has evidently led also to the use of the term *"interior"* as a term of reference for the rest of Guatemala; the same term is to be found as the standard term used by the port dwellers of Panama City and Colón in Panama for the people who live throughout the rest of that republic.

Being a coastal people living in a town which is unconnected by highway with the rest of the country, it is not surprising that a good deal of their time is spent on the water. Fishing is one of the main pursuits, and travel of any distance is done almost wholly by dugout canoes, called *dorys*, or by commercial motor launch when going to Puerto Barrios or one of the major centers in Belice. On land, travel is on foot; neither pack animal nor ox cart are used. Horses and mules are limited, where used, to the travel and transport of the "Span-

---

phology and syntax are mainly Arawak, and whose vocabulary is Ignerian Arawak, with Galíbi (Cariban family), Spanish, French, and English overlays. Only the phonology shows considerable change from what we know of Dominica Carib, both of the seventeenth century and in its most recent form, at the end of the nineteenth century. . . . But virtually nothing is known of Saint Vincent Carib at any period; and it cannot be assumed without further evidence that all, or even part of the changes are due to retention and transmission of the Africans' phonetic habits."

[61] 1951.

iards" and the Maya Indians. The *Morenos* have evidently taken over the use of the tumpline, or *mecapal*; we say "taken over" because it is evidently borrowed from the local Indians; there is no Carib word for the tumpline, according to informants. The use of the *mecapal* is generally restricted to the men, however, and they use it as little as possible, since they try to avoid doing local agricultural work which would require the transport of large loads in from the fields. The women generally carry burdens on their heads, although a few have adopted the tumpline.

The dory (the English term seemed preferred, although the Spanish term *cayuco* was occasionally used), then, is the principal mode of transport, and is used also by Ladinos and Indians as well. For trips of any length a triangular sail may be erected in the dory, otherwise they are paddled with a graceful paddle shaped smoothly from the narrow round handle in a straight line down to the wide flat blade, rounded at the end. Young boys early learn the art of managing a dory. These dugouts are long, narrow, and round-bottomed, and small ones (perhaps ten feet long) are made by and for the boys; one sees them carefully paddling along the shore at all hours of the day and not infrequently capsizing. Large ones may be thirty feet or more in length.

Aside from the language, the basic economy of the *Morenos* reflects their distinctive culture perhaps more than any other aspect of their activities. Whereas the Guatemalan Ladino is an agriculturalist and perhaps a business man, the *Moreno* man does not like to do agriculture. Agriculture is done, but it is divided between the women and the men; the women carry the greatest part of it, in that they are responsible for the cassava planting; the men take over the smaller harvests of corn and rice. From the man's point of view, the more desirable work is fishing or hiring out as a laborer in nearby Puerto Barrios; rarely will he hire out as agricultural labor. The distinction between the Ladino and *Moreno* heritage goes deep, for the agriculture done by the women is basically not that of Europe or Middle America, but that of the tropical forest of South America; it is a cassava agriculture as opposed to corn. Thus has its peculiar Indian heritage carried strongly over into the contemporary life of this "Ladino" community. Over the years of having been in contact with Ladinos and Indians, however, the *Morenos* have adopted a certain amount of rice and corn cultivation, but cassava still remains the major crop.

The agricultural implements are about the same which are to be found in many Ladino communities throughout Guatemala: the ax, machete, and digging stick with a metal point used especially for corn planting. The cultivation cycle begins as soon as the rains let up in March or April. At that time men and women go out, sometimes in groups, to cut down a new bit of the forest for the year's planting. The trees and brush are left to dry for five to seven weeks, and then burned over. It is for this reason that an extremely wet season in which there is no period of dryness is very damaging to agriculture; if they cannot burn, there is no easy way to get rid of the forest growth which has been cut down. Under such conditions planting is restricted to those areas which are already cutover from previous years, and unless these are very low, they tend to be very unproductive. A given piece of land may be used more than a year, particularly if it is in cassava; but this still means that some new land should be cleared each year.

Cassava, the main crop (referred to by informants as *yuca*) is usually planted between April and June; it then takes six or seven months to mature. At this time the root is pulled from the ground and cut from the plant; the plant is left, and in another six to seven months another tuber is removed. This may be done three times or more, until the ground ceases to produce good tubers. One can usually tell by looking at the leaves whether the ground is still good enough to produce another tuber. While most of the fields are in cassava, more corn is planted than rice. The corn is planted in April and May, and a green corn harvest is gathered at the end of June; the major harvest is reaped in September and October. A second corn planting, called the *matahambre* (literally, "killing the hunger") may be done in December for harvest in April. The *Morenos* also grow a little sugar cane, mainly for their own use, some bananas, plantains, and pineapple. Most of their auxiliary foodstuffs are purchased, however, and not produced by them. They grow no tobacco, rubber, coffee, or cacao. As a matter of contrast, the neighboring Indians of Mayan heritage produce principally corn, while the *kuli* people produce somewhat more rice than either corn or cassava.

In agricultural work there is a certain amount of division of labor between the sexes. The men will do the heaviest part of the cleaning of the cultivation patch, but if the planting is to be in cassava, it is then left to the women to do the actual work of planting and cultivating. If it is in corn or rice, the men often will do the work themselves. Those who can, and need to, will employ help for the work. It was reported that among the people of the town there was practically no exchange labor, but that it was fairly common among those who lived along the thinly populated coastal region to the east and west. Among the women, however, there is a *Club San Miguel* in which the various members help each other out in the preparation of the ground for the planting and in the cultivation. One informant said that the *Moreno* men used to spend more time in agriculture work than they do at present, and used to know more about it; for example, he said, they used to know that cassava field work should be done with the moon. The planting should be done between third quarter and new moon, while harvest should be carried on from new moon to full moon. But no one pays attention to such things any more, he said. This belief about the moon is widespread in the Ladino area as well. Another Ladino custom which seems to be promoted locally by the Church is the use of the *rogativa*, although it seems rather unnecessary in view of the amount of rain which falls in the region anyway. The informant said, however, that every May the priest went with the people "into the bush," carrying a small saint, and singing and praying.

If agriculture is a subsistence activity relying principally on women, fishing tends to depend upon the men. Fish form a large portion of the local diet as the only meat available usually is pork; there is practically no cattle kept around Livingston. Fishing is done principally with nets and lines. One type of line is the drop line where a lead weight is placed on a string and two hooks are attached to it. This is used to catch fish, such as snappers, which are 15 or 16 feet deep. Another line, the *juricán* (Sp.), is dragged behind the dory for larger catches such as the kingfish. The nets used are made locally by the men of purchased string. The most common is the *chinchorro*; five or six men will take it out in a dory away from the shore dropping it in a line parallel to the shore. When it is out in a straight line, the dory will double back on the shore side, dragging the net and closing it. The catch thus made will be divided among the participants, with the owner of the net getting one half and the other half being divided equally among the remaining participants. The *atarraya*, or casting net, is also used by the *Morenos*, but not as commonly as the *chinchorro*.

A net is usually made in separate sections; a man will commission different people to make him the sections, and they will then be joined together to produce the final product. A finished *chinchorro* usually weighs about 150 lbs. In the making of the net the Spanish measure, the *brazada*, is used; the sections made separately are usually two by ten *brazadas*. (The *brazada* is the distance between the fingers of the two arms when laterally outstretched.) A skilled net maker can produce his product in the dark of night, sheerly by feel.

The same informant, who complained that the young people are paying no attention to the moon phases in agriculture, said the same was true with respect to fishing. The fish are best during the week when the moon changes phases. It is also better near the end of each of the four seasons of the year, but best of all between spring and summer. In fall and winter it was necessary to go farther away from the immediate coast, up to the community of Sarstún or up the Río Dulce to Lake Izabal. It is best after the last quarter and especially good if the moon is up, since the fish come in with the tide. Much fishing is done at night with lamps and at high tide. Between the months of March and October turtle fishing is good; special nets are used for this. While fishing is a man's task, the selling of the fish is usually left to the women. They will carry the product to Puerto Barrios or as far as Zacapa. If it is sold directly on the beach or short distances away, the men may handle the sale.

The handicrafts of the *Morenos* are limited pretty much to those connected with fishing and cassava. Men make the dorys and the nets and a special cassava squeezer, the *wowla* (C.). The *wowla* is basically similar to the cassava squeezer to be found today in the tropical forests of South America; it is a long tube-like basket into which the shredded cassava is placed. It is then hung from the ceiling, and a person sits on a stick placed through the bottom; this serves to squeeze the juice from the cassava. Since this juice is poisonous, it is a necessary part of the preparation to remove it. Aside from the *wowla*, there is no basket work done by the *Morenos*. All the rest of the specialized work is similar to that found in any Ladino town: there are both Ladino and *Moreno* tailors, shoemakers, carpenters, and seamstresses. There is no spinning, weaving, leather work, or pottery production. Indeed, pottery is not even used by the *Morenos*, and according to the informant, there was no Carib word for pottery utensils. Two types of drums are made for use in the local fiestas: a small two headed drum tied to the waist, and a long single headed drum especially for the *jan'hunu* (C.), a Carib dance.

One of the principal reasons given for the decline in the amount of agricultural work done by the men was that when the banana shipments began in Puerto Barrios, men were drawn over as labor. They did not have time to carry on all the old agricultural work and hire out as well. Even the fishing suffered badly. The work in Puerto Barrios today is mainly that of stevedoring and cargo handling. It was reported in Morales that very few *Morenos* go to the actual banana plantations to work; they prefer to remain on the coast, and Puerto Barrios offers them good work. For a while, from about 1920 until the Second World War, the United Fruit Company was fomenting the production of bananas among the *Morenos* themselves, and purchasing their product. This stopped, however, and has not been resumed; it did serve to increase the amount of land placed under banana and plantain cultivation by the Caribs. It was the strong complaint of one of the writer's informants that the work in Puerto Barrios was taking the *Moreno* youth away from his traditional subsistence work. While he deplored this, in that no one "liked to work" anymore, and the youth (as he expressed it) *"ni es macho para trabajar, ni es buey,"* nevertheless he was very fearful of the results of the possible shutting down of the port operations, since so few of the young men knew how to take care of themselves or a cultivation. There was probably considerable exaggeration in the old man's concern, but there is plenty of evidence that with a continued economic call of the port, the Carib culture is going to suffer strongly. In the past century it was the practice of the Carib men often to go off for months at a time to cut mahogany; but they would return from time to time, and their labor was "in the bush." The work at Puerto Barrios is an urban work, and urban troubles are likely to result.

In Livingston there is one type of mutual work association which is evidently very popular among the *Morenos*. These are the *manaquero* clubs (*manaca* is the palm leaf, and the *manaquero* is a person who cuts leaves; since most of the homes of the *Morenos* have palm leaf roofs, this term is applied to people who form house-building clubs). There were three such clubs in existence in Livingston at the time of the survey: the *Club Manaquero Paris* the *Club Manaquero Cehuéch*, and the *Club Manaquero Admirable*. There used to be others. While the members of the clubs evidently provide a certain amount of aid to one another when sick or in case of death, the principal task is in aiding the construction of homes. When a member wishes to build a house, he informs the president, who in turn calls a meeting at which a time is set when the men will help, and the future house owner will have food ready. While the members of the clubs are said to generally be people of higher status in town, the poorer people also tend to help one another in house building, although they may not be organized into such clubs. On some occasions a poor man who is not a member of a club may ask the president of one of the clubs if the club members will help him, and the help is given. The work of building a house is divided into two parts. The first part involves the gathering of the materials, which are then left a month or so to dry; and then the house itself is put up in one day. While the *kuli* people help themselves in this kind of work (although apart from the *Morenos*), the "Spaniards" usually pay to have a house put up. Two informants claimed that these clubs are of fairly recent origin, at least within the living generation, but that such mutual help is a very old practice and probably goes back beyond the first formal organization of the clubs. The most recent of the clubs was formed about five years ago.

Another phase of the *Moreno* economy which tends to distinguish them from their Ladino contemporaries of European descent is the general concept of land usufruct. In general, no one owns agricultural land around Livingston. Until the passing of the Agrarian Reform Law, all the land belonged to the municipality and anyone used it who wished to. With the type of shifting cultivation practised, there was no real advantage to owning land, since the land was only good for a few years at a time. It is interesting to note that when the Agrarian Committee was set up in Livingston to divide up the land, no *Moreno* was a member of it; it was composed entirely of Ladinos.

The main trade in Livingston goes on in the stores. There is a municipal market, but it goes all the time and is not a weekly affair, such as is to be found elsewhere in the country among the Indians. Many purchases are made in Puerto Barrios, but the Livingston stores themselves are kept well stocked by the local "Spanish" and Chinese merchants.

Most *Moreno* homes are divided into two rooms, a *sala* and a sleeping room. With the exception of the materials used in the preparation of the cassava (a shredder and the *wowla*), the implements are pretty similar to those found in Ladino homes elsewhere. The raised *fogón* or fireplace is used in a separate kitchen structure; metal and enamel ware but no pottery is used. The wooden *bateas*, such as are found throughout Central America, are also made by the men here. There are no Spanish type ovens, but they do use the large wooden *morteros* for hulling rice. Both men and women do this work. The *Morenos* sleep on cotton cots or in cotton hammocks; they do not sleep in the *tabanco* (shelved-over ceiling in a *rancho*) nor on the ground. The furniture is basically Ladino, and its simplicity depends upon the poverty of the family concerned. The wealthier live in a material environment which differs little from Ladinos of equal wealth elsewhere in the republic. There were no special drinks reported nor any special foods outside of the preparation of cassava and fish.

In the political organization of Livingston a basic difference from other Ladino towns (but one that has little to do with the fact that the population is Carib) is that the principal official of the town is the Ladino Port Captain. He is appointed by the national government and brings his own assistants with him. He is in charge of the port and of immigration; but because of his rank, he is considered to be the major official present. The municipal body itself is no different basically from those to be found elsewhere in the Ladino regions of the country. The major variation of interest lies in the relative distribution of power between the *Morenos*, who are demographically overwhelmingly preponderant, and the "Spaniards", who in fact may fix the elections and placement of officials if they so wish. According to the local informants, when the capital of the Department of Izabal was at the town of Izabal, the Livingston officials were *auxiliares* and were *Morenos*. With the coming of the 20th Century, more "Spaniards" began to move into the town, and in the 1920's the capital of the department was moved to Puerto Barrios. The *alcaldes* during the succeeding period were not paid, however, and *Morenos* usually continued to carry the job. However, when Ubico came in, the municipal system was changed, the salaried post of *intendente* was substituted for that of *alcalde*, and immediately Ladinos were appointed to the new position. Even with the re-establishment of the elective system in 1946, "Spaniards" continued to hold the municipal spots in Livingston until 1954 when the first *Moreno alcalde* in two decades took office. In this period, in which the *Morenos* were somewhat excluded from the municipal structure, they were usually given one municipal position "just to keep them satisfied," as one informant put it. During the entire period, however, one series of positions has been consistently given to the *Morenos*, the *alcaldes auxiliares* in the *Moreno barrios*. These *auxiliares* served in the same way they do in other towns in the republic, except that they were more meaningful in Livingston in view of the fact that for a long time they were the only *Moreno* officials. At the time of the study the *alcalde* and three of the *regidores* (called *municipales* locally) were *Morenos* and two *regidores* were "Spaniards." There was little doubt that this was something of an experiment from the Ladino's point of view and may well have been carried on as an attempt to gain political support. The fact that the Agrarian Committee, when formed locally, was composed entirely of "Spaniards" suggests that the "Spanish Ladino" politicians did not entirely trust the *Morenos*.

Of the various social groupings to be found in Livingston, there are three and possibly four endogamous groups: the *kuli* people, *Morenos*, and the "Spanish" all tend to marry within their own group. There are some informal alliances between Ladinos and Indians.

The mere fact that the official census bureau of the country has chosen to consider the *Moreno* population as Ladino does not mean that either the *Morenos* or the "Spanish" living in Livingston fail to make this distinction. The "Spanish" consider the *Morenos* as a rather peculiar group; peculiar because they choose to retain a distinct language, because they do not like to go inland, because they are not overly fond of agricultural work, and because they do not seem to get into fights. As one "Spaniard" expressed it, "they are perhaps the loudest people when they get into a fight, but they never attack one another nor do they kill each other with machetes; they just yell." To some "Spaniards," this lack of desire to chop one another up is one of the most curious traits the *Moreno* manifests. The "Spanish" viewpoint about *Morenos* does not stop with this, however; the *Moreno* also retains certain customs from which the "Spaniard" is excluded, such as certain fiestas, and which must therefore be regarded as mysterious and savage. Some wild tales of orgies "across the river" (where no "Spaniard" could watch well) were told to the writer; he could not substantiate them. It is an accepted Ladino idea that the Black Carib language is a jumble of African words which have undergone violent alteration through the addition of Spanish and English (and perhaps some Carib Indian) words. So far as African traits go, the writer was able to identify no specifically African cultural trait among the Caribs during his brief visit there; there may well be some, especially with respect to the Carib fiestas; but at present there have been none identified.

Thus the *Moreno* is a group apart from the Spanish. The same is true of the *kuli* people. They too are evidently endogamous, but the writer gathered no information on attitudes towards this group, nor on their attitudes towards others. Since there are very few of them, they do not play a very important part in the social structure. It is likely, however, that they may be considered as an ethnic group which is at the same social level, or slightly lower, than are the *Morenos*.

While the Ladino tends to look down on the Moreno, the latter in turn looks down on the Maya Indians. The Indian tends to get into more costly fights, he thinks, and one must take care in handling him. The Indians use the town principally as a trade center, however, and very few live in it (only 2.7% of the town population was considered as being Indian in 1950, whereas 55.4% of the total population of the *municipio* of Livingston was Indian).

Within the *Moreno* group there are clear distinctions of relative social status, and according to one informant, these were often thought of in terms of classes, although there were no names for them. The upper group was composed of the "decent" people, the middle of the "ordinary" people, and the lower, of people who acted badly. The criterion of distinction was mainly a matter of moral behavior, the informant felt, not one of wealth.

Marriage and common-law unions among the *Morenos*, while tending to be endogamous within the ethnic group, are somewhat exogamous with respect to the *barrios* of the town. There are cases of marriage within a *barrio*, an informant reported, but it was much more common for people of different *barrios* to marry. While statistical data is, as usual, lacking to confirm the information, it was reported that relatively few people in the community are formally married. Residence tends to be neo-local, but until such time as a new house may be built, a couple may live with either set of parents. Separations are very common and extramarital or extraunion intercourse is evidently fairly common. Although the land on which the members of a family legally plant belongs to the municipality, it has been customary for a piece being worked by a particular family to remain with that family and to be informally inherited by the next generation. It was reported that the prohibition of intercourse, common-law, and formal marriage between first cousins was fairly strictly observed. According to one informant, the relative freedom of separation, which is present today among the *Morenos*, has been developing during the past fifty years, principally since the growth of Puerto Barrios.

The *compadre* system is fairly important among *Morenos* and "Spanish" alike. Among the former, children of *compadres* are not supposed to marry, indicating an extension of the incest regulations to cover the artificial kin tie as well. Both Protestants and Catholics obtain *compadres* for the baptism of children, while the Catholics obtain a single *compadre* for confirmation. If a child is orphaned, however, he will be taken care of by his parents' siblings and parents, not by the *compadres*. As is suggestive of the relative social status of the three groups, it was reported that requests for *compadres* will go from Indians to *Morenos*, and from *Morenos* to Spaniards, but requests in the reverse direction are very rare. In general, however, *compadres* are sought from within the same ethnic group.

Formal religion among the *Morenos* seems to adhere pretty strictly to the dictates of the particular formal Church to which each belongs, within the variations of the general Ladino pattern. There are certain ceremonies which are of uncertain connection with the formalities of the Catholic or Protestant religions and which are strictly customs of the Black Caribs; the informants disagreed, however, as to the extent to which these should be identified as being part of Christian Church festivals and to what extend they should be regarded sheerly as customs of the *Morenos* and not related to the churches.

It was reported that the great majority of the *Morenos* in Livingston were Catholic. The principal events on the Christian calendar are Holy Week and Christmas. For the latter some Ladino customs are practiced, such as *corrida de cintas* and bullfights, but the writer received the impression that these were not very important to the *Morenos* and that they did not occur with great frequency. For Holy Week there is an *Hermandad de Jesús*, composed of men, which collects money from the townspeople for the Holy Week celebration. There is also a women's church group which sweeps the church building, lights candles, washes the clothes of the saints, etc. There is also a *Comité Pro-construcción de la Iglesia* which is composed principally of *Morenos* but to which Ladinos originally belonged. One informant indicated that within his lifetime there had been various other fiestas celebrated from time to time: *Concepción*, *Guadalupe*, *San Juan*, *San Isidro*, and *Carnaval* were all celebrated for varying periods of time.

House saints are kept by many families, but those which are particularly celebrated are *Esquipulas* and *"la Virgen"* in October. This latter celebration involves the image of the *Virgen* visiting a different house each night during the month of October; it goes only to the homes of the married people and is sponsored by a group of women calling themselves the *Matronas*.[62] Other home observances include the novena held at the time of death, in which only women participate, in extreme Ladino style. It was said that there was an old custom by which dancing was done at all funerals, but that this is not done today.

Informants mentioned two main celebrations which are restricted to the *Moreno* group entirely, the *jan'hunu* and the *hugühügu*.[63] No mention was

---

[62] This particular combination of traits, the travelling saint and the *Matronas*, is more characteristic of the countrymen of Nicaragua than it is of the Guatemalan Ladinos.

[63] The pronunciation of these is as follows: *jan'hunu* is pronounced with Spanish values for all the letters except the *j* and *h* which have the English values; the ' is a glottle stop.

made to the writer during his brief stay of the rites and practices described by Taylor[64] for the British Honduras group, and unfortunately no inquiry was made into this phase of the culture. The only mention Taylor makes of a ceremony which might correspond to the two described by Livingston informants is the *uanaragua*, which he mentions in his glossary as a "masquerade held between Christmas and New Year."

The *jan'hunu* is organized in November before the time for the fiesta in December, but certain phases of it, such as practicing the dances, begin as much as three months early. While the Christmas fiesta is celebrated on the 24th of December, the *jan'hunu* begins on the morning of the 25th. It lasts until the end of the month or the 1st. of January. There is no organization which lasts over from one year to the next. The whole period is a general holiday and is celebrated throughout the *Moreno* population. The *jan'hunu* consists of special drum music, played by three drummers, singing led by men and in which the women join, and masked dances held by the men only. The informant said the same fiesta was held in both British and "Spanish" Honduras.

The *hugũhũgu* fiesta, held during the same period as the *jan'hunu*, is danced specifically by the women, although it was reported that sometimes the men participated in it as well. The men always played the drums for it. Practicing for the dance begins in November. A number of different groups may celebrate this fiesta simultaneously. The *hugũhũgu* is sometimes held across the river and occasionally at other times of the year. As was mentioned above, there was some disagreement between informants as to the degree to which these dances were to be thought of as being related to Christmas.

Unfortunately, the survey failed to explore the many aspects of Black Carib spiritual life described by Taylor. In view of the close relations maintained between the peoples of the British Honduras coast and those of Livingston, it seems very likely that much of what Taylor found in his study would be duplicated in Livingston.[65] In view of the rather urban setting in which the Livingston *Morenos* live and work it would be of interest to have more comparative material on these subjects.

The writer could not uncover any very unique beliefs or practices with respect to sickness and curing among the *Morenos*. None of the more typical Ladino illnesses such as *susto, ojo, pujo, hijillo*, or *pasmo* brought any particular response from informants. It was said that a few "believed" in witches, but that some people "did not believe in anything." There are a few *curanderos* who, because their work was prohibited by local authorities, now practice secretly. They

---

The writer is by no means sure of the pronunciation of the second of the two words which is transcribed herein in the way his Black Carib informant thought it would be written for a Spanish speaker. Since no time was devoted to linguistic study, the writer apologizes and suggests that the above spellings be regarded as symbolic in their entirety for the words involved.

[64] 1951, pp. 102–137.

[65] Taylor, 1951, pp. 35–6, notes that he made at least two trips to Livingston and found nothing of particular note which led him to think that the local culture was very divergent from that which he was studying in British Honduras.

are not practical curers, according to informants, but tend to call upon the supernatural. There is considerable belief in spirits, but on this subject the informants did not become voluble on short notice. The Ladinos in town with whom the writer spoke said they had never heard of witchcraft among the *Morenos*; in view of the Ladino readiness to believe that such superstitions exist in other ethnic groups, this is probably indicative that there is in fact very little witchcraft.

There was much said by some of the informants to suggest that the culture of the Black Carib of Livingston is undergoing a considerable change at present. How much of this can be attributed to reflective sentimentality on the part of informants, and how much on accurate observation, is difficult to know without study. There seems to be good reason to suppose that the conditions existing in Puerto Barrios and the type of labor carried on there would have a considerable effect on the culture of the *Moreno*. On the other hand, historical reports indicate that it has been common, at least into the last century, for the Black Carib men to work away from their home community (usually in mahogany cutting) and to return periodically. The women were usually in charge of the agriculture. Therefore, the degree to which Puerto Barrios as such is having a differential effect on the contemporary Black Caribs must be studied not only in the light of their history, but by a careful analysis of the differences in the fact that Livingston is a large town, and that the labor in Puerto Barrios is a different kind of labor from that more common in the past century.

The Black Caribs of Livingston form a part of a coastal society which is gradually becoming more related to the Ladino culture of the nation as a whole. The regular contacts with other Black Caribs up and down the coast serve to constantly reinforce distinctive customs in which the other Guatemalan Ladinos do not share; on the other hand, the increasing force of the growing "Spanish" population of Guatemala is having a strong effect on the *Morenos* and is bound to have more in the future.

With its four cultures of such different origins (Maya Indian, Spanish Ladino, Black Carib, and India Indian), Livingston offers a facinating anthropological laboratory for the study of culture contact and change. The survey on which the present description is based was all too brief to gain anything but superficial impressions of the nature of the life of the population.

IV. COMMUNITIES VISITED ON THE SURVEY

While the usual practice in this series of reports has been to provide a brief description of each of the towns visited on the survey, the fact that some thirty towns were visited in Guatemala leads us to condense the individual descriptions and achieve some generalizations concerning the towns. Here the towns visited on the survey are going to be described in terms of local regions. These local regions are not necessarily homogeneous within themselves, but the grouping of towns is made because of apparent cultural or social similarities. This means that some towns are described separately, since they do not fall within a clear-cut group.

1. THREE LADINO TOWNS OF THE WESTERN HIGHLANDS: ZARAGOZA, SAN CARLOS SIJA, AND ESQUIPULAS PALO GORDO

The western highlands is an Indian region, and for the most part Ladinos live in it as minorities in Indian communities (such as in Joyabáj) or in some few cases in separate communities in which they form the dominant ethnic group. The three communities named above are of this latter type, as the 1950 Census data will confirm:

Municipio	Department	Percentage of Indians		
		In the department	In the entire *municipio*	In municipal capital
Zaragoza	Chimaltenango	77.5%	21.3%	2.1%
Palo Gordo	San Marcos	72.1%	17.2%	6.6%
San Carlos Sija	Quezaltenango	68.0%	40.5%	23.5%

The Ladinos within each of these communities live as the dominant ethnic group, but as an island in a sea of Indians. Thus their inter-communal relationships are in great part determined by the fact that most neighboring communities are composed predominantly of Indians. The Ladino founders of these towns did not follow the trend followed by most Ladino settlers in the country; instead of seeking out the temperate or hot regions, they settled in high mountain valleys and the *altos*: Zaragoza is about 6,650 feet above sea level, Palo Gordo about 7,700, and San Carlos is 8,300 feet. In all three communities there have long since been established fairly clear-cut relationships between the Ladinos and the Indians who live in the surrounding regions. Among the other points of importance in these relations is that the Ladinos are almost all monolingual, speaking only Spanish, whereas the Indians in the immediate region (at least the men) are bilingual. Also similar for the three is that the countryside surrounding the three is scattered with houses. While there are small nuclei of population, much of the rural population lives out in its own land, and not crowded in small *aldea* centers. Two of the towns, San Carlos Sija and Zaragoza, traditionally date back to the early colonial times; the inhabitants of both are supposed to be descendents from immigrants coming from towns of the same name in Spain, Exija and Zaragoza. It is amusing to note, in view of the pride in which the inhabitants hold their Spanish traditions, that both towns have reputations as being the home of thieves and robbers. San Carlos Sija, through the early years of this century, had the reputation of being the home of the most skillful and active horse and mule thieves in all of western Guatemala, while it was related to the writer a number of times that Zaragoza was settled by gypsies who were still "bad" people. These traditions are not repeated to perpetuate them, but simply to point out a peculiar similarity between the two. The history of Palo Gordo, however, goes back to the time of independence; it was said that the town was founded by three Ladino families, and was set up as a *municipio* in 1825; there is no tradition as to where these original families came from.

In all three towns, ox carts are not extremely common, even though in the writer's opinion the countryside would permit such transport. The Ladino women of all three towns carry water jugs (*cántaros*) on their head. In all three it is the men who bring in the firewood, whereas among the Indians it is often the women who have this task.

In view of the Spanish traditions of these towns, their agriculture is thoroughly mixed. Wheat is grown in all three, and in San Carlos it is the most important crop. In all three *milpa* is planted and is of some importance. The wooden plow is not used at all in Zaragoza, only slightly in San Carlos, and to a limited extent in Palo Gordo. The hoe is the principal cultivation implement in all three towns. In all three towns, the general economic pattern is one of small landholdings.

In both Zaragoza and San Carlos the predominant architecture is *adobe* walls with tile roofs; in Palo Gordo, however, most homes in the center are made of boards.

2. A LADINO *ALDEA* IN THE WESTERN HIGHLANDS: CHITATUL

The community of Chitatul is of particular interest, not because it is large, nor because it is representative of any sizable population, but because it is an example of what can happen in Ladino culture if Indians have economic equality. Chitatul was included on the survey because Sol Tax visited the town in 1935 and reported it with some interest.[66] Tax received the impression that Chitatul was a fairly unique case of a Ladino town in which the Ladinos did not play the role of upper class over a giant Indian population, such as he was used to seeing in most of the western highland towns, but where they were themselves the actual workers, the peasants. This was a very different situation than was found among most of Ladinos with whom Tax was familiar, people who were commercial town dwellers. Another difference he suggested was that the Chitatul Ladinos had been here since "time immemorial," whereas most of the other Ladinos had come in only during the past one hundred years or so.

As is clear from the data gathered in Zaragoza, San Carlos Sija, and Palo Gordo, the survey strongly supports Tax's supposition that where the Ladinos work (but specifically as small landholders) they can form rather strong communities and do not have to rely on their commercial superiority over the Indians to sustain them. Oddly enough, however, while the data from these other towns supports Tax's general idea, the data from Chitatul did not provide strong support. Chitatul, instead of providing a case of noble Ladino peasantry, seemed to provide a case of the degree to which Ladinos could become acculturated to certain of the material culture and other Indian traits without taking over any of the integrative qualities which makes the Indian community cultures function as meaningful wholes. It is impossible to say how much of this may be due to events which have occurred since the time of Tax's visit, but there is some indication that certain important changes have taken place since that time.

Chitatul is probably more similar to the community of Aguas Escondidas,

---
[66] 1935, pp. 74–75.

which Redfield characterized as being (in comparison with that of the neighboring Indians) culturally "shallow."[67] In both Chitatul and Aguas Escondidas, the Ladinos had taken over the use of the Indian *temescal* (sweat bath) as a curing device (and in the latter place there were even some who had *temescales* of their own, a thing reported in no town in the present survey); in both the Ladinos used the *mecapal* as a regular means of carrying things; and in both the Ladinos submit to local Indian political authorities. In addition to these common traits to be found in both towns, the general social relationships described by Redfield for the two ethnic groups in Aguas Escondidas would seem to apply in most respects to the relationships in Chitatul. In Chitatul, however, there is an important economic difference. According to the informant, none of the Ladinos are purely agriculturalists; all have some other occupation as well, and, in general, tend to look upon agriculture as an essential but auxiliary mode of subsistence. Thus one is a carpenter, another a blacksmith, another a mason, others run *cantinas* (small rustic drinking establishments), others make rope and rope products; and as a specialty of the community as such, a great many people purchase and keep pigs which they slaughter for sale in the nearby markets. Thus, the Chitatul people probably do not fix Tax's original estimate of them as well as do the Aguas Escondidas Ladinos.

There was agreement between two informants that in Chitatul during the past ten or fifteen years the Indians have been moving in and buying up land which once was Ladino. We have what appears to be a reversal to the trend of history in which the Ladinos move in on Indian territory. According to one informant, the purchase of land by the Indians is part of an Indian movement from the scattered homesteads of the country to the city; from the more isolated *aldeas* they move to Chitatul (which is on an automobile road); from there into the departmental capital, Quiché; and some of them move on into the national capital. The writer did not have the opportunity to confirm this observation.

While there is some feeling of social superiority on the part of the Ladinos with respect to the Indians, they have evidently had to adjust their lives to retain this position. It was reported, for example, that the Indians did their planting just after the rains, a practice which is generally common throughout the highlands, except in certain regions where there is a good deal of sub-surface moisture. The Ladinos in Chitatul, however, plant before the rains, because if they did not it would not be possible for them to hire Indians to work for them; if they waited until after the rains, the Indians would all be occupied. The scarcity of Indian labor has become so acute in recent years that young Ladinos have taken to hiring out as field hands.

Chitatul differs in an important respect from the three Ladino communities described in the previous section; while in those towns the Ladinos spoke Spanish, and the Indians were bilingual, in Chitatul the Ladinos are bilingual, speaking both Spanish and the Indian language, *Quiché*. This indicates an aspect of ethnic relations seldom found in the western highlands. The Alta Verapaz has

[67] Redfield, 1945, p. 298.

traditionally been the principal region of the country in which the Ladinos have learned the Indian language.

The town of Chitatul itself is laid out along the road between Quiché and Chiché. It is a linear settlement about two kilometers long and composed of about twenty Ladino families. Within the entire land area assigned to the *aldea* there are four *cantones* set in a line along the road. Local political control, what there is of it, is exercised through two *auxiliares*, named annually by the municipal government in Quiché, who are inevitably Indians. It was reported that the Ladinos tried to evade the responsibility of these posts. There are no public buildings in the *aldea*, except a small *capilla* in the cemetery. The houses are of *adobe* and tile, and the landscape is rolling and badly eroded. The soil is fairly hard, a reason given by the local Ladinos for refusing to use the plow in agriculture.

The informant commented, with respect to the Chitatul people, that it was usually the Indians who more readily accepted new things. There had been an agricultural extension agent available locally for a period, but none of the Ladinos would pay any attention to him.

3. THE LADINOS OF A WESTERN HIGHLAND INDIAN *MUNICIPIO*: JOYABAJ

Most of the Ladinos of western Guatemala are town dwellers who handle the commerce of their *municipios*. There are, however, some communities that combine the characteristics of the Ladinos who are themselves agriculturalists (such as in the four towns just described) with those communities in which the Ladinos comprise a minute urban minority. Joyabáj is such a case. Of the total population of 21,381 (1950) in the *municipio* only 5,640 (26.4%) are Ladinos, but of this Ladino population 923, or only 16.4%, live in the municipal capital. The great majority of the rest are agriculturalists who live in the *cantones*. In Joyabáj itself, however, the Ladinos composed 73.3% of the town population.

Joyabáj provides an interesting example of a number of phases of Ladino life and history which are of some importance. In the first place, the community is located on one of the upper tributaries of the Motagua. As will be noted shortly, the Motagua Ladino culture is an important development, and to some degree the Ladino population of Joyabáj is an extension of this Ladino culture. Second, Joyabáj and the *aldea* of Chitatul both lie on what was evidently an important colonial trade route running northwest from the capital and from the upper Motagua Valley. There is thus running through the southern part of El Quiché a belt of towns with low percentages of town Indians (Joyabáj 26.7%, Zacualpa, 12.1%, Chinique 22.2%, Chiché 32.9%) with the Ladino town of Quiché on the west of the Ladino *municipio* of Granados on the east. This belt, it should be noted, runs through a region which is Indian in terms of the distinctions made earlier in this paper.

Third, the land area of the *municipio* falls into two climatic zones which serve as a basis of distinction for the main areas of residence of the two ethnic groups. *Tierra caliente* (warm land) includes six *cantones* which fall in the lower valley lands in the southern portion of the *municipio*, while *tierra fría* (cold land) includes eight *cantones* which lie in the *Sierra de Chuacus* which forms the north border of the *municipio*. Within these two regions, the Ladinos have most of the *tierra caliente* land, while the Indians have most of the *tierra fría*. Although most of the lower lands belong to Ladinos, many of the Indians work these lands, some as renters, others as field laborers. It might be noted that the town of Joyabáj, located at an altitude of about 5,000 feet, is in the valley and is considered to be *tierra caliente*; the writer and his companion found themselves well chilled in this so-called warm land.

Joyabáj, then, provides an example of a community in which the Ladinos not only retain social supremacy through holding the political and commercial strings of the town, but through owning and actively exploiting the best lands in the *municipio*. The situation is a result of an evidently long history of Ladino occupancy during which time there have developed not only a fairly distinct but rigid (in contrast with the Chitatul and Aguas Escondidas situation) caste system, and within the Ladino portion of which there are social status distinctions which go a long way towards, and probably form, distinct social classes. There is no doubt that the town Ladinos who acted as informants for the survey distinguished themselves from the rural Ladinos whom the writer stopped to talk with and who lived in a fairly obvious state of poverty. The town itself is long, located on a *loma* of land, and is divided into three *barrios* set like sausages on a string; the central *barrio*, "El Centro," tends to be the locale of the residences of the *gente buena*, whereas the *gente mala, de menos categoría*, and the Indians live in the *barrios* La Democracia and La Libertad to the west and east of the center. Some of the distinctions made between the two ethnic groups have already been described with respect to the political and religious organizations in Joyabáj; for both, the two groups remain quite separate.

It is one of the vagaries of the development of the road system in Guatemala that to reach Joyabáj, which is a scant fifty kilometers from the capital city, requires a trip covering more than 210 kilometers. It is necessary, literally, to go the other three sides of the square to reach this town. It may be for this reason that it has never particularly attracted the attention of ethnographers; it is isolated, but it is too near to be exciting. This is unfortunate in view of the fact that it is one of the few Indian *municipios* that has preserved the old fiesta custom of the *palo volador*.

4. THE LADINOS OF THE UPPER MOTAGUA: GRANADOS, PALENCIA, AND SANSARE

In all the towns described so far we have been dealing with Ladino populations which are either minorities within an Indian *municipio*, or of *municipios* which are Ladino islands within the Indian area. Now we are suddenly moving into a region which is either mixed in its total population or predominantly Ladino. The three towns grouped together here are not so classified because they show any remarkable similarity, but rather because they seem to be leftovers after other Ladino towns have been classified into regions. For lack of some other explanation, we may for the moment attribute this to the fact that they are all on the upper tributaries of the Motagua River which in turn carries in its middle section a fairly strong type of Ladino culture. Each of the towns has felt some influence from the middle Motagua, but each has also been on the transition into another area of influence.

From Joyabáj, it is a drop of about 3,000 feet down the Motagua to the municipio of Granados. This town had a population of only 339 people in 1950, of which 238 were recorded as being Ladino; the *municipio* in all had a population of 5,865 of which only 12.9% were Indians. Granados is located in very rough, dry country 1,100 feet above the river; much of the ground is rocky and in many places the topsoil is so thin that agriculture, according to our informants, is extremely difficult. They claimed that the soil was so bad that it was next to impossible to grow corn, and only *maicillo* thrived. It is true, also, that *maicillo* composed the principal part of the crops observed. Visiting a community like Granados makes one wonder, if it does not sound too facetious, who actually conquered whom in the conquest of Guatemala. Although Indians in many cases live in places where it is hard to scrape a living from the ground, Granados is as rough and arid a spot as one could choose for a place to live. As is the case in Joyabáj, the land of the *municipio* is divided into *tierra caliente* and *tierra fría*. The *tierra fría* is the higher, more difficult land from which only one crop a year may be taken; in *tierra caliente*, two crops of corn (where it can grow) can be taken out.

The people of Granados are generally poor; there were no particularly wealthy looking homes in evidence, even though informants told us that the richest people of the *municipio* lived here in town. Most of the land is in small holdings, although there are a few fairly large *fincas*. The town itself has the appearance of an *aldea*. The houses are scattered along a single street up the side of the hill; there is a slightly widened flat area which is referred to as a *plaza* in front of the *municipalidad* building, and off to one side stands a fountain. As was evident from the census figures, the overwhelming part of the population lives in the rural areas. The people of Granados are trying to give their town some of the more classic attributes of a municipal center; the church is under construction and they are trying to sponsor a weekly market on the *plaza*. Mail to Granados, oddly enough, does not come up directly from Guatemala City, some fifty miles to the south, but down from Salamá by bus to the town of El Chol, a few kilometers above Granados, and then by foot the remaining distance. The trip to Salamá is by air, or by rail to El Rancho and then by bus overland. Thus it takes usually five days for a letter to travel by a circuitous route to go a distance of fifty kilometers.

While it is not possible to say with certainty, the writer gained the impression that the population of the municipio of Granados was poor Old Ladino and much New Ladino; with an important exception, the same general population types which will be described shortly for the middle Motagua Valley. Both to the north, in the Rabinal—Salamá Valley, and to the south, in the region of the northwestern part of the Department of Guatemala, there are Modified and Traditional Indian communities, but along the Valley of the Motagua itself the Ladinos have long since become predominant.

Southeast of Granados, about 18 kilometers as the crow flies, and east and slightly north of Guatemala City, lies the Ladino community of Palencia. The population of this *municipio* in 1950 was 13,409, of which 2,593 were Ladinos living in the municipal capital and another 352 (or 2.6% of the total) were Indians who lived outside of town. For practical purposes, Palencia may be considered as a completely Ladino *municipio*. The countryside around Palencia is fairly well watered and there are various sections of irrigated land through the *municipio*. The altitude of the town is about 4,000 feet, and the countryside is rough but much of it permits effective agriculture. The town itself is generally spread out along a long triangle of streets with the "center" at the apex most distance from the road which leads into the community.

Most of the land in the town area used to belong to a Paulist convent which was located there (the buildings still stand and serve as the residence of the priest), but it was divided among the people at the time of Barrios; much of the remaining land at that time belonged to a few large *fincas*, but in the intervening years much of this has been divided among heirs so that today there are very few holdings of any size. Much of the irrigation which continues in use today was started by the Paulist fathers. The area around Palencia today specializes in the production of *güisquiles*.

Palencia is evidently composed of a fairly old population of Ladinos (although whether it dates back beyond the republican period is uncertain) who, through the gradual dividing up of lands through inheritance, have been reduced to a medium to poor economic status. There remain a few *fincas* which are small but on which a number of the people work. While Granados is somewhat isolated from Ladino contacts north and south, Palencia is close enough to Guatemala City that there is and presumably has been considerable contact between the people of the *municipio* and the city. The city provides the principal market for the *güisquiles* cash crop and other horticultural products coming from the fields, and there is daily bus service.

In the southern part of the Department of El Progreso, in one of the tributary valleys of the Motagua, lies the town of Sansare at an altitude of 2,500 feet. Like Granados and Palencia, it is made up principally of medium to poor Ladino small landholders. Of the entire municipal population of 4,381, only 36 were classed as Indians in the 1950 Census; 1,127, or about 26% of the population live in the municipal capital. Unlike the other two towns just described, Sansare is laid out basically on a rectangular grid pattern. Tradition in the town has it that the community was originally founded by Jesuit fathers, probably in the 17th Century. While Granados seems to remain restricted to the Motagua Valley in its orientation, and Palencia has been influenced by contact with Guatemala City, Sansare shows influence from the Indian culture of the Jalapa Department. For example, the term for the *macana*, or digging stick, is *huisute*, which comes from the Pocomam language.

Like Palencia, Sansare has a crop which is produced particularly for cash; in this case, it is *yuca*.[68] It is sold in Guatemala City and is exported as far as El Salvador. The Sansare people evidently, like many Ladino peoples of the upper Motagua region, are predominantly independent agriculturalists.

In general, these upper Motagua towns share certain features based more on the socio-economic organization than on specific lines of local Ladino tradition. They are composed mostly of small landholders, and there seems to be no very large class of wealthy people; all three have tended to specialize in the production of a particular crop, although this is partially determined by the nature of the environment in Granados.

5. THE LADINOS OF THE MIDDLE MOTAGUA: SAN AGUSTIN ACASA-GUASTLAN, TECULUTAN, GUALAN, AND SAN JERONIMO

As one moves down into the middle Motagua River Valley, and out on the open plains, a somewhat different socio-economic picture appears. The particular pattern found evidently extends beyond the valley proper, since from the data collected on the survey the town of San Jerónimo, located on the other side of the Sierra de las Minas, manifests a similar orientation. San Jerónimo, it will be noted, lies not in the drainage of the Motagua but in that of the Río Salamá which empties into the Usumacinta River.

The towns of San Agustín and Teculután are similar in so many ways that they may almost be considered together for present purposes. Both lie on the left bank of the Motagua set in the arid valley floor. Through each winds rows of trees and greenery following the path of irrigation water. Both *municipios* have three types of land and a related social structure. There are the irrigated valley floor lands which are owned almost in their entirety by the upper class families of the towns and worked by laborers. There are then stretches of arid, unirrigated, valley floor lands; and finally there are *montaña* lands in the hills of the Sierra de Las Minas which forms the northwest wall of the department. In these lands work numerous small landholders. With this, it is possible to see the essential social difference between these towns and those of the upper Motagua; here there is a distinct upper class, the epitome of what we have been calling in these pages the "Old Ladino." These families control the irrigated lands and have done so, presumably, for generations. There are also smaller landholders, but for them the best available land is to be found on the mountain slopes. As a necessary complement to an upper class which owns large agricultural lands, there is also a large laboring class who work these lands and, in some cases, rent them. When the upper class here is called "wealthy," the term is used relative to the peoples of this and the upper Motagua region; this upper class is not to be compared with the large *finca* owners who have holdings further down the river, in the Alta Verapaz, or in the south coast. This is a local upper class, a group

---

[68] Not the cassava of Livingston.

which probably used to exist also in the upper Motagua towns in bygone years. In this region, however, they have maintained their holdings intact and with them, their wealth.

San Agustín is an old town and still retains a fairly large Indian population within its municipal boundaries. Of the total population of 11,013 registered in 1950, 36.4% were Indians; only slightly over a tenth of these lived in the town itself. Of the total population, 2,546 lived in the municipal capital (23.1%). The municipio of Teculután is much smaller than San Agustín; it has a total population of only 2,209, of which 867 (39.2%) live in the town. There are only 123 Indians in the entire *municipio* and none of these live in the town. It may be seen from these figures that of the two towns, Teculután would seem to have a relatively larger upper class, whereas San Agustín, with its high Indian population, probably has more labor at its disposal. The Indians of San Agustín may probably be considered as Ladinoized, since they are reported to retain no language of their own and no clothing differences were noted.[69] They are distinguished today by the upper and middle class townspeople as the people who live in *ranchos* or simply as "*los indios.*"

In Teculután the upper class was said to be composed of descendents of old families which became established in the colonial period, but that even here the redivision of lands through inheritance has led to a spreading out of the fortune over a number of people. Control of the critical source of wealth, however, the irrigation system, remains in the hands of the people who own the irrigated lands, the "inheritors," as they are known locally. In San Agustín the system is similar; there the owners of irrigated lands elect a *juez de agua* who makes decisions concerning the distribution of water.

The town of Gualán may also be considered a middle Motagua community, but it manifests certain differences from the two just described. Gualán also evidently has an old population, but the type of *finca* differs considerably, and the amount and type of Indians vary. While the valley floor *fincas* of Teculután and San Agustín are devoted to sugar and fruits, the *fincas* of Gualán tend more to specialize in coffee and even in cattle. There is also important irrigated sugar, fruit, and vegetable production in this *municipio*, but the *fincas* have tended to spread into the *montaña* land. With this there have developed to some degree an element of the semi-absentee landowner, so that the upper class of Gualán involves not only the local Old Ladinos, which are also found in other parts of the middle Motagua, but also an element of the cosmopolitan upper class which tends to have headquarters in the capital city rather than in a provincial region. The laborers on the *fincas* are predominantly Ladino, but there is also an important Indian element, much of which is migratory during the coffee harvest season, and which comes in from the Chortí region. It was reported that there were no resident Indians in the *municipio* who could be classified as Traditional.

The present population of Gualán (1950) is 16,367; of which only 10.7% are

---

[69] Stoll, 1938, p. 2, reports that this population was Pipil speaking but it is not clear whether the language was still in use at the time of his studies (1878–1883) or not. The vocabulary he gives is from Salamá.

Indian; 2,898 people live in the town of Gualán. The town is much more tropical and gives the impression of being somewhat less arid than did either of the two other towns described in this region. While there are a number of *fincas* in the region, there is also a fairly large population of small landholders and renters. By the time one has reached Gualán on a trip down the Motagua Valley he has reached the region where one may seriously consider travel by river in preference to land travel by horseback. The dugout canoe, which becomes increasingly important as one approaches the Atlantic coast, is important in the Gualán region.

So far as the writer could tell, the principal differences to be noted between the society and culture of Gualán, in comparison with that of Teculután and San Agustín, stem principally from the variations in economy and social structure.

The town of San Jerónimo geographically belongs to the Salamá Valley. Culturally and socially, however, it seems to fall well in with the towns of the middle Motagua. Like the *municipios* already described, the lands of San Jerónimo are divided into two principal types, the irrigated valley lands, also called *tierra caliente*, and the upper montaña lands, *tierra fría*. In terms of communication, the road winding over the Sierra de las Minas down to El Rancho on the Motagua is as important or more so than is that which goes via Rabinal to the capital city. San Jerónimo, like the towns in the Motagua Valley, has an upper class which is (probably) Old Ladino, but it is relatively small. Much of the land, however, is held in smaller holdings, and the upper class group is somewhat dependent upon commerce as well as agriculture. The upper class, less land based, does not have such control over the irrigated sections. The regulation of irrigation water is in the hands of the *municipalidad*, not of the owners of irrigated lands. In terms of general socio-economic groups, San Jerónimo is more similar to the towns of the upper Motagua than to those in the middle Motagua.

San Jerónimo had a population of 3,900 in 1950, of which 935 (24.0%) were Indian, and a town population of 824. At an altitude of 3,200 feet, it is shut in from the west by the Indian region which centers in Rabinal, to the north by the mountains of southern Alta Verapaz, to the south and west by the Sierra de Chuacus and Sierra de las Minas. All four towns included in this section are laid out on a generally rectangular grid pattern, although San Jerónimo somehow developed a triangular plaza.

6. THE LOWER MOTAGUA: MORALES

The lower Motagua region presents a very different feeling than is received as one moves up the river. Instead of a hot arid region, it is moist with a great deal of rainfall. As a result, the region, like almost the entire Atlantic coast of Central America, did not appeal to the Spaniards. Even in 1893, the entire Department of Izabal had a population of only 7,401, while the municipio of Gualán, the first of the arid valley spaces, had a population of 9,362. The population of Izabal, specifically in the section to the southeast of Lake Izabal, is New Ladino. In 1950 the census recorded 12,219 people in the municipio of Morales, of whom 3.9% were classed as Indian; in the town itself there were 2,143 people.

The town is located immediately adjacent to the United Fruit Company plantation known as Bananera, and is stretched out along the railroad right of way. Such communities, which are not unusual in the United States, are fairly rare in Central America, simply because the railroads are not so common. In keeping with its location in the Atlantic coast region, the buildings are almost entirely of wood boards with corrugated roofs.

The population of Morales comes from *"el interior,"* the up-country. Evidently very little movement has come from the Atlantic coast itself and there are very few Negroes. The banana plantation labor comes from Guatemala, Honduras, and El Salvador. An interesting indication of the recent movement of an old culture trait is seen in the report that the use of the wooden plow, an old Spanish implement common in the middle Motagua Valley, has been gradually increasing in the Morales area.

The writer could not clearly identify a series of social classes in Morales. Numerous factors have played a role in either inhibiting their development or in obscuring their nature if they are present. Basically there are three kinds of population in the region: the independent small landholders of the municipio of Morales; the labor on the banana plantation; and the employees and management of the plantation. Within the community of Morales, the management plays no particular social role, although the labor is important commercially. The community is formed around services for the plantation workers and the independent landholders. Since this population is new, there has been very little time for extreme wealth distinctions to develop. Much of it has probably come from the plantation labor; and others, such as the Chinese merchants, have come in for trade. Thus the social structure can, on the basis of a brief visit, be better described in terms of what is not present than in terms of a delineation of the nature of what is present. There seems to be no strong upper class, certainly no significant Old Ladino group; outside the banana plantations there is very little laboring group in the *municipio* itself. There are doubtlessly townspeople who never have been and never will be agriculturalists who may consider themselves somewhat better than the small landholders, but this is a small group and not extremely significant.

The river and its tributaries are important modes of travel in the municipio of Morales. Almost everyone living in the *caseríos* brings their produce to the rail stations by river. Most of the residences are strung out along the river banks, since water provides such an important means of transport. The rail line serves the purpose of taking people out of the region entirely to Zacapa or Puerto Barrios. The community of Las Quebradas, which used to be the municipal capital in the last century, is now the locale of an important plywood industry.

7. THE LADINOS OF THE EASTERN HIGHLANDS: SAN JOSE LA ARADA, ESQUIPULAS, SAN MANUEL CHAPARRON, AND MATAQUESCUINTLA

The term *oriente* to the Guatemalan usually conjures up a picture not dissimilar to that brought to the North American by the "wild west." It is reputed to be an area of individualism, of Ladinos, and of rough living. From the data collected on the survey, the east or *oriente* may be divided into at least four major regions: the Motagua Valley, the eastern highlands, and the southeastern highlands, and the southeastern coast. Subdivisions of the Motagua Valley have already been outlined, and the southeastern regions will be described in the next sections. Of these various regions, the traditional role of the *oriente* is probably to be found in the southeast highland region; the eastern highland region is an area which comprises principally the departments of Jalapa and Chiquimula, and which (as of 1950) were composed of 50.5% and 62.1%, respectively, of Indians. These two departments are not, then, to be characterized as "Ladino" but as mixed departments, and as is the case in the far west, a consideration of the Ladino population thereof must take into account these Indian majorities.

As may be seen on the map, there is a channel of Ladinos which breaks through along the border of Jalapa and Chiquimula and runs from the Motagua Valley down into the southeastern highlands. In this channel is located the municipio of San José la Arada. San José, with a population of 4,325, was recorded as having 797 Indians. The town itself numbers only 708 people, of whom 92.8% were called Ladinos. The town gives the appearance of a small community which has gone somewhat to seed, but has retained a frank charm in the process of doing so. The plaza, surrounded by low one-story white buildings, is unkept, and the church is in need of paint.

Apparently, on the basis of information provided by informants, the interpretation of the census as to who was Ladino and who Indian did not follow closely the local forms of classification. One informant said that the majority of the municipal population (although not necessarily that in the town) was Indian, and another, that there were Indians in all the *aldeas*. They seemed in agreement that this Indian population is what we have been calling Ladinoized Indians; they spoke no Indian language and retained no particular Indian clothing. What this indicates is that the channel down from the Motagua Valley, which we have believed to be Ladino, may not be so much Ladino as it is ladinoized. The entire population is generally classified in terms of *pobre* and *acomodado*; the former includes almost all the Indians and various Ladinos, while the latter is restricted to a small group of Ladinos who are probably what we would consider as Old Ladinos. One informant felt that a third group existed between this upper class and the lower, since the latter were principally agriculturalists. The middle group was composed of people who worked directly in stores or as craftsmen, such as masons, carpenters, and so on.

There is some irrigated land around the town, and the people who own it elect a *juez de agua* who is in charge of distributing the water and settling disputes. This is clearly the same general pattern of local irrigation control by the owners which exists in the Motagua Valley. Most of the land, as is the case in the upper Motagua Valley, is in small holdings, but much of it is also located in the rough hill regions and not extremely good for agriculture. In the lower lands there are two plantings a year. There is, evidently, a fairly large number of people who have no lands or whose lands are too poor for effective agriculture. According to one informant, people from this population group had in recent years taken over political control in the town from the old upper class.

The town of Esquipulas, famous because of the fact that the shrine of the Black Christ is located there, provides a situation which is slightly different from that found in San José. Whereas the Indian population of San José is Ladinoized, that in the municipio of Esquipulas should better be classified as Modified. Some 36.6% of the municipal population of 11,942 is recorded as Indian in the 1950 Census; 2,844 people, 25.0% of whom are Indian, live in the town. The population of Esquipulas, according to informants, in some part drifted in from Honduras. A portion of them, it is clear, live off the pilgrim trade which keeps *pensiones* full for at least half the year. It is probably significant that Esquipulas, as the greatest pilgrimage center in Central America, should have a different saint as the patron of the town. *Santiago*, and not the Black Christ, is the patron saint of the town, and the fiesta in its celebration is sponsored by a Ladino municipal committee and an Indian *cofradía*. The two main celebrations, during which pilgrims come to visit the shrine of the Black Christ, are referred to locally as *ferias*, not as *fiestas*.

The community of Esquipulas lives in general very much like other communities, except for the fact that there is a population which depends almost entirely upon the pilgrim trade. The town is laid out on a general rectangular plan and is divided into five *barrios*, three of which are inhabited generally by the wealthier and the two others are inhabited principally by the poorer agriculturalists and laborers.

San Manuel Chaparrón is a small *municipio* to the south of the Indian town of San Luis Jilotepeque. San Luis has been the scene of fairly intensive studies of Ladino-Indian relations.[70] San Manuel was included on the survey because it appealed to the writer as being an almost completely Ladino town (as opposed to a mixed town as San Luis), but one in which the culture of the Ladinos should be similar to that in San Luis. The population of San Manuel in 1950 was 3,251, of which 11.8% were Indian (as opposed to the 60.3% of the San Luis population which is Indian). The town itself has a population of only 737. As was the case in the western highlands, there are certain cultural similarities between the Ladinos in San Manuel and the neighboring San Luis Indians. The same general concepts of sickness hold, although there is little doubt that the concepts as described by Gillin[71] are somewhat watered down; the differences are, however, a matter of degree and not of kind. The San Manuel Ladinos were reported to look to the San Luis Indians for *curanderos*, the same situation which holds between Ladinos and Indians in the west. One informant indicated that there was a recognized difference between the Indians of San Luis, among whom the women wear a distinctive dress and who speak the Pocomam language, and the people who are called Indians in the municipio of San Manuel, and who live in a few local *aldeas* and have neither language nor clothing distinctions. There is some contact between the Ladinos of San Manuel and those of San Luis; the writer's informant in San Manuel had worked in the *municipalidad* in San Luis at the time that Tumin and Gillin were there.

---

[70] E.g. Gillin, 1951; Tumin, 1952.   [71] 1948, 1951.

San Manuel, scattered out more or less in a grid pattern, is set in the middle of a rough, arid 3,100 foot plateau, covered with black scrub trees and bushes, and the surface of which is composed of powdery black and white volcanic sand and ash. The land is divided up into both large and small holdings; and informants agreed that there were three social classes present, the large landholders, small landholders and the laborers.

Mataquescuintla is an old community. Only 3.8 % of the *municipio* population of 11,259 were recorded as Indian in 1950; 2,189 people lived in the town proper. It is laid out in the grid pattern in the bottom of a 5,000 foot valley surrounded by hills. While it is connected by road with Jalapa, Barberena, and Guatemala, only the last is passable throughout most of the year. The surrounding region is dotted with fairly good sized *fincas*, many of which are devoted to coffee. It seems likely that a good portion of the population should be considered as New Ladino, since the census of 1893 assigns a much higher percentage of Indians to Mataquescuintla than is assigned in 1950. This population is probably an important part of the coffee labor today. In the town proper there is a fairly substantial population of Old Ladinos, however, and like Gualán, there are also some semi-absentee owners who may form a cosmopolitan upper above this group.

8. THE LADINOS OF THE SOUTHEASTERN HIGHLANDS: ATESCATEMPA, QUESADA, BARBERENA, PETAPA

Arbitrarily, for so must such a delineation be, we may say that the southeastern highlands compose the highland portions of the departments of Jutiapa, Santa Rosa, and the southern portion of the Department of Guatemala. This region differs from the eastern highlands in that where there are remaining Indian populations they are generally Ladinoized Indians. The writer knows of no community or remnant of a Modified Indian population, not to speak of a Traditional Indian group, in this region. This highland area is generally lower than that of the eastern highlands, and becomes gradually lower as one moves towards the El Salvador border.

The community of Atescatempa has long been a Ladino community; with a municipal population of 5,904 in 1950, the town had a population of 1,017. Its social structure is basically similar to that of the middle Motagua Valley; there is a limited amount of irrigated lands and these are controlled by some 16 families. There are two types of land besides the irrigated, the *planos* and the *montaña*, basically the same distinction which is found elsewhere. A point of importance here in the southeastern region is that on the upper portions of the *montaña* cattle are usually grazed. Atescatempa is somewhat unique in that it has within its boundaries one of the few lakes of Guatemala, and while small, it is an important fishing center in season. The Ladinos of Atescatempa consider themselves to be quite distinct from the Ladinoized Indians of some of the neighboring *municipios* which lie to the south and west. There seems fairly clearly to exist an Old Ladino group here, perhaps basically similar in general structure to the middle Motagua region.

The town of Quesada is even "more" Ladino than Atescatempa, if possible.

According to the census, 30 of the total population of 5,794 are Indian. Quesada is unique among the towns visited on the survey in that it is established on a large area of communal lands. Until the latter part of the last century, most of the land in what is now the *municipio* belonged to a large *finca*. For some reason, the *finca* was broken up and the people of the then *aldea* of Quesada purchased the *finca* by pooling their funds. A certain portion of the lands were set aside as communal, and the remainder were divided up among the community members. As a result, the main social distinction, which exists today, is that which stands between the descendents of the families who made the original purchase and who, as inheritors, have land of their own and the right to use the communal lands, and those people who have moved in since and have no lands of their own. Very little land is irrigated, and so no social distinctions have developed about this point. There are, however, evidently relatively few people in the *municipio* who do not have access to the communal lands for planting, if they do not have lands of their own. Those who have no private land usually go out for coffee harvests to other regions, but return to work as *mozos* here. There is some specialty in the production of tobacco in the *municipio*, and since two crops of corn may be taken out, a second is frequently planted following the tobacco harvest in September.

Quesada is laid out on the rectangular grid pattern and gives the appearance of being a neat and orderly community. It would warrant study from a number of points of view, particularly because it seems to be a recent stabilization of a community society through the establishment of the communal lands and the organization of the inheritors of the land.

The municipio of Barberena, the largest in the Department of Santa Rosa, has a population of 15,768. It counts among its rural dwellers almost 1,800 Indians, but the remaining population is Ladino. The town itself has only 2,098 inhabitants. Barberena, like Mataquescuintla, has a number of fairly large *fincas* as well as smaller ones. It produces a good deal of coffee and as a result has a fairly large labor force resident in the *municipio*. Local estimates placed about a quarter of the population as landholders, another quarter as renters, and the remaining half as *colonos*, or farm laborers. Almost all the Indian population are *colonos*. In general, there seem to be no socially important differences between the poor Ladinos, who doubtless in their majority are New and/or Mobile, and the Indians, who are Ladinoized. An unexpected settlement pattern, which it was not possible to confirm, was reported by one informant. He stated that the local upper class lived around the edge of town, and not in the center as is the classic Spanish colonial and Latin American pattern.

There is evidently no important difference recognized between particularly high and low lands within the *municipio*; the whole region is considered as *tierra templada*. The region is too high (3,800 feet) for a double corn harvest.

The municipio of San Miguel Petapa, located just north of Lake Amatitlán, is a case of one of those communities which has declined in importance rather than grown. In the census of 1893 Petapa had a population of over 13,000 people; in 1950, there were 2,147. Of these, 1,359 lived in the town. Petapa was an important town in the colonial period and has evidently seen a decline only recently.

In 1893 it was the third largest *municipio* in what is now the Department of Guatemala, although the size of the town population itself has not changed substantially since that time (1,374 in 1893 to 1,359 in 1950). One reason for its decline may be the fact that it suffered greatly in the earthquake of 1917. At that time most of the homes were made of *adobe* brick, and most of them fell.

There are three *fincas* within the municipal area, but most of the townspeople work on their own land or rent land, or, prior to the Agrarian Reform, used municipal land. There is a certain amount of irrigated land in the *municipio*, but it is pretty well divided up or in fincas. The informant felt that two social grades could be distinguished among the people who lived in the *municipio*, a medium wealthy group and the poor; there are no rich people living there he said.

Many towns of the southeast highlands share certain characteristics with those of the Motagua Valley; there are present both Old and New Ladinos. However, there seems to be a larger proportion of the latter in the southeast. Another important difference is that the landscape itself has not offered the extensive irrigation possibilities which were available in the middle Motagua. Where irrigation has been possible, it has been used, but there seldom has been enough of it to form a strong Old Ladino class.

9. THE SOUTHEAST COAST: GUAZACAPAN AND THE *BARRIO* SAN SEBASTIAN

From the point of view of a survey of this kind, the southeast coast region is an area which is relatively isolated. A good road takes one into the principal coastal town of Santa Rosa, and then stops. As a result, it was not feasible to include a town in the survey in the coastal region of Jutiapa. The only community included on the survey was the town of Guazacapán which, after having been surveyed, appealed to the writer as being somewhat atypical of the region in many ways.

Guazacapán is located at an altitude of about 1,000 feet, on the coastal plain which slopes down from the piedmont to the sea. The *municipio* itself had a population of 5,251 in 1950, of which 57.4% were classified as Indian. The majority of the population, about 64%, live in the town. A situation which makes Guazacapán rather unusual for the country as a whole is that the majority of the Indians live in the town and not in the country. It is, basically, the same situation which we find in the *barrio* of monimbó in Masaya, Nicaragua; there is a *barrio* of "urban" (in that they live in town) Indians. Guazacapán shares this unusual feature with the neighboring municipio of Chiquimulilla and with that of El Adelanto in Jutiapa; elsewhere in the southeast, where there are surviving Indian societies, they live principally outside of the municipal capital.

These *barrio* Indians are outstanding examples of Ladinoized Indians. In Guazacapán the Indians are confined principally to the *Barrio de San Sebastián* and some also live in the *Barrio de San Pedro*. The Indian language is now retained by only a few of the older men; neither the women nor any of the younger people speak it. There is no "typical" costume worn by either sex. The Indian community is endogamous; its members do not even marry the Indians of the neighboring municipio of Chiquimulilla. When asked in what ways he felt that his group differed from the Ladinos, the writer's Indian informant said that the Indians lived in a different *barrio*, were more religious, and were poorer. There are various other differences as well; the houses in the Indian *barrio* are generally of *bajareque* with roofs of straw; the Ladino houses are generally of *adobe* and tile. The Indian homes are built with the aid of friends; the Ladino homes are built by a mason or contractor.

Among the Ladinos themselves there are evidently recognized classes, although there is no strong residential pattern associated with them. An upper class of large landholders and merchants, a middle class of shopkeepers and medium landholders, and a lower class of small landholders, agricultural workers and renters. The Indians are evidently considered as a caste apart, for the informant describing the class system kept the lower Ladino class distinct from the Indians.

Guazacapán, as a *municipio*, has a very small area and has not had the population growth witnessed by the two towns (Taxisco and Chiquimulilla) on either side. From the writer's knowledge of the region, there are to be found a considerable number of immigrants in the entire southeast coast and piedmont region who have come during the last fifty years. This population is principally Ladino, and in many cases families which would elsewhere be considered as Old Ladino. They are often people who have been somewhat unsuccessful or poor elsewhere, and have moved to the coast to see if they could do better. Most of them have probably come out of the adjacent eastern and southeastern highland region.

10. THE CENTRAL SOUTH COAST: SIQUINALA AND LA GOMERA

The central south coast of Guatemala comprises principally the Department of Escuintla. Although almost 16% of the departmental population was classified as Indian in 1950, the great majority live in a limited number of *municipios* in the north, specifically Santa Lucía Cotzumalguapa, Palín, and Escuintla itself. The remainder is almost entirely Ladino. The municipio of Siquinalá is actually atypical in that 22.4% of its population of 5,578 were classed as Indian. Siquinalá, however, is near the piedmont, and in this department the relative number of Indians decreases markedly as one goes towards the coast. The town itself, now with 773 people, has seen practically no growth since 1893 when the population was 734; in this it is an extreme, but not unusual since other towns in the central Escuintla region have seen relatively slight urban growth during the period. The population of the *municipio* has just about doubled in this time.

There are generally two social classes recognized in the town, the *sociedad* and the *popular*. The *sociedad* includes both the Old Ladino residents, landholders, and the more wealthy merchants. The *popular* includes both a Ladino lower class and a Ladinoized Indian population which tend to distinguish themselves from each other. Evidently a great proportion of the increase in population in the areas outside the town has been *finca* labor which has come down to the region during the past three and four generations from the highlands. As such, there are numerous Indians who may have come from Modified or Traditional

Indian settlements but which now fall into the Ladinoized Indian or New Ladino categories. The region also sees a considerable influx of annual migratory labor. One large cane plantation, it was reported, has as many as 1,500 men coming in from the highlands every season to cut sugar cane; and the coffee *fincas* always draw a large group of families, women and children as well as men, from the highlands. Perhaps one quarter of the *municipio* is in small landholdings and the remainder is in large *fincas*. The social structure then involves a combination of the cosmopolitan upper class, the local upper and Old Ladino class, and the combination of the lower class elements just described.

At the time of Barrios the town owned *ejidal* lands, which were divided into smaller holdings. These are the lands which now form the major *fincas* of the *municipio*; they were gradually sold, and bought up into large holdings. The town itself is laid out in the rectangular grid pattern, but oriented now along the main coastal highway which runs directly through it. The houses of the more wealthy are of vertical boards and corrugated roofs, while those of the poorer, around the outskirts, are the pole and palm leaf *ranchos*.

As one moves towards the Pacific Ocean, the towns tend to take on a slightly different appearance. Instead of having the main buildings built one immediately next to the other, in the Spanish pattern, they tend to be spread out in the same manner as are *ranchos*. Thus in La Gomera, while many of the houses are of vertical boards, the town presents a very different appearance than does Siquinalá. The houses are set precisely on the street, but there is a yard between, and palm trees provide shade for much of the town.

There seems to be no particularly wealthy upper group in La Gomera. The town has 392 people at present, an increase over the 216 which were reported in 1893. The *municipio* in all has 3,891, most of which are *finca* laborers, small landholders, or renters. There are a number of large *fincas*, but the owners form part of the cosmopolitan upper class and are not residents in La Gomera itself. In the town the group which comes closest to forming an upper class are the small merchants and the entrepreneurs in lumber, transportation, and so on.

The population of La Gomera impressed me as having a relatively high component of negro ancestry. If so, it is probably one of the few population groups in Guatemala which show any particular retention of such traits.

11. THE MODIFIED INDIAN COMMUNITIES OF THE SOUTHWEST COAST: PATULUL, SAN ANTONIO SUCHITEPEQUEZ, AND SAN RAFAEL TIERRA DEL PUEBLO

In order to survey communities in the southwest coast which contained Ladino populations, it was necessary to visit Indian towns. The southwest coast departments of Suchitepéquez and Retalhuleu are composed principally of Modified Indian populations; within each municipal capital there is a population of Ladinos which may or may not form an actual majority, but which generally is considerably larger, proportionally, than are such Ladino populations in the western highlands.

Of the three communities listed above, the first two are municipal capitals;

the last is an *aldea* of Indians. This entire region has been included in McBryde's monograph on the economic geography of southwestern Guatemala[72] and so there is little which needs to be added here on that count.

Patulul and San Antonio Suchitepéquez may be discussed together. Both are *municipios* which have a majority of Indians in their total populations (62.7% and 74.5%) but in the municipal capitals of which the Ladinos form the majority (57.2% and 68.9%). Both are located at the base of, or in, the piedmont at an altitude of about 1,200 feet (no altitude reading was taken in San Antonio). Both are in a coffee region and much of the Indian and poorer Ladino population live and work as *colonos* on the *fincas*. Among the Ladinos of Patulul there were a few older families which formed something of an upper class, but as is the case throughout the piedmont region from Escuintla west, there is also a cosmopolitan upper class of *finca* owners. The Indian population of Patulul tends to be concentrated in one of its five *barrios* and on the outskirts of the town.

The Ladino population of San Antonio is similar to that already described for other parts of the south coast; most of it comes from other regions. The informant, who arrived 34 years ago, said that when he first knew San Antonio it was much more Indian than it is now. While there has been some change of Indians to Ladinos, most of the Ladino population has come in from elsewhere. The Indians who have tried to change over, he said, have been accepted neither by their Indian families nor by the Ladino society; they must go elsewhere to live.

The Ladinos of this piedmont region have not had to learn an Indian language; most of the Indians, except a few of those who have recently arrived from the highlands, are bilingual. The *aldea* of San Rafael Tierra del Pueblo is an example of such an Indian community. The population has been established for some time, living (in this case) on land that belongs to the municipio of Mazatenango; for this reason, the name, *tierra del pueblo*. This community was included on the survey because it had been described to the writer as a Ladino community; in fact, it was composed wholly of Modified Indians, all of whom spoke *Quiché*, while most of the men were bilingual. The *aldea* was completely rural; the center consisted of no more than a church, the school, the auxiliary *juzgado*, and three or four homes. There were no evidences that anything in the way of social class existed.

Unfortunately, too little study has been given to the Indians of this piedmont and coast region. We have no accurate information on whether much of this Indian population has been here for a matter of decades or a matter of centuries, although it is well known that some portion of the piedmont Indian population was brought down to work on the coffee plantations.

12. A SOUTHWEST LADINO PIEDMONT COMMUNITY: FLORES COSTA CUCA

The community of Flores Costa Cuca is something of an exception to the general picture of southwest coast communities drawn in the last section. Like Patulul and San Antonio, Flores is located in a *finca* region, but at an altitude

---

[72] 1945.

of about 2,000 feet. It is, as a result, literally submerged in coffee *fincas*. The Ladino population has also been submerged in the Indian population which lives throughout the surrounding region. Nevertheless, of the entire municipal population of 5,425, 51.9% are Ladinos and of these only 398, or 14.1%, live in the municipal capital. There is thus located in the middle of the Modified Indian *finca* population a rural Ladino population.[73]

There are evidently four or five Old Ladino families in town who have small *fincas* nearby from which they make a good living; most of the rest of the population work on the nearby *fincas*. There are very few small landholders except that most people have taken possession of the plot of land on which their house is located. Many also move down to the lower part of the *municipio* and neighboring coastal *municipios* to rent land on which they plant *milpa*. Even though much of the population is land poor, they are what should be considered as Old Ladinos. The only social distinctions are: (1) between those two or three dozen people who are members of, and related to, the few landowning families and who are "better educated;" and the "*más humilde*" Ladinos; and (2) between the Ladinos in general and the Indians.

The town itself was one of the prettiest visited in the course of the survey. Laid out in the rectangular grid system, it was made up of whitewashed board buildings, and impressed the survey team as being extremely neat and well ordered. This may, in part, have been due to the fact that on the day of their visit the Bishop of Quezaltenango was in town confirming children.

13. A MIXED TOWN OF THE COASTAL BORDER AREA: CATARINA

In many ways the town of Catarina should be discussed together with Patulul and San Antonio Suchitepéquez; it is a *municipio* located at about 1,000 feet above sea level with a total population of 8,808, of which 49.5% are Indian. In the town itself the population is 642, of which 40.5% are Indian.

Here, as in Escuintla, the coast itself is almost entirely Ladino, and as one moves towards the piedmont, the relative number of Indians increases. Tradition has it that Catarina was a *municipio* until 1871, at which time Barrios changed it into an *aldea* of Malacatán; in 1925, it again was made a *municipio*. The original population is said to have come down from San Pedro Sacatepéquez. In the intervening years, however, Ladinos have come in from various other parts of Guatemala and from Mexico. The Indians are Modified, the women wear the typical yellow skirt of San Pedro and speak Mam. The men and many of the women are bilingual.

Due evidently to the fact that the population of Ladinos is recent and still mobile, there has not developed a strong "*sociedad*" or upper class here. There are medium wealthy merchants and small farmers, cosmopolitan *finca* owners, and there may be crystallizing an "Old Ladino" group. The principal large holdings are devoted to cattle raising, and there are a few people who live as *colonos*

---

[73] The writer has not been able to locate any satisfactory historical data on the town from the more readily available sources, and so does not know when it was created as a *municipio*. It is mentioned neither in the 1893 Census nor in Reyes, 1951.

on the farms. The majority of the people were reported to be small landholders or land renters. This region has seen a considerable population movement back and forth across the border with Mexico. There are people of Mexican origin to be found here, and Guatemalans to be found on the other side.

V. DISCUSSION

In the preceding sections we have presented data on the general culture of the town and country-dwelling Ladinos of Guatemala. We have seen some of the ways in which their culture is similar to that of the Indians of the country, and have discussed some of the relationships which exist between the groups. Our purpose in this, the final section, is to bring some of the data together to give some structure to our somewhat fragmented picture.

One factor which has pressed itself upon us in preceding sections is the degree to which Ladino culture and society may be described in terms of geography. Some of the regions involved are obvious: the Motagua Valley, the lower eastern highlands and south coast. Even ladinoization has to some degree followed geographic lines: the Pacific piedmont is the principal area of Modified Indians. This series of correlations between geography and culture have a solid historical base; there is no need to call upon mystic hypotheses of geographic influences. The Ladinos did not care[74] for the *altos* of the western highlands; the lower areas permitted at least two crops a year, and with irrigation sometimes three. The Spanish liked specifically temperate climates; they did not colonize the low Pacific coast nor the tropical forests of the Atlantic.

The contemporary populations of Ladinos to be found along the Pacific coast and in the tropical area of southeastern Izabal do not, in general, date back to the colonial period. The Spanish had only enough men in such regions to keep a port open. These regions have been opened up by Ladinos of recent generations and by foreign enterprises.

From this it seems that we may classify Ladino settlement and expansion into at least two periods and types: the settlement and areas occupied by Spaniards; and the more recent movement of Ladinos. From the data available, the Spanish settlements seemed to have concentrated as follows:

(1) The Motagua River: the area on both sides of the river was settled by Spaniards from the Izabal-Zacapa border up as far as the tributaries in the Department of Quiché. This particular series of settlements provided a long semicircle, running from northeast to the west.

(2) The Sacatepéquez and Guatemalan valleys and plateaus: the first Spanish capitals were in the temperate highlands of Sacatepéquez and Guatemala; these reached out to the northeast to meet those of the Motagua Valley.

---

[74] Saying that a population group did not "care" for something, of course begs the question. However, we are going for the present to leave our description in this form; we do not know whether they did not "care" for the *altos* because the climate did not agree with them, because the Indians made it more difficult to gain adequate labor for enterprises, because the area seemed too rough and foreboding for a conqueror, because the hills would not give as high a yield as did the more temperate areas or for some other reasons.

(3) The eastern highlands: following the north-south Chiquimula corridor there developed the trade route into El Salvador, and with it a Ladino corridor (much later the railway came through the same region). This brought the Spanish around the Jalapa and Chiquimula highlands, leaving them predominantly Indian, into the somewhat lower southeast highlands.

(4) The southeastern highlands: why this particular area became a region of Ladino settlement must remain for the present a matter of speculation. Whether there is something to the idea that the non-Maya cultures were less resistent to overtures to acculturation, or whether this ladinoization is actually a fairly recent event and to be correlated with the development of coffee in highland Santa Rosa and western Jalapa, the writer does not know. In any case, with the exception of the north-south belt of mixed *municipios* running across Jutiapa, this region is principally Ladino today.

(5) Scattered western highland settlements: finally there are scattered towns through the western and northern highlands, such as San Carlos Sija and Zaragoza; the history of these exceptions to the general Spanish settlement patterns must be sought individually.

This general pattern of settlement, with the possible exception of the southeastern highlands, can be traced today in both the culture and the society of the contemporary inhabitants. Culturally, there are a number of traits which (in the Ladino culture) follow this areal distribution: the wooden plow, the *trapiche*, and the hooked machete (*calabozo*). Socially, this is the region in which is found what we have called the Old Ladinos; the "irrigation aristocracy" is most clearly developed; and (although not the only region) it is a region in which Ladinoized Indians remain as sl. er members of the lower class. In the eastern highlands and on the borders of the region elsewhere, there are communities of Modified Indians.[75]

The importance of these colonial settlements in Guatemala as a whole was not merely that they were the locales in which the Spanish society settled and from which Ladino society generated, but they were also the centers from which the Spaniards carried their culture to the Indians. In this process of directed culture change, there were two general distinct geographical results: first, some traits gradually spread over the entire Maya highlands, such as Catholicism, sodalities, the structure of the centralized political system, sickness concepts (*ojo, pujo, pasmo, empacho*, hot-cold ideas), agricultural crops (vegetables, fruits, grains) and tools (the hoe, machete), and domesticated animals. Second, some traits followed what appeared to be limited colonial distribution patterns. Certain of these patterns are fairly well defined. The introduction of wheat and sheep was limited by climate and followed the higher altitudes. Sugar cane and the sugar press (*trapiche*) followed the lower and temperate altitudes, but also went specifically in a line extended from the upper Motagua overland to Huehuetenango. The wooden mortar follows pretty much the distribution of rice and to some extent *maicillo*. Other traits, specifically the idea of raising a grind-

---

[75] This region, it seems clear, forms part of a greater "colonial Ladino" region with portions of El Salvador; at the time of writing this has not been explored.

ing stone off the ground so that one stands while grinding corn instead of kneeling, the hooked machete[76] and the wooden plow have a distribution which duplicates that of the *trapiche*. The eastern and Motagua regions form a Ladino end of this distribution, and Huehuetenango forms an Indian end.

The more recent expansion and movements by Ladinos has followed a rather different pattern and in it has entered a new factor. The Spanish settlement was simply a case of Spaniards coming in with their traits and introducing their traits into a region through settling there or through directed culture change through such agents as the priests. By the time this general pattern was becoming established and was developing into a Spanish-American pattern through the concomitant adoption of Indian traits (the gradual dependence upon *milpa* crops, the adoption of the digging stick for working tougher terrain, the *rancho* type house among the poorer and for extra buildings) and adjustment to the local environment, the population was beginning to grow. The last half of the 19th Century can probably be set as the time that the Ladino society began to expand. This was due to two different causes: the population was growing through natural increase and some migration, and first coffee then bananas were introduced as plantation crops. These factors brought population movements among both the Ladinos and the Indians (although they were not always voluntary among the latter).

Among the Ladinos new areas began to fill up:

(1) The coastal region and piedmont of the southeast, specifically the departments of Jutiapa and Santa Rosa; and the coastal area of Escuintla, and probably to a lesser degree the lower coast of the remaining southwest coastal departments.

(2) The Atlantic lowland region of the southeastern half of the Department of Izabal.

(3) LaFarge mentions a third region which was opened up to Ladinos in this period, Huehuetenango. "During the last part of the 19th Century, there was a steady, concerted movement, with government backing, to establish Ladino colonies in the fertile lower parts of the Cuchumatán district, hitherto undisturbed Indian territory. The new townships of Quetzal, Barillas, and Nentón were thus created, while the older village of Santa Ana Huista was 'captured.' "[77]

From the point of view of contemporary Ladino distribution, however, another important movement was beginning, the migration (by force initially, later by custom) of Indians seasonally down to the coffee farms to work. One *finquero* describes how, early in the century, it was necessary literally to catch the Indians and bring them down annually; but each year a few would stay on, finding the economic security of the *finca* life somewhat better than the cultural security offered by highland isolation. In this way the southwestern and central piedmont gradually began to fill up with Indians who, in the process of resettlement, usu-

---

[76] The distribution of the hooked machete in the west is based on the survey by Goubaud, Rosales, and Tax (1944), in which they specify that the hooked machete in the west is called the *luk* and has no distributional connection which they could find with that in the east. However, on the present survey, we found the western extension of the *calabozo* to be at least to Joyabáj which suggests, since the intervening distance is not extreme, that there may once have been a connection in the distribution.   [77] LaFarge, 1940, p. 283.

ally changed from Traditional to Modified. Another phase of Indian movement began in the 20th Century as the pressure of a growing Indian population in the limited highland agricultural regions began to be felt. This was a movement, ever so slight though it may have been in the beginning, began to send people to the Pacific coast. It was generally Indians who were partially ladinoized, either individually or through living in constant contact with Ladinos, who packed up and moved south. Some did not make a permanent move, but started the seasonal migration for coastal plantings. The Ladinos in the highlands, feeling identical pressures, used identical solutions. Some went to the coast permanently, others initiated lowland planting (as was the case with the Palo Gordo and Palencia people) in addition to their highland cultivations.

So part of the "Ladino expansion" of the last century has really been combined with a process of ladinoization of migrant Indians. Those who came in large numbers and settled in colonies on the coffee *fincas* (as around Patulul, San Antonio) or in communities on the high coast (such as San Rafael Tierra del Pueblo) tended to retain enough of the general orientation of the Indian culture to settle in a Modified Indian status.[78] Those who went individually or went into enterprises in which they were thoroughly mixed with Ladinos, as on the plantations of the United Fruit Company and on the cattle *haciendas* of the low coast, became individually ladinoized and their children were New Ladinos.

The Ladino expansion has characteristics which are identifiable both socially and culturally. Socially, the groups to which we have referred as New Ladinos and Mobile Ladinos form the major part of the expansion. The Mobile Ladinos are those who come from a Ladino cultural background, principally from the east; the New Ladinos are those who have come out of an Indian background. These people, settling on the south coast, have concentrated principally in Escuintla and adjacent Santa Rosa; they have also been in movement in the southeast highlands, particularly in Santa Rosa. To the west, their movement has been limited by the coffee development and the consequent Indian migration in the piedmont of the western departments; there has been neither motivation nor space for Ladino expansion.

Culturally, the entrance of New Ladinos brought new syncretisms, such as the combination of the three cooking stones used by Indians on the ground, with the raised fire platform. Among Ladinos of the east, it has been customary to use a raised platform with a clay ridge called the *hornilla* set in a horseshoe shape on the platform. As the Indians from the west became Ladinos, they adopted the raised platform, but instead of using the *hornilla*, they placed their traditional three stones on top of the platform, thus in effect bringing the floor up to them.[79] Also, there evidently has followed a re-emphasis in familiar relationships. It was reported from some towns on the south coast, for example, that the marriage of first cousins, which was permitted (although not encouraged) among poorer people in the Old Ladino region, tended to be prohibited, although they still occurred. On the other hand, the relative number of common-law unions is evi-

---

[78] McBryde, 1945 pp. 33–35, provides data on the pre-coffee coastal situation.
[79] The Chortí Indians (see Wisdom, 1940, p. 132 and Fig. 5) use the *hornilla* on the floor.

dently much greater among the south coast Ladinos than among those of either the eastern or western highlands. Possibly, as reaction to the weakening familiar and kin unions, the extension of the incest prohibition to the children of *compadres* was reported in the same region. In the Old Ladino communities in the Motagua and the coast, it was reported that such unions were permissible.

Another aspect of the society of the new regions was that there usually did not exist the medium landholder class which formed the majority of the Old Ladinos of the Motagua and east; instead, the land was kept generally in large holdings and there was a wider social gap between the *finquero* or *hacendado* on the one hand and the Mobile and New Ladino labor on the other than was the case between the Old Ladino medium holders and the New Ladinos of the east and Motagua. The social situation, the wider gap plus the presence of a large proportion of Mobile Ladinos and New Ladinos who were also mobile, provided an area of potential political discontent which was fanned into flames by the government of 1950-1954.[80]

Besides these two major areas of Ladinoism, characterized by the social and cultural movements of the Spanish and the Ladinos, there are other factors which entered the picture of Ladino regional culture. One of the most important of these has been the fact of indigenous differences. It is not always possible to predict ahead of time if a given trait will react in the same manner when placed in two different cultural settings or not. We do know, however, that in some cases the nature of the Indian culture has tended to produce variations in the resultant Ladino culture. There are two general types of variations: those which occur wherever the Ladinos have close contact with the overwhelming Indian population of the west, and those which seem to be based on differences which may have been regional within the Indian culture. The tendency towards patrilocal residence noted in the Ladino towns of the western highlands would seem to be in some measure a result of the fact that these Ladinos live within the Indian region. The Indians themselves tend to be patrilocal. The use of the small wooden stool carved crudely in the shape of an animal is Indian, but is to be found in Ladino homes. The use of Indian curers, midwives, and curing techniques of course is dependent upon the presence of the Indian society and culture.

Regionally, there are certain traits which may be traceable to indigenous differences in the far southeast and east, but for the moment we can only speculate concerning them, since we have no supporting evidence. It cannot be decided here what the origins of these variations may be, but it is worth while pointing out that they exist. Among these are: the carrying of the water jug on the hip or on the hip and on the head, instead of only on the head; the use of the *bajareque* wall for house walls; the use of the *hornilla* instead of three cooking stones; and the use of the *tapesco* platform, the *aporreador*, outdoors for beating beans and *maicillo*.[81] The distribution of the term *espanto* for *susto* is limited to the Poco-

---

[80] See Newbold, 1954.

[81] The *aporreador* would seem to be Spanish in origin, since it is found all the way down through Nicaragua and occasionally in Panama; however, it is possible that it was associated with the Meso-American Indians of Mexican connection instead of Mayan connection; this is pure supposition, however.

mam and Chortí regions of eastern Guatemala; why one Spanish term should be used here, and another elsewhere is not clear.

It will be evident from this rather brief survey of Ladino culture in Guatemala that, at some phases, there is a difference of degree instead of kind between the Ladino culture and the neighboring Indian culture. This is particularly apparent in those phases of life where the beliefs and practices of the two ethnic groups overlap, such as in medicinal beliefs and practices. Thus *espanto* or *susto* are found in both cultures and (except in the central highlands) are associated with soul loss in both. The Indians, however, have a further elaboration, in certain places, of the kidnapping of the soul by a spirit; while the Ladinos have reduced the *susto* in the central highlands to a mere form of shock.

In matters of subsistence agriculture it is practically impossible to draw the line between contemporary Indian and contemporary Ladino. Of course, owners of the larger landholdings are not concerned with subsistence crops and so are not included in the generalization. Where one finds Indians using only a hoe and no plow, the Ladinos within the same region tend to follow the same practice (e.g., the Chimaltenango highlands); where the Ladinos use a wooden plow, so do the Indians, providing their land permits. Where the Indian plants with digging stick, so does the Ladino. And there is no ethnic distinction whatsoever with respect to the plants cultivated, only regional and local differences. Of course, when one enters the realm of social relations and general value system, then the great differences start to appear.

REFERENCES

(The titles listed here are those which are referred to in the course of the text; those in the Selective Bibliography which follows are a distinct set chosen as illustrative works concerning the Guatemalan Indian.)

HOC, Heritage of Conquest; the Ethnology of Middle America. By Sol Tax and Members of the Viking Fund Seminar on Middle American Ethnology. Glencoe, Illinois. 1952.

MCMMACA, Microfilm Collection of Manuscripts on Middle American Cultural Anthropology, University of Chicago, Chicago.

EMQ, Estadística, Mensaje Quincenal, Dirección General de Estadística, Guatemala.

Adams, Richard N., 1952. Un Análisis de las Creencias y Prácticas Médicas en un Pueblo Indígena de Guatemala. Publicaciones especiales del Instituto Indigenista Nacional, No. 17. Guatemala.

―――――, 1953. Cultural Survey of Panama, Part Two, this volume.

―――――, 1954. Cultural Survey of Nicaragua, Part Three, this volume.

Billing, Otto, John Gillin, and William Davidson, 1947–1948. Aspects of Personality and Culture in a Guatemalan Community: Ethnological and Rorschach Approaches. Journal of Personality, Vol. 16, No. 2 (1947) and No. 3 (1948), pp. 154–187, 326–368.

Behrendt, Richard F., 1949. The Uprooted: a Guatemalan Sketch. The New Mexican Quarterly Review, Vol. 19.

Bunzel, Ruth, 1952. Chichicastenango, A Guatemalan Village. Publications of the American Ethnological Society, XXII. New York.

Cámara, Fernando, 1952. Religious and Political Organization. In HOC, pp. 142–162.

Census, 1893. Censo General de la República de Guatemala; Levantado el 26 de Febrero de 1893 por la Dirección General de Estadística. Guatemala.

———, 1921. Censo de la Población de la República; Levantado el 28 de Agosto de 1921. Dirección General de Estadística. Guatemala.

———, 1950. Sexto Censo de Población, April 18, 1950. Guatemala. (Preliminary volume issued in 1953.)

de la Fuente, Julio, 1952. Ethnic and Communal Relations. In HOC, pp. 76–94.

Dirección General de Estadística, 1953. Departamentos, Municipios, Ciudades, Villas, Pueblos, Aldeas y Caseríos de la República de Guatemala. Guatemala.

El Espectador (newspaper), 1954. Extensión de tierras expropiadas por departamentos, desde enero de 1953 a mayo de 1954. (A graph prepared by the Agrarian Department). Año 1, No. 240, June 24, 1954, Guatemala.

Foster, George, ed., 1951. A Cross-Cultural Anthropological Analysis of a Technical Aid Program. (Mimeographed) Smithsonian Institution, Washington, D. C.

———, 1953. Relationships Between Spanish and Spanish-American Folk Medicine. Journal of American Folklore. Vol. 66, No. 261, pp. 201–217.

Gillin, John, 1948. Magical Fright. Psychiatry, Vol. 11, No. 4, pp. 387–400.

———, 1951. The Culture of Security in San Carlos; A Study of a Guatemalan Community of Indians and Ladinos. Publication No. 16 of the Middle American Research Institute, The Tulane University of Louisiana, New Orleans.

———, 1952. Ethos and Cultural Aspects of Personality. In HOC, pp. 193–212.

Goubaud, A., J. de D. Rosales, and Sol Tax, 1944. Reconnaissance of Northern Guatemala, 1944. MCMMACA No. 17.

Holleran, Mary P., 1949. Church and State in Guatemala. Columbia University Press, New York.

INCAP, 1953. Publicaciones Científicas del Instituto de Nutrición de Centro América y Panamá. Boletín de la Oficina Sanitaria Panamericana, Suplemento No. 1. Oficina Sanitaria Panamericana, Washington, D. C.

International Bank of Reconstruction and Development, 1951. The Economic Development of Guatemala. Report of a Mission. Washington, D. C.

King, Arden, 1952. Changing Cultural Goals and Patterns in Guatemala. American Anthropologist, Vol. 54, No. 1, pp. 139–143.

LaFarge, Oliver, 1940. Maya Ethnology: The Sequence of Cultures. In The Maya and Their Neighbors. D. Appleton-Century Company, New York.

McBryde, Felix Webster, 1945. Cultural and Historical Geography of Southwest Guatemala. Institute of Social Anthropology, Publication No. 4, Smithsonian Institution, Washington, D. C.

Maldonado Juárez, Luis Felipe, n.d. Las Tasas Demográficas. Dirección General de Estadística, Guatemala. (A mimeographed course in vital statistics.)

Newbold, Stokes, 1954. A Study of Receptivity to Communism in Rural Guatemala. Guatemala. (Mimeographed).

Orellana Gonzales, René Arturo, 1950. Estudio Sobre Aspectos Técnicos del Censo de Población. Facultad de Ciencias Económicas, Universidad Autónoma de San Carlos de Guatemala, Guatemala.

Paul, Benjamin D., and Lois Paul, 1952. The Life Cycle. In HOC, pp. 174–192.

Redfield, Robert, 1939. Culture Contact Without Conflict. American Anthropologist, Vol. 41, No. 3, pp. 514–517.

———, 1945. Ethnographic Materials on Aguas Escondidas. MCMMACA No. 3.

Reyes M., José Luis, 1951. Datos Curiosos Sobre la Demarcación Política de Guatemala. Guatemala.

Roberts, Robert E. T., 1948. A Comparison of Ethnic Relations in Two Guatemalan Communities. Acta Americana, Vol. VI, No. 3–4, pp. 139–151.

Siegel, Morris, 1941. Resistances to Culture Change in Western Guatemala. Sociology and Social Research, Vol. 25, No. 5, pp. 414–430.

Stoll, Otto, 1938. Etnografía de la República de Guatemala. Traducida del Alemán con Prólogo y Notas por Antonio Goubaud Carrera. Guatemala.

Tax, Sol, 1935. Miscellaneous Notes on Guatemala. MCMMACA, No. 18.

———, 1937. The Municipios of the Midwestern Highlands of Guatemala. American Anthropologist, Vol. 39, No. 3 (Part 1), pp. 423–444.

———, 1942. Ethnic Relations in Guatemala. America Indígena, Vol. II, No. 4, pp. 43–48.

———, 1952. Economy and Technology. In HOC, pp. 43–65.

Taylor, Douglas MacRae, 1951. The Black Carib of British Honduras. Viking Fund Publications in Anthropology, Number Seventeen, New York.

Tumin, Melvin M., 1952. Caste in a Peasant Society. Princeton University Press, Princeton, New Jersey.

Wagley, Charles, 1949. The Social and Religious Life of a Guatemalan Village. American Anthropologist, Memoir Number 71 (Vol. 51, No. 4, Part 2).

Wisdom, Charles, 1940. The Chorti Indians of Guatemala. The University of Chicago, Chicago.

SELECTED BIBLIOGRAPHY OF STUDIES OF GUATEMALA INDIAN COMMUNITIES

The following bibliography is prepared to aid those who may not be familiar with the Guatemalan Indian to gain some insight into the lives of the ethnic population which comprises over one half of the country's population. Many students have worked in Guatemala and many excellent studies have been published in scattered sources. The present bibliography does not pretend to honor all this work; for example, the entire microfilm series (MCMMACA) is omitted because it is not of ready accessibility to most people who might be interested. The selection has been guided by the following points: (1) is the data about a community, and do the sources, when taken together, provide the reader with some idea of the life of the members of that community; (2) are the sources generally available in Guatemala as well as elsewhere. The titles are grouped by Indian community or region. If the title is listed in the references, it is not repeated here, only the reference being given.

The Northwest Highlands

Community: *San Miguel Acatán*. This community was studied by Morris Siegel who has published a series of articles; three of these are now readily available in the volume, Readings in Latin American Social Organization and Institutions, Edited by Olen E. Leonard, and Charles P. Loomis (Michigan State College Press, 1953). These articles are: "Religion in Western Guatemala; A Product of Acculturation;" "Problems of Education in Indian Guatemala;" and "Resistance to Cultural Change in Western Guatemala."

Community: *Santiago Chimaltenango*. Studied by Charles Wagley who has published two monographs: Wagley, 1949; and Economics of a Guatemalan Village, American Anthropologist, Memoir No. 58, 1941.

Community: *Santa Eulalia*. The second town studied by LaFarge, published in a volume by the same name by the University of Chicago, 1947.

Community: *Todos Santos.* The religion and certain general customs are described by Maud Oakes in her "Two Crosses of Todos Santos" (Bollingen Series XXVII; Pantheon Books, 1951); Raymond Stadelman collected data on the agriculture, published in "Maize Cultivation in Northwestern Guatemala" (Contributions to American Anthropology and History, Vol. VI, No. 33, pp. 83–263, Carnegie Institution of Washington, Washington, 1940.)

The Western Highlands

Many studies have been carried on in the midwestern highlands, but unfortunately only Bunzel's work gives general, although restricted, coverage. Tax has various volumes proposed on Panajachel, and both Rosales and Paul have much data on San Pedro la Laguna.

Community: *San Pedro la Laguna.* Benjamin Paul has published: "Life in a Guatemalan Indian Village," (in Patterns for Modern Living, the Delphian Society, Chicago, 1950); "Symbolic Sibling Rivalry in a Guatemalan Indian Village," (in American Anthropologist, Vol. 52, No. 2, pp. 205–218); and "Mental Disorder and Self-Regulating Processes in Culture; A Guatemalan Illustration" (in the volume, Interrelations Between the Social Environment and Psychiatric Disorders, Milkbank Memorial Fund, 1953, pp. 51–67).

Community: *Chichicastenango.* The principal work is that of Bunzel (1952), although Tax has numerous notes in the MCMMACA series.

Community: *Panajachel.* The economy of a Guatemalan Indian village has been carefully analyzed by Tax in his "Penny Capitalism, A Guatemalan Indian Economy," (Institute of Social Anthropology, Publication No. 16, Smithsonian Institution, Washington, 1953.) He also has extensive notes in MCMMACA.

Community: *Magdalena Milpas Altas.* Besides Adams (1952) there are two articles on this Modified Indian community, by the same writer: "Informe Preliminar Sobre la Organización Social de Magdalena Milpas Altas, (in Antropología e Historia de Guatemala, Vol. III, No. 2, 1951, pp. 9–16); and "A Survival of the Meso-American Bachelor House," (in American Anthropologist, Vol. 54, No. 4, 1952, pp. 589–593). Further work, as yet unpublished, has been done by Raymond Amir.

The Eastern Highlands

Community: *San Luis Jilotepeque.* This town has seen intensive study at the hands of Gillin (1948, 1951) Billig, Gillin, and Davidson (1947–1948), and Tumin (1952), and so far is probably the best described social system in Guatemala. For students of Ladino culture this is fortunate because the writers have interested themselves in both the Ladino and the Indian issues.

Region: the *Chorti of the Department of Chiquimula.* One of the first full scale ethnographies (and probably the only one as opposed to a community study) on any Guatemala Indian group is that of Wisdom, (1940).

Besides these studies on special cultures and regions, the volume, *Heritage of Conquest* (HOC in reference list) is to be recommended as an attempt to synthesize our knowledge of Meso-America in general. It covers much of Mexico as well as Guatemala, but does provide various points of view. Tax (1937) is still a valuable introduction to the Indian communities of the western highlands. For the Black Carib, the work of Taylor (1951) is the only major publication to date, and the reader is referred to it for further bibliographical references.

Part Five

EL SALVADOR

WITH APPENDIX BY EDWIN JAMES

1955

EL SALVADOR

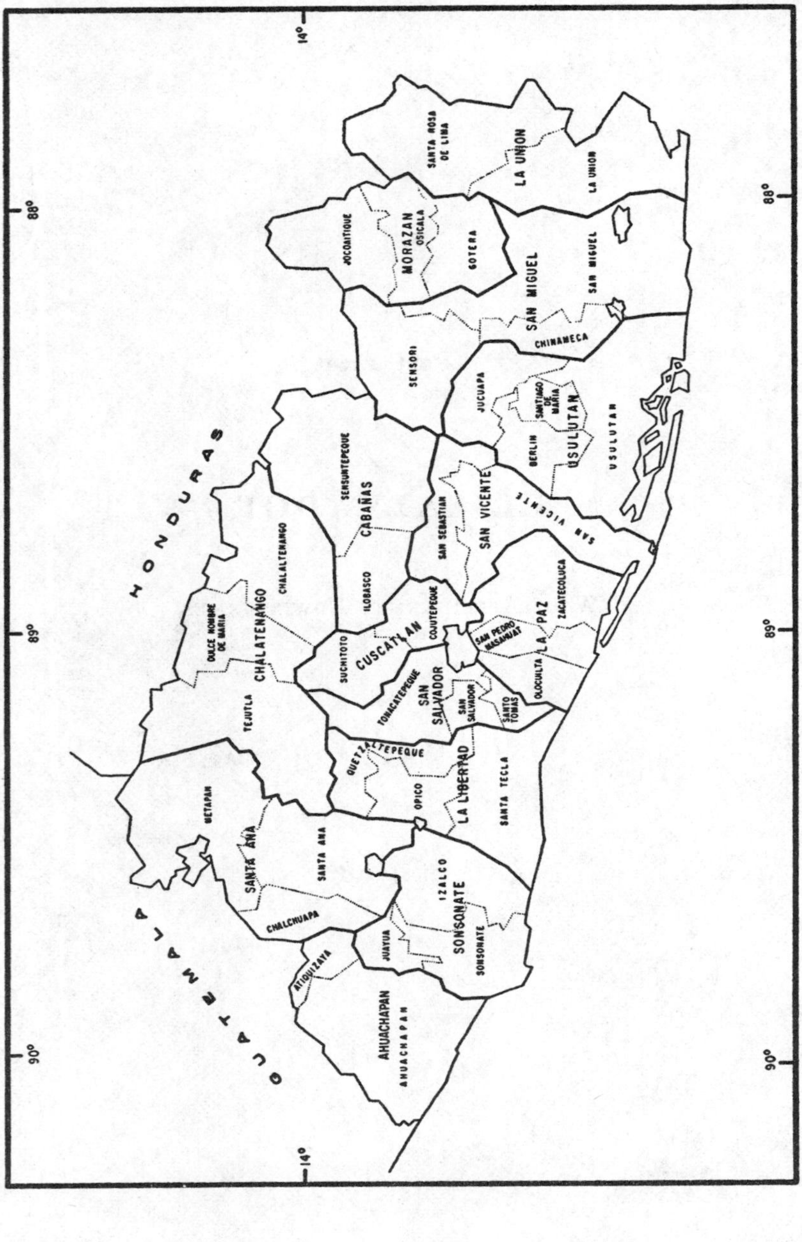
HONDURAS
GUATEMALA
14°
88°
89°
90°
SANTA ROSA DE LIMA
LA UNION
LA UNION
MORAZAN
JOCOAITIQUE
OSICALA
GOTERA
SAN MIGUEL
SAN MIGUEL
CHINAMECA
SENSORI
JUCUAPA
SANTIAGO DE MARIA
USULUTAN
USULUTAN
BERLIN
SAN VICENTE
SAN VICENTE
SAN SEBASTIAN
SENSUNTEPEQUE
CABAÑAS
ILOBASCO
CHALATENANGO
CHALATENANGO
DULCE NOMBRE DE MARIA
TEJUTLA
CUSCATLAN
SUCHITOTO
COJUTEPEQUE
SAN PEDRO MASAHUAT
LA PAZ
ZACATECOLUCA
OLOCUILTA
SANTO TOMAS
SAN SALVADOR
SAN SALVADOR
TONACATEPEQUE
QUEZALTEPEQUE
LA LIBERTAD
OPICO
SANTA TECLA
METAPAN
SANTA ANA
SANTA ANA
CHALCHUAPA
IZALCO
SONSONATE
SONSONATE
JUAYUA
ATIQUIZAYA
AHUACHAPAN
AHUACHAPAN

INTRODUCTION

The present study of El Salvador is the fourth in a series of general cultural area studies of the countries of Central America. As in the others in the series, the purpose has been to explore the culture and society of the country from a superficial point of view, to provide a general framework for examination of the culture of the *campesino*, and to point out some of the blanks in our knowledge concerning an important population group.

In a way, this study is the most difficult which the writer has attempted in this series. El Salvador, small, densely populated, with numerous small regional variations, dominated economically by a basic *finca* and *hacienda* economy, and hitherto little studied by social scientists, provides a confusing picture to the newcomer. Much time has been saved by the availability of Baron Castro's work on the growth of the Salvadorean population, a volume which is without parallel in the other Central American countries.[1] This book has brought together much of the scattered information from numerous historical sources which the present writer had neither the knowledge nor time to explore in a study of the present type.

As in other studies in this series, a variety of communities were visited and comparable data collected in each. This report is based on both the field information and those published sources which were available to the writer. Mr. Norman Craig helped in the interviewing in the western part of the survey. In addition to Mr. Craig, the writer is indebted to many other people for various kinds of aid: Dr. Juan Allwood Paredes, Director General de Sanidad; Dr. Alberto Aguilar Rivas, Dr. Julian Rodríguez; Dr. Joaquín Santos; Dr. Mario León U.; Dr. Alvaro Aldama; Mr. Fritz Loenholdt; Sr. Félix Choussy; Sr. Jorge Larde y Larin; Sr. Salvador Schapps y Sra.; the staff of the Biblioteca Nacional; Dr. Jorge Boshell; the Asociación Algodonera, and Asociación Cafetalera. Dr. George Foster kindly made available some notes on sickness and curing practices which he collected in San Salvador in 1951; and Mr. George Dudley gave permission to use material published earlier by the writer in the IBEC Housing Company's report on the Valle de la Esperanza. Transport on the survey was made available through the courtesy of the Dirección General de Sanidad. To all these people I want to express my gratitude, but of course I accept responsibility for the ideas and opinions expressed herein. Most of all, the writer is indebted to the numerous persons in the towns and countryside who served as informants. As has been the custom in these studies, their names shall remain unmentioned.

This report includes as an appendix a series of case histories, together with a brief analysis of sickness patterns collected by Mr. Edwin James in the *cantón* El Jícaro, San Matías. So far as the writer knows, Mr. James' work is the first descriptive endeavor of this type in El Salvador.

May, 1955　　　　　　　　　　　　　　　　　　　　　　　　　　　　　　　R. N. A.
Guatemala, C. A.

---

[1] Baron Castro, 1942.

TABLE OF CONTENTS

	Page
Introduction	415
I. The Population of El Salvador	419
II. The Culture of the Salvadorean Town and Country Dweller	428
1. Land, Labor, and Agriculture	428
2. Production, Transport, and Commerce	441
3. The Domestic Establishment	449
4. Family and *Compadrazgo*	455
5. General Social Structure	462
6. Local Political Organization	468
7. Religious Activities	472
8. Sickness and the Spirit World	478
III. The Indians of El Salvador	485
1. The Identification of the Indian and the Problem of Ladinoization	486
2. The Distinctive Culture of the Salvadorean Indians	491
IV. The Cultural Regions of El Salvador	500
V. Communities Visited on the Survey	507
1. Ladino Towns of the North: Texistepeque, Tejutla, Tejutepeque, and Guacotecti	507
2. Indian Communities of the Southwest: Ataco, Izalco, Jayaque, Panchimalco, and Santiago Nonualco	509
3. Towns of the Center Belt: San Matías, Tonacatepeque, Moncagua, and the Valle de la Esperanza	511
4. Towns of the East: Santa Elena, Conchagua, El Sauce, and Cacaopera	512
References	514
Appendix: Concepts of Sickness and Practices of Curing in the *Cantón* of El Jícaro, San Matías; A Series of Cases, Collected by Edwin James. 1954	515

I. THE POPULATION OF EL SALVADOR

The history of the Salvadorean population has been treated at some length by Baron Castro.[2] Our purpose in this chapter is not to repeat this work, but to supplement it with certain of the data which was not available to that writer, particularly the 1930 and 1950 population censuses, and to draw upon some of the information which may aid us in delimiting socio-cultural regions of the country.

The population of El Salvador was recorded as 1,855,917 in the Census of 1950, and the population density calculated as 93 per square kilometer in 1952. Baron Castro has indicated that the growth of the national population has been somewhat unequal. The earlier population was concentrated somewhat more in the central and western areas, and the eastern area has been catching up in recent years.[3]

The reason for this unequal growth is probably due in part to some recent migration into the eastern area as it has been more and more opened up for *hacienda* agriculture. However, there is evidence which suggests that the differential growth in the two areas, the west and central on the one hand, and the east on the other, may be due to the differential increase of the two principal ethnic groups, the Indians and the Ladinos. If we use the relative growth figures for the period 1778 to 1950 obtained from comparative census reports in Guatemala,[4] we find that the Indian population of that country has grown approximately 4.8 times, while the Ladino population has grown approximately 16.1 times. If we apply these figures to the 1796 census data from El Salvador for the respective ethnic groups, we find that on the basis of this growth differential alone, the percentage of the total population east of the Lempa rises from 17.7% in 1796 to 27.9% in 1950. The use of these estimates are, of course, far from exact, and there are obviously factors at work in El Salvador which have not been present in Guatemala. Nevertheless, the use of the differential growth rates would make the center and western part of the country grow relatively more slowly because the greatest part of the Indian population has been located in that section. The Indian population in the east was vastly outnumbered by Ladinos even as early as 1796[5] (see Table 17 in chapter on Indian Population).

---

[2] 1942.

[3] As Loenholdt has pointed out (1953, p. 12), Salvadoreans tend to think of their country in terms of three regional divisions: the west, which includes the departments of Santa Ana, Ahuachapán, and Sonsonate; the center, including the departments of La Libertad, Chalatenango, San Salvador, Cuscatlán, Cabañas, San Vicente, and La Paz; and the east, including the departments of Usulután, San Miguel, Morazán and La Unión.

[4] Adams, n.d. (c).

[5] The population of the east in 1796 was 25,401 Ladinos, 9,888 Indians. Applying respectively 16.1 and 4.8 to these gives us a hypothetical population for 1950 and 409,000 Ladinos and 47,300 Indians or a total in the east of 456,400; in the center and west, the 1796 figures were 52,624 and 73,122; applying the same factors, we get approximately 831,000 plus 350,000 or 1,181,000 for 1950. 456,300 is then approximately 27.9% of the total hypo-

This general growth information is available only in departamental terms. By comparing the 1930 and 1950 censuses, we can get more precise growth differential for recent years. During this period, there was an over-all increase of 32.8 % in the country's population. By districts,[6] however, this growth varied from a low of −6.6% in San Pedro Nonualco, to a high of +73.4% in the district of Opico. Of the total of 38 districts in the country, only ten had an increase larger than the national average, and only 3 of these were as much as 10% larger. The other 28 districts had population gains under the national average, and 16 of these had gains which were more than 10% less than the national average. The area of least relative gain was the entire coastal section of the west and the center, and a belt running through the center of the country from the coast to the Honduran border (the departments of La Paz, San Vicente, Cuscatlán, and the district of Dulce Nombre de María in Chalatenango). Only two districts west of the Lempa, Jucuapa and Gotera, showed such relatively low increases.

Table 1.—Variation of percentage of total population in each of the standard regions of El Salvador 1768 to 1950 (*Sources: Baron Castro, 1942; Censuses of 1930 and 1950*)

Region	1768–70	1878	1930	1950
East	17.7%	24.7%	28.0%	29.1%
Center	54.8	50.7	48.8	48.5
West	27.5	24.7	23.2	22.5
Total	100.0	100.1	100.0	100.1

There were three general regions of relatively high gain. The greatest were in the districts of Opico and San Salvador and there was also a slightly higher than average gain in the intervening district of Quezaltepeque. The second was that of most of the eastern coastal and low inland area, with particularly high gain in La Unión. And third, a somewhat higher than average gain appeared in the adjacent northwestern districts of Metapán and Tejutla. As will be noted later in the report, the areas which showed gain were areas which were predominantly Ladino, while most of the area showing little gain is occupied by Indians.

This general picture may be viewed in another way, but in a cruder geographical breakdown, by the average annual increment of population per department over the period of 1930 to 1950.[7] During this period, the average annual increase for the entire country was 13 per mil. In the coastal departments of the southwest and center, the average increases were: Ahuachapán 9.0 per mil;

---

thetical population of 1,637,300. The fact that the actual population in 1950 was over 200,000 larger than this sum indicates that conditions in El Salvador and Guatemala are not parallel, but the hypothesis of a differential growth in ethnic groups does seem to account for at least part of the differential growth geographically.

[6] A district is a political administrative unit which stands between the *municipio* and the department in size. See chapter on political organization.

[7] Data from *Boletín Estadístico*, II Epoca, Número 2, March and April, of 1952.

Table 2.—General population data

Districts	Total population 1930	Total population 1950	% increase	1952 Density per Sq. Kl.	Rural percentage 1930	Rural percentage 1950	Change
Ahuachapán	62,728	73,706	17.5	72	65.1	72.5	7.4
Atiquizaya	16,305	20,940	28.4	179	56.5	62.9	6.4
Santa Ana	100,990	131,468	30.2	176	58.6	62.2	3.6
Chalchuapa	30,344	39,063	28.7	118	65.6	69.2	3.6
Metapán	23,186	31,924	37.7	41	88.6	84.0	−4.6
Sonsonate	44,740	52,961	18.4	113	53.1	50.2	7.1
Izalco	42,836	51,507	20.3	99	64.5	71.4	6.9
Juayua	12,641	15,859	25.4	120	59.9	67.0	7.1
Chalatenango	40,774	51,196	25.6	76	67.0	69.0	2.0
Tejutla	27,519	37,047	34.6	40	81.0	81.2	0.2
Dulce Nombre de María	14,923	17,615	18.0	45	65.5	73.4	7.9
Santa Tecla	84,243	91,239	8.3	93	55.6	60.6	5.0
Quetzaltepeque	16,168	21,635	33.8	89	66.2	68.0	1.8
Opico	17,949	31,130	73.4	92	75.2	78.6	3.4
San Salvador	129,592	220,929	70.5	1475	19.1	13.6	−5.5
Tonacatepeque	38,091	48,830	28.6	103	70.5	71.7	1.2
Santo Tomás	23,442	26,693	13.8	139	63.4	69.4	6.0
Cojutepeque	59,613	62,020	4.0	202	68.8	72.6	3.8
Suchitoto	23,750	28,079	18.2	73	78.2	81.8	3.6
Zacatecoluca	42,965	51,830	20.6	91	63.3	70.2	6.9
San Pedro Nonualco	13,657	12,759	−6.6	143	47.1	57.1	10.0
Olocuilta	14,768	16,653	12.8	78	46.2	58.0	11.8
San Pedro Masahuat	14,242	15,501	9.5	64	48.5	57.9	9.5
Sensuntepeque	32,321	42,350	30.7	68	83.2	85.0	1.8
Ilobasco	26,697	35,278	32.1	90	82.0	85.1	3.1
San Vicente	53,505	58,861	10.0	81	63.8	68.4	4.6
San Sebastián	24,219	28,716	18.5	71	67.9	71.6	3.7
Usulután	51,437	73,104	42.2	64	59.8	70.3	10.5
Jucuapa	22,955	25,353	10.4	103	56.4	62.6	6.2
Alegría*	50,914	63,892	25.5	143	72.0	72.9	0.9
San Miguel	66,778	94,330	41.3	82	63.7	63.9	0.2
Chinameca	35,607	45,214	27.0	144	56.0	64.4	8.4
Sensori	24,197	31,690	31.0	57	87.3	88.8	1.5
San Francisco Gotera	35,453	43,348	22.3	75	74.8	78.2	3.4
Osicala	24,681	31,976	29.6	90	79.2	85.6	6.4
Jocoaitique	15,527	21,405	37.8	32	80.4	88.8	8.4
La Unión	31,035	50,981	63.6	53	54.3	65.7	11.4
Santa Rosa de Lima	43,533	58,734	34.9	67	86.1	87.5	1.4
Republic	1,434,361	1,855,917	32.8	93	61.7	63.5	1.8

* Alegría is now divided into Santiago de María and Berlín.

Sonsonate 9.1 per mil; La Libertad 9.9 per mil; La Paz 3.9 per mil; San Vicente 6.1 per mil. All other departments varied from 12 to 14 per mil except the Department of La Unión which showed an increment of 19.4 per mil and San Salvador which showed one of 22 per mil.

EL SALVADOR

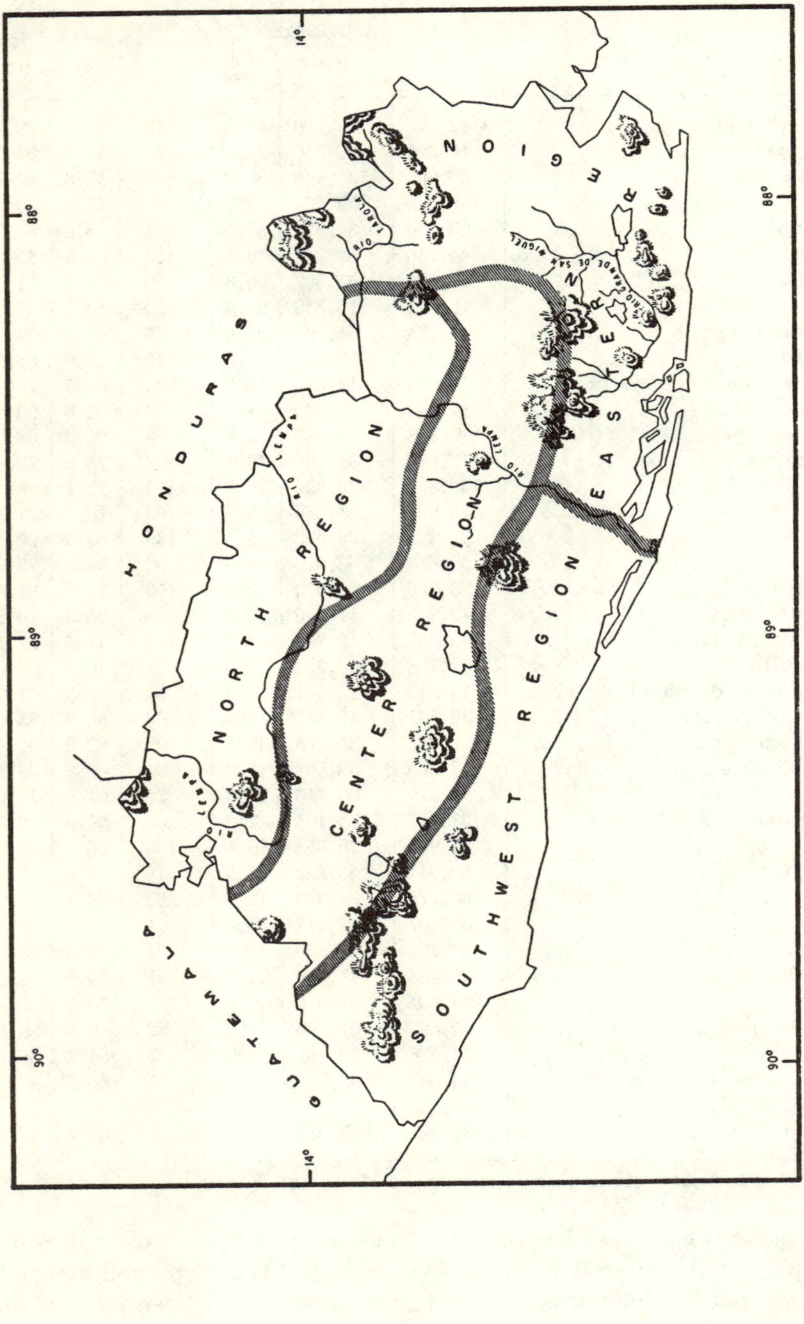
HONDURAS
GUATEMALA
NORTH REGION
CENTER REGION
SOUTHWEST REGION
EAST REGION
RIO LEMPA
RIO TOROLA
RIO GRANDE DE SAN MIGUEL
88°
89°
90°
14°

Population growth means, of course, greater population density, and in El Salvador this has a very special meaning. It hardly needs repeating that the density of population in El Salvador, calculated at 93 per square kilometer for 1952, is the greatest in continental America, and poses for the country increasing problems. However, the relative distribution of this population varies. In looking at the map of population density by *municipio* provided in the 1950 Census, certain general zones of heavy density appear. Running across the country from west to east is a belt of heaviest population. Beginning on the Guatemalan border, it includes the adjacent portions of the departments of Santa Ana, Ahuachapán, and Sonsonate; the northern portions of La Libertad and La Paz, most of San Salvador, southern Cuscatlán, a belt across central San Vicente, and the upland section of Usulután. This belt extends to the coast area at two points, in Sonsonate and Usulután. There are certain scattered isolates with similarly heavy density in Chalatenango, Morazán, and La Unión. These areas generally have over 100 people per square kilometer.

The general area somewhat less densely populated, that is, with between 50 and 100 people per square kilometer, comprises the Department of Cabañas, and the adjacent eastern half of Chalatenango. This region extends across the Lempa, and comprises also the northernmost part of the Department of San Miguel. In addition, most of central San Miguel and the area of La Union adjacent to the border falls in this category.

The least densely populated regions are the far northwest (districts of Metapán and Tejutla), and scattered portions of the coast of La Unión, San Miguel, Usulután, San Vicente, and most of the southwest coast, excluding Sonsonate.

Population density is greatest, of course, in areas of urban growth, and in most countries of Central America there has been a gradual tendency for urban population to grow relatively more rapidly than the rural populations. El Salvador poses something of a problem in this, however. It has been pointed out in the 1950 Census[8] that between the censuses of 1930 and 1950 the percentage of population considered as rural has increased for the country as a whole by 1.8 %. It will be noted in Table 2 that an increase in rural percent was registered in every district except Metapán and San Salvador. The areas showing the greatest relative gain in rural population over urban are south central and south east coast. Aside from those showing urban gain, the areas showing the least rural gain are in the departments of Chalatenango and Cabañas.

It is not entirely clear why this registered increase of rural percentage occurs in El Salvador. There are a number of possible reasons upon which we can speculate until further research is possible.

(a) It is possible that the definitions of "rural" and "urban" differed between the two censuses, and that the registered figures do not actually represent a movement in population. We have no data on the formulation of the 1930 Census, however.

(b) There may have been a gradual movement out of departamental urban centers into *fincas* and *haciendas* in search of work. This seems most likely in terms of people moving

---

[8] p. xi.

from urban centers of one region to rural centers in other regions. It is of interest to note on this point what Squier wrote on the settlement pattern at the time of his visit to the country:[9] "San Salvador... is relatively the most populous of the Central American states. It has, indeed, a relatively larger population than most of the states of the United States.... The traveler, however, would not be apt to receive this impression in travelling through the country since comparatively few of the people live outside of the numerous villages which dot over the state in every direction. The inhabitants of these towns have their little patches of ground at distances varying from one to five miles from their residences...." This suggests, even though it is open to various interpretations, that a hundred years ago there was a greater tendency for Salvadoreans to live in nuclear communities and not in dispersed *aldeas*.

Table 3.—Number of families in terms of number of people per family, in rural and urban populations, 1950 (*Census*, 1950, *Table* 28)

Number of people in the family	Number of urban families	%	Number of rural families	%
1	12,686	8.9	11,408	5.1
2	21,002	14.8	22,446	10.0
3	22,809	16.1	30,478	13.6
4	22,323	15.7	33,935	15.1
5	19,244	13.6	33,092	14.7
6	14,911	10.5	28,430	12.7
7	10,577	7.4	22,581	10.0
8	7,112	5.0	16,054	7.2
9	4,618	3.2	10,665	4.8
10 or more	6,390	4.5	15,082	6.7
Non familiar groups	399	.3	48	—
Total	141,980	100.0	224,219	99.9

Such a movement, it should be noted, tends to increase the relative rural component in both the area of emigration and that of immigration. People leaving a municipal capital in one zone means that the relative number of rural dwellers in that zone increases; the arrival of the immigrants in a rural zone elsewhere also means a relative increase of the rural component in the new zone.

(c) Another possibility is that the vegetative growth rate has been greater in the rural areas than in urban centers. Unfortunately, there are available to the writer no vital statistics on this point which provide a breakdown for rural and urban components. However, there is little doubt that the rural family tends to be larger than the urban.

Table 3 shows that for urban families the mode is 3 persons per family, while for rural it is 4. Taking the total census figures, the average urban family has 4.78 persons, while the average rural family has 5.25 persons. These data, without supporting vital statistics, cannot assure us that the rural growth increment is greater than the urban, but it seems possible that such is the case. Another possible interpretation of this data will be taken up in the chapter on the family.

---

[9] 1855, p. 326.

This registered relative increase in the rural population needs further study. Salvador has seen increasing industrial development and population growth which should be forcing people to the cities. Yet this trend reverses that found in most of the other Central American countries. If we may for the moment assume that the 1930 and 1950 Censuses were measuring the same thing, it seems likely that the increased rural component stems from one or both of two factors: the increased agricultural activity on the south coast may have called more people to rural residence; and the possibility of a greater vegetative growth in rural areas than in the urban.

With respect to the 1950 figures, the areas with the greatest rural components are the northwest and the northeast. The districts with the greatest urban components are scattered, but generally located in the south; there is also a heavy block in the southeast. The only districts in the north which have somewhat lower rural percentages than the rest are Chalatenango (69.0%) and Dulce Nombre de María (73.4%).

The data presented thus far on certain demographic characteristics of the population provide us with a tenative basis for the delineation of certain zones of demographic differences. Table 4 outlines certain such zones and indicates the ways in which they differ on the basis of the information available.

(1) *The Northwest.*—This includes the neighboring districts of Metapán and Tejutla. Certain characteristics of this zone, such as the low change in rural-urban proportions and the relatively high total population growth over the period 1930 to 1950, carry down through the northern *municipios* of the Department of La Libertad.

(2) *The Southeast.*—This includes the coast and adjacent low interior valleys of Usulután, San Miguel, and La Unión. There is some variation in this zone as between the Usulután and San Miguel-La Unión coasts, and the immediately adjacent border region. The border region has the very high rural component characteristic of the northeast, while the Usulután coast has a rural component somewhat greater than that of San Miguel and La Unión. The municipio of La Unión also has a density which is much higher than that of the rest of the zone.

(3) *The Southwest.*—This includes the coastal areas and adjacent piedmont and highlands of the coastal departments to the west of the Lempa River. While consistent in a low rate of total population increase and a relatively high increase in the rural component, there is some variation in population density in this zone. While the density is generally low, the piedmont and highlands are much more heavily populated than the coast, and specifically the districts of Sonsonate and Zacatecoluca have a greater density. Also, Zacatecoluca and Ahuachapán have a generally higher rural component than does the rest of this zone.

(4) *The Central North.*—This includes the districts of Chalatenango, Ilobasco, Sensuntepeque, and Sensori. Dulce Nombre de María is also included in this zone, but it provides a number of points of variation with the rest of the zone: lower total population increase, higher rural component increase, and together with Chalatenango, a lower rural percentage.

Table 4.—Population zones of El Salvador according to differences in population density, population growth, and rural component. (*See key for explanation of symbols*)

Zone	Population density 1950	Rate of increase of total population: 1930–50	Rural percentage in 1950	Change in rural percentage between 1930 and 1950
1 Northwest	Low	++	High	− to 0
2 Southeast	Low to medium, with local areas being high	++ to +++	Usulután coast is medium; border is high; low in between	+++ (? in San Miguel)
3 Southwest	Low (high in Sonsonate, medium in Zacatecoluca)	0	Low (medium in Zacatecoluca)	++ to +++
4 Central north	Medium	+	Medium (high in San Miguel)	0 (− − in Dulce Nombre de María)
5a Center belt the west	High	−	Low to medium	+
5b Center belt west center	High	++ to +++	Medium except in San Salvador	0 to + Except − in San Salvador
5c Center belt center	High	0	Medium	+
5d Center belt east center	Medium to high	0 to +	Variety generally medium	+ (Except 0 in Berlín and Santiago de María)
6 Northeast	Varied	0 to ++	High	++ in the center of the zone, but lower on periphery

Key for Table 4
Population density:
    Low: 0 to 50 persons per sq. km.
    Medium: 50 to 100 " " "
    High: over 100 " " " "
Rate of increase of total population, 1930 to 1950:
    +++: +63.6% to +73.4%
    ++: +32.8% to +42.2%
    +: +25.4% to +32.7%
    0: −6.6% to +22.3%
Rural percentage in 1950:
    High: 78.2% to 88.8%
    Medium: 67.0% to 73.4%
    Low: 13.6% to 65.7%
Change in rural percentage between 1930 and 1950:
    −: −5.5% to −4.6%
    0: −0.2% to +2.0%
    +: +3.0% to +5.0%
    ++: +6.0% to +8.4%
    +++: +9.5% to +11.8%

(5) *The Center Belt.*—This broad zone lies between those northern and southern zones just described. It tends to break down into four subzones which vary principally in terms of total population increase over 1930 to 1950, and in size of the rural component.

(5a) *The West:* This zone includes the districts of Santa Ana, Chalchuapa, Atiquizaya, and Juayua. It has a generally low total increase in population with a low to medium rural component.

(5b) *The West Center:* This includes the districts of Opico, Quezaltepeque, Tonacatepeque, and San Salvador. As might be expected, it is actually not a coherent zone itself, since the capital *municipio* differs profoundly from all the rest in the country. In the various respects, some of the districts can usually be placed more conveniently with one of the neighboring zones. Opico, for example, falls into the northwest zone in change in rural component, with San Salvador in total population gain, and stands by itself with respect to size of rural component.

(5c) *The Center:* This includes the districts of Cojutepeque, Suchitoto, Ilobasco, San Sebastián, and northern San Vicente. This region has a low total population increase and a medium sized rural component. The district of Tejutepeque has a much higher rural component than the rest of the zone.

(5d) *The East Center:* This includes roughly the districts of Berlín, Santiago de María (which together formerly composed the district of Alegría), Jucuapa, and the northern two thirds of Chinameca. This is also a zone with some internal diversity. Particularly the old district of Alegría varies from the rest in that it has seen little change in the rural component. Jucuapa has a much lower population growth than does the rest of the zone.

(6) *The Northeast.*—This zone, like the west center, shows great internal diversity from one *municipio* to another. It is consistent in having a high rural component; but in density, total growth, and growth of the rural component, there are many local differences. It includes the Department of Morazán and the districts of Santa Rosa de Lima, Sensori, and northern San Miguel.

The characteristics of these zones permit certain suppositions with respect to recent population movement. The entire southwest shows in general a high increase in the rural component. Since this has not been accompanied by a high total increase, it suggests that there has been an urban exodus from these zones to other zones. The most obvious recipient of this migration is the southeast where both a high total population increase and a high rural increase has been recorded. This fits, of course, with the fact of more intensified coastal agricultural developments in this southeast zone. Depending upon proximity, however, there has also doubtless been significant immigration to other regions as well.

The northwest and central north zones are both areas of fairly high total growth. However, there has not been a high increase in the rural components in these zones. This suggests that either there has been an unusually high vegetative growth in this area, or that there has been some immigration and that it has been to both rural and urban areas.

The slight, but probably significant increase in rural component in the west zone of the center belt probably indicates that there has been some slight urban emigration.

This general picture of the demography of El Salvador, is of course, limited both by the extent of the information available and by its specificity. As a general picture, however, it makes it perfectly clear that El Salvador cannot be considered as a country of unified demographic qualities. There are distinct zones of varying changes and, as we will have occasion to note later, these zones have a certain reality in terms of the distribution of socio-cultural differences and historical economic developments.

II. THE CULTURE OF THE SALVADOREAN TOWN AND COUNTRY DWELLER

1. LAND, LABOR, AND AGRICULTURE

As in all Central American countries, the basic economy of El Salvador is agriculture. Also, as elsewhere, this includes both national production of cash crops and subsistence production. In the present chapter we are going to try to fill in certain data concerning agriculture and the related subjects of land and labor. At present there is an excellent preliminary survey of the agricultural economy of the country available (Loenholdt, 1953), and a detailed discussion of the crops and certain other phases of agriculture (Choussy, 1950). The present survey attempts to supplement certain data and focus certain of the information which is already available in these other studies.

The degree to which the Salvadoran population is dependent upon agriculture is indicated in Table 5. Fifty-three percent of all chiefs of families are engaged in agricultural activities, and excluding those with no economic activity, 69.0% of all chiefs of family work in agriculture.

Of the population 10 years and older, which is classified as being economically active, the following breakdown is provided by the census: There are 653,409 economically active persons 10 years and older; of these, 411,098, or 62.9% are engaged in agricultural activities. The breakdown for the 411,098 was as shown in Table 6.

An employer is defined by the census as a person who "directs some private enterprise in which he employs one or more persons."[10] In the course of the survey, it became evident that among the subsistence agriculturalists, many did, from time to time, employ help in their work. However, the group classified as employers in Table 6 refers presumably only to those who regularly and constantly employed one or more persons. If this is the case, Table 6 gives us a very good idea of the relative number of people who may be regarded as regular employers, of employees in agricultural activities, and of those who are subsistence agriculturalists. Excluding those who are employers and those on whom there was no data, it is extremely interesting that the remainder is divided almost

---

[10] See Census 1950, p. XX.

half-and-half among salaried employees and self-employed. Unfortunately, we have no breakdown by department or district for these groups to provide statistical information on regional variation.

Among those who are classified as salaried employees in agricultural and livestock work, only 6,098, or about 3%, are people who work in tasks auxiliary to specifically agricultural and livestock activities (i.e., cooking, office work, etc).

In considering the people classed as salaried employees, it should be noted that the census was taken in the month of June and that it was most likely that

Table 5.—Category of occupation of chiefs of families, 1950

Total No. of Chiefs of Families	366,199	100.0%
Economic Activity in which Chiefs of Families Are Engaged:		
Agriculture	196,469	53.6
Industry and manufacture	30,887	8.5
Commerce	17,256	4.7
Other, including services	40,212	11.0
None	81,375	22.2

Table 6.—Employment status of economically active persons of 10 years and older working in agriculture and livestock, 1950

Status	Men	%	Women	%	Total	%
Employers	11,592	2.9	140	1.1	11,732	2.9
Salaried employees	193,725	48.7	10,292	77.6	204,017	49.6
Self-employed or work for family with no cash remuneration	190,505	47.9	2,701	20.3	193,206	47.0
No data	2,013	.5	130	1.0	2,143	.5
Total	397,835	100.0	13,263	100.0	411,098	100.0

the many women participating in coffee and cotton harvests were not included as economically active. During these harvests, of course, many women are so engaged. In eleven of the towns visited on the survey, it was reported that women commonly worked in coffee and/or cotton harvests, and nowhere was it specifically stated that they did not participate in this kind of work. Thus the woman labor force is a seasonal thing and probably highly migratory. In three southwest coast communities of the survey, Ataco, Jayaque, and Panchimalco, it was reported that the women worked regularly in subsistence agriculture. In Santiago Nonualco and Tejutepeque it was said that they did this at times, to help out occasionally when needed. In Cacaopera, both men and women of the Indian population worked regularly in the cultivation and harvest of henequin. Most of these communities were Indian; in general, however, it does not seem to be a custom for the Ladino women to participate in the subsistence agriculture.

If one takes into account the seasonal migrations of labor and the increased labor force at the times of harvest of coffee and cotton, the number of agricultural laborers must increase substantially. These seasonal migrations do not seem to follow a very specific pattern. The main coffee regions are the western and southwestern hills and piedmont, and the uplands of Usulután and adjacent San Miguel. There is considerable movement from the east reported from Cacaopera, Conchagua, and the Valle de la Esperanza, to the west to participate in this harvest even though the same harvest is going on in the Usulután-San Miguel area. The west also receives people from the north during this period; the departments of Chalatenango, Cabañas, and Cuscatlán provide a considerable supply of labor.

While the coffee harvest seems to initiate both north-south and east-west movement, the cotton harvest evidently draws people more from north to south. The writer encountered no cases of people from either the east or west going to the other region for this. El Sauce provided labor for the La Unión coast, Cacaopera provided it for the southern San Miguel region, and Santa Elena provided it for plantations in the immediate vicinity. Cotton, a relatively new intensive production (although it has been produced at other periods in the history of El Salvador), seems to be establishing a somewhat different migratory pattern from that of coffee. Whereas coffee has traditionally drawn upon people from diverse regions, these people usually return to their own homes for their own crops and retain their principal residence there. The call to the cotton plantations, however, has been answered more by landless people, and the migrations have taken a somewhat more permanent form. The principal regions of cotton production have been Usulután, San Miguel, and La Paz,[11] and in these departments much of the labor is derived from what are now local sources. In only two communities, outside this main cotton zone, Tejutepeque and El Sauce, was it reported that people went to cotton harvests.

There are other crops which draw on migrant labor, but so far as I know coffee and cotton are the principal ones which draw upon both men and women. Sugar cane harvest is principally the work of men.

While the small scale independent agriculturalist often participates in salaried labor, the reverse is also true; *colonos*, resident salaried laborers, also participate in small scale subsistence agriculture. Of the 174,204 land exploitations recorded in the 1950 *agropecuario* census,[12] 33,398 or 19.2% were lands provided for *colonos* to work. Of the 174,204 holdings, 125,487 or 72% were under 3 hectares in size, and of this group, 32,426 or 25.8% were run by *colonos*. The major regions

---

[11] See the annual reports on area under cultivation in cotton, *Boletín Algodonero*, 1945–1954. In 1952–53, for example, 86% of the land in cotton was in these three departments, although in recent years other departments have tended to increase their area under cultivation, so that in 1954–55, 77.5% of the land was in these three departments. See also, Choussy, 1950 pp. 279–289.

[12] See *Boletín Estadístico*, Epoca II, Número 10, of July and August 1953.

in which *colonos* are used are the four western departments of Santa Ana, Sonsonate, Ahuachapán, and La Libertad, and in the adjacent departments of San Vicente, Usulután, San Miguel, and La Unión. In view of this departamental distribution, it seems likely that the northern parts of Santa Ana and San Miguel are probably also low in *colono* numbers. The *colono* land exploitation for the country as a whole averaged 1.04 hectares in size, but 68.6 % were under one hectare in size.[13]

The provision of land for *colonos* by landholders, however, is by no means a universal practice. Statistically, this is clear by comparing the total number of such exploitations, 33,398, with the number of salaried employees in agriculture, 204,017. It was commented by some landholders that they did not care to provide land for *colonos* because it meant that the *colono* would be using his time for something other than working for the *patrón*.

The relationship which holds between the laboring population and the property holders seems to vary from one area to another in the country, but the data from the survey did not clarify the picture. In the Valle de la Esperanza in the east the relationship was clearly one of extreme superordination and subordination. The laboring group was of a completely distinct social class and practised divergent customs (separations and shifting of spouses was common). In Jayaque, however, the landholding class, while distinct, did not seem to retain itself in such a superordinate position. There was no question that there was a distinction in practices between the groups, but the landholders themselves were a local population and were more of a local upper class.

On the basis of the information collected on the survey, it appears that the socio-economic classes parallel generally those to be found in Guatemala. There is, socially and economically on the top, a class of people whom we may call cosmopolitan upper class. In El Salvador, this group is more powerful both politically and economically than in Guatemala. From the point of view of landholding, this group comprises a very small but extremely wealthy group of urbanites who live for varying periods on their *fincas*, but who are basically an urban, sophisticated group, all but socially disconnected from the laboring population of their properties.

There then follows a much larger group of medium landholders, the members of which are relatively wealthy, but whose economic position is much more dependent upon the annual status of their crop. While the holdings of the cosmopolitan upper group may be seen in the principal coffee *fincas* of the Santa Ana and eastern region, the medium landholders are much more widely dispersed. Some of the coffee holdings around Jayaque are in the hands of this class. The northern area of Santa Ana, Chalatenango, and probably Cabañas, are predominantly in the control of these medium holders. They are to be found, varying in importance, over much of the east, north, and probably the center and level coastal area of the southwest. The relationship of the medium holder to the

---

[13] *Ibid.*, pp. 19–20.

salaried worker is perhaps closer, but not much gentler, than that between the large landholder and the laborer.

Next in the socio-economic scale is the small landholder and renter, or better called, the subsistence farmer. While both the large and medium landholders are probably included in the 11,732 employers indicated on Table 6, the subsistence farmers and members of their families doubtless comprise the vast majority of the 193,206 self-employed persons. It is not possible, on the basis of present information, to estimate what percentage of this population also engage in salaried work in harvest labor, but it seem likely that a fairly large proportion of them are so involved. On the coffee *fincas*, two to three times the normal labor force can be used during harvest time. Furthermore, it must not be assumed that the subsistence agriculturalist is always a landholder. In many cases he rents much or all of the land on which he raises his crops.

The lowest socio-economic category is composed of the laborers and *colonos*. The Census of 1950 records 197,919 people (189,254 men, 8,665 women) as having the occupation of salaried agriculturalist. This includes both resident *colonos* and *jornaleros*, non-resident laborers. At present, the writer has no way of estimating what proportion of this population are *colonos* and *jornaleros*.

While the greater proportion of the agricultural population lives outside of the towns, 31,312, or 15.9% of the 196,469 heads of family recorded as being in agricultural work, lived in municipal capitals. And this 31,312 composed 22.1% of all urban heads of families. In comparison, 165,157, or 73.6% of the 224,219 rural heads of families, were engaged in agriculture.

Turning now to the problem of land distribution and utilization, the census provides some data.[14] That available to the writer is classified in such a way as to make it impossible to determine the distribution of subsistence plots as opposed to medium and larger holdings. However, the census does provide some indication of the relative amount of land in certain classes of holdings. The results of the official *agropecuario* studies have been classified in terms of four types of holdings: (1) *Fincas*, which include all coffee plantings, and all other plots of permanent cultivations such as bananas, fruits, etc. which are over one *manzana* in size; (2) *Terrenos*, which include all lands dedicated to annual crops such as corn, beans, cotton, and all plots of under one *manzana*, except those dedicated to coffee; (3) *Haciendas*, which includes all holdings dedicated to livestock which are 60 *manzanas* or larger; and (4) *Granjas*, all such holdings devoted to livestock which are under 60 *manzanas*. The land under exploitation in the country is divided in terms of these categories (Table 7).

Something of the importance of cattle in the entire national economy may be seen by comparing the relative amount of land devoted to it in comparison with the number of such exploitations. While only 7.6% of the landholdings under exploitation are devoted to cattle, they occupy 62.5% of the land. On the contrary, the class of holdings called the *terreno*, which it may be assumed includes

---

[14] See *Boletín Estadístico*, Epoca: Número Extraordinario of July of 1952, and No. 10, of July and August 1953.

almost all those occupied by subsistence farmers, comprises some 82.2% of the holdings, but occupies only 27.5% of the land.

The relative size of landholdings has been discussed by Loenholdt[15] with respect to certain specific cultivations. For all types of holdings, however, the *agropecuario* census provides the information given in Table 8.

The *agropecuario* census provides the data on the nature of land usufruct of the small holdings in the country (Table 9).

Table 7.—Distribution of land under exploitation, 1950

	Size of holdings in hectares	%	Number of holdings	%
For Livestock Production.........	956,290.37	62.5	13,293	7.6
Haciendas.....................	791,095.97	51.7	3,662	2.1
Granjas.......................	165,194.40	10.8	9,631	5.5
For Agricultural Production.......	574,051.71	37.5	162,024	92.4
Fincas........................	143,463.60	10.0	17,693	10.2
Terrenos......................	420,588.11	27.5	144,331	82.2
Total.........................	1,530,342.08	100.0	175,317	100.0

Table 8.—Relative size and number of *agropecuario* units in El Salvador, 1950[16]

Size of the *agropecuario* unit	Number of units	%	Area in hectares	%
Under 1 hectare....................	70,416	40.4	35,204	2.3
1 to 2 hectares....................	35,189	20.2	48,015	3.1
2 to 5 hectares....................	34,868	20.0	106,971	7.0
5 to 10 hectares...................	14,064	8.1	99,441	6.5
10 to 50 hectares..................	15,524	8.9	328,811	21.5
50 to 100 hectares.................	2,107	1.2	147,640	9.6
Over 100 hectares..................	2,026	1.2	764,231	50.0
Total...........................	174,204	100.0	1,530,313	100.0

It will be seen from the above table that the great majority of plots are exploited by their owners (this includes, presumably, lands both worked by the owner or by salaried employees of the owner). Of the small holdings, however, approximately one half are exploited by non-owners, specifically renters and *colonos*. The distribution of *colonos* was mentioned earlier. Land rented out is found mainly in the eastern departments of Usulután, San Miguel, and La Unión;

---

[15] 1953, pp. 8–9.

[16] The figure of 174,204 for the number of units and the other data is taken from *Boletín Estadístico*, II, No. 10, July and August, 1953. It does not agree with the figure of 175,317 given in Table 7.

somewhat less in the northern departments of Morazán, Cabañas, Chalatenango, and the south center departments of San Vicente and La Paz; and least of all in the west.

It is not possible to judge adequately on the basis of this data between two types of renting. One, that by the landless subsistence farmer is done on a small scale and worked by the individual renter; and the other, that by an entrepreneur, involves renting a large holding or a series of medium holdings, hiring labor, and growing a large cash crop. This latter practice, also found in Nicaragua, is increasingly popular in El Salvador for cotton cultivation, because of legal restrictions on the number of years one may grow that crop.

Rental payments by subsistence renters may be classified into four types: (1) fixed cash payment for a given unit of land; (2) fixed crop payment for a given unit of land (*censo*); (3) crop payment in proportion to the harvest (sharecropping); (4) labor payment for use of land (*colono*). Of these, sharecropping seemed

Table 9.—Form of exploitation of landholdings in El Salvador

	Total number of exploitations		Number of exploitations under 3 *manzanas*	
	Number	%	Number	%
Exploited by owner	107,875	61.8	63,335	50.5
Exploited by renter	32,931	18.9	29,726	23.7
Exploited by *colono*	33,398	19.2	32,426	25.8
Total	174,204	99.9	125,487	100.0

to be the least important. While it is still found with varying frequency in the rest of Central America, it was reported from only one town on the survey, Tonacatepeque. The *colono* system has already been discussed. The most common types of rental, aside from the *colono* system, are the fixed cash payment and the fixed crop payment. The first of these is merely the payment of a fixed amount of money for the right to utilize a given piece of land for a specified period of time or a specified number of harvests. The *censo* system, in which a fixed amount of the crop is paid as rent, is distinct from the fixed cash payment since the value of the crop will vary from year to year and from one period of the year to another. In general, the *censo* payment system seems to be utilized more in the western and central regions, although it was also reported from Moncagua and Conchagua. In the former community, the payment was referred to as a *carretaje*, literally, a cart load. Cash payment was reported from parts of the Valle de la Esperanza, Santa Elena, El Sauce, and Cacaopera in the east, and from Guacotecti and Tejutla in the north.

The amount paid in *censo* varies from one part of the country to another, just as does the value of the measurement used. Choussy[17] has pointed out

---
[17] 1950, p. 26.

the extreme divergence which exists in the value assigned to the "*medio almud*," or the twenty-fourth part of a *fanega*. One *fanega* equals approximately 400 lbs. of grain corn. The *censo* payment for corn is generally about 1 *fanega* of the crop per *manzana* of land rented. In Santiago Nonualco, it was expressed as 1 *fanega/manzana*, with the *fanega* having a value of about 360 lbs.; in Texistepeque, rent was calculated as 1 *arroba/tarea* (or 16 *arrobas/manzana*, or approximately 400 lbs.); in Conchagua it was rated as a straight *fanega/manzana*. There is probably much greater variation both in the measure used and the size of payment than was indicated by the survey. While cash rent is for an entire year, the payment of the *censo* is usually for one crop only, not for the whole season which, depending upon the land and conditions, might permit two or even three crops. However, it was said in Conchagua that a lower *censo* was paid for the second planting, 20 *almudes* instead of 24.

The amount of *censo* varies, also, with the crop planted. Information on this variation was not collected from all communities visited on the survey, but the

Table 10.—Example, from Santiago Nonualco, of variation in value assigned to *medio-almud* and tarea for different crops in *censo* payment

Crop	Value of *medio-almud*	Value of land unit	Amount paid in local terms	Amount paid per *manzana*
Corn	*almud* 15 lbs. (24 *almud* equal 1 *fanega*)	*manzana*	1 *fanega/manz.*	360 lbs.
Sorghum	*medio* 20 lbs.	*manz.* 4 *tareas*	4 *medios*/6 *tareas*	53.3 lbs.
Beans	*medio* 18 lbs.	*manz.* 7 *tareas*	1 *medio/tarea*	126 lbs.
Rice	*medio* 8 lbs.	?	10 *medios/tarea*	?

case of Santiago Nonualco will provide an example of how extreme this variation may be (Table 10).

It should be noted in passing that it was reported from Ataco that frequently, because the harvests were so small, renters of land were not asked to pay anything for the use of *milpa* land. This, while perhaps not a common practice, may be found in other areas of limited and low production *milpa*.

Work on small plots is carried on principally by the subsistence farmers themselves, the *colonos*, renters, and owners. Aid in field work is generally paid for. Exchange labor, still common in some parts of Central America, seems to all but have disappeared in El Salvador. It was reported from seven towns but of these it was said to be of some importance only in San Matías and Santiago Nonualco where it is still used among the poorer people who cannot afford to employ labor. In the other towns (Tejutla, Tejutepeque, Panchimalco, Santa Elena, and El Sauce) it was said to be used very rarely.

Concerning the agriculture of El Salvador, Loenholdt has provided an analysis of the large scale production of the principal crops. He classifies production into export crops (coffee, henequin, cotton, sesame, etc.) and basic food crops (corn, beans, rice, sorghum, sugar cane, etc.). In his work,[18] he provides data on the amount of land devoted to these two types of crops for seven years between 1935 and 1950. According to these data, basic food crops occupied between 66 and 73 % of the land in all years reported; however, it is of interest to note that during years when less total land was in production, the proportion of this land in basic food crops also decreased. Loenholdt notes[19] however, that since much of this basic food production comes from small subsistence plots for consumption, it does not enter the commercial channels and consequently is not recorded in crop production registers.

Subsistence or basic food crops are produced in two different agricultural complexes, which for convenience we may refer to as the plow complex and the *chuso* or digging stick complex. With some exceptions, plow agriculture is characteristic in level or rolling areas; also, lands under plow cultivation are usually used continuously, year after year, without rest. Digging stick agriculture, sometimes called *siembra de estaca*, is generally found in rough, broken, and rocky areas where a plow cannot effectively be used. These lands, with certain exceptions, are used for a short time, then left to rest. The areas of digging stick agricultural, in which lands are not left to rest, are those in which the available land is so restricted that the farmer has no alternative but to continue using what he has. The towns reporting this situation to be present were Izalco, Ataco, Santiago Nonualco, San Matías, Tejutepeque, Santa Elena, and Moncagua. Only in the last of these, was a type of crop rotation said to be used. It was said that two crops a year could be taken from the lands, but that it was the custom to alternate a piece of land so that one year a first crop would be harvested, and the next year it would rest during the period of the first cultivation, and be planted for the second harvest. During those alternate years in which the first harvest was being extracted, the second planting might be made, but in sorghum instead of corn.

In the rest of the towns, the general pattern of land rest for digging stick lands was to use the land for one to three years, depending upon the quality of production and the availability of land, and then to leave it to rest for two to seven years, depending, again, upon how much land was available and how long it took for the weeds to grow. As is the case elsewhere, the usual criterion which is used to indicate that a piece of land is again ready for cultivation is a tall growth of weeds. In only one town, Tonacatepeque, was it reported that land under plow cultivation was also left to rest; there, both types of land were left to rest every other year. The worst land, as indicated by the method necessary to work it, encountered in the survey was that in El Sauce; there it was reported that digging stick land could be used for only one year, and then it had to be left for from six to seven years to rest. Another form of rest, reported from other countries, but only from Texistepeque in El Salvador, is the sowing of recently used digging stick lands in pasturage grass instead of allowing weeds to grow. This method has been a common method in certain places elsewhere in Central America to

---

[18] Loenholdt, 1953, p. 20.   [19] 1953, p. 33.

open up new land for pastures; here, however, it seems to be a regular pattern, with the pasturage grasses being burned out at the end of four years, and the the land being returned to digging stick cultivation for two years or so. It is the writer's impression that this is a doubtful practice, since many grasses are so tough that mere burning does not stop them from returning to choke out the new crops.

Differences between the two cultivation complexes are also reflected in the implements used. The plow cultivation, of course, involves the wooden plow drawn by oxen. The usual method of planting is for one man to drive the oxen and for another to follow, dropping the seeds and covering them with his foot. In some places, the land is plowed again, between the furrows, providing a heavy cover for the seeds. In Izalco, however, it was reported that some followed the plow with a digging stick, making the hole for the seeds with that implement. If oxen are not well trained, it requires a third person to lead them. Cultivation of plowed plots is occasionally done with the *azadón*, or hoe, more commonly with a machete, and in Texistepeque it was said that a few used metal cultivators moved by oxen. Plow cultivation was reported to be at a minimum in the two towns visited in the northeast and in Ataco because the land was so steep and broken that it could not profitably be used.

Digging stick agriculture uses the *chuso*, a wooden pole to which has been attached a metal point or a piece of broken machete blade. The digging stick goes under various names: besides *chuso*, the most common are *macana* (various towns), *pico* (Ataco, Tonacatepeque), *pujaguante* (Tejutla), *estaca* (Tonacatepeque), *huisucte* (San Matías), *huisute* (Cacaopera), *barreta* (El Sauce). While plow agriculture returns to the same lands year after year, the *siembra de estaca* is usually shifting agriculture and depends upon a periodic change of locale, even though land limitations in El Salvador force many people to re-use the same land constantly. The usual practice, however, is to leave the land a few years for the weeds to grow up; when this has happened, the weeds are cut down in February or March and the land burned over in preparation for the planting in May. For this pre-planting cleaning various types of machetes (discussed below) are used. Machetes are also used for whatever cleaning must be done during the actual period of cultivation. As a result, the machete, in its various forms, is a much more important adjunct to digging stick agriculture than it is to plow agriculture.

Besides having correlations in land used and implements, the differentiation of these two types of agriculture is reflected in the crops planted and in the socio-economic status of those who participate in them. The digging stick agriculture is basically a corn affair, although in parts of El Salvador, as in certain other regions of long use, *maicillo* has also become of considerable importance. To a lesser degree, rice and sugar are produced with the digging stick methods. Plow agriculture produces relatively more rice, but also, of course, produces much corn. Of greater importance, however, is that the digging stick agriculture is, almost by definition, that which is carried on in less desirable lands, and therefore is relegated to people whose socio-economic status prohibits them from having lands for plow agriculture. It is a fairly standard type of cultivation for *colonos*, since they are usually assigned lands which the landowner cannot use effectively in terms of plow cultivation, be it with a wooden plow or a more modern plow. Historically, of course, the digging stick is the indigenous method, while the plow is that introduced by the Spanish. This differentiation is still to be seen in Izalco, where even though the plow is used, the digging stick is used to make holes for the seeds following the plow.

With respect to machetes, there is a fairly distinct distribution of different types. Basically, the machetes of El Salvador may be classified into three types: the *corvo*, the long, straight blade; the *cuma*, a shorter, wider blade than the *corvo*, with a hook on the end; and the *calabozo*, an even shorter and wider blade than the *cuma*, also with a hook on the end. The last two of these have variant forms usually known as *pando* when the blade is bent so that the machete may be more easily used for cutting down weeds at the ground level. The *corvo* in El Salvador is used as an implement for cleaning out heavy brush, cutting wood, and as a weapon. It is most common all through the southern part of the country and in the west. Of the northern towns in the survey, it was reported in use only in Guacotecti.

The *cuma* and *calabozo* are distinctly agricultural implements. The *cuma* is most common throughout the western and central part of the country. The *calabozo* is more common in the western part, and is also found across the north center and northeast. Where the *cuma* and *calabozo* are both found in use, the latter is used more for pre-planting cleaning and in much the same way as is the *corvo* (reported from Tejutepeque, Tejutla, and Texistepeque). In the west, the *calabozo* goes under various names. In Cacaopera, it is called the *forolito*; when bent, it is referred to simply as *machete pando*; in Conchagua and El Sauce, the term *cuma* is used to refer to the *calabozo pando*, while in the former place *jorolo* is the term for *calabozo*.

In general the use of mineral and other artificially prepared fertilizers is not characteristic of subsistence agriculture but is restricted almost entirely to large scale agricultural production. Even the use of animal manure was reported from only four towns (Izalco, Santiago Nonualco, Texistepeque, and Tejutepeque), while folding in of the remains of the previous year's crop leftovers was reported as being done only in San Matías. In a number of places it was said that the previous year's refuse was gathered together and burned.

Attempts to get rain usually take the form of *rogativas* (also called *rogaciones* and *peregrinos*). These were reported from about one-half the towns visited, but were neither particularly Indian or Ladino, nor showed any particular regional distribution. The patron saints are usually used for the *rogativa* processions.

Agricultural work occupies much of the year. Loenholdt wrote: "The cultivation of corn in El Salvador can be considered an *all-year round process*, as, in the course of one year, three and sometimes four crops of corn are produced..."[20] While it is important to realize that in certain places more than one annual crop

---

[20] Loenholdt, 1953, p. 38. Italics mine.

is taken, it is of perhaps greater importance to realize that the number of harvests varies greatly from one place to another. The tables which Loenholdt provides on the extension of land and production in the second, third and fourth harvests demonstrate clearly that these are of very limited importance. According to his figures for 1950, 88% of the total corn production was harvested from the first planting, 10% from the second, and 1% from the third and fourth combined. It is a mistake, then, to think of the Salvadorean subsistence farmer as being occupied throughout the year in planting and harvesting one crop after another. For the most part, subsistence agriculture depends upon one or two harvests. Three crops are to be found only in areas which are irrigated (usually not available to subsistence farmers) or in which there is much subsurface moisture, or *humedad*, as it is called locally. No town visited on the survey had four harvests annually, and the writer did not encounter the use of the term *shupan* given by Loenholdt for the fourth crop.[21]

The relation between the first and second planting is at times complex. Of the communities visited, nine reported having two harvests of corn (and sometimes beans) a year (Izalco, San Matías, Tonacatepeque, Texistepeque, Cacaopera, Santa Elena, El Sauce, Conchagua, and parts of the Valle de la Esperanza). The standard pattern in these towns was as follows:

First planting: May (usually after the first rains)
First harvest: August
Second planting: August to September
Second harvest: between October and January, depending upon local conditions and other occupations of farmer

In San Matías, however, one planting was said to be more customary. Three towns reported that only one harvest of corn was possible, although two of beans was possible (Ataco, Panchimalco, Guacotecti):

First planting: May, or after the first rain
Doblar (bending the ear on the stalk so the rain cannot enter and rot it): August
Tapiscar (harvest): October to December

In only Jayaque, Izalco, and Santiago Nonualco was it reported possible to take out a third crop a year, and in all three it was said that the terrain on which this was possible was very restricted. In Izalco, it was only possible in limited irrigated lands. In Jayaque, third crops were taken out on certain rented lands nearer the coast where irrigation was possible; and in both communities land in which subsurface moisture was present were so used. The third crop is usually planted in December or January, but in Santiago Nonualco it was not harvested until April, or just before the planting of the new crop. Jayaque provides a good example of the variation which may be found in certain areas with respect to the number and importance of harvests. Two types of land were used (mostly outside the *municipio* itself), *parcelas secas* and *parcelas húmedas* (dry

---

[21] Loenholdt, 1953, p. 38; on page 40, the same term for a fourth crop of beans.

pieces and moist pieces). In the *parcelas secas* it was customary to plant a single crop of corn, and follow this up with a second planting in beans. In the *parcelas húmedas* the first two crops were similar to those on the *parceles secas*, but a third was usually planted in potatoes or legumes.

In two towns it was reported that second crops were possible but that there were varied practices in connection with them. The cases of the alternate use of lands between the first planting and the second in Moncagua was mentioned earlier. In Tejutepeque, it was said that the second crop was only possible on lands under plow cultivation; digging stick lands produced only one crop a year.

There is a certain variation in terminology with respect to these various harvests. The first planting was called *milpa* in Santiago Nonualco and San Matías; *primavera* in El Sauce and Conchagua; and simply *de invierno* in Santa Elena, Moncagua, and Cacaopera. Elsewhere, for the most part it was simply called the "first". The term *tunamil* (*tunalmil* in Tejutla, *tunasmil* in Texistepeque) is fairly standard for the second crop through most of the western and central part of the country, and especially along the southwest highlands and coast. In the west, it was called *de verano* except in Cacaopera where the term *tunamil* was also used, and in Conchagua where *postrera* was used. The term applied to the third crop, where possible, varied. In Jayaque, the term *apante* was applied to the third crop, whether it came from irrigated or *humedad* land; in Guatemala, this term is usually restricted to irrigated land. In Izalco, *tempante* was applied to the irrigated lands. In Santiago Nonualco the expression *tunamil de humedad* was applied to the third harvest which was possible from those lands with sufficient moisture to permit the final crop.

The use of one, two, or three crops, applies, of course, to the cultivation of corn, beans, and other crops which have a short growing season. Certain of the important crops, however, do not mature in short periods, and consequently only one crop a year is possible over most of the country. Sorghum is usually planted in May, and is not ready for harvest until the end of the year. Sugar cane, where planted, is a year long crop, and El Sauce was the only town on the survey which reported two rice crops a year.

It is not necessary here to deal with the distribution of crops in El Salvador, as the subject has been covered by more qualified persons in readily available publications.[22] In the course of the survey, the writer did not encounter the community specialization in certain crops which is to be found in Guatemala. Only in Cacaopera, where much of the population, especially the Indians, devote their efforts to the production of henequin was any clear-cut specialization evident. Elsewhere, there was usually a complex of basic crops, such as corn and sorghum; corn, sorghum, and beans; corn and rice; or corn, rice, and beans. In various areas, of course, sugar, coffee, etc.; are of importance, but generally these are under production on larger landholdings and are not a part of subsistence agriculture. There is little doubt but that sorghum is tending to replace corn in certain regions where the land is badly worn out.

---

[22] Choussy, 1950; Loenholdt, 1953.

2. PRODUCTION, TRANSPORT, AND COMMERCE

As elsewhere in this monograph and series, our subject is the rural and country dweller. Consequently, when we take up the subjects mentioned in the title of the present chapter, we are not embarking on a study of Salvadorean national and international economy, but certain aspects of the economy which are peculiar to the town and country dwellers.

El Salvador is the most "lived on" country in Central America, and as a result, there is little wild life left to attract the hunter. In Izalco occasionally deer or *tepescuintle* were killed, and for this there were still some *escopetas de chimeneas* (muzzle loaders) as well as .22's in use. The only *municipio* visited in which hunting is of any importance was El Sauce. Deer, certain birds, rabbits, *tepescuintles*, armadillos (*cusucos*), lizards (*iguanas* and *garrobos*) are the principal animals hunted. Practically none of the catch is sold regularly; it is eaten in the home.

Fishing is of greater importance, but limited in variety. Four towns in the north (Tejutla, Tejutepeque, Cacaopera, and El Sauce) and three in the south (Izalco, Santiago Nonualco, and Conchagua) reported some fishing. Except in the case of Conchagua, where coastal fishing is done, all fishing described was done in rivers. Usually, it was restricted to the catching of crayfish, crabs, and small fish, although near El Sauce larger fish were caught. The most common fishing method was with the *atarraya*, or throwing net, and hook and line. In Izalco, a basket shaped net attached to a circular stick, called *lumpe*, was also used for crayfish. Fishing in the Lempa, below Tejutla, both the *chinchorro* and *trasmayo* nets are also used. In that region, fishing is done from log rafts, pushed by a pole (*picador*). Although their use is prohibited, vegetable poisons and gunpowder are both used. The principal poison is that which goes under the usual name of *barbasco*, and is taken from the root of a certain vine; in Tejutepeque, it was said that this plant was similar to the *camote*. In El Sauce the bark of a tree called *pescadillo* was said to be used for this purpose. In Tejutla, lime was also used to poison the water. The use of gunpowder is evidently not extremely common as it is expensive, heavily punished, and there is some realization of the damage done by its use. In Santiago Nonualco, it was said that explosives were used in coastal fishing. Much of the fishing in Conchagua is done under a government fishing cooperative. Dugout canoes are used, called *cayucos* or *botes*, and the *atarraya* and *manga* (a *chinchorro* type net) are the principal nets.

The writer encountered very little mineral exploitations in the course of the survey. Conchagua was the only town in which it was reported that lime (*cal*) was produced in any quantity, and there it was made by burning shells. Also in that *municipio*, at two points along the coast, Tamarindo and Güisquil, it was said that there were salt flats from which salt is produced for sale.

There are numerous home industries in El Salvador, and many of them are intimately related to regional economy. Some, however, are principally for home production or at best for local sale. Weaving has all but disappeared from the Salvadorean home. Izalco and Panchimalco were the only towns visited in which women still weave, and in both cases it was to produce certain items of dress for Indian women. In Izalco, the belt loom is still used to make 3″ wide belts, but the skirt material used by the Indians is no longer produced locally. In Panchimalco, however, skirts, carrying cloths, and head cloths are still being produced. The Panchimalco loom is a belt loom, but one of the broadest which the writer has seen anywhere in Central America. Most belt looms are used to make cloth which at best is 1½ to 2 feet wide; the Panchimalco loom produces cloth which is easily a meter in width. The designs used are highly formalized into single stripes or plaids. There are three types of skirt materials produced, two for women up to middle age, and one for elderly women. The former are a fine plaid of red, blue, and yellow, while the latter is similar except there is no yellow. There is a little more variety in the head cloths, but the general design is also a plaid. The material used is commercially purchased cotton. Until ten or 15 years ago, according to informants, spinning was still done. Each house had a garden with some cotton "trees" in it (a tall plant, 2 to 3 meters high), and the spinning was done with a stick spindle in a *guacal*. Most such spinning is done for members of the family or on order.

Of much greater importance in the lives of the townspeople and countrymen are the various fiber industries. These are of three principal types: hat making, string products, and leaf and wicker products. Hat making is carried on in a number of places; Cojutepeque and the Masahuat region were mentioned by informants of being of particular importance. The hat production of Cojutepeque provides a case of extensive specialization at the local and regional level. The palms from which the hats are made are grown on the coast. They are brought to the Cojutepeque market and possibly other interior valley markets. Women from the villages, rural areas, and other towns then come to the markets, purchase the palms and take them home. Tejutepeque was one of the towns in which the women then braided the palms into long braids (*trenzas*). These are then sold to the hat makers in Cojutepeque, or wherever they may be located. Recently, two hat makers have set up shop in Tejutepeque and make the hats by machine. In Tejutepeque, and presumably in other regions, the production of braids by women is a fairly important economic activity.

String products are usually made of *mescal*, or henequin fiber. Cacaopera is one of the centers of this production. There considerable land is devoted to the cultivation of henequin, a very satisfactory plant because it gives two harvests a year for three or four decades. The Indians of Cacaopera specialize in this production, but many Ladinos of the region are also involved in the same activity. The henequin is locally dried and the fiber separated out. From this, string is produced, and in turn, hammocks, *alforjas* (the twin string bags, made like saddle bags, which are the regular companion of the countrymen), *redes* (the large net bags used for carrying crops), and various other products. In Cacaopera both men and women evidently participate in all phases of the production, from the harvest of the henequin to the fabrication of the final product.

No leaf and wicker production center was visited on the survey. Nahuizalco is perhaps the most famous, and there baskets, *petates* (large woven mats), and *sopladores* (fire fans, of restricted use now) are made. In Tejutla, it was reported that a few men and women of some of the rural areas made baskets for sale outside, and in Ataco and Panchimalco a few baskets are made, but principally for local use. A great deal of these products are sold over much of El Salvador and some supply part of the market of southwestern Honduras.

Another important local industry which supplies the needs of the country is pottery making. There are three general types of pottery production centers. Some such as San Salvador, produce on a large scale in factories and sell over most of the country. Some towns such as Quezaltepeque, San Juan Nonualco, and Guatejiagua, supply fairly large adjacent regions. And some supply only local needs and frequently do not take care of these. Certain centers in eastern Guatemala, particularly San Pedro Pinula and San Luis Jilotepeque also export pottery into the adjacent parts of El Salvador. Pottery is an essential part of the Salvadorean domestic scene, and its production, distribution, and sale is a subject which needs a great deal more study. Pottery production on a limited scale was reported from the *caserío* Las Chorchas of Tejutla, *cantón* Las Mesas of Texistepeque, and from San Matías and Panchimalco. Rather more important was the production of Tonacatepeque, in which it was said that four families were producing *cántaros*, *ollas*, and *comales*, and that of the *aldea* of Bañadero in Guacotecti whence the pottery is sold in the departmental capital of Sensuntepeque. Pottery, when made for local and regional consumption, is usually handmade by the women, but men participate in some of this production, such as in Tonacatepeque.

Another fairly important type of local specialization is the production of certain items of clothing, principal among which are men's trousers. Two centers of production came to the writer's attention, Tonacatepeque and Nueva Guadalupe. In Nueva Guadalupe there are a large number of women who make men's trousers. These women work in different ways. "Some work with their own sewing machine, do their own cutting, and consequently receive the major profit from their work. Others who have no machine of their own hire themselves out to families who pay for the work. In some families there is a division of labor with certain members, possibly a brother or a sister who do the cutting and other relatives who do the sewing. It is claimed that between four and a dozen pairs of trousers can be made by an individual in a day, not including the cutting time."[23] Cloth for the trousers is usually taken on credit from local stores or from San Miguel dealers. With the money earned with the week's work, the cloth is paid for and credit taken on new cloth. The men usually take the products out for sale to other towns on Friday or Saturday, and return with the earnings on Sunday or Monday. Trouser making is considered as the *"patrimonio"* of the town.

The situation in Tonacatepeque is somewhat different. There, instead of working independently, the women are hired by entrepreneurs. The cloth is supplied to the women, who then make the trousers at home, and the finished product is

---

[23] Adams, 1952. Under the government's development plan for the Valle de la Esperanza much of this work is being coordinated into a cooperative organization.

turned back to the entrepreneurs for sale. The informant estimated that there were about six such enterprises going with perhaps 15 women sewing for each of them.

Besides specialized sewing of the type just described, every town counts a number of professional seamstresses who make both men's and women's clothes. Dressmaking is usually not a business in the sense that the trousers making is. Dresses are made on order, and as often as not the person making the order must supply the material. Similarly, many towns have professional tailors who make men's suits.

An industry still of considerable importance is making yokes and ox carts. One such workshop was visited in an *aldea* of the town of Chinameca. Six men worked in the carpentry shop, a chief carpenter, three specialists on carts, and two more on beds and other things. They could produce three to four carts a week. All the wood was purchased locally from *fincas*. Most towns, of course, have a few carpenters for the regular work of coffin making, doors, etc., but such small industries as that just described usually serve most of the immediate region.

Another industry which is to be found over much of the country is the production of *panela*, crude sugar blocks. In only three towns visited on the survey was it reported that there was no production of *panela* whatsoever. In four more it was said to be of very minor importance, and in seven it was an industry of some importance. In all cases, the *trapiches* in use were powered by oxen or, in a few cases, motors. More primitive types of *trapiches* were not encountered. "The production of *panela* involves bringing in the cane, pressing it, boiling it, pouring it in molds, wrapping the resultant *lajas* by pairs into *atados*, and marketing it. In these processes, a man may sell his cane, take it to the *trapiche* for pressing, or press it in his own *trapiche*; the larger producers of *panela* send the *lajas* to day laborers who are employed to wrap them."[24]

In addition to those described, there are various crafts and industries which form an intrinsic part of the way of life of the Salvadorean. Tile making and brick making are essential to the construction of many Salvadorean homes. Masons, specialists in *adobe* making, *adobe* laying, and the construction of *bajareque* walls, are to be found in almost all towns and rural areas. Besides tailors, seamstresses, and hat makers, there are also shoemakers located in many of the towns.

The local production of goods is not always a matter of full time professional work, however. There are many minor industries which are usually carried on by women in their homes. The production of starch from *yuca*, vinegar from fruits and other local produce, small wooden pill boxes, pottery figurines for the city and tourist trade (especially in Ilobasco), ice cream (by those storekeepers who have refrigerators), chocolate (from locally produced *cacao*), pickled vegetables, candy, candles, and paper flowers are some of the ways in which the women of the towns, and a lesser degree of the countryside, augment their income. These

---

[24] Adams, 1952.

industries are of special importance when one takes into account the rather high percentage of Salvadorean families which have no male chief of household.

In general, while El Salvador is perhaps more industrialized than other Central American countries, it nevertheless depends to a great degree upon the local production of such specialists for most of the goods utilized in work and daily living.

The transportation of people and goods in the country is gradually changing as better roads are opened up. While El Salvador boasts a border-to-border paved highway, nevertheless, most of the area along the coast and adjacent to the north border are still inaccessible except occasionally by jeep, or by mule and foot. Also, within the reach of good roads, few town and country people can afford motorized vehicles for work between their land or job and home. As a result, much travel and transport is still done by ox cart, mule, horse, or by foot. Trucks have been replacing the ox cart for carrying produce from *fincas* and town centers to the central points of export or internal distribution, but within the rural areas, the rural and town dwelling people still rely heavily on slower forms of transportation.

Transport of goods on foot is still used extensively in the rural areas, even near large towns. The farmer who has a small plot of land, and must bring in his corn harvest, and cannot afford the rental of an ox cart, will carry it in on his back. In some areas, the use of the *mecapal* (head tumpline) is still to be seen, and in Cacaopera, among the Indian population, is still the standard mode of short distance transport. In the towns along the coast (except in Santa Elena and Ataco), it was reported to be used only by the older people and by the poor; only in Panchimalco was it said to still be fairly common. Its use in Ataco has practically disappeared, and the men now carry on the shoulder and the women on the head. In Cacaopera and Conchagua both men and women use the *mecapal*, and this was said to have been the case in earlier times in Ataco. Elsewhere, it seems to be more of a man's carrying method. In the north, the *mecapal* was said to still be used in Tejutla, Tejutepeque, and Guacotecti. Its use seems to have all but disappeared throughout the entire center belt of the country. The term *mecapal* is generally used everywhere the tumpline is found, except in Cacaopera where the Spanish term *bambador* was used by informants. Women generally carry loads, particularly *cántaros* (water jars), on the head, but the Indian women of Cacaopera carry with the tumpline, as do those of Panchimalco in steep paths, and the women of El Sauce and Tejutepeque sometimes carry the *cántaro* on the hip.

Horses and mules are used through most of the country as a means of travel, when they can be afforded, but they are most important in the areas where roads are not yet adequate for either bus or truck service. In general, both are found, but mules are preferred in rough country such Ataco, Cacaopera, and El Sauce, while horses are used when the terrain is a little easier. Horses are preferred for riding, and in El Sauce, women ride both side saddle and astride.

The ox cart is still one of the most important means of heavy transport throughout the country. They are least common in those areas where the land is too steep or broken for their effective use. Tejutla, Cacaopera, El Sauce, and Ataco have few for this reason. Also, where their use to take out *finca* and *hacienda* products has been superseded by trucks, such as in Jayaque, they are disappearing. Most of the interior valley of El Salvador is not too broken for ox carts, and they are used extensively both by large farmers and small. While many farmers do not have their own carts, both large and small will rent them when needed.

Not only are carts used for taking produce from *haciendas* and *fincas* to centers, but they are used extensively by the townspeople for the local importation of fire wood, carrying water in regions where there is a regular or periodic scarcity, carrying building materials (*adobe*, rocks, tiles, wood, etc.), and numerous other odd jobs.

An interesting side light on the replacement of the ox cart by the truck was provided by an informant in Jayaque. Years ago he had been an ox cart driver, renting out his services to the *finca* owners and others of the region. As the truck became more important, he learned to drive and became a truck driver, engaged in the same traffic.

The ox carts of El Salvador fall into two distinct types. There is a line running north and south which begins a few miles to the west of the Lempa River on the coast, continues north roughly parallel to the river, then cuts northwest towards Ilobasco, but east of Tejutepeque, and then continues more or less north to the Honduran border. To the west of this line, the ox carts have spoked wheels and the yokes are generally plain. To the east, the ox carts have solid wheels, and the yokes are out in a fairly stylized form. The stylization of the yoke actually is to be seen slightly to the west, of the line, but in a modified form, in Tejutepeque and Zacatecoluca; but the solid wheel follows more or less the line described above. This dividing line applies to most of Central America. To the west and throughout Guatemala the spoked wheel is found; to the east, through most of populated Honduras, Nicaragua, and Costa Rica, the solid wheel is in use.

For carrying produce, the standard method in El Salvador is the *matate* or open string net. The writer saw no use of leather bags such as are found in parts of Nicaragua, Honduras, and Panama. Only in one place (Guacotecti) were shallow leather bags seen, used to carry pottery *cántaros* of water by horseback. Throughout the country men use the *alforjas*, twin string bags, and the *tecomate*, gourd canteen for water. Water carrying by oxcart is generally done now with *toneles*, fifty-gallon gasoline cans attached to the cart. In Izalco, however, are still to be found carts carrying vertical wooden kegs, such as are also used as water tanks for some of the homes. For the most part, pottery *cántaros* are used for water carrying but in certain parts of the west and through the center belt, especially around the capital city, metal *cántaros* are used by many. Although they are more expensive than their pottery counterparts, they are unbreakable, and if they spring a leak, they can be patched. They do not cool the water as does the pottery, however. The metal *cántaro* has been in use in El Salvador for at least fifty years, but its point of diffusion is not at present known. To carry other produce on the head, woman generally use *canastas* (small or medium sized baskets) and *canastos* (large, flat, baskets).

The sale of economic goods in El Salvador is done principally by means of stores and markets. With little doubt, the greater part of town commerce is done through stores. Of all the towns visited on the survey, only Guacotecti had no stores at all; that town is so close to the departamental capital of Sensuntepeque that the local residents go to the capital for all their buying and selling. As elsewhere in Central America, the stores usually carry a wide variety of goods, ranging from cloth and clothing, to agricultural implements and soft drinks, and are often in charge of a family, with either the wife or husband or both serving customers. Many establishments are run by women. The Census of 1950 reports that in the occupational category of *"Vendedores y Similares"*, for the entire country there were 5,347 men and 7,784 women. The women comprised 7.2% of all the economically active women, while the men comprised slightly under 1% of all the economically active men. These figures indicate, then, that both absolutely and relatively the women participate more in selling activities than do men.

There are usually three main sources of supplies for stores. Of first importance are the national or regional wholesale houses which send out salesmen and to whom the storekeepers go to replenish their stocks. Second, there are ambulatory vendors who market products which they themselves or members of their families have produced (such as the trousers salesmen of Nueva Guadalupe). And finally, there are the local subsistence agriculturalists who will sell part of their crop to local dealers, or who supply these dealers to repay credit provided earlier. Similarly, women will sell the products of their chickens, fruit trees, or small home industries. The store thus acts not only as a means of local distribution of goods produced elsewhere in the nation or imported from outside, but also as a distributional center for products produced within the locale or region.

The distribution of local, regional, national and foreign products is also the main function of the market. There are two distinct types of markets in the country, those which are housed in a municipal market building, and those which take place along a street or public square. The first of these is referred to as *mercado* while the second is a *plaza*. Of the towns visited on the survey, seven had neither *plaza* nor *mercado*, five had one and five had the other. There was no significant regional distribution of these differences.

The extent of the network of commerce implicated in a local market may perhaps be seen by a brief survey of the Jucuapa market (Valle de la Esperanza) made during one of the slack days during March of 1952. From this it was possible to distinguish 124 distinct types of items (such as onions, soap, etc.) being handled by distinct vendors. The provenience of these items was as shown in Table 11.

Of the distinct items for sale, Jucuapa and the immediate region provided about ⅖ of the total. It should be noted here, however, that most of this came from the immediate region to the west of Jucuapa because the region immediately to the east supplied another market, that of Chinameca. Another

1/5 of the total came from San Salvador, the national capital, and was composed in great part of fabricated goods. Of the remainder, 2/5 came from eastern El Salvador, 1/5 from central and western El Salvador, and 2/5 from other countries. The vendors themselves were local people for the most part. But 3/5 of the types of goods handled came from outside the immediate region and almost one half came from other countries or from east of the Lempa. Whether this is characteristic of other parts of El Salvador is not clear, because Jucuapa at this time still was recuperating from the damage suffered from a powerful earthquake some ten months previously.

Mercados vary greatly in size, depending upon the amount of local commerce. Perhaps the smallest formal *mercado* observed was that in San Matías which was composed of two *ranchos* and was used by local people only, and then only on Sundays. Large *mercados* are to be found in numerous centers of regional importance and sometimes take up an entire block or more. The *plaza* is, his-

Table 11.—Provenience of articles in Jucuapa market, off-day, March, 1952

Provenience of items	No of distinct items	Percent
Jucuapa and the Valle de la Esperanza	49	39.5
El Salvador, east of the Lempa, excluding the Valle de la Esperanza	19	15.3
El Salvador, west of the Lempa, excluding San Salvador	10	8.1
San Salvador	27	21.8
Three neighboring Central American countries (Nicaragua, Honduras, Guatemala)	14	11.3
Extra-Central American	5	4.0
	124	100.0

torically within any locale, the prelude to a *mercado*. In a number of places where *plazas* were in session informants said that there was in the planning stage (which is an indefinite length of time) the construction of a regular *mercado* building.

With only one exception, the principal market day is Sunday, and if there is a second, it is Thursday. The exception was El Sauce where Tuesday was the day of the *plaza*. The reason given for this is that Tuesday is the *"día de San Antonio,"* the local patron saint. Generally, when there is a regular *mercado* building, selling goes on throughout the week, but with more people buying and selling on Sunday or Thursday. Some of the *plazas* operate in a similar manner. In Santa Elena, there was a wooden structure for the sale of meat, but other things were being sold irregularly under the large ceiba tree which stood to one side of the center of the public square. In Izalco, vendors may be seen daily along one side of the public plaza.

Historically, the presence of a market is probably explained in part by the fact that El Salvador lies in the pre-columbian Meso-American region where market exchange was a principal part of the economy. However, it is of interest to note that in the towns in which Indians still form a significant portion of the total population, markets are not necessarily present. Ataco and Jayaque have small *plazas* only, and Panchimalco and Conchagua have neither *mercado* nor *plaza*. The absence of markets is sometimes due to the presence nearby of a much more important center, such as is the case between Guacotecti and the departmental capital of Sensuntepeque. The fact that most of the local population is a laboring group and not independent producers might be related to the lack of extensive markets in Ataco, Jayaque, and Conchagua. The absence of any market in the northwestern towns visited (Texistepeque, Tejutla, Tejutepeque, and Guacotecti) may be coincidental, since there are markets in the departmental centers.

3. THE DOMESTIC ESTABLISHMENT

Squier noted in 1855 that in travelling through El Salvador one would not get the impression of a large population because "comparatively few of the people live outside of the numerous villages which dot over the state in every direction".[25] The situation today is much changed, and if the evidence of the relative growth of the rural population is correct, it is continuing to change. Much of the rural population today, especially outside the principal *finca* and *hacienda* regions, is dispersed over the countryside, sometimes forming irregular and indefinite village groups, but more commonly a series of semi-isolated homesteads In general, the nucleated village is much more common in the center and southwest than it is in the center north or through the eastern region. Where there has been development of *fincas* and *haciendas*, such as in the coffee zones and in the southeastern *hacienda* area, villages have also been established for the laboring population. The northeast and north center, particularly, seem to be regions of dispersed *caseríos*.

In house construction, there is considerable local divergence from one community to the next, but little of regional significance. In general, walls of *bajareque* (wood frame with a mud or rubble fill) are very common and so is *adobe* brick. According to the census of urban housing, taken in 1950,[26] there is a general tendency for *adobe* houses to be more common in the towns of the northern departments, and *bajareque* in those of the southern departments, but it must be emphasized that there are exceptions to this, both in terms of departmental statistics and great local variation within most departments. In general, houses of poles and straw (*ranchos*, or *pajizas*) are a rural phenomenon, but they are also to be found in many of the towns among poorer families and located usually on the edge of the town. The use of *adobe* in the rural areas is generally uncommon. Homes in the *cantones* are usually either of poles or *bajareque*, and only in some limited local regions does *adobe* construction predominate. It was reported in El Sauce that rural homes were generally of *adobe*, but that there were also some of poles.

In many parts of the country, where earthquakes occur with some frequency,

---

[25] Squier, 1855, p. 326. [26] Censo, 1953.

there is an increasing tendency to turn to *bajareque* because it is more resistant to the shakes than is *adobe*. However, it was reported in Cacaopera that recently there has been a trend there to shift from *bajareque* to *adobe* because the latter is cheaper. In regions where wood is scarce and its importation is costly, there is little doubt but that *adobe* is a more economical construction than *bajareque*, so long as the right kind of earth is available.

The other walling materials which are of some importance in the towns and countryside are wood and brick. Brick, of course, is very costly, both to purchase and to use in building, and so is principally limited to somewhat wealthier people of the towns and the houses constructed at the expense of *finqueros* and *hacendados*. Wood homes, both rural and urban, are to be found in some places, principally where wood is still fairly abundant. For the most part, this restricts its use to coastal and occasional highland communities.

In the towns, tile roofs are almost standard. Only in Sonsonate, La Paz, Morazán and La Unión does the percentage of urban houses with straw roofs reach 10% or more of the total, and the highest of these is Sonsonate with 14.1% of straw.[27] There is some use of corrugated metal roofing, but this too is relatively limited; even in the capital city of San Salvador under 3% of the buildings have this type of cover.

The construction of homes is generally done by paid labor. Carpenters and masons are ordinarily employed, and helpers in such numbers as may be necessary. House building as a communal or voluntary aid venture is now very restricted, and so far as the writer knows, is only found in the construction of *ranchos*. Izalco was the only community in which it was reported that the construction of a home involved the inviting of many friends, the preparation of food by the women, and the sponsoring of a small fiesta with food, drink, and music in return for the help rendered. And this, of course, was strictly within the Indian community.

Most *ranchos* are still constructed with the use of vines to join the poles for the frame work.[28] There is doubtless some *bajareque* constructed in this manner, but the writer did not have the opportunity to explore this subject. While there is scattered use of tile roofs with walls of poles, in general the *rancho* is composed of poles and straw or palm, depending upon which is more prevalent locally. Along much of the coast and through the lateral interior valleys one frequently finds that *rancho* roofs extended to the ground on one or two sides of the structure. In some cases there is a pole wall in addition to this, and in some the roof actually replaces the construction of such a wall. It has been suggested that the reason for this is that such a roof protects the house from certain prevailing winds and rain.

Ranchos and most country homes (aside from *finca* and *hacienda* houses) are usually of a single room. Where construction is of *adobe*, one is apt to find more

---

[27] Censo, 1953.

[28] In Moncagua the term *taquesal* was applied to *ranchos*. This is the only place where the writer encountered the word in El Salvador. In Nicaragua, *taquesal* is applied to the type of construction which is called *bajareque* in El Salvador, and *bajareque* in turn is applied to a section of the house. See Adams, Nicaragua, n.d. (b).

than one room if the family can afford it. According to the urban housing census,[29] the great preponderance of town houses are also of one room. A type of town residence of considerable importance in El Salvador is the *mesón*, a building in which each room is rented out to a different tenant. *Mesones* are of particular importance in the departments of San Salvador and Santa Ana (where they account for over 60% of all urban domiciliary units) and to a lesser degree in La Libertad, Sonsonate, San Miguel, and Usulután. Elsewhere, they are of minor importance. They may be considered as a specifically urban phenomenon of the larger cities. It should be noted in passing that the Salvadorean Instituto de Vivienda Urbana is taking steps to remedy this situation with housing projects. The *mesón* is relatively unimportant outside of the major cities, even though it is found in some of the middle sized towns.

Even though most homes are of one room, it is a common practice in much of the country (particularly the center, north center, northwest, and posibly also the west) to place kitchen work outside the room. It may be in a separate shelter, but more commonly it is under an extension of the main roof, either one built for this purpose, or in the regular *corredor* of the house. In the towns this *corredor* is usually at the back of the house, but in the country homes it may be placed anywhere that it is convenient.

Before leaving the subject of housing, it should be mentioned that in the areas where *fincas* and *haciendas* are common, rural houses are often technically somewhat better made than when constructed by countrypeople who do not have the economic resources for more expensive materials. The use of brick houses, for example, on some *fincas*, or the use of *bajareque* houses in a region where almost all private housing is of poles and straw, represent from some points of view better housing. It should also be noted, however, that while some of the *finca* and *hacienda* housing is technically better, in some cases it does not provide any better general living conditions than private houses. A technically better house is not necessarily more livable than one built according to the needs of the occupant.

As is the case in the rest of rural Central America, the furnishings in the Salvadorean country home are usually homemade or fabricated by local carpenters. The *taburete*, a leather-seated and sometimes leather-backed straight chair, is to be found over most of the country. The *butaca*, a leather covered reclining-chair, was seen in the western part of the country, but its distribution is not clear because the term *butaca* is used in some places to refer to a small bench or stool. None of the reclining-chair type *butaca* were seen in the east. Simple wooden straight chairs are also common, as are small stools, some of which are called *zancudos* (mosquitos). In poorer homes, particularly in the countryside and in *ranchos*, benches of boards and sometimes of logs are to be found. For sleeping, among the poorer people the *tapesco*, made of a series of sticks, is common; the very poor sleep on the ground. Beds, usually of string, but also sometimes of leather thongs, are very common among those who are slightly better off, and in the particularly hot areas *tijeras* (folding canvas cots) are also used. On top of the *tapescos* and the string beds it is common practice to place a *petate* (woven

[29] Censo, 1953.

mat) or a few sacks. In *ranchos* in Izalco, San Matías, and formerly in Panchimalco, it was said that some slept in the *tabanco*, (attic of poles), but this was not said to be common elsewhere. *Tabancos* exist almost exclusively in *ranchos*, and they are not to be found in all of them. The use of hammocks for resting is quite common except along the southwest coast and adjacent highlands. When specifically used for sleeping, such as was reported from El Sauce and Conchagua, it was said that only men slept in hammocks, while the women used the string beds. In Cacaopera, however, it was said that hammocks were in common use by Indians for sleeping, while Ladinos there preferred beds. The hammock is also used frequently by men who are travelling from one place to another, such as in seasonal migrations for work. Sleeping facilities on the *fincas* for migrant labor varies from rooms for families, to dormitories, to nothing. In the last case, the people usually sleep in the *cafetales*.

Still to be found everywhere that *tabancos* are in use is the ladder made of a single log (*guarumo* in El Sauce) with steps cut in it.

Aside from a place to rest, the home is the center of domestic activities, one of the principal of which is the preparation of meals. Before the grains from the fields can be prepared, they must be processed. To remove the rice from the stalk, it is necessary to beat the stalks against some solid surface. For this, three types of surfaces are used. One is the *garrita*, a horizontal set of poles of a couple of inches in diameter, set about two and one half feet above the ground. The poles are usually about six or eight feet long. Two or three men will beat the rice against this platform the grains falling out onto a hide or some other surface below. Another type of stand, used not only for rice but also sometimes for sorghum and beans, is the *aporreador* (called *cacaste* in Moncagua). This too is a surface of sticks, but the sticks are usually finer, under an inch in diameter, the total surface is usually about one meter on one side with three sides protected by a raised wall. The third surface used is the ground itself. The writer could not determine from the survey any specific distribution of these three methods. The *garrita* was reported in Texistepeque, Jayaque (by those who grew rice on the coast), Santiago Nonualco, Guacotecti, and Cacaopera, and was observed along the coastal road west of the Lempa and in the region of Sensuntepeque. The *aporreador* was either seen in or reported from, the Valle de la Esperanza region, Moncagua, El Sauce, Izalco, and on the main highway just east of the Lempa. Beating rice on the ground was reported from Ataco, Panchimalco, San Matías, and Tejutla.

The storage of grains in the home is most commonly done in a *troja*, a low *tapesco* surface inside the house. In this corn is usually stored in the husk. An older method, still reported from Izalco, Santiago Nonualco, and Tejutla, is the storage of grains, especially corn and rice prior to husking, in the *tabanco*. In the western part of the country, among those who can afford it, the metal silo is coming into favor. It was reported in Texistepeque, San Matías, and Izalco as being common, and in limited use in Tejutla and Tejutepeque. It was not reported from the eastern part of the country. For storage of grain as such, some board boxes are in use.

The actual removal of corn from the cob and grains from sorghum is usually done by beating the corn on the ground with a stick, and by beating the sorghum either on the ground or on the *aporreador*. The husking of rice is done with the large wooden mortar and pestle, the *piladera*. The *piladera* is used everywhere that rice is husked in the home. In some towns, motor driven machines are established and the women may bring the rice in and have it husked. This, and the lack of locally grown rice, are the principal explanation for the absence of *piladeras* in certain localities. The *piladera* was also said to be used for coffee in Tejutla.

Both corn and sorghum are usually converted into *nixtamal*. For this, lime is used through most of the country, but in the far northeast wood ash was preferred (El Sauce and Cacaopera), and such was also the case in Panchimalco. In Tonacatepeque both lime and wood ash were said to be used, depending upon the taste of the individuals concerned. In Santa Elena, lime was used, except in the preparation of certain foods.

For grinding the *masa* from the *nixtamal*, the grinding stone is still the main implement used. Throughout El Salvador the grinding stone is set on two forked posts (*horquetas*; *horquitillos* in Izalco), and a bowl, usually a large gourd (*taro*) or metal pan, is set on a third forked stick for the *masa* to fall into. In some places (reported specifically from El Sauce and Conchagua, but seen occasionally elsewhere) a wooden frame substituted for the sticks, and went under the name of *molendero*. In general, the stone used does not have three legs as is the case with the stones in Guatemala, but is rough bottomed.

The general pattern in El Salvador is that the fire is on a raised platform, usually referred to as a *poyo* or *fogon alto*. These are of two main types, the *poyo de lodo* or *poyo de tapesco* which consists of a *tapesco* platform on which mud has been placed, and on top of which the fire is built; and the solid *poyo* of abode brick, stone, or occasionally brick. On top of the *poyo* is a horseshoe shaped ridge of clay within the arms of which the fire is built. This is called the *hornilla*. In Indian towns a floor fire was fairly common, but Tejutepeque and Santa Elena were the only Ladino towns in which it was reported. Where the floor fire is used, it is generally built between three stones (*tetuntes* in Jayaque), the standard Indian method found over most of Guatemala. However, there are some exceptions to this. In Panchimalco, the floor fire is very common, but the *hornilla* is built on the floor. Similarly, in Santa Elena and in Cacaopera, both the three stones and the *hornilla* are used. The writer found no case of the three stones being set up on the raised *poyo*, but in lieu of this, it was reported in Santiago Nonualco, and observed near San Matías, that three solid mud cylinders were set on the *poyos* sometimes. These were called *sapos* (frogs) in Santa Elena.

Besides the cooking fire, scattered over all of El Salvador is the common dome shaped stone and mud oven of Spanish origin. In general, the oven is present in those homes where baking is done for sale. However, in some areas where homes are dispersed, most houses have one.

For cooking, pottery (*comales*; *ollas*; *cajetas*, a small *olla*; etc) is the principal type of ware. Among the townspeople it has been replaced to some degree, but in general its cheapness and availability make it preferable to commercial enamel and metal products for the countrypeople and poorer townsmen.

The fire fan, produced in Nahuzalco, was reported to be in common use in Izalco and Ataco, in limited use in Panchimalco and Santiago Nonualco, rarely used in Texistepeque, San Matías, Tejutla, Tonacatepeque, and Tejutepeque, and not used at all in the towns east of the Lempa. It is clearly a remnant of the older Indian culture and not a part of the Ladino kitchen equipment.

Very little data was collected in the course of the survey concerning types of foods prepared. *Tortillas* and *tamales* are the principal corn foods. The term *nacatamal* was reported not to be used in Izalco and Texistepeque, but was used for the simplest type of *tamal* in Tejutla. A small sweet *tamal*, the *tamalito de cambray*, was reported from Izalco, and a triangular *tamal*, the *tamal pisca*, from Santiago Nonualco. *Atol* was also reported from this last site. The making of *chicha* and clandestine liquor was reported from a number of towns all over the country. The specific substances used for *chicha* are corn, sorghum, rice, wheat, pineapple, and sugar. Of these, corn and sugar are probably the most important, particularly for distillation into *clandestino*.

In certain of the *fincas*, food is prepared in a large *finca* kitchen and served out to the laborers and their families. The usual meal consists of one or more very large *tortillas* with a helping of beans on top. Under these circumstances, the wives and women of the laborers do not prepare food nor keep a hearth going.

The clothing of the Salvadorean is fairly simple. Women's dresses are made by seamstresses, some of whom are to be found in almost every town, and by factories. Men's clothes are made both in scattered clothing specialist areas, such as Nueva Guadalupe and Tonacatepeque, and in factories. In certain regions, notably around Cojutepeque, the women use the black head cloth, *paños*; these become less important as one moves away from this region, although they are common for a church head covering. The *enagua* skirt, still to be found in Indian communities, occasionally is seen on old women in the Ladino populations, but it may be said to have been superseded for this population as a whole.

Over much of the country, especially in the warmer regions, boys often go naked until somewhere between four and 10 years of age. In general, they are dressed simply with trousers around the age of four to six, but in the far southeast, a naked boy eight or ten years old was observed herding cattle from horseback. While girls are usually not allowed to go naked, poorer women in the towns and country generally show little embarrassment at going uncovered to the waist when occupied in some work, such as washing clothes.

In general, countrypeople, and a good proportion of townspeople go barefooted, especially during work.

The Salvadorean domestic establishment still retains a strong portion of Indian heritance in cooking and food preparation, although the origin of certain of the items, such as the *hornilla*, is problematic at present. In clothing, there is very little which may be said to be aboriginal, even among the surviving Indian communities.

4. FAMILY AND *COMPADRAZGO*

In spite of the extensive migration of Salvadoreans to Honduras and other neighboring areas, the country itself maintains a fairly even balance of men and women. The urban areas, as is to be expected, show a preponderance of women, and the rural areas have relatively more men. From the figures in Table 12, it was evident that at least in terms of total departamental figures, there is slight variation in man-woman ratio from one part of the country to another, but the differences are not so great as is found among some population components such as in Panama.[30]

Table 12.—Woman-man ratio in the Departments of El Salvador, 1950

Department	Ratio: Women/100 Men		
	Total	Urban	Rural
Ahuachapán	97.6	112.9	91.6
Santa Ana	99.8	115.1	92.0
Sonsonate	99.6	113.2	92.0
Chalatenango	98.3	104.9	96.2
La Libertad	97.6	113.1	90.2
San Salvador	111.1	118.0	97.6
Cuscatlán	105.7	121.7	100.8
La Paz	101.5	113.9	95.2
Cabañas	100.5	119.1	97.8
San Vicente	103.9	120.3	97.3
Usulután	100.1	118.0	94.6
San Miguel	100.1	111.7	96.6
Morazán	100.0	106.3	99.4
La Unión	99.7	108.0	97.2
Republic	102.1	115.0	95.3

From this table it is clear that there is generally a relatively lower number of women in the rural areas of the west and southwest (Ahuachapán, Santa Ana, Sonsonate, and La Libertad), while there is a relatively greater number in the center, north, and northeast (Cuscatlán, Cabañas, San Vicente, Morazán, La Unión). In urban populations, the center departments (San Salvador, Cuscatlán, Cabañas, San Vicente, and Usulután) have relatively more women, while the north and far east have relatively fewer (Chalatenango, Morazán, and La Unión). This general picture suggests that variations in the man-woman ratio should not have any very drastic effect on the general form of family structure.

The size of the Salvadorean family was alluded to earlier in the section on population. It will be remembered that urban families have an average of 4.78 persons while the rural families have an average of 5.25. This may be interpreted in part as being due to difference in natural increase, but it is also open to inter-

[30] Adams, n.d. (a).

pretation that the difference is in part due to the relatively fewer men in the urban area. The families might generally be of the same size except that many of them (one third in the urban areas, one fifth in the rural) have no male head.

Basically, the Salvadorean family has the same form as does the family in the rest of the Ladino population of Central America: it is bilateral and neo-local. The residence pattern has some variations, however, specifically in some Indian communities. The standard pattern is for a couple to set up a new residence apart from that of either of the parents. In Panchimalco, however, it was reported that patrilocal residence is standard; that is, a couple regularly takes up residence at the home of the parents of the man. As a result, in Panchimalco, many of the households have two or even three generations living in them. Neo-local residence was reported from all the other Indian populations included in the survey except Jayaque. There it was said that some households were patrilocal but most were neo-local. Some patrilocal residence, evidently irregular, was reported from Tejutepeque, and in El Sauce it was said that temporary patrilocal residence, followed by neo-local, was common. Temporary matrilocal residence was reported as an alternative in both Tejutepeque and Cacaopera.

The degree of relationship which is permitted in free unions and marriage varies somewhat. In general, it was reported from towns in the east and center that first cousins were not permitted to form an alliance, and if it did occur, it was rare. In Guacotecti, Cacaopera, Santa Elena, and El Sauce, however, it was said to be of no importance whether such alliances took place or not. The only town in the east where this was specifically reported as being prohibited was Conchagua, a town in which a good proportion of the population is Indian. On the contrary, however, in Izalco it was said to be permitted but not common, and in Santiago Nonualco that it occurred but that it was prohibited.

The extension of the incest prohibition to include children of godfathers was reported from seven towns, again mainly in the west, but more scattered. Alliances between *hermanos espirituales* was reported as being permitted in Ataco, Santiago Nonualco, Texistepeque, Tejutla, Cacaopera, and El Sauce. The informants in Guacotecti and Santa Elena said they knew of no such cases. It was generally prohibited in all other towns except Moncagua from which there were no data on the subject.

There was practically no evidence anywhere of a recognized rule for community endogamy except in Panchimalco. There, however, it was more a case of ethnic endogamy since it was said that there was a tendency for Indians to marry Indians. In Izalco it was said that there was intermarriage between Indians and lower class Ladinos. In general, it seems likely that considerable movement of population over El Salvador, due to varying calls for labor and population pressure in some regions, has broken down whatever tendency may once have existed for community endogamy except possibly among the Indian population.

Marriages and common-law unions are about equally common. Table 13 gives relative percentages by department on the civil status of the population 14 years old and older as reported in the 1950 Census.

These data clearly indicate that there is regional variation in this matter. Ahuachapán, Santa Ana and Sonsonate have high percentages of free unions and low percentages of marriages. Chalatenango, Cuscatlán, and Cabañas show the reverse. Usulután and San Miguel also have a fairly high free union percentage and a low married percentage. The writer suspects that the figure for Santa Ana is probably more representative of the southern section of the department than of the north. It seems likely, on the basis of other similarities, that Metapán is more similar to Chalatenango in this matter than to the more southern coffee region of Santa Ana.

The causes behind the relatively high rate of common-law unions are far from

Table 13.—Civil status of persons 14 years and older, 1950

Department	Single	Married	Common-law union	Other	Total
Ahuachapán	42.6%	18.3%	34.3%	4.8%	100.0%
Santa Ana	45.1	19.0	31.0	4.9	100.0
Sonsonate	41.9	17.7	33.6	6.8	100.0
Chalatenango	40.9	42.0	10.4	6.7	100.0
La Libertad	43.8	24.1	25.5	6.6	100.0
San Salvador	48.6	23.0	22.3	6.1	100.0
Cuscatlán	42.3	36.9	11.7	9.1	100.0
La Paz	44.4	25.1	22.3	8.2	100.0
Cabañas	42.5	39.1	9.8	8.6	100.0
San Vicente	46.8	29.2	15.8	8.2	100.0
Usulután	47.2	18.1	27.7	7.0	100.0
San Miguel	44.7	20.1	28.0	7.2	100.0
Morazán	41.5	26.1	24.2	8.2	100.0
La Unión	41.2	24.3	27.0	7.5	100.0
Republic	44.6	24.3	24.2	6.9	100.0

clear. There are a number of factors which are cited from time to time, and which in certain situations may be operative. The high cost of wedding fiestas was cited in Guacotecti as a reason why some people do not go through the formalities. This reason might well hold in regions such as this north center area in which formal marriage is more common. But it does not seem like an adequate reason for those areas such as the southwest where the large majority of couples are unmarried. A more cogent reason was given by an informant in Chinameca; there, he said, there was a fairly high rate of separations, especially among people who had not had children, and a formal marriage was felt to tie people together and make such separations more difficult. This reasoning does not stand up too well, however, in view of the evidence that marriage seems to make little difference with respect to separations (see data given below). The writer feels that an understanding of the free union situation must begin with the acceptance of the idea that it is a custom among some segments of the population not to get married. How such a custom was initiated in a Catholic country is a historical problem which we cannot attempt to solve here.

It can be noted among men that there is practically no difference between the urban and rural populations with respect to the percentage of persons in free unions. Among women, however, there is reported to be a slightly higher percentage of the rural women than of the urban women in this civil status. In most of the country the rural population shows a slightly higher percentage of free unions than does the urban population. Only in the north and center departments of Chalatenango, San Salvador, Cuscatlán, Cabañas, and San Vicente is the urban greater than or equal to the rural in this respect.

The presence of a high percentage of free unions in itself is indicative of a possibly unstable family situation, but more critical evidence rests in the nature of the family itself. As Tables 14 and 15 will indicate, one third of all urban and one fifth of all rural families in El Salvador have no male chief of household.

This data is highly meaningful. While it can be interpreted that some of these families are headed by widows, only 5% of the total population of both sexes in the republic are widowed, and of these slightly less than half are men, and of the entire group there is no reason to think that they are all heads of households. A comparison of the above table with Table 13 and Table 14 shows that there is little correlation as between those departments which are high in households with female heads and those in which there are free unions.

Furthermore, while the rural area consistently shows a lower percentage than does the urban in households with female heads, the rural areas have, if anything, a somewhat higher percentage of free unions than do the urban. Regionally, the southwest is the area with the relatively highest percentages of common-law unions, and this same region in the rural areas shows the lowest percentages of households with women chiefs. Of the four departments with high urban percentage of households with female heads (Cuscatlán, Cabañas, San Vicente, and Usulután), three (Cuscatlán, Cabañas, and San Vicente) have a low percentage of common-law unions.

The problem of the unbalanced family is doubtless related to other factors. The facts of labor mobility and population pressure are very likely correlates. The small town and the rural dweller, unless he is a member of the permanent labor force of a farm or owns enough land, is forced to migrate. Such migration may be seasonal for certain harvests, such as coffee, sugar, cotton, etc., or permanent or semi-permanent to other parts of the country in search of work or to other countries in search of land and/or work. Northern Honduras has seen the arrival of thousands such immigrants over the past years. Labor migration is the subject of some study in El Salvador now, and little can be added here. From the point of view of family structure, however, younger men who move do not necessarily take women along with them.

The fact that households with female chiefs are consistently more common in towns than in the countryside is doubtless related to the common situation of having more women than men in the towns. Table 12 provides data on this for

EL SALVADOR

Table 14.—Relative percentage of rural and urban men and women 14 years and older who live in common-law union, 1950

Department	Percentage of people 14 years and older in common-law unions			
	Urban		Rural	
	Men	Women	Men	Women
Ahuachapán	25.5%	28.6%	33.8%	42.0%
Santa Ana	27.4	26.7	31.0	36.7
Sonsonate	29.5	29.1	33.7	39.6
Chalatenango	9.3	10.9	10.0	10.9
La Libertad	23.4	22.6	24.7	29.5
San Salvador	23.4	22.2	20.2	22.3
Cuscatlán	16.0	16.4	9.6	10.7
La Paz	20.8	20.6	21.3	25.2
Cabañas	14.6	14.0	8.5	9.4
San Vicente	15.2	14.9	15.0	17.3
Usulután	24.7	23.7	27.3	31.5
San Miguel	25.4	25.6	27.3	31.2
Morazán	21.0	24.9	23.1	25.9
La Unión	24.9	26.6	25.6	29.1
Republic	23.2	23.0	23.3	26.7

Table 15.—Percentage of households with men and women heads in urban and rural areas of El Salvador, by departments, 1950

Department	Percentage of families which have men and women as heads of households in urban and rural areas					
	Urban Head of household			Rural Head of household		
	Men	Women	Total	Men	Women	Total
Ahuachapán	66.9%	33.1%	100.0%	82.6%	17.4%	100.0%
Santa Ana	68.0	32.0	100.0	82.3	17.7	100.0
Sonsonate	66.2	33.8	100.0	82.5	17.5	100.0
La Libertad	68.0	32.0	100.0	82.8	17.2	100.0
Chalatenango	71.0	29.0	100.0	80.7	19.3	100.0
San Salvador	68.4	31.6	100.0	79.1	20.9	100.0
Cuscatlán	60.0	40.0	100.0	76.9	23.1	100.0
La Paz	64.2	35.8	100.0	76.6	23.4	100.0
Cabañas	61.3	38.7	100.0	80.1	19.9	100.0
San Vicente	59.5	40.5	100.0	77.6	22.4	100.0
Usulután	60.0	40.0	100.0	77.2	22.8	100.0
San Miguel	65.5	34.5	100.0	78.2	21.8	100.0
Morazán	65.3	34.7	100.0	78.5	21.5	100.0
La Unión	67.2	32.8	100.0	78.8	21.2	100.0
Republic	66.3	33.7	100.0	79.6	20.4	100.0

El Salvador, and it is consistently true of other Central American countries as well. However, the dynamics behind the presence of these households needs much more exploration.

There is the possibility that the registered relative increase in the rural population may stem in part from urban men migrating to rural areas for work but leaving their families either permanently or temporarily.

Another aspect of the problem is revealed in a coffee *finca* in the Valle de la Esperanza region of Usulután and San Miguel.[31] There the writer had the opportunity to compare the family structure of three different situations: the coffee *finca*; urban Chinameca; and the refugee camp composed of people left homeless by the earthquake of May, 1951. By comparing family relationships and informants' data from these three settings a number of points became evident: (1) Of 23 families on the *finca*, 6, and in some cases large ones, had a woman chief of household. Of the 17 families which had male chiefs of household, 7 were cases in which all or most of the children were those of the women by another man. This suggests that the census data on women heads of households may even underestimate the situation of unbalanced families and separations, because it necessarily omits those families in which the woman has shifted from one man to another. So the separation picture is even more critical than that portrayed by the census. (2) The families in the refugee camp were originally residents of the principal towns hit by the earthquake. If instability and lack of balance were a delicate matter among these families, it is to be expected that the refugee camp situation, in which work was hard to get, would cause the families to split. Of the some 180 families in the camp at the time of the study, 99 were composed of a man and his legal or common-law wife and various other dependents. In an equal number of these familes, however, there were relatives who were connected only through the wife, such as being children of the woman by another man. In only 21 were there such dependents who were related through the man (e.g. children of the man by another woman). There are two points of importance to take from this. First, something over 50% of the families were stable enough to survive the shock of the earthquake and retain their balance. This means that although instability and unbalance do exist, there is also a body of the population which can remain stable. Second, these data, combined with that provided earlier on the population as a whole, clearly indicate that there is a very significant proportion of family units in which the most significant connecting relationships exist through the woman. We find, for example, many cases of homes in which there is a woman, her daughter, and her daughter's children, and no husbands.

This last point is of great importance, not because the entire population is like this, but because there is a significantly high percentage. It results in the situation that even though the patterned residence at the time of marriage or beginning to live together may be neo-local, the subsequent departure of the man of the family leaves it a domestic establishment based on the fact that the

---

[31] Adams, 1952a.

woman lives there. It is, if you like, matrilocality-by-default. Among these families, there is a certain amount of movement of men; they may come in to live for a while, and then drift off to another town or region, and live with someone else. Sometimes they do and sometimes they don't feel responsibility for their children who remain with the mother.

This type of family, localized about the woman, is probably more common, specifically in those areas in which it is reported that there is a high percentage of households headed by women (see Table 15). It must also be kept in mind that such a family organization is also related to the situation where a couple are living together and they are raising children which one of them (usually the woman) has had by another person. From the census data, this type of woman-centered family is more common in towns than in rural areas, and from field data, it was much more common in the *fincas* of the Chinameca-Jucuapa area than in the adjoining towns. Census data (as reproduced in Table 15) indicate that the *fincas* of the west are not necessarily similar in this respect, as the percentage of women heads of households is very low. However, it seems likely that most of the center belt and east resemble the Chinameca-Jucuapa situation.

The solidarity of the Salvadorean nuclear family was reported in some places (Texistepeque and Chinameca) to be increased after the birth of children. This does not, however, seem to hold in all cases in view of the numerous cases in which the woman has retained her children and the man has gone elsewhere.

From the point of view of the gradual stabilization of the family the situation at present does not seem to have much to offer. Children brought up in homes in which their own father may long since have left are not likely to create families which are balanced and stable. Furthermore, the fact that it is the custom, the common thing, to have families of this nature provides constant reinforcement for their perpetuation. Combine with this the fact that neither the landholding nor the labor situation are basically changing to provide the basis for increased balance, there does not seem to be much reason to think that stability will increase in the near future.

This discussion of the nature of the Salvadorean family has not provided any final answers to the issues of instability and unbalance. It has, we hope, served to point out the extent of the problem and some of the factors inherent in the situation.

Turning now to another type of bond, the *compadrazgo*, we find that this relationship is of considerable importance in El Salvador as it is elsewhere in Central America. It was mentioned earlier that in seven of the towns it was reported that the incest prohibition was extended to include *hermanos espirituales*. Some consistency was also reported in that in eight of the towns it was said that the same godfathers were never obtained for both baptism and confirmation, and in three more it was said that such was done only occasionally. Only in Guacotecti and Santa Elena was it said to be customary to get the same godfather for these different events. No such consistency was reported with respect to finding the same godfather to serve for the various siblings in a family, however. The Indians of

Ataco and Izalco usually tried to do this, and the Ladinos from Santa Elena were reported to observe the custom. Elsewhere, however, it was said to be an irregular practice, certainly not a fixed custom.

In the choice of *compadres*, wealth and/or higher social position was reported to be of importance, especially among the poorer people, in all towns of the center and west except San Matías, Tejutepeque, and Guacotecti. In the east it was specifically said to be of importance only in Moncagua and El Sauce. In most places in the center and west it was said that *compadres* were frequently sought out from among people who were respected or from among friends. Only in Texistepeque was it specifically stated that close relatives were sometimes asked.

In general, the impression the writer received in the course of the survey suggested that the *compadre* relationship was not in itself an extremely strong one. Its specific functions seemed to provde for a means of relating people of different social status, and to strengthen a relationship which may already have existed through kindship or friendship. The irregularity of the inclusion of *hermanos espirituales* within the incest prohibition is probably indicative of a general weakness in the relationship.

5. GENERAL SOCIAL STRUCTURE

The basic picture of the social structure of El Salvador is similar to that which has been described elsewhere for Guatemala,[32] but with certain differences in emphasis due to a more rapid process of ladinoization, a more highly developed large scale agricultural pattern, and the related density of population. Notes on the nature of the Indian population will be found in Chapter III. In the present chapter, we are going to concentrate on the Ladino population as such.

The social class structure of El Salvador is comprised of four distinct groups: cosmopolitan upper, local upper, local middle, local lower.

The cosmopolitan upper class is that small group of usually wealthy persons who own, or are related to families which own, a large percentage of the land under cultivation and who usually make their residence in one of the major cities or occasionally or periodically on their landholdings. They are a part of an international social organization. The local upper consists of that group of landholders who live in the smaller towns, frequently live on their farms or in a municipal capital, comprise what is known locally as the *sociedad*, *gente de primera categoría*, *los acomodados*, *los más arriba*, etc. Their wealth varies over a wide range and its significance is often relative to the particular set of local circumstances. For example, in Tejutepeque, the informant felt that there was no *sociedad* present in the town, that the upper group locally must be considered as *medios*. From the point of view of the present classification, the group to which he referred as *medios* may probably be considered as the local upper class. When he said that no *sociedad* was present, he was referring to what we have called the cosmopolitan upper.

The local middle class is usually composed of town-dwelling small business-

---

[32] Adams, n.d. (c). Unless otherwise specified, the same terminology is followed in both studies.

men, employees, artisans, small to medium landholders who are able to make a reasonably good living off their land without resort to renting or labor, and who are able to employ a few *mozos* to aid them in their work. This group may be said to be small everywhere except in the major cities. They are fewest in the rural areas except in those regions where small to medium landholdings are fairly common.

The local lower class varies in its composition depending on the local economy. It is composed of *colonos*, landless renters, owners of tiny parcels of land which frequently do not suffice to support the owner, and the day laborer. It is the overwhelming majority of the population in most rural areas, and probably composes between 40% and 80% of most of the town populations. This group is frequently referred to as *los pobres, la gente humilde, gente más baja, gente del pueblo*, etc.

From the point of view of local significance, the cosmopolitan upper exerts an important influence in that his need or lack of need for labor controls the immediate destinies of much of the lower class population. Similarly, those who live on a large farm as *colonos* very often live in houses provided by the landowner and eat food prepared in his farm kitchen. In terms of numbers the large landowners are not important, but as foci of power, they cannot be underestimated. While this holds particularly true for rural areas, in which large farms are to be found, it is also reflected in the social structure of the nearby towns. Whether town resident or not, the cosmopolitan upper's town associates inevitably in great part are members of the local upper group. The attitudes and opinions of these two groups are usually parallel, although the local upper is often considered by the cosmopolitan upper to be provincial. Local business depends upon the wealth brought to the area by the landholders, and local businessmen usually try to conform to their needs and desires. In this way, the interests of the cosmopolitan upper is consistently represented through the local upper in those areas where the former is of importance, and the local upper is supported in both his economic and social class position by his links with the cosmopolitan upper.

The potential importance of the cosmopolitan upper for the economic wellbeing of a town was expressed by the informant in Tonacatepeque. He mentioned that it was most unfortunate that most of the land in the *municipio* was in small to medium holdings because there was no one rich enough to help the town. Were there *haciendas*, the town would be the recipient of funds and would benefit thereby. In fact, of course, the use to which such funds are put when available varies greatly with the type of persons in the municipal and district government. There is no doubt, however, that the wealth of the town is dependent upon the wealth of the rural area surrounding it.

The local upper is a critical group in every community. This is the nucleus of educated people to whom the middle and lower class members turn to for help in financial matters. The attitude expressed by members of this class towards the lower class varies somewhat depending upon the economic relations between the two and the degree to which the members of the lower class are Indian or have recently become Ladinos. Usually, two contradictory attitudes are expressed depending upon the subject under discussion and type of person with whom it is being discussed. One is an expression of a feeling of superiority: people of the lower class are ignorant, dirty, undependable, dishonest, and perhaps biologically inferior. The other, to be found more commonly in those regions in which there is no distinct cosmopolitan upper class, is one of equality: that the *acomodados* and *humildes* are really one, that there are few differences between them, that it is just a matter of some being better off, even though intermarriage is almost unheard of. The writer has had these two attitudes expressed to him by the same informant concerning the members of the local lower class. The two attitudes reflect two different phases of the relationship between the members of these classes.

The first concerns the relationship between an individual of the upper class with the members of the lower class in general, i.e., as a laboring population, or as clientele in his store; and individually with respect to certain members of the lower class who have demonstrated themselves to have certain of the qualities mentioned earlier. The second usually concerns the relationship which is related to communal matters, frequently religious matters, and often face-to-face personal interrelationships. Where there is a cosmopolitan upper group present, the feeling of equality is usually weak if existent at all. The local upper usually strives to be a part of the cosmopolitan group, and the lower group is usually economically at the bottom of the ladder, day laborers and *colonos*.

In most towns, the local upper is composed of residents of fairly long standing whose families have been of some prominence in the history of the community. This is especially true in those regions where there have not yet been established large landholdings with a cosmopolitan upper group. This is the group which we have elsewhere called the "Old Ladino."[33] It is usually an endogamous population which maintains significant power in local social control. Marriage alliances outside of the local community are with people of the same social class of other communities.

Outside of the towns, the local upper class consists of basically the same population group, but merely those who, for one reason or another, prefer to live on their lands. Frequently, members of this class will have homes both on their lands and a house in the town, and will spend part of their time at each.

While the local upper class may be considered to be basically similar in both town and country, the local middle class shows marked differences. The town middle class is usually composed of small businessmen, *técnicos* (mechanics, for example), drivers, the group known as *empleados* or employees hired to do nonmanual labor, and a few farmers. In the countryside, this group consists of the people who own enough land to permit them to hire a few laborers as aid during the season of heavy work, or even to keep one or two laborers employed full time. The rural or agrarian middle class person may in some cases appear to be little different from a member of the lower class. He works in his own fields, lives in a house which differs little in style but may manifest some slightly greater luxury than that of the poorer person. However, he is independent of others, he has enough land to provide him with necessities, and except in time of marked crop failure, need not consider working as a laborer.

---

[33] Adams, n.d. (c).

Thus, the town middle class person approaches more the concept of the middle class usually held by western sociologists, while the country middle class person diverges from that concept.

The lower class, which forms the great body of the population, varies from those who are *colonos*, dependent upon a large farm for food, housing, and cash, to small landholders who do not have enough to live off of and who consequently must spend part of their time as day laborers or rent land. This latter group may in general be distinguished from what we have designated as a country middle class, in that the middle class is not entirely a subsistence farming population; much of what they raise is intended for sale. Among the lower class, however, the farmers are basically subsistence farmers, and the sale of their produce is forced upon them by an immediate need for cash.[34]

In the towns the lower class includes day laborers and people involved in the small home industries. Among this group are many women who must support themselves and their children with the sale of home made starch, vinegar, candy, cigarettes, and various of the other industries described in an earlier section.

Socially, there is neither such a clear nor sharp line to be drawn between the middle and lower class as between the middle and upper. The survey shows considerable variation from one community to another, and from a specific locale to another. The degree of separation which exists between the members of the various classes also varies with the history of the particular place, the personalities of the upper class members, the economic relationship which holds between the classes, and recentness of ladinoization of the lower class.

Social mobility in the towns and countryside from a lower to a higher class goes according to much the same process which is involved in changing from Indian to Ladino. It is very difficult for a person of a lower class to move up the social scale within his own residence areas. He is too well known for his antecedents and the place he holds in the local picture. However, movement to another town or a city permits him to move up. Education, of course, plays a basic role in this ability to move. The town middle class is generally somewhat literate as is, of course, the upper. Hence, a person from the lower class need change certain of his customs prior to moving up the scale.

There are, however, numerous points of common ground between the lower and middle class. Concepts of sanitation are generally the same; preferences in clothing styles basically similar, although the poorest resort to rags; and concepts of personal morality insofar as marriage and marital fidelity are concerned are similar. As a result, it is possible for a lower class person to move elsewhere, learn some trade, such as that of driving a truck, elementary accounting, or set up a small business (if he can get the capital), and he is likely to be considered locally in his new residence as a middle class person.

The lack of a traditional label for the middle class in El Salvador, as in most of Central America, does not mean that it is of little importance. It does mean, however, that its importance is at present limited. Since the end of the long

---

[34] It will be noted that these views diverge from those of Guandique, 1950, p. 116. Prof. Guandique considers the middle class to include only the urban group.

Martínez dictatorship of the 1930's and early 1940's, there has been no radical reversal in politics in El Salvador such as occurred in neighboring Guatemala; the middle class has been growing more slowly into a position of importance. The relatively stronger and smaller cosmopolitan upper class in El Salvador has in part been responsible for this lag, and the memory of the excesses of the attempt in the early 1930's to establish a Communist controlled population still remains with the Salvadorean people.

Within the towns, there is frequently a classic residence distribution of the members of the classes. In seven of the towns it was stated that the *acomodados* tended to live nearer the center of town, while in another they tended to live in only two of the four *barrios* which composed the town. Similarly, the poorer people and the poorer houses (those of poles and straw) were to be found at the edge of town and sometimes in specific *barrios*. It should be pointed out that this distribution is not universal, however. A number of towns reported that there was no distinguishable residence pattern in accordance with either wealth or social position. These cases were usually those in which differences were not too great, such as in San Matías.

The relationship which holds between the town dwelling and country population in El Salvador is of some interest, particularly in view of the relative increase in rural population indicated by the comparative census figures of 1930 and 1950 (see Chapter I). As elsewhere in Central America, the towns act not only as commercial centers of the surrounding rural area, but they are also the centers for legal and political business and for religious activities. Towns usually serve fairly distinct regions. The neighboring towns of Chinameca and Jucuapa in the Valle de la Esperanza provide an interesting case of this regional influence. The two towns, scarcely four kilometers apart, are joined by a fairly good road. But both are capitals of districts as well as of *municipios* (see section on political organization), both are supplied by distinct local regions, and both are jealous of their autonomy. Each of the towns lies in a distinct department, and the departmental line serves roughly as the dividing line between their respective zones of influence. The market in Jucuapa depends for its local products almost exclusively upon the territory which lies within the Department of Usulután, while that of Chinameca depends upon an area lying within the Department of San Miguel. There are certain exceptions to this. There are some rural centers which administratively fall under the municipio of Chinameca, but which are directly connected by road to Jucuapa, and not so connected to Chinameca. These rural centers use Jucuapa as their commercial center and not Chinameca.

An important component of the population of many of the towns is the laboring population. It is easier to gain work from a town center than from an isolated country homestead. As a result, in most towns there is among the lower class a regular population of laborers who travel out from the town to coffee, cotton, or sugar harvests in other parts of the country, and return to look for work locally when finished. It is probably in considerable part this population which accounts for some of the relative increase in rural populations over the past 20 years. The towns offer limited opportunities for work, but do provide centers from which people may look for work. Women, particularly, who must support families have more opportunities in a town than in the country. The towns consequently serve as a place where people, who may from most points of view be considered as rural, may seek means of livelihood. If there is an increase in *hacienda* or *finca* activities, then they can move out from the towns; if there is a reduction in this kind of work, they can move back into the towns.

Social life in the towns generally revolves around the social class distinctions just described. The importance of the classes, in actual social intercourse, is modified or emphasized, depending upon local events and those in the world at large. However, there are occasionally local institutions which provide crystallization of these social differences. One such institution is the social club. These clubs usually develop in larger towns. Jucuapa, prior to the earthquake of 1951, had three such clubs, each one specifically composed of persons from one of the three distinct local classes. The clubs, known locally as *casinos*, provided places for their members to have parties, meet for social intercourse, and to give permanence to the distinction between the classes. The *Casino Jucuapense*, composed of local upper class people, and the *Casino Democrático*, of middle class people, each had a *rocola* (juke box), while the *Casino Juvenil*, a lower class club, could not afford one.

In the town of Santa Elena there was one such club, called *El Vencedor*, which has a building with billiard tables. It was called locally a "sports club" because it also had a soccer team. In practice, according to informants, in spite of its name, it served more as a social club than as a sports club... unless billiards be considered as a sport.

In Tonacatepeque a very different sort of organization was reported. There, the *Sociedad de Obreros "Juan Pablo Londoña"* was said to consist of lower class men. Headed by a directive council of ten men, they held celebrations of anniversaries and birthdays of the members, but served to look for work for members who were unemployed or needed additional work. Unfortuntely, the writer did not have the opportunity to explore this organization more thoroughly; but it is the only one of its kind which he has encountered during the course of his surveys in Central America.

The only kind of clubs which were almost universal among the towns visited on the survey were sports clubs. These usually consisted of a soccer team, a basketball team, or both. Some towns had two such clubs, but most had only one. In all cases, they were composed of young men.

It is probably significant that in only one town was there encountered any sort of permanent civic club or organization devoted to the bettering of the town. This also was in Tonacatepeque, where a *Comité de Ornato*, composed of some 15 men and women of the better class, collected money to improve the park, streets, and cooperate with the endeavors of the programs of the government being sponsored through the nearby Public Health Demonstration Area. There were in a number of towns local *comités* for the only political party, PRUD. However, these seemed generally inactive and the informants showed little interest in them.

6. LOCAL POLITICAL ORGANIZATION

El Salvador is divided for administrative purposes into 14 departments, 39 districts, and 260 *municipios*.[35] As elsewhere in the present series of studies, our interest is with the structure of the political organization at its lower levels, specifically that of the *municipio* and subdivisions of the *municipio*.

The Salvadorean *municipio* is the basic unit of the national administrative and territorial hierarchy. Fundamentally, it is the same administrative unit to be found in Nicaragua, Honduras, and Guatemala. Prior to 1952 the officers of the *municipio* were appointed, but under a new law, they are now elected.[36] These officers consist of an *alcalde*, a varying number of *regidores*, and a *síndico*. The *alcalde* is the mayor, the chief officer of the *municipio*. The *regidores* are aldermen, and together with the *alcalde* and *síndico* form the city council. The number of *regidores* varies between 2 and 8, depending upon the size and the category to which the town is assigned by the national government. Of the towns visited, five had 2, five had 4, one had 5, two had 6, and one had 8 *regidores*. Theoretically, a *ciudad* is supposed to have 8, a town classed as a *villa*, 6, and one classed as a *pueblo*, 4. In fact, there are differences among towns in this respect. Conchagua, not a district capital, had 8 *regidores*, while Tonacatepeque, which is such a capital, had 5. The *síndico*, or syndic, is the *municipio's* legal representative. He also has such duties as verifying land measurements and examining land disputes.

According to the national municipal code, the law by which the *municipios* are governed, each *regidor* is supposed to oversee certain phases of the municipal responsibilities in the local territory. These are: public instruction, jails, public works, water supply, butcher shops, public plazas, streets, general sanitation, decoration of the town (during fiestas, for example), markets, the slaughterhouse, public lighting system, the cemetery, and weights and measures. The *regidores* do not stay in the municipal building, and aside from attending regular monthly meetings and special sessions, are theoretically only called in when something concerning the phase of activity assigned to them is under discussion. Each *regidor*, or each pair, is assigned a group of these responsibilities. However, during the interviews, no one ever knew to whom the various things were assigned. They always had to be looked up in the session book. As was the case in Guatemala, these responsibilities are more honored as labels than as active posts. There were even cases of having a *regidor* assigned to oversee the public lighting system (because the *Ley Municipal* said it was necessary) when there was no public lighting system in the town. The situation seems to be one of a traditional respect for the authority which says that these responsibilities must be looked after, but also traditional lack of interest in them.

The *alcalde*, *regidores*, and *síndico* together make up the town council. Usually, they meet on the fifth of each month (in Ataco on the last day of the month)

---

[35] In 1950.

[36] Appointing municipal officials was reinstituted by the Martínez regime. Earlier in the century, municipal officials were elected.

to discuss current business. The actual daily business of the municipality is carried on mainly by the *alcalde* and a group of employees (*empleados*). The *alcalde* is the only paid official. He receives 6.5% of the taxes collected in *municipio* as salary. Formerly the *alcaldes* were paid a fixed sum by the national government, but recently the present system was instituted in order to encourage the local official to collect the taxes from the people within his jurisdiction. The employees of the *municipalidad* always include a secretary and a general handyman. Most groups of employees are more complicated than this, however. The number and variety depend upon the size of the *municipio* and its wealth. Perhaps the most extensive such group among the towns surveyed was that in Izalco. There, besides the secretary, there were stenographers, a municipal treasurer, a bookkeeper, an errand boy, a janitor, an administrator of the market, a *guarda rastro* (man in charge of the slaughterhouse), an administrator of the *Baños de Tecuzal* (some local natural baths which lie within the *municipio*), and the municipal police. Among the other employees which were found in one place or another were a plumber, a custodian of the cemetery, a man in charge of the electric light plant, and a man in charge of the public water supply. In many towns there is no municipal treasurer and, in those places, the *alcalde* acts in that capacity. Where there are few employees, the *policía municipal* or *guarda municipal* may also act as errand boy and janitor.

This general organization represents a departure from the type of municipal organization which existed during the period when the Indian population was larger and more distinctive. There are remnants of the older organization still to be found, however, and three such cases (Ataco, Cacaopera, Panchimalco) were encountered on the survey. In Ataco, besides the regular municipal officers and employees, there was also a group called the *Patrulla Civil Municipal* composed entirely of Indians. This group consisted of 2 *mayores*, 2 *alcaldíos*,[36a] and 8 to 12 *alguaciles*. This group was split into two parties, each headed by a *mayor* and assisted by an *alcaldío*, together with from 4 to 6 *alguaciles*. The two parties served alternately for half a week each. Their specific duty was to report at the *municipalidad* building in the evening, spend the night, and act as a patrol of the town during the night hours. During the day they dispersed to their private tasks. The members of the *patrulla* are appointed for an entire year and receive no pay.

In Cacaopera a slightly different system of turns has survived. There, there are four *mayores de las llaves*, four *mayores auxiliares*, and eight *alguaciles*. These are split into four parties of one *mayor de las llaves*, one *mayor auxiliar*, and two *alguaciles*. Each of these parties reports for one week out of four for general service in the *municipalidad*. They are not paid, and are also named by the *alcalde*. In Cacaopera, however, it was said that this *comisión especial*, as it was called, was composed of both Ladinos and Indians. These are the only survivals of the old system of serving turns which I encountered in municipal capitals.[37]

These offices just described are those which are filled in the *cabecera municipal*,

---

[36a] Not to be confused with *alcaldes*.
[37] Other notes on the Indian political system will be found in chapter on Indians.

the town in which the municipal government is located. A *municipio*, however, is a piece of territory, and the territory as such is divided into rural segments called *cantones*. The term *valle* is used in some places instead of *cantón* when referring to these rural units. The same variant appears commonly in Nicaragua[38] and reflects the tendency to locate rural settlements in valleys. People may live scattered out over the *cantones*, or live in small villages or settlements which go under the names of *aldeas* or *caseríos*. It is standard practice for the *alcalde* of each *municipio* to name certain officials within the *cantones*. Usually, these posts consist of a *comisionado propietario*, *comisionado suplente*, and a group of *alguaciles*. The *suplente* acts both as second in command and as substitute for the *propietario*, while the *alguaciles* are the helpers. The function of the *comisionado* and his helpers is to carry out orders of the municipal council in the *cantón*, report events of the *cantón* on the weekly visit to the *municipalidad*, and to generally maintain law and order. Among the things included in the weekly report (usually brought in on Sunday, but on Monday in some towns) are births and deaths which have occurred during the period.

The number of *alguaciles* which a *comisionado* will have depends upon the extent of the area of the *cantón* and the size of its population. The largest number encountered on the survey was in Tonacatepeque, where there were 14; elsewhere there were between 3 and 12. None of these rural officers receive any salary, and they are appointed for a period of one year. In Panchimalco, the old system of turns is still found among these rural officers. There, there are 3 *comisionados* and 12 *alguaciles*. They are split into three parties of one *comisionado* and 4 *alguaciles* and each party serves for a period of four months of the year. This was the only case encountered of the turn system among the rural officials. Also in Panchimalco there is no survival of older elements within the system of municipal offices of the town itself. The *comisionados* in the rural *cantones* were said always to be Indian because Indians knew better how to deal with the people.

Within the towns themselves, there were few cases reported of distinct territorial subdivision administrations. About one half the towns visited were divided up into *barrios*, but in almost all cases (with the exception of some *comandantes de barrios* mentioned below) there were no distinctive officers responsible for these *barrios*. They were essentially social units, and not political units.

All the officers described thus far have been civil officials. Beside these, there are judiciary officers and military personnel appointed in the municipal capital. There is in each municipal capital a *juez de paz propietario* and a *juez de paz suplente*, the second of which serves as a substitute for the first. They handle all the civil cases which come up within their jurisdiction. On the military side, there are two types of functionaries. In each *municipio* there is a *comandante local*, and he names a *comandante cantonal* in each *cantón*. The *comandante cantonal* usually has as assistants a *comandante segundo* or *suplente*, two *cabos* (corporales), and some eight soldiers. All these men are civilians, appointed for a specified time as military officers in their areas. They wear no uniform. Their main functions

[38] Adams, n.d. (b).

are to serve as police in the rural areas and to recruit annually the necessary quota of young men for the national army. In addition, in certain places there are also posts of the *Guardia Nacional*. These are manned by regularly uniformed soldiers of the national guard who also act as police for the region. These men are dressed as soldiers, carry rifles, and may be seen walking in pairs in all parts of the country.

The *comandante local* sometimes also names *comandantes de barrios* within the town. This was reported from both Tejutepeque and Tonacatepeque. This permits him to have aids working not only in the rural areas, but also among the townspeople.

While the *municipio* provides the critical local government, there also exists another administrative and territorial subdivision, the *distrito*. The Salvadorean district is composed of a number of *municipios* (between 3 and 18). The *alcalde* of the municipal capital which also serves as the district capital is also the *jefe del distrito*, or *alcalde distrital*. The person holding this post acts as a general overseer of the activities of the municipal *alcaldes* under his jurisdiction. The town which serves as the district capital is also the seat of the *Juez de Primera Instancia*, the next superior court over the various justices of the peace.

The *municipio* in El Salvador is usually responsible for certain activities which go on in the town. The most common and important of these is the market, if there is one, the slaughterhouse, the upkeep of the streets and plazas of the town and the roads of the *municipio*, and the upkeep of the cemetery. While the upkeep of the roads and the cemetery is still done through voluntary labor in some of the other countries, these tasks are done with employed labor in El Salvador. The system depends upon the collection of local taxes, all of which are transmitted to the national government. The national government then takes a percentage of this income, and places it in the national bank on deposit in the account of the *municipio* from which the taxes originated. This money is then drawn upon by the *municipio* to employ men to repair the roads and give the twice annual cleaning to the cemetery. In some cases, the payment of the cemetery cleaners is made with funds taken from the income from the sale of burial plots. The cleaning of cemeteries belonging to *cantones* is a voluntary affair among the residents of the *cantón*. Evidently the municipal government does not pay too much attention to these affairs.

The taxes upon which the *municipio* must rely for its welfare are numerous, but because they also represent the income of the national government, not a great deal remains for municipal use. Among other things, income is derived from a road tax, rental of posts in the market, taxes on stores of various classes, on *pulperías* (small stores), pharmacies, on mills, on coffee buying agencies, on coffee and rice *beneficios,* on *trapiches,* on social clubs (such as the Jucuapa *casinos*), on ox cart licenses, licenses on both private and public dances, on each head of beef and pork slaughtered, etc. If the town has electric light owned by the municipality, then of course there is income from that source.

The *municipios* of El Salvador no longer are the owners of large extensions of municipal or *ejidal* lands. While many were at one time in control of much of the municipal territory, these lands have long since been sold off and are now in private title. It was reported in Tejutla that the *ejidal* lands there were repartitioned in 1912, and divided up among the Indians of the *municipio*. Within a few years, however, many of the individual holders had begun to sell their parcels.

Even though El Salvador is under a constitution which calls for an elected president, the period of the writer's familiarity with the country was a political "off season" and he saw little indication of small town and rural interest and participation in political parties and allied activities. There was only one party, the PRUD, and during the writer's visits it manifested little activity. The civil administration, however, gives one the impression of considerable homogeneity when comparing it with the parallel situation in Guatemala. In the latter place, there is still a great deal of variation in municipal organization from one *municipio* and one region, to another. In El Salvador, the variations are of little significance except historically, as they appear as survivals of an older period.

7. RELIGIOUS ACTIVITIES

Like the rest of Ladino Central America, El Salvador is predominantly Catholic. Protestant congregations of varying sizes were reported in all western and central towns visited except San Matías, Tejutepeque, and Guacotecti. In the eastern towns, they were only reported from a rural *cantón* of Moncagua and within one urban *barrio* of El Sauce. In none of the towns surveyed did the writer encounter any evidence of conflict or especially bitter feelings between the Catholics and the Protestants. In one case, El Sauce, the Protestant converts were evidently limited to certain families of one *barrio*, and there was some bitter feeling between the *barrios*; but there was no indication that the differences in religion were responsible for this inter-*barrio* feeling.

In order to describe the religious practices of the Catholics of El Salvador, it is convenient to distinguish between three types of activities: those in which individuals or family groups alone participate; those in which larger segments of the community participate, but the members of which are not necessarily tied by bonds of kinship; and those in which the entire community or representatives thereof participate.

Among those practices which are essentially private, restricted in participation to individuals or family groups, are family worship of a saint, pilgrimages, and prayers for the dead. Most homes in both the towns and countryside of El Salvador have pictures of one or more saints or holy figures. It was reported in four of the towns surveyed that it was a fairly standard practice for the members of the family, especially the women, to offer prayers to the most important of these saints on their day. The most common practice is to hold a novena, invite intimate friends, and provide a repast on the final night of worship. In some places, prayers are simply offered on the saint's day. In six of the towns it was reported that some families observed these practices, but some did not; and in two, San Matías and Tonacatepeque, it was said to be most uncommon for the families to have home worship even though most had either pictures or small images of the saints in their homes.

Pilgrimages, or *romerías*, to shrines were reported to be common from all towns except Tejutla. With a few exceptions, most such pilgrimages are to centers within a fairly short distance of the home, that is, one could go and return in the same day if one so desired. In the west, the centers of this type which were mentioned were Santa Ana, Coatepeque, and Jicalapa; in the central part of the country, San Juan Talpa, Zacatecoluca, San Vicente, San Ramón, Cojutepeque, Guayabal, Tonacatepeque, and Suchitoto were said to be of importance. And in the east, Ciudad Barrios, San Miguel, Guatejiagua, El Sauce, and San Alejo were mentioned to be of local importance.

Another type of pilgrimage center is that which draws upon people of a much larger region. San Antonio del Monte, near Sonsonate was the most important of these, and Chinameca and Jucuarán may be said to be similar but less important. All the towns surveyed west of the Lempa, except Tejutla, reported that people went in varying number to Sonsonate. Few went from the most distant towns, Tejutepeque and Guacotecti. No town east of the Lempa, however, reported that anyone went, and in one it was said that the people had never heard of the shrine. Chinameca is not so important a pilgrimage center as Sonsonate, but it was reported from two towns fairly distant (Tonacatepeque and Panchimalco) that people went there. Jucuarán is a secondary center of importance east of the Lempa; it was reported pilgrimages were made there by people of Cacaopera, Conchagua, and nearby Santa Elena.

Clearly the most important single shrine, however, was none of those in El Salvador, but Esquipulas in Guatemala. All but three of the towns visited reported that people visited Esquipulas, and this included those five towns visited east of the Lempa, the most distant from the shrine. Of the thirteen towns in which it was said that local people visited Esquipulas, five said that relatively few went, but the remainder said that many made the trip. The five which said that few went were scattered from west to east (Jayaque, Panchimalco, Santiago Nonualco, Moncagua, and Conchagua), and so it seems to be more a matter of local preference than merely of distance.

Besides all those which sent pilgrimages to Esquipulas, two towns reported visiting shrines in other countries. In Guacotecti, it was said that pilgrimages were made to Tomalá in Honduras, and in El Sauce, the pilgrimage to El Viejo in the Department of Chinandega in Nicaragua was said to be important.

Private religious practices also take place on the occasion of the death of a member of the family. While baptism is generally not observed with a fiesta in the home, and marriages are usually accompanied by a gathering of family and friends, only death occasions an extensive home religious ritual. A novena is usually held in the home of the deceased immediately following the death. Sometimes intimate friends are invited to participate in all nine nights of prayer, but probably more common is the practice of restricting the prayer to members of the family for the first eight nights, and inviting in others for the final night. When this is the case, the last night usually involves serving coffee, bread, or some other refreshments.

As is the standard Ladino practice in the other Central American countries, it is usually a woman who leads the prayers at the novena. In three of the towns in which Indian populations are still prominent (Jayaque, Santiago Nonualco, and Cacaopera) it was said that both men and women led the novenas, but in Santiago Nonualco, it was specifically stated that it was only among the Indians that men did this; among the Ladinos, only women led. There were two exceptions to the general Ladino picture. In Tejutepeque, it was said that men did, very occasionally, lead novenas, and in Conchagua, it was stated specifically that some Ladino men led the prayers, but that the Indian men did not. The situation in El Salvador with respect to this matter generally conforms to that which is found in Guatemala and Nicaragua: a woman leading a prayer session is indicative of ladinoization, whereas in Indian communities the men were regularly the leaders in religious affairs. However, as has been noted, there are exceptions in El Salvador. In three towns in which other Indian customs have survived to a varying degree, women lead in the novenas: Ataco, Izalco, and Panchimalco, and in two towns of those mentioned above men are said to occasionally lead among the Ladinos.

In all towns, it is customary to repeat the novena following a fixed time period after the death, to hold a Requiem Mass, or do both. In two towns only (Ataco and Izalco) was it reported that a second novena was not held, and that only a Mass was held on the anniversary of the death. In Ataco it was said that annual Masses were held if the people could afford it, but in Izalco, evidently only the first anniversary is so observed. Elsewhere, a second novena was always held. In most places, it was customary to hold this one year following the death, but in Texistepeque, it was customary to hold it one month after; in Cacaopera and Moncagua, 40 days after; and in El Sauce, six months after the death. In two towns, Tonacatepeque and Guacotecti, it was said that if the family could afford it, a novena was held annually for nine years following the death. In some of the towns it was said that the more wealthy would have a Mass at the end of the year in addition to the novena, and in a few cases, that the Mass would be repeated annually.

Within almost every community of any size, there is an important type of religious activity in which certain segments of the community participate. These are the *hermandades* and *cofradías*. Were more information available, it might be possible to distinguish some consistent difference in the use of these two terms, but on the basis of the data acquired in the survey, they appear to be almost interchangeable. These sodalities are basically associations of persons organized for sponsoring of the fiesta of a certain saint or holy day. As elsewhere over much of Spanish America, there has been a trend in recent years away from the custom of placing the entire annual burden of expense for a fiesta on a single *mayordomo* of one of the sodalities to dependence upon contributions of all the members. Together with this trend has been one away from the older organization of the sodalities, involving *mayordomos, capitanes, priostes, mayores*, etc. to the directing council type of administration involving a president, vice-president, treasurer, etc. The situation in most sodalities described to the writer fell somewhere between these two extremes. They depend principally upon voluntary contributions, but in some cases these contributions were in fact provided in great part by one man. And even though the officials acted like a directing council, the older names were still retained.

In most of those towns where there is still a distinctive Indian population, the sodalities of the Indians are usually regarded as being distinct from those of the Ladinos. Santiago Nonualco was the only Indian town in which it was said that the sodalities included people of both groups. While the characteristics of these groups peculiar to the Indians will be taken up in the chapter devoted to the Indians, much of the organization is parallel in both groups. Basically, the Ladinos take less active interest in these organizations than do the Indians, and among Ladinos, women are much more active than men.

The most important sodalities encountered in the survey were those of the *Guardia de la Santísima* and *Hijas de María*. These were reported to exist in nine towns, and in all cases except one, they were composed only of women. The exception was the *Guardia de la Santísima* in Tonacatepeque where it was said that it was a man's sodality. The specific holy day celebrated by the *Guardia* varied, but often it carried the additional task of helping in the general upkeep of the church. In Texistepeque, *Corpus* was the annual holy day celebrated, and the members prayed the first Thursday of every month in addition to this. In Tejutla the members of the *Guardia* arranged that some of their members would pray every day in the church, and made a point of attending all holy processions. The *Hijas de María*, as is the case in most places, was composed of unmarried girls. When they got married, they left the sodality. In San Matías it was said that the *Hijas* organization there disintegrated a few years ago through lack of interest.

Also of considerable importance are the sodalities of the *Virgen del Carmen* (four towns), *Sagrado Corazón de Jesús*, the *Virgen de Guadalupe*, and *Cristo Rey* (three towns each). The sodalities of the *Virgen del Carmen* were composed of women in two towns, and of both men and women in the other two. *Cristo Rey* was a man's sodality, while the *Virgen de Guadalupe* was a woman's. The *Sagrado Corazón* was a man's sodality in two towns and had both men and women members in one. Besides these, there were various other sodalities such as those of the *Virgen de los Remedios*, *Virgen de Fátima*, *Virgen del Tránsito*, *Jesús Nazareno*, etc. In all, excluding the Indian *cofradías* and *hermandades* which usually involved both men and women, 25 of the sodalities were composed of women, 8 of men, and 4 of men and women. This reflects an important facet of Ladino life, in that in such social activities as these, men and women seldom work together. Not only do the women play a greater role in the active religous life, but they do so alone. When the men do participate, they usually do it as a distinct group.

While more information would be necessary to verify this, it seemed that the organization of these sodalities varied somewhat regionally. In the east and center, the pattern seems to be for each group to name a *mayordomo*, a man, and a *capitana*, to be in actual charge of the planning. In the west, however, the presence of a directing council seemed to be more common. In those organizations where a *mayordomo* was appointed, he frequently held the post indefinitely, until he, the priest, or the members became dissatisfied with his work.

Except in El Sauce, where it was reported that there were no sodalities organized, most Ladino towns had between two and four such groups. The number and activity of sodalities in any one community seems dependent upon a number of factors. Among the most important are: the energy and time devoted by the priest; whether or not there exists either or both an Indian population or an old local upper class population to provide constant support for the groups; and whether or not the population of the town is fairly stable with respect to emigration. The writer got the impression that one of the principal reasons for the lack of such groups in El Sauce was that there was such a large and constant movement of people to Honduras in search of work or land.

In general, the image of the saint to which the members of the sodalities are devoted remains in the church. The presence of a special *cofradía* house in which the saint is kept is, insofar as the survey information indicated, restricted to certain Indian communities. The use of a piece of land for harvesting a special crop for the benefit of the sodality is also a trait which seems now entirely restricted to a few Indian communities. The Ladino sodalities are financed entirely by contributions.

While sodalities are generally voluntarily formed groups of people devoted to the worship of a particular saint, there are some which act either in a dual capacity or specifically as a mechanism to promote the physical upkeep of the church building. Every town, whether there is a resident priest or not, faces the problem of cleaning the church, making periodic repairs, and generally caring for the property. In Ataco, Jayaque, and San Matías, the women's sodality of the *Guardia* took this responsibility. In Jayaque there was organized a special sodality of men, the *Sociedad de Adoradores*, which also shared this work. In Guacotecti each of the sodalities is expected to contribute.

Perhaps the most important religious event in which the entire community participates is the annual *fiesta titular*. Only in the Indian communities is the responsibility for all or part of this still left in the hands of the sodalities. In most towns, the standard practice is for the *alcalde* to name a *mayordomo* or committee which is in general charge and names various helpers. In Tejutla the *alcalde* and the priest together call a town meeting to name a *mayordomo*, and the person named frequently holds the post for a number of years, until he wishes to be relieved of it. In Tonacatepeque, a *Comité de la Fiesta*, with *mayordomo* and *capitanas*, is named every August to prepare for the fiesta in the following December. This group, however, handles principally the civic aspects of the fiesta, while the organization of the religious part is in the hands of the priest. The same situation exists for the *Comité Pro-Fiesta* in Conchagua. In Tejutepeque, the committee which is named also has charge of disposal funds for the religious aspects. In Guacotecti, the fiesta is almost entirely religious and is in the hands of a semi-permanent *Junta de Fiesta Titular*. Usually, responsibility of those in charge include collecting contributions to finance the affair, as well as planning for the various events which are to take place in the course of the celebration. In most places, the funds are solicited by persons assigned the task. In Tejutepeque, the custom of sending the saint out on *demanda*, a practice found in some of the other countries, is used. Three months prior to the fiesta, the saint, San Rafael, visits many of the homes in all the *cantones*, and each house pays for the right to have the saint visit. In this way, funds are gathered to pay for the fiesta. During the entire year, also, a *cuadro*, or picture, of one of the virgens is circulated throughout the *municipio*, and also collects money. While this practice was not observed in any other town visited on the survey, it was reported in Santa Elena that the town of Ereguayquin sent a saint on *demanda* annually. This does not seem to be as widespread a custom as it is in some of the other countries, however. The municipality of Santiago Nonualco reported a somewhat different mode of financing the civic and recreational aspects of the *fiesta titular*. On all municipal transactions, a 4% tax was imposed. The money from this tax was turned over to a *Comité de Testigos* who were responsible for safeguarding it, and it was then used for the fiesta.

The *fiesta titular* in most towns involves not only religious observances, but a commercial fair, games and sports, dances, and sometimes parades. Among the customs which are commonly observed are the *palo encebado, toro de fuego, carrera de cintas, carrera de caballos*, fire crackers and rockets, and social dances. The *corrida de toros* was reported from only one town, Jayaque, and cockfights were said to be prohibited, but practiced in private in one town, and in a community near to one of the towns surveyed in the west. Three towns said that they had floats (*carrosas*). Masked and costumed dances in which historical dramas were enacted were found only in Indian communities. In Moncagua it was said that the Dance of the Moors was held, but the participants wore no masks and it consisted more of a recitation than a dance. The social dances were often sponsored by the *municipalidad* and admission was usually charged. This effectively made it a middle and/or upper class affair.

While most towns have but one patron saint, two on the survey, Conchagua and Moncagua, reported having two *patrones*. In each case, one of the two fiestas was treated as the principal fiesta, and the other was observed mainly as a religious event.

Besides the *fiesta titular*, the various sodalities in the towns sponsor other smaller fiestas during the year. But the only other fiestas which seemed to be of some importance everywhere were Holy Week and Christmas. Holy Week was not observed in some towns, except through an increase in praying. Christmas, however, usually involved other customs. The most important of these is the *posada*, wherein images of Mary and Joseph seek a place to stay over a fixed period prior to Christmas Eve. The usual custom is that people who wish to house the saints ask the person in charge (sometimes it is a sodality, sometimes it is the priest), and so the route of the saints through the town is fixed beforehand. In four towns, the search for a *posada* lasted from the first until the 24th of December (Panchimalco, San Matías, Tonacatepeque, and Tejutepeque); in three others, it was said to last only the nine nights prior to the 24th (Texistepeque, Santa Elena, El Sauce). In Ataco a variant form was reported. From the first until the 14th of December, the Virgen made the visit alone; this was known as the *alborada*. Then from the 16th until the 24th, the images of Mary and Joseph together seek *posada*. The visits of the Virgin during the *alborada* is accompanied by some party making, while the visits during the *posada* are somewhat more serious affairs. In three towns, Santiago Nonualco, Guacotecti, and Conchagua, it was reported that the *posada* custom was not observed.

A Christmas custom reported only from Guacotecti and Santiago Nonualco (both places where the *posada* was not observed) was the *pastorela*. This consisted of a group of children dressing like shepherds, carrying staffs, and going out to sing around the town on Christmas Eve.

Unfortunately, the writer did not explore the extent to which the custom of arranging a *nacimiento* was observed.

While on the subject of fiestas, it should be noted that although inquiry was made through the course of the survey, the custom of the *gritería*, such as is observed in the Pacific belt of Nicaragua, was not reported from any town visited.

Effective support from the priesthood seemed somewhat stronger in El Salvador than in some of the other countries. Of the towns visited, eight had resident priests, and in the others, a priest was said to come whenever called or regularly every other Sunday. The writer heard no complaints voiced, as was the case in Guatemala, that there were not enough priests, and that the towns had been forgotten. This, however, may be due to the fact that distances are shorter and the survey was made basically along passable roads. It may also reflect less concern about the priesthood.

8. SICKNESS AND THE SPIRIT WORLD

Our concern in this chapter is not with human ailments as they are perceived by the medical profession, but as they are conceptualized by the town and country people of El Salvador. Further than this, we will not deal with illnesses which are treated much in the same way by cosmopolitan people and countrypeople, but those specific aspects in which the folk conception of illness is distinct from that of the western physician. There is little doubt that many people in El Salvador are familiar with many, if not all, of the various ideas about to be described. But in the writer's experience, there is little realization on the part of the population who do not share in these ideas that they have unequal distribution and that they form a fairly coherent body of beliefs. We are fortunate to have available a brief but intensive study by Mr. Edwin James of sickness concepts from one rural area of the *municipio* of San Matías. So far as the writer knows, it is the only such systematic study to come out of El Salvador, and for this reason, if no other, it warrants inclusion as an appendix to this study. While most of the data provided in the present chapter take certain concepts and look into their variety and distribution, Mr. James' study provides us with a cross section of these and other concepts as they are integrally conceived in a single community.

The Salvadorean town and country person generally has little opportunity to have recourse to adequate medical facilities. While the government is taking pains at present to remedy this situation, there is little doubt that there also exist for them various other possible means of seeking a cure for their sicknesses. In the towns themselves and for the rural people living nearby, one of the most important curers is the pharmacist. Most of the towns visited had pharmacies and in some cases the pharmacist even advertised his ability as a curer. There is evidence that pharmacists are becoming of even greater importance since the advent of antibiotics. Their recommendations have even greater chance of success. In many cases the pharmacist is not particularly trained, but accumulates his knowledge through some years of recommending various remedies. His clients casually report back to him on the success of certain of the remedies and the failure of others, and through this long trial and error method he does in fact often attain a fair competence in diagnosing and prescribing for the most common local ailments.

Of equal importance with the pharmacist, but probably complementary to him in function, are the local *curanderos* or *parcheros*. The types and importance of these lay curers vary tremendously over the country, and insofar as the writer could tell, their presence is dependent upon local history and conditions and there is no particular regional distribution with respect to their use or disuse. *Curanderos*, as elsewhere, tend to specialize. Among the most important are the following:

(a) Specialists in bone setting and massaging. Sometimes these two specialties are combined, and sometimes they are distinct. A competent bone setter usually commands a good deal of local respect. His work is only occasionally associated with mystical appurtenances and he either demonstrates obvious skill or makes obviously bad jobs. Massaging is usually part of the bone setting process, but there are also specialists who do this type of work in connection with other illnesses which require it as a part of the cure. One of the principal illnesses thus treated is *empacho* (see below).

(b) Curers of childhood illnesses. These curers are usually empirical midwives, *parteras*, and handle certain illnesses connected with childhood. Of principal importance are *caída de mollera*, *ojo*, and *pujo* (see below). It should be mentioned, however, that in the communities visited, the mother evidently played a more prominent role in this curing than in the other countries surveyed to date. This reflects a lesser degree of specialization than has been reported hitherto.

(c) Specialists in psychological and mystical illnesses. These are of various types and their presence is related to the presence or absence of certain disease concepts within a locality. There are *parcheros* who specialize in curing *susto* in Tejutla, but as will be noted, most communities do not conceive of *susto* to be very significant, and have no such specialists. There are also some *parcheros* who behave very much like, and are sometimes called, witches. They elaborate charms and potions, place lizards and snakes in people's stomachs, cure them of this, etc. But these too depend upon local credence for their practice. In a very few places it was reported that there were or had been recently, practicing spiritualists. Yet another type was the family reported from Tejutepeque which was reputed to sell secret "waters" and salves which could instantly heal wounds.

Perhaps the point of greatest significance concerning the types of curers and their practices in El Salvador is that there seemed to be little consistency over the country as a whole. In this the culture gives much evidence of undergoing a confusing change, with older methods and practices taking on new elements, and newer techniques adjusting to older concepts of sickness. In general, this situation bodes well for the introduction of scientific practices. Such introductions can be made much more successfully if the older practices do not seem to be satisfactory; and the variety of curing specialists indicates that there is not complete satisfaction with the older methods.

The one community which reported the retention of an integral system of curing, quite divergent from that of the rest of the country, was the Indian community of Cacaopera. There it was reported that a regular part of curing was a preventative procedure which involved ritual sacrifice of a chicken as well as other elements. The curer, or *zajorin*, is said to pay the saints in order to both cure and prevent certain illnesses. This payment involves the provision of a chicken by the patient. Theoretically, the individual must provide this payment every year as a preventive measure, and another yet if they get sick. Unfortunately, time did not permit further exploration into this aspect of the Cacaopera Indian culture.

The illnesses or conditions on which data was collected on the survey were: *pasmo, aire, empacho, ojo, pujo, tuna fuerte, susto, flato, caída de mollera*, and *hijillo*. While specialists in curing show considerable variation, the illnesses themselves show a remarkable consistency over much of the country.

In seven of the towns visited in the survey (scattered over the country) *pasmo* was consistently considered to be the result of getting something cold in the stomach. It was said to come mainly from eating cold food, even a piece of cold bread. In Ataco it was said also to come from getting cold feet. In two towns (Tonacatepeque and Moncagua) it was intimated that cold foods were also bad foods. In Texistepeque, it was also said that eating bitter food would cause it. In Tonacatepeque there was some distinction made between people getting sick of *frio* or *calentura* resulting from poor preparation of food, and another type of *pasmo* which occurs in children, which is also derived from bad feeding and causes the child to be weak and unhappy. In referring to "cold" food, the informants were evidently not specifically thinking in terms of the well-known hot-cold distinction in quality of foods. *Pasmo* seems to be derived in these towns from food which is actually cold in temperature. The hot-cold quality distinction which has been reported to be of such importance from many other areas was not reported by survey informants to be of comparable importance in El Salvador. In most places where information was solicited, only a very sketchy idea of which foods were cold and which were warm or hot could be given. The only town in which an actual list was forthcoming, Texistepeque, gave a classification which varies in some important respects from those commonly found elsewhere: hot foods are fish, crabs, shrimp (usually cold foods elsewhere); cold foods are fruits, i.e., papaya, *melón, guanaba, lima, naranja*. However, information collected by George Foster[39] from a *partera* in San Salva-

[39] Foster, Ms.

dor, and the intensive study made by Edwin James (see appendix of present study) indicate that hot-cold differences are well recognized. Foster's data referred specifically to the diet of the post-parturient mother, while the material gathered by James related to certain illnesses. In this discrepancy between the survey data and that collected through more intensive study, the latter is probably more correct.

Returning to *pasmo*, four towns reported somewhat divergent concepts related to this term. In two, Izalco and Tejutepeque, it was said to be of two types, *pasmo de sol* and *pasmo de luna* (overexposure to the sun and the moon). In Izalco, this overexposure was said to cause a headache, while in Tejutepeque it was said to make some part of the body swell up. This latter may be related to the idea expressed in Jayaque, that *pasmo* attacks open cuts and wounds and makes them worse. This idea of the susceptibility of open wounds is most commonly expressed with respect to *hijillo*, described below. The other divergent concept is that already described for Tonacatepeque.

The cure for *pasmo* usually consists of herbal teas (made from the bark of the *piquilita* tree, from *alcatán*; mainly bitter herbs) when it is a matter of cold in the stomach. In the case of the *pasmo de sol* and *pasmo de luna*, the Izalco people prepare a mixture of toasted mint leaves, cloves of *chichapinza*, a fine oil, and then this is rubbed on the head to alleviate the headache. Swollen limbs are cured with massages and medicines of various types.

Integrated with the general *pasmo* concept is that of the effects of *aire*, *mal aire*, or *viento*. The specific result of exposure to a cold breeze or air after one has been indoors or been working and sweating is to give a stiff neck. More serious results were said to be trembling and crossing of the eyes (Tonacatepeque) and defecating blood (Tejutla). In Guacotecti it was specifically said that *aire* was the cause of *pasmo*. Cures involve taking herb teas, slowly twisting the head back to its normal position, and a purge of castor oil.

Another related disease concept is that of *empacho*. This illness is usually thought of as a form of indigestion. Diverse causes were ascribed in different communities visited. Among the most important were (a) eating late or fasting for too long a period; this could cause the stomach to form a bow; and (b) eating badly cooked food, bad food, or cold food. Also, a nursing mother who is sweating will pass it on to her child through the milk. The most common cures involve massages, purges, and herb teas. In Izalco a divergent concept was provided: there it was said that some fruits will make certain people sick. One cannot predict which fruits will be bad for him without trying them out. When it is found that a person is made sick in this way, the fruit in question is cooked to an ash, and a tea made from this is drunk. After this, it is possible for the person to eat the fruit with no ill effects. In three towns, Santiago Nonualco, Tonacatepeque, and Moncagua, it was said that *empacho* is mainly a childhood malady.

A pair of illnesses which are closely related over much of El Salvador are *pujo* and *ojo*. *Pujo* is an infant diarrhea, usually involving a need to defecate and an inability to do so. It may be caused in the same way as is *pasmo* (by too much heat or cold; reported from Tejutla and Cacaopera), but most commonly it is the result of the force emanating from a particularly "strong" person. Strength in a person is differently conceived from one community to another. In some it is a thing that a person is born with and that one either has or has not. In others, it may come from certain conditions, such as when a woman is pregnant, or when a person has been out in the sun, *asoleado*, or has been working and sweating. When the *pujo* is a result of too much heat or cold, its cure is similar to that of *pasmo*. In Cacaopera, it was said that burning lemon leaves and having the child breath the smoke was a cure. This was reported here and elsewhere as also being a cure for *hijillo* (see below). The cure for *pujo* resulting from exposure to a strong person is the same as that for *ojo*.

Ojo is a more generalized infant illness which results from being seen by a strong person. Giving *ojo* is usually interpreted as an unintentional event, the strong person not meaning to do any harm to the child. However, in some communities, Tonacatepeque, Izalco, and Guacotecti, it was said that it is often done with evil intent, and in the last named place it was identified with *daños*, damages done intentionally by a bad person. A child which has been *ojeado* cries, has fever, and is generally ill. Basically, there are three techniques of curing. One is to place an egg under the bed or hammock of the child; the *ojo* causes the egg to cook and is thereby removed from the child. In *cantón* El Jícaro[40] of San Matías and Panchimalco it was reported that the egg was also rubbed over the body of the child prior to this operation. Another cure is to wrap the child in the sweaty clothes of the person who caused the *ojo*, and/or to have the person who caused it hold the baby and rock it. The third cure, and probably the most common, is to prepare a mixture (this also should preferably be done by the person who is responsible for causing the *ojo*) involving some combination of rue, *aguardiente*, incense, garlic, olive oil, chewed tobacco, and have this rubbed or spit on the child. In El Sauce, an aberrant form of *ojo* causation was reported: there, an adult who was *ojeado* as a child was the person thought to be responsible for causing *ojo* in a child.

The strength which a person has as a cause of *ojo* and *pujo* goes under a special name in parts of El Salvador. The term *tuna, tunar*, or *tuna fuerte* first reported from the *cantón* of El Jícaro by James, was also reported to be used in the communities of Ataco, Santiago Nonualco, Tejutla, and Cacaopera. Elsewhere, informants said they did not recognize the term. The best description of *tunar* will be found in the cases provided by James in the appendix to this report. Basically, it is the strength which certain people have which enable them to cause *ojo, pujo* in others, and which also protects them from certain illnesses. This term was not reported in the Guatemalan survey and, so far as the writer knows, is an essentially Salvadorean product.[41]

---

[40] James, Appendix to this report.

[41] Having had the benefit of James' study, *tuna* was looked for in Guatemala (Adams, n.d. (e)) and it was found only in the border town of Atescatempa. The origin of *tuna* or *tunar* is not clear. The word means "idle and licentious life," or leading such a life, according to Appleton's Dictionary. Its use in the present context might be derived from the expression *humor fuerte* which refers to the same quality of strength; or to *lunar*, a skin blemish, the presence of which was said to give a person the strength to cause *ojo* in Guazacapán, Guatemala.

In two towns a similar term, *tunal*, in the expression *cae el tunal*, was used with respect to the illnesses of *caída de mollera* and *susto*. There seemed to be no conceptual relation with the terms *tuna* and *tunar*, however. *Caída de mollera* is a standard illness of infants over all of El Salvador. It is essentially the same illness found in all other countries of Central America, and results from the fontanelle of the infant falling and choking it. The standard treatment is to hold the child upside down by the feet and tap the bottom of the feet to make the *mollera* fall back in place. Additional variant forms of curing involve putting rue on the feet, massaging, rubbing the child with oil, and blowing smoke on it. Infant diarrhea was also attributed to *caída de mollera* (reported in Izalco, San Matías, and Tejutla). The cause of the falling of the *mollera* is said to be the result of rough handling of the child or lack of care on the part of the mother. In the two towns where it also goes under the name of *cae el tunal*, frightening the child also causes it.

Fright, or *susto*, itself has a rather spotty distribution over El Salvador, and at least three concepts concerning it. Basically, the illness is simply something which results after one has been frightened. One concept is that just described, where it results in *caída de mollera* in infants, and is cured in the ways described. Another is that it happens also to adults, but that it is cured simply by drinking a tea made from the *hierba de susto* (Tejutepeque and Santiago Nonualco). And finally the most complex and classic type of *susto* is that reported from Izalco and Cacaopera, where the fright involves the loss of one's soul and the cure involves regaining the soul. In Izalco the fright was said to result from one of a number of things, seeing a person unexpectedly, an animal, one of the spirits (see below) or the spirit of the *Señor del Monte*. Evidently, the *Señor del Monte* is responsible for taking up the soul when lost. To cure the person, he is taken to the place where the soul was lost, he is beaten three times, and each time his name is called out. If the *susto* occurred without the person knowing where it happened, then he is taken to church and prayed over. In Cacaopera, the soul of a person lost through *susto* is said to be involved in some sort of "conquista" on the saint's lands, and a *pago a los santos* is required to cure him.[42]

The distribution of *susto* indicates that it is an illness which either has never been of great importnce in El Salvador, or is one the importance of which declines with the advance of ladinoization. All communities east of the Lempa reported not even knowing of the illness. The variety of ways which it is viewed indicates that it is a zone in which *susto* is an alternative and not an essential part of the sickness concept pattern.

A kindred ailment, *flato*, was reported from three towns in the east (Cacaopera, Moncagua, El Sauce) when informants were asked about *susto*.[43] *Flato* does not

---

[42] The combination of soul loss with *susto* in these modified Indian communities seems to conform with the hypothesis advanced in an earlier study (Adams, 1952b., p. 102) that Indians under a certain degree of ladinoization, specifically Modified Indian communities, may make this combination, while it is not necessarily made either in Traditional Indian nor in Ladino communities.

[43] Unfortunately the writer did not encounter this until he was making the last visits and consequently does not know whether it is present in the west or not.

necessarily seem to be related to flatus, but is a nervousness which may be derived from a variety of emotional experiences. Fright and extreme grief were given as two common causes, and the principal symptoms were insomnia, general nervousness, and stomach discomfort. People were said to die of it, and in Conchagua it was said that *curanderos* could cure it. In Cacaopera a concoction of spices and *aguardiente* were given the patient before and after meals to alleviate it.

Hijillo appears through El Salvador consistently in much the same form that it is found in the far eastern part of Guatemala. Basically, it consists in a person with an open wound or scratch, or with a cold, or in some places just sick of anything, going near a corpse. The *hijillo* is bad air which emanates from the corpse and aggravates whatever condition the person may have. Having a cold or wound is conceived as a weakening condition which when present permits the *hijillo* to have an effect. If a person is not sick, *hijillo* is not thought to affect him; and some people who are particularly strong (who have *tunar fuerte*) may not even be susceptible when sick. Going near a corpse includes visits to a cemetery or a wake. Some claim that there is no cure for *hijillo*, others that whatever cure one would use for the illness which made the effect of *hijillo* possible was the only cure. In four towns (San Matías, Tejutla, Cacaopera, Santa Elena) it was said that the use of lemon leaves would cure it. In the first two towns the leaves were supposed to be burned and the smoke inhaled; in the last two, the leaves were to be cooked and placed on the wound. Conchagua was the only town in which the informant claimed not to have heard of *hijillo*.

Illness attributed to witches, sorcerers, and spirits was reported in about half the towns in which inquiries were made on the subject. Asking about witchcraft in a survey as brief as the present one can hardly be satisfactory since if it is present there is often a reluctance, either because of embarrassment or fear, to speak of it to a stranger. It was reported as being present to some degree in all the southwestern Indian towns and in Texistepeque, San Matías, Santa Elena, and El Sauce. Three types of witchcraft were specifically mentioned: (a) that which involves the control of a spouse, lover, or rival in love and sexual relations; (b) making a person ill by putting a toad, lizard, snake or some other animal in his intestines or stomach; and (c) making a person go crazy. Such activities are said to be carried on by both men and women although in certain places it may be attributed to people of one sex only. The practices of witchcraft are usually referred to as *malos oficios* or *daños*.

There are various spirits which are regular inhabitants of the Salvadorean countryside and play a role in the loves and welfare of the inhabitants. The greatest abundance were reported from Izalco (probably because the informant was particularly interested in the subject). The most common was the *cadejo*, the nocturnal dog who as often as not was considered to be a friend of the lost drunk and protector of night travellers. As causes of illness, the *Señor del Monte*, of Izalco as well as the other spirits (the *cipitillo*, *siguanava*, the *sombrerón*) which might give one *susto*. The spirits of the dead are called upon at times, usually by spiritualists. In Izalco one informant claimed that he knew of various cases where spiritualists had been able to marry living women to ghosts, and that the women had been able, *mirabile dictu*! to conceive children by their phantom husbands; one woman had been married to the ghost of Nicaragua's heroic poet, Rubén Darío. James[43a] describes a number of cases of resorting to spiritualism. The presence of spiritualists was generally denied in the towns visited, but in view of the data collected by James, it is not possible to say just how important they may be in the lives of the town and country people.

Finally, getting back to hard ground, informants in eleven towns reported that children commonly ate earth. In three other communities it was said to occur, although rarely, and in one only did the informant claim that it was not present.

This brief survey of certain of the concepts of sickness and practices of curing indicates that El Salvador has a healthy set of folk illnesses. While the curers seem to be less consistent in type than in certain other countries, the illnesses themselves and the method of treating them provide as broad a range and variety as are to be found elsewhere. Certain of the Indian towns, particularly Cacaopera and Izalco, provide a more abundant lore than do most of the communities visited, and certain illnesses, especially *susto*, seem spotty in distribution; but, in general, there are ample concepts with country-wide consistency to provide the Salvadorean with many alternative ways of analysing his internal problems.

III. THE INDIANS OF EL SALVADOR

In the previous chapters we have described in brief certain of the more prominent aspects of the Ladino culture of El Salvador. In this chapter on the Indian population, we are going to try to indicate in what ways there exists a significant population of people who observe certain distinctive customs and are thereby differentiated from the Ladino population. Salvadoreans will generally agree that there are Indians with a distinct culture still living in their country; the costumes and crafts of Panchimalco, Nanuizalco, and Izalco are obvious evidence of this. But a problem of some magnitude remains to be solved because it is obvious that there are other communities which share in this Indian culture, although in a highly modified degree. They are much more ladinoized than are the three towns just mentioned.

Before going further into the subject, a word of caution is in order. In this discussion, as in others in this survey series, the word *Indian* is used in a strictly cultural sense. When we refer to a person or a community as Indian, we are saying nothing about their racial or genetic inheritance; by the same token, when we say that a particular community is *not* Indian, we are not saying anything about racial characteristics. We are concerned here wholly with behavior, with socially shared habits and ways of life, not with biological or genetic questions. The term *Ladino* is used, as in Guatemala and adjacent parts of Central America, to denote the population group which is not Indian, i.e., that group which shares a variety of customs and habits which are partially of Indian and partially of

---

[43a] In Appendix at end of this report on El Salvador.

Spanish or some other origin, the whole of which constitute what today is the Spanish-American culture of a given nation. Similarly, when we use the word *ladinoized*, we are referring to the degree to which a given community or individual has taken over the habit patterns of the Salvadorean Spanish-American culture.

1. THE IDENTIFICATION OF THE INDIAN AND THE PROBLEM OF LADINOIZATION

A completely satisfactory identification of the Indian of El Salvador is far beyond the capacity of the present survey. Our purpose is to draw out a general picture, to provide a framework for thinking about the Indian which will permit

Table 16.—Estimated number of Indians in certain towns visited in the survey

Municipio	1950 Municipal population (Census)	Proportion reported as being Indian by informants	Estimate of number of Indians
Ataco	6,711	80% of total, rural and urban	ca. 5,400
Izalco	22,255	20–30% of total, about 75% of urban	ca. 5,000, almost all urban
Rural	16,289		
Urban	5,966		
Panchimalco	10,338	80% of urban, almost all of the rural	ca. 9,750
Rural	8,253		
Urban	2,085		
Santiago Nonualco	12,460	75 to 90% of total	ca. 9,300 to 11,200
Jayaque	3,819	Majority of rural are Indian; majority of urban are mestizo	ca. 2,000 to 2,500
Rural	2,032		
Urban	1,787		
Conchagua	4,444	About 50%	ca. 2,200
Cacaopera	9,562	About 6,000; 200 of whom live in the town	ca. 6,000

one to judge with some systematic basis the degree to which a given community is Ladino and to what degree it must be considered as a distinctive Indian group. Towards this end, our discussion will be based in great part on the characteristics observed and recorded in seven towns: Izalco, Panchimalco, Cacaopera, Ataco, Conchagua, Jayaque, and Santiago Nonualco. A segment of the populations of each of these *municipios* were reported by informants to be "Indian." We go on the assumption that when a population group is called Indian, there is some set of characteristics which distinguish them from the population which is called Ladino. Table 16 provides an estimate of the number of people in each of these *municipios* that informants considered as Indian.

In the course of visiting these communities, it became amply clear that the degree to which a distinctive culture had been retained varied greatly between one and another. In Jayaque and Ataco, for example, there were no distinctive clothes seen; everyone dressed in the same general style. Whereas in all the other towns there was some difference, if even in only a small part of the population.

In some of the towns, an Indian language was still spoken among at least some of the older inhabitants, whereas in others it was reported that the last use of an Indian language disappeared over 50 years ago. And there were other differences, as will be related shortly. But in all these towns the informants said that there was a portion of the population which was Indian.

In order to answer the question, "How many Indians are there in El Salvador," we have two problems: (1) What do we mean by Indian? and (2) How many people are there who fit into this definition of Indian? The major part of this chapter will deal with the first of these. Before turning to the problem of definition, however, let us glance briefly at some historical notes concerning the Indian and some estimates concerning their present numbers.

Baron Castro quotes census data for the year 1796 (see Table 17) from which it is possible to calculate the accompanying percentages.[44]

At this period, about 160 years ago, the heaviest body of the Indian population

Table 17.—Percentage and distribution of Indian and Ladino population in 1796

Region	Total population	Indian percent of total	Distribution of Indian population No.	%	Distribution of Ladino population No.	%
Santa Ana	11,001	64.2%	7,129	8.6	3,872	5.0
Sonsonate	24,684	62.8%	16,495	19,9	8,189	10.4
San Salvador	68,659	57.0%	39,164	47.2	29,495	37.8
San Vicente	21,402	48.2%	10,334	12.5	11,068	14.2
San Miguel	35,289	28.0%	9,888	11.9	25,401	32.6
Total	161,035	51.6%	83,010	100.1	78,025	100.0

was concentrated west of the Lempa. The Ladino population, on the other hand, was more evenly distributed, and in particular, there were relatively more Ladinos than Indians east of the Lempa.

Modern estimates of the size of the Indian population vary tremendously. Baron Castro[45] gave an estimate of 20 % in 1942. At that time, the results of the 1930 Census had not yet been published. When they were published, they gave the startling figure of 5.6 %.[46] It is impossible to know now precisely what the census takers had in mind in 1930, but there is considerable evidence that they were not thinking about the Indians in the terms employed in the present study. Table 18, which provides the data of the 1930 Census, recorded that in the Department of Morazán there were 6 Indians. The data from the present survey indicate that in the municipio of Cacaopera alone there are upwards of 6,000, and other evidence indicates that there are probably over 3,000 more in the nearby municipio of Lislique.[47] The 1930 figures state that there are 34 Indians

---

[44] 1942, p. 235. The totality of these regions comprise the entire area of modern El Salvador.

[45] 1942, pp. 526–7. [46] Census, 1942. [47] Lothrop, 1937, p. 129.

in the Department of La Unión, and data from the present survey indicate that there are possibly over 2,000 in the municipio of Conchagua alone. We can only conclude that whatever the 1930 Census is talking about, it is not the same thing we have in mind.

If we speculate for a moment, and take the very crude growth rate of 4.8 times for the Indian population between 1778 and 1950 in Guatemala, and apply it to the 1796 figure for the Indian population of El Salvador (83,010), we arrive at approximately 398,000. Comparing this figure with the total population of 1950, 1,855,917, we find that it is about 21.4% of the total. Even making allowance for the fact that the period of time involved is some 20 years under that for Guatemala, this percentage is remarkably close to the 20% estimated by

Table 18.—Number and percentage of total population which was Indian, according to the Census of 1930

Department	Number of Indians	Percent of Total
Santa Ana	4,051	2.6
Ahuachapán	20,572	26.1
Sonsonate	34,764	34.7
La Libertad	8,749	5.9
San Salvador	11,334	—
Chalatenango	15	—
Cuscatlán	21	—
La Paz	3	0.0
San Vicente	0	—
Cabañas	12	—
San Miguel	7	—
Usulután	5	—
Morazán	6	—
La Unión	34	—
Total republic	79,573	5.6

Baron Castro. Furthermore, if one can place any reliance on the estimates given by informants in the six *municipios* visited (see Table 16), we immediately have a figure of over 40,000 Indians from these seven towns alone. In view of the fact that there are obviously many other *municipios* with sizable Indian populations, the estimate of Baron Castro seems quite reasonable. For the country as a whole, we might assume for the present that there are something under 400,000 people that could be classified as Indian.

Now let us return to the problem of defining more precisely what we mean by Indian; just what differentiates these people from those whom we call Ladinos. First, we must keep in mind that when we say that a trait differentiates a particular group from the general run of the Ladino population, we are saying nothing about the origin of the trait. As will be seen, some of the most important traits which distinguish Indian populations today were actually introduced by the Spanish or grew out of a synthesis of the Spanish and Indian cultures. Also, a number of important traits (such as digging stick agriculture) which were contributed by the Indian cultures are now shared by Indians and Ladinos alike and do not serve to differentiate contemporary Indian groups.

In going over the data gathered from the various towns, there were a number of traits, some specific, and some general, which seemed to distinguish these seven Indian populations from the Ladinos. Table 19 gives a résumé of these. The choice of these traits and not some others has been dictated by the nature of the survey. Questions were asked about only certain aspects of the culture of

Table 19—Presence of certain distinctive Indian traits in the seven communities visited in which Indians were reported to form a significant part of the population

Characteristic	Cacaopera	Panchimalco	Izalco	Conchagua	Ataco	Jayaque	Santiago Nonualco
Use of the *mecapal*	men and women: common	common	some men still use it	men and women: common	men and women: common	only a few old people	only the very poor
Cooking fire on floor of house	common	fairly common	common	fairly common	common	fairly common	present, but not common (?)
Certain religious activities distinct from Ladino customs	yes	yes	yes	yes	yes	yes	no
Distinctive woman's dress	yes	yes	yes	yes	no	no	only among old women
Retention of an indigenous hand industry	yes	yes	yes	no	no	no	no
Survival of elements of a distinct political organization	yes	yes	yes	no	yes	no	no
Indian language still used	yes	yes	yes	no	no	no	no
Number of characteristics which are distinctive for the community	7	7	7	4	4	3	3

the communities, and based on these inquiries, the traits listed were distinctive. From many points of view, the traits are not "equal in value," that is, some are of greater importance than others. However, from one point of view, that of having survived, these traits have proved themselves to be somewhat comparable. Later in this chapter, the relative importance and intensity of these traits will be discussed in relation to the general similarities and differences between Indian and Ladino culture.

Before launching into the description, however, we are going to put the conclusions before the evidence and make some comments concerning the differences shown in Table 19. From the data there, the towns tend to fall into two groups: (1) those (Cacaopera, Panchimalco, and Izalco) which have retained something of all seven of the traits listed, and (2) those (Conchagua, Santiago Nonualco, Jayaque, and Ataco) which have retained only three or four of them. In the survey of Guatemalan Ladino culture, the writer proposed a classification of Indian groups in accordance with the degree of their ladinoization.[48] Three categories, or better said, points on a continuum, were suggested and characterized by certain rule-of-thumb characteristics: (1) *Traditional Indian;* those communities in which there is still considerable monolingualism. In these communities both men and women usually have retained a distinctive Indian dress. (2) *Modified Indian;* those communities which are generally bilingual and in which the women, but not the men, have retained distinctive dress. (3) *Ladinoized Indian;* those communities which are monolingual Spanish or in which an Indian language is only retained by a very small and aged portion of the population, and in which no distinctive Indian dress remains.

With some adjustment, these categories will help us to talk about the Salvadorean Indian. There is, so far as the writer knows, no Traditional Indian community in El Salvador. The three towns of Izalco, Panchimalco, and Cacaopera, however, can fall into the category of Modified Indian, and the remainder into that of Ladinoized Indian. In El Salvador, the characteristics of the survival of the language is not as satisfactory a criterion as it is in Guatemala, but its retention at all is evidently significant. Of perhaps greater importance is the survival of elements of an older political organization and the retention of hand industries.

The remaining four towns, Conchagua, Ataco, Jayaque, and Santiago Nonualco are easily classified along with the Ladinoized Indian communities of Guazacapán and Chiquimulilla of Guatemala, and Monimbó of Nicaragua.

It should be noted that when speaking of Modified and Ladinoized Indian communities, we are speaking about communities as such, population groups, not about specific individuals who may leave their Indian milieu, take over the habits of a Ladino, and thereby become a Ladino. Each of the Indian towns under discussion has lost and is losing, to a greater or lesser degree, characteristics which distinguish it from the general Ladino culture. The process or series of processes by which this occurs we call group ladinoization. When a single person becomes a Ladino through separation from the Indian culture, we call it individual ladinoization.[49]

The process of ladinoization obviously does not stop with the change to Ladinoized Indian. When either individuals or communities make the final shift, divesting themselves of all distinctive Indian behavioral traits, they step into a category which we have called New Ladino.[50] The New Ladino population is somewhat distinguished as a rather deculturated group; that is, they have given up most of their Indian traits, but they have moved into the lower class of the Ladino population which does not share in much of the traditional upper class Spanish-American heritage. Their culture has distinctive elements, however, for example, whereas the upper class may manifest extremely strong family ties, the

---

[48] Adams, n.d. (c). [49] Adams, n.d. (c). [50] Adams, n.d. (c).

New Ladino is frequently characterized (especially in El Salvador) by very weak familiar ties.[51]

The New Ladino population is one of the most important population components in El Salvador. Over many years of ladinoization, the Indian population has gradually been contributing more and more people to this population. Individuals from it arise and form important elements in the emergent middle class and bring to the middle class the culture which, of all, is most uniquely that of El Salvador. There is little doubt that the majority of Indians in El Salvador today are Ladinoized, people who are on the border of becoming New Ladinos.

Now let us return for a minute to the original question: How many people are there who fit into the definition of Indian? When we say that there are probably something under 400,000 Indians in El Salvador, we obviously do not mean that there are that many people living in Modified Indian communities. Without taking our definition into the field for another study, however, we cannot state with any precision how many of the postulated Indian population are closer to the category of Modified and how many are closer to that of Ladinoized. Sheerly as a guess, the writer would estimate that there are probably between 50,000 and 100,000 people who live in communities which could be classified as Modified. The rest probably consist of Ladinoized Indian communities which vary from those like Ataco or Jayaque to those like Santiago Nonualco.

2. THE DISTINCTIVE CULTURE OF THE SALVADOREAN INDIAN

Contemporary systematic descriptive studies of the Salvadorean Indian population may be said to be non-existent. There are some works which have interested themselves in certain specific aspects of the culture, but they are in general unsystematic and may be classed as studies in folklore.[52] It is to be hoped that intensive study may be started in certain of these regions, particularly in the southwest and in the Cacaopera-Lislique region. As the brief description to follow clearly indicates, much of the culture is changing rapidly.

While there is reason to think that the culture of certain of the communities under discussion were divergent at the time of the conquest, particularly Cacaopera and Conchagua, there is little evidence from the present survey to indicate that the earlier linguistic groupings have survived in terms of distinctive cultural units today. For the purposes of general discussion, then, the communities will be treated together, and contemporary divergences will be indicated as they occur.

The only distinctive aspect of settlement pattern which seems to hold for most of the communities visited is that the Indians tend to remain as a unified population. They either live in specific *barrios* of the town, such as is the case in Izalco and Santiago Nonualco, or tend to occupy certain *cantones*, such as in Cacaopera and Izalco, or are occupants of an entire *municipio*, such as in Panchimalco. Only in Conchagua was it reported that Ladinos and Indians lived

---

[51] It is most likely that much of the population which shows such weak structure, discussed in Chapter II, Section 4 of the present report, would be classified as New Ladino.

[52] Gonzales Sol, 1945; de Baratta, n.d.

mixed in both the town and countryside. The settlement pattern of Ataco, Jayaque, and Conchagua has been generally formed by the fact that the greater part of the *municipios* are in middle to large landholdings and many of the Indians live as *colonos* on the farms.

The basic economy of the Indians shows little differentiation from the general Ladino pattern. The types of tools used follow the general distribution described in an earlier chapter, the crops, except in Cacaopera, show no divergence from the Ladino pattern, and the form of labor is little different. Exchange labor, for example, was reported to be no more common among Indians than among Ladinos. It is practically non-existent in both groups. Only with respect to the role of the woman in agricultural work is there a significant difference. While women over much of El Salvador serve as hired labor in certain kinds of agricultural work, particularly the harvest of coffee and cotton, the participation of the woman in the field labor of the subsistence economy seems to be retained as basically an Indian trait. In only one Ladino town, Tejutepeque, was it reported that women very occasionally worked in subsistence agriculture. In four of the Indian towns, however (Ataco, Jayaque, Panchimalco, and Cacaopera), it was said that they commonly participated, and in Santiago Nonualco it was said that they did on occasion. In Izalco and Conchagua it was said that they did not do this kind of work.

Only in Cacaopera, where the Indian population concentrates much of its attention on the cultivation and processing of henequin, is the economy anything different from the general run of Ladino communities. And in Cacaopera, Ladinos also participate in this work. The economy of Ataco, Jayaque, and Conchagua are highly influenced by the presence of the *fincas*, and in Ataco it was said that there was very little subsistence agriculture practiced for this reason.

The handicraft production is still important in a number of the communities. Although Nahuizalco was not included in the survey, the products of this town are distributed over most of western El Salvador. Weaving is still carried on in Panchimalco and Izalco. In the latter place, only a narrow belt loom is used, but the art is still of considerable importance in the former. *Guacales* are painted in Izalco, baskets and fiber bags made in Panchimalco, and various henequin products come out of Cacaopera. Until recently, it was reported, hats, baskets, and *petates* were made in Conchagua, but only one old man still practices the the work now.

Neither Ataco nor Jayaque have retained (if they ever had) any such specialty, nor has Santiago Nonualco, but the coastal region of La Paz has a number of towns where specialities are carried out.

For the transportation of goods, Spanish methods have been taken over to a great degree. Horses, mules, and ox carts are all used but so also is the *mecapal*. As is noted on Table 19, both men and women use it in Ataco, Conchagua, and Cacaopera, and it is used with some consistency in Panchimalco. Only in Santiago Nonualco and Jayaque was it said to be in very limited use. Again, this probably reflects the fact of the coffee *finca* economy where transport is done in a different way.

All the towns except Panchimalco and Conchagua had a market or *plaza*. This cannot be considered as distinctively Indian any more, however, since it is also an important part of the Ladino culture.

In family organization little data were collected, but it seems that the form of the family follows generally that of the Ladinos. Only in Panchimalco was it reported that patrilocal residence was standard, and in Jayaque that it was observed by some. Elsewhere neo-locality was the rule.

In the home, an outstanding trait which is retained by the Indian communities is the floor fire. This was very uncommon or non-existent in Ladino communities. Many Indians do use the raised *poyo*, but the floor fire is still very common in Ataco and Izalco (in the *cantones* of the former), fairly common in Jayaque, Panchimalco, Conchagua, and Cacaopera, and uncommon but present in Santiago Nonualco. Except in Panchimalco and Conchagua it is the standard practice to build the floor fires between the traditional three rocks. In Panchimalco, however, the *hornilla* is built on the floor. In Conchagua, both the three stones and the *hornilla* are found in use with the floor fire.

Panchimalco also varies from the standard pattern of using lime in the making of the *nixtamal*. Wood ash is used in preference to lime.

The fire fan, an instrument of Indian origin, is today found only in western El Salvador, but is not restricted to Indian communities. While of Indian origin, it seems now to have become a minor regional trait in Ladino culture.

The writer found no survival of distinctive Indian man's dress in El Salvador. Women, however, have retained an older style in five of the seven towns visited. There was nothing distinctive reported from Jayaque or Ataco, but in Panchimalco the skirt is woven by the women themselves, and in Santiago Nonualco, Conchagua and Cacaopera, a similar skirt, the *enagua*, of commercially woven cotton is used. In Izalco the Indian *corte* material woven in Guatemala is used as a wrap-around skirt, according to informants. The women of Izalco no longer weave their skirt material. The *enagua* skirt is a pattern stemming from at least the last century and is of Ladino origin. It is still seen occasionally in various parts of the country on older women. In the other towns in which it was reported, however, it evidently is distinctive of the Indian population. The skirt used in Cacaopera, perhaps somewhat wider than the standard *enagua*, is called merely *falda*.

From one point of view, the retention of distinct or semi-distinct Indian political and religious organizations is the most significant indication of the Indian society being a separate social component of the general population. Of the two, the political organization is much more affected by the dictates of national municipal law and organization. Three of the communities (Jayaque, Santiago Nonualco, and Conchagua) reported no distinct political organization. Three (Ataco, Panchimalco, and Cacaopera) have retained elements of a former organization as an adjunct to the official municipal organization. These have already been described in the section on political organization. Izalco, however, has grown under a distinct form of political control.

There is among the Indians of Izalco a *cacique*, a man who acts as mouthpiece and general contact man with the outside political world. The position of *cacique* is not part of a hierarchy or extensive political system such as is found in Traditional Guatemalan Indian towns. It stands quite alone, and is related neither to other political posts nor to the system of religious *cofradías*. Also, the man holding the position of *cacique* does so sheerly on the basis of strength of personality and the fact that outsiders, specifically Ladino politicians, turn to him over issues of the political activity of the Izalco Indian population. The post of *cacique* has been important at least since before the 1930's. During the development of the Communist efforts in the late twenties and early thirties, the *cacique* of Izalco played a leading role in organizing the Indian population behind the movement. When the movement was overthrown, this man was publicly hung in the Izalco plaza.[53]

The principal function of the present *cacique* is to represent the Indian population before the national government, and to provide a voting block for the politicians who win him over. Evidently the Izalco *alcalde* (the entire municipal official body is Ladino) does not have recourse to the *cacique*. Municipal affairs are carried on effectively through the normal channels of the municipal police and the *comisionados*. The precise functions of the *cacique* within the Indian community and how he operates and maintains his power were not ascertained. Unfortunately, he was absent during the day the writer visited Izalco.

A situation which comes close to paralleling this is that encountered in the town of Monimbó in Nicaragua. Monimbó also has a person who functions as does the Izalco *cacique*, but in Monimbó he is a part of local political organization within the community and not a separate and disparate element as in Izalco. This suggests that at one time the functions held by the Izalco *cacique* may have been vested in an officer of the Indian political system, but something (perhaps the downfall of Communist movement) acted to separate him from the older organization.

In religion, all towns except Santiago Nonualco manifested certain elements which indicate the retention of certain values which are not maintained by the general Ladino population. The elements which are of particular concern to us are those which have to do with the social organization which supports the religious activities. Perhaps the most integrated of the systems was that reported in Izalco. At its head is an *alcalde del común* held by one of the elders or *principales*. One informant said that the group of *principales* together was called the *milicia*. The *principales* carry *varas*, or sticks, with silver heads during ceremonial occasions. These *varas* are otherwise kept in the special *cofradía* houses. Besides being head of the general Indian religious organization, one function of the *alcalde del común* is to obtain permission from the municipal *alcalde* for religious observances and fiestas.

The actual sponsorship of fiestas in Izalco is in the hands of Ladino *hermandades* (of the type described in the chapter on Religious Activities) and Indian *cofradías*. There are eight Indian *cofradías*, but whether they are all of equal

---

[53] Schlesinger, 1946.

importance was not ascertained. Each is supported by people living within one section of the town.

Cofradía	Section of Town
Santa Teresa	Barrio de Santa Teresa
San Sebastián	Barrios de San Sebastián
Santa Cruz	Barrio de Santa Cruz
Virgen de Belén	Barrio de San Juan
San Juan	Barrio de San Juan
Virgen de los Remedios	Barrio Cruz Galana
Jesús Nazareno	Those living on the edge of town to the east
Virgen de la Asunción	Those living in the south (Barrios Cruz Galana?)

The *cofradías* are supported financially through voluntary contributions of the members and through the cultivation of special lands known as *tierra del santo*. The work of *cofradía* is not limited to the time of the fiesta since beans and corn must be sown, cultivated, and harvested from these lands. Some members of the *cofradías* plant such crops on their own land, while others use the *tierra del santo* which actually belongs to the *cofradía*. The products are used exclusively for the saint.

Most *cofradías* also have a special *casa de cofradía* or *casa del santo*, a *rancho* in which there is an altar on which the saint is kept, and a few benches for persons who wish to come in and pray. The *mayordomo* in charge of the *cofradía* is responsible for the house and the saint. Unfortunately, time did not permit an adequate exploration into the functioning of the *cofradía* system of Izalco. It is quite distinct, however, from the Ladino *hermandades* of which there are three. One each is responsible for Holy Week, Christmas, and the patron saint, *la Virgen de la Concepción*.

It can be seen even from this brief picture that the religious organization in Izalco has much which resembles those found in Traditional and Modified Indian towns of Guatemala, and the elements are derived from the same colonial base.

The religious organization of Cacaopera varied somewhat from that in Izalco, but was basically the same. There are eleven saints cared for by the Indians of the *municipio*. For each, there is a *cuadrilla* composed of four *mayores* (men) and four *tenanzas* (women). Each *cuadrilla* also has a person designated as *vaquero* who is responsible for the *animales de la Virgen* which are kept on a piece of property in the *cantón* Agua Blanca, and called the *Hacienda de la Virgen*. This piece of land for keeping animals is parallel to the *tierra de santos* of Izalco, but in this case the profits from the livestock go to help the fiesta and provide meat. While the saints of Cacaopera *hermandades* are evidently kept in the church, there are a number of *casas de "recibimiento,"* special houses where the saints are taken from time to time and prayed to.

Until 1936 the Indians occupied most of the municipal posts in Cacaopera, including that of *alcalde municipal* then called the *alcalde de vara*. By that time, however, more Ladinos had begun to move into the town and they took over the municipal government. Before this happened there was a tie-up between the political and religious organizations. The *primer mayor* of the *hermandad* groups was called the *alcalde huanco* and on January first of each year he was given complete authority in the town and could jail or free anyone he wished. The *primer mayor* was always the leading *mayordomo* of the *hermandad* of the patron saint, the *Virgen del Tránsito*. The entire group of *mayores*, besides being responsible for their particular saints, were also generally responsible for the upkeep of the church, lighting candles, etc.

The Cacaopera situation reflects a rather recent survival of the tie-up between the religious and political organizations of the community. The destruction of this relationship was obviously due to the assumption of municipal control by the Ladinos. With this, the Indian *hermandades* veered off to more purely religious functions. As in Izalco, the Ladinos of Cacaopera have their distinct *hermandades*. A recent introduction by the *sociedad* was a sodality for the *Virgen de Fátima*. Evidently the only fiesta in which Ladinos and Indians participate jointly is that of the patron, the *Virgen del Tránsito*. The religious aspects of this fiesta are handled by the Indian *hermandad*.

The towns of Ataco and Conchagua have Indian religious organizations which are similar to those just described, but without the superstructure of an Indian *alcalde-principales* organization such as exists in Izalco, nor with saint's lands to support the fiestas. In Ataco, there are five Indian *cofradías* the members of which are called *cofrades*. They name each year as officials within the organization a *mayordomo, diputados, mayordomitos* (all men) and *capitanes* (women). Also within each *cofradía* the older men are referred to as *principales* and play the role of general masters of ceremonies. The principal *cofradía* is that of the *Virgen de la Concepción*, the patron saint. This *cofradía* has a special house in which a second image of the saint is kept (the main image stays in the church). The *mayordomo* of this *cofradía* lives in the *cofradía* house during this period of tenure.

In Conchagua there are four *mayordomías* as they are called. While the *mayordomo* in charge may continue over various years, the woman *mayordoma* is changed each year. Again, these organizations are distinct from the purely Ladino *hermandades* such as the *Hijas de María, Guardia, Corazón de Jesús*. Both men and women belong to the *cofradías* and play roles in their operation. In the others, only men or only women are members.

The situation in Panchimalco in terms of organization is not very different from those just described. There are two major *cofradías* and many smaller ones (the informant was not sure, but guessed there to be around a total of 20). The officers of the *cofradías* are called *priostes, munidores*, and *aposentadores*. Each year a *mayordomo* and a *mayora* are appointed. There are no *cofradía* houses and the saints remain in the church throughout the year. It is customary for the *cofradías* to rent out land (they own no *tierra de santos*) and for the members to plant and harvest wheat from which bread is made for the fiesta. The funds of the *cofradías* are controlled by the *alcalde* who retains their books. So far as the writer knows, there are no Ladino *hermandades* in Panchimalco. The Ladino population is very small.

Jayaque provides one of the most interesting cases of distinctive Indian religious activity in the form of a relationship which has been established for many years with the town of Cuisnahuat, about 20 km. away in the Department of Sonsonate. Besides a group of Ladino *hermandades*, there are two Indian *cofradías* for the two patron saints, *San Cristóbal* and *San Sebastián*. Of these, *San Cristóbal* is the most important for the Indians. It is headed by a *mayordomo mayor*; male assistants are *mayordomitos*, and female are *capitanes*. In Cuisnahuat, there is a similar organization for the patron saint, *San Lucas*. Each year, the patron saint of one town goes to visit the other on his day. Thus, on the day of *San Cristóbal*, the *cofradía* of San Lucas of Cuisnahuat brings *San Lucas* to Jayaque. The image is placed beside *San Cristóbal* in the *cofradía* house of the latter and remains there during the five days or so of the fiesta. Similarly, in November, on the occasion of the fiesta of *San Lucas* in Cuisnahuat, the *cofradía* of San Cristóbal takes out the saint and makes the pilgrimage to the other town, places *San Cristóbal* beside *San Lucas* in his *cofradía* house, and remains during the days of that fiesta. On the trip over, the first night is spent at a place called La Peña, and the next day they are met there by the people of Cuisnahuat who come out to greet them and accompany *San Cristóbal* to the fiesta. The members of San Lucas and San Cristóbal *cofradías* refer to each other as *compas*, from the term *compadre*; the two saints are also supposed to be *compadres*, and for this reason, each makes the annual trip to visit the other.

There is little doubt that this ceremonial relationship between the saints and the people of Cuisnahuat and Jayaque is essentially the same as the *guancasco* ceremonies reported heretofore only from the Lenca region of Honduras. It is interesting that it has been retained in this coffee region of El Salvador where many of the other Indian traits have gone by the wayside. This custom, it must be noted, should not be confused with the custom of sending a saint out on *demanda* to visit other communities and collect funds for his fiesta. This is a ceremonial relationship binding the members of the two towns together.

The nature of the survival of distinct Indian religious organization obviously varies considerably from one town to another, but it is evidently one aspect of the culture which has adjusted to much change. The evidence is clear that religious organization here, as is still the case in some Traditional Indian communities of Guatemala, was tied to the political organization at one time, and there is little doubt that the schism has affected the strength of the religious system. Nevertheless, in one form or another, religious practices have been retained, although in an increasingly attenuated form, while many other traits, such as the Indian language, have all but disappeared.

Aside from the organization of the fiestas and social groups which underlie them, the use of masked and costumed dances also characterizes all but one of the Indian communities visited on the survey. Only Conchagua did not report the use of these dances.[54] These dances are basically similar to those still common in Guatemala. They are usually historical representations concerned with

---

[54] Although the informant in Conchagua said there were no dances observed now, Gonzales Sol (1945) reports that three such dances are held, or were held at that time.

the story of the conquest, of the history of Charlemagne fighting the *turcos* or *moros*, the *Baile de Pluma*, the *Baile de Negritos*, the *Baile de Toros*, etc. Various aspects of these dances have been described elsewhere.[55] Of importance here, however, is that the masked dance seems essentially a trait of the Indian culture and is one which is being temporarily carried into the general Ladino culture. A recitation and dance, but without masks was reported from Moncagua, but there was no Indian population there evidently responsible for it. It seems likely that such survivals may continue for some time in scattered parts of the Ladino population, but their presence alone should not be mistaken for an indication of the existence of an Indian population.

From this brief survey of some of the distinctive characteristics of Indian culture, it is possible to state some general propositions concerning the differences and similarities between Indian and non-Indian groups.

(1) Indian and Ladino cultures are dependent upon essentially the same agricultural crops, technology, and general economy. The crops and technology are derived historically from both aboriginal and Spanish sources. Digging stick and wooden plow agriculture go on side by side, and whether one or the other is used depends in great part upon the nature of the terrain and the relative wealth of the farmer.

(2) The distinctiveness of the cultures of Indian communities vary. We have three communities on the survey, Izalco, Panchimalco, and Cacaopera, which have retained more distinctive traits than have the other four, Conchagua, Ataco, Jayaque, and Santiago Nonualco. This proposition, of course, is another way of saying that the rate of ladinoization varies from one community to another depending upon what combination of influences have been focused on a particular place during its history.

(3) The characteristics which distinguish Indian communities from Ladino communities are of two basic types: (a) individual items of survival which are usually replaced by other traits in the Ladino culture; (b) complex items of survival which have an integrative function in the Indian community and which therefore cannot be replaced by traits of the Ladino culture but which disappear with no basic replacement. In the first category are traits such as the use of the *mecapal* (to be replaced by ox cart, mules, horses, trucks, and carrying on the shoulder, etc.), cooking between three stones on the floor (to be replaced by cooking on a raised platform), distinctive woman's dress (to be replaced by the general Ladino fashions), etc. There are doubtless other traits of this type which were not ascertained in the survey.

Into the second category are those traits which because of their integrative character (i.e., they function to retain a distinctive way of social life) usually disappear without replacement. The most important of these are community specialization in production or industry, a distinctive political organization (whether modified to be an appendage of the Ladino municipal organization or not), distinctive social organization for religious observances, and the Indian

---

[55] See Gonzales Sol, 1945; and de Baratta, n.d.

language, which is of course replaced by Spanish. If one aspect were to be selected out as decisive in denoting whether a Salvadorean community could be labeled as retaining an Indian distinctiveness, it would probably be the issue of religious differences. The retention of "Indian *cofradías*" as opposed to "Ladino *hermandades*" is not merely a case of differences in religious custom, but reflects a distinction between two social groups. Similarly joint activity of men and women in religious ritual with more activity being carried on by men is clearly different from the Ladino situation where it is replaced by specific activity of men or women, with more activity being carried on by women. In the seven towns visited on the survey, only one, Santiago Nonualco reported no distinctive retentions in the field of religious activity. It might be postulated that Santiago Nonualco is on the "last legs" of Indianism.

A distinctive political organization is also very important. Empirically, however, we have seen that such an organization tends to disappear before the religious organization disappears. The reason for this is fairly obvious. The adequate functioning of a Ladino municipal system could be impeded were there a competing organization in the Indian community. For the Ladino organization to function, then, the Indian system must either be made inoperative or integrated into the Ladino system. In Ataco, Panchimalco, and Cacaopera, the remnants of the Indian organization have been integrated into the Ladino municipal system. The system of working turns, or the existence of a special "patrol" or body of Indian minor functionaries, work as a part of the Ladino municipal system. In Izalco, history has taken a slightly different turn, and the Indian political organization has been destroyed, but there has been established at some time in the past status, that of *cacique*, which permits the Indians to continue as an integral political body. The *cacique* status has meaning both with respect to the Indian community and with the outside Ladino world. As long as some recognition of the distinctiveness of the Indian community is extant in the Ladino political organization, there can be little doubt that the community does exist as a distinctive social entity.

The retention of hand industries of specialized production, perhaps even more than political organization, is subject to destructive influences. The establishment of a *finca* economy in which the Indian population one way or another enters the laborer status is bound to have a destructive effect on such specialties. It is probably significant that the three Indian communities in which an *hacienda* or *finca* pattern had become established had no such distinctive industries: Conchagua, Ataco, and Jayaque. Of equal importance, however, is that local specialization, unlike religious or political organization, is not necessarily always present in an Indian community. In the Traditional Indian communities of Guatemala local specialization is not universal; it occurs here and there.

The Indian languages have almost disappeared from El Salvador. Where they are retained, bilingualism is the rule. A distinct language, involving as it does different thought patterns, acts as a strong supporter of other cultural differences; in this way, language is an important integrative trait. Unlike other such traits, however, it cannot disappear without equal replacement in the form of another language. Spanish has taken over in most cases now, and the Indian languages remain as survivals of a previous age.

From the point of view of El Salvador, it is probably reasonable to define the conditions of Modified and Ladinoized Indians in terms of the relative retention of integrative traits. Empirically, of the communities visited on the survey, we can classify as Modified Indian those in which there has been a retention of political and religious distinctions: Cacaopera, Panchimalco, and Izalco. The communities in which only the distinctive religious traits are retained, we can classify as Ladinoized since the disappearance of political organization differences indicates that the differences between dealing with Indians and Ladinos on the political level have ceased to have functional importance: Conchagua, Ataco, and Jayaque. Where both political and religious differences have disappeared, such as in Santiago Nonualco, we are faced with a problem which is more academic than practical. Because they are called "Indian" and because of the retention of certain traits which we can consider as Indian (*mecapal*, fire on floor, distinctive woman's dress among a few older people) we may call them "highly ladinoized" Indian, but from the point of view of practical dealings, they may equally well be considered as being on the border between Indian and New Ladinos, members of the lowest Ladino social stratum.

IV. THE CULTURAL REGIONS OF EL SALVADOR

It was mentioned earlier that Salvadoreans tend to think of their country as being divided into three major sections, the west, center, and east. Loenholdt, on the basis of ecological and agricultural studies, has postulated a different division whereby the east-center-west division is crosscut by a north-center-south division.[56]

The following is a brief résumé of Loenholdt's classification:

North Region: One third of total area; a strip between 25 and 50 kilometers deep along the Honduran border; "Rough, hilly, ... not particularly suited for general agriculture."

Center Region: One half of total area; a rough plateau of between 1,500 and 3,000 feet; it is the area of greatest agricultural development and heaviest concentration of population.

South Region: One sixth of the total area; flat, level, south coastal plain; little developed but has great agricultural potential.

To these two classifications may be added a third categorization based on general terrain. El Salvador may be classified in terms of mountains, interior valleys, and coastal plains. The mountains of the country are in four main areas: (a) the volcanic chain running east from the Guatemalan border in a broken belt through the Department of San Vicente; (b) the continuation of this volcanic range on the other side of the Lempa, in a block in northern Usulután

[56] Loenholdt, 1953, pp. 12–13, and map at end of volume.

and central-west San Miguel; (c) the end of the Cordillera de Merendón which runs north and south out of Chiquimula (Guatemala) and Ocotepeque (Honduras), and which forms the north shed for the Lempa in the northwest corner of the country; (d) a similar extension of the Honduras highlands which break into the northeast corner of the country in the departments of La Unión and Morazán. Two major river basins of the country serve to separate these mountain blocks. The Lempa, and its tributaries, have produced a great interior plateau or valley which breaks out of the Honduran border in Ocotepeque, on the west, and out of the Department of Morazán (El Salvador) in the east, creating an interior valley which waves east and west across the northern border of the country, and which drains out to the Pacific. In the east, the Río Grande de San Miguel, together with other rivers draining into the Gulf of Fonseca, have chopped up the drainage area to the east of the Lempa into a series of broken intermountain valleys. Finally, along the entire south coast runs a flat coastal plain, rather narrow in the area where the western volcanic range comes close to the sea, widening out at the mouth of the Lempa, and continuing as a wide plain through the southeast to the Gulf of Fonseca. It is only really broken by the volcano of Conchagua which rises singly in the far southeastern corner of the country.

The cultural regions of the country have been determined by the history of population movement and growth, and the history of ladinoization. These histories, in turn, have been highly influenced by the geography and regions just described. Neither Ladinos nor Indians in El Salvador have followed a single line of geography. In the latter part of the 18th century, the greatest part of the population was located in the mountainous areas. On a gross departmental basis, the comparative distribution by percentages are as shown in Table 20. Whereas the combined departments of Sonsonate, San Salvador, Cuscatlán, and La Paz accounted for 56.2% of the total population in 1768–1770, it accounted for only 35.2% in 1950. The most underpopulated sections in the earlier period were those which followed the interior valley of the Lempa (San Vicente, Cabañas, and Chalatenango accounted for only 8.7% of the population). Another census taken in 1807[57] indicates that in the eastern section of the country, of the total of eight parishes, 19,513 out of a total of 36,343 people, or almost 54%, came from the three mountainous parishes of Chinameca, Gotera, and Osicala. The other main concentration was around the town of San Miguel itself, and accounted for another 19.0% of the total. At that time, Osicala (which included Cacaopera) had a larger population than did lowland San Miguel.

This preference for the highlands was found among both Ladinos and Indians, but was much more marked among the latter. In the census made of the Partido de San Salvador (which did not include Sonsonate) in 1807, distinction was made between various ethnic groups, and it is interesting to note that in only one area did the group called *Españoles* (as opposed to *mestizos* and Indians) outnumber the Indians; this was in Metapán, the far northwest corner of the country and

[57] Baron Castro, 1942, p. 244.

in the upper valley of the Lempa. Only 2.9% of the total population was classified as *Español*, but of this group one third were said to live in Metapán. One of the heaviest concentrations of Indians at that time was in the region surrounding Lake Ilopango; San Salvador, Olocuilta, Zacatecoluca, and Cojutepeque accounted for almost 65% of the Indian population.

On the basis of these general data, the population zones (outlined in the chapter on population) and the contemporary cultural data, it is possible to distinguish certain regions of culture.

The North Region.—This region generally includes the contiguous districts bordering on Honduras, west of the Lempa, and the district of Sensori to the

Table 20.—Comparative distribution of population, 1768–1770 and 1950.
(*From Baron Castro, 1942, p. 223, and Census, 1954*)

Department	Percentage of Total Population	
	1768–1770	1950
Ahuachapán	5.6%	5.1%
Sonsonate	13.5	6.5
Santa Ana	8.4	10.9
La Libertad	3.4	5.2
San Salvador	20.1	16.0
Cuscatlán	9.1	4.9
La Paz	13.5	7.8
Cabañas	1.3	4.2
San Vicente	3.3	4.7
Usulután	6.0	8.7
San Miguel	4.4	9.2
Morazán	4.7	5.2
La Unión	2.6	5.9
Total	100.0%	99.9%

east. The area had been highly mestizoized by the time of the census of 1807, and today there may be said to be practically no remnants of an Indian population. This is geographically the interior Lempa valley and culturally the extension of the Ladino corridor which comes down out of eastern Guatemala. Elsewhere[58] we have referred to this type of population as Old Ladino, to distinguish them from New Ladinos, which have only recently ceased to be Indian, and this term probably serves equally well here. Demographically, the region falls into two general divisions, the northwest and the north-center (see chapter on population). Culturally too this subdivision makes sense since in the north-center there is probably a more distinct New Ladino population than in the northwest. The informant in Texistepeque said that there were practically no Indians in the *municipio*, while further east, in Tejutla, 25% of the population was said to be racially Indian but to retain no distinctive Indian customs.

[58] Adams, n.d. (c).

EL SALVADOR

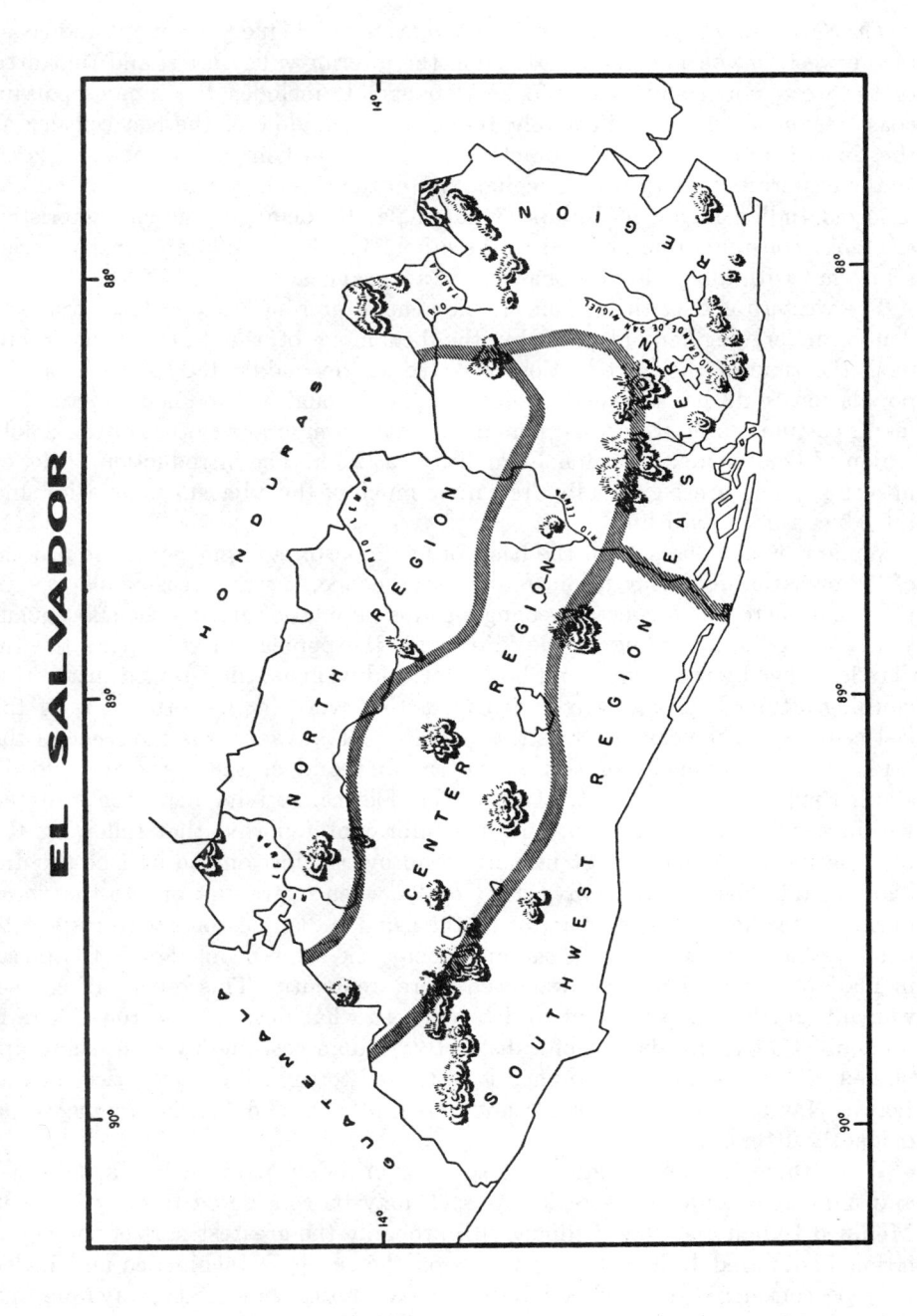

The Southwest Region.—This region includes the highlands, piedmont and coast of the western volcanic chain, excluding the interior valley areas and that area to the west, north and east of Lake Ilopango. It includes the famous balsam coast region which was still purely Indian in the middle of the last century at the time of Squier's visit. For practical purposes the Lempa may be considered as the eastern boundary of this region, and in the west it continues into the Ladinoized Indian region of Jutiapa, Guatemala. Its demographic characteristics are fairly constant from one end to the other, but the population density varies somewhat with a high in Sonsonate and Zacatecoluca.

The western end of the region, in the general area of Zacatecoluca, was evidently undergoing ladinoization by the beginning of the last century,[59] but until the time of the introduction of coffee in the middle 1800's much of the population could have been considered as Traditional or Modified Indian. The men's costumes used were very similar to the contemporary clothes of the Sololá region of Guatemala, and monolingualism was high. The introduction of coffee into the upland areas gradually drew upon much of the adjacent population and introduced it to *finca* life.

While it is not possible on the basis of available data to pin point the process of ladinoization following the introduction of coffee, it seems reasonable to suppose that there was a constant change in this population during the subsequent years. By 1930, according to one informant, the population still spoke the Indian language by preference, and both men and women still retained distinctive clothing although probably modified from that worn in the latter part of the last century. In the early 1930's, this region of El Salvador was the scene of the attempted development of *comunismo criollo*,[60] and of the stern and bloody elimination of the movement. Much of the political activity had been centered within the Indian population, and one informant reported that following the termination of the movement he noticed an overt effort on the part of the Indians to take over Ladino ways. Previously, when migrants came to the *fincas* during coffee harvest, they manifested the usual Indian customs with respect to language and dress. Following the movement, the same people began to appear in Ladino dress and Spanish was used more frequently. This report, of course, warrants further investigation to determine to what degree it is true. There is no doubt that today the use of a distinctive Indian costume by men has disappeared and its retention by women is restricted to certain communities such as Izalco, Nahuizalco, Panchimalco, and a few others. The Indian languages are evidently little used.

While there are many Ladinos in this region today, particularly in the cities and municipal centers, the region as such may be considered to vary between Modified Indian and New Ladino, with probably the greatest part of the population Ladinoized Indian. Of the towns on the survey Panchimalco and Izalco may be considered as Modified Indian communities, but Ataco, Jayaque and Santiago Nonualco are clearly Ladinoized Indian.

The Center Belt.—This region includes the interior valleys and low mountains

---
[59] Baron Castro, 1942, p. 254. [60] Schlesinger, 1946.

from Chalchuapa, on the Guatemalan border, to the east, and includes roughly the districts of Chalchuapa, Santa Ana, Opico, Quezaltepeque, northern Santa Tecla, San Salvador, Tonacatepeque, Suchitoto, Cojutepeque, Ilobasco, San Sebastián, most of San Vicente, Berlín, Santiago de María, Jucuapa, and much of Chinameca. The region is broken into two parts by the Lempa. This center belt region from many points of view should be considered as a number of distinct subregions, and may be described as such. It is the area of greatest population density of the entire country; it contains the major cities with attendant consequences of urbanization; it is (according to Loenholdt) the area of greatest agricultural development, and varies from the extensive coffee *fincas* to subsistence agricultural holdings; and ethnically it is an area of varied ladinoization. Unfortunately, not knowing of its importance prior to the survey, luck dictated that only three towns in this region were included in the survey: San Matías, Tonacatepeque, and Moncagua. Supplementary information was available from a previous study of the Valle de la Esperanza,[61] but no data was gathered either in the far west nor between Lake Ilopango and the Lempa.

In general, the population of this region may be considered as New and Old Ladino. The former predominates in numbers, particularly in the region around Lake Ilopango; this region was still predominantly Indian at the time of the 1807 Census. Whether the Cojutepeque population could better be considered as New Ladino or Ladinoized Indian can only be decided through further research. It was my impression from observation on various trips along the highways of this region that the population could be considered as New Ladino; there are a few distinguishing traits which might be indicative of a Ladinoized Indian population, however, such as the reported retention of "typical" dances[62] in Cojutepeque and the extensive use of the black headcloth by women. The same situation holds in the *municipios* immediately adjacent to San Salvador; Gonzales Sol also reported such dances in Mejicanos, Villa Delgado, Barrio Paleca, Barrio San Sebastián, and Cuscatancingo. In comparing the population data on this area (see Table 4), it may be noted that in terms of total population growth, it has acted more like the Indian southwest region than has most of the center belt. This may be another indication that it is still more of a Ladinoized Indian population than New Ladino.

In the far western part of the area the introduction of coffee evidently served to ladinoize whatever Indian communities may have survived as distinct entities into the end of the last century. Sixty-five percent of the Santa Ana population was already reported as being mestizo in the 1807 Census.[63] However, like the Cojutepeque region, this region also showed a low total population increase.

In the far east, the region occupies the volcanic highlands of Usulután and San Miguel, and is also an important region of coffee production. The majority of the population is New Ladino, but there is an important Old Ladino component. This far eastern section of the center belt is probably similar in structure to the far western portion.

---

[61] Adams, 1952a.   [62] Gonzales Sol, 1945, table at end of volume.
[63] Baron Castro, 1942, p. 254.

The center belt region may be considered as a unit mainly as a matter of convenience, and in that it does manifest some demographic consistency. The population density is high except in the area immediately bordering the Lempa, the rural component is of average size, and there has been only a slight change in the urban-rural proportions between 1930 and 1950.

Portions of this area, defined in terms of administrative political units, are probably better considered as parts of the adjacent regions. The northern sections of Santa Ana, Opico, Quezaltepeque, Suchitoto, and Ilobasco, can probably be thought of as part of the north region. On the south, the distinct presence of Indian communities in the highlands serves as a fairly clear break with the center belt.

The Eastern Region.—The eastern region forms the entire remainder of the area east of the Lempa. It can be broken into three fairly distinct subregions. The southern portion is flat coastal plains, and is composed principally of Ladinos with occasional enclaves, such as Conchagua, of Ladinoized Indians. The region has long been predominantly Ladino, but in recent years there has been some immigration of New Ladinos from the southwest as *hacienda* agriculture has developed. This coastal area includes the low inland plateau of San Miguel itself.

In the north, there are two subregions, the distinct Indian enclave of Cacaopera and Lislique, and the remainder of the area, a broken low hilly country occupied mainly by Ladinos. As in the south, this population is generally of long residence, but due to increasing population density in some portions of the area, there has been extensive emigration to Honduras. There may be scattered communities of Ladinoized Indians in this region, but none were specified to the writer in the course of the survey.

The east never had, apparently, a very large indigenous population. Of those which were recorded in 1807, 40% lived in the northeast mountain area, another 40% in what is now the Department of San Miguel, and only the remainder occupied the entire coastal and adjacent border region.[64]

This regional picture has been determined principally by the combined factors of early Indian areas, Spanish and Ladino settlement preferences, and recent *finca* and *hacienda* developments. The main Indian areas of today, the southwest and far northeast, are two of the main areas in which Indians were found throughout the latter part of the colonial period and in the republican era. Spanish settlement concentrated in the center belt and the western interior Lempa Valley where at least by the end of the colonial period there were very few Indians. Evidently neither Spanish nor Indians were attracted to the hot coastal plain, and it tended to become an Indian area only along the balsam coast when the extraction of the balsam was an important source of economic support for the Indian population of the adjacent piedmont and mountains.

As elsewhere, Ladinos have sought out regions in which two crops are generally possible, and left to the Indians those areas where one crop was the rule. This pattern shifted, of course, with the introduction of coffee, for this crop was

---

[64] Baron Castro, *ibid.*

best grown specifically in upland regions which in some cases had been left to the Indians. Thus the mountains of the southwest, which had been predominantly an Indian area, became an area of *fincas* and the Ladinos came into the region as agricultural enterpreneurs and business men, but not particularly as agricultural settlers on the land.

The intense growth of the Salvadorean population has tended to blur certain of these earlier geographical lines, particularly in the longer center belt. There, where the land varies from broken uplands to inland valleys, the combined Ladino and Indian populations grew side by side and the Indians of the Lake Ilopango region were subjected to a more intensive process of ladinoization than were those of either the southwest or the northeast. This, combined with the development of coffee in this region, has provided a complicated socio-cultural picture which the present study cannot hope to untangle.

V. COMMUNITIES VISITED ON THE SURVEY

1. LADINO TOWNS OF THE NORTH

Texistepeque (1950 Population: 1,096 urban, 8,249 rural)

Although located in the Department of Santa Ana, Texistepeque belongs to the region of Ladino settlement of the north. It is located on the road from Santa Ana to Metapán and the railroad also provides a means of transport. The population may be said to be Ladino, although the informant stated that there were perhaps ten *"olleros"* whom he thought were Indian because they made pottery. Most of the land is evidently in middle sized *haciendas*, and some of them have resident *colonos*. While much of the agricultural work is done with the wooden plow, the digging stick is still used in the rougher portions of the *municipio*, and the metal plow and cultivator have been used on some of the farms recently.

Apparently Texistepeque has been the recipient of various Guatemalan immigrants in years past, both Indian and Ladino. The present population is clearly divided between a local upper *hacendado* class, many of whom are residents in the town, and the *colonos* and laborers. The upper group is practically endogamus with respect to the lower. What middle class may be said to exist is composed principally of employees of the *hacendados*. The men of the upper class as well as the women tend to participate in church work. *Mayordomías* and saints' lands used to exist, but died out some years ago, and the main activity in the church has been sponsored by women's groups and the upper class men who regard it as important.

The town is laid out in the usual grid pattern, and the construction is predominantly *adobe* and tile. It was said that the earth there is not very good for making *bajareque*, but the reason for this was not given. In the *cantones*, there are both *adobe* and tile homes and *ranchos*.

Tejutla (1950 Population: 885 urban, 3,905 rural)

This is an extremely old town. While there was at one time an important Indian population here, it has become culturally ladinoized and now forms part of the lower class Ladino population of the *municipio*. The town is on the road leading from San Salvador to Nueva Ocotepeque, near the Honduran border. It is on an important line of commerce and travel between the two countries. There is considerable migration to the south in coffee harvest season, and many of the women participate in the cotton harvests within the *municipio*. The landless population both work on the *haciendas* and rent lands.

Most of the land here was *ejidal* prior to 1912, but at that time it was divided up as private farms for the population. Much of it remains today as subsistence agricultural enterprises, but some of it has been sold off into larger holdings which comprise the present *haciendas*. As in Texistepeque, both the wooden plow and digging stick are used for cultivation.

The town supports a secondary school with only a small subsidy from the national government. The salaries of six teachers are paid from a fund to which the parents contribute. Aside from a small annual subsidy, the government was also said to provide twenty scholarships a year for children of the rural areas to come to the school.

The construction in both the town and country is principally *adobe*, *bajareque*, and tile, although there are some *ranchos* in the rural areas.

Tejutla is both a district and municipal capital.

Tejutepeque (1950 Population: 843 urban, 3,400 rural)

While included here as a part of the north region, Tejutepeque lies more or less on what might be considered to be the border of the north and the center belt. The population is Ladino, although it was said that a few Indians have moved in recently from San Rafael Cedros near Cojutepeque. The town is accessible over a poor road running out of Ilobasco.

Almost all the land in the *municipio* is in medium sized holdings and belongs to about 10% of the population. There has been some tendency in recent years for the holdings to be split up among descendents of the original holders, but this has not altered the proportion of the landless. Of the *campesino* population about half rent subsistence plots from the *haciendas* and half work as laborers; many of the latter are *colonos*. The wooden plow and digging stick are the main cultivation implements. It was said that even the rocky lands in which it is necessary to use the digging stick were used year after year. Many people go to the coffee *fincas* for the harvest, and some have emigrated to the north coast of Honduras to work on the banana plantations.

There are two general classes recognized, the landholding group and those who must rent land or work as laborers. The informant said there was no extremely wealthy group present, i.e. no cosmopolitan upper, and there was no obvious evidence to dispute this general picture. The town does not have much commercial activity and so probably does not support much of a middle group.

Construction in town is mainly *adobe* and tile, but in the *cantones*, *bajareque* walls and straw roofs are also common.

Guacotecti (1950 Population: 133 urban, 1.991 rural)

Guacotecti gave the impression of a town which has had all the life drained out of it, and such seems almost to be the case. There are no stores in the town at all, the houses are scattered here and there, and the plaza, a lovely green area, was empty of people. The town is located so near to the departmental capital of Sensuntepeque that the residents evidently consider it as almost a residential suburb.

The population is agricultural, but most of the land is in small to medium sized holdings and the majority of the population must rent land or work as laborers. Many leave here annually for the coffee harvest in the area of Berlín and Santiago de María. The land of the *municipio* is extremely broken and, as a result, much of the agricultural work is done with digging stick and the plow is somewhat less used than in other parts of the region.

There are no Indians in the *municipio*. The informant tended to classify the local people into three groups, laborers, small agriculturalists, and the wealthy. This would seem to provide an example of an agrarian middle class, if there is indeed a social distinction between the small agriculturalists and the laborers. It seems likely, however, that the distinction is a local one which may have significance because of the absence of a commercial town class.

2. INDIAN COMMUNITIES OF THE SOUTHWEST

Ataco (1950 Population: 3,102 urban, 3,609 rural)

This town is located at an altitude of 4,000 feet in the mountains which rise to the south of Ahuachapán. It is in a coffee *finca* zone and almost all the land in the area is in middle and large sized coffee holdings. As a result, the great majority of the population are *finca colonos*. There is very little subsistence agriculture carried on, but where it is, the digging stick is the main instrument of cultivation. The land is too hilly and the people too poor to use the ox plow. Many of the laborers live in the town and many on their own small residence plots scattered around the *municipio*. The *colonos*, of course, live in homes on the *fincas*. Ataco itself serves not only as a residence area for the day laboring population, but as a secondary commercial center for the *fincas* of the region.

The population of the *municipio* is primarily Ladinoized Indian and this population forms the lower class of the area. There is, in addition, a small class of business men in the town. The upper class is represented both by a local upper class of Old Ladino families, and the cosmopolitan upper of *finqueros* who live either on their *fincas* or in the cities.

Izalco (1950 Population: 5,966 urban, 16,289 rural)

This community is one of the best known Indian towns of the country. It is particularly interesting because, unlike most of the Indian communities of the area, the Indian population of Izalco is concentrated in the town itself and is not scattered out in the rural *cantones*. It was reported that there was only one *cantón* of the *municipio* which was Indian; the rest were Ladino.

The Izalco Indian population is agricultural and cultivates coffee besides the subsistence crops. They go out to their holdings daily from the homes in the *barrios*.

The town itself is divided into fairly distinct *barrios*. The section of town which is divided into the classic grid pattern is mainly Ladino. The Indian *barrios* are mainly composed of houses scattered along irregular dirt paths.

Izalco is located on the main highway between San Salvador, Sonsonate, and Acajutla. The Indian population is in no way isolated so the relatively slower ladinoization which is evidently taking place there may be due to the fact that the population has been able to retain its economic integrity, and has not been converted into a *colono* or day laboring population.

Jayaque (1950 Population: 1,787 urban, 2,032 rural)

Jayaque, like Ataco, is a *municipio* devoted almost entirely to the cultivation of coffee in *fincas*. Jubsistence agriculture is carried on mainly by people who go either to the interior valley or to the coast to do their planting. Also, like Ataco, the population is predominantly Ladinoized Indian. The town population is mainly Ladino, and in great part is devoted to the commerce attendant to the *fincas*. The rural population, however, is Indian.

The landholders in the *muncipio* are generally people of the local upper class. This group seems to blend pretty much with the commercial group, so that it is hard to distinguish between the local upper and the local middle group. There are a few *fincas* which belong to outsiders who live in San Salvador.

Most of the construction in town is *bajareque* or board walls and tile roof. There has been a tendency in recent years to use brick both in the town and in the construction of *colono* houses on the *fincas*.

Panchimalco (1950 Population: 2,085 urban, 8,253 rural)

This community is located but a few miles from San Salvador, but on the south side of the mountains. It is set on the side of the slope and the topography of the town is thoroughly broken. There are a few Ladino families living in Panchimalco, but in general the population is Indian.

Panchimalco is somewhat aberrant among the Indian towns of El Salvador for a number of reasons. In the first place it is one of the few towns in which weaving continues to provide an essential article of clothing, the woman's skirts, as well as the head cloths and carrying cloths. The costume itself is essentially Spanish or Ladino in origin, not of the wrap-around *corte* type still used in Izalco. In the Panchimalco kitchens it was reported that unlike almost all other Salvadorean communities, both Indian and Ladino, wood ash is preferred to lime for the making of *nixtamal*. Also, on the flooi fires of Panchimalco, the *hornilla* is used, not three stones. While markets are indicative of an Indian tradition, Panchimalco has no market and has never had one so far as the informants knew. These variations are perhaps small in themselves, but when one considers them all together, they suggest that either the origins of Panchimalco or the course of its history must have varied somewhat from the other Pipil Indian towns of the southwest.

The land of the *municipio* is divided up into fairly small holdings, but even with this, a great proportion of the men have no land of their own. Many rent pieces of land, and many seek work in construction jobs in "Los Planes," a suburban residential area of San Salvador located on the top of the mountain above the town. Many families spend November to January working in coffee harvests, both nearby in Los Planes, and in Santa Ana, Santa Tecla, and elsewhere.

Santiago Nonualco (1950 Population: 2,304 urban, 10,156 rural)

This *municipio* is located partially in the piedmont and partially in the upper coastal plain. It is an old predominantly Indian *municipio*, and the surrounding area is occupied by a similar population. The Indians of Santiago and probably those in the other towns of the area are highly ladinoized. A few customs remain to distinguish them from the Ladinos of the towns, but in general they are considered as Indian not so much because they manifest extreme differences in custom, as because they are retained as a distinctive social group.

While perhaps a quarter of the land of the *municipio* is in large *haciendas*, the majority of the people work in subsistence farming, either depending principally on this, or combining it with work on the *haciendas* and in the coffee and cotton harvests. A few must rent land for this purpose and fewer still are *colonos* on the local *haciendas*.

The town itself has a *sociedad* of Ladinos and a class of local businessmen. In the countryside there is what appears to be an agrarian middle class of small to middle sized landholders, but the distinctiveness of this class was not clear from the data gathered on the survey.

3. TOWNS OF THE CENTER BELT

San Matías (1950 Population: 561 urban, 2,086 rural)

San Matías is a small, sleepy community located in the broken plateau which lies in the drainage of a tributary of the Lempa. The population is Ladino, but generally very poor. A large proportion are evidently land renters, but the writer could not ascertain what the general pattern of landownership was.

In the town itself there is a small local upper class, but it is evidently neither very wealthy nor cosmopolitan. There are generally two classes, a local upper group and the great majority of the population composed of land renters and laborers. Land is not plentiful in the *municipio*, and consequently it is being used quite constantly with little rest. The poverty of the population is reflected in the fact that among the poorer, exchange labor is still resorted to as a means of carrying on agricultural activities, and most rural homes are the simplest, one room, *ranchos*.

San Matías reflects some of the problems inherent in the overpopulation and long occupation of this center belt region. There is not enough land, and what there is is either in *hacienda* production (there is one *hacienda* in San Matías) or overworked in subsistence production.

Tonacatepeque (1950 Population: 2,413 urban, 5,282 rural)

Whereas San Matías reflects the problem of land poverty of the central belt, Tonacatepeque reflects a different problem. Here, most of the land is divided into small and medium sized holdings and through low production, the *muni-*

cipio is generally poor. The majority of the population work as labor for these local landholders and as sharecroppers.

Tonacatepeque is an old town and has a local upper class, the *sociedad*, the property holders of the *municipio*. They tend to live in two of the four *barrios* of the town. There is also a fairly well formed middle group, people who are not particularly rich but who "live well." There were thought by the informant to be a few Indians in the rural part of the *municipio*, but they were only to be distinguished by their imperfect use of Spanish.

This town is perhaps more characteristic of the center belt than San Matías. The proximity to San Salvador is reflected in considerable travel to that center; the town also receives electric current from the capital. The construction is basically *bajareque*, in both town and country, while tile roofs are standard in town. In the country, straw roofs are more common.

Moncagua (1950 Population: 790 urban, 6,775 rural) and the *Valle de la Esperanza*

These towns, Moncagua, Chinameca, Jucuapa, San Buenaventura, Nueva Guadalupe, and Lolotique, provide a good idea of the general nature of the Ladino culture of the eastern end of the center belt. The region is occupied by various large holdings in coffee *fincas* and *haciendas*, but much of the land is in medium holdings. The coffee is concentrated primarily in the uplands of the volcanic area, while as one moves off to the north into the broken land of the interior valleys, the medium and smaller holdings become more important.

All phases of the class system are found in these communities. Everywhere there is a large lower class of *colonos*, laborers, and small subsistence agriculturalists. In both towns and the countryside there is a distinctive middle class of small landholders, artesans, businessmen. Some towns, such as San Buenaventura, and probably Lolotique, stop with these two, but in the bigger towns, there is a distinctive local upper class of wealthier businessmen, the old families and *sociedad*. The social clubs in Jucuapa reflect the crystallization of these differences. Then there are representatives of the cosmopolitan upper class, the *finqueros* who live either on their *fincas*, often have houses in the town too, or residences (their own or their families) in the capital.

The fact that much of this region was struck by a severe earthquake in the early 1950's caused it to be a center of national interest, and considerable study has been devoted to some aspects of its way of life.[65] There are very few people in the region who could culturally be called Indian. The area is, however, basically Ladino. It is vastly overpopulated and even with the annual and seasonal work in the *fincas* and *haciendas*, there is a regular emigration, mainly to Honduras.

4. TOWNS OF THE EAST

Santa Elena (1950 Population: 3,218 urban, 6,061 rural)

Santa Elena is a Ladino community located in the semi-broken upper coastal

---

[65] See the IBEC report of which Adams, 1952a, is an appendix.

belt. Local tradition says that the area was originally an *hacienda*, and that Indians never formed a very important part of the population. There is no doubt but that today the population is Ladino.

There are no *haciendas* or *fincas* in the *municipio*, except for a small portion of the piedmont section on the north which is in coffee. The rest of the land is divided into small holdings. With this, however, there is not sufficient land to go around, and about half the population do not have enough of their own for subsistence agriculture. This population rents land and participates in the migrations to the coffee harvests immediately to the north and to the cotton harvests in the coastal plain to the south.

The entire *municipio* of Santa Elena is evidently dependent upon a single source of water, a large spring which rises in the middle of the town and which has been under municipal control for many years. People from the rural areas come in with oil drums tied on ox carts for their water supply, and domesticated animals are walked in daily for their drink.

As might be expected, from this general economic picture, there are only two social classes, the town *primera sociedad* and the *gente del pueblo*, town and country small landholders and renters.

The town is near the departmental capital of Usulután and most of the major commerce is carried on there.

Conchagua (1950 Population: 1,164 urban, 3,280 rural)

This community is located high on the volcano of Conchagua which rises out of the coastal plain in the far southeast corner of the country. The greater part of the *municipio*, which includes an extensive coastline, is in *haciendas* and *fincas*, and most of the population are laborers, *colonos*, and land renters. It is evidently customary in this region to provide the *colonos* with land for the cultivation of subsistence crops. Perhaps three-fifths of the townspeople also work as *hacienda* and *finca* laborers.

About one half of the population is Ladinoized Indian. They evidently do not live in distinct *cantones* or *barrios*, but are generally mixed with the Ladino population. This situation is fostered, of course, by the fact that the *haciendas* seldom pay any attention to such social differences, and the residence pattern is dictated by other concerns. Apparently whatever social distinctions existed between Indians and lower class Ladinos is fast breaking down as there is intermarriage between the two groups.

El Sauce (1950 Population: 855 urban, 5,084 rural)

El Sauce is located in the broken northeastern lowlands near the Honduran border. It is a Ladino community which is said by tradition to be one of the oldest in the department.

All the land is in small and medium sized holdings, but there still is a large proportion, perhaps half, of the population which must rent land or work as laborers. The shortage of land has led to extensive emigration to neighboring Honduras. The distinction between the medium landholder and the subsistence agriculturalist and laborer is clear-cut. As is the case over much of eastern Salvador and adjacent Honduras, the class division is emphasized by the members of the local upper class carrying pistols.

Like Santa Elena, El Sauce is a descendent of the early Ladino population which moved into eastern El Salvador. The Indians long since ceased to play any distinct role in many of these communities.

Cacaopera (1950 Population: 837 urban, 8,725 rural)

Cacaopera is the center of the one remaining Modified Indian population in eastern El Salvador. It is located in the low, broken mountains of northeastern El Salvador. While the Indians form the majority of the rural population, Ladinos now form the larger part of the town population. There have long been a few Ladino families in the northeast, but in recent decades there has evidently been an immigration into Cacaopera. Ladinos handle most of the store commerce and, as was related earlier, have in the past twenty years taken over the control of the municipal government.

Cacaopera is basically a region of small and medium sized landholders, and as yet, most people have land. There is some seasonal migration to the departments of San Miguel and Santa Ana for coffee harvest, but the people evidently do not participate in the coastal cotton harvests. Those without land are divided between renters and laborers. The Indians and many of the Ladinos of Cacaopera spend much of their time in the production of henequin and henequin products. It was said that the Indians particularly preferred henequin cultivation to extensive subsistence agriculture because it was much easier. Apparently only the Ladinos plant food crops for sale.

While there is ready distinction made between Indians and Ladinos, the term *humilde* seems to be used for members both of the Indian population and the lower class Ladinos. The town has a *sociedad*, but because so many are recent arrivals they are not necessarily all old families. Generally, there is no intermarriage between Indian and Ladino, although there are cases of people of the two groups living together.

REFERENCES

Adams, Richard N., 1952a. "Investigaciones en el area del terremoto realizadas de marzo 4 a marzo 15, 1952." Appendix 4 in *Una nueva Vida para el Valle de la Esperanza; un Plan de Desarrollo Preparado para el Ministerio de Obras Públicas*, El Salvador, pp. 61–70. IBEC Housing Corporation, New York.

———, 1952b. "Un Análisis de las Creencias y Prácticas Médicas en un Pueblo Indígena de Guatemala." *Publicaciones Especiales del Instituto Indigenista Nacional, No. 17.* Guatemala.

———, n.d. (a) Cultural Survey of Panama, Part Two, this volume.

———, n.d. (b) Cultural Survey of Nicaragua, Part Three, this volume.

———, n.d. (c) Cultural Survey of Guatemala, Part Four, this volume.

de Baratta, María, n.d. *Cuzcatlán Típico*. 2 Vol. San Salvador.

Baron Castro, Rodolfo, 1942. *La Población de El Salvador*. Madrid.

Dirección General de Estadística y Censos, *Boletín Estadístico* [A periodical issued about six times a year]. San Salvador.
Census, 1942. *Población de la República de El Salvador. Censo del 1o. de mayo 1930.*
―――――, 1953. *Primer Censo de la Vivienda Urbana, Feb. de 1950.* San Salvador.
―――――, 1954. *Segundo Censo de Población, junio 13 de 1950.* San Salvador.
Choussy, Felix. 1950. "Economía Agrícola Salvadoreña," *Biblioteca Universitaria*, Vol. XVIII. San Salvador.
Foster, George, ms. Field notes on El Salvador, 1951.
Gonzales Sol, Rafael, 1945. *Fiestas Cívicas, Religiosas y Exhibiciones Populares de El Salvador.* Talleres Gráficos Cisneros, San Salvador.
Guandique, José Salvador, 1950. "Noción y Aspectos de la Clase Media en El Salvador." *Materiales para el estudio de la clase media en América Latina*, IV. Washington, D. C., pp. 113–119. (Mimeo.)
Johnson, Frederick, 1948. "Central American Cultures: An Introduction." *Handbook of American Indians*. Vol. 4, *The Circum-Caribbean Tribes*. Bureau of American Ethnology, Bulletin 143. Washington, pp. 43–68.
Larde y Larin, Jorge, 1950. *Recopilación de Leyes Relativas a la Historia de los Municipios de El Salvador.* Publicación del Ministerio del Interior.
Loenholdt, Fritz, 1953. *The Agricultural Economy of El Salvador.* San Salvador (Mimeo.)
Lothrop, S. K., 1937. "Central America: Ethnology," *The Encyclopedia Britanica*, Fourteenth Edition, Vol. 5, pp. 128–130. New York and Chicago.
Schlesinger, Jorge, 1946. *Revolución Comunista.* Guatemala.
Squier, E. G., 1855. *Notes on Central America.* New York.

APPENDIX

Concepts of Sickness and Practices of Curing in the *Cantón* of El Jícaro, San Matías; A Series of Cases, Collected by Edwin James, 1954

Introduction

The purpose of this study is to explore the practices and beliefs of rural folk regarding sickness and health in order to reveal the core of beliefs around which these activities are oriented. Health education can follow more easily when one understands what people already understand. The cases to follow were collected during house and field visits to the *cantón* of El Jícaro between the months of June and December, 1953. The study was originally undertaken by Miss Winnifred Weeks at the suggestion of anthropologist Richard Adams. Since Miss Weeks had to leave El Salvador unexpectedly, I undertook the work in her place. My approach was that of a foreigner who was interested in the way of life of the people; I did not stress the subject of health during the informal interviews and conversations, and for the most part the information which follows came up in the course of regular conversation. In the main, the field notes were written up following the visits, not during the work. The families represented in the following cases were not selected scientifically, but are those which selected me; that is, those who indicated that they were comfortable with my presence were those whom I visited. In some families, which were genial, the evident feeling that the visitor might not agree or might know better stopped the flow of information.

At the time of the study no health program had been initiated in El Jícaro. The *cantón* was composed of about 112 families, scattered over the *caseríos* of El Jícaro, San Lorenzo, Las Hamacas, Chinalta, La Ceibita, Capulinera, El Timón, and the Planta on Río Sucio. The families visited in the study lived in El Jícaro and a section of El Timón. The majority of the population derive its income from the *hacienda* San Lorenzo. The main subsistence crops are rice, beans and corn and there is almost no garden production. The homes are generally *ranchos*.

The informants' families were as follows:

AR (father), JP (mother), daughters of 2 and 14, and sons of 8 and 11.

DC (father), MHC (mother), daughters of 6 months and 8 years, and a son of 7 years.

JE (father), RF (mother), and one daughter of 15 years; other children are maintaining their own homes elsewhere.

JR (father), LD (mother), daughters of 15 months, and 3, 10, and 13 years, and a son of 5 years.

DP, a single man of about 70 years, who lives alone.

Cases

The material which follows is presented pretty much as it appears in the field notes.

July 2, 1953

(1) Passing through the corral of *hacienda* San Lorenzo I saw a number of men gathered around a calf laying in the shade. The calf's ear had been largely cut away and it was bleeding profusely. On inquiry it turned out that the ear had been cut off intentionally by one of the men with his machete. This was done, he said, in order to see if the calf had *sangre roja*. Asking further, it was explained that if the blood were *chele* (light colored) the calf was sure to die; if it were red, the calf would be able to recover from the sickness he had. The blood proved to be red, and *fuerte*, too. The men assured each other that the calf would recover and we left the animal laying in the mud with the ear covered with blood and flies.

I mentioned this incident to JP, and she said that she could tell the state of the blood by the same method. She confirmed that *chele* and *roja* qualities were signs of condition of the blood. To her, *chele* blood meant *sangre debil* and red blood meant *sangre fuerte*.

(2) JP says to cure *mal de estómago*, one may suck on the bark of the *palo de sicuaite*, or boil the bark and drink the tea.

(3) JP says to cure *cangrinas* (boils), the bark of the *palo de quina* may be rubbed on the boil, or a tea made and drunk.

In both this and the previous cure, the tea is made of *tres por tres dedos* of bark.

(4) JP says to cure *orín tapado* one should cook *patas de grillo* (cricket feet) in water; *se destapa el orín ligero*.

(5) JP says that there are people here who can do *daño* to one; but not right here in El Jícaro. There is a woman farther down who knows about such things; she is very intelligent. JP would not elaborate on where "farther down" was.

July 15, 1953

(6) JP says that *artritis* or *calentura* are evidenced by aching bones and muscles, especially in the arms. It is caused by bathing very late or at night. Bathing late in the day *hace daño a uno*; *se quita la fuerza del cuerpo*. She does her own bathing after doing the washing in the morning.

(7) JP says that sweeping or cleaning the house in the late afternoon also does *daño*. One should not throw the garbage and dirt out but keep it in a corner until the next morning and throw it out then. It would be very dangerous to throw it out in late afternoon or evening.

July 22, 1953

(8) LD says *mal de ojo* is when the eyes become red and pus comes out; to cure it, one puts a drop of the father's urine in the eye. Both children have it, and this is the cure she uses.

(9) MHC says bathing should not be done at night or when the moon is new. Her husband will not bathe when he comes home late in the afternoon, even though he is quite dirty; it is too dangerous. One afternoon a rainstorm had soaked her husband when he was working in the field and as a result he became very ill. He had chills and a fever for some time afterwards. She confirmed that the house can only be cleaned in the morning or one will be in danger.

August 19, 1953

(10) RF spoke of the young child of MHC, her neighbor, and mentioned that they both fear it has *daño*. The child has *tunar débil* since it was born before it should have. She feels that the *daño* came from another person who has *tunar fuerte*. The fact that such a person is sweating makes it worse. RF sent some leaves of rue to the child as a cure.

(11) RF says *mal de ojo* is when the eyes are inflamed, red, and hurt; one wants to rub the eyes, and there are red *granitos* in them. To cure it, one may wrap a *venda* (a rag) wet with *aguardiente* in another cloth, and place it on the eyes and forehead. The eyes must be shut or it will burn. The *guaro* stings the eyes and she considers this to be good. This process may be repeated daily until the *mal de ojo* is gone. *Guaro* (*aguardiente*) is *cálido* and makes the eyes hurt. The inflammation of the eyes is *cálida* also. She is using this remedy at present on her daughter.

(12) MHC's daughter, when not in the arms of its mother, is in a hammock

made of a henequin sack. Under the cloth on which the child lies is a booklet called *"El Milagro."* This booklet, explained MHC, is to ward off dangers and sicknesses. If a sickness comes to the family, and especially to the *"sietilla"* (the child), a prayer is read from it, and this cures the sick person. The child, when in the hammock, is never without the safeguard of the booklet; it is responsible for keeping the child alive so far.

(13) While the writer was eating lunch with DP, a very feeble dog came over for a handout. Instead of food, the *chucho* received a severe thrashing from DP and left. In a few moments, it returned and lay down; DP beat it again, and it left. When this was repeated for the third time, the old man turned and said that he was afraid the dog would die in front of his house (where we were seated) and leave the sickness with him.

September 2, 1953

(14) RF says that *mal aire* and *daño* from a person with *tunar fuerte* are similar; they result in a sick stomach, lack of hunger, perhaps diarrhea and headache. *Mal aire* is encountered in the streets and strange places. It is often in the form of a *puño de aire*, a gust of cold air which strikes one suddenly. The result of this gust is often sickness of the stomach and fever. *Daño* comes from very strong people (*gente muy fuerte*), especially the local policeman. When a person has *daño*, it is just like having any other illness. To cure these troubles, a cross made of two branches of rue is placed on the top of a glass of water. This is allowed to sit for about an hour *para que despida el gusto al agua*, so that it savors the water. The resulting tea is taken by the sick person. Rue is better and has a numbing effect on the mouth if the leaf is chewed. RF says the rue has the quality of *cálido*.

(15) RF says a person with *tunar débil* is one with *sangre no muy cálida*, and such a person is susceptible to sicknesses and frightens easily. On the other hand, a person with *tunar fuerte* is not susceptible to sicknesses, has *sangre cálida*, is *brava* (tough, hot tempered), and does not frighten easily. The policemen, for example, are always of *tunar fuerte* because of their bravery and strength.

(16) MHC says her child is sick, does not wish to eat, cries a great deal, and has diarrhea. It was caused by *daños* given by a policeman who passed near the house, walking fast and sweating. The child apparently did not see the policeman, nor touch him, but he is responsible for the sickness. MHC maintains that the policeman has very strong blood and gave the *daño* to the child who had *tunar débil*. I asked her how she was so sure that the policeman was the cause of the child's condition, and she said she used the following proof. She rolled a chicken egg all through the child's hair and touched it to every part of his body. The child lay in its hammock, and she put a *guacal* on the floor under the hammock. The *guacai* contained a little cold water and into this she broke the egg and stirred it around (*se pica el huevo*). She left this under the child for a few hours and then examined it. Upon finding the white no longer clear and the yolk slightly hard on the outside it was a clear case of *daño*. The *daño* had affected the egg and caused it to be partially cooked. If the egg had not cooked,

then the child would not be suffering from *daño* caused by the policeman. He did it since he was the last one to look at the child before it got sick. To cure this, a mixture is made of the herb *memoscada*, ground cigar butt (best if picked up from the street), three pinches of cloves, and some bits of garlic. This mixture is mixed with saliva from the child, chewed, and smeared over the child's body.

(17) MHC says all her children were quite susceptible to *susto* but are seldom affected now, except for the youngest. The other children are all seven years or over. *Susto* almost always elicits crying or fright on the part of the child immediately. The crying and fright come right away, not a long while afterwards. The child may cry for some time, even days, if the *susto* is not recognized and cured quickly. *Susto* may be caused by the appearance of a sweaty stranger, a sudden motion, or just the entrance of a stranger. Her older child always used to be *asustado* when strangers were around. To cure *susto*, three sprigs of the herb called *hierba de susta* are boiled; the solution is allowed to cool, then mixed with cold water. The child is bathed in this (not in the afternoon), and then drinks three mouthfuls of the water. Also, if caused by a stranger, he may hold the child, *chinear*, and this will cure it. Or if caused by a sweating stranger, the child may be put to bed in a sweaty shirt of its father.

September 23, 1953

(18) DP says that coconut water is *fresca* and acid; it is bad for one who has just stopped working and is still hot. I was advised not to drink from a coconut offered me by VM because I had just come up the hill out of breath. VM did not push the offer but seemed indifferent to the idea expressed by DP. DP said the *fresco* quality of the coconut is bad for one who is hot. The acid quality also damages the stomach of a hot person. Cold water is also *fresca* or *fría* and bad to drink after working, except in small amounts. Meat is also *ácida*, and should not be eaten after working.

(19) DP says that the blood is *cálida* usually, but it can change. Some people have *sangre fuerte* and others *sangre débil*. One with strong blood is successful with women, isn't frightened, and does not get sick. He is fearless and healthy. A person with weak blood is often sick, affected by *daño* from one with strong blood, and may lose his appeal to women. People with weak blood may be born with it, or get it simply from not eating well. However, it can be changed, especially by eating certain kinds of strong foods. Two dishes which are almost certain to strengthen the blood are: (1) *pijón* soup, made of potatoes, *güisayotes*, and *pijón* cooked together in a little water. All three things are very *cálidas*. (2) Two *reales* worth of chocolate, a *medio litro* of milk, a well beaten egg, and two *reales* worth of *guaro*. Mix the chocolate in the milk, and add the egg and *guaro*.

(20) LD was sweeping around her grinding stone about three in the afternoon. I asked her if this was not dangerous, and she said that it was bad to sweep at night or with the new moon. Bathing must be done early in the day or you will get *daño*.

October 14, 1953

(21) MHC and DC say that *fuego* is a series of very red pimples, apparently found mostly on children. The cases I saw were around the face and neck. MHC and DC did not know where it came from . . . perhaps from unknown persons. It causes the body to become very hot and one must give a purge to cure it; with this the *cosas chucas* and the heat leaves the body. Also, a child may be bathed in water from the leaves of the *paraíso* tree. The *paraíso* is *helado*, and this helps cool the body.

(22) I burned myself the other day and asked MHC how to cure it. She immediately suggested putting kerosine on it. "The kerosine hurts some, but it cures the burn quickly."

(23) DC mentioned that her child had inadvertently drunk some kerosine the other day thinking it was water. After spitting out what he could, DC gave him some lemon juice in water as a remedy. Both the lemon juice and the kerosine are *cálidos*, but the boy was not sick afterwards.

(24) LD has two children who have red boils on the upper part of their bodies. This is *fuego*. LD says it is in *andancia*, i.e. spreading, through the community, going from house to house touching the children. LD went to the sanitary unit in Quezaltepeque, and was given a small tin of sulfathiazol salve. It seemed to work and LD concluded that it must have been very *caliente*. She thought the salve should also work well for the burn in my arm since it too was *caliente*.

October 28, 1953

(25) JP mentioned that *daño* and *mal aire* are very common. Goya, the daughter of LD, is sick after having been taken along when her mother went washing. The *daño* came from *mal aire* in the street. JP suggested the best cure is to wrap the child in its father's clothes at night.

(26) LD said the symptoms of *daño* or *mal aire* in a child are crying, vomiting, and fever. LD thinks her child got it the same way that JP mentioned.

(27) LD says *cálido* foods include coffee, cheese, eggs, beans, chicken, corn on the cob, and meat; *helado* foods include fruits, yuca, water, and roosters.

(28) LD says to cure a headache one may take the patent medicine, *Mejoral*. *Mejoral* is *caliente*, and one must fight fire with fire. However, the common cold is *frío*, and also needs something *caliente*.

November 4, 1953

(29) MHC says *pujo* is when a child cannot defecate, when he has gas in his stomach. This case was caused by a sweaty stranger who went by the house emiting gas. *Pujo* in the child can be cured by gathering the rubbish of the house, putting it in the cooking fire, and then placing an armadillo shell in the fire. The child is held nude over the fire. The armadillo and his shell are *cálidos*.

(30) MHC says *daño* from *tunar fuerte* caused her child to become very sick with fever and chills and to lose his appetite. When he was smaller, he used to be visited by his uncle who did *daño* to the child because he was of strong blood.

The uncle cured the child regularly by holding him and giving him good herbs. But it was very dangerous for the child every time the uncle came to visit.

(31) MHC says that rats go through the house at night and try to get at any food they can. One must keep the food out of reach or one will get the disease of *galico* from the saliva they leave on the food.

(32) MHC maintains that there are very few spiritualists in El Salvador. However, she told of one she knew about. About a year ago a man was found dead, reportedly killed by a car. The wife of the dead man was suspicious and went to this spiritualist to really find out the cause of his death. The spiritualist interviewed the widow and in the session put her into contact with her dead husband, who said he had been murdered by a vicious enemy. He would not give his name because this would endanger the rest of the family. The spiritualist collected a fee of 40 *centavos*, a sum "fixed by God."

(33) MHC said her infant is now generally better and out of danger. She went on to explain that the child was born at seven months, and the number seven has therefore been dangerous for it. Seven weeks was a very dangerous time, and it was sick then. It is now past its seventh month, and there will be no more danger until the 17th month, following that, the 27th, etc. However, the danger gets less as the child gets bigger.

November 25, 1953

(34) MHC said that cures for *pujo* include such foods as cheese, boiled eggs, and coffee. *Hierba de pujo*, an herb, she has also used. Generally only *cálido* foods should be taken. *Pujo* strikes both young and old, and the remedies are the same for both.

(35) MHC says that coughs (*tos ferina* and *tos chifladora*) are very dangerous for the children. They cough so much at night that they cannot sleep. Whooping cough is cured with the flower *chula* or *chulita blanca* which is taken as a tea. *Tos chifladora* is cured with the flower of the *veranera* taken as a tea and rubbed on the chest.

(36) MHC says one of her children died of a burn once. She had left the baby on a bed which was lighted with two candles, one on either side. Upon returning to the house, she found that one of the candles had toppled and set the bed clothes afire. She tried many remedies on the badly burned child, including a mixture of kerosine, lime, and salt. But the child died anyway because it was time for it to die. She had suspected this because she had felt the child being pulled from her arms many times previously. Other cures she tried were lard and an herb, *barraja de la tierra*.

(37) MHC spoke of HD, a spiritualist who recently died. She had gone to him many times because she has a bad heart. HD had an "understanding with God" which enabled him to work. She thinks that he was poisoned by a doctor.

Summary and Interpretations (By Richard Adams)

These cases bring out a number of basic ideas concerning the causes of illnesses. Many illnesses, especially among children, are caused by a strong force such as *daños*. *Daños* may come as *mal aire*, but more often come from a person with *tunar fuerte*. A person with weak *tunar* or weak blood is specifically susceptible to this. *Malos aires* and *daños* are generaly treated with things which are *cálidas*. *Susto* in a child is also related to this concept. The cure of a frightened child and one with *daño* both include wrapping it in the sweaty clothing of the father, presumably on the principle that the father's superior strength may be given to the child in this way. Similarly, *pujo* is related to this same cause, and is cured in a similar way.

The concept of contagion is fairly common: contagion from food eaten by rats, from whatever is ailing a dying dog, and the *fuego* which was said to be going from house to house infecting the children.

The general condition of the individual, his basic susceptibility to illness, was seen as a function of many things: the time and condition of his birth, which might make certain subsequent periods dangerous; his own age, since he increased in strength as he got older; the time of day (sweeping and bathing should not be done in late afternoon or evening); the phase of the moon; the qualities of the foods eaten, whether they were *cálidos*, and therefore conductive to strong blood, or *helados* and not so conductive, and whether they were bitter or acid. There is some evidence of a balance being conceived as a state of well-being for the individual; certain illnesses which are thought to be *cálidas* are cured by the use of *helado* or *fresco* remedies. On the other hand, the concept of "fight fire with fire" was also expressed as a guide for curing certain troubles such as pink eye and burns.

Instead of a specific set of distinct ailments, the material from El Jícaro seems to point to a generalization of certain disease concepts, particularly the effect of *daños* in their various forms. The system of principles is basically simple, and the specific forms of the illnesses seem almost interchangeable: constipation (*pujo*), fright, crying, fever, chills, and stomach trouble, can all result from the same general cause of something *cálido* or strong approaching a person who is weak.

Of possible importance in this material is the lack of certain things: there is no mention made of recourse to *parcheros*, only to spiritualists occasionally; no mention is made of two extremely standard illnesses found elsewhere, *mal ojo* (which would fit perfectly well into the specific disease pattern of strength and weakness), and *caída de la mollera*.

In general, the illness concepts and practices revealed by Mr. James' study in El Jícaro point to much simpler basic system than that found among Modified Indians of Guatemala studied by Adams (1952a). This, perhaps, is another aspect of the general deculturated character of the Ladino culture of the countryman. Complicated western medical concepts have entered but little (if the idea of contagion may be said to be derived from this source), while older patterns have become generalized and simplified. While old curers seem to play little role in the curing, neither has western medicine entered with additional doctors and clinical facilities. Thus more curing is done on the basis of home cures with only occasional recourse to spiritualists or to the distant clinic.

Part Six

HONDURAS

With Appendix by Doris Stone

1955

HONDURAS

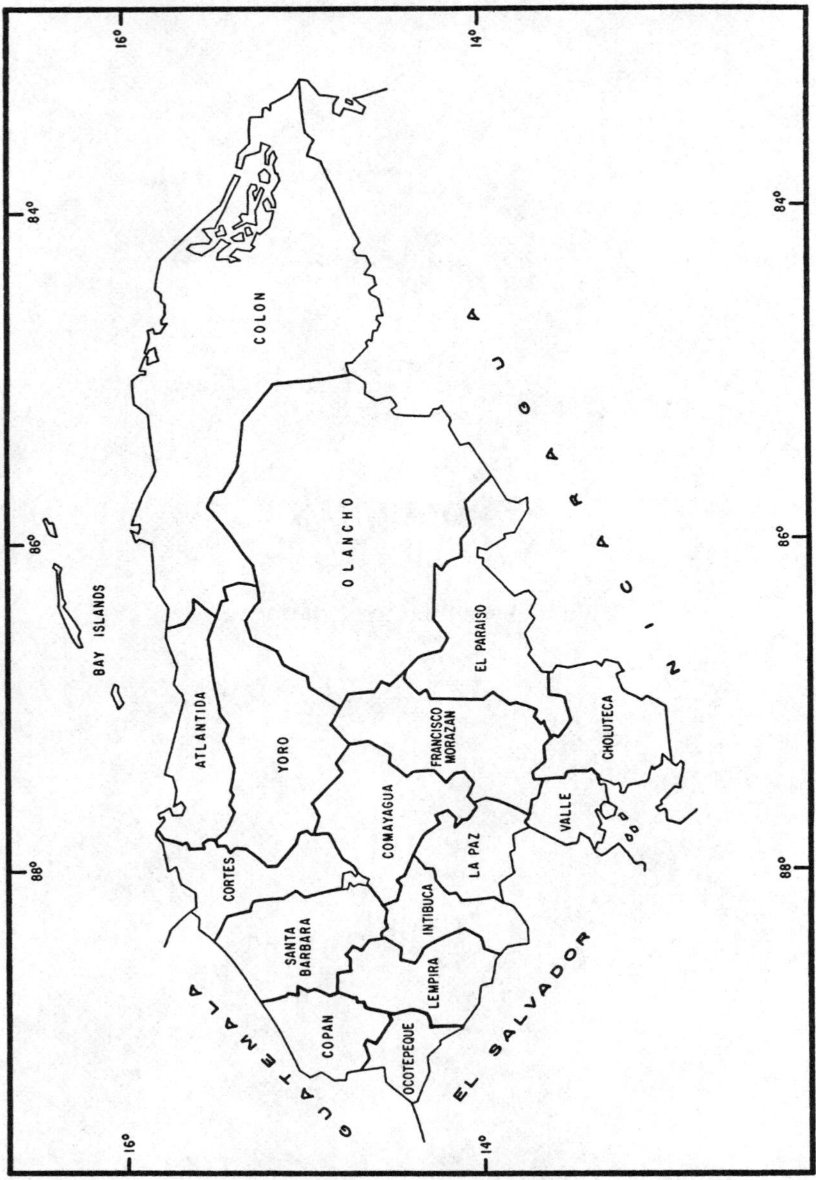

16°
14°
84°
86°
88°
BAY ISLANDS
COLON
OLANCHO
ATLANTIDA
YORO
EL PARAISO
FRANCISCO MORAZAN
CHOLUTECA
COMAYAGUA
VALLE
CORTES
LA PAZ
INTIBUCA
SANTA BARBARA
LEMPIRA
COPAN
OCOTEPEQUE
NICARAGUA
EL SALVADOR
GUATEMALA

INTRODUCTION

The present monograph is the last of a series of country studies which the writer has made in Panama, Nicaragua, Guatemala, El Salvador, and Honduras. The emphasis in this, as in the previous studies in the series, has been on the Ladino culture of the country. The Honduran Indian population has been little represented in formal study, however, so some space is devoted to the delineation of this population. The Black Carib of the north coast are here dealt with briefly, since their culture is essentially similar to that of the Black Carib of Guatemala and British Honduras which has been described by Taylor and in an earlier monograph in this series. The field work on which the present study is based was carried on in the months of February and March of 1955. While the road system in Honduras is improving rapidly, it is still more feasible to reach some sections of the country by air than by road. As a result, eight of the towns surveyed involved air trips, and two, those in the Bay Islands, boat trips. Otherwise, all travel was done by car or horseback. Due to the dispersal of the Indian populations of Colón and their difficulty of access, no attempt was made to include them in the present study. Fortunately, we have ethnographic accounts concerning them, even though the work is somewhat old and does not touch on many of the phases of the culture which interest us.

Travel by car was made possible by SCISP, and the writer is deeply indebted to Dr. Zepeda of that Organization for his help in arranging transportation and other phases of the work. To Dr. Gaspar Vallecillo and Srta. Ernestina Caballero, also of SCISP, the writer is indebted for help in the course of the survey and their company on the trip to Quimistán and Ilama. Dr. Manuel Cáceres Vijil, Minister of Health, and Dr. M. A. Sánchez, Director General of Public Health, kindly provided letters of introduction. Miguel Figueroa, of SCISP, accompanied the writer as chauffeur on most of the automobile trips and provided excellent company. Mr. Clair Butterfield, of SCIDE, helped the writer in various ways, as did Dr. Jesús Núñez Ch., Director of the Institute of Anthropology and History. Dr. Joaquín Núñez, stationed in La Ceiba, arranged to take the writer to the town of Corozal, and helped greatly with his knowledge of the coast. The Summer School staff of Danlí was most courteous in helping the writer gain some information he needed, and the Agricultural School staff in Catacamas was most courteous in providing him with a place to stay while there. Sr. Carlos Zúñiga Figueroa, Director General of Census and Statistics, and Mr. Edgar Elam, technical advisor to that office, kindly made copies of the census available to the writer and provided him with certain other useful materials. The Standard Fruit Company provided transportation between Corozal and La Ceiba. Mr. E. S. Whitman of the United Fruit Company helped the writer with data on the arrival of the negros in the north coast. Prof. Rubén Angel Rosa kindly provided copies of some of his publications. Mrs. Doris Stone, beside preparing the appendix to the present report, has helped the writer through this entire series of reports by providing him with copies of her available publications. The text has benefited from critical reading by Mrs. Stone and Miss Chapman.

Of course, the greatest debt is to the numerous informants in the towns visited who gave of their time and knowlcdge to answer the writer's questions. It is the policy of the study to provide anonymity for these people.

R. N. A.

November, 1955
Guatemala

TABLE OF CONTENTS

	Page
Introduction	525
I. The Geography and Population of Honduras	529
II. The Culture of the Ladino Town and Country Dweller	539
1. Land, Labor, and Agriculture	539
2. Production, Transport, and Commerce	556
3. The Domestic Establishment	561
4. Family and *Compadrazgo*	567
5. General Social Structure	572
6. Local Political Organization	577
7. Religious Activities	584
8. Patterns of Sickness and Curing	597
III. The Indians of Honduras	603
1. The Indian Population	603
2. The Lenca of the Southwest Highlands	608
3. The Indians of East-Center Santa Bárbara	617
4. The Indians of Southwestern El Paraíso	621
5. The Jicaque Indians of Central Yoro	623
6. The Identification and Acculturation of the Indian	624
IV. Notes on the Black Carib of the North Coast	631
V. The Antillean Population of the Bay Islands	634
VI. The Communities Visited on the Survey	644
1. The South Coast: Yusguare, Nacaome, La Venta	645
2. The Central Highlands: Güinope, Jacaleapa, Zambrano, Guaimaca, La Libertad	646
3. The Southwest Highlands: Marcala, La Esperanza	649
4. The Northwest: La Misión, San Francisco de Yojoa, Quimistán	650
5. The Far West: Dulce Nombre de Copán, Nueva Ocotepeque	652
6. The North and Northeast: Yoro, Olanchito, Catacamas	652
VII. Discussion	654
References	659
Appendix: The Torrupán or Jicaque Indians of the Montaña de la Flor, by Doris Stone	661

I. THE GEOGRAPHY AND POPULATION OF HONDURAS

There are various studies available concerning the general topographical and climatological configuration of Honduras;[1] for the purposes of the present essay, it will be sufficient to define certain major regions of the country as they are outstanding from the point of view of population.

Geographically, about 63% of the land area of Honduras is mountainous.[2] The remaining area may be classified in terms of four major types of regions: (1) the southern coastal area on the Gulf of Fonseca, a hot region of irregular rain; (2) the north coast belt, extending from the Guatemalan border to the region of the mouths of the Río Aguán and the Río Negro, a tropical region of considerable rain fall; (3) the northeast coastal plains which, unlike the north coast, extend far inland and geographically are part of the neighboring coastal region of Nicaragua; also a region of high rainfall; (4) and the numerous interior valleys, the most important of which are formed by the following rivers and their tributaries: Río Choluteca, Río Chamalecón, Río Ulúa, Río Aguán, the Ríos Guayape and Patuca, and the Río Negro. The entire interior of the country is composed of a rough landscape of mountains cut by these rivers.

The mountains, for present purposes, may be defined in terms of three major groups: (1) The southwestern highlands, consisting of the ranges in the departments of La Paz, Intibucá, Lempira, and Ocotepeque, and the lower broken ranges cut by interior valleys in the departments of Santa Bárbara and Copán. These mountains are set off by the upper tributaries of the Río Ulúa (the Río Jicayua, Río Grande de Otoro, and Río Humuya), the Río Chamalecón and the Río Lempa and its tributaries on the south. This mountainous region may be subdivided into the higher and more rugged portions in the departments bordering on El Salvador, and the lower eroded hills of Copán and Santa Bárbara. (2) The second mountainous region of importance, geologically related to the southwestern region, is the central highlands, the ranges which circle Tegucigalpa. These mountains are set off from those of the southwest by the relatively low watershed between the upper reaches of the Río Goascorán which empties into the Gulf of Fonseca on the south, and the Río Humuya, a tributary of the Río Ulúa to the north. On the east, the Río Choluteca and various tributaries of the Río Patuca separate it from the ranges which form the Nicaraguan highlands and spurs which go out to the Atlantic coastal region. On the north, this mountainous region is separated from the hills further to the north by the Río Sulaco and tributaries of the Río Guayape. (3) The north central mountains include the related chains to the north, the Montaña de la Flor, and the mountains overlooking the Atlantic seaboard. On the west they are bordered by the Río Ulúa and its tributaries; on the east, by the Ríos Guayape and Negro; and on the northeast, by the Río Aguán.

---

[1] See, for example, Archer's summary in Census, 1954c, pp. 3–12 on geography, and pp. 12–16 on population, and references cited on page 16.
[2] Tosco, et al, n.d.

HONDURAS

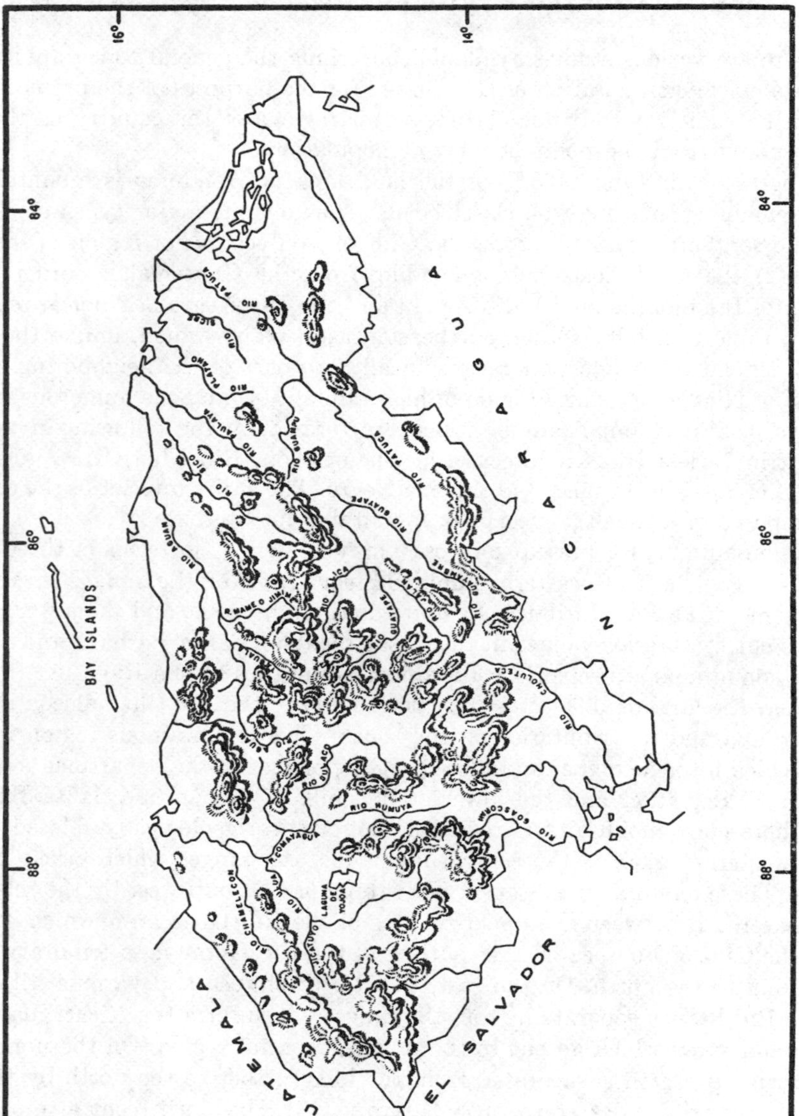
16°
14°
84°
86°
88°
BAY ISLANDS
NICARAGUA
GUATEMALA
EL SALVADOR
RIO PATUCA
RIO SICRE
RIO PLATANO
RIO PAULAYA
RIO GUAMPU
RIO AGUAN
RIO GUAYAPE
RIO TELICA
RIO GUAYAMBRE
RIO CHOLUTECA
RIO SULACO
RIO HUMUYA
R. COMAYAGUA
RIO ULUA
RIO CHAMELECON
LAGUNA DE YOJOA
RIO GOASCORAN

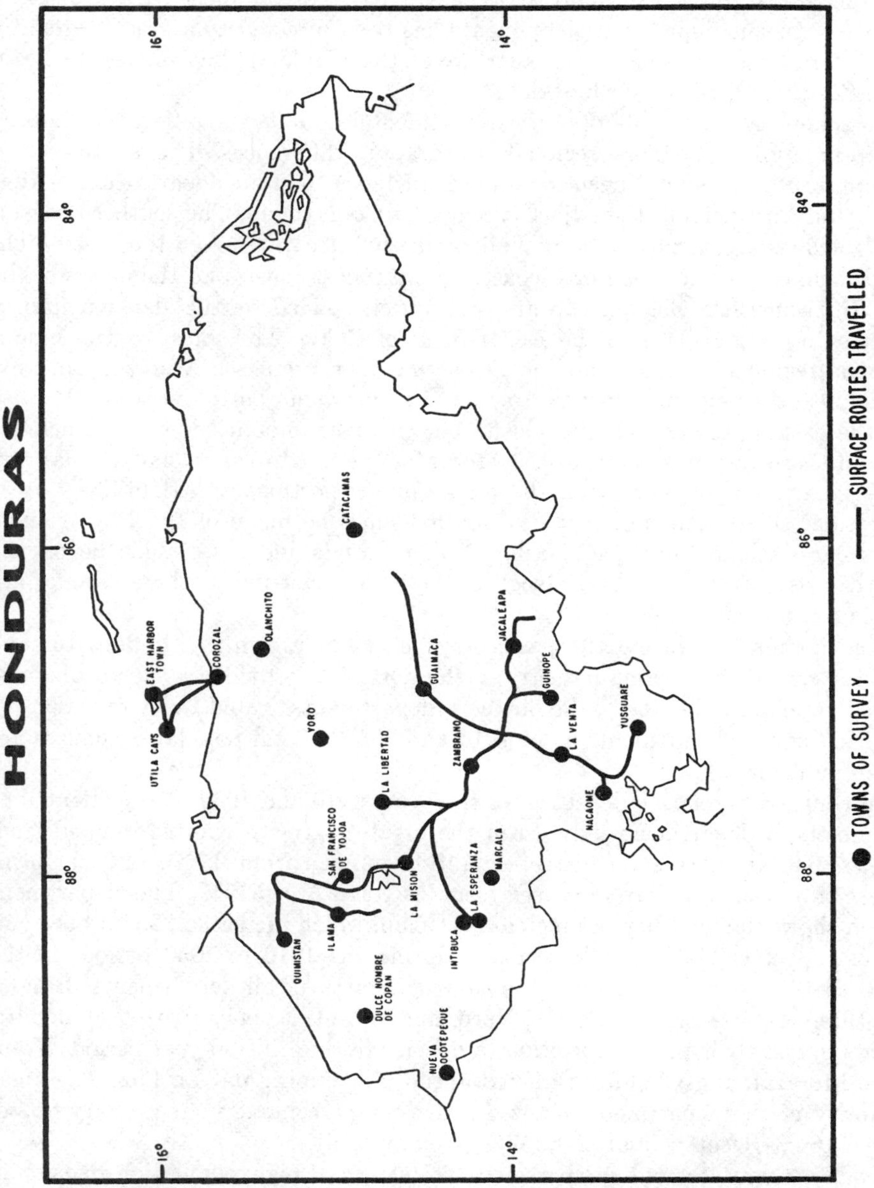
HONDURAS
16°
14°
84°
86°
88°
UTILA CAYS
EAST HARBOR TOWN
COROZAL
OLANCHITO
CATACAMAS
YORO
GUAIMACA
JACALEAPA
GUINOPE
ZAMBRANO
LA VENTA
YUSGUARE
NACAOME
LA LIBERTAD
SAN FRANCISCO DE YOJOA
LA MISION
MARCALA
LA ESPERANZA
INTIBUCA
ILAMA
QUIMISTAN
DULCE NOMBRE DE COPAN
NUEVA OCOTEPEQUE
TOWNS OF SURVEY
SURFACE ROUTES TRAVELLED

In order to understand the contemporary population distribution in Honduras, it is necessary to have in mind these basic areas. For the most part, the settlement of various population components has been directed to a great degree by the interior valleys, and the settlement of the highlands has tended to be in terms of these three major blocks.

In some cases the contemporary departmental boundaries within the country conform crudely to these regional topographic differences. The southwestern mountain region, as has been mentioned, includes the four departments of that area, and also includes the adjacent region of Comayagua. The southern coastal belt includes the departments of Valle and Choluteca, although there are highland regions in both. The north coast, the northeast coast, and the deltas of the Río Ulúa and Río Chamalecón are pretty well defined by the departments of Cortés and Atlántida, and the Department of Colón. The south central mountainous region is centered on the Department of Francisco Morazán, and extends into the neighboring departments of Comayagua on the west, El Paraíso on the east, Choluteca on the south. The northern mountainous area includes the northern portions of Francisco Morazán, the northwestern half of Olancho, the Department of Yoro, and the mountainous portions of Atlántida.

Besides these mainland regions, mention must be made of the Bay Islands, three large islands and neighboring smaller islands and cays which lie off the north coast of the country. Geographically and culturally, these islands are distinct from the mainland.

The population during the past forty years has grown in all departments, but the rise of the banana industry in the north has provided a spectacular rise in the population density of the northern departments. Table 1 gives the density for each of the departments as of 1910 and 1950. (Total population figures are given in Table 7.)

In comparing relative densities for the years 1910 and 1950, it is evident that the northern departments have seen the greatest growth. Cortés jumped from 6.0 to 30.9, an increase of 650%; Atlántida jumped from 2.7 to 14.9 or an increase of 552%, and Yoro increased from 2.4 to 12.7, or 529%. The department which shows the next highest increase is Colón, which increased 325%; however, almost all of Colón's growth occurred during the 1910 to 1930 period; in the 1930 to 1950 period, it showed the slowest growth of all departments. Besides the three departments of Cortés, Yoro, and Atlántida, only two other departments upped their relative position in density during this 40-year period: Francisco Morazán and Choluteca moved ahead of Lempira and La Paz. The great majority of the departments showed a density percentage increase varying between 161% (Ocotepeque) and 257% (Comayagua).

Today, there are four main regions of relatively high population density in the country, and none of these are excessive if taken in comparison with the densities of El Salvador. The two western border departments of Copán and Ocotepeque have densities of 29.9 and 27.1, respectively; Cortés has a density of 30.9; the Bay Islands have a combined density of 31.0; and the south coast and Francisco Morazán departments stand at 41.7, 25.4, and 24.0. In the Department of Francisco Morazán, however, lies the national capital, and the relative high density may not be considered to be significant for the whole department, but only for the area of the capital. It is likely that most of the department could be considered to be more like the density of Comayagua, were it not for the presence of the capital.

The remaining western departments show a fairly even density varying from 18.8 in Santa Bárbara to 21.9 in La Paz. The departments of Comayagua, Yoro, Atlántida, and El Paraíso show relative similar densities (varying from 11.4 to 14.9), suggesting that except for the presence of the city of Tegucigalpa, most

Table 1.—Population density by department, 1910 and 1950
(*Calculated from Census*, 1952)

Department	Population per Km² 1910	Population per Km² 1950	Total percent increase
Colón	0.4	1.3	325%
Olancho	1.8	3.4	189
Yoro	2.4	12.7	529
Atlántida	2.7	14.9	552
Comayagua	5.1	13.1	257
El Paraíso	5.8	11.4	196
Cortés	6.0	30.9	650
Santa Bárbara	7.8	18.8	241
Intibuca	8.9	19.3	217
Francisco Morazán	10.3	24.0	233
Choluteca	10.9	25.4	233
Lempira	11.6	21.2	183
La Paz	12.3	21.9	178
Copán	13.4	29.9	223
Ocotepeque	16.8	27.1	161
Bay Islands	18.8	31.0	165
Valle	19.5	41.7	241
Republic	4.9	12.2	249%

of the north and central highlands would show a fairly even density. The population of the Department of Olancho is located almost entirely in its southwestern half and so, while lower than that of the rest of the departments in the central highlands, its density may be seen as a tapering off as one moves towards the northeastern coastal region.

The relatively greater growth of the northern departments is due, of course, to the development of the banana plantations and the attendant growth of the second city of the republic, San Pedro Sula, as a commercial center of first importance. In the earlier days of the banana industry, the Atlántida coast and adjacent region of Colón were relatively important in the development of this economy, but in recent years the greatest concentrations have been in the neighboring portions of the departments of Cortés and Yoro, the center of the United Fruit operations, and in the far eastern portion of Yoro, around Olanchito, the principal Standard Fruit center of production. Because of the coincidental location in the two extremes of the Department of Yoro of these two production centers, the statistics for the department as a whole are affected rather violently. If one visits the town of Yoro, there is no indication that any such rapid growth of population is under way. Similarly, the figures for the Department of Atlántida are highly influenced by the zones around Tela and La Ceiba, two principal shipping centers for this industry.

The relative growth of population is due evidently both to a variation in natural increase and in migration to the centers of plantation production. With respect to the latter, only four departments were registered as having less than 90% of their citizen populations as native born to the department (1950 Census),

Table 2.—Birth, death, and natural increase, by department, for 1952

Department	Birth/mil	Death/mil	Natural increase
Cortés	48.2	13.1	35.1
Atlántida	46.7	12.4	34.3
Santa Bárbara	44.6	15.4	29.2
Comayagua	43.5	11.8	31.7
Francisco Morazán	41.9	15.7	26.2
Copán	41.2	11.4	29.8
Ocotepeque	40.0	10.7	29.3
Yoro	39.5	8.6	30.9
El Paraíso	39.5	15.2	24.3
Lempira	37.2	16.1	21.1
La Paz	37.0	17.3	19.7
Valle	36.6	8.6	28.0
Intibucá	36.1	18.9	17.2
Colón	34.1	8.5	25.6
Olancho	33.7	8.2	25.5
Choluteca	32.7	8.2	24.5
Bay Islands	31.9	6.3	25.6

and three of these were Cortés (77.4% native born), Yoro (80.3%) and Atlántida (81.8%). The other departments showing a significant number of native citizens born outside of the department of residence were Francisco Morazán (89.0% native born), Copán (90.8%), Santa Bárbara (93.9%), and Comayagua (94.6%). Perhaps indicative of the importance of migrant populations is the absolute number of Salvadorean-born persons reported in the census. Cortés and Yoro had the greatest absolute number registered, with 6,464 and 3,147, respectively, higher than any of the departments neighboring on El Salvador.

The departments showing the greatest number of persons native born to their department of residence are the block along the southwestern border of the country: Ocotepeque (99.5%), Lempira (98.4%), Intibucá (98.8%), and La Paz (98.7%).

Data on natural increase is limited, but there are figures available for the year 1952.[3]

[3] Census, 1954c.

Even though these figures must be taken with considerable caution, they tend to support the general picture provided by the gross growth data over the past years. Cortés, Atlántida, and Yoro all have fairly high growth rates, although those for Cortés and Atlántida are based principally on a high birth rate, while that for Yoro is based equally on a low recorded death rate. The three southwestern departments of Lempira, Intibucá, and La Paz show a consistently middle sized birth rate (36.1 to 37.2), a high death rate (16.1 to 18.9), and consequently a relatively low rate of increase (17.2 to 21.1). The adjacent western departments of Copán and Ocotepeque, however, which diverged considerably in the rate of growth (Copán being quite high, Ocotepeque being quite low; see Table 1) show very similar figures for births and deaths. The difference here seems due to the fact that almost 10% of Copán's Honduran population are emigrants from other parts of the country, and it also has a high absolute number of both Guatemalans (4,309 in 1950 Census) and Salvadoreans (1,799 in 1950 Census), whereas less than 1% of the Honduran population of Ocotepeque are emigrants from other departments, and there were said to be only 1,028 Salvadoreans and Guatemalans there in 1950.

In general, the birth rate seems relatively high in the country as a whole, and in comparison with Guatemalan figures[4] the reported death rate is suspiciously low.

The populations of the northern departments show great extremes in the percentages for rural and urban populations.

An "urban" population is defined by the Honduran census as being that population which lives in a municipal or district capital. It may be seen from Table 3 that Yoro and Atlántida stand almost at opposite extremes in this matter, the former with 80.3% classed as rural, and the latter with 45.4% so classed. Even leaving out of consideration these three divergent northern departments, the remaining departments of the country do not show any great systematic difference with respect to rural percentages. There is evidently a tendency for there to be a slightly higher rural population in the southern departments (none are under 70%). However, there does not seem to be a variation as between highlands and Pacific coastal region as is the case in Nicaragua where there is a consistently higher rural component in the highlands;[5] nor is there a higher rural component among the departments with a significant Indian population (Lempira, Intibucá, and La Paz) as is the case in Guatemala.[6] Choluteca, a predominantly Ladino (Spanish-American) coastal department, has one of the highest rural components in the country.

Nor is there any evidence that there has been a significant change in recent years in the rural-urban proportions. On the basis of figures given for estimated total population from 1926 through 1952[7] there has been a very slight variation in rural percent ranging from 68.9% to 71.0% over that 27-year period, and even this reported variation has not been consistently in one direction.

The consideration of urban and rural components in terms of populations which do or do not live in municipal or district centers of course has little rela-

---

[4] Adams, n.d. (c). [5] Adams, n.d. (b). [6] Adams, n.d. (c). [7] Census, 1954c, p. 29.

tion to the usual sociological and economic concepts. Archer, in a study of this matter in Honduras,[8] has provided an estimate of rural and urban components of the country in terms of defining as urban any town population of over 2,000 people. This excludes 165 towns or 61% of all communities considered urban in the administrative sense. In addition, however, there are four towns of over 2,000 which are not municipal or district capitals, the total aggregate of which amounts to about 22,000 people. From this recalculation, he estimates that 81.1% of the population of the country may be called rural, while only 18.9% is urban. It should be noted that three of the four towns which he considers as

Table 3.—Total population with rural and urban percentages for 1950 (*Census*, 1952)

Department	1950 Total population	Percent rural	Percent urban
Intibucá	59,362	81.3	18.7
Yoro	98,700	80.3	19.7
Choluteca	107,271	80.0	20.0
Lempira	90,908	78.8	21.2
El Paraíso	82,572	76.8	23.2
Valle	65,349	76.7	23.3
La Paz	51,220	74.5	25.5
Ocotepeque	45,673	71.4	28.6
Copán	95,880	70.8	29.2
Olancho	83,910	69.9	30.1
Santa Bárbara	96,397	69.9	30.1
Colón	35,465	66.2	33.8
Comayagua	68,171	64.8	35.2
Cortés	125,728	63.9	36.1
Bay Islands	8,058	60.3	39.7
Francisco Morazán	190,359	52.4	47.6
Atlántida	63,582	45.4	54.6
Republic	1,368,605	69.0	31.0

urban, but which are not administrative capitals, are in the banana growing center of the Department of Cortés.

Except for the excessive growth manifested in the northern departments, and the extreme variation in the relative size of rural components manifested there, Honduras shows considerable consistency with respect to these characteristics. It is possible to block off certain general regions which show demographic consistencies, however, and some of these have cultural significance as well.

The west may be divided into three general areas: (1) The adjacent departments of La Paz, Intibucá, and Lempira. These departments were recorded as being fairly consistent in natural increase characteristics, an above average, but not extreme, rural component, and similar population densities. The Department of La Paz, geographically, is part highlands and part interior valley. The

[8] See Census, 1954c, pp. 13–15.

eastern portion is in the low Comayagua Valley, while the west forms a relatively high highland block. Evidently none of this region has seen any great increase in population size due to emigration of either Honduran or foreign groups. This region was the scene of small early colonial settlements, the town of Gracias being of special importance, but is also one of the main areas of highland Indian survival. (2) The far western departments of Copán and Ocotepeque stand together in certain respects, but vary culturally. Both departments have a relatively high density, and both are recorded as having similar rates of natural increase. As was noted, however, Copán has been the recipient of considerably more emigration, both national and foreign, than has Ocotepeque. Also, Copán numbers among its population a significant number of Chortí Indians, the greater part of which live in the area neighboring on Guatemala. Ocotepeque, on the other hand, has few remaining Indians of any kind. The capital of Ocotepeque lies on an upper tributary of the Lempa, and as such probably has commerce with neighboring El Salvador as with Honduras. (3) Santa Bárbara and the neighboring highland portions of the Department of Comayagua form a region of lower mountains and interior valleys. The area in general is lower than that of the departments of La Paz, Intibucá, and Lempira, and the altitude of the capital city, Santa Bárbara, is only about 750 feet. This region retains isolates of Indians, has seen a fairly rapid growth and has received a fair number of emigrants, both national and Salvadorean.

The fact that the departments of Valle and Choluteca are both predominantly south coast departments suggests that they should show numerous similarities. On the basis of available population data, however, there seem to be as many differences as similarities. Valle is the most densely populated department of the country with 41.7 persons per km^2; Choluteca is also more densely populated than most departments, but the density of 25.4 is considerably under that of Valle. Both departments have relatively high rural components, but that of Choluteca is excessively high, while that of Valle is more similar to El Paraíso or neighboring La Paz. Both departments have approximately the same percentage of Hondurans native to the department (Valle, 97.6%, Choluteca, 97.1%) and both have received a significant number of foreigners. Valle has some 1,350 Salvadoreans, while Choluteca has about 500 Salvadoreans and 950 Nicaraguans.

The central highland region, for practical purposes, may be said to extend through the Danlí region of El Paraíso even though that area is severed from the rest by the middle Choluteca Valley. The presence of the national capital in a principal portion of the region, the central and southern portions of Francisco Morazán, precludes evaluations of statistical data concerning the population dwelling in the smaller towns and countryside.

The north highlands is in general a region of scattered isolated settlements. Some of these in the western portion of the Department of Olancho are served today by air, but much of the region is almost unpopulated. The Montaña de la Flor Indian population is an exception which illustrates the rule; this population has retained itself in a cultural isolation, in part because there has been little conflict from an encroaching Ladino population. The Sierra de Nombre de Dios and the neighboring Cerros de Cangrejar form the northernmost portion of this general mountain block and are little populated.

About one third of the total land surface of Honduras lies in the departments of Colón, the southeastern half of Olancho, and the far eastern portion of El Paraíso. In the Department of Colón, the total population is recorded as 35,465, but of this 73% live in the seven *municipios* surrounding the coastal city of Trujillo. The remaining municipio of Iriona was recorded as having only 9,599 people in 1950 and includes probably three quarters of the entire area of the department. In the southeast half of Olancho there are probably little more than 10,000 people. The greater portion of this region are flat Atlantic lowlands. The Montes de Jalapa and Montes de Colón extend from Nicaragua into El Paraíso, and there are low rugged mountains lying between the Guayape and Patuca Rivers and between the Guampú and Negro Rivers. In these latter two ranges are scattered groups of Paya Indians, but as one moves down to the coast, there are Sumu and, near the coast itself, the Miskito Indians.[9] This region, generally referred to as "La Mosquita" by the Hondurans, has been penetrated from time to time by travellers, government officers, mahogany cutters, and pirates, but it remains today of little importance in Honduran national economy.

The north coast, the Ulúa-Chamalecón Valley, and the Aguán Valley may be considered as a single basic region. Long of little importance except as a means of entry into the highland and southern regions, this is today the most important economic area of the entire country. In 1952, bananas, principally from this region, formed 66%[10] of the exports of the country. The departments of Cortés, Atlántida, and the neighboring portions of Yoro, have shown the greatest population growth of any departments in the country, and the city of San Pedro Sula has grown to be the second center, and possibly the most important economically. The population of this coast is highly varied, and includes, besides Hondurans from the interior of the country, Salvadoreans, Black Caribs, Antillean Negroes, and Antillean whites. In a sense, a different Honduras has grown up on the north coast; the population is not particularly oriented towards Tegucigalpa, but towards the Caribbean.

In the essay to follow, special sections are devoted to certain of the more unique cultural groups of the country. In the chapter on the culture of the Ladino town and country dweller, we will basically be considering mainland Honduras, and more specifically the interior and south coast. The Atlantic littoral and island population, Black Carib and Antillean in a significant degree, will be discussed apart. While the Lenca Indian population of Lempira, Intibucá, and La Paz will generally be considered with the rest of the interior population, special chapters will be devoted to the characteristics which set that and other Indian groups off from the rest of the Honduran population.

---

[9] See Conzemius, 1932, and Johnson, 1948, map 5.
[10] Census, 1954c.

II. THE CULTURE OF THE LADINO TOWN AND COUNTRY DWELLER

1. LAND, LABOR, AND AGRICULTURE

Of the total land area of some 112,088 km² of Honduras, it has been estimated that approximately 63% is in mountains and 37% in coast and interior valleys.[11] Of the mainland departments, it is estimated that the most mountainous departments are those of the southwest block, La Paz, Intibucá, and Lempira. Of the total area, according to the 1952 *agropecuario* census, 22.4% was held in farms, only about 8% was under agricultural cultivation, and of this about half was resting. The general breakdown of the use of farm lands is as shown in Table 4. It may be seen from this that only about 19% of all lands occupied for *agropecuario* purposes are actually under cultivation at any one time. Of this, a little over one third is in what are called permanent crops (i.e., bananas, coconuts, fruit

Table 4.—Land use of farm land in Honduras, 1952 (*Census*, 1954b)

Land under agricultural cultivation 895,831 hectares		35.7%
Transitory crops	296,411 hectares	11.8%
Permanent crops	174,653 hectares	7.0%
Resting	424,767 hectares	16.9%
Land in pasturage	822,562 hectares	32.8%
Land in forest	528,551 hectares	21.0%
Land in *monte*	198,814 hectares	7.9%
Land in other use	61,646 hectares	2.5%
Total land in farms	2,507,404 hectares	99.9%

trees, etc.), while the rest is devoted to the transitory crops, those which must be seeded annually (i.e., corn, beans, sorghum, rice, sugar cane, etc.). The importance of cattle in the general economy of Honduras may be seen by the fact that approximately one third of the total farm land is in pasturage. While only 21% of the farm lands are recorded as being in forest, in fact, some of the pasturage land is also forest land but is classified as pasturage.[12]

With respect to the distribution of farms, Table 5 gives the percent of area of each department which is so occupied. With one startling exception, the Department of Valle, those departments with the greatest area in farms are generally those with the greatest population densities: Cortés, Copán, Choluteca, and Ocotepeque all have approximately half or more of their land in farms. Why the Department of Valle, with the highest population density in the country, should have only 37% of the land area registered as being in farms is difficult to say. Of the Valle farm lands, 47.5 are actually under agricultural cultivation or resting; the national figure for such lands, it will be remembered, was 35.7%.

The distribution of farms by size is shown in Table 6. According to this in-

---

[11] Tosco, at al., n.d., p. 23. [12] Census, 1954, p. xvii.

formation, 57.0% of the farms (those under 5 hectares in size) occupy about 8% of the farm area of the country; on the other extreme, 1.7% of the *fincas* (those over 100 hectares) occupy 46.3% of the *finca* area. Honduras clearly has a broader

Table 5.—The land area of each department occupied by farms (*Census*, 1954b)

Department	Total area in Km²	Area of farms Km²	%
Atlántida	4,251	965	22.7
Colón	25,505	439	1.7
Comayagua	5,196	1,495	28.8
Copán	3,203	1,761	55.0
Cortés	3,954	1.970	49.9
Choluteca	4,211	3,011	71.5
El Paraíso	7,218	1,967	27.2
Francisco Morazán	7,946	2,829	35.6
Intibucá	3,072	1,077	35.1
Bay Islands	261	102	39.4
La Paz	2,331	929	39.8
Lempira	4,290	1,655	38.6
Ocotepeque	1,680	831	49.5
Olancho	24,351	1,092	4.5
Santa Bárbara	5,115	2,316	45.3
Valle	1,565	588	37.6
Yoro	7,939	2,048	25.8
Republic	112,088	25,075	22.4

Table 6.—Distribution of farms by size, 1952 (*Census*, 1954b)

Size of farms	Farms Number	%	Land area Hectares	%
Less than 1 hec	15,394	9.9	9,991	0.4
From 1 to 4 hec	73,617	47.1	192,241	7.7
From 5 to 9 hec	28,092	18.0	201,554	8.0
From 10 to 19 hec	18,620	11.9	259,213	10.3
From 20 to 49 hec	13,752	8.8	417,317	16.6
From 50 to 99 hec	3,865	2.5	265,929	10.6
From 100 to 499 hec	2,317	1.5	451,855	18.0
Over 500 hec	478	0.2	709,304	28.2
Total farms	156,135	99.9	2,507,404	99.8

distribution of land in use than does El Salvador, where 80% of the farms are under 5 hectares and these farms occupy 12.4% of the farm area.[13]

Land usufruct in Honduras takes a variety of forms. There are three basic

[13] Adams, n.d. (d).

types of land title: private property, *ejidal* properties, and national lands. It is evidently customary throughout Honduras to indicate land one is claiming by fencing it in, whether it is one's private property or *ejidal* lands.

There are two kinds of private holdings, those which belong to a single individual, and those which are titled to a group of people, and referred to as communal lands. Many communal lands originated in colonial land grants to families or groups of families and the titles have remained in the families. These communal lands should not be confused with communal lands in other countries where a land area will belong to an entire community. In Honduras the term "communal," when applied to land, usually refers to private property held by a number of co-owners; these co-owners do not necessarily form a community but are part of a larger community. In some cases, communal lands are of more recent origin, having been purchased by a group of friends. So far as the writer could determine, there was no great difference in the agricultural technology used in communal lands and others. Some communal lands are held as cattle *haciendas*. Data from the survey indicated that communally held lands were more common in the northern interior of the country. Such holdings were reported from Quimistán, Ilama, San Franciso de Yojoa, Yoro, and Catacamos, but from none of the towns to the south. In Olanchito it was said that the colonial grants had long since been subdivided by generations of inheritors. The area held communally in Catacamos was said to have been purchased from the municipality some time past. The Quimistán communal land was a colonial grant and is used principally as *hacienda* land; much of it was rented out and the owners are town dwellers. The retention of land on a communal basis of course requires constant agreement among the co-owners, and seems on the surface to be a fairly fragile system of landholding.

In only two communities was it reported that land called "communal" belonged to the community rather than to a limited set of co-owners. In San Francisco de Yojoa, according to the informant, the municipality purchased some land about 1904 as communal land for the *municipio*. This land was distinct from *eijdal* lands which were granted the *municipios* by the government; it was purchased property. However, almost immediately upon purchase, about five people fenced the communal land in, and have retained usufruct of it ever since. In Marcala, the municipality purchased an *hacienda* in 1902[14] and holds it as "communal" property; this land is handled like *ejidal* land although its legal status is different.

Ejidal lands are those which are the property of a municipality. This type of land title is also a colonial survival but one which is continued today officially. In other countries of Central America, *ejidal* land titles have been lost and the system of tenure survives only in a weak form. In Honduras, however, 30% of the farm land of the country is so held, and in many cases, serves to provide the municipalities involved with a small but steady income. From Table 7 it may be seen that the region with the greatest amount of land in *ejidal* holdings is the southwest mountain block of Lempira, Intibucá, and La Paz, where over 50% of the farm land is so held. The departments with the smallest *ejidal* lands are the

---

[14] Bonilla, 1931, p. 1.

Bay Islands, where they are practically non-existent, and Yoro and Olancho where they form about 15% of the farm land.

In general, *ejidal* lands are assigned to individuals, and are treated as if they were private holdings. The people using them may cultivate them, leave them to rest, rent them out in one form or another, or even ignore them. It is customary in most places to rent out *ejidal* land at L.0.25 per *manzana* per year; this is often referred to as the *manzanaje*. In Catacamas, it was said that the rate was L.0.50 for cultivated land, and L.1.00 for uncultivated land. This variation, depending upon the condition of the land, is made to discourage persons from renting a large area and not placing it under cultivation. The *ejidal* land of the town of La Misión is also handled differently. This land is held in common with the neighboring community of Taulabé. Both communities are *aldeas* of the district of Siguatepeque, and all lands within the two *aldeas* are *ejidal*. This land is divided up among the inhabitants of the communities, fenced in, and used or rented out as if it were private property. No *manzanaje* is paid. If a newcomer arrives in the community, a meeting is held by the residents, and a decision is reached as to whether or not a portion of the remaining *ejidal* land will be assigned to him. Without approval of the community, the newcomer cannot use this land.

National lands are those which are under neither private nor *ejidal* title. For the most part, national lands consist of the more mountainous regions of the *municipios*, and the large expanses of unpopulated territory of Olancho and Colón. These lands are available for use by anyone who wishes to move in and cultivate them. Title may be had to them, but in most cases, this is not bothered with. In the *agropecuario* census, the land which is considered as "used" is usually national land. Over 25% of the farm lands of Atlántida, Colón, and Olancho are of this type, and about 10% of those of Yoro, Cortés, and El Paraíso. Elsewhere, such occupancy involves a small portion of the total land in farms. National lands provide a ready means of expansion to accommodate a growing population, but in most interior departments the national land is rough, mountainous, and precludes the use of the plow.

While title may be held either privately or by a municipality or district, the land usufruct involves a number of other forms. Private or *ejidal* lands may be worked by the individual to whom they belong or are assigned, or that person may assign them to a *colono* or rent them to someone else. The assignment of *ejidal* land to a *colono* is rare, simply because most *ejidal* land is in middle sized and small holdings. For example, 24% of the *ejidal* land area of the country is in holdings of under 10 hectares, and 66% is in holdings under 50 hectares. In private property, on the other hand, only 7% is in holdings of less than 10 hectares, and only 25% in holdings less than 50 hectares.[15] With respect to the use of the term *colono*, the compilers of the *agropecuario* census found that it was used in certain parts of the country in its usual Central American sense of a person who was assigned land by a landowner, and in return for which he provided labor for the landowner. In some places, however, it seemed to be used in the sense

[15] Census, 1954b.

of being any occupant, or user, of land for which there was no title. Unfortunately, the census does not mention where this latter usage was found.[16] The writer did not encounter this variation in terminology during the course of the survey.

The rental of land is carried on in three main ways: payment in an absolute amount of cash, payment in an absolute amount of crop, and payment in a relative amount of crop, or sharecropping. Payment of a fixed rental, whether in crop or cash, seems to be the increasingly preferred form of rental. In San Francisco de Yojoa land was rented for either L.10.00 per *manzana* per year, or for

Table 7.—Distribution of *finca* land area by form or usufruct and department (*Census*, 1954b)

Department	Area of farm in hectare	Property	Ejidal	Rented	Sharecropped	Colono	Used	Total
Atlántida	96,580	30.4	34.0	5.0	0.1	0.4	30.1	100.0
Colón	43,856	16.6	37.8	2.3	*	0.1	43.2	100.0
Comayagua	149,477	57.5	31.6	5.4	0.9	0.3	4.2	99.9
Copán	176,109	60.9	30.2	4.4	1.1	0.9	2.5	100.0
Cortés	197,041	55.8	26.8	6.8	0.6	0.4	9.6	100.0
Choluteca	301,110	73.3	20.5	3.8	0.8	0.9	0.6	99.9
El Paraíso	196,684	60.6	24.5	2.2	0.7	1.1	10.8	99.9
Francisco Morazán	282,902	73.8	21.2	2.7	1.2	0.3	0.8	100.0
Intibucá	107,646	40.3	54.7	3.9	0.1	0.3	0.6	99.9
Bay Islands	10,246	86.6	0.1	6.5	4.9	0.1	1.7	99.9
La Paz	92,915	19.2	77.6	1.6	0.5	0.6	0.5	100.0
Lempira	165,497	40.0	54.1	4.6	0.1	0.1	1.0	99.9
Ocotepeque	83,101	71.0	23.5	3.6	0.4	1.3	0.2	100.0
Olancho	109,178	56.4	15.8	1.7	*	0.1	25.9	99.9
Santa Bárbara	231,555	54.6	33.3	5.2	2.2	0.7	4.0	100.0
Valle	58,762	57.8	28.4	7.1	4.3	1.5	1.0	100.1
Yoro	204,745	62.9	14.7	11.7	0.7	0.6	9.3	99.9
Republic	2,507,404	57.2	30.1	4.7	0.8	0.7	6.5	100.0

* Less than 0.1%

1½ *fanegas* per *manzana*. In Quimistán the rates were L.6 or 7, or 2 *fanegas*. In both these communities the *fanega* was calculated as 800 ears of corn. In La Misión, the *fanega* was set at 480 ears, and the rent was L.4 or 5, or one *fanega* per *manzana* per year. In Nueva Ocotepeque, it was reported that the preferred form of payment is in cash at the rate of L.25.00 per *manzana* per year, but that some still pay in crop.

Sharecropping seems to be on the decline. While some form of sharecropping was reported from five communities, the form of payment varied greatly. In La Venta, a *tercio* or *mitad* (i.e., one third or one half) of the crop was paid. In Zambrano, the people who went down to the Comayagua Valley to rent land were said to pay 6 *medios* of corn for every 3 *fanegas* harvested; there are 25 *medios* in a *fanega*, consequently, this amounts to paying slightly under $\frac{1}{12}$ of produce

[16] Census, 1954b, p. xvii.

in rent. In Guaimaca, it was said that about 5% of the crop was paid. In Dulce Nombre de Copán, a *quinta*, or ⅕ of the crop was the payment, but this was being replaced by straight cash payments. In Yoro, it was said that a *carretaje* was paid, but the writer failed to ascertain what proportion this was. The term *carretaje* was also used in La Misión to refer the crop payment for a given piece of land.

This great variety in forms of sharecrop payments suggests that if there ever was any consistency in it, it is disintegrating into a series of alternatives now. Data from the *agropecuario* census, reproduced in Table 8, indicate that the departments in which sharecropping is of the least importance are the southwestern highlands (Ocotepeque, Lempira, Intibucá, and La Paz) and the north coast and eastern regions (Atlántida, Colón, and Olancho). The reasons for the lack of sharecropping in these two separate regions are probably different. In the north and east there is ample national land for use and it would be hard to interest anyone in sharecropping when free land is available. In the block of Indian departments in the southwest, however (Lempira, Intibucá, and La Paz), most land is worked privately and sharecropping does not seem to be a custom among a population of small landholders. The writer does not know why Ocotepeque is low in sharecroppers. According to Table 8, the departments in which the greatest number of farms are sharecropped are Santa Bárbara and Choluteca. In the survey, it developed that both towns visited in these departments reported that sharecropping was of no local importance.

Tables 7 and 8 give the distribution of forms of usufruct in terms of land area and number of farms. These data, taken from the *agropecuario* census, classify land usufruct patterns into six types: property under private title (including both individual and communal) which is worked by the owner: "property"; property under *ejidal* title, but worked by the person to whom it is assigned: "*ejidal*"; property which may be either private or *ejidal*, but which is rented out for a payment in absolute cash or crop value: "rented"; property which may be either private or *ejidal*, but which is sharecropped: "sharecropped"; property which can be either private or *ejidal*, but most likely the first, and which is assigned to a *colono*: "*colono*"; and property which is occupied with no rental payments or title, most of which is probably national land: "used". The farm area rented, sharecropped, and worked by *colonos* comprises only 6.2% of the total farm area of the country, while holdings worked by their owners and by *ejidal* "owners" occupies 87.3% of the farm area. In terms of the number of farms, sharecropping seems to be of relatively little importance, being for the most part under 1%. Yoro has the highest percent of land rented out, but in most departments it is rather small. *Colonos* were reported as being relatively unimportant from the point of view of land occupied; except in El Paraíso, Valle, and Ocotepeque, they accounted for under 1% of the total everywhere.

These tables are worth study because they suggest a variety of patterns which exist in the different departments. Atlántida and Colón, for example, each have relatively little in private property, but much of the farm land is simply used. This probably reflects, in part, the lack of formal title, either private or *ejidal*, found among the Indian populations of parts of those departments. In Olancho, however, the other department with a high percentage of land in "use", and probably also Atlántida to some degree, it probably reflects the fact that there are emigrants who have moved into the area and who are working national lands.

In Table 8, "farm" is defined as all the pieces of land controlled by a single individual; as a result, there are various mixed forms, e.g., a person who owns some land and works some *ejidal* land, or works some *ejidal* land and rents some land. For the purposes of the present discussion, all these mixed forms have been

Table 8.—Distribution of farm producers by form of usufruct and department (*Census*, 1954b)

Department	Number of farms	Property	Ejidal	Rented	Share-cropped	Colono	Used	All mixed forms	Total
Atlántida	3,495	15.1	18.1	7.6	0.6	2.0	47.9	8.8	100.1
Colón	3,961	1.7	20.4	0.8	0.2	0.3	70.3	6.4	100.1
Comayagua	8,471	8.2	51.3	10.2	4.3	1.5	7.7	16.9	100.1
Copán	13,049	12.6	27.0	22.6	5.8	7.7	4.2	20.1	100.0
Cortés	6,688	9.9	31.1	10.9	5.4	4.1	26.0	12.7	100.1
Choluteca	13,245	40.8	16.6	11.0	6.5	8.6	2.8	13.6	99.9
El Paraíso	10,540	20.5	33.7	2.6	3.3	6.8	18.6	14.4	99.9
Francisco Morazán	17,269	30.0	35.5	5.5	4.5	1.5	2.3	20.7	100.0
Intibucá	9,239	11.3	54.7	7.4	0.5	1.4	0.8	23.9	100.0
Bay Islands	947	79.5	0.4	4.1	5.0	*	3.8	7.3	100.1
La Paz	7,583	4.3	76.3	4.3	1.8	2.6	0.4	10.2	99.9
Lempira	15,017	14.9	47.0	7.5	0.1	0.4	2.3	27.8	100.0
Ocotepeque	6,632	41.3	20.3	8.5	0.6	7.9	0.3	21.2	100.1
Olancho	10,461	27.3	23.8	2.4	0.1	0.3	34.5	11.6	100.0
Santa Bárbara	13,794	18.1	28.4	7.1	12.9	3.2	10.4	20.0	100.1
Valle	7,292	22.8	26.3	15.1	3.7	15.7	3.0	13.4	100.0
Yoro	8,452	33.6	24.8	10.4	4.1	3.5	14.9	8.8	100.1
Republic	156,135	21.3	33.9	8.6	4.0	4.1	11.0	17.1	100.0

* Less than 0.1%

brought together under the classification of "all mixed forms." The reader who wishes to pursue the subject further is referred to Census, 1954b.

Turning now from tenancy and land usufruct to the agriculturalists themselves, data from 1950 population census reproduced in Table 9 reports that 82% of the economically active population are engaged in agricultural work. Of the total of 530,736 people so engaged, 75.5% worked for themselves or for their families; only 24.5% worked as salaried employees. This contrasts strongly with the situation in El Salvador where approximately 50% of the economically active agricultural population worked on a salaried basis.[17] The rather high percentage of persons regarded as being economically active is due to a very wide definition given this category by the Honduran census (1952). While this makes an intercountry comparison of the size of the economically active component of the pop-

[17] Adams, n.d. (d).

ulation impossible, it seems likely that the relative percentages of such groups said to be involved in agriculture are somewhat comparable.

The percentage of agriculturally occupied people is greater than the national average of 82 % in all departments except Francisco Morazán, Atlántida, Cortés, and the Bay Islands. The percentage of persons engaged as salaried employees, however, seems to vary from the south to the north. Except for the Department of Ocotepeque, all the southern departments (Choluteca, El Paraíso, Valle, La Paz, Intibucá, and Lempira) have a percentage of salaried workers below the national figure of 24.5 %. The northern departments, on the other hand, tend to go above the national average. Two outstanding exceptions to this are the Bay Islands and Colón, both of which have the lowest percent of salaried agricultural workers of any of the departments in Honduras. In Colón, most agriculturalists are independent for the simple reason that there are practically no large agricultural enterprises and there is ample available land. In the Bay Islands, however, land is severely limited and a significant portion of the population is engaged in fishing, while many others ship off as sailors and ship's officers from time to time. The census reports that only 13 % of the economically active of the Islands are fishermen, but this may not be representative as many gather both coconuts and fish. The reportedly high percentage of salaried labor in the Department of Atlántida may be due in part to the fact that Black Carib men work in the principal ports as dock hands as well as on their holdings in the area.

The landholding and exploitation patterns in Honduras, outside of the banana industries which saw their development in the past seventy years, have been highly influenced by the fact that there has generally been ample land available. The writer could see no "agrarian" problem in the country except in a few specific regions where large tracts of land have been taken over into single holdings for grazing or lumbering. Even in these regions, as in Zambrano, there are nearby regions, such as Comayagua, where there is land available for cultivation. Within this general picture, there have not developed any large scale interior agricultural industries; coffee, which in Guatemala, El Salvador, and Costa Rica, is generally done on large landholdings, is cultivated in Honduras in great part by small and medium landholders.[18] As a result, Honduras, except for the north coast banana plantations, is basically a country of independent agriculturalists. In this way, it may be considered as similar to the southeastern and eastern highlands of Guatemala.

Since there has always been ample land available, if a real land shortage is felt in any given region, there is usually a nearby region where one may get either free national land, or rent private or *ejidal* land. The developing banana industry found this to be the case and had to resort to the importation of considerable numbers of Antillean negroes to provide labor for the plantations. Even in recent years, while many interior Hondurans have gone to the north coast, many also go north to get land to work and not as salaried labor. The same holds true for migrant Salvadoreans. There has evidently been a relative increase recently of

---

[18] According to the Census, 1954b, 63% of all coffee farms were under 10 hectares in size, and these farms produced 37% of the coffee of the country.

Hondurans going from their interior towns to the north coast in search of labor, but many of these go only in the agricultural off-seasons.

Besides those going to the north coast for work on the banana plantations, seasonal migrations to the centers of coffee production are of some importance in Honduras, but not to the same degree that they are in El Salvador and Guatemala. Most migrants for coffee come from nearby regions. People from Güinope and Jacaleapa go to El Paraíso for the harvest; Indians and Ladinos from Inti-

Table 9.—Employment status of economically active persons working in agriculture and livestock, by department, 1950 (*from Census*, 1952)

Departments	Total economically active	Total engaged in agriculture and livestock	%	Independent producers and employers	Familial unsalaried labor	Total independent and familial	Salaried labors	Total %
Atlántida	28,357	18,349	66.7	23.0%	31.1%	54.1%	45.9%	100.0
Colón	16,917	14,256	84.2	34.2	52.7	86.9	13.1	100.0
Comayagua	30,726	25,935	84.5	27.7	43.5	71.2	28.8	100.0
Copán	42,423	36,162	85.3	29.2	44.3	73.5	26.5	100.0
Cortés	63,237	45,843	72.5	28.7	40.8	69.5	30.5	100.0
Choluteca	51,694	45,729	88.4	31.6	48.4	80.0	20.0	100.0
El Paraíso	40,877	35,834	87.6	30.2	47.2	77.4	22.6	100.0
Francisco Morazán	79,388	52,758	61.5	30.6	46.0	76.6	23.5	100.1
Intibucá	28,874	26,344	91.2	31.0	49.7	80.7	19.3	100.0
Bay Islands	3,550	2,397	66.5	37.3	53.1	90.4	9.6	100.0
La Paz	23,847	20,127	84.4	30.2	48.9	79.1	20.9	100.0
Lempira	44,648	40,667	91.1	32.4	48.9	81.3	18.7	100.0
Ocotepeque	22,400	18,900	84.4	24.9	38.7	63.6	36.4	100.0
Olancho	39,234	34,696	88.4	29.0	47.0	76.0	24.0	100.0
Santa Bárbara	46,003	38,581	83.8	29.3	43.2	72.5	27.6	100.1
Valle	32,933	28,867	87.6	32.3	51.0	83.3	16.7	100.0
Yoro	52,285	45,318	86.7	31.8	42.5	74.3	25.8	100.1
Republic	647,393	530,763	82.0	30.1	45.4	75.5	24.5	100.0

bucá and La Esperanza have been going to the harvests in the departments of Comayagua and Santa Bárbara. It was reported that people from the community of Salamá go to coffee harvests elsewhere in the Department of Olancho. Nowhere, however, was there found to be the extensive migrations which are common in some of the other countries.

Labor in subsistence agriculture is done principally by the family members. Table 9 indicates that 45% of the entire economically active agricultural force is composed of people who work for some member of their family with no financial remuneration. In the *agropecuario* census, of the 521,941 agricultural workers reported, 77.9% worked without salary, i.e., for themselves or their families.[19]

[19] Census, 1954b.

Of this independent group of 406,136 people, 47.3% were recorded as women, and 25.6% were recorded under 15 years old. In the 115,805 people reported as salaried labor, 9.6% were women, and 7.0% were recorded as being children under 15 years old.

The writer frankly does not know what to make of the *agropecuario* census figures that indicate that such a large number of women work in familial agriculture. Excluding the Black Carib population of the north coast in which women traditionally perform the major part of the agricultural work, only six communities on the survey reported that women participated to any serious degree in subsistence agriculture. In two of these, Intibucá and Marcala, it was specifically the Indian population which participated thus, although the rural Ladino women of La Esperanza were also reported to participate in such work. In Yoro it was said that both Ladino and Indian women helped some in the work, but not to any great degree. Yusguare was the only town in which it was specifically reported that women consistently aided their husbands in the fields, and in Nueva Ocotepeque it was said they did horticultural work, but in almost all the other communities on the survey it was said specifically that they did not do subsistence agricultural work. In some of the towns where women did not participate in subsistence agriculture, they did go to coffee harvests as paid labor. According to the description given in the *agropecuario* census,[20] people recorded as being agricultural labor were those who had worked at least a total of three days during the week prior to the taking of the census. From this description, there should be no question as to what is meant when the census reports that so many women participated in the work, and yet it conflicts strongly with the results of the survey. One explanation for this may be in a differentiation between town and country women. In a number of places it was reported to the writer that women in the *aldeas* and *caseríos* often assisted in the agricultural work, while the women of the towns frequently did not. Since much of the survey concerned the town populations, it may be that informants interpreted the questions related to this subject as concerning specifically the town women. Informants reporting on Guarita and San Esteban specifically said that *aldea* women did such work, but that town women generally did not. Another possible reason for the divergence may lie in the fundamental concepts of precisely what is involved in a woman's participation in agricultural work. Without further exploration into the interpretation placed on the survey question by informants and the interpretation of the census takers, the question must remain unresolved.[21]

Subsistence agriculturalists have two resources for extra labor if they need more help than their families can afford: exchange labor and hiring help.

In Table 10 it may be seen that almost 17% of the hired male labor recorded in the *agropecuario* census worked on farms which were under 5 hectares in size, and almost 29% on farms under 10 hectares.

Exchange labor, or *mano vuelta* as it is usually called, was reported to still be

---

[20] Census, 1954b, p. xviii.

[21] The same discrepancy occurred between the writer's data in the Guatemalan survey and the data given in the Guatemalan census. See Adams, n.d. (c).

common in six of the towns surveyed (Jacaleapa, Yoro, San Franciso de Yojoa, Ilama, Indian population near Marcala, Intibucá, and also from two other towns, San Esteban and Salamá) and present, but not common, in five others (Catacamas, Guaimaca, Yusguare, La Venta, and Dulce Nombre de Copán). In Dulce Nombre it was said to survive only among the very poor people, and in Yusguare, mainly among land renters. It was said to have been fairly common until recently in Quimistán, where it was referred to as working *en sociedad* but it has been dying with the older generation. It should be noted that of the six towns in which it was reported to be common, three, Ilama, Intibucá, and the Marcala Indian population, are specifically Indian. There seems little doubt that exchange labor is giving way to salaried labor. Even in those communities where exchange labor was said to be common, it was seldom reported as being more common than employing help.

The relative importance of employed labor in subsistence agriculture is per-

Table 10.—Percentage distribution of 104,664 salaried male laborers according to size of farm (*Census*, 1954b)

Size of farm	Percent of salaried male labor	Average number of men per farm
Under 1 Hec.	1.0%	1.7
1 to 4 Hec.	15.8	2.3
5 to 9 Hec.	12.0	2.6
10 to 19 Hec.	13.5	3.1
20 to 49 Hec.	15.0	3.4
50 to 99 Hec.	7.9	4.1
Over 100 Hec.	34.8	18.9
Total.	100.0%	4.1

haps best reflected in the fact that of the 156,135 farms, large and small, covered in the *agropecuario* census, only 25,671, or 16.4%, hired any labor at all. Of the farms under one hectare in size, only 4.1% hired any help, and of those between one and five, 9.7% hired help. This means that for the subsistence agriculturalist, hired help is a rare bird. Doubtless during planting and harvest time a greater percentage of help would show up, but at the time the *agropecuario* census was taken in March, there was little.

The agricultural technology of Honduras is basically similar to that of the neighboring countries in Central America. There are two basic complexes, that of the digging stick and that of the two-ox plow. Whereas in Nicaragua, El Salvador, and eastern Guatemala, these two complexes co-exist, the one being used in rough, rocky, or mountainous country, and the other on level areas, this parallel situation is found basically only in southern Honduras. In the northern departments the wooden plow is very little used. This distinction may be seen in both survey data and *agropecuario* census data.

On the survey, all the towns visited lying in the northern half of the country reported that the plow was little use or not used at all: Dulce Nombre de Copán,

La Misión, La Libertad, San Francisco de Yojoa, Ilama, Quimistán, Yoro, Catacamas, Olanchito, and Corozal. The only community in the south which reported the plow to be of relatively little importance was the Indian town of Intibucá. The digging stick is found in use throughout Honduras. Only one community on the survey, Jacaleapa, reported it little used, and the reason for this was that most of the lands of the *municipio* were level enough for the plow. Two types of digging stick are used, the plain wood pole, usually made out of durable heart wood, and the pole with a metal blade, either triangular or a piece of old machete, inserted in one end. So far as the writer can tell, there is no particular regional distributional pattern as between the use of these two types. There are regional

Table 11.—Number of wooden plows per 1,000 *fincas* by departments (*Census*, 1954b)

	Number of wooden plows per 1,000 *fincas*
Atlántida	2.3
Colón	6.1
Comayagua	278.0
Copán	186.5
Cortés	19.0
Choluteca	193.5
El Paraíso	480.0
Francisco Morazán	537.0
Intibucá	226.0
Bay Islands	2.0
La Paz	120.0
Lempira	177.2
Ocotepeque	337.0
Olancho	224.0
Santa Bárbara	21.1
Valle	287.3
Yoro	7.2
Republic	225.5

differences with respect to the term used for the digging stick. The term *pujaguante* is found very commonly through the southern and central portions of the country (Corquín, La Esperanza, Intibucá, La Venta, Yusguare, Zambrano, Guaimaca, Catacamas, Dulce Nombre de Copán, San Francisco de Yojoa, Yoro, and San Esteban). Three other terms are also used, however, each manifesting a general regional distribution. The term *macana* was reported from most of the communities in the south and southwest (Nueva Ocotepeque, Guarita, La Esperanza, Intibucá, Güinope, and Yusguare). The term *barreta* was used in communities of the northeast and north (Yoro, Salamá, Olanchito, Corozal) but was also reported to be used in the south coastal area of Nacaome and from Duyere. The term *huisute* was reported from three towns running in a line northeast: La Misión, Ilama, and Quimistán. The word *huisute* evidently comes from the Pocomam Indian language as it is so reported by Gillin and was found in the eastern mountain region in the Guatemalan survey.[22] All the other terms are of Spanish origin. In La Esperanza, there is yet another alternative term, *chusa*, used for the digging stick. There is some distinction in terminology between one town and another with respect to whether the stick has a metal or wooden point. In Intibucá and La Esperanza, *macana* refers to the wooden pointed variety, while *pujaguante* refers to the metal pointed one; in Salamá and Olanchito, *barreta* refers to either wooden or metal points, while in Yoro, it refers to the wooden point, and *pujaguante* refers to the metal point. *Pujaguante*, in general, seems to refer to metal pointed sticks, and in the towns where reported, *huisute* referred to this type.

Other implements of importance in the agricultural economy are the varieties of machete, the hoe, and the ax. The machete, while going under a variety of names, is of two basic types: the curved or hooked machete, and the straight machete. The curved machete follows more or less the same distribution as does the wooden plow. It is used in all the southern communities, but is used rarely or not at all in Quimistán, San Francisco de Yojoa, Yoro, Salamá, Guaimaca, Catacamas, San Esteban, Olanchito, and Corozal. In Catacamas and Quimistán, it was specifically stated that this machete was used only by the immigrants who have come into the regions from El Salvador. In the western part of the country, this machete usually goes under the name of *machete de vuelta* (Ilama, Dulce Nombre de Copán, Quimistán, where it is also referred to as *calabozo*, Guarita, Corquín, and Nueva Ocotepeque). Elsewhere, it usually is called *machete de taco* (Yusguare, Nacaome, La Venta, Güinope, Zambrano, La Misión, La Libertad, Guaimaca, and by the Salvadoreans in Catacamas). In Jacaleapa this machete was referred to as the *corvo*, a term which in Guatemala usually refers to the straight machete.[23] In the neighboring towns of La Esperanza and Intibucá, the curved machete was called *machete corte*.

There is a variant form of the curved or hooked machete of equal importance which is bent to make it more convenient for cutting low to the ground. In the western towns this generally is called *machete de pando* (Marcala, La Esperanza, Intibucá, Corquín, Nueva Ocotepeque, San Francisco de Yojoa, and Ilama), while in other places it is referred to as the *cuma* (La Venta, Güinope, La Libertad, and La Misión). It may be noted that in San Francisco de Yojoa, the regular curved machete is said not to be used, but the bent variety is used.

The other main variety of machete is the straight bladed machete which frequently goes under the name of *colins* (after the manufacturer, Collins). While the curved machete is specifically an agricultural implement, the straight machete varies in function. In the northern towns where the curved machete is not used, the straight one is used as an agricultural implement. It goes under a variety of names: *tunca* (Yoro, Salamá), *pata de cabro* (Salamá), *guarisama* (Quimistán), and just plain *machete*. The straight blade however, is also used over much of the southern part of the country, as a brush and wood chopping tool, and of equal importance, as a weapon. Except possibly in the Pacific coastal towns, it is not used in the actual cultivation.

[22] Gillin, 1951, p. 14; Adams, n.d. (c). [23] Adams, n.d. (c).

The hoe shows a distribution which corresponds in some degree to that of the curved machete and wooden plow. It is used throughout the wooden plow area in conjunction with the plow as an instrument of cultivation. It extends beyond this area, and was reported in Dulce Nombre de Copán, La Misión, and Quimistán in general use with the digging stick. It is also used along the north coast littoral by the Black Carib for their cultivations. In the north interior, however, it seems to be little used, and was so reported from Ilama, San Francisco de Yojoa, Yoro, Catacamas, and Olanchito. In Catacamas it was said to be used only in horticultural plots, and in Yoro and San Francisco de Yojoa its use was said to be just starting. The only community in the south which reported that it was not used was Yusguare.

Before leaving the subject of agricultural implements, it should be noted that the differential distribution of the plow, the different types of machetes, the digging stick terminology, and the *azadón*, probably reflect the older colonial tradition of the south and southwest, as opposed to the north. The south central highlands and the southwest highlands, in these respects, are part of a continuing belt of similar traits which includes the greater part of populated Nicaragua, El Salvador, and the Old Ladino region of Guatemala.[24]

There is considerable regional and local specialization in crop production in Honduras. Throughout the interior of the country, corn, and usually beans, form a basic staple which is produced for local consumption. In the south, particularly in the piedmont and interior Lempa Valley, sorghum is increasingly becoming an important crop. Wheat, which used to be of some importance in the southwest mountain section, has evidently been on the decline, both because it has proved a difficult crop and because the coffee has been more profitable. Potatoes have become a specialty of the towns in the southwest corner of the Department of El Paraíso, and tobacco has long been one of the principal products of the Department of Copán. While bananas and related crops are produced in some quantities over most of the country, the large plantations of the north account for the greatest production. Coffee production, which began in the last century, has tended to concentrate in certain highland regions. The most important of these are Santa Bárbara and adjacent Lempira, northern Comayagua, the region around the town of El Paraíso, and that around the town of El Corpus in Choluteca. Coffee production is of secondary but increasing importance in Copán, Olancho, Yoro, and the Marcala section of the Department of La Paz. *Yuca*, both the bitter and the sweet, are cultivated in Honduras, the former specifically by the Black Caribs of the Atlantic littoral, and the latter by the Ladino and Indian populations of the interior. No distinction was made in the *agropecuario* census between these two varieties of crops, so the extent of the bitter variety inland is not certain from that source. The sweet *yuca*, the non-poisonous variety, is a specialty of certain towns in the highlands, such as Zambrano. Cotton is as yet of relatively little importance, but it is grown to some extent in the south

---

[24] See Adams, n.d. (b); n.d. (c); and n.d. (d).

coast. Sugar cane is grown in small quantities over much of the country, and rice in various temperate regions.[25]

The extent of local crop specialization in Honduras is similar to that of Guatemala, and strikingly dissimilar to the situation in El Salvador where small scale specialization is uncommon. Among the towns visited on the survey where the small and medium agriculturalists specialize were: Zambrano, where *yuca* is grown by most people; Güinope, where potatoes and orange trees are important; Jacaleapa, where beans are produced in some quantity; Guaimaca, Marcala, La Libertad, and Yoro, where coffee is grown; Dulce Nombre de Copán, in the tobacco area of Copán; and Ilama, where henequin is grown for the fabrication of fiber products. Besides these, the Bay Islands specialize in coconut production, and the Black Carib specialize in bitter *yuca* production.

As was mentioned earlier, with exception of the banana plantations of the north, Honduras has indulged little in the development of large scale farms for the production of agricultural crops. Cattle production in *haciendas* has been important through most of the history of the country, and there are large regions which are being exploited for lumber. Most of the highlands of Honduras are not extremely high and a great part, south of the Atlantic coastal departments, from Olancho to the west, are covered with stands of pine of varying age. As a result, the agricultural production in the country has remained principally in the hands of small and medium landholders, and as such, has seen regional specialization in that form. The availability of land in general has not forced people to produce only the necessary subsistence crops.

The general availability of land has also relieved most communities of the necessity of squeezing everything possible out of their lands. As a result, there are probably not as many areas under continual cultivation as in El Salvador. The communities where it was reported that two crops of corn were regularly taken out were mainly in the center and north (Quimistán, Ilama, San Francisco de Yojoa, La Misión, La Libertad, Guaimaca, Catacamas, Yoro, and Olanchito); only in Nacaome in the south was it said that two crops were customary. However, it is not uncommon for two bean crops to be taken out, and the *agropecuario* census reports that the second is slightly above that of the first. In this region the second corn crop was only 13% of the size of the first.[26] Specialty crops are often planted two or three times. The most exaggerated example of this, encountered in the survey, was the reportedly successful production of four potato crops in some parts of the municipio of Güinope. The *primera* was planted in April, the *postrera* in August, the *veranera* in November, and finally in irrigated areas, the *de riego* was planted in February.

The terms of reference for the two crops are generally simply *primera* for the first, and *postrera* for the second. A few variations were reported on this. Besides that just quoted from Güinope, the second crop in La Libertad was referred to as *chuasco* and not *postrera*. In Dulce Nombre de Copán the first crop was called

[25] These data are taken from the survey, from Census, 1954b, and from Ortiz, 1953.
[26] Census, 1954b.

de invierno and the second *tunasmil*. This was the only reported use of *tunasmil* in the Honduras survey; it is a term which is quite common in neighboring Guatemala and El Salvador. The importance of the second corn crop varies regionally. For the country as a whole, it was reported in the *agropecuario* census as being 25.2% of the first crop. In the south coast (Choluteca and Valle) and in the northeast (Santa Bárbara and Cortés) it was approximately 50% or larger; these are, of course, lower regions. However, in Olancho, in which there is also much lower land, the second crop was only 2.5% of the first. Where a second crop is not taken, it does not mean that the land inevitably goes unused, however. In Jacaleapa it was said that when the corn crop was finished in August, it was not uncommon to use the field for a second crop of beans. In Dulce Nombre de Copán, it was said that two crops a year were taken from the fields, and that three consecutive crops were taken out before the land was left idle; however, during these three crops, the land was usually rotated between corn and tobacco so that two consecutive crops of corn were not taken.

There was great variation among the towns surveyed as to how long a piece of land was left to rest. *Montaña* land everywhere is left to rest periodically; in those places where land is used continuously, it is usually level land (whether or not a plow is used). An exception to this general picture is to be found in La Misión where it was reported that because there was a limited amount of land, most of which was in the *montaña* anyway, it was used almost continuously. In most places, land was used one to three years, and then allowed to rest anywhere between one and five years. It will be remembered that of 895,831 hectares reported under cultivation in the 1952 *agropecuario* census that almost half (47.4%) was resting, while of the remainder, 19.4% were in permanent crops and 33.2% were in transitory crops (see Table 4). And, it is not unlikely that some of the land included in the category of *monte* in the census was also land under rest.

The reason for resting land in most of the highland region is the obvious one that the land gives better after the rest. It is customary to allow the land to lie idle until the weeds or *monte* have grown fairly high. In the tropical Atlantic lowlands and the similar climatological regions of Olancho and Colón, the problem is not so much one of the land wearing out quickly, as one of the agricultural technology being too ineffective to combat the appearance of weeds after a plot of land has been cleared for a year or so. As a result, in Catacamas for example, where the land is extremely fertile, the land use pattern is similar to that reported from La Venta on the Pacific piedmont. The land is used from two to three years, and then rests from four to five.

Planting generally starts in May after the appearance of the first rains. In the corn agriculture, the first harvest may take place anywhere between August and November, depending upon the length of the local growing season, whether it is traditional to double the corn on the stalk, and whether a second crop is planned or not. In Zambrano, Güinope, Marcala, La Esperanza, Intibucá, and the *montaña* of Ocotepeque, a single corn crop planted in May will be taken out sometime in November, December, or as late as January. In La Misión, San Francisco de Yojoa, Quimistán, Dulce Nombre de Copán, Ilama, and Yoro, the *primera* planted in May will be taken out in September or October, perhaps as late as November, and a second crop planted and harvested between January and March. In Olanchito and Catacamas, the May planting was harvested between August and September, and the second planting took place in September and October and was harvested between November and January. In Nacaome, La Venta, and Guaimaca, the first crop took from May to August, and the second three more months, beginning sometime between August and October.

Nowhere else in the Central American survey did the writer encounter so many towns in which the second harvest took place as late as February or March, bringing it very close to the beginning of the new planting. This may explain in part why seasonal labor is rather hard to come by in Honduras. In Guatemala and El Salvador, the corn and bean harvest is usually out of the way by November or December at the latest, and the independent farmer then has a few months in which he may find it profitable to search for temporary work. In those parts of Honduras where the second harvest is late, however, the independent producer simply has little available time between the end of one season and the beginning of the preparation of fields for the next.

The reason behind the excessive length of the total cultivation period in such towns as Dulce Nombre may be that the technique of doubling the corn sometime before the harvest is practised in both the first and second harvests. Elsewhere, so far as the writer knows, in those regions where two or more harvests are taken out the corn is harvested as soon as it matures and it is not ordinarily doubled on the stalk. In other communities, where the growing season is longer, it is customary to double the corn sometime prior to the harvest, and then leave the actual harvest until some later time when it is convenient. Thus, under either one or two harvests, the crop is usually gathered prior to the end of the year. When the extra technical step is included, however, it naturally prolongs each crop so that the final harvest may not terminate until March.

As techniques to promote the growth of crops and assure their success, the Honduran countryman makes relatively little use of either irrigation or fertilizer. In only five towns was it said that some irrigation was used. In Güinope, irrigation permitted a fourth crop of potatoes for some people; in Nueva Ocotepeque, it was used for various crops (corn, sugar cane, onions) along the main river; in Yoro and Ilama there was said to be a little, specifically for sugar and occasionally for corn; in Intibucá, irrigation was used by some specifically for garden crops (beets, cabbage). Animal manure was said to be used as fertilizer in garden cultivations in Catacamas and La Esperanza and in the potato land in Güinope. In Jacaleapa and La Esperanza it was used together with crop leavings by some in the regular plow cultivation fields. The only place reporting the use of artificial fertilizer was Nacaome, and there it was said not to be used by the resident town and country population but only by Salvadorean entrepreneurs who have rented or purchased land in the region.

The use of *rogaciones*, special masses, processions, or both, asking for rain for the crops, was reported from fourteen towns of the survey, but in three (Olanchito, Guaimaca, and La Esperanza) they were said to be rare. In some places the patron saint is taken out (*San Juan Bautista* in Quimistán, *Santa Ana* in La Libertad), in others a certain saint, not the patron, is used (*la Virgen de la Merced* in Intibucá, *Dulce Nombre de Jesús* in Catacamas, *San Sebastián* in Nueva Ocotepeque), and in most of the others it was said to make little difference what saint was used. In Nueva Ocotepeque, it was said to be customary to place the saint out in the sun so that he could witness personally how hot and dry it was. Evidently, the presence of *rogaciones* is not completely dependent upon whether or not there is enough rain as they were said to be held in Corozal on the north coast where, presumably, there is ample annual rainfall. Olanchito, while near the north, is evidently in a zone of relatively little rain.[27] In the center of the country, in the same zone of low rainfall as Olanchito, lie Zambrano and Güinope, and in both these places it was said that *rogaciones* were not common.

2. PRODUCTION, TRANSPORT, AND COMMERCE

Besides being engaged in agricultural pursuits, the Honduran of the interior is involved one way or another in a variety of economic activities: hunting, fishing, hand industries, transport, marketing, and purchasing. The present chapter will describe briefly some of the principal aspects of these phases of the economy. The data on the north coast Black Carib and the Bay Islanders will be left for later chapters.

Hunting plays a relatively minor part in the economic activities of the Honduran. It tends to be of somewhat greater importance in the north and northeast, and in the southwest highlands. The principal weapons are the antique cap shotgun, the cartridge-type shotgun, and the .22 rifle. A Ladino informant in La Esperanza said that the Indians of Intibucá used the bow and arrow[28] and the same was reported of the Indians of the Department of Lempira. The bow has been prohibited in some places because it also was serving as a weapon against enemies, but this has evidently not entirely stopped its use. Also in the Department of Lempira it was reported that traps, particularly a weight-fall called the *copachol* and a spring-trap, the *sada*, were used for catching smaller animals.

The principal animals hunted are deer, coyotes, pumas, agoutis, *pisotes*, *mapaches*, rabbits, iguanas, armadillos, and peccaries. In Olanchito it was said that hunting was done mainly at night, using a light to attract the animals.

The importance of fishing varies, naturally, with the access to bodies of water in which there are fish. In the rivers and the sea of the south coast fishing is fairly common. Fishing is most important during the dry season; during the wet season, most of the fishermen are occupied in agricultural pursuits. In the sea, a large *chinchorro*-type net, referred to as the *manga*, is used, as well as the hook and line. In the river above Yusguare, the *atarraya* net and a large river weir, the *tranca*, are used. In both the rivers and the ocean, gunpowder and vegetable poisons are prohibited, but used to some degree. The use of poisons is perhaps more common in the sea than along the rivers because the most common local poisons,

---

[27] See Census 1954b, *Mapa Pluviométrico (provisional)*, p. 11.
[28] Stone, 1948, p. 212, describes the bow and arrow used.

which go under the name of *pate*, are abortifacients and domestic cattle suffer greatly from them after drinking the water. In Yusguare, two types of *pate* were mentioned, one coming from a vine, and the other from the bark of the *guanacaste* tree.

As one moves into the highlands, the variety of fish decreases, and in many places little more than crayfish are taken from the streams. The *atarraya*, hook and line, and gunpowder continue to be the principal materials used. While it was said that poisons were known, they were little used. In Nueva Ocotepeque, the vegetable poison called *barbasco* was said to be used, and water was also poisoned by throwing lime in it.

Near the north coast, the general pattern of fishing changes slightly in that most of it is done in the wet instead of the dry season. The same general techniques are used, gunpowder, the *atarraya*, the *manga* (in Catacamas), and a non-abortifacient poison from a vine, *pate*. In addition, it was generally said that the hook and line were little used, and in Yoro, that men fished with a bow and arrow. In both Yoro and Quimistán it was said that a three-pointed harpoon was used. In the latter place, a river weir called the *nasa* is used, but the writer did not determine whether it was the same as the *tranca* of Yusguare or not.[29]

Some minerals are exploited in various parts of Honduras by the town and country people. Lime extraction was reported to be of some importance in Jacaleapa, Guaimaca, Nueva Ocotepeque, La Misión, Yoro, and Catacamas. Salt is gathered on the south coast in the Department of Valle, and it was reported that quite a number of people along the upper reaches of the Guayape River devoted some of their time to panning gold.

The Honduran countryman, while increasingly dependent upon products of factories for certain of the articles of daily living, still is basically dependent upon products derived from hand industry. Some of these products, such as pottery and foodstuffs, generally come from the immediately surrounding region; others, such as certain articles of clothing and various string and fiber products, receive wider distribution through a pattern of regional trade.

Pottery forms an essential part of the kitchen equipment in most Honduran homes. Most communities have a few women scattered in the rural areas who make enough to satisfy the local demand. In some places there are certain communities, usually rural, in which women specialize in handmade pottery production. Pottery was produced in this manner in the *aldea* of Saque in La Libertad, in El Nance, San Jerónimo, and Jagalteca near Olanchito, and in the *aldeas* of Galeras and Malaria near Ilama. In the Indian communities of the southwest highlands, such specialization in pottery production is evidently more common. Most of the pottery for the Indians in the Intibucá area, for example, is made quite close to the town. Around Marcala, it was said that most of the Indian towns produce pottery for their own use, and the town of La Campa in the Department of Lempira is famous for its pottery. While most pottery is distributed locally within a small region, there are certain exceptions wherein the ware is transported some distance. In Yusguare, for example, there is very little pottery

---

[29] *Nasa* in Panama refers specifically to a basket trap; see Adams n.d. (a).

produced and most that is used is purchased in Choluteca and comes from the municipios of Apacilagua and Orocuina in Choluteca, and Langue in Valle. Similarly, Zambrano people make no pottery at all and their source of supply is the *aldea* Protección in Comayagua; in Dulce Nombre de Copán, much of the pottery used comes from La Campa in Lempira. Wide distribution of pottery between country towns seems, however, to be the exception and not the rule. In general, there are enough local countrywomen, either in particular *aldeas* or scattered through the *municipio*, to supply the local needs. Nueva Ocotepeque was the only town visited in which it was said that there were men potters, and they used the wheel.

Clothing is usually produced by seamstresses and local tailors, but the communities near towns depend upon machine-made products a good deal. Yusguare people, for example, buy most of their clothes in Choluteca and while there are seamstresses in La Venta, much of the local clothing comes from either Tegucigalpa or Choluteca. In general, the more isolated the community, the more dependent it is upon local seamstresses and tailors for clothing. Almost everywhere, however, there are some of these specialists. Among poorer people, much of the clothing is homemade.

Among the products of hand industry which have the widest distribution are those of fiber. These are generally of two types, the string and rope products of *mescal*, or henequin, and the plaited or woven fibers of palm or other plants. As is the case with pottery, there are many communities in which a few people make their own rope and string, but unlike pottery, this production seldom suffices for the local needs. As a result, unless there is a regular local industry, the goods must be imported. The principal articles produced in the henequin industries are *matates* (net bags), hammocks, harnesses for horses and mules, whips, string, rope, and the *alforjas*. Of palm and similar fibers, *petates*, or woven mats, and baskets are the principal products.

The trade in fiber products as indicated by the survey data suggests a rather peculiar distribution pattern. A surprising amount comes from El Salvador; Yusguare, Marcala, and Dulce Nombre de Copán all receive either rope or basketry products from this source. On the other hand, Ilama, which is one of the main towns of Santa Bárbara specializing in such production, has a very good reputation for the quality of their henequin work, and Nueva Ocotepeque receives some of this produce even though the latter town is almost on the Salvadorean border.[30] In Olanchito, it was said that rope products came from as widely separated places as the departments of Olancho and La Paz. The baskets made in Intibucá were transported not only to Tegucigalpa for sale, but also appear in the market in the city of San Miguel, El Salvador. This rather confusing picture can hardly be representative of the state of affairs of this trade, and further study should be made in the field.

There are some local industries which are found in many communities. Tile making is one of the most important of these. To a lesser degree are to be found shoemakers and leather tanners. There still survive in some places drum makers,

---

[30] Doris Stone (in correspondence) says Ilama products also reach Costa Rica.

and women in many of the rural regions make their own cigarettes as well as occasionally some for sale.

Travel and transport in Honduras cover the entire range from human pack animal to air travel. Among the Indian populations of the southwestern mountains, Santa Bárbara and Olancho, as well as among certain Ladino groups and possibly ladinoized Indians scattered elsewhere (Duyere, Salamá, Yoro) the *mecapal*, or head tumpline, is still used. In some places, such as in Quimistán, Ilama, La Misión, and Guarita, it was said that only the poorest people still used the *mecapal*; everyone who could afford it had pack animals or access to ox carts. In general, where used, the *mecapal* is restricted to men; among the Paya of Olancho the tumpline has been reported to be used by women[31] and among the Lenca of the southwest highland region men and women carry things in a string bag which may be carried as a tumpline.[32] Women generally carry *cántaros* of water on their head, but this custom is dying out in those towns where a central water supply has been installed.

The *alforja*, woven twin string bags, are carried by men through most of southern and central Honduras. In these regions too, the *tecomate*, gourd water flask, is used by men for travel and when working in the fields.

Human transport, even in regions where it is quite common, is often a means of bringing goods to the house, where it can be repacked on a mule, or to a roadhead where it can be transshipped by truck. The most common form of transport in the country is probably mule and horseback. Ox carts are found over most of the country, but in practice their use is often restricted to the main roads and to the towns. Much of Honduras is so broken that it makes ox cart transport difficult. While carts were reported from many towns visited on the survey, they were said to be really in common use only on the south coast and around some of the larger towns. The ox cart most commonly in use in Honduras is the solid wheel type. Except for some locally variant forms in Jacaleapa, the solid wheel cart was standard except for the region of the far west, generally the departments of Ocotepeque and Copán where the spoked wheel was standard. This line of division is an extension of the line which cuts up through El Salvador through the Department of Cabañas of that country.[33]

Due to the generally broken nature of the country, travel and transport by mule and horseback may probably be said to be the most important next to foot travel. In the rougher sections mules are generally preferred for transport, but horses will often be kept for travel and, among the Indians of the southwestern highlands, are preferred for transport as well. Mules naturally involve a greater investment since they do not reproduce, and the Lenca Indians evidently regard them as economically unsound. Among that Indian group, however, even horses are restricted to the wealthier. The use of donkeys is not widespread, although Comayagua is said to be famous for them. They are found most commonly in the departments bordering on Nicaragua, in the south central highlands, and in Olancho.[34]

---

[31] Conzemius, 1927–28, p. 282. [32] Stone, 1948, p. 210; and in correspondence.
[33] Adams, n.d. (d). [34] Census, 1954b, and survey data.

To transport produce by pack animal, usually one of three types of containers are used: the *árgana*, or large leather sack; the *matate*, or string bag; and the *costal* or *saco de yute*, the regular woven grain bag. *Arganas* were reported from only four towns, Nacaome, La Venta, Güinope, and Guaimaca (no data were gathered on this in Yusguare or Jacaleapa). Stone reports also that the Lenca use leather sacks at times in human transport,[35] but the writer's informants in Intibucá said that they were not used for animal transport. The leather sack would seem to have a distribution related to Nicaragua, as it is common in the highlands of that country, but was reported as being absent from most of western and northern Honduras. The *costal* and *matate* are to be found over most of the country, although the former is probably more common in the north. The term *aparejo* was used in Dulce Nombre de Copán for *matate*.

Besides horses, mules and burros, the ox was reported by Ladino informants to be used as a beast of burden in certain parts of the southwestern highlands. In La Esperanza the informant said that it was fairly common in Intibucá, but an informant in Intibucá denied that such was the case.

The truck and freight-passenger busses today are very important for any long distance transport. The latter, called the *baronesa*, goes almost anywhere that there is a semblance of a road throughout the interior of the country. On the north coast the fruit companies and national railroads are an important means of transport, and over much of the country there is a regular air service. The airlines of Honduras serve not only the larger producers, but are a standard means of travel for many of middle wealth. The departments of Olancho, Yoro, the southwestern highlands, and the north coast are the regions in which this service is most important. The writer found people in Olancho who regularly used the air service to go to the north coast for temporary periods of work. Airline rates are high, however, and wherever there are roads, trucks are taking much of their freight business. For example, much tobacco used to be flown out of Dulce Nombre de Copán, but recently trucks have been doing it more cheaply.

The use of boats is confined principally to the north coast, the south coast, and the larger interior rivers of the east. The dugout, called *vaciada* in Nacaome, *cayuco* in the interior, and going under a variety of names depending upon its size and use on the north coast, is a standard means of transport in these regions. In the middle and upper sections of the main interior rivers, such as on the Chamalecón and Ulúa, the *cayuco* is used mainly as a means of ferrying oneself across the river, but not as a means of transport up and down the river.

The marketing of produce and other goods is done mainly through stores. In only eight of the towns visited, or reported on, were there municipal market buildings, and in one of these (Olanchito) it had never developed into much more than a place where meat was sold. Three of the remaining seven (Güinope, Nueva Ocotepeque, and Olanchito) had no special market day. In Nacaome and Dulce Nombre de Copán, Sunday was the day of greatest commercial activity, and the rest had two or three main days (Marcala: Sunday and Thursday; Intibucá: Saturday, Sunday, and Thursday; Corquín: Friday, Saturday, and Sunday). It

---
[35] Stone, 1948, p. 210.

is of interest to note that except for Güinope and Olanchito (and Yoro where they were completing a new market building at the time of the survey), all the towns in which markets were held were near the Salvadorean or Guatemalan border. Of the towns near these borders, all had markets except Quimistán, which is adjacent to a non-market region of Guatemala, and La Esperanza, for which the Intibucá market serves. La Esperanza had a market building, but since the Intibucá market filled the needs of the town, it is used as a school building.

Without doubt the principal market area of Honduras is the southwest highland area in which is located the Indian population. In Marcala, it was reported that there were also markets in neighboring Santa María and Tutule. Marcala also has an annual fair which used to be of great commercial and religious importance. In recent years, however, such regional commercial endeavors have been declining, and a new priest in the town has been trying to build it up again in terms of a time of religious pilgrimage. In the departments of Intibucá and Lempira, people from nearby towns go to the Intibucá market. Except for these Indian towns, the market (where it is found) is generally subsidiary to the commerce carried on in the stores. Stores everywhere act as retailers of goods produced elsewhere in Honduras, as well as various local and foreign-import items. More enterprising storekeepers act as agents for selling local produce. While stopping in a store in Yoro, the writer overheard a truck driver inquiring how much the store owner was paying that day for coffee. Stores also act as important credit centers for the poorer town and country people of Honduras. The Banco de Fomento has discovered, in trying to establish supervised credit for small agriculturalists, that there is some open reluctance to use the bank. The explanation given in both La Libertad and Catacamas was that they are accustomed to getting their credit from local storekeepers who do not try to supervise how it is used. In communities of any size, the storekeeper is banker, buyer, and seller.

Stores in Honduras are generally classed as *tiendas* or *pulperías*. The *pulpería* is the smaller enterprise of limited stock, while the *tienda* is the larger. There are few *farmacias* as such scattered over the countryside, but every town has a store which handles the sale of medicines. In one southwestern town, for example, informants assured the writer that there was no *farmacia* in town. One of these informants made this assurance at the very time that he was selling medicines in his store which was devoted almost exclusively to such products. He was also acting as advisor and empirical doctor for people who came asking about their ailments. The term *botiquín* is often applied to these small stores which deal in medicines.

As elsewhere in Central America, much of the marketing and storekeeping is done by women. While a man may own a store and supervise it, he will often be occupied in other ventures, such as agriculture, and the actual running of the store will be left to his wife, daughters, or an employed girl.

3. THE DOMESTIC ESTABLISHMENT

Most Honduran town and country homes consist of one or two-room houses. In the rural areas, they are at times set off by a fence, while the towns present the usual Central American picture of houses set together or joined by *adobe* walls. The principal construction forms are walls of *adobe* brick, *bajareque*, boards, or poles. Except in some of the coastal areas and in regions of extensive wood supply, the roofs in the towns are almost always of tile, and those in the rural areas are either tile or straw. In the north coast region, corrugated and palm roofs are common, and wood shingles are found from time to time in certain parts.

The use of *adobe* house walls seems more common in the south central and southwest areas, and in the northeast. In general, *adobe* in these regions is limited pretty much to the towns themselves. It was the principal wall material in Nacaome, La Venta, Güinope, Jacaleapa, La Esperanza, and Catacamas, and was also important in Guaimaca. When one moves out of this general region, *adobe* gives way to *bajareque* as the principal wall material in the towns. *Bajareque* was the principal material in Zambrano, La Misión, La Libertad, San Francisco de Yojoa, Ilama, Quimistán and Yoro. In Olanchito and the north coast towns, board buildings are among the most common urban structures.

While *bajareque* is most important as an urban building form in the central and northern interior towns, it is found over most of the country in rural construction. Even in the areas where *adobe* may be important in the towns, *bajareque* will usually be more important outside. The *bajareque* construction is the same as that found in El Salvador and Guatemala, being a mud and rubble fill between a double wooden framework.

The use of *ranchos*, *chozas*, or *pajizas*, houses with pole walls and either straw or leaf roofs, is found all over the country. In some regions they are very rare, and in some, *bajareque* walls with straw roofs are more common. This use of *ranchos*, however, varies both with the wealth of the population, their background, and the climate. *Ranchos* are usually used by the poorer people in the population. Nowhere in the country are they the standard housing. They are also used as temporary housing by people who would otherwise live in a house of *bajareque* and tile. The people of Zambrano, for example, have houses of *bajareque* and tile in the town, but many of them go down into the Comayagua Valley to rent pieces of land for cultivation. While there, they build themselves *ranchos* in which to live. In some regions, Ladinos will generally live in tile roofed homes, while the neighboring Indian population will live in *chozas*. Such was reported in Jacaleapa and Ilama, but in both cases it was stipulated that the correlation was not exact; that is, some Ladinos also lived in *chozas*, and some Indians lived under tile roofs. In some places, such as was reported in Yoro, there is no ethnic correlation in house types. Both Ladinos and Indians who are poor live in *ranchos*.

While *ranchos* are seldom of more than one room, the kitchen space in Honduran homes is often separate from this room. It is common practice for the cooking fire to be located apart, in the corridor of the house or in a small annex to the house. The practice of having the cooking fire in the single house room is to be found under certain circumstances, specifically in most Indian communities (reported to be the case in Jacaleapa, Marcala, Intibucá, Yoro). However, among the poorer Ladinos in some other communities the same practice is found, although it is usually restricted to those who live in *ranchos*.

The relation of wealth to house type is obvious, but it affects Indians as well as Ladinos. In the northern part of the Department of La Paz in the Marcala sector, it is reported that the Indian population is more wealthy than those of the south. This is due specifically to the fact that coffee cultivation has been adopted in the northern part and has brought an increase in income. As a part of the change this is bringing into the area, it was said that some Indians are now putting their cooking space outside the main room of the house.

The furniture of the town and country home also varies with wealth, but there is also a rural-urban distinction, and in some places, differences related to ethnic differences. There are seven basic types of sleeping arrangements used in Honduras: the bed with a mattress; the bed of string, leather thongs, or metal strips, on which is placed a *petate* or a hide; the canvas cot, referred to as *cama de lona* or *tijera*; the bed of poles, called the *tapesco*, also on which is usually

Table 12.—Percent of people using different types of sleeping arrangements, according to 1950 Census (*Census*, 1952)

Persons		Bed and mattress	Bed and *petate*	Canvas cot	Hammock	*Tapesco*	On the ground	Total
Rural	944,152	2.2%	73.9%	10.0%	3.6%	8.8%	1.6%	100.1%
Urban	424,453	11.2%	72.6%	10.8%	1.9%	2.4%	1.1%	100.0%
Total	1,368,605	5.0%	73.4%	10.3%	3.0%	6.8%	1.5%	100.0%

placed a *petate* or hide; the *tabanco*, a ceiling of poles on which people occasionally sleep but which is more important as a storage place; the hammock; and the ground, also usually on a *petate* or hide. In the 1950 Census, information was collected on some type of sleeping apparatus used.

While the classification used in the census telescopes some of the distinctions which we made above, it makes clear that the bed with a *petate* (whether the bed is of string, leather, or metal, and probably including those on which skins may be placed) is used by about three-quarters of the people. This should not be misunderstood to mean that all these people have their own bed. On the contrary, it is likely that a very large percentage of the people recorded as sleeping in a bed are children who sleep with either one or both of their parents.

As between towns and the countryside, the principal distinction lies in a greater use of beds with mattress in the former, and a greater use of hammocks and *tapescos* in the latter. If we take the bed with *petate* (and its variations) as the principal sleeping arrangement, the census points out some regional variations in the secondary forms. The hammock, for example, is of special importance on the north and south coasts. The departments of Valle and Choluteca account for 27.7% of all hammocks, and the departments of Cortes, Yoro and Atlántida account for 36.5%. These departments taken as a whole, then, account for

64.2% of all the hammocks used in the country. Similarly, the canvas cot is found most commonly in the north and east. Cortes, Yoro and Atlántida account for 36.1% of the total; Olancho, Colón, and El Paraíso, for another 22.1%; and the Department of Francisco Morazán for 18.5%. These departments, as a whole, account for 76.7% of the canvas cots used in the entire country. The *tapesco* is generally found in all departments, but the Department of Copán has an especially large number, 15.5% of all those in the country. The bed with mattress is principally an urban item, characteristic of the wealthier people. There is one area, however, in which it may be said to be a standard culture trait: the Bay Islands. 88.7% of the Bay Islanders sleep on beds with mattresses; the department with the next highest percentage is Francisco Morazán, and there only 17.7% of the people use it. Excluding the Bay Islands, then, the bed with mattress may be considered to be a trait of only the wealthier people, and more specifically of town dwellers.

The hammock, while used for sleeping in the regions noted, is also found in other parts of the country, but used specifically for resting, much as we would use a living room sofa. The only regions in which the hammock is most uncommon are those high mountain communities where it is fairly cold. The hammock is also most important for travel, because the countryman can carry it along and string it up anywhere. In a country where inns are rare outside of the principal towns, this is a necessity.

The *tabanco* has disappeared from most Honduran homes. It was reported to still be found (particularly in the poorer homes) only in five of the towns visited, and these were widely separated (Nacaome, Jacaleapa, Nueva Ocotepeque, Quimistán, and Yoro). Where it is found today, it serves principally as a place of storage. In Yoro, however, it was stated that in some Indian families the *tabanco* was used for sleeping, and in Nueva Ocotepeque, that some of the poorer people used it in this way.

The major items of furniture in the homes of the town and country, aside from whatever sleeping arrangements may be present, are benches, chairs, and tables. The classic chair is the *taburete* with a leather seat. It is found today over all the interior and south coast of Honduras. In some places, where leather is scarce, the seat is made of string, leather strips, metal strips, or even simple boards. These chairs also may go under the name *taburete*. The *butaca*, a reclining chair made of two pairs of cross sticks, and also usually made with a leather seat, is less common than the *taburete*. It was reported from most of the towns of the country, but was said to be in limited use or not found at all in the south coast (Nacaome and Yusguare) and in the southwestern highlands (Marcala, Intibucá and La Esperanza). In Yusguare, as in parts of El Salvador, the term *butaca* is used to refer to a small bench. Various types of benches are also used, some of boards with legs, others simply of a large log with a side flattened (*trozas*). In the better off homes of the towns, regular furniture is used, produced either by a more skilled local carpenter or brought in from one of the larger towns.

As was mentioned before, it is customary in most Ladino homes to have the kitchen space apart from the main room or rooms of the house. In the wealthier homes, there is a special room for the kitchen; in the poorer, it is put in a shelter on the side of the house or in the corridor; and in the poorest it may be found in the single room of the house. The fire is customarily on a raised platform or *fogón alto*. In the wealthier this is a large surface of stone or brick. Among the poorer or as a temporary medium, a *tapesco* will be built, mud laid on top, and the fire built on this. On top of these surfaces the *hornilla*, horseshoe shaped ridge of clay, is built and on this the pots and *comales* are placed to do the cooking.

The main variation in the placing of the cooking fire is found among the Indian groups and among some of the poorer Ladinos. In most of the towns visited it was reported that some people had the fire on the floor. In three of these towns (Intibucá, Jacaleapa, and Yoro) it was specified that it was the Indian population which retained this practice. In the remaining towns, however, it was more a matter of wealth, and a distinction between urban and rural dwellers. In Nacaome, the distinction was made between the *fogón*, which referred to the floor fire, and the *hornilla*, which referred to the raised cooking surface. The floor fire, where used, is usually correlated with the one-room *rancho*. For a *rancho* to have separate kitchen often means that there must be a second *rancho*. Fires on the floor are found using both the *hornilla* and the three stones (*tenemastes* in Intibucá). While there seems to be some distinction in the use of one as against the other of these with respect to whether or not the population involved is Indian, general poverty or isolation also seems to be a factor.

The use of ovens is fairly general over the entire country. In some communities they are restricted to people who specialize in bread for sale, and in Jacaleapa and Yoro it was said that the Indian populations did not use them much. In Intibucá, however, predominantly an Indian community, the *horno* was said to be fairly common, although Stone[36] reports that they are actually rare in the region as a whole. In the Ladino population of La Libertad the oven was said to be little used because built into the *hornilla* was an extra opening, the *jurón* or *juraño*, which permitted some baking to be done. The writer did not explore the presence of the *jurón* in other places.

The preparation of some grains for cooking varies somewhat regionally. The corn grain is removed by hand and by the graining machine, but most common is to place it (husked) in a net, and to beat it with a pole. This method is evidently being replaced in Nacaome by a method which is being introduced from El Salvador. This involved leaving the ears unhusked, placing them on the ground and then beating them. Sorghum, rice, wheat, and beans are variously treated. Along the south coast and in Nueva Ocotepeque and La Libertad, it is evidently somewhat customary to place the sorghum on the ground and beat it as one would corn. Elsewhere, a *tapesco*, about waist high, is used. This is usually called the *aporreador*, but in Dulce Nombre de Jesús the term *toldo* was used for it. The sorghum is placed on this, a hide put underneath, and the sorghum beaten. The grain then falls out on the hide. The *aporreador* is also commonly used for rice,

---

[36] Stone, 1948, p. 206.

but the rice is beaten against it. In Nueva Ocotepeque, a special type of platform for rice is constructed of heavier poles, similar to that used in El Salvador.[37] Where grown, wheat is treated in much the same way as is sorghum. In Nueva Ocotepeque, instead of beating wheat out on the *aporreador*, it was threshed by the standard European method of having mules trample over it. Beans are usually removed from the shell by beating them with a pole, either on the *aporreador* or on the ground. In many places now the beating of rice has been stopped and machines in the towns serve the purpose.

For preparing corn and sorghum, the standard method involves grinding the grain on a stone by hand, preparing it with either lime or wood ash in *nixtamal*, and its formation into *tortillas* or *tamales*. The standard method of using the stone over almost all of Honduras is to place it on a slightly slanted table surface and to grind while standing up. This table surface goes under at least three common names, and a fourth, *arteza*, reported only from Catacamas. The term *molendero* is generally used in the south (Nacaome, Yusguare, La Venta, Güinope, Zambrano, Marcala, Intibucá and La Esperanza). It was also reported from Catacamas. In the far west the term *tablón* was reported from Corquín and Dulce Nombre de Copán. Elsewhere, the term *tablero* is evidently standard for this. The only towns in which any divergent method of holding the stone was reported was in Nueva Ocotepeque, in which the standard Salvadorean *horquetas* were also said to be used, and in La Venta where the *horquetas* are an alternative to the *molendero*.

The stones themselves vary from being carefully worked with three legs (some of which are said to be imported from El Salvador), to crude rocks collected locally and prepared for use by the man of the family. In Dulce Nombre de Copán, it was said that the stones came from neighboring Esquipulas in Guatemala, while in some of the central and northern towns, it was reported that they were produced in San Antonio de Cortés and that some were brought from Tegucigalpa. The writer could determine no particular differential distribution with respect to whether the stones had legs or not.

There does seem to be a rather distinct regional differentiation with respect to the use of lime or wood ash for making the *nixtamal*. Wood ash is preferred by the Indians of the southwest highlands, although in Marcala it was reported that the best trees for making the ash are disappearing and some are turning to lime in preference to a poorer ash. On the south coast wood ash is evidently preferred, although in Nacaome it was said that the townspeople tended to use lime. In Jacaleapa, it was said that the Indians used ash, but the Ladinos used both. Ash was also said to be preferred by the Indians and Ladinos of Ilama and Yoro, and by the general population of Guatemala, Catacamas, and San Esteban. In Salamá, it was said to be a matter of taste, and both were used.

Lime was said to be the preferred or only material used in the western towns of Nueva Ocotepeque, Dulce Nombre de Copán, and Quimistán, and in the central towns of Zambrano, Güinope, La Misión, La Libertad, and San Francisco

---

[37] Adams, n.d. (d).

de Yojoa. In Nueva Ocotepeque, it was reported that some of the poorer people used wood ash, and in Quimistán, that ash used to be used some years ago, but that most have converted to lime.

It should be added that the commercial hand grinder of corn has been introduced into various parts of the country, but in general, it is used for the initial grinding, and then the corn is passed over the stone for the final grinding.

The removal of rice from the husk is usually done in a *mortero* or *pilón*. The term *pilón* is evidently used only in the south of the country, having been reported from Nacaome, Yusguare, Jacaleapa, and Marcala. Elsewhere, the term *mortero* seems to be standard. The *mortero* is the common large wooden trunk set on end with the upper end hollowed out. It is also commonly used to grind up coffee. The writer found no other use to which this implement is put. The work with the *pilón* was said to be done principally by men.

The storage of corn and other grains varies with no discernible regional pattern. In some places, the corn is stored in the husk in *trojes* of poles set on a *tapesco* a few inches off the ground. These *trojes* are usually in one corner of the house, or in a shed on the side of the house. Some people use large board boxes for grain storage, and among the more wealthy in some places cylindrical metal silos are used. Where there are *tabancos*, they are regularly used for storage.

In kitchen equipment, pottery still holds first place, but some communities are making more and more use of metal containers. Basically, pottery is much cheaper and in the more isolated communities more readily accessible.

The production of *chicha* and clandestine *aguardiente* is reported from most parts of the country. Since the fabrication of these drinks is entirely forbidden, it is impossible to be sure to what extent they are produced secretly. The principal towns in which it was reported that they were not produced in any quantity were those in the central south highlands, and in the northwest.

Clothing among the Ladinos of Honduras is basically simple. Men wear the usual western dress, with variety being provided principally by poverty. The women tend to wear single piece dresses. The principal variation is to be found among the Indian women of the southwestern highlands and up into Santa Bárbara. This dress will be discussed later in the section devoted to the Indian population. The town and countrywomen generally show little embarrassment at going bare to the waist when washing clothes or engaged in other similar activities.

4. FAMILY AND *COMPADRAZGO*

The town and country family of interior Honduras is basically similar to that found over the rest of Central America; it is bilateral and neo-local. A temporary patrilocality was reported in only four towns, La Libertad, Catacamas, Olanchito, and Intibucá. In the first two places patri-neolocal residence was said to be the general rule; a couple newly married would go to live temporarily in the home of the boy's parents until such time as the young couple could economically separate themselves from the parent's home. In Olanchito this was said to take place only in some cases but that straight neo-local residence was the rule. In Intibucá it was said that patri-neolocal residence was the rule, but that in some cases, matri-neolocal residence occurred. In these cases, the couple would go to live in the home of the girl's parents until such time as they could afford to set up a separate household.

Of the 19 towns in the interior in which data was gathered on the subject, marriage or unions between first cousins were said to be prohibited in 13 and permitted in six. In La Libertad, the comment was made that if such marriages were prohibited, there would be few people to marry, since almost everyone was already related in one way or another. The extension of the prohibition to *hermanos espirituales* (children of *compadres*) was reported from 9 towns, but there was no evident correlation, either negative or positive, between first cousin prohibition and *hermanos espirituales* prohibition, nor is there any apparent geographic significance with respect to them. In the Guatemalan survey[38] there was a suggestive correlation between permissive first cousin marriage and no tendency toward patrilocality. This tendency does not show for the Honduran towns. Nor is there any correlation between permissive first cousin alliances and a reported high degree of common-law unions. There is a possible correlation between reported high degree of separations and permissive first cousin marriage, but the data are far from conclusive. For the record, the breakdown is as follows:

	Separations Common	*Separations Uncommon*
First cousin marriage permitted	La Venta Güinope Jacaleapa Quimistán	La Libertad
First cousin marriage not permitted	Yusguare Yoro	Intibucá Olanchito San Francisco de Yojoa Nacaome La Misión

Unfortunately, data is missing on over a third of the towns involved, and these might well throw the suggested correlation out. It may be noted, however, that the La Libertad case (and this applies also to the Antillean whites of the Bay Islands) presents a special situation in which there has been considerable intermarriage within the community so that prohibition of first cousin marriage might mean prohibition of the only available persons. In both cases, unions are evidently stable, however.

Formal marriage, under Honduran law, must first be enacted in the municipality as a civil affair, and then, at the discretion of the individuals, in the church. Formal marriage, either as a civil affair or combined with the religious ceremony, takes place in only about half the unions made.

Table 13 indicates that of the entire population of 14 years and older, 22.7%

---

[38] Adams, n.d. (c).

Table 13.—Civil status of people 14 years and older by department, 1950 (*Census*, 1952)

Department	Percent of people				
	Single	Married	Free union	Separated, divorced, widowed	Total
Atlántida	54.7%	19.1%	23.8%	2.4%	100.0
Colón	57.5	18.6	20.9	3.0	100.0
Comayagua	46.6	28.1	21.4	3.8	99.9
Copán	45.0	23.8	26.5	4.7	100.0
Cortés	54.5	17.5	24.5	3.5	100.0
Choluteca	48.6	18.8	27.7	4.8	99.9
El Paraíso	55.1	17.0	24.7	3.2	100.0
Francisco Morazán	57.6	18.7	19.7	4.0	100.0
Intibucá	44.3	28.4	23.2	4.1	100.0
Bay Islands	52.4	34.5	7.1	6.0	100.0
La Paz	48.9	25.8	20.2	5.2	100.1
Lempira	48.8	27.7	18.8	4.7	100.0
Ocotepeque	46.3	33.2	17.0	3.4	99.9
Olancho	51.6	22.4	22.5	3.5	100.0
Santa Bárbara	48.8	26.0	21.2	3.9	99.9
Valle	54.6	20.2	21.7	3.5	100.0
Yoro	52.8	15.2	28.5	3.5	100.0
Republic	50.6	22.7	22.3	4.3	99.9

Table 14.—Relative percentage of civil status of people living together, by department, 1950 (*census*, 1952)

Department	Married	Free union
Yoro	34.9%	65.1%
Choluteca	40.5	59.5
El Paraíso	40.7	59.3
Cortés	41.6	58.4
Atlántida	44.4	55.6
Colón	47.2	52.8
Copán	47.2	52.8
Valle	48.3	51.7
Francisco Morazán	48.7	51.3
Olancho	49.9	50.1
[Republic	50.4	49.6]
Intibucá	55.0	45.0
Santa Bárbara	55.1	44.9
La Paz	56.1	43.9
Comayagua	56.5	43.5
Lempira	59.6	40.4
Ocotepeque	66.1	33.9
Bay Islands	83.0	17.0

were married, and 22.3% were living in free union. To make clearer the differences in these data by department, Table 14 gives the relative percentages of people living in free unions as opposed to those who are married in the entire population of people living together. From this it is evident that there is considerable regional difference. The Bay Islands, of course, stand completely apart from all the rest of the country, and culturally cannot be considered part of it. Apart from the Islands, however, the northern departments as a group, together with El Paraíso and Choluteca in the south, have the highest percentages of free unions. Those with the greatest percentages of marriage are

Table 15.—Average number of people per family, rural and urban, by department, 1950 (*Census* 1952)

Departments	Number of people per family	
	Urban	Rural
Atlántida	5.72	5.83
Colón	5.44	5.71
Comayagua	6.29	6.23
Copán	5.35	5.71
Cortés	6.03	6.11
Choluteca	6.74	6.66
El Paraíso	5.74	6.44
Francisco Morazán	6.44	6.28
Intibucá	6.05	5.60
Bay Islands	5.82	5.46
La Paz	6.21	6.26
Lempira	6.20	5.62
Ocotepeque	4.98	6.36
Olancho	6.53	6.26
Santa Bárbara	6.08	6.61
Valle	4.98	6.16
Yoro	5.95	5.71
Republic	6.00	6.12

the southwestern departments, including Santa Bárbara and Comayagua. Unfortunately, we have no such statistical data on separations or family stability. The 1950 Census makes no sex distinctions with respect to chiefs of households, and consequently we cannot determine how many families have female chiefs, and how many male chiefs. On the basis of survey data, separations were said to be rare in Nacaome, the rural Indians of Marcala, Intibucá (Indian), La Misión, La Libertad, San Francisco de Yojoa, and in Olanchito. In Ilama they were said to be commoner among Indians than Ladinos (one of the few cases that this circumstance has been reported), and in Nueva Ocotepeque, separations were said to be more common in the *aldeas* than in the town itself.

The size of the family, according to 1950 Census returns, does not vary consistently between the rural and urban population. In this, Honduras differs considerably from El Salvador where the rural family average is considerably higher than the urban. It is probably significant that the departments of Valle and Ocotepeque, the only two predominantly Ladino departments which border on El Salvador, also show a distinct variation in this respect. In Valle the rural family average is 1.18 times the urban, while that for Ocotepeque, is 1.38 larger. This is to be compared with the national average in which the rural family average is only 0.12 larger than the urban. It is interesting to note that Intibucá and Lempira, departments which are somewhat Indian, the rural average is below that of the urban family. Intibucá is 0.40, while Lempira is 0.58. These two departments have the lowest rural family size relative to the urban families.

Unlike El Salvador, where the relationship between formal marriage and family stability is far from clear, there does seem to be considerable correlation between Honduran towns in which separations were reported to be few, and in which formal marriage was said to be more important than free unions. Olanchito, San Francisco de Yojoa, La Misión, La Libertad, and Nacaome, all reported both these traits to be present. On the other hand, only Ilama and La Venta reported relative high degree of formal marriage with separations fairly common, and Indians of Intibucá and Marcala were reported as having few separations but also few marriages. However, in both these latter places, it was stipulated that among the Indians marriages were more common than among Ladinos. In Dulce Nombre de Copán, Quimistán, Yoro, Catacamas, Guaimaca, Zambrano, Güinope, Jacaleapa, La Esperanza, and Yusguare, both separations and high degree of common-law unions were reported. While far from conclusive, these data suggest that the marital situation in the towns and countryside of Honduras is more influential in family stability than is the case in El Salvador. The principal exception in Honduras seems to be among the southwestern highland Indian population where even though there is relatively more marriage than among Ladinos, there is nevertheless a little, and marriage is fairly stable. The high percentage of free unions (one half of all unions) indicates that, like El Salvador, this form of relationship is fairly standard and well established. As in El Salvador, the writer found comments in Honduras to the effect that, "It is easier to be *amancebado* . . . one doesn't get taken to jail for it!" reflecting the legal problems one may become involved in through leaving, not supporting, or perhaps, beating one's wife.[39]

The *compadrazgo* in Honduras does not seem to differ from that observed elsewhere in Ladino Central America. Godfathers are sought for baptism, confirmation and marriage. On the 19 interior towns, 9 reported that it was customary to try to get the same godfather for all the siblings in a family, 6 reported that it was of no importance whether the same served or not, and 4 said that different godparents were sought. There was no discernible regional pattern involved in this. Only three towns reported that it was the standard practice to look for a *compadre* from among the people of a better

---

[39] *Amancebado* is the most common term for the free union relationship; in Olanchito it was jestingly referred to as *amaclinados*, and in the Black Carib community of Corozal, as *amachinados*.

class or from among the more wealthy (Yusguare, Jacaleapa, and Olanchito); seven others reported that this was an alternative way of choosing a godfather (La Venta, La Esperanza, Nueva Ocotepeque, La Libertad, Quimistán, Yoro, and Catacamas). In these seven, and in all the rest, *compadres* were said to come usually from among friends or family members. Six towns reported that family members were sometimes sought (Nueva Ocotepeque, San Francisco, Quimistán, Dulce Nombre de Copán, Olanchito, and Intibucá). Almost all towns reported that it was customary to seek out distinct godfathers for baptism and confirmation, but that the godfather at marriage might be the same as that of baptism. Almost everywhere the *compadre* relationship was reported to be one of great respect. The only place where it was reported not to be of particular importance was in Texiguat.

5. GENERAL SOCIAL STRUCTURE

As in the case throughout Central America, the family forms the basic element in the larger class structure of the country. There are in the country four fairly distinct classes among the Ladinos; in addition to these classes, there are distinct socio-cultural groups which tend to stand outside this class structure. In any given community, usually only two or three of the distinct social classes are identifiable, and there is seldom more than one, if any, of the extra-structural groups.

The principal Ladino classes are: "cosmopolitan upper;" "local upper;" "local middle;" and "lower." The local definitions and appelations for these classes will be described below. The principal non-Spanish American groups are the Indians of the interior, the Indians of the northeast region, the Black Caribs (or *Morenos*) of the north coast, the Antillean whites of the Bay Islands, and the Antillean Negroes in scattered parts of the north coast, and various elements of European extraction. The definition of the relative position of these non-Spanish American groups in the total social structure is easiest in the interior towns where the only such groups are usually Indians of various degrees of ladinoization. On the north coast, however, where various of the groups are in residence, the definition is more complex, and not enough time was devoted to the subject on the survey to provide a clear picture of the situation.

While the criteria used to characterize members of the distinct social classes in Honduras are various, the classes themselves may be said to rest on two particular elements: wealth, and age and importance of family. The other characteristics (education, morals, place of residence, participation in certain groups, etc.) may be said to be more or less dependent upon these two characteristics. It will be noted that these two characteristics were also evident as the principal framework of the system in Guatemala.[40]

The group which we refer to as the cosmopolitan upper class is evidently quite small in Honduras. This is due in great part to the fact that most people are independent producers and there are relatively few great landholders.

---

[40] Adams, n.d. (c); Tumin, 1952.

Of considerably greater importance is the group which we call the local upper. This group consists of members of local families which are wealthy and/or old and respected. These families have their main residence in a town or departmental capital. If there is no adequate high school (*colegio*) locally (and there frequently is not), the children of these families will usually be sent to the national capital for further education, and in a few cases, will go on to professional school, either in medicine, dentistry, the law, or more recently, engineering. These local upper families have traditionally fed and continue to feed the political and administrative posts in the national government.

A superior position in the local social ranking in a small town may be had through membership in one of the older "good" families, and it may also be achieved through accumulation of a certain amount of wealth and adherence to certain of the customs observed by the older families. The writer rarely got the impression that the "old families" formed an upper group which excluded the entrance of other families. This may have been the case in some of the older towns in which there has been no recent socio-economic change of particular note, such as the introduction of coffee planting. The retention of a fairly exclusive local upper class has also depended to a great degree upon the size of the general population and of that class. In some of the larger towns, such as Olanchito, the appearance of a new wealthy family does not mean that the family will have an immediate position in the local upper class. Rather, there is a much larger middle group into which it goes. This middle group, as a developing middle class, is of considerable importance in parts of Honduras, and may probably be assumed to be of increasing importance.

One way in which the growing importance of the middle group and a relative decline in importance of the upper class has been reflected is in the disappearance of many of the old exclusive local social clubs, and the appearance in some places of the socially broader clubs. *Casinos*, or social clubs, were found to be still functioning in only one town visited on the survey, Olanchito. In La Libertad, a *Club Social Libertad* existed until about ten years ago, but it fell apart through lack of interest. In Nacaome, until a few years ago, there existed a *Club de Leones*, an affiliate of the national and international Lions Clubs, which started a clinic. This too was composed of members of the upper class of the town. It too is now defunct. In Marcala, there is a Lions Club which was recently organized by a group of men from Tegucigalpa. In forming the club locally, only members of the local upper class participated. In Marcala, this local upper class is still quite distinct as the entire Ladino population is small and somewhat endogamous. In Olanchito, however, where a Lions Club has been started, members have been recruited from both the upper and middle groups. The growing middle group in Olanchito has been much more active in many local affairs than has the older upper group, and the Lions doubtless were impressed by this. In Marcala, however, such a middle group does not seem to have become distinct as yet.

The local upper class usually goes under the names of *la primera, la sociedad, los acomodados*, and are usually considered to be *más civilizados, más inteligentes*, *de mejores costumbres, educados,* and generally more wealthy than people of the lower brackets. This group may be considered to be generally locally oriented, preferring their provincial town residence to that in the national capital. The cosmopolitan upper class, sometimes referred to locally as *la capitalista, la primera clase, los hacendados,* are often found to prefer residence in the capital city or in their *haciendas.* They may or may not participate in the social life of the local town, but as often as not, their *hacienda* is distant from the town. Such was reported to be the case in Nacaome, where some of the major land exploiters are Salvadoreans who live in San Salvador; in Zambrano, where the major part of the land is held by a single individual who passes time variously in the *hacienda* or in the city; and in Yoro, where of two major *haciendas,* one *hacendado* was said to live in Tegucigalpa and one in Yoro. This should not be interpreted to mean that none of the *hacienda* owners live in the provincial centers. Some members of the local upper class people are large landholders. In Quimistán, most of the so-called communal lands are so held, and the co-owners generally live in the town.

Within the town itself, the local upper group will often live near the center. In many cases, however, this is either not really convenient due to the topography, or has not been followed out in fact for other reasons. In Marcala, for example, the old families are found scattered from one of the two principal plazas to the other, but relatively few actually live on the main plaza. In Dulce Nombre de Copán, the town is so hilly, that a level area, of whatever location, is preferable to trying to live near the plaza. In any case, the local upper group is basically a town-dwelling group, and the majority are not found as residents outside the town limits. This seems to be a fairly well observed custom over most of Honduras. In Quimistán, as was already mentioned, the *hacienda* co-owners are generally town residents. In Nacaome, it was said that of the town's population, perhaps 30 % could be considered as of the *primera* or *sociedad,* but that none of the rural resident population fell into this category. The same general picture was specified in Dulce Nombre (where many of the local upper actually own *haciendas* in other neighboring *municipios* and not in the jurisdiction of Dulce Nombre), San Francisco de Yojoa, La Libertad, La Venta. In Yoro it was said that a very few of the *primera* did live in *aldeas,* but that in general, they were town dwellers. Even in the Indian community of Intibucá, it was said that the Indian town dwellers tended to marry among themselves and were in some cases better off than the rural Indians. This cannot be considered as part of the general class system under discussion here, however, but only an interesting parallel.

What may be regarded as the upper class in a specific locale may be either one or the other, or both, of the two groups which we have here distinguished. In towns of any size, and particularly in the older towns, the upper class locally is entirely or predominantly what we have called the local upper. There are few cosmopolitan upper class people at all, and few of these actually live in municipal centers. In poorer and smaller communities, such as Zambrano, probably La Misión, and Yusguare, there is practically no local upper class.

In some cases the upper class is represented by the little seen cosmopolitan upper *hacendado*, whereas in La Misión there are perhaps a few people who are a little more wealthy, such as the storekeeper in Yusguare, but they hardly comprise an upper class, either local or cosmopolitan. They do reflect a culture which is somewhat distinct from the main body of agriculturalists, but they do not form much of a group within the town.

Below the upper classes, there may be an intermediary group or middle class, composed of newcomer entrepreneurs, small storekeepers, poorer people who may nevertheless have been fairly well educated. This class usually includes such people as school teachers who were termed by one informant, *"intelectuales."* The importance and distinctiveness of the middle group is closely dependent upon the nature of the upper class. Where there is no functional upper class within the community (Zambrano, La Misión (?), and Yusguare), the middle group serves as an upper class, but no one, neither they nor the other people of the community, confuse them with the upper classes as found in other communities. Where the upper classes are distinct, the middle class varies depending whether the upper is an old, family-based, social grouping, or whether it is a simpler wealth-based group. In the former case, the middle group is composed of most of the people of better education and wealth who cannot enter the somewhat closed upper group. In the latter, they blend with the upper group, and their actual position varies with the individual's wealth, public activity, and education. This type of middle group is doubtless the more common, and also includes people who are full time agriculturalists. This population is often difficult to distinguish because their actual holding in lands may vary from one region to another, and their relative position will also vary with the general range of wealth locally.

The lower class, as elsewhere the largest social group in the country, is generally termed *la segunda* or *la tercera* (depending upon whether two or three classes are distinguished locally), *el populacho, gente humilde, el pueblo, los pobres, mengales, de solemnidad, pobrería,* etc. It includes, of course, the vast population of laborers, small landholders, land renters, *colonos*, and squatters. Within any community, certain distinction is made on the basis of customs and wealth within this group, but in all cases, they are felt to be distinct from the upper classes. Into this group in many places go the ladinoized Indians and Ladinos who were of recent Indian descent. Between these people and the Ladinos of a longer Ladino tradition there is often felt to be some distinction, but the importance of this varies locally.

The relationship between the local upper class and the lower is generally one of depreciation by the former, and a respectful but quiet independence by the latter. The lower class *hondureño* did not strike the writer in general as occupying the inferior position in terms of attitudes which are to be found in certain other parts of Central America. While this varies, the difference is probably in part due to the difference in landholding which is to be found in Honduras and the other countries. It will be remembered that only about 25% of the Honduran agricultural population are laborers. The rest are independent agriculturalists, mainly landholders, but also including land renters. The large landholder, then, and the local upper class person may look down on the lower class person, but the lower class does not necessarily return this with submissiveness.

The major variations from this general picture occur in those regions in which there is a distinct or heavy Indian population or where most of the land area involved is in *haciendas* and consequently most of the lower class stand in a position of being laborers. In the case of the Indian regions, the relationship varies with the degree to which the Indians have retained a distinctive culture and the degree to which they are considered merely the lowest portion of the lower class. In situations such as in Intibucá, the Indians have retained an integral culture, distinctive in important ways from the Ladinos. The Indians in this situation are not, then, merely a lower class, but a distinctive sociocultural group, a situation essentially similar to that found in Guatemala. In other regions, however, such as Texiguat, probably some of the Santa Bárbara area, and many of the Indian communities around Yoro, the Indians are highly ladinoized in culture and are more distinctive for their poverty than for separate customs. In such situations, the Indian tends to assume a most subordinate role, even though possibly an independent producer. They have the disadvantages of the lower class Ladinos in matters of low education, little wealth, and lack of traditional family lines, and combined with this, manifest certain customs from their Indian tradition which are well watered down and appear to the eyes of the upper class as akin to stupidity.

The independence of the lower class Ladino is to be seen in numerous stories about his reactions to governmental orders and officials. The refusal to accept Banco de Fomento loans because they entail supervision of the cultivation is only one of these. The Zambrano people who prefer to journey a number of times annually to obtain rented lands in Comayagua to being entirely dependent upon jobs on *haciendas* is another.

In the years since the initiation of the banana industry, the north coast has provided a fairly reliable source of work for people from all over the country and from neighboring countries as well. People with no land and those who may not have quite enough have for some years now looked to the north coast as an area to which they could turn in times of bad harvest or during slack seasons. This has brought to the north coast people from all parts of the country, but it may be interpolated, people who for one reason or another found their own lot at home unsatisfactory. In view of the fact that there is generally a good deal of land available for cultivation, although by no means always good land, the possibility suggests itself that the population which has congregated with some permanence in these plantation centers may, through selectivity, be the least independent of the Honduran countrymen. The temporary laborer is another thing, of course, because he goes only for short periods as a fill-in during the regular agricultural season.

The roles and attitudes which accompany membership in one of these general class groups naturally vary somewhat from one community to another, but of considerable importance is the degree to which the members of the two main classes, the upper and the lower, participate in certain local activities. In general, the local governing bodies are made up of the local upper class. Where such a class is non-existent or weak, these functions may either be performed by an outsider or by certain people of somewhat more prestige locally. Akin to this governing role is the participation in certain fairly rare organizations which have to do with maintaining or bettering the schools of the community. The case that comes to mind (and the writer knows of none other exactly like it in Honduras) is that of Marcala. In that community there are two funds, the *Fondo de Instrucción Pública de Ladinos* and the *Tesorería de Indígenas*. Each of these funds is controlled by a committee composed of a *gerente, tesorero, fiscal,* and three *vocales*. The *Fondo* belongs exclusively to the Ladinos of the community, while the *Tesorería* belongs exclusively to the Indians. In 1954, the former had total assets of about $10,000, and the latter of about $2,750. These funds were used to make loans out to the members of the respective groups. The interest on these loans was devoted to keeping up the schools, paying extra salaries for the teachers, etc. The actual administration of these funds is handled by the local municipality. The committee of the Ladino fund is composed almost exclusively of people of the *primera*, as are most of the main posts in the municipality.

The Ladino fund in Marcala was started some 70 years ago, and continued with various ups and downs during the following years.[41] The impulse to continue high school education, however, and to maintain the fund consistently came from the upper class. A similar support for a secondary school was reported from Olanchito, but there the system was evidently run along more conventional lines, with tuition being paid for the support of the school.

The two major classes tend to be endogamous, as do the two major ethnic groups of Ladinos and Indians. Intermarriage is uncommon, and when it occurs, usually one of the members has come from another community and his antecedents are not too clear. The local upper class tends to be quite endogamous, however, and in some places, such as Nueva Ocotepeque, this has produced a class of people within which there has been a good deal of intermarriage.

6. LOCAL POLITICAL ORGANIZATION

The territorial demarcation of Honduras in 1951 involved a division of the country into 17 departments. These 17 departments were in turn subdivided into either *municipios* or districts. The writer has been unable to ascertain any consistent reason for this alternative system of districts and *municipios*, although their differential role on the local and national scene are obvious. At the time of the listing of political units in 1936,[42] the system was different. At that time, each department was divided into between two and six districts; in turn, each of these districts was divided into sub-units, the *municipios*. Basically, the 1936 system was the same as that which still functions today in El

---

[41] Bonilla, 1931.   [42] Census, 1936.

Salvador. By 1951,[43] however, this straight pyramidal system had changed so that a given district no longer included in its jurisdiction a number of *municipios*. Rather, certain territorial units were called districts and others were called *municipios*. The changes between 1936 and 1951 involved a marked reduction in the number of units referred to as districts, and a lesser reduction of the number of *municipios*:

	1936	1951
Number of Districts	68	31
Number of *Municipios*	273	245

Furthermore, according to the Organic Law of Districts published in 1948, the districts were classified into three types:

(1) Departmental Districts: those territorial units in which the principal town was a departmental capital. In 1951 there were nine departmental districts and the Central District (the national capital). Seven of the towns which were departmental capitals were not district headquarters, but municipal headquarters. (The departments with no departmental district were: Bay Islands, Yoro, El Paraíso, Valle, Intibucá, Lempira, Ocotepeque).

(2) Sectional Districts: those territorial units which were important as ports. In 1951 there were five Sectional Districts: Amapala, Danlí, Choloma, Puerto Cortés, and Tela. However, there is some inconsistency in this matter because the area of San Marcos de Colón and San Lorenzo are not rated as sectional districts but as local districts; and Guascorán and Nueva Ocotepeque, the road exits to El Salvador, are rated merely as *municipios*, and not as districts at all.

(3) Local Districts: all other territorial units which, because of their commercial importance, are considered too important to be left in the status of *municipio* and have consequently been given the rank of district. In some cases the only explanation to be found for the fact that some territorial units are considered as local districts and not as *municipios* seems to be that they are survivals of the previous period when they were districts with jurisdiction over neighboring *municipios*, and that for some reason they have not been reclassified yet as *municipios*. Thus, it is possible to understand the commercial importance of Olanchito, El Progreso, or Siguatepeque, but it is difficult to rationalize Naranjitos, San Nicolás, or Reitoca as being so important. The distinction between districts and *municipios* is not made on the basis of population size. The departmental districts and districts based on commercial importance seem to make the most sense, even though it cannot be said that the selection has been made consistently. The greatest concentration of districts is in the Ulúa River Valley and certain adjacent regions and tributaries, and in the Department of Francisco Morazán. In the former area there are a total of eleven districts, and in the latter, six. Thus, over half of all the districts in the country are to be found in these two areas. The regions in which there are few or no districts are the south-

---
[43] Census, 1951.

western highlands (the departments of Ocotepeque, Lempira, and Intibucá have none, and Copán and La Paz only one each), the north central highlands (there are none in northern Comayagua and in central Yoro), and in the northeast (Juticalpa is the only district in Olancho, and Trujillo and Sonaguera are the only ones in Colón).

There is a tremendous difference between the forms of administration in these two types of subdepartmental units. Basically, the *municipio* is administered by elected local officials; the district is administered by officials who are appointed by the national president. The differences in these local administrations will be treated first, and then the elements common to both.

The officers of a district are appointed directly from the national capital by the office of the chief executive of the country. These officers are: *jefe de consejo*, two *vocales*, a *fiscal*, and a treasurer. The actual government of the district is in the hands of this *consejo*. Unlike the municipal system, in which there are a varying number of *regidores*, the number of *vocales* does not vary; it is fixed by law at two. The *jefe de consejo*, as the title indicates, is chief of the council and of the district. The two *vocales* are his advisors, and the *fiscal* is the district attorney and legal representative of the district. The actual exercise of government is carried out through various employees named by the council.

In the survey, two communities which were district capitals were visited, Quimistán and Olanchito. Of the two, the Olanchito district structure was by far the more complicated of the two. In the *Gobernación*, i.e., the office of the *consejo*, there were a secretary, three recorders, a typist, an archivist, a secretary for the police, a sergeant of police and five *agentes de policía*, a chauffeur, and a janitor. Also under the control of the *consejo* were the employees of the branch of welfare, hygiene, and health: a cemetery guard, a slaughterhouse guard, a man responsible for issuing licenses for slaughtering animals, a man employed to oversee the slaughtering, a man responsible for the condition of the market (of which the slaughterhouse was part), and two men to collect garbage. The activities in "development and public works" included the electrician who was in charge of the electric plant, an assistant and an apprentice, an inspector of light and water, an assistant, a person in charge of collecting the taxes on light and water, and a gardener in charge of the park. In general charge of funds, besides the centrally appointed treasurer, were an assistant treasurer, a bookkeeper, a tax collector for the town, and a fee collector for the garbage disposal service. In addition to all these people were the various persons connected with the educational system, an inspector, school directors, urban teachers, and rural teachers.

It was explained to the writer by one of the members of the *consejo* that the reason that districts, rather than *municipios*, were set up was that certain areas were much more productive and consequently provided more income for the nation in terms of taxes on exported products. The handling of such funds could not be entrusted to elected municipal officials; it was necessary for the central government to have direct control over the situation. It is true that the annual district budget for Olanchito was considerably above that which one would find in the great majority of the *municipios* of the country. For 1954–55 it was over $84,000. The greater portion of this budget was derived from the local district tax imposed on the export of bananas; since Olanchito was the inland center for the Standard Fruit Company operations, the town stood to gain tremendously from this export. In view of handling this kind of money, the explanation continued, it was impossible to entrust local government to elected officials who spent a good four months out of every year in electioneering.

The district political structure in Quimistán was considerably simpler than that in Olanchito. Instead of the extensive series of posts found in the latter place, there were simply the members of the *consejo*, a secretary and his scribe, a treasurer and his recorder, and a man who acted in the dual capacity of tax collector and local policeman. Off hand, there seemed to be little reason why Quimistán should be classed as a district rather than a *municipio*.

In *municipios*, instead of the basic *consejo*, there exists what is called the *municipales* or group of elected municipal officers. This group includes an *alcalde*, between 2 and 7 *regidores*, and a *síndico*. The *alcalde*, or mayor, corresponds to the *jefe de consejo*; the *regidores*, or aldermen, correspond to the *vocales*, and the *síndico* corresponds to the *fiscal*. The responsibilities of the municipal *alcalde* and *síndico* are practically parallel to those of the district *jefe de consejo* and *fiscal*. The function of the municipal *regidores*, however, varies somewhat from that of the district *vocales*. The *regidores* in a municipal organization usually act in the capacity of chief of police. In all the *municipios* visited, only one *regidor* was on duty at a time. The usual practice was for the incumbents to take turns of a month each. Thus, if there were 2 *regidores*, they would serve alternate months; if there were six, they would each serve only two months out of the year. In some cases, the turns were set at 15 days each. In Nueva Ocotepeque, where there were 7 *regidores*, a man would serve 15 days, and then be free for three months.

While the officials of the district *consejo* were full time government employees and received a salary, most municipal officers receive no salary. In addition to these elected officers of the *municipio*, there is regularly also a group known as the *consejeros* who are named by the *alcalde*. These *consejeros* (there are usually four of them) act in one or both of two capacities. They usually act as substitutes for *regidores* should one of the latter be ill or unavoidably absent from his duty or from a council meeting; and in some few cases they act as extra members of the elected town council in the deliberation on local matters. This second function is evidently fairly rare. The choice of the *consejeros* is up to the *alcalde*, and as often as not, *suplentes*, alternates, are named for each *consejero*.

The number of employees that any particular municipality has, of course, varies with the demands made on the office and on the wealth of the *municipio*. To be found in almost all municipal offices, however, are a secretary, at least one scribe, and very often a *conserje*, or janitor. In addition to these, there is usually one person employed as *policía municipal*. In some towns this man also carries the functions of runner and tax collector for the municipality, while in others these tasks are given to distinct persons. The *policía municipal* is under the direction of the incumbent *regidor*. Among the other employees which a *municipalidad* might have, are: treasurer, *fiel de rastro* (responsible for the slaughterhouse; this post in some places is also held by the *policía municipal*), someone responsible for keeping the statistics, someone responsible for registering people and issuing the *cédula* (national identification card), someone in charge of keeping the streets clean and disposing of garbage, and in Yoro, someone responsible for the municipal tower clock.

The officials and employees in the district and municipal capital are different. Functionally, the district officials are acting completely in the capacity of representatives of the national government, and annually, the *jefe de consejo* must submit a fairly full report to the president concerning the activities of the district, specifically concerning financial matters. The *alcaldes*, however, are not directly responsible to the president. In the first place, they are elected by the local population and not named by the president. And in the second place, as representatives of the national government, they are responsible directly to the governors of their respective departments, and indirectly to the national government. This means, of course, that local autonomy is greater in the *municipios* than in the districts. However, as elsewhere in Central America, this does not mean that there is extensive local autonomy in the *municipios*. Even though the local *alcaldes*, *regidores*, and *síndicos* are elected, they are nevertheless responsible to the departmental governor, and they act in the capacity of the national government's principal local official.

Below the district and municipal organizations are the rural officials. The general system functioning all over the country, in both *municipios* and districts, involves the naming of an *alcalde auxiliar* in each *aldea* and in the principal *caseríos*. The distinction between *aldeas* and *caseríos* is not clear to the writer. *Aldeas* are ordinarily larger, i.e., they have larger populations, and in some cases (such as La Misión, Zambrano, and Corozal) are distinctive towns. *Caseríos* are generally smaller and often highly dispersed homes in a rural area. However, while *aldeas* almost always have one or two *auxiliares* (usually with *suplentes*, or substitutes, named), many *caseríos* also have the same officials. Some *aldeas* have regular *cabildos*, buildings for the auxiliary officers to work in. La Misión has such a building. Others, as is the case in Zambrano and Corozal, have no *cabildo*. In some *aldeas*, there may be more than one or two *auxiliares*. Zambrano has five such men and they serve turns of a week each. In La Misión, however, a larger community than Zambrano, there is only one *alcalde auxiliar* and a *suplente*. The main function of the *alcaldes auxiliares* is to keep public order locally and to carry out orders of the *alcalde* of the *municipio* or of the *jefe de consejo* if it is a district organization.

Many of the towns visited on the survey had *auxiliares* appointed from the town as well as from the rural areas. These were usually referred to as *auxiliares de barrio*, since in most cases one was named from each of the town *barrios*. Such was the case in Güinope, Jacaleapa, Dulce Nombre de Copán, Yoro, Catacamas, and in the outlying *barrios* of Olanchito. In Ilama, two *auxiliares* were named from each of the two *barrios*. In Guaimaca, however, there were no *barrios* recognized in the town and four *auxiliares* and three *suplentes* were named annually from the general population. In La Esperanza six were named from the general town population. In Marcala a slightly different *auxiliar* situation exists. There, two *varaltas* and six *auxiliares* are named from the general town population; one *varalta* then acts as chief of three *auxiliares*, and the two teams take turns working in the *cabildo* for two-week periods. The situation also varied considerably in Intibucá. There, most of the Indian population lives in the outlying rural *aldeas* and *caseríos* of which there are 20. In each of these, two *auxiliares* are named. From each rural unit, then, one of the *auxiliares* stays in the *caserío* and the other serves in town. Thus the municipal *cabildo* theoretically has the services of 20 *auxiliares* at all times, and each *caserío* also has a resident *auxiliar*. The two *auxiliares* take turns serving in their own *caserío* and in the town *cabildo*. The Intibucá case is the only one which the writer encountered in Honduras in which the rural *auxiliares* come into town to serve.

Besides the municipal and district officials, almost all municipal and district capitals have a judiciary official, the *juez de paz*. In most places there is a single *juez de paz* to handle both civil and criminal proceedings, but in some there are separate judges for each. These justices are named by the Supreme Court of Justice of the country. In certain centers around the country are the higher courts in which sit the *juez de letras* (corresponding to the *juez de primera instancia* in other countries). Although the writer was told in some places that the criterion used for classifying a given territory as a district or a *municipio* was related to the presence or absence of the *juez de letras*, there is little evidence to support the idea.

There are also scattered over the country military commandant posts. Usually an officer and a few soldiers are stationed at such a post. The actual local control exercised in Zambrano is done from a post in which there is a *jefe de resguardo* and ten policemen serving in a permanent station. The *alcaldes auxiliares* in Zambrano are, for practical purposes, subordinate to these police officers. Elsewhere, where regular commandant posts are established, there will also be *subcomandantes* named in the more important *aldeas* and *caseríos*.

The maintenance of a local municipal government, with one exception, is dependent financially on taxes gathered in the *municipio*. The exception is the upkeep of the school, which is usually aided by a subsidy from the national government. In general, however, taxes collected locally provide the basis upon which municipal work is done. Taxes are of various types. Those on stores, fiestas, etc., are fairly standard throughout the country. In those communities where there is a significant local production for export, such as bananas in Olanchito, and tobacco in Copán, the local government places an export tax on the produce leaving the *municipio*. Where the tax situation is effective, taxes may also be placed on imported goods. Two taxes which are standard, and which the *municipio* or district shares with the national government, are the *vialidad*, or road tax, and the school tax. The *vialidad* amounts to an annual payment, usually of a Lempira or more per person, which may be paid or which may be taken out in two days of road work. In Olanchito, it was said that only 25% of the *vialidad* receipts remained in the district; the rest was sent to Tegucigalpa. Since so much of the *vialidad* is sent to the national government, there is seldom enough left locally to pay for all necessary local road repair. As a result, it was reported in almost all the towns visited that everyone is expected to do work on the roads locally. One of the functions of the rural *alcaldes auxiliares* is to call up the man when the time comes to repair one of the *caserío* roads. Similarly, a charge is usually made for the use of a burial plot in the cemetery, but actually very little money accrues from this and the residents are usually called upon either once or twice a year (one time usually being just prior to the Day of All Saints in November) to clean the cemetery.

The municipal and district governments seem generally to be in the hands of the members of the local middle and upper classes where such exist. In some places, such as Guaimaca, there is really no group of residents of great wealth, the *alcalde* appears in general to come from the same economic group as do the majority of the townspeople, but in such communities as Quimistán, Nacaome, Marcala, Yoro, and Catacamas, there is little doubt but that the local officialdom is selected from the local upper class. In those communities where there is a significant Indian population, this varies. In Intibucá, where the population for practical purposes is entirely Indian, the entire municipal body is also Indian. In Ilama, however, where there are both resident Ladinos and Indians, the pattern has evidently developed for the *alcalde, síndico*, and two of the *regidores* to be Ladino, and the other two *regidores* to be Indian. All the *auxiliares de barrio* are Indian, but the rural *auxiliares* may be either, depending upon which group is more prominent in a given *aldea* or *caserío*.

The school system in Honduras, while under the Ministry of Education, is dependent upon the local school tax which is levied locally. In La Venta this tax was reported as being L.3.00 per year per person. The receipts from this tax, however, go principally to the national government. As a result, if a local community wishes to either improve their own school, or to have additional or secondary schools, they must raise much of the money locally. We described earlier the method by which this has been done in Marcala. In Olanchito a secondary school is supported largely by local funds together with the aid of a subsidy from the government. In the Department of Olancho, there is a departmental school tax which is used to support the secondary school in the departmental capital of Juticalpa.

The selection and assignment of teachers in the primary schools is, however, a function of the Ministry of Education and not of the local communities. This has brought about an unfortunate situation among some of the English speaking communities of the Bay Islands where it has long been a tradition to provide the children with a full six-year primary education in schools heretofore run by the islanders. In the past two or three years the Ministry of Education has refused to allow the islanders to hire their own teachers, and assigned to the islands regular primary teachers. In some places, such as on the Utila Cays, this has meant that the school has been reduced from a four or six year school to a one or two year school because the ministry cannot afford to send enough teachers and refuses to allow the islanders to hire any extra. The situation has been aggravated by the fact that some of the Ladino teachers sent over from the mainland have had personal problems and often failed to fulfill the minimal teaching role assigned to them.

In general, local government in Honduras, while deviating in particulars, follows the same general pattern of territorial and administrative hierarchy as is found elsewhere in Central America. Local autonomy is at a minimum, and in most cases not encouraged. The peculiar situation exists in the *municipio*-district division where a *municipio* that may develop economically to the point where it is financially productive is threatened with total loss of what autonomy exists. It might be changed from a *municipio* with elected local officials to a district with appointed local officials. The tendency to discourage local initiative is also to be seen in the handling of the Bay Islands school situation, where more extensive education offered by the islanders themselves is refused in favor of inferior education provided by the government. The political territorial division also causes some peculiar situations. The central district, for example, that in which the national capital is located, is extremely large and includes many rural communities. Some of these, as is the case with Zambrano, lie at a considerable distance from the national capital and yet all the people in the community must go all the way to Tegucigalpa to pay their taxes.

7. RELIGIOUS ACTIVITIES

The population of Honduras is predominantly Catholic. There are a number of small Protestant missions and many communities, possibly most, have one or a few families of one or another of the evangelizing Protestant sects. The only area which is predominantly Protestant is the Bay Islands in which almost the entire English speaking population is of that religion. Characteristics of this group will be taken up in Section V. Of the mainland communities visited, only five (including the Black Carib community of Corozal) reported that no Protestants were present (Zambrano, La Libertad, San Francisco de Yojoa, and Ilama), while of the remaining, seven had Protestant *capillas*, i.e., church buildings. In most communities, the number of Protestants were estimated at between 2 and 30 families. Dulce Nombre de Copán evidently had the largest number: there informants estimated that 25 to 30 % of the total town population were Protestant. In the present survey, we will not concern ourselves further with the Protestant population, except in the later discussion of the Bay Island group.

The Catholic religion begins playing a role in the life of the Honduran with baptism. Baptism, so far as the survey data indicate, is a standard practice everywhere in the country. In those towns in which there is no priest, it is sometimes the custom to wait until he comes for a fiesta and then to have all the children born since the last fiesta baptized on that occasion. Such is the case in Zambrano, Güinope, La Misión, and Ilama. In some of these communities the priest comes only once a year and so all baptisms must be saved up until that time. In all but three mainland communities (Zambrano, La Libertad, Yoro) it is customary to have a family fiesta following the baptism.

Marriage, too, is usually followed by a fiesta and is often done at the time of the priest's visit during the local fiesta. As a result, in those communities where marriages are held during the titular fiesta, the families frequently make no effort to have a special celebration, since the whole community is involved in celebrating anyway. In most communities, however, it is customary to have a party for the couple and guests in the home of one of the parents. In six of the towns (Nacaome, Yusguare, Güinope, Dulce Nombre de Copán, Marcala, and Corozal) it was said to be the custom to hold this in the house of the bride's parents; in three others (Jacaleapa, Nueva Ocotepeque, Intibucá) the house of the groom's parents was said to be preferred. Elsewhere, it was said to be of little traditional importance which house was used, the decision usually being made on the basis of which family was the wealthier, which had the greater prestige, and which house was more comodious for a party. In La Esperanza it was said that parties were held in the homes of both parents simultaneously. In some places it is evidently the custom to have the party in a rented *salón* since the homes are sometimes too cramped for such an event. In Olanchito it was reported that the growing custom in the middle and upper classes is to have some soft drinks in the home of the bride's parents, and then move on to a *salón* for a dance; in La Venta, a rented house may be used for the whole affair.

While the baptism ceremonies are brief, and marriage a matter of taste, the ceremonies following death are regarded as an absolutely necessary obligation. Immediately following death it is customary to initiate the novena, nine nights of prayer usually held before the saint in the home. In all but seven towns, additional novenas are held some time during the subsequent months, and usually also at the end of the year. In six towns (Nueva Ocotepeque, Quimistán, Dulce Nombre de Copán, Ilama, Marcala, and Corozal) only the novenas at death and on the anniversay are held. In San Francisco de Yojoa only one, at the time of death, is held. In many towns poverty will prevent some from holding further novenas, but this is evidently a variation from the standard practice. In all towns it is the practice to hold a second novena six months after the death. In Güinope, various novenas are held, one at death, one at six months, one at a year and on each anniversary for nine years. In Zambrano it was said that the ideal custom was to hold novenas at death, three months, and six months, but that due to the cost very few people followed the pattern. In two towns, Quimistán and Catacamas, it was said that following the locally prescribed novenas, it was customary to hold a single night of prayer on each subsequent anniversary. Two southern towns, La Venta and Nacaome, have the practice of holding a novena at 40 days after the death; in La Venta this is followed by another at six months, and in Nacaome by another at a year. There are other variations on these patterns, such as in Yusguare where on the final night of the first novena the prayer goes on through the entire night, or in La Venta and Nacaome where a second novena is held 40 days after the death.

Participation in novenas is generally a woman's role, but there are some variations on this pattern. In the three southern towns, Nacaome, Yusguare, and La Venta, it was said that men participate actively in the novenas, and that in all three cases some men actually led them. In Nacaome, it was said that in town only women led novenas, but that in the countryside some men did also. As will be noted, this varies from the usual Ladino pattern in which women lead novenas and in many cases are the only participants. It may well be that male participation in this region is indicative of a recent change from Indian to Ladino, and the retention is a survival of the Indian custom.

The other principal variation on the usual Ladino pattern is to be found in the Indian populations. In La Esperanza, for example, a Ladino town, and among the Ladinos of Ilama, women are the leaders and the principal participants in novenas. In Intibucá and among the Indians of Ilama, however, the men are the main leaders, and both sexes participate. The transition may be seen in Marcala and Intibucá. In the former community, the Indians of the surrounding area have both men and women leaders, and in Intibucá, women are just beginning to act in this capacity. In Ladino communities the degree to which men participate in the praying seems to be principally a matter of local tradition. In some communities they do, in others they do not. The writer could not detect that there was any particularly consistent relation between social class and male participation in these activities.

The novena is usually a social event in the local community. Guests, usually those who are counted among the closest friends, are invited, sometimes to each night of praying, but usually to the final night. Minor refreshments, often little more than coffee, will be served. In some few communities a Mass will be held in the church on the final night, or on the anniversary, but this is an expensive affair, usually depends upon the presence of a resident priest, and is consequently limited to the wealthier people in parochial centers.

The customs of having music, dancing, or a home fiesta upon the death of a child is tending to disappear in Honduras as in the other Central American countries, but it is still practised to some degree in most communities. Only seven communities (Quimistán, Ilama, La Esperanza, Güinope, Zambrano, Guaimaca, and Catacamas) reported that there was no survival at all of the practice. In Yusguare, La Libertad, and Yoro, it was said to be fairly rare although still to be found. In seven towns (Dulce Nombre de Copán, San Francisco de Yojoa, La Libertad, La Misión, La Venta, Jacaleapa, and Olanchito), it was said to consist principally of refreshments and music, that dancing was not part of the event. In Yoro, Nueva Ocotepeque, Guarita, Intibucá and Texiguat (all except the last two restricted to the poorer elements of the rural population) dancing was said to be a part of the celebration. The only two places where dancing was reported to be a standard and regular part of the fiesta was among Intibucá and Texiguat Indians. Both these communities are Indian, although the latter is considerably ladinoized. While the use of music and/or dancing at a funeral observance has been prohibited in some towns, the disappearance of this custom is evidently not due merely to such formal prohibitions. In Yusguare, for example, it has not been prohibited, but it was reported that the people have been losing interest in it. In Olanchito, where the local custom consists principally of having music on the way to the cemetery, the informant noted that many of the people who have come into the region from other parts (this is a banana plantation center) still practise the custom of the full fiesta.

Besides the religious and auxiliary ceremonies related to the life cycle, the Honduran home is frequently the scene of religious prayer to the saint of the house. As in most other Central American homes, there is usually an image or picture of a saint in each house. The surroundings for this imagery may simply be a table or wooden crate, or in more wealthy homes, be a fairly elaborate home altar. The attention accorded to the family saint varies from community to community and as among families in any given community. In some places it was reported that it was customary to hold a regular novena for the nine nights prior to the annual day of the saint (Nacaome, Guaimaca, Marcala, San Francisco, Catacamas); in others, a single night of prayer, a *rosario* or *velorio*, is held, and in yet others, whether a single night or a novena is held depends upon the wealth and preferences of the particular family. Where a full novena is held, it is often the custom to invite friends in on the final night for a small fiesta; in these cases, music may be included and coffee served. They do not ordinarily turn into wild parties as the occasion is a serious one, and they are most commonly observed by the women. The men participate probably less than they would in novenas held for the dead. In some towns it was reported that certain saints are favored. In Yoro and Marcala, for example, it was said that San Antonio was the favorite saint; in Ilama, both Esquipulas and San Antonio were favored.

The pattern of making pilgrimages to shrines is common over most of the interior of Honduras. The two shrines of greatest importance are Esquipulas, just across the border in Guatemala, and the shrine of Suyape, outside of Tegucigalpa. Pilgrimages to Esquipulas are an old pattern in Honduras, and all towns in the central and western highlands reported that local people made annual trips there. Interest in the Suyape shrine is newer, and a number of towns reported that it has only been in recent years that people have started to go there. Of the towns visited on the survey, those in the south central highlands, and the corridor through to the Atlantic evidently have people who make the trip. Towns in the north highlands, specifically Yoro and Olanchito, and those in the far west (Nueva Ocotepeque, Dulce Nombre de Copán) together with others which were physically nearer (La Esperanza and Ilama) said that no pilgrimages were made to Suyape. While Esquipulas and Suyape were said to be visited by 15 and 14 towns, respectively, there were also a number of secondary or regional pilgrimage centers. Taulabé (San Gaspar) is an important shrine for the Indians of the southwest highlands.[44] People from Marcala, Inti-

---

[44] Stone, 1948, p. 215 records that "Many of these Highland Indians make a yearly pil-

bucá, and La Esperanza were said to go there with regularity. Ilama, which itself sends people on pilgrimages to Esquipulas and other nearby centers, also houses the shrine of the *Virgen de Lourdes*. The town of Tomalá receives visitors to the shrine of the *Virgen de los Remedios* not only from towns in western Honduras, but also the informant in Guacotectí in El Salvador said that local people made the pilgrimage. The *aldea* of Quezailica of Santa Rosa de Copán is the locale of another Esquipulas shrine to which people from as far as Quimistán go. Perhaps the most important regional shrine is that of Moroceli in the Department of El Paraíso. Towns in all the neighboring departments reported that local people visited the *Señor de las Aguas* there.

Besides these shrines of regional importance, there are numerous others which are also visited by people of a given region, but are usually little visited by people outside the immediate region. Among these are the towns of Santa María (in La Paz), Esquías (Comayagua), Liure (El Paraíso), Dulce Nombre de Culmí (Olancho), Sonaguera (Colón), Yojoa (Cortés), and Yoro. Besides Esquipulas in Guatemala, a number of other foreign shrines are visited by people of communities which are near the borders. Sonsonate and Citala (in El Salvador) were visited by people of Nueva Ocotepeque; El Viejo (in Nicaragua) by people of Nacaome, and El Sauce (in Nicaragua) by people of Yusguare.

The pilgrimage pattern is essentially a Ladino and Indian pattern. It is not followed, naturally enough, by the Protestants of the Bay Island, but also it was reported in Corozal that the Black Caribs did not make such visits. While the writer is not familiar enough with the pilgrimage customs to know the motives behind all such visits, in some places they are made to comply with promises made to make the pilgrimage if a particular prayer is answered.

The pilgrimage patterns should not be confused with another custom, the *guancasco*, wherein saints of neighboring towns visit each other on their respective fiesta days. This custom, first described by Stone,[45] is taken up again in a later section of the present paper which deals with the Indian population and its customs. It should be noted here, however, that in neighboring Guatemala a parallel custom is shared between Ladino and Indian communities.[46] The visiting of saints, of course, involves a parallel visiting of the peoples of the towns. This does not, however, constitute a pilgrimage in the same sense as it is being discussed here.

Perhaps the most important single religious activity in any Central American community is the town fiesta. As is customary elsewhere, every Catholic Honduran town has a patron saint which is celebrated with an annual fiesta on the day of the saint. The general rule is that each town has but one such saint, but quite a few towns either recognize two patrons or celebrate a major fiesta in addition to that of their patron. The titular fiesta of a town is usually the

---

grimage on April 24, the day of San Gaspar, the patron of Taubelve in the relatively low hills south of Lake Yojoa." The present writer has not heard the use of the name "Taubelve," but assumes that the reference is to "Taulabé," the name used in the town itself and so recorded on the maps and in Bonilla, 1952.

[45] Stone, Ms. [46] Gillin, 1951, pp. 97–104.

principal annual fiesta, and except for Holy Week, Todos Santos, and Christmas, may be the only fiesta in the year. The sponsorship of this fiesta, then, generally involves the most complicated religious organization in the town.

In the towns visited by the writer in the survey, the form of sponsorship was similar in almost all interior towns, but there were no two towns quite alike. We can analyze the various forms of religious organization in terms of two criteria: under whose or what authority is the organization established; and is the activity of the organization basically carried on by a coordinated group or by separate individuals. On the basis of these two criteria, the towns present an apparently random distribution. In terms of the authority under which the organization is established, there are four principal forms and combinations of these. A fiesta can be organized by people appointed by the municipal or a submunicipal (e.g., *aldea*) authority, by the priest, by a town meeting, or by a permanent religious society; it may also be organized through a combination of any two of the first three forms. The people who actually do the work of collecting money for the fiesta may be organized into a group (i.e., a committee, a commission, or a *gremio*), or they may operate as individuals (i.e., *mayordomos*, *comisionados*); or the fiesta may be financed and organized by both a group of some kind and by other individuals who carry on specific tasks which, in the course of their operation, are not coordinated with the work of the group.

Taking these up in the order of the authority upon which the sponsorship is based, there are five towns in which sponsorship depends entirely upon the authority of the *municipalidad*. In San Francisco de Yojoa and La Libertad the *alcalde* or *municipalidad* names annually a group (*comisión* in San Francisco, *gremio* in La Libertad) of men who take the responsibility of collecting funds for the fiesta and for making the arrangements, such as contracting with the priest, buying fireworks, etc. In La Libertad there are four such groups named, two from the town proper and two from the rural sections. Each of these *gremios* is composed of about seven members, a president, vice-president, secretary, treasurer, and three *vocales* or members. Each of the four *gremios* takes the responsibility for one day of the fiesta; this includes having the proper religious observances and recreational elements (discussed below). On the day following the fiesta, each *gremio* presents an account to the *alcalde* in which the amount of money collected and the expenditures are stated. If there is any money left over, it is either given to the church or held in hand for the next year's fiesta. In San Francisco there are usually two major fiestas. For each of these, the *municipalidad* names a *comisión* of eight people, four of which are from the town and each of four of which are named from one of the principal *aldeas*. Each group of eight names one of their members as treasurer, and the group as a whole undertakes to collect funds for the fiesta and to make the necessary arrangements and contracts. In the year prior to the survey neither of the fiestas were held, however, because the entire town was so occupied in political activities that there was not enough interest to undertake the effort necessary to arrange for the fiesta.

In the *aldea* of Zambrano there is no municipal organization, only the *alcaldes auxiliares* named from Tegucigalpa. These *auxiliares* take the responsibility each year for collecting the funds for their annual fiesta of *Concepción*. This is the only community fiesta of the year, and there is no recreational side to it, so the entire activity of preparation involves simply collecting sufficient funds and contracting the priest.

The town of Dulce Nombre de Copán is essentially dependent upon the municipal sponsorship for the two main fiestas celebrated, but they combine an older *mayordomía* system with the committee system. As will be noted in various other towns, there is a division of labor in Dulce Nombre between those activities involved in the religious aspects of the celebration and those for the recreational aspects. For both the main fiestas the *municipalidad* names a *Comité de Festejo* which is responsible for the diversions during the celebration. This committee collects funds from the people of the town and the *aldeas*. For the Masses and processions, however, there is an entirely distinct system. There exist in Dulce Nombre four *mayordomías* composed of a *mayordomo* (man), *mayordoma* (woman), and a helper for each. Each of these four *mayordomías* is responsible for the celebration of a specific fiesta (distinct from the two major town fiestas) which is entirely religious (San Francisco, San José, Santa Lucía, and San Antonio). For the two major town fiestas, however, they have the additional responsibility of collecting funds for the Masses and processions. For this they must obtain permission from the *municipalidad*, and then go through the *municipio* collecting money. Upon the termination of their collections, they must report to the *municipalidad* how much they have taken up and are turning over to the church. These *mayordomos* retain their positions indefinitely, but unfortunately it was not ascertained how they were selected. However, the performance of their task was clearly dependent upon the approval of the *municipalidad*.

There were also four towns in which the principal authority behind the sponsorship of a fiesta is the priest. There was no case in which the entire organization of the activities was left only up to a single group. In one town, La Esperanza, it evidently fell entirely on the shoulders of individuals, while in three others it was shared between groups and individuals. La Esperanza stands in a rather unusual situation in that it is immediately adjacent to the Indian town of Intibucá in which a number of intensive religious fiestas are celebrated. The Ladino population which occupies La Esperanza has evidently concluded that there is enough religious celebration on the diversion level, and restricts its activities to more religious activities. There are two big fiestas in La Esperanza, *Concepción*, the patron saint, and *Nuestra Señora de la Esperanza*. Each runs for a given period, and the two are consecutive: *Concepción* runs from 8 to 17 December, and *Nuestra Señora* from 18 to 25 December. Prior to this period of two and a half weeks, the priest either requests or accepts as volunteers two to four families to celebrate one night of the fiesta. Thus on each night from the 8th to the 25th, a family fiesta is held in some few houses of the town. At these family sponsored gatherings guests are invited, and the entire evening is devoted to prayer. So far as I could discover, there exists hardly any organization specifically set up for the fiestas aside from an arrangement of families to take care of the various nights.

Three towns have a combined group and individual organization under the priest's authority for fiesta sponsorship. In Ilama, the priest named a semipermanent group known as the *Consejo de Fábrica* which was in charge of collecting and opportioning funds for the fiesta. This *consejo* was composed as follows at the time of the survey: president: the priest; vice-president: an Indian; treasurer: a "white"; secretary: an Indian; 2 *vocales*: both "white".

While the term *"fábrica"* evidently stems from an Indian usage[47] this organization in Ilama is composed of both Indians and non-Indian with reportedly no distinction being made in membership. To accompany the saint on money collecting trips (discussed below), a single *mayordomo* is appointed. In Jacaleapa, the priest named a *mayordomo* annually to collect money for the two major fiestas, and a directive council to arrange for the diversions. In Olanchito, the priests named various people annually to take care of the various religious fiestas, and for the additional fiesta of *Corpus Cristi*, a group was named which was responsible for setting up altars at the four corners of the plaza at which the procession stopped in its course.

Six towns combined appointment by the priest with that by municipal order to sponsor fiestas. In Yusguare, two separate commissions were named. One, named by the *alcalde*, was responsible for going to the *aldeas* and collecting money for the lay phase of the fiesta, and the other, named by the priest, was responsible for the same task, but to collect funds for the religious part. Basically, the same pattern existed in Nacaome, but the writer could not determine whether the commissions named there were organized in themselves, or merely consisted of separate individuals named by each of the authorities. In Catacamas the municipality named a *gremio* of men in each *aldea* as well as one among the businessmen of the town, each to be responsible for one entire day of the fiesta. In addition to this, the priest named separate groups of women who collected funds which were then distributed between the religious and laical aspects of the celebration. The chief of each of the men's *gremios* was called a *mayordomo*. In Yoro a similar system existed, but combined the committee system with the *gremio* system. There the *alcalde* named a committee (president, vice-president, secretary, treasurer, and 20 or more *vocales*) which had the responsibility of collecting funds from the townspeople and for soliciting funds from natives of the town resident in the national capital or elsewhere. The funds so gathered were split between religious and lay needs. Besides the committee, however, the priest named a *mayordomo* and a *mayordoma* to be responsible for each of the *aldeas*. Theoretically, the entire population of any specific *aldea* comprised a *gremio*, all residents were *mayordomos*, and the two named were the *mayordomos primeros*, or chief *mayordomos*. In practise this meant that the *mayordomos pri-*

---

[47] In La Campa and Gracias, Department of Lempira, the *Consejo de Fábrica* is that group of Indian officials that is responsible for guarding the sacred equipment which is used in the church and religious aspects of the fiestas.

meros were the only ones who did any work in the matter of collecting funds, and the other *"mayordomos"* were just contributors. The contributions from the *aldeas* were given entirely to help defray religious expenses. The departmental capital of Nueva Ocotepeque also divides the titular fiesta sponsorship between the local municipal government and the priest. There the *alcalde* named a *Comité de Festejos* to handle the entertainment, and the priest named three *mayordomos* to accompany the saints on trips through the *municipio* collecting money for the religious expenses. For another fiesta, *Concepción*, the *alcalde* and priest each named committees to handle the preparations.

Besides the municipal and clerical sponsorship of fiestas, there is a third form which was reported from three communities: the town meeting. In Quimistán, which is a district and hence has no elected government, a meeting of the townspeople is called annually two months before the titular fiesta. In this meeting a committee (president, vice-president, *fiscal*, treasurer, and 10 to 20 *vocales*) is named which forms various sub-commissions to collect money in the *aldeas* and in neighboring *municipios*. In the *aldea* of La Misión the same sort of community meeting is held, and the residents are formally asked by the *alcalde auxiliar* whether they wish to hold a fiesta, and when the usual affirmative response is given, he names, with their approval, a treasurer, a *comisionado* from each of the neighboring *caseríos* to collect funds, and two or three other *comisionados* to make arrangements for the fiesta, and the money is handed over to the treasurer who, in turn, pays the expenses contracted by the second set of *comisionados*. In Marcala the municipal authorities call a town meeting and name a committee to arrange the fiesta. However, there the priest also names a separate committee to collect funds for the religious portions.

Besides these types of sponsorship, certain cases of sponsorship by *mayordomías* or sodalities were found in the course of the survey. In Güinope there exists a permanent group of *mayordomos* who make the annual selection of persons to compose the *Consejo de Festejos*. While the *mayordomos* are men, the *consejo* was said to be composed of both men and women. The *mayordomos* themselves each come from one of the six *barrios* of the town and each *barrio*, together with the women's sodality of the *Corazón de Jesús*, are responsible for certain days of the fiesta. The 1st and 2nd days are the responsibility of the barrio del Centro; the 3rd and 4th, the barrios of La Cruz and Arriba; the 5th and 6th, the barrios of Ocotal and Abajo; and the 7th is the responsibility of the sodality. The community of La Venta is also dependent upon sponsorship by *mayordomos*. There are two, one each for two of the major fiestas, and the two together handle the third major fiesta. In each case, the responsible *mayordomo* names three or four helpers who aid him in collecting funds and arranging for the fiesta. In the Black Carib community of Corozal, there is an *hermandad* (sodality) of women who take care of the entire sponsorship of the annual titular fiesta.

The situation in Intibucá is basically dependent upon *hermandades* and a separate permanent Indian organization for the principal annual fiesta which involves the *guancasco*. Since this is distinctively an Indian affair, a description of it will be reserved for the later section on Indians.

There is considerably more to the sponsorship of a fiesta than the mere organization behind it. Religion may be a thing of the spirit but its activities require cash. In about half of the towns visited it is the custom to get at least some of the necessary funds by sending one or more of the saints out on *demanda*, i.e., a visit through the *municipio*, and sometimes to other *municipios*, to collect money. The usual practice is to send the saint out with one or more individuals who are referred to as *mayordomos*. A month seems to be the average time for such trips (Yusguare, Duyure, Guaimaca, Salamá), but the time varies from one locality to another; Nueva Ocotepeque 15–20 days; La Libertad, 8 days; Dulce Nombre de Copán, 6 months; La Esperanza, the entire year; Corozal, two weeks. In most towns the saint makes the trip through the rural area of the *municipios*; in many cases it was said that they used to go to other *municipios*, but that this has been prohibited in recent years. A few communities reported that the saint still visited nearby *municipios*. The visit of the saint involves the maintenance of good relations with the neighboring communities. In Quimistán, it was said that in former years it was customary for the saint to visit the town of San Marcos, but that in recent years there had developed some bad feeling between the towns and the practice was stopped. Some communities said that they did not observe the *demanda* custom (La Misión, San Francisco de Yojoa, Güinope, Yoro, and Quimistán). The usual *demanda* involves the saint leaving the church at some determined time, and making a visit to various houses in the *aldeas*. It spends one or more nights in various homes along the way. While in a home, neighbors come to visit, pray, and leave an offering for the saint. The owner of the home where the saint rests, is expected to give an especially substantial contribution.

Whether or not a given community observes the custom of sending one or more saints out on *demanda*, it is usually customary to collect additional funds through asking each resident for a contribution. This is the way that the committees obtain funds for the lay aspects of the fiestas and is also common for those individuals and groups responsible for the religious parts.

While the titular fiestas are usually the fiestas of greatest importance in a given community and are usually arranged in one of the general ways described above, the custom of maintaining permanent sodalities is also found. It should be noted at the outset that the sodality pattern is not as strong in Honduras as in some of the other countries in Central America. Such societies were reported from only six communities. In Guaimaca it was said that there used to be one, but that it had died, and in Marcala, informants reported that the priest intended to initiate one. In Jacaleapa, Nueva Ocotepeque and Corozal there was one sodality each, in La Libertad two, and in Olanchito and La Esperanza three. In all except one case the sodalities were associations of women. The exception was the *Sociedad de Franciscanos* in Nueva Ocotepeque in which both men and women were members. In La Libertad it was said that there were plans to initiate the society of *Los Caballeros del Santo Entierro*, to be composed exclusively of men.

The functions of religious societies vary somewhat. The *Sociedad Catequista* (unmarried women) of Jacaleapa and the *Sociedad Católica* of La Esperanza had as their principal function the maintenance and upkeep of the church building and the religious artifacts therein. The *Sociedad de Franciscanos* of Nueva Ocotepeque and the *Hermandad Católica* of Corozal took over the responsibility of part or all of the celebration of the titular fiesta. For the most part the remainder were composed of devotees of a particular saint. The *Hijas de María* (La Libertad and La Esperanza), composed of girls, followed the same pattern as in other countries. They prayed nightly during the month of May. The other groups, the *Guardia de la Santísima* of La Libertad, *Hermandad Franciscana* and *Cofradía del Santísimo Sacramento* of Olanchito, and the *Hermandad Santísima* of La Esperanza are all involved in a certain amount of praying and religious observances.

Fiestas themselves are of two general types, the purely religious, such as those in La Esperanza and those sponsored by the sodalities, and those which combine religious observances with recreational aspects. The religious observances usually consist of one or more Masses and processions, together with *novenas, rosarios*, or other evening prayers. On the recreational side, the most commonly reported features were the *carrera de cintas* (13 towns), the *palo encebado* (7 towns), and social dances. Of course, most fiestas which have an entertainment phase involve considerable drinking and setting off fireworks. Other features which were reported from four towns or less were the *corrida de toros* (bull baiting), the *carrera encostalda* (sack race), horse races and donkey races, *futbol* games, popular dances, gambling (prohibited in some places), the *descabezada de gallos o patos*, and the *triángulo*. In Yusguare, the bullfight was reported as being called the *garrochada*, and was the same type as is found in Nicaragua, involving riding the bull. Popular dances are distinguished from social dances in that the latter are usually for only the upper and possibly middle classes, while the former are for the lower class people. The beheading of chickens and ducks is the survival of an old colonial custom whereby a fowl is hung by its feet from a frame and riders on horseback, going full speed under the frame, try to grab the head of the fowl and to yank it off. It was reported as a contemporary custom in Intibucá, Olanchito (actually in a neighboring *aldea* where one of the Olanchito fiestas is held), Guaimaca, and Catacamas. It was reported to have been a custom up to between 5 and 30 years ago in Nueva Ocotepeque, La Libertad, La Misión, Quimistán, Yoro, and Ilama. Honduras is the only country in Central America where the writer has encountered the survival of this custom.

Besides these customs, there were some others which were reported in individual towns. In Jacaleapa, the *Viejos Enmascarados* consisted of a group of men costumed as women, masked with commercial paper masks, who danced to *marimbas* on the street corners on *Sábado de Gloria* of Holy Week, collecting money for the Holy Week celebration. In Yoro, the *mojigangas* were two masked characters who danced before the bullfight. They were evidently clowns. This custom stopped, however, when bullfighting was given up a year or so ago.

As has been indicated, none of these customs appear in all fiestas, and in some cases, some of them are carried out in fiestas other than the patronal. The beheading of chickens in Guaimaca, for example, is not done on the day of the patron saint, *Santa Rosa de Lima* (30 August), but on the days of *San Juan* (24 June) and *San Pedro* (29 June).

The use of masked historical or representational dances seems to have disappeared from most communities. It is an essential part of the *guancasco* of Intibucá, but aside from its appearance there is uncommon. It was given up in Ilama only recently and the masks are still to be seen in the municipal building. Doris Stone has moving pictures of the dance. In the Black Carib town of Corozal the Dance of the Moors and Christians is still held, but masks are not used. Stone (in correspondence) reports the use of masks generally common in Black Carib towns, however. The use of a drum in the religious aspects of the fiesta was reported from five towns; the drum together with the *chirimía* (flute) was reported from one town (Catacamas) and has disappeared recently in a few others.

There are two customs associated specifically with the celebration of the Christmas fiesta over much of Honduras, the *posada* and the *nacimiento*. Of the 14 towns in which inquiry was made, *posadas* were held in 10 and *nacimientos* in 11. The *posada* involves taking the images of Joseph and Mary on a visit around the town for a number of nights prior to Christmas. The trip is supposed to be the search for a lodging place, and each night they stay in a different house. In general, it begins nine nights before Christmas and ends on Christmas eve. Two towns, however, varied this pattern. In Quimistán, it was held on one night only, the *Día de los Reyes,* the sixth of January, and on that evening the saints stopped at six or seven houses. In La Esperanza, where it will be remembered one of the principal fiestas is going on prior to Christmas, the *posada* begins on the 18th of December and lasts until the fiesta of Carnival at the beginning of Lent. During this period not just Joseph and Mary, but the entire Holy Family visit almost every house in town.

The custom of the *nacimiento* involves setting up a *crèche* in the home. There is usually some competition between the better families as to which can provide the more elaborate setting and the more expensive figurines. In La Libertad the competition has been recognized so that there is an annual contest in which a group of judges decide which of the *nacimientos* is the best. As an integral part of the *nacimiento* custom in seven of the towns, and reported as being rare in two more, is the robbing of the Christ child figurine from the *crèche*. This is usually done sometime just before Christmas. The figurine is returned on the sixth of January and a fiesta is given. The practice varies as to whether the person who stole the figurine or the person from whom it was stolen sponsors this fiesta, and whether it is held in the home of the robber or the home of the owner. In Yusguare, there is the custom of having the figurine reappear in the door of the church on the sixth of January or sometime in February, usually the second. The owner must then buy it back from the church and throw a big party. This combines helping the church and having a good party. In Catacamas and Jacaleapa the robber must pay for the fiesta, but it is held in the house of the owner of the figurine; in Guaimaca, the robber holds the fiesta in his own home. Among Marcala Ladinos it was said that the custom of the *nacimiento* is giving way to the Christmas tree.

In most Christian communities one of the constant and regular problems which faces the inhabitants is the maintenace of the equipment and plant of the church. Where there are resident priests, this is usually under their control and they have assistance in menial tasks in accordance with the financial facilities and local traditions of the community. In La Esperanza, for example, money is collected for this purpose by the *Sociedad Católica*, a woman's association in the town, and in Guaimaca, the *Pro-Junta Católica* fulfills this function. In eight of the communities included on the survey there were resident priests, and in five cases there were two.

Most communities, however, do not have resident priests and are visited by the parish priest one or more times a year, depending upon the importance of the community and the amount of territory which the priest must cover. In these communities some other arrangement must be made to care for the church. In Zambrano, a small *aldea*, there is evidently no organization at all for this purpose. There is a local man who keeps the keys of the church, but it is opened only on special occasions. In Ilama there is an employee, a janitor called the *esclavo* (slave), who is paid by the *Consejo de Fábrica*, to care for the church. In Quimistán and San Francisco de Yojoa, the welfare of the church building is in the hands of a committee. In the former place the *Comité Pro-Reconstrucción de la Iglesia* is collecting funds for a new church, and in the latter, the *Comité Pro-Iglesia* collects funds for upkeep. There are two evidently older methods which survive in the southern part of the country. One of these is the appointment of two (or possibly more, although no such cases were encountered in the survey) *mayordomos* who took the responsibility. In Yusguare a man and a woman (specified as a *señorita*) are in charge of the church structure and keep the keys. They maintain their position until they, the town, or the responsible priest sees some reason for there to be a change. It was reported from Duyure that the same system is in effect, but that two *señoritas* are so responsible. The shouldering of this charge by the women of the community seems to stem from a colonial pattern which was reported to survive in stronger form in three other communities. The most highly crystallized form was found among the Indians of Intibucá and reported from the Indian community of La Campa in Lempira. The Intibucá system involves two separate teams of 16 women each (one, the *capitana* is the leader) who alternate each month. One such team is called in each Saturday to clean the building and put pine needles on the floor. The Ladino community of La Venta also reported that this responsibility was held by a group of women, but there it was said that the organization was quite informal.

In general, religion in Honduran communities seems to be about as important as it is in other Ladino populations in Central America. The organization of the efforts in some cases does not seem so highly structured, but the same differential between men and women appear in the same general ways. One difference which may be important is the greater survival of certain of the customs which are evidently of colonial origin. Principal among these is the observance of a child's death with a fiesta, involving music, dancing, eating, and/or drinking, and the survival of the beheading of chickens and ducks, a trait which seems to have been lost in the other countries. With respect to traits which appear only briefly in Honduras, mention should be made of the *gritería* held on the day of *Concepción* in December. This custom, which is common through most of the coastal belt of Nicaragua, was reported to be observed today in some communities near the Nicaraguan border in Honduras. It used to be observed in Yusguare and was said to still be observed in Choluteca.[47a]

8. PATTERNS OF SICKNESS AND CURING

As is the case in the rest of Central America, the Honduran town and country dweller relies on a considerable amount of traditional knowledge for the diagnosis and curing of bodily ailments. As in the other studies in this series, the present survey collected data on certain of these concepts and practices. In the following discussion, we will first take up some of the more prominent traditional illness patterns, and then discuss the types of curers called upon for healing.

Empacho. *Empacho* was one of the most consistently reported illnesses from the point of view of conception and curing. Generally, it was attributed to eating too much, or eating at the wrong hour, usually too late. If one was tardy in returning from the fields and ate his meal, *empacho* could result. In some places it was also attributed to eating bad food. It was sometimes (in five towns) referred to simply as bad indigestion. The diagnosis usually involved calling a specialist who would feel the wrist and forearm of the individual, and from this determine whether the particular stomach ailment was in fact *empacho* or something else. If it was determined that the patient did have *empacho*, then the cure involved a massage of the forearm by the specialist and, in most cases, the administration of a purge. The purges were usually specially concocted from herbs. In some places an enema was also administered in these cases. In three communities slightly variant interpretations were given the illness. In Dulce Nombre de Copán, it was said to result simply from hunger, not necessarily from excessive or poorly eating. In Yoro, it was explained as being *chibolas* (little lumps) in the blood, like "dead blood in the veins." In Catacamas it was said to result from having been in the sun too long, and also from eating green fruit. Even with these variations, however, the general pattern of *empacho* as being some sort of digestive trouble and related to the veins of the wrists and forearms is highly consistent through much of Honduras, as is the cure by massaging and

---

[47a] Adams, n.d. (b), describes the custom for Nicaragua.

purging. While the use of the purge was not mentioned by six informants, it was reported as specifically not being a part of the cure only in Corozal, the Black Carib town.

Pasmo. Pasmo is another intestinal ailment, but its definition is not so clear as is that of *empacho*, nor is it so widely recognized. In the south, parts of the southwest, and in the area running up to the Department of Cortés (Yusguare, Nacaome, La Venta, Zambrano, Guaimaca, Intibucá, La Libertad, La Misión, and Ilama) it is defined as something resulting from the cold. In some towns it was said to derive specifically from eating something cold, or having cold attack the stomach. In others, it was a generalized cold of the body, resulting perhaps from being chilled while bathing or something of the kind. The usual cure in these cases where it is interpreted as chilling or cold is to give either hot food or some herbal remedy which is regarded as having the quality of being warm (for example, sassafras, anise, *apasote, raíz de guaco*, or *té de manzana*). The characteristics attributed to *pasmo* in other communities varies. In some places it is regarded as being essentially similar to *empacho* (Dulce Nombre de Copán and Nueva Ocotepeque) and as such is the result of eating bad food, and is to be cured by taking a laxative. In La Esperanza it was not specified as being related to cold, but was said to be a pain in the stomach, and the cure involved putting ashes, eggs, various herbs and other things on the stomach. In Catacamas, the term *pasmo* was said to refer to nervous contractions caused by strong emotions. This interpretation sounds similar to that usually referred to as *flato* (see below). *Pasmo* of whatever interpretation was said to be unknown by the informants in Güinope and Corozal, and to be of very little importance locally in Jacaleapa and Yoro and specifically among the poorer people of the lower class in Olanchito. In only two towns, La Venta and Intibucá, was it said to be customary to look for a *curandero* to cure *pasmo*; elsewhere, the cure was evidently well enough known that where there was specialization, it was restricted to old women.

Vista fuerte, Ojo and *Pujo*. These three things are closely related. *Ojo* and *pujo* are two usually distinct childhood ailments which are felt to be the result of *vista fuerte*. The basic concept is that certain people are born more powerful or stronger than others, and certain other people are more powerful for temporary periods (e.g. during pregnancy, menstruation, just after finishing working in the sun), and that this quality of power when brought close to a child can make the child sick. In Yusguare, La Venta, La Libertad, San Francisco de Yojoa, and Catacamas, this power is referred to specifically as *vista fuerte*, that is, the strong glance. When *ojo* results from this, the symptoms are usually fever and a variety of other things; when *pujo* results, the specific symptom is diarrhea.

Ojo can easily kill baby animals, and many such deaths are so attributed. In San Francisco de Yojoa it was said that it usually killed the children as well because there was no medical attention locally. Practice as to whether a curer was called was irregular and there seemed to be no specifically regional pattern as to whether it could be cured with or without a *curandero* or doctor. In those towns in which a specialist was not said to be necessary, and in a few in which it was, the person who was responsible for the strong glance was usually an essential part of the curing process. Either he (or she) had to hold and rock the baby, or some of the clothes of the person had to be made available so that the child could be wrapped in them. Among the other standard cures are putting one or more of the following things on the child: *barbasco*, earwax, *aguardiente*, rue, anise, or tobacco. These things are usually mixed together and rubbed on the child's back or head. This type of cure was reported from Yusguare, La Venta, Güinope, Jacaleapa, and Guaimaca. In Yusguare, the child so rubbed was then wrapped in the sweaty clothes of the strong person, and if the trouble really was *ojo*, this cured it. Presumably if the fever did not leave, it was not *ojo*. In La Venta the treatment also involves blowing *aguardiente* suddenly in the face of the child to shock him. In Guaimaca, the method of placing an egg under the child's bed is used; if the egg "cooks" in a few minutes, the case has both been diagnosed as *ojo* and cured. In Ilama, informants said that *ojo* came not so much from merely *vista fuerte* as from a person who envied a child's beauty. The cure was said to be to pass an egg over the child's head. Rosa[48] also reports the use of the egg in Ilama, in a way which is essentially similar to that found over much of Guatemala. *Ojo* was said to be prevented by putting red ribbons or cloth on the child, a coral bracelet, or a lizard's tooth on a string on the wrist or neck. In Nacaome, a child could be protected from the strength of a strong person if that person held it very close.

Only six towns reported that *pujo* resulted from *vista fuerte* (La Venta, Güinope, Guaimaca, Marcala, La Misión, and Ilama). In six more, *pujo* referred simply to diarrhea in children, and was variously cured with pharmaceutical or home remedies. The causes in these latter cases varied. In Yusguare, it was said to come when the weather was particularly warm and was cured with a purge. In Zambrano it was merely said to be endemic and was usually cured with the juice of bitter oranges, or lemons; in Nueva Ocotepeque and Olanchito, it was cured with bismuth; in La Libertad it was said to be caused by chilling. In Olanchito, Dulce Nombre de Copán, and Corozal, the term *pujo* was said to be unknown.

The concept of strength affecting someone finds expression not only in the illnesses of *ojo* and *pujo*, but in others. In La Venta, *pasmo* was said to occur only to weak people; if one was strong, nothing would happen. The effects of *hijillo* (described below) are usually specifically harmful to people who are weak, or in a weakened condition due to some other illness. And the condition *flato* (described below) was said in Intibucá specifically to affect weak people.

Susto and *flato*. For practical purposes, the illness known elsewhere as *susto* or *espanto* does not occur with any frequency in Honduras. The only community which reported anything which could be regarded as equivalent to the *susto* found in Guatemala was that in Dulce Nombre de Copán, near the Guatemalan border. There it was said to be quite common that a person, when frightened by an animal or something else, would grow sick; this involved the loss of his soul, and the cure had to be effected by a *curandero*. In Yusguare the informant said

---

[48] Rosa, 1940.

he knew of one case wherein a man had been frightened in the hills behind the town; the fellow thought he would die of the fever that resulted. Elsewhere, *susto* simply does not seem to be a part of the culture. In Jacaleapa the informant said that in former years some cases were known, but that it had disappeared, and in Catacamas it was said that very rarely people became sick from surprise, and that they called a *curandero* to cure them with herbs.

In five towns, however, another nervous ailment, *flato*, was reported. *Flato* is a condition which occurs when a person is strongly affected emotionally by some loss or sadness. If a very dear friend dies, if a person is badly frightened, or if a person becomes very angry and agitated with a friend then he will become sick with *flato*. In Yoro and Intubucá it was said that it could only be cured by calling a *curandero* who, in the latter place, cured it with herb teas. In Yoro it did no good to call a doctor for this kind of ailment. In Guaimaca and La Misión t was cured with herb teas, specifically rue, *alcotán*, and *moroporán*. In La Misión, however, it was said that this really did not cure it, but simply alleviated it. In San Francisco de Yojoa, it was said that there was no specific way to cure it; one just had to wait until they got over it.

Hijillo.[49] *Hijillo*, or *bajo* as it is called in Olanchito and Catacamas, is an air and/or odor which emanates from dead things, specifically human corpses. It has the capacity of making a person ill, especially when that person is already sick with a cold, cough, if he has an open wound, boils, or is simply a weak person. It was reported in essentially this form from all towns except San Francisco de Yojoa in which the informant said he knew of no cases. In Nacaome the informant said he did not know of any human being suffering from *hijillo*, but that plants, especially the watermelon, suffered from it. In Catacamas, the effects of *bajo* tended to last for a day or two. If a person had visited a corpse, or slaughtered cattle, he was not supposed to bathe for a day since bathing tended to chill one and thereby weaken him. To aid in ridding oneself of the effects of *bajo*, the informant there recommended putting the plant rue, which is supposed to smell like the dead, under the pillow at night. In La Esperanza, where it is quite cold, *hijillo* was said not to be very dangerous because corpses did not disintegrate so rapidly. For Ilama both the writer's informant and Rosa[50] reported that the *flor de muerto* served as an effective cure for *hijillo*.

Caída de mollera. The falling of the fontanelle in infants was generally recognized as a fairly serious ailment over most of the country (data was not gathered in all towns, but in all nine where inquiry was made it was reported to be present). As elsewhere, rough handling of an infant is said to cause the fontanelle to fall, threatening to choke the child. The cure is to hold the child up by the feet, tap him across the sole of his feet, in some places to shake him a little, and in some places to put mineral oil on the head or in the mouth and some on the fontanelle. In Yoro it was said that it was wise to call on a *curandero*, an old woman or the midwife, to do this.

Witchcraft, Malos Oficios. Witchcraft was reported as being known in almost all the communities visited on the survey. In some cases informants said that there

---

[49] Rosa, 1940, p. 33, refers to this as *egio* or *egido*, for Ilama.   [50] *Ibid.*

were no witches or persons practicing the occult art in the town itself, but that in the *aldeas,* or in some other known town there were such people. In general the terms *brujo* and *brujería* are felt to be reserved for the very strongest type of sorcerers, those who can turn themselves into animals, for example. As such, most informants denied that there were *brujos,* but said that witchcraft was well known in terms of the preparation of love potions, of spirit witches who would throw things at a person. Also, these witches could make people sick, specifically make them go crazy and act in odd and unpredictable ways. In a few communities it was specified that the persons who practiced such activities were referred to as *curanderos,* that it was not unknown for such an individual to cause a person to become ill, and then to be employed to cure the illness. In Yoro it was reported that when local personnel were inadequate to handle a case of witchcraft, it was customary to go to the north coast and get a "negro". The negroes were said to be especially effective in this type of curing. Unfortunately, the informant could not be more specific as to what kind of negro this was, whether an English speaking Antillean negro, or a Black Carib.

Earth eating. Of the 21 towns on which data was collected on earth eating, all reported that children did eat it, but in varying amounts. In 11 towns, it was reported that children had died of it. In general, no consistent explanations were given concerning the interpretation of why this practice existed. In Marcala, Nueva Ocotepeque, and Yusguare it was thought to be related to worms; in Dulce Nombre de Copán it was said that "the blood makes some use of this earth."

The above illnesses were the ones which were covered on the survey. No mention was made of the *tunar fuerte* of El Salvador.[50a] The concepts of hot and cold foods as related to illnesses resulting from being overheated and/or chilled were mentioned in Jacaleapa and La Libertad, but only in the Black Carib community of Corozal could the writer obtain anything like a satisfactory listing of foods in terms of these qualities. Among those foods considered as cold were coconuts, pork, fish (specifically salted; fresh fish was not so cold), *yuca,* banana, and salt; among the hot foods were oranges and beef. It was said there that a person who was hot or had a cold should not eat things which were cold. In other places the qualities of heat and cold, while applying to some foods, seemed to be of greater importance in terms of curing herbs. Various herbs were sought for specific illnesses because they had either cold or warm qualities. Outside of this, the hot and cold idea seemed to be utilized more in its absolute sense. In Guaimaca, for example, whitlow or felon, a condition in which the fingers become abscessed, was said to result from putting an overheated hand into cold water. In La Libertad if a person was very agitated, it was said to be bad for him to eat things which were cold; and in Jacaleapa, chills were said to result from getting cold when one had been hot before.

Curing in the town and countryside of Honduras is carried on by a variety of people. It is difficult to classify them since the writer could not discern that the people themselves made many clear distinctions. Basically, it is possible to dis-

---

[50a] See Adams, n.d. (d), and the appendix therein by James.

tinguish: the trained medical personnel, specifically doctors, since nurses are extremely scarce; empirical personnel who make something of a practice of curing, pharmacists, *curanderos*, *parcheros*, midwives, spiritualists; and empirical personnel who "know how" and are called in more as experienced persons who are particularly good at handling certain kinds of illnesses. Actually, the personnel in the last two categories tend to blend together and, except for the midwives who go under various terms such as *partera*, *comadrona*, and *matrona*, little distinction is made in terms of terminology. In some places the terms *curandero* and *parchero* are interchangeable; in others, the former tends to refer to the professional, while the latter refers to the person who "knows how". In La Misión the writer was told quite definitely that there were neither *parcheros* nor *curanderos*, but upon questioning concerning specific illnesses, he was told that there were some people who knew how to cure *empacho* and who were called in such cases, that there were others who could cure *ojo* and *pujo* and were called, and yet others who could cure *caída de mollera*. Thus, even in those communities where there are "no *curanderos*" recognized formally, there may be and probably are people who are known for their ability to handle certain forms of illnesses.

The medical doctor is still something of a rarity in the countryside. It is extremely unlikely that one will be found in any communities which are not at least departmental capitals, except in the banana zone where the fruit companies have taken over the responsibility of providing adequate medical services for their laborers. Where doctors are available, they seem to be used with considerable frequency. One indication that available medical services are so used is that, in a number of communities, some illnesses which are interpreted in a traditional manner were said to be taken both to empirical curers and to medical doctors if available. In Intibucá, *pasmo* was said to involve calling either a *parchero* or a doctor; on the other hand, it was never said that a medical doctor would be sought to cure *empacho*, *flato*, or *caída de mollera*.

Empirical curers are of various types. While few towns reported having *farmacias*, almost every town which had a store of any size had a place where medicines were sold. In these stores the storekeeper acted as consultant and curer. The individual with an ailment would come for advice, and the storekeeper would advise and sell the remedy on the basis of his accumulating experience. While there are doubtless some storekeepers who use this as a commercial lever, it would be both unwise and untrue to accuse all of doing this. Aside from the storekeepers themselves, there are occasional people who are felt to be very *"inteligente"* i.e., they know how to cure many things. In La Venta, for example, it was said that there were no *curanderos* in town but that in the nearby town of San Antonio las Flores there was a person who knew a great deal about curing and to whom many of the people went when they needed such help. Similarly, there was no one in La Misión who warranted even the name of *curandero* or *parchero*, but there was in neighboring Taulabá a person *"muy inteligentes"* to whom many went. This type of curer, like the storekeeper, usually does not resort to mystical or occult practices, but relies mainly on an empirical knowledge of the functioning of the human body, of the most common local ailments, and his experience and previous fortune in curing. He is not infrequently dubbed "doctor" locally and is usually quite happy to have this title used.

Sometimes these people who are *"inteligentes"* are also referred to as *curanderos*, but that term is often reserved for private individuals who may be known only locally and occasionally indulge somewhat in mystical curing techniques. Thus in some places the *curandero* tends to be equated with the sorcerer. However, even more cosmopolitan local people tend to accept the curer because they are usually the only people available to do curing of any kind. As was mentioned, the term *parchero* is often used interchangeably for these persons. While the curers mentioned in the last paragraph are usually men, the *parcheros* and *curanderos* may be either men or women. *Curanderos* tend to blend into the "people who know how". Just as the latter usually know how to cure specific illnesses, such as *empacho*, *pasmo*, *pujo*, *ojo*, *flato*, etc., so do the *curanderos* tend to specialize somewhat. Among the principal specialists are the massaeurs who can cure *empacho*. Not only are they called to do the massaging, but they also diagnose and recommend the purges to be used. The midwives, of course, are another type of specialist. They usually are called in on childhood ailments, specifically *caída de mollera*. *Pujo* and *ojo*, depending upon the community, may have specialists also. Also for children's illnesses, where specialists may not be available, it is not uncommon to find that certain old women have a reputation for being able to handle certain troubles.

While spiritualists were found to be of varying importance elsewhere in Central America, the only one reported to the writer in the course of the survey in Honduras practiced in Tegucigalpa. However, this subject was not explored in all communities so it may be that their presence was overlooked.

In general, Honduras shows a fairly well developed series of traditionally explained illnesses and an active empirical curing system. *Empacho*, *ojo*, *hijillo* and *caída de mollera* are found to be common. *Pasmo* and *pujo* are not so common and, where present, have a variety of interpretations attached. *Flato* is widespread and the interpretation is fairly consistent; *susto* seems limited to the area immediately adjacent to Guatemala and all but absent elsewhere. Where doctors are operating, they seem to have no particular problem as yet from resistances developing in the local curing patterns. This is probably in some part due to the fact that there are few of them, but it may also be indicative that the system as such is receptive to new elements. While cases were encountered in which it was said that doctors would not be called for certain kinds of illnesses, the writer did not have the feeling in general that there was a strong potential resistance to medical practice.

III. THE INDIANS OF HONDURAS

1. THE INDIAN POPULATION

Doris Stone has remarked that, "Honduras is a country of acculturation, perhaps one of the greatest examples of such in America. . . . . The majority of the Spanish colonists who settled in Honduras took Indian wives and their children absorbed and passed on customs and lore from both sides of their forebears."[51] While we do, indeed, find in most of Honduras an amalgamation of the two major traditions, it is possible and useful to distinguish certain groups which still think of themselves as Indian and which are still called Indian by the Ladino population. In this chapter we are going to delineate the principal areas in which Indians are still the dominant population and to estimate the numbers of these people who still exist as separate population components.

The distribution of the principal Indian groups at the time of conquest and during their subsequent history is still a subject of study. For the interested person, the following sources will provide a general picture: Conzemius, 1932, Johnson, 1948a, 1948b; Stone, 1948, von Hagen, 1940, 1943. In the present discussion, we will leave the Black Carib out of consideration; they are not a group indigenous to Central America and for convenience' sake, they will be discussed in a separate chapter.

The contemporary distribution of the Indian population is a result of elimination, amalgamation, acculturation, and fleeing into refuge areas. There are nine principal Indian population groups (see map).

The estimated size of these populations for 1950 is as follows:

The Lenca of the Southwest Highlands. This is the largest of the contemporary Indian population. Stone[52] quotes Honduran government figures for this population as follows:

Department of La Paz	18,589
Department of Intibucá	32,707
Department of Lempira	5,659
Total	56,955

Unfortunately the date for these figures is not given, but it may be assumed that they refer to the data taken from the Census of 1935.[53] The total population of Indians given in that census was 89,655, or 9.3% of the total population of the country.

On the basis of data from informants concerning Indian *municipios*, the present writer used the 1950 census figures to arrive at the following estimates for the size of the Indian population for 1950.

Department of La Paz	26,230
Department of Intibucá	44,425
Department of Lempira	34,250

In comparing these figures with those given by Stone, the departments of La Paz and Intibucá represent an increase of 136% and 138% respectively over the 1934 census data. The estimate for the Department of Lempira, however, is

---

[51] Stone, 1951, p. 113.   [52] In Johnson, 1948a, p. 62.

[53] Census, 1936, refers to this census, but the writer was not able to locate a copy of the census itself during his stay in Honduras.

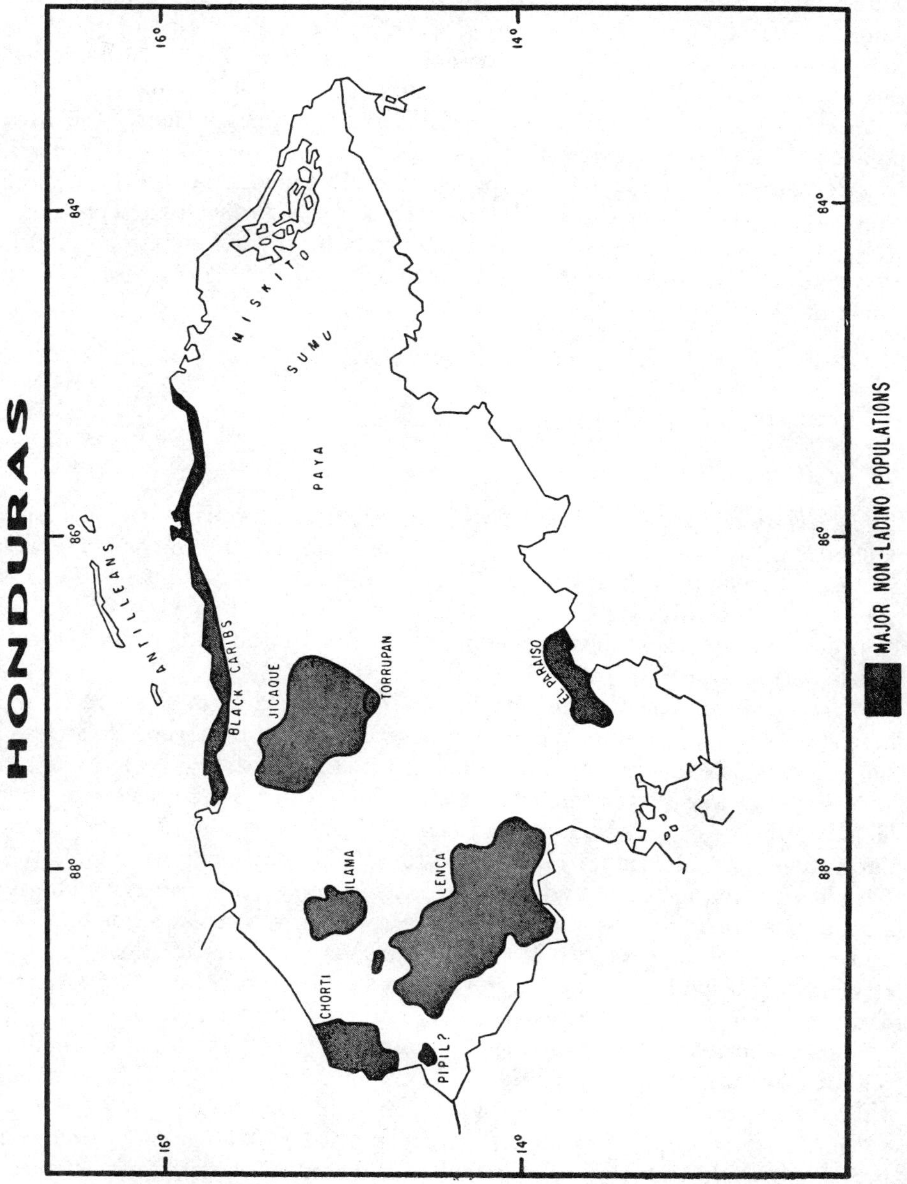
HONDURAS
16°
14°
84°
86°
88°
ANTILLEANS
BLACK CARIBS
MISKITO
SUMU
PAYA
JICAQUE
TORRUPAN
EL PARAISO
ILAMA
LENCA
CHORTI
PIPIL?
MAJOR NON-LADINO POPULATIONS

excessively large. The writer was not able to visit that department during the course of the survey, and his estimates were taken from local school teachers whom he was able to interview during a special teacher summer school session. As a result, he does not trust the Lempira estimate as much as he does those for the other two departments. Stone[54] also points out that the Department of Lempira was an early center of Spanish colonization, and consequently the Indian population of that department was ladinoized earlier than those in the other two departments. For present purposes, then, it would probably be more accurate to apply a factor of 1.37 (between those for the other two departments) to the 1935 census figures to arrive at an estimate for this population in 1950. This gives us 7,760. For the three departments as a whole, then, the 1950 estimate would be as follows:

Department of La Paz	26,230
Department of Intibucá	44,425
Department of Lempira	7,760
Total	78,415[55]

The Chortí of Copán. We have no specific estimates available for this Indian population. On the basis of data gathered from informants and the 1950 census figures, it probably includes some 12,500 people. The great part of the Chortí group are in neighboring Guatemala in the Department of Chiquimula. The 1950 Guatemalan census gives a figure of 70,096 for the Indian population of that department.

The Indians of East Central Santa Bárbara. The writer is not sure to what linguistic group this Indian population may once have belonged. It is close to the region which the Jicaque once occupied in the Department of Cortés, but could as easily be an extension of the Lenca group which live to the south, or the Chortí to the west. The estimate of the size of this population is based on estimates given by informants taken with the 1950 census figures: 5,000. While there is a concentration of Indians in the neighboring *municipios* of Ilama and Chinda, there are various scattered to the southwest, west and north.

The Jicaque of Yoro and the Montaña de la Flor. Estimate for this population component was made as were the previous, on the basis of local informant's estimates, combined with 1950 census data. The figure arrived at is 8,400.

Bonilla reported in 1942 that the Montaña de la Flor population was reduced to about 300, and Stone estimates the 1955 population at 200.[56] The remaining of the present estimate may be considered as highly ladinoized.

The Matagalpa (?) of El Paraíso. This group is called Matagalpa by Johnson,[57] an estimate of the contemporary population, based as before, gives a figure of 15,150 for this group in 1950.

---

[54] Johnson, 1948, p. 62. [55] Stone today (in correspondence) gives an estimate of 75,000.
[56] Bonilla, 1942; Stone, Appendix, *infra*.
[57] Johnson, 1948a, p. 61, Map 5, Stone (in correspondence) says this identification is based on place names and Lehmann, 1920.

The Pipil of Ocotepeque. The writer is neither sure of the fact that these are Pipiles, nor of the estimates of their present population size. The municipio of Dolores was said to be the main contemporary concentration. The writer estimates that there are perhaps 400 people in this component.

The Paya of Olancho and Colón. Conzemius estimated in 1928[58] that there were something over 600 Paya Indians. The writer sees no reason to increase this estimate for the intervening years.

The Miskito-Sumo of Colón. Von Hagen[59] quotes a Honduran commission report of 1928 which gave the figure of 2,246 for the Miskito between the Río Negro and the Río Coco. Johnson[60] reports some few Sumo in the region as well, and Stone[61] estimates the contemporary Indian population to consist of 5,000 Miskitos and 50 Sumos.

Besides these major groups, there are numerous isolates of Indians scattered in *aldeas* through much of the highland area of Honduras. Some of these, those which came to the writer's attention in the course of the survey, are: Yaruca (Atlántida); Tatumbla (Francisco Morazán); the *aldea* of El Cerro in Yusguare, made up of people from Liure; the barrio of San Andrés in Ocotepeque Viejo, probably Pipiles; and the municipio of Atima and the *aldea* of Machuloa in Santa Bárbara. It is impossible from the data available to estimate either the number of such isolates or the size of the populations involved. The writer suspects, however, that these groups probably do not add up to a very significant quantity and, in any case, are highly ladinoized.

On the major populations of Indians, then, we have the following estimate (rounded of to hundreds):

	Population	Percent
Lenca of the Southwest Highlands	78,400	62.4
Chortí of Copán	12,500	10.0
Indians of East Central Santa Bárbara	5,000	4.0
Jicaque of Yoro	8,400	6.7
Matagalpa (?) of El Paraíso	15,100	12.0
Pipil of Ocotepeque	400	0.3
Paya of Olancho and Colón	600	0.5
Miskito-Sumo of Colón	5,100	4.1
Total	125,500	100.0

This total figure of 125,500 is 9.2% of the total population in 1950 of 1,368,605. The 1935 Census gave the Indian percentage as 9.3%; the 1940 Census[62] gave

---

[58] Conzemius, 1927–28. [59] Von Hagen, 1940, p. 258. [60] Johnson, 1948, Map 5.

[61] Stone, in correspondence, from government and missionary sources.

[62] Quoted in International Labor Office, 1953, p. 53. Colindres, 1942, quotes the figures as follows: total population, 1,107,859; Indian population, 105,000. Colindres' distinction between various contemporary "tribes" such as Chorotega, Miquirano, Goajiro, and the Opator are somewhat meaningless to the present writer. Bonilla, 1942, gives a figure of 85,000 for the entire Indian population; she probably arrived at this figure by excluding some of

an Indian population of 105,732 out of a total population of 1,107,859, or 9.5%. Since the estimates upon which the present general figure is made are crude, there is no reason to take seriously an evident growth or diminution of the relative size of the Indian population; rather, the closeness of the estimates probably means simply that the censuses and the estimates are probably talking about the same thing.

Of these major indigenous groups, all are ladinoized to some degree, and a great many to a great degree. In the pages to follow, we are going to describe briefly four of these groups, those of the southwest highlands, El Paraíso, Santa Bárbara, and Yoro. No data was gathered during the survey on the Chortí; it may be anticipated that they are essentially similar in culture to their neighbors on the Guatemalan side of the border, and the reader is referred to the work of Wisdom (1940) for a detailed description of this. For a description of the most traditional of the Jicaque, the reader is referred to von Hagen (1943) and to the more recent work by Doris Stone described in the appendix to the present report. Aside from Adams (n.d. (d)) there are ethnological studies on neither the Pipil population of El Salvador nor those who live in Honduras. On the Paya the reader is referred to Conzemius, 1927–28; on the Miskito-Sumo, Conzemius (1932) and von Hagen (1940) are two good sources to which may be added various studies made in Nicaragua.

2. THE LENCA INDIANS OF THE SOUTHWEST HIGHLANDS

The main chronicler of the contemporary Lenca Indians is Doris Stone, and she has provided us with a general description of the culture of this population group.[63] The present notes are provided principally to add to the data provided in previous work and to give a background for the comparative analysis on the acculturation of the Honduran Indian which follows in a later section. The writer visited two centers in the Lenca area during the survey, Marcala and La Esperanza-Intibucá. Marcala is basically a Ladino town set in the center of the Indian area of the Department of La Paz. Data was gathered there not only on the Ladinos of the community, but on the Indians of the surrounding regions. The towns of La Esperanza and Intibucá are physically a single town. The former is mainly Ladino and is the departmental capital of the Department of Intibucá, and the town of Intibucá is mainly Indian. In addition to the notes gathered during these visits, data was collected on some specific topics from a number of school teachers from the Department of Lempira. They were attending a summer school in Danlí, and the writer spent an evening with them. It is from these data that the following description is composed. The town of Intibucá was the only place in which Indian informants were used, and so it is from there that most of the information is taken.

The general area occupied by what are now generally considered as Lenca

---

the highly ladinoized populations such as the majority of the Yoro population and possibly also those of southwestern El Paraíso.

[63] Stone, 1948.

Indians include the highlands of the three adjacent southwestern departments of La Paz, Intibucá, and Lempira. On the east, the Department of La Paz is actually divided into two fairly distinct regions, the eastern portion which includes part of the Comayagua Valley, the watershed, and the upper valley of the Río Goascorán. This portion of the department is Ladino. The western section, which includes most of the highlands, is inhabited principally by Indians, although they tend to thin out as one approaches the lowlands of the Río Torolá on the south border. Marcala is a Ladino town set in this Indian region. The Indian population continues practically uninterrupted through the highlands of the Department of Intibucá. On the south border there are few of them, and they thin out as one approaches the Department of Comayagua on the north. There are occasional Ladino communities, such as La Esperanza itself, but they are few. In the Department of Lempira, they occupy the northern part of the highland mass which composes the southern part of the department, and much of the valley of the Río Mejocote. The very northern *municipios* of Lempira are again Ladino.

In the municipio of Intibucá most of the houses are scattered over the countryside. Very few Indians live in the town itself and even the so-called *barrios* of the town are actually nearby rural settlements. These *barrios* (Lempira, Maniadero, El Terrero, Llano de la Virgen, and El Molino Viejo) are not referred to as *caseríos*, the term which is used for the rural territorial units into which the rest of the *municipio* is divided. The community of Chinacla in La Paz was described by informants in Marcala as what Sol Tax has called a "vacant" town; that is, the town itself has a very small permanent population, but many of the Indians in the surrounding rural area have town houses to which they come during business or fiestas.

The Indian language in this region has practically disappeared. In Guajiquiro it is reported that some people still speak Lenca, and the informants from Lempira said that they believed that there were still some towns there in which it was used. The writer found no one who said that an Indian language was still spoken in the Intibucá area.

The Lenca Indian is basically an agriculturalist. The main crops which he cultivates vary somewhat with the altitude of his fields, but corn and beans are the principal cultivations. Plantains, wheat, sugar cane, citrus, fruits, wheat, potatoes, and sweet potatoes are also of varying importance. In recent years, especially in the area north of Marcala, the cultivation of coffee has been of increasing importance. Informants in Marcala claimed that the Indians in the northern towns were generally better off since that area was specializing in coffee. The recent increase of coffee and its relatively high price on the international market has channeled more wealth into the north of the department than in the south.

The agricultural technology of the Lenca does not vary in any great degree from that of the Ladino. The principal difference is that the Lenca do not make much use of the wooden plow. Sowing is done mainly with the digging stick of one form or another, and with the hoe. The generally high altitude of the area occupied permits only one crop a year. Potatoes do give two crops and there is some irrigation used for garden crops. Sorghum has evidently not entered the area in any significant amount, and rice is of very minor importance. Land is seldom used more than one year, and is left to rest for three or four years. Most families have a few cattle and the animals are occasionally turned to pasture in old *milpa*, thus providing a minimum of animal fertilizer. The principal form of land usufruct is *ejidal*. While for the country as a whole, 46.1% of the *finca* land is private and 24.6% is *ejidal*, in the total *finca* area of the three departments of La Paz, Intibucá, and Lempira, 24.0% is private and 51.6% is *ejidal*. Stone[64] describes cases of communal land usufruct but the writer did not encounter this in the brief interviews of the survey. In any case, the *ejidal* lands are worked free of charge. Labor in the fields is carried on by both men and women in Intibucá and in the communities around Marcala. Exchange labor was reported as still being fairly common, mainly between pairs of men. There is evidently a considerable amount of annual migration to other areas for labor; some of these movements turn out to be permanent and the families do not return to Intibucá. Whole families go to coffee harvests in Comayagua, La Libertad, and Santa Bárbara; some men go to mines in Santa Bárbara and to the city of Tegucigalpa; quite a few go to the north coast for periods of work on the banana plantations. Some of the families from Marcala go to Comayagua to rent land for cultivation in much the same way that the Ladinos from Zambrano do.

There is still a good deal of hunting done by the Lenca. Stone reported the use of the bow and arrow; many also use old shotguns of the cap type, and both fall and spring traps.

Among the handicrafts, there is neither spinning nor weaving of cloth, but net and basket products are still fairly important. Pottery is made throughout the area, that of certain towns, such as La Campa in Lempira, being especially well known. Women's clothes are sewn at home or very occasionally made by seamstresses. Men's clothing is usually bought readymade. While the regular wooden *trapiche* (sugar press) made of wood and moved by oxen is used, there also survives the *sangarro* type of two horizontal rollers turned by hand.

Much of the domestic picture has been described by Stone. The main points which we wish to mention here for the sake of future comparison is that the fire is usually on the floor of the house between three stones, called by the term *tenemaste*; a few also make *hornillas*, and Stone notes that in some settlements there is a porch at the rear which serves as a kitchen;[65] this last, it will be noted, is specifically a Ladino style. The grinding stone, reported by Stone to be of various types, was said by the writer's informants to be generally crude. They are used on a *molendero*, or special table surface. Wood ash is preferred to lime for *nixtamal*; it was said that strong ash came from green wood, while the older the tree, the more the ash lost its power. There are very few ovens, and the wooden mortar is used for coffee and the little rice which may be purchased. Stone has described the women's dress in some detail. The only point to be added here is that

---

[64] Stone, 1948, pp. 212–213.   [65] Stone, 1948, p. 208.

in addition to the skirt and blouse type she described, the writer noted that many women were wearing one piece dresses which were made to look as if they were skirt and blouse; from a short distance away the two look identical. Most of these dresses are a faded matching color, but the writer noted in the market in Intibucá that some women were using flowered prints, checks, and even plaids. Over the head a *pañuelo* is almost always worn when out. The skirt is called the *nagua* or *enagua*, the same term used elsewhere in Central America for the older style Ladino skirt and now used almost exclusively by Ladinoized Indians. The informants on the Department of Lempira said that the *pañuelo* was not too commonly used there.

While the town of La Esperanza has no market place, Intibucá does. To this market come people from all the neighboring *municipios* of the department. The market is set up in a building which occupies one half of the plaza in front of the municipal building. While it operates every day, Thursday, Saturday, and Sunday are the principal market days. Markets are fairly important over much of the Lenca area. Informants in Marcala reported that there were markets of some importance in Santa María, Tutule, Marcala, and Santiago. The main days in all these towns were Thursday and Sunday. In Opotoro, while there was no formal market as such, there was said to be a general movement into the town on business on these two days. People from Intibucá were said also to go to the markets in Marcala, Jesús de Otoro, and Siguatepeque, the last of these being the major commercial outlet for products of the entire Department of Intibucá. Certain of the Lenca products, mainly baskets, are sold in Tegucigalpa, and carried down to Cacaopera and the San Miguel markets in El Salvador.

While relatively little information was gathered on family organization, both Ladino and Indian informants in Marcala, La Esperanza, and Intibucá agreed that Indian families were generally more stable than Ladino unions. It was said that there was a slightly higher formal marriage rate among Indians, but that whether married or living in free unions, they tended to retain a family unity which was lacking in many Ladino homes. Stone[66] reported that temporary matrilocal residence was the general practice; the writer's informant in the town of Intibucá said that temporary patrilocal residence was customary although some did observe matrilocal residence. In any case, a couple eventually, after a year or two, goes to a house of its own. There was a tendency reported for town dwellers to marry among themselves, and for the wealthier Indians to marry into families of similar economic status. *Compadres* were generally sought from within the Indian population, not from the Ladinos living in La Esperanza.

Ladinos in general tend to be somewhat depreciatory concerning the Indian population. In Marcala the Indians were grouped roughly together with the *"pueblo"* or general lower class population. However, Ladino informants in Marcala insisted upon referring to themselves as "mestizo" in the racial sense, claiming descent in part from the Indians, and Ladino informants in both Marcala and La Esperanza tended to show considerable objectivity concerning the

[66] Stone, 1948, p. 214.

Indian population; the main comments of a depreciatory nature concerned the heavy drinking of the Indians, their machete fighting, and their dialectic Spanish. There is practically no intermarriage between the two groups, although Ladino men will have children by Indian women. In La Esperanza it was said that in such a union, the Ladino would not live with the Indian woman. If the child was brought up by the mother, it was an Indian, whereas if the father chose to take it with him to La Esperanza, it would be brought up as a Ladino. Ladinoization of individual Indians seems to be a gradual although regular process. It was said that some Indians from Intibucá have moved across the line into La Esperanza and have become Ladinos, and some have become highly ladinoized while retaining their residence in the town of Intibucá.

The religious organization, which is fairly complex and will be described shortly, has evidently been completely separated from the political organization in the Indian towns. Intibucá itself, an Indian town, has a regular political organization staffed entirely by Indians. It is basically similar to that found in Ladino towns, and includes an *alcalde*, seven *regidores*, a *síndico*, and seven *consejeros municipales* named by the incumbent municipal officers. There are also the usual group of employees, a secretary, scribe, treasurer, and a *policía local*. The *regidores* each serve a term of a month and act as the chief of police. The *consejeros* are chosen on the basis of their ability and maturity, and many of them continue as councilors through changing municipal bodies. In each of the *caseríos* are two *alcaldes auxiliares* who alternate serving a month in town and a month in their rural area; the *regidor* in town has charge of those who are serving their time in the town. None of the municipal officers are paid.

As in the towns of La Esperanza and Intibucá there are separate *municipalidades*, so at one time a similar situation was planned for Marcala. Sometime in the second half of the last century the Ladino who held the leading position in the community built a separate building in the town as the *cabildo indígena*, i.e., the municipal headquarters of the Indians. Other Ladinos in the town fought this measure, however, as they felt there should be but one municipal government for both Indians and Ladinos, and that the Indians should not have a separate organization. This group was successful so that the building was never used for its original purpose and today is used as an extra school building. It still retains the same name, however, and is referred to as the *cabildo indígena*.

While the municipal officers are elected by the municipal population, there was some evidence of the survival of a group of elders who actually make the selection of who were to occupy these municipal offices. This group, known as the *principales*, was said to be the same as the *consejeros* of the municipality; they met twice a year, once in May to name the religious officials, and again in October to select the new municipal officials. They do not act entirely alone in these matters, but hold a series of meetings with all the men of the *municipio* who can attend. Thus it is not a matter sheerly of their selection, but of an agreement reached in a general meeting in which they are probably the most influential participants. The writer could not get a consistent picture from informants as to how much the municipal elections were settled ahead of time in these general meetings, and how much there was still a possibility of running competitive candidates.

There is considerable evidence that the actual control of the Indian population varies in form from one community to the next. The fact that Intibucá is immediately next door to the departmental capital of La Esperanza has probably had the influence of having the Intibucá organization function more or less along the accepted lines of Ladino municipal government. In Chinacla, in La Paz, however, the situation seems more to revolve around a single man who is considered as headman in the community. Stone says that in some towns the *cacique*, as such a headman is usually called, received his office through inheritance.[67] Where there is any sizable number of Ladinos, such as in Marcala, the system fits the usual Ladino pattern completely.

The religious organization of the Lenca of the southwestern highlands has evidently undergone differential acculturation. Unfortunately, the main data collected on this subject was for Intibucá alone, although it will be noted some comparative information is available from La Paz and Lempira. The situation in Intibucá cannot be considered as necessarily typical of all the communities in the area, but certain items of it are found elsewhere.

There are to be found in Intibucá today what appear to be two fairly distinct sets of religious organization. One, the older, stems from a development which evidently has undergone considerable readjustment through the years. This organization is responsible for a series of religious celebrations through the entire year, has a permanent staff operating at all times, and has as an annual climax to the observances of the patron fiesta of the *Virgen de la Candelaria*. The other organization is evidently a newer development on the more common Ladino pattern of the sodality, and so far as the writer could tell, generally operated as a distinct entity.

The second of these organizations involves the existence of four *hermandades*. Three (*Santísima, Corazón de Jesús,* and *la Sagrada Familia*) have male leaders and one (*la Virgen del Carmen*) has a female leader; the members were of both sexes. Informants said that anyone who so wishes could join these sodalities. In each, there are two *mayordomos* (of the appropriate sex) who are the leaders, secretary, a treasurer, and four *munidores*. So far as the writer could ascertain, the only connection that these *hermandades* had with the older organization was that the choice of the *mayordomos* (who held office for two years) was made in the same manner and in the same meetings as was the choice of the principal officers of the older organization. The *hermandades* have no special buildings, and their saints are kept in the church. The main job of the members is to collect money for the sponsoring of their respective annual fiesta.

Stone writes that the *cofradía* system which probably formed the basis of the older system was abolished about 1880.[68] Since that time, the major religious organization of Intibucá has evolved into a permanent complex organization

---

[67] Stone, 1948, p. 212.   [68] Stone, Ms.

which maintains constant vigil over the religious property of the community and sponsors a whole series of fiestas during the year.

On the far north side of the town of Intibucá lies a large rectangular plaza. On one side of this stands a building which is known as the *Cabildo de Auxiliaría*. In this *cabildo* is a small crude altar, a chest in which is said rest the land titles for the lands of the community, and various equipment which is used in the course of the fiestas. Some of this equipment is used only during the fiesta known as the *guancasco*. The organization of personnel which operates in the *cabildo* is fairly complex and is named annually. At any one time all the following people are supposed to be on duty, either in the *cabildo* or in carrying out special tasks:

Present at one time	Total number of alternates
1 *Alcalde de Varalta*	3
1 *Regidor*	2
16 *Comisionados*	48
5 *Alguaciles*	10
1 *Mayor de Arca*	2
1 *Autor*	2

Thus there are three *acaldes de varalta*, the first, second, and third, and they alternate usually a month at a time in their responsibility for the *cabildo*. The *regidor* and the *comisionados* have to sleep in the *cabildo* during their periods of responsibility. The writer could not ascertain the distinction between the *alguaciles* and the *comisionados*; they both seemed to act as general messenger boys and guards of the *cabildo*. The *mayor de arca* was specifically responsible for the *baúl del arca*, the trunk in which were kept the land titles for the *municipio*. The *autores* were the only officials who did not change annually. They might be considered as the "priests" of the organization. It is they who make the orations at the annual fiestas, having them well memorized, and each time they come to the *cabildo* they kneel before the altar and pray. The *regidores* have the responsibility for the care of the *milpa comunal*. This is land which has been set aside from the rest of the *ejidal* lands and on which is grown corn and beans used in the fiestas or sold to get money to buy candles, *cacao*, *dulce*, and other things necessary to make the *chilate* (an *atol* of corn with *cacao*) for the *guancasco* and for the celebration shortly after the naming of the new *alcaldes de varalta* each May. The *regidor* who is "on duty" is responsible for calling together enough men to do the necessary cleaning, planting, cultivating, and harvesting of the products from the *milpa comunal*.

In addition to these men, there are two groups of 15 women each, called *tenacinas*, who are called on alternate months to the *cabildo* and then sent to the church to clean it and spread clean pine needles on the floor. In charge of each group is a *capitana*. It was said that the only women eligible for this work were unmarried women, "those who are not occupied."

The situation described for the town of La Campa in Lempira varied somewhat from this general picture. There was an *hacienda* devoted to the saints, and there was a *consejo de fábrica*, a council in charge of the *"fábrica"* or religious equipment used in the *fiestas*. The municipal *síndico* was evidently in charge of the land titles there, however. Each of the saints had a fund of money which the respective *mayordomos* would take and use during the year; the interest (i.e., crops, etc.) would serve to pay for the *fiesta* for that saint, and the capital would revert to the next *mayordomo* for the next year.

In Intibucá, besides the alternating officials, there are a series of *mayordomos de los santos* for the saints in the church. These are not, according to the informant, the same as the four pairs of *mayordomos de las hermandades*. There are two *mayordomos de los santos* for each of the saints in the church. The organization of the *cabildo* celebrates each of these saints, and the *mayordomos* among themselves arranged that there shall be two of them present in the church at all times. The writer is not sure that the following list is complete, but it was quoted to him by the first *Alcalde de Varalta* as being the *fiestas* which were celebrated:

1 January	New Year
6 January	*Día de los Reyes*
15 January	Esquipulas
2 February	*Virgen de Candelaria* (patron saint and *guancasco*)
19 March	*San José*
variable	Holy Week
month of May	*Virgen Auxiliadora*
13 June	*San Antonio*
15 August	*Virgen del Tránsito*
8 September	*Virgen de las Mercedes*
month of October	*Virgen Auxiliadora*
1 November	*Todos los Santos*
2 November	*Día de los Difuntos*
8 December	*Virgen de Concepción*
(13–22 December)	(*guancasco* in Yamaranguila)

From the data provided by informants, the writer gathers that each of these saints and days has a pair of *mayordomos*. Each of the fiestas was described as being basically similar and consisting of the following phases:

(1) From 9 to 10 a.m. a Mass is held in the church.
(2) The crown of the saint is brought to the *cabildo* after the Mass, together with the equipment which is usually kept in the *cabildo* (*varas*, drums, flute, mask for a dancer known as the *grasejo*, red pendons carried by two *pendoneros*).
(3) The game of *carrera de patos*, wherein riders try to pull the head of a duck hung by the feet from a frame overhead; the *grasejo* and *pendoneros* dance at this time. This lasts about three hours.
(4) The crown of the saint is returned from the *cabildo* to the church.
(5) A *rosario* is held in the church about 3 p.m.
(6) Refreshments are provided by the *alcaldes*, and the visitors leave offerings of corn in the church. The offerings are collected by the *alcaldes* to help defray the expenses of the *fiesta*.

The writer had conflicting reports locally as to whether a *carrera de patos* was held each time a fiesta was held or not; Stone (in correspondence) says it occurs only for the *guancasco*. One informant insisted that it was, and another claimed that a further responsibility of each of the *mayordomos de los santos* was the raising of the ducks for use in this game.

While most of the *fiestas* sponsored by the *cabildo* are only one day in length, that of the patron saint in February is 9 days long. It is during this *fiesta* that the *guancasco* is held.[69] On the 2nd of February the image of *San Francisco de Asís*, the patron saint of Yamaringuila, a neighboring town, arrives in Intibucá accompanied by various of the *cabildo* officials of that town. *San Francisco* spends the next nine days in the *cabildo* in Intibucá visiting with *Candelaria*. During the first two days the *carrera de patos* are held and the *grasejos* and *pendoneros* of the two towns dance together. In the following days, Masses and *rosarios* are held daily and people from the countryside bring in the offerings of corn, candles, etc. Upon the conclusion of the fiesta, *San Francisco* returns home. On the 13th of December, the *Virgen de la Candelaria* makes the trip to visit *San Francisco* in Yamaranguila for a similar series of celebrations. Stone interprets the origin of the *guancasco* as an annual meeting between the towns to assure one another that each would observe peace during the following year. This is a reasonable interpretation in view of the extremely warlike reputation the Lenca and their neighbors have gained during their known history.

The *guancasco*, or visiting of patron saints between two towns, has been reported from various other towns in Honduras. The informants from Lempira reported that it was held between Gracias and Mejicapa (13 December in Mejicapa, 19 January in Gracias), two *barrios* of Erandique (in Gualmaca on 24 September, in Erandique on 20 January), and formerly between La Campa and Colohete (8 December in Colohete, and 24 February in La Campa); and there was a three way *guancasco* held between La Campa, Belén, and San Sebastián, but today while all three come to La Campa, La Campa goes only to Belén. In the Department of La Paz, informants said that reciprocal visits of saints were occasionally made between Chinacla and Marcala, Santa Elena and Marcala, and Santiago and Marcala. There were two images of *San Miguel*, the patron of San Miguel, and one in particular was used for these visits. The informant in Jacaleapa said that such visits were made between the towns of Texiguat and Liure (to Texiguat on 4 October, and to Liure on 2 February) in southwestern El Paraíso. It may be noted in passing that this reciprocal visiting of saints, the real *guancasco*, should not be confused with the trips a saint makes on *demanda*, when it goes out to collect funds prior to its fiesta. The reciprocal visiting has been reported, so far as the writer knows, in only two areas outside of Honduras. One of these is between the Indian town of San Luis Jilotepeque and the Ladino towns of Ipala and Santa Catarina Mita in eastern Guatemala,[70] and between the Indian communities of Jayaque and Cuisnahuat in El Salvador.[71]

---

[69] See Stone, Ms., for a description of the event. [70] See Gillin, 1951, pp. 97–104.
[71] Adams, n.d. (d).

It is unfortunate that the Lenca Indians, a group of considerable number and of an interesting culture, should have gone so long without intensive study devoted to them. It is no reflection on Stone's own work to say that it is limited, and the data gathered in the course of the present survey add but little to that which she already published. In both cases, the information derives principally from the departments of Intibucá and La Paz, and we know little from first hand observation concerning the situation in Lempira. It is to be hoped that in the near future ethnologists will take an interest in this remnant society.

3. THE INDIANS OF EAST CENTER SANTA BARBARA

Ascending the Rio Ulúa from the plains of the Department of Cortés, one enters a rugged, cutover country. The Ulúa itself continues almost to the departmental capital of Santa Bárbara, and then splits into two major tributaries, the Río Jicatuyo which comes down from the west, and the continuation of the Ulúa itself which comes out of the southeast from the Department of Lempira. Along these rivers and some of their tributaries there are still to be found today enclaves of Indians. Probably the most important are those who compose the majority of the population of the communities of Chinda and Ilama, and a small portion of populations of neighboring Gualala, Petoa, Colinas, San Marcos, and Trinidad. Further up the Ulúa, above Santa Bárbara, is the Indian municipio of El Níspero which for practical purposes is probably one with the general Lenca region of the southwest highlands. On a tributary of the Río Jicatuyo lies the municipio of Atima, and directly across the river from the city of Santa Bárbara itself, lies the *aldea* of Machuloa; in both these places are Indians. Ilama was visited on the survey and the road carries one through Chinda and Gualala, so it was possible to have at least a look at the latter towns. The data which is given in the present section concern specifically Ilama, however. It is the largest center of Indians of this region, even though the contemporary Indians of that *municipio* probably do not exceed 2,500 in number.

The original affiliation of this enclave of Indians is not clear. Ilama itself is a very old Indian town; Rosa claims that it was founded prior to the conquest.[72] There is no Indian language spoken today and the present writer does not know of any vocabularies which have ever been collected there. There are three logical possibilities as to the former affiliation of these people: Chorti, Lenca, and Jicaque. It is also possible that they were a Mexican language speaking group, but their isolation from other such groups makes this the sheerest speculation. Archaeologically the region under discussion was one of the easternmost extensions of Maya culture. Johnson[73] places the entire Ulúa Valley in the Chortí language area. Jicaque is a possible affiliate if von Hagen's extension of the Jicaque area through the entire Department of Cortés and to the Sierra de Omoa is correct. This Santa Bárbara group would almost be immediately adjacent to the area he assigns as once having been Jicaque.[74] However, Stone believes that the term "Jicaque" has little linguistic significance historically,

---

[72] Rosa, 1940, p. 13.   [73] Johnson, 1940, Map.   [74] Von Hagen, 1943.

that it merely referred to various non-Mexican languages.[75] The possible affiliation with what is today called the Lenca is based principally on geographical and tenuous socio-cultural connections. The Santa Bárbara groups lie in the valleys of rivers which go directly up into the Lenca area. It is only about thirty kilometers up the Ulúa Valley from Ilama to the northernmost Indian *municipio* of the Lenca region, El Níspero. Socially, there is an important contemporary connection between the Lenca region and Ilama and the neighboring part of Comayagua in that the Intibucá Indians make regular pilgrimages to the shrines in Taulabé and Ilama. Also, the term *guancasco* was known and used by informants in Ilama. The possible affiliation with the Chortí on the basis of present evidence is even more tenuous. The term *huisute*, which is Pocomam for digging stick, is used in Ilama. This points to a westward connection, but since Wisdom gives no word for this implement, I do not know whether it is the same or not.[76] It is also possible that the Santa Bárbara population was Pocomam. In any case, we cannot come to any satisfactory conclusion at present concerning their former affiliation, and their importance today is as an Indian enclave which is fairly ladinoized.

Ilama and other Indian communities nearby differ in an important respect from many other Indian communities in Honduras. Instead of being located in highland refuge areas, they are located on one of the principal transportation routes of the country. The main road from San Pedro Sula to the departmental capital of Santa Bárbara follows the Ulúa Valley and goes directly through Trinidad, Chinda, Ilama, and Gualala. It is certain that this route was traversed by numerous Spaniards, and that it has served as an important channel of goods and people moving from the highland area of the south to the north coast. In view of this, the survival of an Indian enclave is remarkable; it is not surprising that it is ladinoized, but it is surprising that it exists at all. Ilama stands at an altitude of 700 feet. On one side is the Ulúa River, and on the other a high ridge of hills. About 70% of the town population is considered as Indian, and in the *aldeas* there are numerous scattered homes of Indians.

While this is a region in which the ox cart could be used, it has not been adopted intensively. The *mecapal* is still used by the poorer people, but most use the horse or mule. Transportation on the river seems to be at a minimum. Informants agreed that the use of *cayucos* in the Río Ulúa was limited almost entirely to crossing the river; there was practically no river traffic going either upstream or down.

The basic economy of Ilama is corn and bean agriculture and henequin production. Sorghum is not planted. While all are agricultural, most of the town Indians and some of the Ladinos grow henequin and convert the fiber into numerous products. Fiber work is carried on through much of Santa Bárbara, and the "Panama" hats of the region are famous. The storekeeper informant in Nueva Ocotepeque spoke highly of the Ilama products and wished he could get

---

[75] In Johnson, 1948a.

[76] Wisdom, 1940, describes the implement which is also the main Chortí planting implement, but does not give the Chortí word.

more of them. The agricultural technology, however, is generally simple. The plow is not used in Ilama, but it will be remembered that the plow is rare or non-existent through almost all the northern half of Honduras, so this cannot be considered merely as an Indian peculiarity. The digging stick is the principal planting implement.

It was reported by informants that the women do not participate in the field work. In the actual fiber industry, however, there is some division of labor. The men produce most of the henequin products, making the string and the net bags (*matates*), hammocks, whips, ropes, and animal harness gear. The women, on the other hand, devote more of their time to the production of palm products, hats of various types and some odds and ends of other products. The men do some hunting but it was said that no bow and arrow is used. In field labor it was said that exchange labor was still common in the *aldeas*.

As is the case in the southwestern highlands, a very high percentage of the lands in Ilama are *ejidal*. In the Department of Santa Bárbara, as a whole, 54.6% of the *finca* land is private and 33.3% is *ejidal*. In Ilama, 28.4% is private and 63.6% is *ejidal*; in the combined *municipios* of Chinda, Ilama, and Gualala, 25.6% is private and 67.2% *ejidal*. In Ilama there is one *aldea*, San Vicente de la Nieve, in which the land is held communally by the residents. *Ejidal* lands are apparently held as if they were private, since it was said that an occupant did not pay for his right to use it and could rent it out if he so desired.

In the town most of the Ladino houses are of *bajareque* and tile, while the Indian homes are usually *chozas*, i.e., walls of poles or *bajareque* with roofs of straw or palm. There are some poor Ladinos who live in the latter type home and some Indians in the former, but in general the correlation between the social distinctions and the house types was said to be high. Inside the home most were said to have the raised *fogón* for the fire, although some few did have the fire on the floor between three stones. For making *nixtamal* both lime and wood ash are used, but the former, while abundant, is more expensive and the latter is preferred.

In dress, the men are indistinguishable from Ladinos; the Indian women still generally use the *enagua* skirt, however.

There is no market place, and all products are sold in stores or sent out of the *municipio* for sale.

While in the southwest highlands Indian unions were said to be considerably more stable than those between Ladinos, in Ilama formal marriage was said to be about equally frequent within each of the two groups and, if anything, the Indian unions tended to be somewhat less stable than did those of the Ladinos. Indians were also said to seek *compadres* from among the Ladinos, a practice which was not reported from the southwestern highlands.

There is separation between Indians and Ladinos reflected in the opinion expressed by one Ladino informant that a person born Indian cannot himself become Ladino because "his tendencies continue to be the same;" this same informant referred to the Ladinos as "whites."

The Indian-Ladino distinction is maintained in the municipal organization.

The town has the usual structure involving the *alcalde, regidores, síndico,* and *consejeros municipales,* but the *alcalde* is usually Ladino, the *síndico,* always so, and the *regidores* evenly divided, two Indians and two Ladinos. The four *consejeros* are all Ladinos. In the town there are four *alcaldes auxiliares,* two from each *barrio,* and all are Indians. In rural administration, the *alcaldes auxiliares* are either Indian or Ladino depending upon which group is predominant in the *aldea* in question.

In the religious life, about the only distinction the writer could find which was Indian was that among the Indians the men still lead novenas while among the Ladinos, the women were those who "knew how." In the organization of fiestas, however, there seemed to be no distinction as to social group. It was said that there were neither purely Ladino nor purely Indian sodalities. The priest is in general charge of religious activities and personally heads the *Consejo de Fábrica* which cares for the funds and arranges for the *fiestas,* and which is also composed of both Indians and Ladinos. At the time of the survey, the vice-president was an Indian, the treasurer a "white," the secretary an Indian, and the two *vocales* were "whites."

Stone reports that she was informed that the *guancasco* was carried on between Ilama and Chinda,[77] and the present writer's informants also assured him that such was the case. Rosa also describes the *guancasco* for these towns[78] and, according to his description, there are basic similarities with the *guancasco* of Intibucá. However, there are significant differences between the two, probably indicative of a recent accretion to the affair and evidently involving a change of emphasis.

The *guancasco* in Ilama involves three towns, Gualala, Chinda, and Ilama. The description as provided by informants was as follows. For a month prior to the first of February, the *Virgen de la Candelaria* leaves Ilama for Chinda, and *Santa Lucía* leaves for Gualala. They spend a month collecting funds, going through the *aldeas,* and then return to Ilama for the major *fiesta* which lasts from the 1st until the 12th of February. However, the saints of Gualala and Chinda do not arrive in Ilama to sit with the Ilama saints during this *fiesta*. The pilgrimages of people who arrive for the *fiesta* come accompanying Ilama's own saints which were out collecting funds and which come back on the first of February. Similarly, between the 5th and 14th of January, the saint, *Esquipulas,* comes from Gualala collecting funds through the *municipio* of Ilama, and returns to Gualala for the fiesta there on the 15th; people from Ilama accompany it back, but do not take an Ilama saint on the visit. And between the 2nd and 14th of August, the *Virgen de los Angeles* from Chinda comes through Ilama collecting funds, and returns to Chinda for the *fiesta* on the 15th of August, accompanied by people from Ilama; but again, no saint from Ilama goes there for the *fiesta*. Thus the *guancasco* of Ilama, Gualala, and Chinda is not a visiting of saints, but an elaborate pattern of going on *demanda,* in which the three *municipios* involved are particularly wedded. In Rosa's description of the affair in Ilama, he says: *Mientras toman el "chilate," el "hablador" u orador que viene de Gualala,*

[77] Stone, Ms. [78] Rosa, 1940, pp. 41–42.

primero, y el de Chinda después, pronuncian sendos y ampulosos discursos en los que ponen de manifiesto las cordiales relaciones que unen a estos pueblos, y excitan a los concurrentes para que nunca se dejen relegadas estas antiguas y tradicionales costumbres. El "hablador" de Ilama contesta a los oradores y ofrece al concurrente el "chilate" con que los vecinos obsequian a sus amigos que les visitan.[79] From this it is clear that even though there is no visiting of saints, the pilgrimages from one town to another are a reaffirmation of friendly relations between the populations involved. The *hablador* of these towns has the same function as does the *autor* of Intibucá. There used to be masked dances involved in the celebration, and some of the masks are preserved in the *municipalidad* although the dances stopped some years ago. The visiting of the saints between these three towns, however, is specifically a matter of going out on *demanda*, going out to collect funds, a custom which is found among Ladinos over much of neighboring Central America, especially in Nicaragua. There is no *carrera de patos* or *gallos* connected with the Ilama celebration although this custom has survived in more ladino communities elsewhere.

From this data, it is obvious that the Indians of Santa Bárbara are much more ladinoized than are many of those of the southwest highlands. While there survive various specific traits which still permit distinction between Indians and Ladinos, such as the use of the *mecapal* and the differences in house types, the principal social distinctions are to be found in assignation of posts in the municipal organization and in the retention of the emphasis on men as the principal workers in religious affairs.

4. THE INDIANS OF SOUTHWESTERN EL PARAÍSO

In the southwestern corner of the Department of El Paraíso is situated an Indian population which is still accessible only by horseback road. The principal *municipios* involved are Texiguat, Liure, Vado Ancho, and Yauyupe; the population is said to spread out along the Honduran side of the border region, however, and include considerable numbers of persons in the municipios of Alauca, Oropolí, and some in San Antonio de Flores. Johnson[80] refers to this group as part of the Matagalpa population which is found scattered today from the municipio of Matagalpa in Nicaragua[81] to Cacaopera in El Salvador.[82]

The writer encountered a splinter of this group living in the *aldea* of El Cerro behind the town of Yusguare; that group, some of whom travel back and forth from Liure to El Cerro, are considered as an Indian population by the Yusguare Ladinos. Further information was gathered from informants in Güinope and Jacaleapa. In the latter place, the informant was a person who had acted as school inspector for many years in the Texiguat region and was married to a woman from the town. The time alloted to the survey did not permit the writer to visit these communities himself, but by a stroke of luck, Doris Stone was in Honduras on a visit during the survey, and planned to visit the Jicaque of the

---

[79] Rosa, 1940, p. 42.   [80] Johnson, 1948a, p. 61, Map 5.
[81] See Adams, n.d. (b), and appendix by Stone in same report.   [82] Adams, n.d. (d).

Montaña de la Flor. (The result of that trip is recorded in the appendix.) The writer discussed the Texiguat-Liure problem with her and she promised that if it were at all possible, she would make the trip there since the writer's informants indicated that there were still some old people who spoke an Indian language. Mrs. Stone was able to make the trip, and has made her notes available for inclusion in the following description.

When she arrived in Texiguat and Liure, she wrote, she was many years too late. It was a difficult trip and no one knew any words in the Indian language. "All said their grandparents had said that in their day *lengua* was spoken. What I did find were *aldeas* without sufficient food, nor decent water, and with certain customs that still cling. Among these are: they make their own thread with a spindle whorl; they sew from their own cotton, but do not weave; they make *petates* and some very crude coiled pottery. They take out the saints to collect funds with drums beaten with sticks and the men go along using some of the alms to buy *guaro*. There is no lore that is not *mestizo*."[83]

As is the case in the southwestern highlands and in the Indian *municipios* of Santa Bárbara, the greater part of the land in the four main *municipios* in which the Indian population is found is *ejidal*. For the entire Department of El Paraíso, 60.7% of the *finca* land is private, and 24.5% is *ejidal*; in the combined municipios of Liure, Texiguat, Vado Ancho, and Yauyupe, only 5.3% of the *finca* land is private, and 90.4% is *ejidal*. In addition, 97.1% of the San Antonio de Flores *finca* land is *ejidal*. Indeed, the *ejidal* land, of these five *municipios* account for 50.5% of the total *ejidal* lands in the entire department. No information was gathered on agricultural technology, but informants agreed that not only was the production of *petates* rather important in Liure, but so also was hat making. In some of the *aldeas* of Texiguat, Santo Domingo for example, henequin is grown and a fiber industry similar to that of Ilama and Cacaopera of El Salvador exists.

In the homes in the rural areas of Jacaleapa, an extension of the area under discussion, the fire is usually on the floor of both Indian and Ladino homes, but in the former it was said that three stones were usually used, while in the latter the *hornilla* was made on the floor. As elsewhere, the grinding stone is raised on a board for use. While the Ladinos of Texiguat were said to use lime or wood ash in the *nixtamal*, Indians were said to use wood ash only. While almost all Ladinos have ovens, they are rare in Indian homes. The Indians evidently tend more to use the *tapesco* as a bed than do Ladinos. In the combined municipios of Texiguat, Liure, and Vado Ancho are to be found about 42% of all the *tapesco* beds in use in the entire department according to the 1950 Census.[84]

The informant in Jacaleapa said that the Texiguat Indians did tend to marry somewhat more than did the Ladinos, and that families were somewhat more stable. Separations did occur, however, and in those cases it was common to find the woman remaining in the house while the man went elsewhere. Neo-local residence was the general practise. While the writer is inclined to believe the

---

[83] Stone, personal correspondence.   [84] Census, 1954a.

report on the stability of the family, the census figures from Texiguat and Liure do not support the informant's contention that the Indians tend to marry. For El Paraíso as a whole, 58% of the people who are living together live in free union; in Texiguat and Liure, however, the free unions account for 71% and 74% respectively of the couples.[85]

In Texiguat it was said that women tended to lead in the Indian novenas, although men did it occasionally; men never did it among the Ladinos. Also there they observe the *fiesta* for the death of an infant; the informant said it included dancing, music, and food. For Holy Week it was said that a group of men put pitch and grease on their faces to make them black, put on special costumes, and went about collecting funds for the *fiesta*; they were called *Judíos*.

In both Güinope and Jacaleapa it was said that there was a *guancasco* between Texiguat and Liure; the Texiguat *fiesta* was held on the 4th of October and that of Liure on the 2nd of February. There was said to be a special building for this ceremony. Informants knew that saints visited back and forth between the two towns but did not know whether this was of the Intibucá type, in which the saint of one town actually attended the *fiesta* of that of the other, or the Ilama type in which the saint simply went on *demanda* and then the townpeople of the other town made a pilgrimage to the locale of the *fiesta*, accompanying the saint on his (or her) homeward trip.

In general, while the data on this population group has the clarity of a bag of dirty potsherds, it seems evident that the group is highly ladinoized. They are considered as Indians by the Ladinos who have been to the area, and they retain a few Indian customs now shared by Ladinos. Their *guancasco* is evidently distinctly theirs within the area and is not shared by the Ladinos.

5. THE JICAQUE INDIANS OF CENTRAL YORO

According to von Hagen,[86] the ancestors of the contemporary Montaña de la Flor population of Jicaque Indians fled to their present place of residence from nearby Yoro in the 1860's. This action served to isolate that small group from the rest of the Jicaque population which is today scattered over much of the large municipio of Yoro and the adjacent municipios of Yorito, Jocón, and Morazán. This Montaña de la Flor group is a very small enclave which has retained itself as a predominantly monolingual group. The rest of the Jicaque, over 95% of the Indian population involved, are much more ladinoized. As was mentioned earlier, the Montaña de la Flor population is described by von Hagen (1943), and a more recent study by Doris Stone will be found in the appendix in the present report. The present section is concerned with some brief notes taken by the writer while in Yoro from Ladino informants and an Indian woman who was visiting the town from the *aldea* of Plan Grande. These notes concern the ladinoized portion of the population, not the enclave in the Montaña de la Flor.

The Jicaque in Yoro are generally known as "tribes" and labelled according to the territory in which they live. Thus there is the *Tribu de la Joya*, the *Tribu*

---

[85] Census, 1954a.   [86] Von Hagen, 1943.

de San Francisco, etc. The term tribe as used here has no relation to the ethnological term, and simply refers to a local territorial population. There are no Indians in the town of Yoro itself. It was said that most of the Indian population is bilingual, speaking both the Jicaque language and Spanish; in the small *aldea* of Plan Grande, all but one were bilingual, and the exception was an old man who spoke only Jicaque. In general, as was the case in El Paraíso, these Indians are probably most marked by poverty. The houses, known as *seta*, are ranchos with pole walls and roofs of leaves. The fire is usually between three stones on the floor of the single room, and the people sleep on the ground, on *tapescos*, or in the *tabancos*. The *mecapal* is little used and the woman, it was said, did not participate much in the agricultural work.

Both men and women were engaged in the production of baskets and henequin products (*matates*, ropes, harnesses), but there is no weaving. Pottery is made by Indian women and by Ladino women. Housebuilding was said to be a voluntary group affair. The informants could not provide satisfactory information on religious organization aside from the fact that the women were ordinarily the leaders of novenas. The priest in Yoro indicated that there was practically no participation by the Jicaque men in formal church activities. At the family level post-marital residence was said to be dictated mainly by economic concerns; few people were wealthy enough to afford the cost of a new dwelling immediately and would usually live in whichever parents' home was larger.

6. THE IDENTIFICATION AND ACCULTURATION OF THE INDIAN

During the long history of the development of the Honduran population, there has been a gradual amalgamation of the population components which were at one time distinct. Presumably two hundred years ago there was no problem in saying who was an Indian, who was a Spaniard, and who was a Mestizo or Ladino. In that period, customs were highly distinct and racial differences served as identifying marks. Today, for practical purposes, racial differences are no longer satisfactory for the identification of anyone. Among peoples who are culturally Indian there are some who appear of white descent; and among those whom we call Ladinos are numerous mestizos and possibly many of racially somewhat pure Indian ancestry. To jump from 200 years ago to today, we must change our entire point of view of definition concerning Indians. Instead of defining them in terms of racial characteristics we must define them in terms of socio-cultural differences: that is, in terms of personal habits which they have and which Ladinos do not have; interrelationships which exist among them and which do not exist among them and Ladinos. It is on this basis that we have distinguished the various groups discussed in the previous sections as "Indian."

It is obvious that sheerly in terms of culture traits, i.e., specific things which are habits, it is difficult to distinguish an Indian group from a Ladino group in many cases. This is due principally to the fact that many traits which were originally Indian are now used by both Indians and Ladinos, and many which were originally European are also used by both groups. The distinction must be sought not merely in a listing of traits, but in terms of distinctive social groupings, of the way the traits are integrated into habit systems and the way these habit systems distinguish components within the total social structure.

Of the Indian groups in Honduras, we are going arbitrarily to exclude from discussion the groups of the Mosquitia, the Paya, the Sumu, and Miskito. Our reason for this is a practical one: the writer has had no personal experience with these groups, and there are no recent ethnographic studies; Hondurans generally accept the fact that the groups involved are Indian, of a very distinct culture, and make some allowance for that fact in their thinking concerning the groups. Here we are going to concentrate mainly on what may be called the interior groups, those enclaves that live in the highlands and interior valleys.

Of the interior groups, superficial examination permits us to distinguish immediately at least two degrees of acculturation: the Jicaque of the Montaña de la Flor stand as a very distinct group from all the other groups described in preceding sections. They are predominantly monolingual, they live intentionally isolated from the rest of the Honduran population, both Indian and Ladino; and they have numerous customs which easily distinguish them from their neighbors. In line with the general terminology which we have used in the previous studies in this series, we will refer to this population group as being culturally *Traditional Indians*; i.e., they are so Indian in custom and social organization that there is not the slightest doubt in the mind of the observer that they cannot in any way be classified as Ladino. An indication of this may be seen in the fact that both Bonilla (1942) and Colindres (1942), in writing brief articles on the Indians of Honduras, devoted a relatively large amount of space to this minute population which in terms of percentages probably composes about one fifth of one percent of the entire Indian population of the country.

All the rest of the interior Indian populations are much more acculturated than is the Montaña de la Flor group. It is possible, however, to make a further distinction between certain of the remaining groups. The basic definition of an Indian which we will use is as follows: an Indian is a person who is a member of a group, the members of which are collectively referred to as Indians by themselves and by Ladinos, and which group maintains certain forms of social organization which serve to distinguish it from other groups which are usually referred to as Ladino. All the groups described in previous sections, the Lenca, the Chortí, Jicaque of Yoro, and the populations in Santa Bárbara and El Paraíso, fit this definition to one degree or another. It is convenient, however, to distinguish two degrees of acculturation, for in some of the groups the degree to which the social organization is different as between the Indian groups and the Ladinos is much greater than in others. Elsewhere[87] we have used the terms *Modified* and *Ladinoized* to distinguish two grades of acculturation. In Honduras the Lenca and probably the Chortí would be considered as Modified, whereas the Santa Bárbara group, that of El Paraíso, and the Yoro Jicaque would probably be considered as Ladinoized. The distinction between a Modified group and the Ladinoized

---

[87] Adams, n.d. (c) and (d).

group is made on the degree to which social organizational forms peculiar to the Indian community exist. Modified Indian communities are more distinct in structure than are the Ladinoized; or to place the emphasis on the other side, Ladinoized communities have lost much more of their distinctive structure than have Modified communities.

Unfortunately, lack of specific data on the Chortí must leave the exact position of this group (in Honduras) in question for the present, but the distinctions

Table 16.—Gross trait listing for four Indian groups in interior Honduras*

	Lenca	Santa Bárbara	Yoro Jicaque	El Paraíso
Use of *mecapal*...................	yes	yes	no	yes
Cook on 3 stones on floor.........	yes	some	yes	yes
Women use distinctive dress.......	yes	yes	?	no
X Survival of indigenous hand industry.........................	yes	yes	yes	yes
X Survival of voluntary and/or exchange labor.....................	yes	some	some	?
X Distinct religious organization....	yes	no	?	some
X Men lead religious *novenas*.......	some	yes	no	some
X Distinct political organization....	yes	some	?	?
X *Ejidal* lands still important.......	yes	yes	?	yes
X Indian language survives.........	some	no	some	no
Gross totals:				
Yes............................	8	5	2	4
Some...........................	2	3	2	2
No.............................	0	2	2	2
?..............................	0	0	4	2
X Integrative features, totals				
Yes............................	5	3	1	2
Some...........................	2	2	2	2
No.............................	0	2	1	1
?..............................	0	0	3	2

* Those features marked with "X" are integrative features.

may be made clear by a comparison of the four groups described earlier in the present section. There are a number of specific traits which empirically seem to stand as somewhat distinctive elements in Indian culture in interior Honduras. Table 16 provides a gross picture of the presence and absence of these for the four groups under discussion. To these may be added others which, when present, add further suggestion of the retention of distinctive culture: the market, such as in Intibucá and elsewhere in the southwest highlands; relatively greater family stability, present in much of the southwest highlands; and the work of women in subsistence agriculture.

Those traits listed on the table are of two basic types. Those which are unstarred may be thought of as surviving distinctive traits which reflect social and/or economic distinctions between the Indian and the Ladino. They have no extreme or immediate significance with respect to differential social relationships which may exist inside of the Indian and Ladino groups. When they disappear, they are replaced by other techniques or methods. Thus the *mecapal* is replaced by carrying by shoulder, horse or mule; cooking on the floor is replaced by cooking on a *poyo*; and an Indian dress for women by Ladino dress. The starred items, however, which for the sake of convenience we have called "integrative" features, are those which act in a specific way to tie members of the Indian community together, to retain a distinctive value system, and to make relations between Indians and Ladinos distinct from those which exist within either group. In general, it may be said that these traits are specifically distinctive because of their integrative function and, when they disappear, they reflect the gradual disappearance of the Indian culture as a distinct entity. In many cases, the disappearance of these traits involves no one-for-one replacement because the basic traits may remain; what changes is the way these traits are utilized in social relationships and the value orientation.

To make more clear the distinction between Modified and Ladinoized Indian communities, let us see how these integrative traits are differentially retained and how they serve to provide clarity to the distinction between the Indian and Ladino community. The survival of an indigenous hand industry does not in itself mean that a community is Indian. But when a community is called Indian, and the people therein are engaged in such an industry, and nearby Ladinos are disproportionately not so engaged, it then means that the industry has a distinctive quality locally of being Indian. Furthermore, the fact that both men and women (which is usually the case) are engaged in a type of activity which is distinct, and which establishes a different relationship between them than would otherwise exist, then the presence of the industry has an integrative quality. Similarly, the survival of some sort of exchange or voluntary labor within a community immediately indicates the presence of certain social relationships among the members of that community which may be absent from a community where such labor is not found. Voluntary labor among the Lenca is very important both at the interfamily level and within the religious framework. In Santa Bárbara it survives mainly among some of the rural people at the interfamily level, and in Yoro in the rural area with respect to *rancho* building. In both the latter places the general weakness of the trait, in comparison with the Lenca situation, indicates the disappearance of a trait which, when present, provided a type of social relationship between people called Indians which did not exist among Ladinos nor between Ladinos and Indians.

Distinctive religious organization involves both important social relationships and attendant values. In Intibucá, and evidently in various other towns of the southwest highlands, there is a highly distinct religious organization which exists for the perpetuation of specifically Indian socio-religious observances. The *mayordomías*, the organization of the *Cabildo Auxiliar*, of the *Consejo de Fábrica* (reported in Lempira), and of the various social positions and functions connected with the fiestas and *guancascos*, all reflect important distinctions between the organization of people who are members of the Indian community and those who are members of the Ladino community. In Santa Bárbara, various of the specific traits of the *guancasco* exist, but they no long stand as specifically integrating features of an Indian community; rather, Ladinos and Indians both participate in them (or at least so it was reported by informants). In El Paraíso, there also existed some form of *guancasco* but data was inconclusive as to what degree it served as an Indian trait. A specific division of labor which changes between the Indian and Ladino system is that of the leading of novenas. The general Indian pattern is for man to lead, and this reflects the dominant importance of men in religious affairs. Among Ladinos, women lead, and again reflects the dominance of women in these activities. Only in Yoro was it reported that men had given up entirely this practice, this reflects a basic change in religious value orientation. Elsewhere, the situation varied from being an alternative situation to one in which the men lead. In this point the Lenca are somewhat more acculturated than was the Santa Bárbara group.

The survival of a distinct political organization is dependent to some degree upon a permissive attitude from the Ladino central government and local Ladinos. In Intibucá, such an organization exists completely independent of any other municipality; in Marcala, however, the existence of such an organization was squashed years ago by the Ladinos. In general, for the southwest area, however, the communities which are predominantly Indian have their own municipal organizations. In Santa Bárbara the political distinctiveness of the Indian has been subordinated to the Ladino system. There, certain posts in the *municipalidad* are supposed to be filled by Indians, thus keeping alive the recognition of Ladino Indian differences, and also the fact that the Indians might go entirely unrepresented were not the incorporation made in such a formal manner.

The retention of a large proportion of the land on an *ejidal* basis again is not a trait which in itself is specifically Indian; there are probably Ladino *municipios* in which a large amount of land is *ejidal*. But in Intibucá and certain of the other southwestern towns[88] a large amount of this land is actually controlled by the *municipio* or local headmen, whereas in Santa Bárbara this *ejidal* land is handled basically as if it were privately held land. A similar control over the land on a community basis was reported from the communities of Taulabé and La Misión in north Department of Comayagua, indicating that this control has been retained in some communities which have been almost completely ladinoized in other respects. Again, the importance of this trait is that people in an Indian community have retained such distinctive integration while those in neighboring Ladino communities have not.

The position of language as an integrative device is obvious. A different language usually reflects a different value system, but at the same time is a basic must for any society. Thus, when a language disappears, it does so only because it has been replaced by another. In this respect, language differs from other integrative features. Language change in general depends upon some forceful

---

[88] Stone, 1948, pp. 212–213.

reason which places the people of one language group in fairly close contact with those of another language group. In this situation, general communication can only be accomplished through one of the two groups becoming bilingual. When one is politically subordinate and relies on the other as an economic support, then the subordinate is bound to become bilingual to some degree. Where Indian monolingualism remains, it is usually because the community has been physically or culturally isolated from Spanish speakers. Such would seem to be the case in Guajiquiro and among the Jicaque. In Lempira and Intibucá, the Indian communities have been in contact with the Spanish since early in the colonial period.

From this review of certain distinguishing features, it may be seen that our distinction between Modified and Ladinoized Indian communities rests on the degree to which distinctive integrative traits have remained in the community culture. The Lenca of the southwest have in general retained a much more dis-

Table 17.—Approximate percentages of Indians in traditional, modified, and ladinoized categories

Location of Groups	Traditional	Modified	Ladinoized
Southwest highlands—Lenca	—	50,000	28,400
Copán—Chortí	—	6,000	6,500
Santa Bárbara	—	—	5,000
Yoro—Jicaque	—	—	8,100
Montaña de la Flor—Jicaque	200	—	—
El Paraíso	—	—	15,100
Ocotepeque	—	—	400
Total	200	56,000	63,500
Percent	0.2	46.7	53.1

tinctive set of traits than have the other three groups under discussion, and this retention has specifically been in the realm of integrative traits.

In terms of numbers, we can do little more than give more gross estimates as to how many Indians would fall into each of these categories. A breakdown might be as shown in Table 17.

The reason for subdividing the Lenca and the Chortí between the Modified and Ladinoized categories is merely that it seems likely that a group of Modified Indians completely surrounded by Ladinos would have some communities which had lost many of the integrative traits. As to what proportion should be considered as Modified and what proportion as Ladinoized, the figures given above are sheer guess work. A higher Ladinoized proportion is assigned to the Chortí because the entire Chortí region in Honduras is a border region to the basic Chortí area which is in Guatemala. For practical purposes, the writer feels that we may probably consider about one half the Indian population as Modified, and one half as Ladinoized.

In terms of regions, there is another way in which it is worthwhile looking at Indian populations. This is in terms of what proportion they are of the regional population of which they are a part. On the map which accompanies this report, we have indicated the general geographical regions in which the Indian populations under discussion are resident. These populations, however, are seldom the sole occupants of these regions. Since the size of the Indian populations are only estimates based on the size of certain municipal populations anyway, it is impossible to indicate how important they are in terms of the total population without merely repeating the estimates of their size. Since these estimates were generally made on the basis of municipal populations, however, to see them as parts of total departmental populations may give some indication of their relative importance. From this it may be seen that Indians form a really significantly large proportion of the total population only in the southwest highlands and Iriona municipio of Colón. The southwest highlands in this case refer to the combined departments of La Paz, Intibucá, and Lempira. Iriona municipio is

Table 18.—Estimated Indian proportion of total population in terms of major administrative regions

Area	Total 1950 Population	Estimated Indian Population	Percent
Southwestern highlands—Total	201,490	78,400	39.0
Intibucá Department	59,326	44,425	74.8
La Paz Department	51,220	26,230	51.2
Lempira Department	90,908	7,760	8.5
El Paraíso Department	82,572	15,100	18.3
Copán Department	95,880	12,500	13.0
Yoro Department	98,700	8,400	8.5
Santa Bárbara Department	96,397	5,000	5.2
Olancho-Colón Departments	119,375	5,650	4.7
Iriona *Municipio* (Colón)	9,599	5,050	52.5

that which forms the vastly greater part of the Department of Colón in terms of geography, and which is between half again and twice as large as the combined area of the three southwestern departments.

Intibucá and La Paz are the only departments which have Indian percentages which even closely approximate those found in the major Indian departments of Guatemala. Seven of the 23 Guatemalan departments have Indian percentages which are over that of Intibucá. This is mentioned to make it quite clear that even in those regions where there are Indian isolates in Honduras, they are generally of insignificant proportion when compared with the concentrated Indian populations of Guatemala.

Before leaving this discussion, a word concerning the groups of the Mosquitia. The Miskito, Sumu, and Paya are three groups which were, so far as we can tell, subject to a considerably different form of acculturative experience than the rest of the Indian groups in the country. The Jicaque Indians have often been thought of as being of generally the same kind of culture as these groups, but because of their location, they were subject to pressures more similar to those felt throughout the rest of the Honduran interior. The distinction between the

Mosquitia lowland groups and those of the rest of the country was very much emphasized by the fact that the Spaniards preferred the interior territory of the Lenca, Jicaque, and other highland groups, and manifested a long term disinterest in that area occupied by the Paya, Miskito, and Sumu. Consequently, the interior groups were subject to a fairly constant pressure towards culture change, some of which was directed by priests, political administrators, and settlers, while the lowland groups were generally free from much of this pressure. This Spanish disinterest in the northeast had the concomitant effect that it left that region open for influences from other colonial powers, specifically England. So the Mosquitia population has undergone a vastly different history from that of the rest of the country.

The classification here used to distinguish Indian groups into the general categories as Traditional, Modified, and Ladinoized, has developed specifically to handle groups which underwent some directed culture change at the hands of the Spanish. As a result, it may not be immediately applicable to the Atlantic coastal groups. The general categories could probably be applied, but the writer would much prefer the opportunity of visiting those groups before deciding whether the application would be useful or not. It is always a temptation to extend generalizations, but where there is no reason to do so, it is wiser to wait.

IV. NOTES ON THE BLACK CARIB OF THE NORTH COAST

Along the greater part of the Honduran north coast, from about Iriona in the east to La Ceiba, and in scattered communities on to the Guatemalan border, are to be found the population component known as the Black Carib, Garif, or locally, *Moreno*. The history of this group has been summarized elsewhere and the general culture has been described for some communities of British Honduras by Taylor, and notes on the Honduran population were reported by Conzemius, and on the town of Livingston by Adams.[89] The present chapter is not going to attempt a summary of all the data on the *Moreno* nor to repeat all the information collected during the present survey. The reader is referred to those sources already mentioned for a general picture. Our purpose here is merely to make a few comments concerning this population as they fit into the general Honduran scene, and to indicate certain traits which were not covered by the description made by Conzemius. In the survey, the writer visited the *aldea* of Corozal a few miles to the east of the town of La Ceiba, and the barrio La Barra, a *Moreno* community in La Ceiba.

The total population of Black Caribs now living in Honduras is not known. Conzemius estimated in his 1928 publication that the total *Moreno* population, including those who lived in British Honduras, Guatemala, Honduras, and Nicaragua, was between 20,000 and 25,000. Unfortunately, the 1950 population census makes no distinction which permits us to have any basis upon which to estimate the contemporary size of the Honduran contingent of Caribs. The only

---

[89] Conzemius, 1928; Taylor, 1951; Adams, n.d. (c).

basis the writer has found is that in the *agropecuario* census which gives data on the number of farmers who grow *yuca*. Now, unfortunately, no distinction was made on this census between the "sweet" *yuca*, which is a secondary crop over all of Central America, and "bitter" *yuca*, which is the basic food crop of the *Morenos*. However, in view of the very heavy concentration of *yuca* cultivation reported for the north coast, it seems not unreasonable to assume that much of it is the bitter *yuca* grown by the *Morenos*. The number of farms growing *yuca* for the combined departments of Atlántida, Colón, Cortés, and the Bay Islands (mainly from the single Carib community of Punta Gorda) is 3,104. However, of this total, 900 are from the municipio of Iriona of Colón which includes almost the entire Miskito and Sumu population of that region. Since *yuca* is an important crop of these groups, this entire number must be excluded from our calculations.[90] Taking the figure of 5.75 persons per family as a reasonable family size (see Table 15 in chapter on the family) for this region, and multiplying it times 2204 (the number of *yuca*-producing *fincas*) gives us an estimate of 12,673 persons who may be Black Carib. The best estimate that we can get on this basis, then, is something between 12,000 and 13,000. It was the writer's impression that the *Moreno* population was somewhat greater than this because the community of Corozal which he visited was itself said to have a population of about 1,000. However, until better data are available, we shall have to be satisfied with this.

The culture of the Black Caribs seems to be fairly uniform over most of the region. There are noticeable community differences, sometimes being due to differential acculturation, sometimes being due to differential economic emphasis. For example, the Carib men of Corozal, like those of Livingston in Guatemala, work as stevedores on the docks of La Ceiba. Everywhere, however, the same language prevails, a great majority are bilingual, and probably a majority are also trilingual, speaking English as well as Spanish and the Carib language. Fishing by the men and the cultivation of bitter *yuca* by the women are the main basic economic enterprises. The men supply almost the entire Atlantic coast with the dugout canoes (*dories*) which form the principal river and ocean front transportation.

Perhaps the principal difference to be found between the structure of the community of Corozal visited in Honduras and Livingston, the Black Carib town in Guatemala, is in the political organization. Political organization in Livingston followed the basic Guatemalan municipal pattern. In Corozal, however, the political organization was that of an *aldea*. There were two *alcaldes auxiliares*, and a *subcomandante*. The real difference in structure, however, lies in the fact that, for practical purposes, the entire political power, both with respect to internal operation and relations with the outside, is in the hands of the *subcomandante*. The Corozal system is basically the old *cacique* system in which a single person of particularly strong local power assumes the position of headman for the entire community. His appointment as *subcomandante* probably followed on

[90] Kirchhoff, 1948, p. 219.

the fact that he had local power, rather than the reverse. He is the local contact man for the national politicians, and while he may not be able to "deliver" 100 % vote, he knows exactly how the vote will go ahead of time.

Family structure in Corozal was said to be quite stable. The percent which is formally married is not high (informants estimated about 25 % of the unions were legal), but since most couples live for a period in the home of the girl's parents, the families exert some pressure to maintain a union. Women are of great economic importance, since they carry the major part of the agricultural work; the men will prepare (clean) a plot of land, but the women do the planting, cultivation, and harvesting.

In Livingston there were formal housebuilding clubs; this was not the case in Corozal, but voluntary help in housebuilding was the usual way of erecting a new dwelling. It was said that they did have such clubs up until about three years ago.

Unlike the Antillean Negroes, with whom they are sometimes confused by people unfamiliar with the region, the *Morenos* are generally Catholic. Novenas are held in the homes; the women are usually inside praying and the men sit outside playing cards and otherwise passing the time. At funerals, music and dancing are customary, it was said, mainly as a means of keeping people awake through the entire night. The Corozal community held the Dance of the Moors and the Christians (as did other *Moreno* communities on the coast, according to informants) during their titular *fiesta*. Passages are memorized by the principal characters, and up to 50 people dress in costumes to participate in it. The event is held on the day of *Esquipulas*, the patron saint of the town. This Moors and Christians dance is the same which was introduced by the Spanish and taken over by many of the Indian groups of Central America as a part of the general Catholic *fiesta* celebrations. It must have been adopted by Caribs, however, in the Republican period, as they did not arrive in Central America until almost the end of the colonial period. In barrio La Barra it was said that the Dance of the Moors and Christians was held, but that it was usually done by Caribs who came over from Trujillo because the local people really did not know how to do it.

The same two celebrations peculiar to the Caribs, which were reported in Livingston, were reported as being of principal importance in Corozal. These were the *jugujugu* and the *yáncunú*.[91] The first of these is a dance without masks in which men and women dance separately all night on December 24th and December 31st. The second is danced during the day of December 25th and January 1st by men only using masks. The *yáncunú* was said by the informant in Corozal to be the "English name" for the dance; the Spanish name was *Los Máscaros*. In barrio La Barra it was said that yet a third dance was held on these evenings, known vulgarly as the *culeado*, more correctly as *la punta*. This is the same dance which is held at a wake for a dead person. On the evenings of

---

[91] The spelling of these terms is more or less in accordance with pronunciation in Corozal. They seemed to vary slightly from the pronunciation used in Livingston, but as in the former volume (Adams, n.d., (c)), the writer makes no claim for the phonetics here used.

24th and 31st of December, it was said that the dancers alternated dancing the *jugujugu* and the *punta*.

As in Livingston, the writer could not ascertain that there was any other specific connection between these Carib celebrations and the Catholic Calendar, except that they were held on Christmas and New Year. They seem to be specifically traditional Carib dances and celebrations.

With respect to other Catholic customs, the Caribs of Corozal were said not to go on pilgrimages anywhere. A crucifix does go out from the church from house to house to collect funds for the two-week periods prior to Esquipulas and Holy Week, but aside from this, there is no visiting of the saints.

In other respects, the Caribs of Corozal are similar to those in Livingston. The members of this littoral population travel a great deal along the coast visiting relatives and friends in other Carib communities, so there is little isolation of any particular settlement and consequently relatively little cultural divergence.

As in Livingston and British Honduras, the Black Carib are retaining a highly distinctive culture and at the same time adjusting it to changing conditions in the society around them. In years past, when the mahogany trade was good, the men would ship off annually to do this work. Today, they participate in stevedoring if they are near a port. But in the process of change, the basic domestic culture and social organization seems to be surviving. While we have no data at all on the Atlantic littoral population, it seems likely that the Black Carib population probably accounts for about half or more of the population which lives specifically on the coast. There is little doubt that the region has been filling up with interior peoples since the introduction of the banana industry over half a century ago, and the future will doubtless see further acculturation of the Carib group through their increasing contact with the Ladino population. At present, however, the Ladinos and *Morenos* are culturally and racially so distinct that it seems unlikely that the Carib culture will be destroyed unless the Ladinos take some specifically political or economic steps to assimilate it. Even under these conditions, the domestic culture and social structure can probably survive many more changes.

V. THE ANTILLEAN POPULATIONS OF THE BAY ISLANDS

The north coast of Honduras has long been subjected to influences from the Antilles. Besides the incursions of pirates in the 17th and 18th Centuries, the Black Caribs arrived at the end of the colonial period to spread in the next few decades over the entire coastal region. About 1836[92] there began a gradual influx of a new and distinct population component into the Bay Island off the north coast. This group was composed of white English colonists (and later also Negroes), who moved in from the Antilles and British Honduras and specifically from the Island Grand Cayman some six hundred miles to the northeast. At the

---
[92] Rose, 1902, p. 20.

time of the first Grand Cayman immigrants, the Bay Islands were under the jurisdiction of Honduras and the English settlers sought Honduras permission to settle there. Although the British government made subsequent claims to the Islands, they ultimately resided with Honduras and the gradually growing English speaking population submitted to Honduran control. Through the subsequent years this population has grown somewhat more slowly than has the population in some parts of the mainland, but has retained a great amount of cultural isolation.

According to information obtained from one Bay Island native, much of the Negro component of the Antillean immigrants subsequently moved to the mainland and other parts of the area. Among other places, they are found in barrio Inglés in La Ceiba, and some moved to the Corn Islands and Bluefields in Nicaragua. With the initiation of the banana industry on a large scale late in the last century, there was some importation of negro labor to the north coast. The writer's informant stated that the members of the older contingent of Antillean Negroes were in general more religious than the later migrants. With respect to the numbers and time of arrival of the later groups there is very little definite data available. The writer inquired of the United Fruit Company if they had any records of such migrations, but unfortunately little seemed to be available. One 30-year resident of the north coast, however, wrote as follows: "... I have been unable to find any printed matter... but there is no doubt that when operations were begun on a large scale on the North Coast there was insufficient labor. As a matter of fact, I find that in an *acuerdo* of January 20, 1914, the Company was authorized to import 1,200 negroes as laborers. I have come across numerous instances of old-time negro employees who claimed that they were brought here from Costa Rica and Panama during the early stages of operations in Honduras. Furthermore, I can remember... that in the early 20's there were a lot of Haitians around Tela, and I think that at one time some of these were imported by the Company. These importations of negroes brought, as a consequence, an influx of an additional number who came on their own."[93] It seems clear, then, that later contingents of Antillean negroes did arrive in the north coast, both as brought over specifically for the banana industry and as private migrants following in the train of possible employment.

This series of migrations, beginning with the people from Grand Cayman in the 1830's and probably to some degree still going on today, has brought to the north coast a large population of English speaking peoples. In addition to the population which is English speaking by birth, a relatively large percentage of the Black Carib population have also taken over English as a third language because of their connections with the Caribs resident in British Honduras. As a result of this situation, the north coast of Honduras presents a generally distinct cultural picture from the rest of the country. Culturally, it is oriented towards the Antilles, either towards Protestant, English language culture or towards Black Carib, Catholic culture. In recent years, more and more Spanish speaking

---

[93] Quoted by Mr. Edmund S. Whitman in a letter to the writer.

Ladinos have been coming into the region and while the Ladino culture, as well as the Spanish language, will probably become dominant in the area, it will be many decades, if not centuries, before this happens. In the meanwhile, the north coast provides us with yet other distinctive population components which must be taken into consideration.

The writer visited two communities of Antilleans in the Bay Islands, East Harbor Town on the Island of Utila, and the Utila Cays, just off the west end of Utila proper. East Harbor Town is the principal (and for practical purposes, only) settlement on Utila, the westernmost of the three islands which form the Bay Island group; the population is divided between Antillean whites and Antillean Negroes. The population of the Utila Cays is entirely Antillean white. From one informant the writer received the following estimates concerning the relative size of the principal population components on the three islands:

	White	Negro	Black Carib
Island of Utila:			
East Harbor Town	60%	40%	—
Utila Cays	100%	—	—
Island of Roatán:			
Roatán	20%	80%	—
French Harbor	50%	50%	—
Oak Ridge	50%	50%	—
Santa Elena	—	100%	—
Punta Gorda	—	—	100%
Various settlements on northwest coast	—	100%	—
Island of Guanaja:			
Guanaja	35%	65%	—
Savanna Bight	30%	70%	—
East End	50%	50%	—
Mangrove Bight	5%	95%	—

These estimates do not take into account scattered groups of Ladinos. There were said to be some in Savanna Bight and in the town of Roatán itself, and of course there are now Ladino school teachers in all communities which have schools as well as some Ladino government administrators.[94]

In the short time available to visit the Islands, it was not possible to collect comparable data on both the white and Negro Antillean groups in Utila. The main Negro settlements are on the Island of Roatán, and Utila was the only Island visited. As a result, we will treat here only the Antillean white population. Informants have told the writer that there is considerable difference between the Negro populations of the various Islands, and some difference in the white populations, but he frankly does not know how to estimate what this may mean in terms of the socio-cultural picture. Lacking further data, the following description will be specifically concerned with East Harbor Town and the Utila Cays.

---

[94] The reader should note that the percentages given are estimates made by a local resident; the informant cautioned not to rely on their precision, and they are given because they are the only data with which the writer is familiar concerning this problem.

East Harbor Town is located on the southeast corner of the Island of Utila. It covers the coastline of a small harbor protected by reefs and closed in at both ends by lagoons. The town itself is divided into what are called districts (neighborhoods) by the inhabitants. The principal districts and the population components therein are as follows (going from west to east):

Sandy Bay	Predominantly Negro
Bobwood Tree	" "
Bobwood Tree Road	" "
Poke-and-go-boy Patch	" "
Methodist Church	" white
Hill Road	" "
Sava	" Negro
Middle Path	Mixed
The Center	Predominantly white
Colomico	" Negro
Holland	" "
Punto Caliente, or Jackson Square	Mixed
The Lagoon	Predominantly white

In general, the whites occupy the eastern portion of the town along the waterfront and the center; the Negroes occupy certain parts of the east and center, but have to themselves certain inland neighborhoods and the western end of the waterfront. Physically, the white population shows intensive interbreeding; there is a great similarity of physical features to be seen among many people. The men are generally medium to tall in height. The writer saw very little evidence of inter-mixture between the negro and white groups. According to local informants, the Utila Negroes first came in around 1880, and have drifted in from time to time since. Prior to the arrival of the English speaking population, there were some Ladino inhabitants, but they disappeared years ago.

The economic opportunities on the islands are limited, especially so on Utila where there is little cultivatable land. As a result, and due to traditional preferences, there has been some tendency for the younger generation of whites to leave the island. Many return, but since a fairly large proportion are occupied in marine occupations, they are away from home a good portion of the time. There is no high school on the island, and families that wish to provide their children with a fuller education send them to La Ceiba, Tegucigalpa, or to the United States.

The main resident occupation of the Utila islander is coconut gathering. All land on Utila is privately held, and *ejidal* lands are of minimal importance on all the islands. According to the *agropecuario* census, there were 132 landholdings on Utila; this would mean, according to the local estimate of the size of the adult male population, that about 50% of the male population have land. The greatest part of these holdings are coconut patches. Among the people who do not own coconut patches it was said that they either work for those who do, or they "borrow" coconuts from those who do have plots; the population is small enough that the "borrowers" are fairly well-known. Years ago bananas were an important local crop, and the local people say that it was from the Islands that the United Fruit Company first shipped their products. Banana cultivation has lost all importance now, however. Most men who have land devote a small portion of it to subsistence crops, and some to cash crops. The agricultural technology is fairly simple. The hoe, shovel, and machete, together with a simple wooden stick for planting beans, are the main implements. Besides some corn and beans, some plant a little bitter *yuca*, pumpkins, potatoes, and the *malanga* (a tuber). The bitter *yuca* is planted sheerly as food for pigs. In recent years tomatoes have been cultivated as cash crops, but the undependability of the mainland market has discouraged many people from promoting this cultivation further.

The coconuts are dried and converted into copra on the island, and shipped to the mainland for sale. Since so little land is under cultivation in food crops on the island itself, the residents are entirely dependent upon the mainland for much of their staples. Some three people raise cattle on the island, and sell the meat locally in the small building called the market, and many people keep chickens. But, in general, the welfare of East Harbor Town depends upon a completely cash economy.

Labor is usually paid in cash when it is work such as clearing of land, planting, etc., but in harvest work payment is usually in some proportion of the yield. In agricultural work, usually one quarter of the crop harvested is paid, while in coconut gathering, about two fifths of the coconuts are given in payment. Antillean white women do not participate in the agricultural work at all.

Informants said that land renting as such was not a custom. If a person had land he was not using, he would let someone else use it for nothing. Such occupants may stay on indefinitely, depending upon their personal relationships with the owner.

On the Utila Cays the main local economic activity is fishing. While many of the men will have coconut holdings on some of the cays or on Utila, this is secondary to the sale of fish to the mainland. Of the eleven cays of any size, only two are occupied; the rest are left in coconuts. Most of the others have been occupied from time to time, but one thing and another has led the inhabitants to regard the now unoccupied cays as haunted or for some other reason undesirable, and at present only Suc-Suc Cay and Lower Cay are occupied with homes. These two, it may be added, are most crowded.

The cay fishermen go out between 2 a.m. and dawn, depending upon how far they intend to go to fish, and return sometime before 2 p.m. The greatest radius they usually go is from 6 to 8 miles from the islands. While most fishing is done individually or at most in pairs, the fishing boats usually stick fairly close together because the fish tend to go in schools and where there is catch for one, there will be some for all. Upon returning to the cay, the fish are placed in crawls, pens set in the shallow water, and stay there alive until early the following Monday morning. At that time, they are removed, killed, split and cleaned, weighed, and sent over on the morning launch to La Ceiba for sale. During most of the year the fish are sold to stores and bring a fairly steady price. The time of greatest sale, however, is just prior to Holy Week, during which time much of the catch is split and dried on poles on the cays, and sent in for shipment all over Honduras. In this way Protestant islanders benefit from mainland Catholic customs.

The fish are usually caught with hook and line. A harpoon with a detachable point is also made and used, and one with a fixed point is usually used to spear fish in the crawls.

Quite a few of the cay men and some from East Harbor Town ship out on merchant ships. Some belong to the National Maritime Union, and a few have gone to the merchant marine academy in the United States. One of the writer's informants had shipped over most of the world at one time or another as an engineer. He usually went out for 6 to 18 months at a time, although he said one could not be too sure once one got aboard, and on one occasion, during the war, he found himself out for three straight years. In general, the islanders who live thus save most of their earnings and when they return, they can live comfortably, depending only upon fishing and coconut gathering for a modest regular income, for periods up to as long or longer than that spent on the sea.

Fishing, and a great deal of the travel between islands and to the mainland, is done in large dugouts, the dories. These boats frequently have a well built in them to keep the fish alive, and those who can afford it have inboard motors set in them. The islanders themselves do not build the dories; the basic reason is that there is almost no wood for the purpose to be found on the island, and as a result, they have never developed the skill. The dories are built by the Black Caribs on the mainland, and by a few Ladinos. In general, however, it is a *Moreno* skill and the islanders are all but completely dependent upon them for the product.

There are few hand industries on Utila aside from the preparation of fishing gear by the men on the cays, the preparation of copra, and the making of clothing by the women. Houses are built by carpenters. The homes are uniformly of boards with either metal or palm roofs. Some in East Harbor Town are of two stories. The houses are all set up off the ground a few feet on poles since a good storm across the island will bring sheets of water across the land which is only a few feet above water level. In general, the house equipment is basically similar to that of the American middle west in late part of the last century: wooden and metal bedsteads, rocking chairs, tables with lace doilies, photographs of family members and colored prints. Cooking is done on wood stoves with built-in ovens. The Antilleans seem to have taken little from the Ladinos in kitchen technology; the writer found no grinding stones, no tortillas. Wheat bread is made from purchased flour, often with coconut water. The women of the island make most of their own clothes and those for the men. One informant showed the writer a very handsome and subdued sports shirt which his wife had just finished; it frankly looked as if it had come directly out of a high class shop window.

Much of the commerce on which the Utila islanders depend is carried on in La Ceiba. There are five stores in the town handling general merchandise, however, and one of these also sells medicine. As was mentioned before, most of the staples are brought over from the mainland and the meat is sold in a separate market run by the cattle producers of the island. In general, the islanders think in terms of dollars and not lempiras, the Honduran currency unit. If one asks how much one gets for his fish, how much coconuts are bringing, how much a dory costs, or how much he can save up on a long marine cruise, the answer is inevitably in dollars.

When the British finally gave up their claim to the Bay Islands in 1861, they promised the contemporary residents that they would continue to be regarded and treated as British subjects, as would any subsequent Britishers who immigrated to the islands. The islanders, however, for the next four decades felt that this applied not only to those who were alive at the time, but to their descendents. In 1902 it came as a bitter shock to many when a British warship stopped at the islands to inform them once again of the nature of the treaty signed with Honduras, and to point out that persons born on the islands since 1861 were not British subjects.[95] Today there are some residents who still claim British nationality, but from the point of view of the Hondurans and British, anyone born subsequent to 1861 on the islands are Hondurans unless they have undergone nationalizing procedures in some other country. The local government of the islands is now entirely under the Honduran system, although for many years subsequent to end of the British claim the islanders were permitted to continue to operate under an inherited set of British laws.

The islands form a department of Honduras, and each of the three islands is considered as a *municipio*. As such, the local officers are elected by the islanders and are local people. The departmental government, with the capital in Roatán, is appointed from the national capital, and usually consists in part of Ladinos, but usually some attempt is made to place a person as governor who is sympathetic to the islander society. At the time of the writer's visit, for example, a new governor was just assuming office; he was the son of an islander and a Ladino, had grown up on Roatán, and had lived his entire life moving back and forth between the two cultures. As such, he was considered as an islander by those of the islands, and yet was a Ladino from the point of view of the national government.

In East Harbor Town the municipal government consisted of an *alcalde*, two *regidores*, and a *síndico*, as well as a justice of the peace, and a treasurer, a policeman, and six *auxiliares* from various of the town's districts. In general, the Spanish terms were used for these offices, and not their English equivalents. The elected officials are white, but the appointed *auxiliares* either negro or white, depending upon the district from which they came. As elsewhere, the roads, cemetery, and slaughterhouse are the responsibility of the municipality.

The administration of the Utila Cays is in the hands of an appointed *alcalde auxiliar* and a *subcomandante*. At the time of the visit, the first of these was an old islander, and the second was, like the governor, half islander and half mainland Ladino.

Families among the islanders are highly stable and almost always involve formal marriage. It will be remembered from the chapter on the family that the

---

[95] Rose, 1904, Chapter 15.

Bay Islands have the highest marriage rate of any department in Honduras; only 17% of the unions are free unions. Residence is almost always neo-local. Cousin marriage is not only permitted but, as one informant said, sometimes necessary because there has been so much intermarriage that one has a multitude of cousins and there may be no non-relative of the proper age. There have been occasional Ladinos who have come to the islands and who have married local women. These men are usually accepted into island society on the basis of their adherence to the general value system of the islanders. The families are most important social units and feel strong ties both with respect to their island property and their ancestry. The *compadre* system is of relatively little importance but, probably through the structure of the Methodist Church, the predominant religious organization in Utila, there is a tendency for many of the men to refer to each other and favored strangers as "brother," as a term of address. A Danish-Venezuelan who has retired to the islands and lives in the home of one of the islanders has established a relationship between himself and his host as an "adopted son"; the writer does not remember whether the "son" or the "father" is older, but both enjoy the artificial bond. If anything, kinship counts for much more among the Antillean whites than it does among the rural Ladinos of the Honduran mainland. Reasons for this are probably not hard to find: extensive intermarriage; a small total society which cannot produce larger sociological units; and a sense of self-protection against and isolation from the culturally distinct Ladinos of the mainland. To these factors may be added the importance of a strong Protestant Church as a broad unifying factor which adds emphasis to familial stability and observance of a moral code.

Voluntary social organizations above the family level, aside from the territorial divisions, white-negro division, and church organizations, are few. There is a lady's sewing club in East Harbor Town which meets once a week, rotating among the homes of the dozen or so members. One informant said that from time to time local chapters of international civic groups have been established in the town, but that they have usually rapidly disintegrated; the slightest dissention puts an end to them.

With respect to other population components, the white islanders generally consider themselves superior. They look down upon the mainland Ladinos whom they consider as generally drunken and undependable machete fighters. Ladinos are accepted into the island society if and when they actually marry into it and demonstrate themselves to be like the islanders with respect to the Protestant moral code. Socially, in general, they consider themselves above the neighboring Antillean Negroes, but this is a rather gentle distinction and on the surface, at least, the best of relations exist between the two groups. On the surface, they treat each other as equals, but as members of separate groups. The Negro group is only slightly subordinate economically, although some Negro women are hired as cooks by white women. This involves no subservient attitude on the part of the Negros, however. Negroes and whites participate in the same churches and schools, but the line is usually drawn at intermarriage and in private parties. Occasionally members of the other group will be invited to private parties, but in general they are held within each group. Antillean whites are equally sensitive about not inviting Ladinos to their parties until they have been accepted by the islanders. The story was told of one islander who started a dance hall, and charged admission. Since anyone could afford it, "everyone" came; the whites did not like this intermingling, and so bought the hall from the owner and put an end to the dances. Although both Negroes and whites will attend the same churches, the writer received the definite impression that clique formation was made within the groups, and as a result, seating in the churches tended to be in bunches of the two groups. One white informant referred to the Negroes of one district of the town as "lower class people" who drank more than the whites did and who tended to fight more among themselves. He made the statement with no rancor, but stated it as a "known" fact.

One further element of the class structure should be mentioned. There is at Punta Gorda, Roatán, a community of Black Caribs and a few families elsewhere in the islands. In East Harbor Town there was said to be one resident family of Caribs who had been there for three generations. In general, according to informants, the Antillean Negroes considered themselves socially superordinate to the Caribs.

Aside from the territorial and class structure, the most important social organization is that which revolves around the Protestant Churches. Writing at the beginning of the century, Richard Rose recorded that there were two denominations active in Utila, the Seventh Day Adventists and the Wesleyan Methodists.[96] At the time of the writer's visit these were still the two strongest groups but the latter was by far the dominant. The writer's informants (whom it should be noted were Methodists) said that there were four main groups and the population was divided among them about as follows (mixed white and negro): Methodist 89%; Adventist 9%, Church of God 1%; Baptist 1%. The last two churches have been irregularly active, and the membership has varied from time to time. Their membership has necessarily been drawn from the other two, and as they get bigger, the others must of necessity get smaller. The Methodist Church is the oldest on the island, the Adventist came some 40 years later, and the Church of God and Baptist were established within the past ten years.

The Methodist Church organization includes the largest portion of the island's population and is doubtless the most complicated of any. The various posts are as follows:

1 Minister: he attends quarterly meetings on the island, but is responsible for some 18 churches on the islands and mainland.
9 Preachers (not a fixed number), local men who have their positions approved by the Minister in Roatán.
1 Society Steward.
1 Assistant Society Steward.
1 Treasurer.
1 Chapel Steward.

[96] Rose, 1904, p. 72.

1 Assistant Chapel Steward.
1 Sunday School Superintendent
1 Assistant Sunday School Superintendent.
1 Assistant Sunday School Treasurer.
1 Librarian.
18 Sunday School Teachers (men and women).
1 Organist.
1 Secretary of the Sunday School.
1 Assistant Secretary of the Sunday School.
5 Leaders of Classes (not Sunday School classes, but weekly classes in religion).

Church services are held in the Methodist Church on Monday, Wednesday, and Friday, and in the morning, at noon, and in the evening on Sunday. Men and women were said to participate equally in the services, but one old resident said that church was not attended as well today as formerly; this was not said with any indication that the informant thought the old days were better because he was one of those who was not attending.

Four times a year the Quarterly Meetings are held. Three main meetings are held during this time. In the morning the preachers get together and have a morning service; in the afternoon all the leaders meet (including most of the people listed above); and in the evening there is a meeting and service for everyone.

Perhaps the principal formal recreation in the island are the weddings, which send the women into a frenzy of preparation, and a few annual celebrations: New Year, Mother's Day, Columbus Day, Thanksgiving, and Christmas. The last and the first are evidently the main holidays. Christmas celebration was said to last from December 20th to January 5th, and the New Year's church service was said to be the best attended of the year. Among the items involved in the Christmas celebration in East Harbor Town is the expenditure of about $1,500 worth of fireworks, a custom which seems to have been borrowed from the Ladinos.

In the short period of his visit, the writer did not discover if there were any patterns of folk illnesses among the Antillean whites. Because of the difficulty of getting to a doctor, there are various specialists on the island. There are some women who act as midwives, and it was said that every woman on the island was the family physician. One man was mentioned as being an excellent bone setter, that the islanders would not think of bothering with a doctor for such a case, since this individual had proven his ability in many cases. There were said to be no spiritualists. Ghosts seem to play some role in the lives of the islanders, as the case of the haunted cays indicates. But it was said that ghosts were more threatening to the people in Roatán than those here. On the other hand, a Roatán informant advised the writer that the Negroes of Utila were much more ridden with ghosts than were those of Roatán.

In general, the islanders seen by the writer in East Harbor Town and on the Utila Cays were a highly courteous, very proud, provincial people. A few manifested some difficulty still in accepting their position as Hondurans rather than

British subjects, but for each one of the conservatives, there were some who favored the Honduran connection. The general relations which exist between the islanders and the mainland Ladinos is unfortunately highly influenced by the nature of the Ladinos who are sent in official capacities to the islands. There was high ill feeling towards some of the Ladino school teachers who, themselves feeling they had been banished to an isolated outpost, drowned their unhappiness in drink, and as a consequence, made themselves thoroughly unpleasant to the islanders and helped perpetuate bad relationships between the Ladinos and islanders in general. Some informants were quite open in their disgust with the ineffectiveness of certain of the agents of the national government. They needed help in certain practical matters, such as in re-establishing their schools, in combating a plague of beetles which attacked the coconut palms, etc., but they felt that the national government neither had the interest in, nor was capable of understanding the problems which faced the islanders.

The general feeling the writer received from his visit is that the island population is culturally distinct, and will probably remain so for generations to come. They present an interesting "ethnic minority" in which a group of English extraction has long been politically subordinate to a Latin nation. The entire orientation of their culture is distinct from that of the mainland Ladinos, and the value systems of the two cultures are profoundly different. So far, the islanders have resisted acculturation and assimilation by the Ladino population. The Protestant orientation of their culture, the retention of their contacts with English speaking people, both in British Honduras and the United States, helps sustain them in this resistance. On the other hand, there is a gradual infiltration of Ladino elements. The political system is completely Honduran in structure; the agricultural technology is at about the same level as that of the Ladinos; certain elements of the diet, such as the staples of rice and beans, are dependent upon and related to the Ladino culture; and Spanish is now mandatory in the schools so that the next generation should be nearly bilingual. From the point of view of the general picture of acculturation, the Antillean islanders may be said to be the least acculturated group under Honduran rule. Most of the Indian populations, with the possible exception of those in the Mosquitia and the Torrupán, are much more Ladinoized than are the islanders.

VI. THE COMMUNITIES VISITED ON THE SURVEY

In each study in the present series one section is devoted to descriptive notes on the towns visited. It is impossible to satisfy all curiosity about the various sites in which data were gathered, so the descriptions are limited to census data and a few impressions the writer received during his visit. The survey was made in 23 towns; in addition to these, some material was collected for comparative purposes from students resident in the agricultural school in Catacamas and the summer normal school in Danlí. From these school teachers and natives of certain regions to which the writer could not go, information was collected on Duyure (El Paraíso), Guarita (Lempira), Corquín (Copán), Salamá and San Esteban

(Olancho). No further notes will be provided on these towns for obvious reasons. Besides these, Intibucá has been described in the section on the Lenca, Ilama in the section on the Santa Bárbara Indians, Corozal briefly in the section on the Black Caribs, and East Harbor Town and the Utila Cays in the section on the Bay Islands. This leaves 18 towns of predominantly Ladino culture which will be dealt with in the present chapter. Principally as a convenience, these have been ordered in terms of certain regions. These regions have little cultural reality and the reader should not be lead to believe that they are cultural "sub-areas" or regions.

1. THE SOUTH COAST

Yusguare (1950 population: 632 urban; 1337 rural)
This is a small town in a small *municipio* located in the flat coastal area behind Choluteca. There are some hills in the *municipio*, but they have been occupied by Indians from the Liure region. The town is easily accessible from Choluteca, but somewhat off the main road. While most of the people of the *municipio* are small scale agriculturalists, many also regularly migrate to nearby *haciendas* to assist in the harvesting of sugar. Most such movement goes on during the local agricultural off-season, from January to April. A few have gone to the north coast but most of these have not returned.

The town houses are scattered along the principal road and are generally of *bajareque* and tile. There are also a few of *adobe*. The town has little evident commercial activity; there is no market and the four small stores carry a very modest stock. The proximity of the departmental capital of Choluteca makes the maintenance of a large local stock unnecessary.

Aside from the Liure Indians who live in the *aldea* of El Cerro, the population of Yusguare is Ladino. There survive a few traits which indicate the Indian background of some of the population, such as the fact that women still participate to some degree in subsistence agriculture, and the use of a drum in sending a saint out on *demanda*. The Nicaraguan custom of celebrating the *fiesta* of *Concepción* with the *gritería* was said to be observed in former years, but now, so far as the informants knew, it was only practised in Choluteca.[97]

Nacaome (1950 population: 3,429 urban; 15,386 rural)
This city is the departmental capital of the Department of Valle. It is located on the arid and hot south coastal plain in a region of scrub growth. As departmental capital, Nacaome acts as commercial center for the various *municipios* of the department. The only all weather road in the department is the international highway which runs from the Salvadorean border to Jícaro Galán, and then one branch continues east to Choluteca and Nicaragua, and the other north to Tegucigalpa. Nacaome and the port of San Lorenzo are the only towns of any size located on the road, so almost all local transport is done with ox carts

---

[97] Adams, n.d. (b).

on the coastal plain region and with mules, horses or by human being in the hilly portions.

Unlike some departmental capitals, the territory of Nacaome is a *municipio* and not a district. Consequently there are housed in the town, an elected municipal government as well as the appointed departmental government. The rural populations are usually referred to as living in valleys, the same terminology to be found in Nicaragua.[98] The *municipio* is thought of in terms of the two distinct environmental sections, the coastal plain and the foothills and mountains rising on the north side. While corn is the major crop in both areas, rice is important on the coast and sorghum in the hills.

The town houses are generally of *bajareque* or *adobe*, while the rural houses are generally *bajareque* or of poles. While there has been some recent influx of Salvadorean *finqueros* to rent land and extract annual harvests, the region is generally not one of immense *haciendas*. There has been some influx of poorer *Salvadoreños* in search either of work or land to rent. In the town itself, as would be expected in a departmental capital, there is a relatively high percentage of families which are regarded as being of the *primera sociedad*, but it was said that in the rural areas there were few if any resident upper class.

Even though it is a departmental capital, the town has only two primary schools and no high school. Choluteca seems to overshadow Nacaome in general, both in schools and commerce.

La Venta (1950 population: 668 urban; 3,144 rural)

This small community is located in the hills overlooking the south coast at an altitude of about 2,000 feet. The land is generally hilly and broken, and the town itself is located on a brief shelf of land. The informants claimed that the original grant of land to the *municipio* was issued by the king in the colonial period, but that in 1917 this title was sent to Tegucigalpa to be revalidated and was lost. The majority of the land is still *ejidal*, however.

Town houses are generally of *adobe* and tile, but those in the "valleys" are either of *bajareque* or poles, but also with tile roofs. Within the town there are a few families which are considered as the *sociedad*, and the informant said they tended to be endogamous. The main class feeling existed, however, between the town dwellers and the rural dwellers.

La Venta is really a highland town, and its orientation at present is in that direction rather than towards the coast. While there are three small stores locally, the people go north to Sabana Grande or to Tegucigalpa for most of the necessary purchases. One reason for this is that administratively the town is in the Department of Francisco Morazán and therefore there is no control exercised from either of the coastal departments.

2. THE CENTRAL HIGHLANDS

Güinope (1950 population: 1,631 urban; 2,314 rural)

Güinope is a clean little town located in the hills of southwestern El Paraíso,

[98] Adams, n.d. (b).

almost on the border of the Indian region centering in Texiguat and Liure. Informants said, however, that there were no Indians resident in Güinope itself. The writer was impressed with the general cleanliness of this town and the fact that people whom he saw on the roads outside were generally well dressed.

The appearance of the town is different from many other highland communities in which the land has been cut over and there may be few if any trees left. Güinope is so full of orange and coffee trees that one seldom gets the impression that he is in a town of any size. The surrounding land is fairly hilly and most transport outside of town is done on mules. There are some ox carts in the town itself, but they are not common. The cultivation of potatoes is an important source of cash income. While men do most of the subsistence agriculture, various families do move east to the coffee area of El Paraíso during the coffee harvest.

Jacaleapa (1950 population: 793 urban; 1,387 rural)

This community lies in the general area of influence of Danlí, the southeastern Honduran center. There are Indians scattered in the rural population but they are so highly ladinoized that within a generation or so it is unlikely that any distinct Indian group will be said to exist. The town itself is fairly open, with a large plaza and houses of *bajareque* or *adobe*. Some *aldeas* are of *bajareque* and in others houses of poles predominate. As is the case elsewhere in the southern towns, sorghum is tending to replace corn for many because of its better yield. Most people work land as subsistence agriculturalists. This was one of the few Ladino communities where it was said that exchange labor was still fairly common.

There are generally recognized to be two social classes, the *primera* and *segunda*, but in the second group the Ladinoized Indians are also included. The town seems oriented principally towards Danlí. There are a few stores active, carrying a fairly good country stock, but the town cannot be considered as an important commercial center. At the time of the survey there were two mixed schools of three grades, and one with the fourth and fifth grades.

Zambrano (estimated population: 900 to 1,200)

Zambrano is an *aldea* of the Central District of the country. It lies on rolling upland and pine country near the border of Comayagua at an altitude of about 4,300 feet. The main part of the community is stretched out along the main highway, and the area is best known for the fact that a large portion of the surrounding territory belongs to the former president, General Carías. Informants estimated that there were perhaps 200 houses in the *aldea*, which would give it a population of somewhere between 900 and 1,200. It was said that the present population moved in to what is now the center about fifty years ago, most of them coming from the immediate surrounding regions.

This *aldea* impressed the writer as being quite poor, and it is so with respect to land. Most of the men rent land in the Comayagua valley and migrate there annually to plant and take up the harvest. Here in the *aldea* most people plant root crops, principally sweet *yuca*. Many are also occupied in gathering pine resin from which turpentine is distilled in a factory located on the edge of the community. In the community the houses are mainly of *bajareque* and tile, but those who go down to Comayagua usually put up a *rancho* for the duration of their stay there.

The community people were in general said to fall into two classes, the slightly wealthier businessmen, and the poorer farmers.

Due to the fact that Zambrano is so distant from Tegucigalpa, its inclusion in the Central District works an inconvenience for the residents. All taxes must be paid and all reports must be made in the capital city, a trip of some two to three hours distant by bus, and considerably longer by foot or horse. Even though administrative control is exercised from the capital, the general orientation of the town is towards Comayagua where the majority go to get land.

Guaimaca (1950 population: 879 urban; 1,482 rural)

This community, situated on barren uplands, is located almost on the border between the departments of Francisco Morazán and Olancho. At present the surrounding region is undergoing lumbering, but the town gave no evidence in its outward aspects that it was benefiting from these activities. The people gave the appearance of being rather poorly off, and none of the homes seen by the writer gave evidence of any wealth. The informants confirmed this impression by saying that while there was some social distinction made between the more *acomodados* and the poorer, the *acomodados* themselves were generally poor. There are some *haciendas* in the region, but their owners are resident either in Tegucigalpa or on the *haciendas*. There are no Indians in the region at present, but the informants were aware of the presence of the Jicaque group in the Montaña de la Flor. Although some of the land is fairly rolling, there is no use of ox carts in the *municipio* and all transport is done by horse or mule.

The houses in town are generally *bajareque* and tile. Since it is distant from any other center, the town evidently serves as a commercial center for a relatively large area. While most of the population are agriculturalists, there are various *haciendas* of cattle. Of the 25 *municipios* and districts of the department, Guaimaca was third in the number of cattle and amount of land in pasturage (Census, 1954b). There is one school of five grades in the town.

La Libertad (1950 population: 1,070 urban; 3,017 rural)

This community in the northern part of the Department of Comayagua is located at an altitude of about 1,500 feet. In the past fifty years, but particularly following the First World War, it has become an important coffee center. As was mentioned earlier in the survey, coffee cultivation in Honduras has generally been carried on in small and medium sized holdings, and La Libertad is a good example of this situation. Fifty percent of the land in coffee are in holdings of under 20 hectares each (Census, 1954b). As a result, La Libertad, with the recent coffee prices, has benefitted by their specialization. There was said to be a three class system based principally on wealth, although the *primera sociedad* was defined to some degree on the basis family lineage. Some Indian families have moved from the departments of Intibucá and La Paz, mainly people who have come up during the coffee harvest and then stayed on.

The town houses are of *bajareque* and *adobe* with tile roofs; the *aldea* houses were said to be similar but to also include some of boards. There are a number of stores in town and the recent increase in local wealth is to be seen not only in the generally neat appearance of the town itself, but in the newly built municipal building and the number of trucks which ply the road south to Comayagua.

3. THE SOUTHWEST HIGHLANDS

Marcala (1950 population: 1,921 urban; 3,238 rural)

The Department of La Paz is divided into two general parts. On the east, including the Comayagua valley section, is the area dominated by the departmental capital of La Paz. This region is predominantly Ladino and has been ladinoized for a long period. The other part, the highland west of the department, is principally Indian and has its center in the town of Marcala. Marcala itself, although in an Indian region, has a population which is predominantly Ladino. It serves as the main commercial and administrative center for the entire western half of the department. The only road leading out goes west to Intibucá, not east to La Paz.

Marcala is a developing coffee region, and the area, particularly that to the north, is benefitting from the increased income which the crop is producing. As in La Libertad, most of holdings are small, and the incoming wealth is somewhat evenly distributed. One informant mentioned that because of this increased wealth the Indians in the north were becoming acculturated more rapidly than were those to the south where coffee was not so important.

The town is located at an altitude of 3,900 feet and the town buildings are of *adobe* and *bajareque*. The population is generally divided into three classes, the *primera*, *segunda* and *pueblo*, the Indians being included among the last. As was mentioned in the chapter on the Lenca, Marcala avoided the development of separate Indian and Ladino governmental structures in the last century, so the Ladinos have retained political control and the town has developed mainly as a Ladino community.

The educational system in Marcala, as was remarked in an earlier section, is greatly helped by two special funds which are handled locally. Their combined capital amounts to a total of almost $13,000, and in 1954 provided over $1,500 extra money for the running of the schools.

La Esperanza (1950 population: 1,959 urban; 922 rural)

This town is the departmental capital of the Department of Intibucá. It is a Ladino town which forms a single large urban unit with the Indian town of Intibucá. The two towns are divided only by a street, and the market of Intibucá serves the population of La Esperanza, while the town of La Esperanza, due to the way the dividing line is drawn, contains the church of Intibucá.

La Esperanza is an old town and at one period was one of the most important cities in the country. Formerly, the main route of transport from El Salvador to Comayagua and Tegucigalpa came through La Esperanza. Today, however, the town lies halfway down a dead-end road to Marcala, and the main transport routes have bypassed it entirely.

La sociedad is very old in La Esperanza, and informants said that fairly strong social distinctions were still made between the upper class and the rest of the population. The situation is socially similar to some of the older Ladino towns in the western highlands of Guatemala where, surrounded by Indians, the upper class Ladinos have retained strong class attitudes.

The *municipio* of La Esperanza itself is quite small and the lower class rural Ladinos, while marked as distinct from the Indians, have taken over some of Indian traits. It was said that the *mecapal* was used, for example, and elsewhere in the country Ladino use of the *mecapal* is most rare.

4. THE NORTHWEST

La Misión (estimated population: 1,000)

La Misión is an *aldea* of the district of Siguatepeque. The population was said to have been one with that of the neighboring town of Taulabé about a century ago, but a priest moved a portion of that population to the new site. Taulabé was formerly a municipal capital, and ill feeling between the two towns has continued at least since that time. The two towns together have a single title to their collective lands and, in both, the residents use them without paying. A newcomer, however, must have the approval of a community meeting before he is allowed to use local lands.

While a Ladino town, La Misión, impressed the writer as having retained features of an Indian community. This may in part be because it has retained an integrated community social structure which is more often found in Indian than in Ladino communities. Also, Taulabé, it will be remembered, is an important pilgrimage center for the Indians of the southwest highlands. There are evidently very few if any Indians resident in the territory of La Misión now; those that are present were said to be similar to Ladinos in almost all ways except that they tended to speak a slightly dialectical Spanish. The writer could not detect the presence of distinct social classes within the community and the informants claimed that there were no consistent distinctions.

Like Zambrano, La Misión has no municipal government, but is run locally by an *alcalde auxiliar*. Unlike Zambrano, however, there was evidently no overshadowing *comandancia* post. The administrative and territorial system of La Misión is similar to that of a *municipio*, even though the structure is sub-municipal. There are three *aldeas* with *alcaldes auxiliares* within the La Misión area which are considered to be subordinate to the *alcalde auxiliar* of La Misión. Ordinarily, one *aldea* would not be subordinate to another in this way.

As an *aldea*, La Misión has only a two grade school and only one teacher.

San Francisco de Yojoa (1950 population: 678 urban; 1904 rural)

This town is located on the side of the mountains rising at the north end of the great Ulúa flood plain valley. The valley floor itself is only slightly above sea level, and San Francisco is at an altitude of about 1,000 feet. The town used to be an *aldea* of the community of Yojoa, in the last century the population has been moving from Yojoa, and San Francisco has been building up, so that now Yojoa is an *aldea* of San Francisco. At present, there is evidence that the same process is again at work, and the community of Río Lindo, now an *aldea* of San Francisco located on the valley floor at the foot of the hills, is growing and may eventually take the lead over San Francisco, commercially and administratively. Río Lindo is located on the main road connecting San Pedro Sula with Tegucigalpa, and consequently is much more in line for development than is San Francisco, located on the mountainside, off the main road. Even at present, the *alcalde* of the *municipio* is a resident of Río Lindo, and not San Francisco, even though he has to appear at the *municipalidad* in the latter place to exercise his functions.

There are said to be three social classes in the town, the *primera* being composed of a few relatively wealthy families which live here in town and in one of the *aldeas*, the middle class composed of the somewhat well-to-do, and the poor. The informants seemed to think principally in terms of economic standing. This was the only community visited in the course of the survey where the writer heard open bitterness on the subject of insufficient lands for cultivation. Their own communal and *ejidal* lands, which belong to the community and municipality respectively, are occupied by a few families which use all of it. The rest of the land, except for a little national mountain land, is privately owned by the few wealthy persons in the community. And there is a standing grudge against the fruit company, since there has been a litigation over some of the valley for some time. Recently the company ceded almost 300 hectares to the community, but the community claims that this is only part of the land due them. No matter what the case may be with respect to the land, there seems to be considerable truth in the matter of there not being enough land locally for the population. The situation has been aggravated by an influx of Salvadoreans in recent years.

Quimistán (1950 population: 522 urban; 2,867 rural)

Quimistán is a very old town located on the middle drainage of a tributary of the Chamelecón River. Today it is entirely Ladino, although it was said that a few Indians had moved in from the Department of Lempira. Most of the lands are in large holdings, mainly communally held, although there is some *ejidal* land. There is a section in the north, which is still in virgin forest and some of this is *ejidal* and open to settlement. Virgin forest, however, is a real problem for the poor Ladino.

The informants denied that there existed "social classes," and said that no distinction was made between the older families and others. Nevertheless, the writer is satisfied that there is easily a dual class system, distinguishing the landless countrypeople and the older *sociedad* of the town, and that there very likely exists a middle group as well.

Administratively, Quimistán is a district and not a *municipio*. Why this is the case, the writer could not determine. Quimistán did not seem to be an extremely wealthy area, and the mere fact of being a border area (with Guatemala) does not seem to be sufficient reason, since there is no main road connecting the two countries.

5. THE FAR WEST

Dulce Nombre de Copán (1950 population: 2,631 urban; 670 rural)

Dulce Nombre is the second largest urban population (not the second largest *municipio*) in the border Department of Copán. It lies in the major tobacco producing region of the country and many of the residents are concerned in the production and elaboration of cigars. The actual size of the *municipio* is small, and many of the landholders, renters, and laborers who live in Dulce Nombre actually work in neighboring *municipios*. The town is located on the tops and sides of a number of hills and is at an approximate altitude of 3,000 feet. The population is Ladino, although there were said to be Ladinoized Indians in the neighboring municipio of Dolores.

Informants said there were three fairly distinct classes, the upper being composed of *hacendados* and "capitalists," the middle of fairly well-to-do people, and the lower of the poor. The town imposes a tax on all outgoing and incoming cargos, and the money so derived helps support the *municipalidad* and part of it is sent to the national government.

Nueva Ocotepeque (1950 population: 4,170 urban; 4,300 rural)

Nueva Ocotepeque is the departmental capital of the Department of Ocotepeque. It was moved to its present site in 1935 following the destruction of the old town by an avalanche. In laying out the new town, an engineer was called in with the result that almost all the streets are boulevards and are about the widest streets the writer has seen in any city or town anywhere in Central America.

Nueva Ocotepeque lies in the far southwest corner of Honduras, only a few kilometers from the border of Salvador and slightly more distant from that of Guatemala. The only highway connection is with El Salvador, and horseback routes lead into Esquipulas in Guatemala. As a result, Nueva Ocotepeque is culturally much more closely related to El Salvador than to Honduras. Commercially, this is reemphasized constantly as it is an important point of exit and entry for both goods and people. There is Honduran air service to the town, and bus and truck service from there to San Salvador. The writer had difficulty in obtaining change in Honduran coinage in the town since most coins in circulation were Salvadorean and Guatemalan.

A fairly distinct class system exists among the Ladinos of the town, with three general groupings being recognized. Many of the townspeople are descendents of Guatemalans or Salvadoreans. There are a few Indians in a *barrio* of the old town, Ocotepeque.

6. THE NORTH AND NORTHEAST

Yoro (1950 population: 2,078 urban; 12,809 rural)

Yoro, the capital of the department of the same name, lies at an altitude of

2,100 feet, far inland on the upper reaches of the Río Aguán in the middle of the area of Ladinoized Jicaque Indians. To the outsider, the town gives the impression of a sudden development of a relative poor area. The town itself is in poor shape, but the park is extremely well kept and the stores are full of such items as radios, refrigerators, and other goods which indicate a fairly high local income. This income, however, is evidently limited to a few of the more enterprising landholders. This does not mean that there is a real land shortage throughout this area. Much of the rural population is Indian and is somewhat reluctant to move to regions in which superior land would be available. Most of the land in the *municipio* is national, very little is *ejidal*.

Although the writer did not visit the areas, informants said that there was considerable virgin forest both on the north and south of the *municipio*. The Indian population does not live in the town itself, but is scattered through various areas of the *municipio* and neighboring *municipios*. The Ladino population of the town was said to fall into three classes: the old and well-known families, educated and wealthy; the middle group of *"intelectuales"* who were educated but not particularly wealthy; and the *populacho*. The term *populacho* included the Ladinoized Indian population, but the Ladino poor generally looked down on the Indians.

There is an active evangelical missionary station in Yoro and two very active North American Jesuit priests. The latter have recently initiated an agricultural cooperative organization which already has about 150 members in about 30 *aldeas*. Most members are small coffee producers.

Olanchito (1950 population: 3,256 urban; 21,045 rural)

Olanchito is one of the principal banana growing centers of the northern region. It is located inland along the Aguán River and, while in the Department of Yoro, is a district and therefore not subject to the departmental government. Of the male agricultural laboring population in Olanchito, 62.6% are salaried; this may be compared to the municipio of Yoro where only 9.8% of the same population is salaried (Census, 1954b). Even though the banana industry is important in Olanchito there is a large population of independent agriculturalists and there is no shortage of land for those who may wish to go on their own. According to the informants, while some local people work on the banana plantations, the majority of that labor has migrated to Olanchito from other regions, mainly from Honduras and El Salvador. Most of the land area is in national lands, and of the valley land, most of it is either owned or rented by the fruit company or held in communal holdings under old grants.

The informants said that there were generally two social classes, the *más civilizadas*, and the *populacho*. There used to be an Indian community in the locale known as Jagalteca, near Olanchito, but early in the century the government encouraged them to move to the town of Yaruca, just over the Atlántida border. There remain today a few families in the old site, but at present the town is mainly the site of an annual *fiesta* given by the Ladinos of Olanchito in which various of the older customs are observed.

The informant felt that the people of Olanchito were very "civilized" now, that they retained none of the "older customs." There is little doubt that to a great degree this is true. The combined influence of the prosperity provided by the banana exports and the greater contact with the outside world, afforded by this commerce, has permitted Olanchito to put aside many of the Ladino customs of the interior. There is little reason, however, to think that this generalization is applicable to the countrypeople who live in the more isolated parts of the district.

Catacamas (1950 population: 2,412 urban; 4,611 rural)

The combined departments of Colón and Olancho include 44.5% of the entire national territory. Of these two departments, Olancho is slightly the smaller in territory, but has 70% of the combined populations. The town of Catacamas is the last major population center in Olancho as one moves out towards the sparsely populated regions of the Atlantic coastal plains. Catacamas is located a short distance west of the Río Guayape where, coming in from the southwest, it makes a complete bend and goes again southwest before making its final turn towards the Atlantic. The valley area is one of extreme fertility and, while vastly underpopulated at present, is beginning to fill up with migrants.

Catacamas looks very much like hundreds of other Ladino towns of Central America. The town houses are mainly *adobe* and tile, while those in the rural region are mainly *bajareque*. There are generally recognized to be two classes, the *primera*, composed of the older families and the more enterprising businessmen, and the *segunda*, which includes the subsistence agriculturalists, small producers, and also some Ladinoized Indians. There is no really distinct town Indian population now, although it was said that previously the barrio La Cruz on the north side of town was mainly occupied by them. The Paya Indians, who live further out towards the Atlantic, refer to the surviving individual Indians around Catacamas as Ladinos, and the Ladinos themselves tend to think of them in the same way.

Outer Olancho, now underpopulated, offers excellent opportunities for development and migration. Catacamas, which is already serving as the commercial center for this development, is likely in the future to grow into a city of some importance.

VII. DISCUSSION

It is convenient to classify the population components of Honduras into four major groups. These are, together with their estimated populations for 1950, as shown on the following page. Of the total population of the country, about 11.0% are not Ladinos. Of this non-Ladino population, 79.6% are highland Indians, 3.8% Atlantic Indians, and 16.6% consist of the culturally diverse Antillean groups.

So far as records and archaeological data indicate, the Jicaque, Paya, Miskito, and Sumu had a fairly similar culture at the time of their first contact with the

1. Atlantic Indians... 5,650
    Paya
    Sumu
    Miskito
2. Antillean Groups.. ca. 25,000
    Antillean Whites
    Antillean Negros
    Black Caribs
3. Highland Indians... 119,800
    Lenca
    Chortí
    Jicaque
    Indians of Santa Bárbara
    Indians of El Paraíso
    Pipil

    Total non-Ladino Groups............................ 150,450
4. Ladinos... 1,218,155

    Total (1950 Census)................................. 1,368,605

Spanish. Of the three groups, the Jicaque is the most difficult to classify, both because of paucity of information concerning them and because of their transitional position geographically between the South American oriented area (Miskito and Sumu are Chibchan languages) and the Meso-American Area (Chortí and Pipil are Mayan and Mexican, respectively). The most recent convincing classification of this group is that by Swadesh[99] on the basis of his lexical statistic studies and in which he relates Jicaque to the Hokan stock of languages, suggesting that Jicaque language began to isolate itself as a separate language from the Chontal some 34 centuries ago. These data are highly tentative, but suggest that Jicaque would be better related to the north, historically, than to the south. An affiliation with the north is more convenient for our present classification because, in the years since the conquest, the Jicaque have lived in the interior Yoro valleys and the Montaña de la Flor refugee group has isolated itself in a highland region. This is the general pattern followed by the Lenca, a transitional group which has not been satisfactorily related linguistically either with the north or the south, but which during the colonial and republican epochs has developed a general Catholic culture similar to those of the highland Indians of Guatemala, especially the Pocomam.

What we have here called the Atlantic Indians are grouped together both on the basis of certain historical similarities and because of their similar reaction to conquest. The Paya, like the Lenca, have not been classified by the linguists with any degree of satisfaction. But their location and general culture, together with the fact that they now extend through the back coastal area of the Atlantic, make their inclusion with the Chibchan-related Miskito and Sumu a convenience. The

---
[99] Swadesh, 1954.

Atlantic Indians differ greatly from the highland Indians today in that they live in much smaller communities, often scattered out along river banks for some distance, and that they have historically been subject to the English and French influences which affected the coast for some period during its history. Unlike most of highland Indians today, the Atlantic Indians are among the principal residents of their region. The highland Indians usually have ladinos as town dwellers or as not too distant rural neighbors.

The Antillean groups are racially extremely diverse, culturally different, but similar in that they are in no way indigenous to Central America and have all come to the coast within approximately the past century and a half. The first arrivals in quantity were the Black Carib in 1796. Shortly thereafter English settlers began to occupy certain parts of the Bay Islands from British Honduras and the Antilles. While some Antillean Negroes may have come in during this early period, it is likely that the most significant influx of this population came at the time of the initiation of the banana industry on the mainland and the building of the attendant railroads.

In general, the Atlantic Indians are probably a population fairly stable in numbers, but one which will easily be extinguished culturally should their habitat ever appear desirable to Ladinos. The Antillean group is, so far as we can tell, a population which is growing in numbers, probably at more or less the same rate as is the Ladino population, and one in which, so far, a rather stable cultural pluralism has been established. That is, there is no strong evidence at present that the Antillean whites, Negroes, or Black Caribs are accepting Ladino culture with any rapidity. Rather, they are making gradual adjustments as necessary, but are retaining their cultural individuality. The highland Indian groups are evidently growing at more or less the same speed as are the Ladinos, but are definitely undergoing ladinoization and heading for eventual assimilation to the Ladino culture. It was suggested in an earlier chapter that over 50% of this highland population is standing on its last legs of Indianism at present; within one to three generations, depending upon the factors present, much of this group will probably be assimilated into the Ladino population. The great part of the remainder, composed principally of the Lenca of the southwest highlands, are not so acculturated as yet and, again depending upon factors present, will become more and more assimilated as time goes on. The introduction of coffee as an Indian crop may play a great role in this process.

While the future of the Indian and Antillean groups are of importance, the most important cultural entity in Honduras is the Ladino population. As Stone has indicated, the Spanish colonists early intermarried with the Indian population, and acculturation has been going on constantly since shortly after the conquest. In the course of the survey, the writer was impressed with the general cultural homogeneity of the Honduran Ladino population. If one excludes from immediate consideration the various Indian enclaves and the north coast and banana regions, there is a surprising consistency in general culture between the social organization within the various departments of the country. Private landholding is relatively high throughout, the general structure of the social classes and proportions of people in each are similar from one region to another, the domestic techniques of food handling and tastes do not differ greatly, the economy is generally locally centered, and the differences in general values and ideology seem slight.

There are some differences, however, and while they are anything but definitive, they are worth pointing out because they contain the possibility that further differences might come to light were more intensive study possible. There are a number of changes as one moves from the south to the north. The retention of communal lands as opposed to private or *ejidal* lands seems commoner in the north than in the south; salaried labor is more common in the north (but this may be highly influenced by the fact of the banana plantations); the agricultural technology reveals a basic difference in the two areas in that the wooden plow is a standard implement where usable in the south, while in the north it is rarely used; accompanying this, the hooked machete, the *machete de taco*, follows more or less the same area of distribution as does the plow, although it is now being introduced into the north by Salvadorean immigrants. Certain terminology also differs between these two general regions: the term *molendero* is generally used in the south, while *tablero* is more common in the north; *macana* is used in the south, while *barreta* is used in the northeast.

Certain differences can also be detected as between portions of the east and portions of the west. In the far west, the spoked wheel cart is used, while in the center and east the solid wheel is used. It will be remembered that this dividing line is one which comes up from El Salvador.[100] In the southeast, the leather sacks, *árganas*, are used to carry things on horse and mule back; this is a trait which is an extension of highland culture of Nicaragua.[101] Weekly markets are evidently fairly limited to the southwestern region, the area bordering on Guatemala and El Salvador, and is probably more a survival of a Meso-American Indian trait than a distinguishing Ladino regional trait. In the southwest corner, the Salvadorean custom of having the grinding stone on *horquetas* rather than on a *molendero* is found. In the far east and northeast, the term *bajo* is used instead of *hijillo* which is common elsewhere. A single annual novena after that held after death is more common in the far west, while multiple novenas are more common elsewhere. *Susto*, the specific illness resulting from fright, and the term *tunasmil* for the second annual crop appear only in the region bordering on Guatemala. The terms *machete de vuelta* (instead of *de taco*) and *machete pando* are evidently western usages.

Aside from these, the south coast itself seems to retain a certain distinctiveness. Novenas at 40 days after death were reported only from that region. Extremely high degree of free unions are present there, and the term *valle*, common in Nicaragua to distinguish specific rural areas, is regularly used. The Nicaraguan trait of the *gritería* on the day of *Concepción* was said to be practiced in Choluteca.

But in all, these differences are generally more suggestive than they are definite. One can perhaps draw a series of lines across the country representing a

---

[100] Adams, n.d. (d).   [101] Adams, n.d. (b).

series of alternative usages, but few of these lines are superimposed, except around specifically Indian areas. More impressive than these broad regional differences are certain local differences which evidently stem from recent ladinoization of local Indian populations. La Misión gives the impression of being only recently removed from the Indian, as does possibly La Venta. Catacamas, Nueva Ocotepeque, Marcala (the town itself), La Esperanza, and Olanchito, on the other hand, seem to be strong old Ladino cultures. In part, this difference in general impression is due to the presence of a strong old upper class which has retained itself as being culturally distinct from the lower class, whether the latter is Indian or not. The survival of such traits as the use of a drum in making municipal announcements or in taking a saint out on *demanda*, the custom of beheading a duck or chicken as a *fiesta* sport, the survival of a *fiesta* upon the death of an infant, of preferring wood ash in the making of *nixtamal* rather than lime, and a variety of other traits, are local survivals of old traits which are now disappearing. Some are thought of as being "Indian" customs, and actually are in terms of having been retained longer by Indian and recently converted Ladinos than by old Ladino social groups. But many of these traits are not Indian in the sense that they were here at the time of the conquest; the infant death *fiesta*, the use of the two headed drum, the beheading of a fowl, are all Spanish introductions.[102]

It may be found practical for certain purposes, as in the previous chapter, to divide Ladino Honduras into regions of Ladino culture. It must be remembered, however, that at least on the basis of the present study, such regions are not extremely distinct. Rather, we may say that there are local regions in which there are local variations in certain things: i.e., the degree to which the local population has retained certain colonial customs or the degree to which a single crop (such as coffee, potatoes, *yuca* or bananas) has developed into a specific local cultivation around which the annual cycle tends to be based. But as broad regions in which basically different social systems are to be found, Ladino Honduras does not offer such distinct differences as are to be found in Guatemala, Nicaragua, or El Salvador. The survival of communal lands and absence of the wooden plow indicate that the northern half of the country was probably rather underpopulated by subsistence agriculturalists through most of its history. As such, it does offer a parallel to the Escuintla region of Guatemala. The presence of certain old towns, however, has served to maintain a class structure which is more similar to south Honduras than to the Guatemalan south coast. Except for the north-south variations and the differential influences of the adjacent Ladino cultures in Guatemala, El Salvador, and Nicaragua, Honduras is similar to Panama where there has been a general acculturation, of varying intensity and rapidity, from one region to another, but without the evident entrance of grossly disturbing factors since the colonial period. The main region of Honduras

[102] Should there be any question on the matter of the beheading of the fowl being a Spanish trait, it may be remembered that the chicken and most varieties of ducks were Spanish introductions, the horse necessary to ride during the game was a Spanish introduction, and the game itself was found, at least until recently, in mestizo communities in the highlands of Perú where the Spanish also introduced it.

for which this is not true is the north coast banana zone. Here, the plantation economy, drawing in thousands of migrants from other parts of Honduras, the Antilles, and from neighboring Central American countries (particularly El Salvador), has set the scene for a changing cultural development. Gradual acculturation cannot be expected under these conditions. The entire social organization is different, as was the case in the similar plantations in northeastern and southern Guatemala.[103] Instead of the classic upper and lower classes, stabilized in a local community, there is an administrative class and a mass of laborers, together with the gradations based on differences in employee status. This is perhaps the only area of Honduras, outside of the city of Tegucigalpa, in which there may be said to be developing a sub-culture on the general Ladino pattern. Unfortunately, the present survey did not explore this culture sufficiently to provide us with a picture of the differences.

REFERENCES

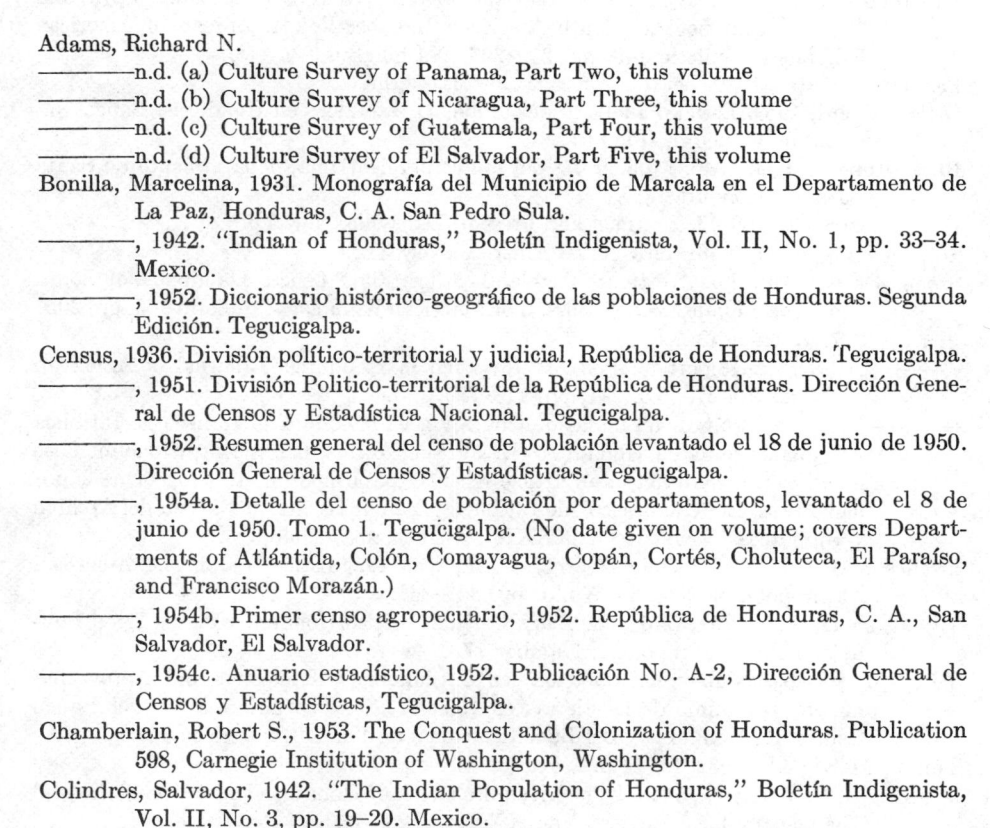

Adams, Richard N.
————n.d. (a) Culture Survey of Panama, Part Two, this volume
————n.d. (b) Culture Survey of Nicaragua, Part Three, this volume
————n.d. (c) Culture Survey of Guatemala, Part Four, this volume
————n.d. (d) Culture Survey of El Salvador, Part Five, this volume
Bonilla, Marcelina, 1931. Monografía del Municipio de Marcala en el Departamento de La Paz, Honduras, C. A. San Pedro Sula.
————, 1942. "Indian of Honduras," Boletín Indigenista, Vol. II, No. 1, pp. 33–34. Mexico.
————, 1952. Diccionario histórico-geográfico de las poblaciones de Honduras. Segunda Edición. Tegucigalpa.
Census, 1936. División político-territorial y judicial, República de Honduras. Tegucigalpa.
————, 1951. División Politico-territorial de la República de Honduras. Dirección General de Censos y Estadística Nacional. Tegucigalpa.
————, 1952. Resumen general del censo de población levantado el 18 de junio de 1950. Dirección General de Censos y Estadísticas. Tegucigalpa.
————, 1954a. Detalle del censo de población por departamentos, levantado el 8 de junio de 1950. Tomo 1. Tegucigalpa. (No date given on volume; covers Departments of Atlántida, Colón, Comayagua, Copán, Cortés, Choluteca, El Paraíso, and Francisco Morazán.)
————, 1954b. Primer censo agropecuario, 1952. República de Honduras, C. A., San Salvador, El Salvador.
————, 1954c. Anuario estadístico, 1952. Publicación No. A-2, Dirección General de Censos y Estadísticas, Tegucigalpa.
Chamberlain, Robert S., 1953. The Conquest and Colonization of Honduras. Publication 598, Carnegie Institution of Washington, Washington.
Colindres, Salvador, 1942. "The Indian Population of Honduras," Boletín Indigenista, Vol. II, No. 3, pp. 19–20. Mexico.
Conzemius, Eduard, 1927–28. "Los Indios Payas de Honduras." Journ. Soc. Amér. Paris. n.s., T. 19, pp. 245–302; continued in t. 20, pp. 253–360.

---

[103] Adams, n.d. (c).

———, 1928. "Ethnographical Notes on the Black Carib (Garif)," American Anthropologist, Vol. 30, No. 2, pp. 183–205.
———, 1932. "Ethnographical Survey of the Miskito and Sumu Indians of Honduras and Nicaragua." Bureau of American Ethnology, Bulletin 106. Washington.
Gillin, John, 1951. "The Culture of Security in San Carlos," Publication No. 16, Middle American Research Institute, Tulane University, New Orleans.
International Labor Office, 1953. Indigenous Peoples. Geneva.
Johnson, Frederick, 1940. The Linguistic Map of Mexico and Central America, in The Maya and their Neighbors, pp. 88–114, Map. New York.
———, 1948a. Central American Cultures: An Introduction. Handbook of South American Indians, Vol. 4. Bureau of American Ethnology, Bulletin 143, pp. 43–68. Washington.
———, 1948b. The Post-Conquest Ethnology of Central America: An Introduction. Handbook of South American Indians, Vol. 4. Bureau of American Ethnology, Bulletin 143, pp. 195–198. Washington.
Kirchhoff, Paul, 1948. The Caribbean Lowland Tribes: The Mosquito, Sumu, Paya, and Jicaque. Handbook of South American Indians, Vol. 4. Bureau of American Ethnology, Bulletin 143, pp. 219–229. Washington.
Lehmann, Walter, 1920. Zentral Amerika. 2 Vols. Berlin.
Ortiz, Edgard, 1953. Estudio analítico del problema cafetalero en Honduras. Banco Nacional de Fomento, Honduras.
Rosa, Rubén Angel, 1940. Monografía del municipio de Ilama, departamento de Santa Bárbara. Honduras.
Rose, Richard H., 1904. Utila: Past and Present, Dansville, New York.
Squier, E. G., 1855. Notes on Central America. New York.
Stone, Doris, 1948. The Northern Highland Tribes: The Lenca. Handbook of South American Indians, Vol. 4. Bureau of American Ethnology, Bulletin 143, pp. 205–217. Washington.
———, 1951. "A Report on Folklore Research in Honduras." Journal of American Folklore, Vol. 64, No. 241, pp. 113–120.
———, Ms. La Significación de las oraciones y celebración del guancasco de Intibucá y Yamaranguilla en Honduras. (In addition to this manuscript, Stone includes much of this material in an article recently published but to which I have not had access: El "Guancasco" de Intibucá y Yamaranguila, in Revista del Archivo y Biblioteca Nacionales, t. XXXIII, Tegucigalpa, 1955.
Swadesh, Morris, 1954. "Time Depths of American Linguistic Groupings," American Anthropologist, Vol. 56, No. 3, pp. 361–364.
Taylor, Douglas MacRae, 1951. The Black Carib of British Honduras. Viking Fund Publications in Anthropology, Number 17. New York.
Tosco, M., y Cabañas, R. en colaboración con C. Simmons y J. Joosten, n.d. Aprovechamiento y dominio de las tierras en 1950–51. Servicio Informativo del Banco Central de Honduras y del Banco Nacional de Fomento. Tegucigalpa.
Tumin, Melvin M., 1952. Caste in a Peasant Society. Princeton.
Von Hagen, V. Wolfgang, 1940. "The Mosquito Coast of Honduras and its Inhabitants," The Geographical Review, Vol. XXX, pp. 238–259.
———, 1943. The Jicaque (Torrupán) Indians of Honduras. Indian Notes and Monographs, No. 53. Museum of the American Indian, Heye Foundation, New York.
Wisdom, Charles, 1940. The Chortí Indians of Guatemala. Chicago.

APPENDIX

The Torrupán or Jicaque Indians of the Montaña de la Flor, Honduras

by

DORIS STONE

Misnomers form an important group in the terminology associated with America, beginning with the very name of the hemisphere and its inhabitants. This unfortunate fact has resulted in the confusion of much ethnological, historical, and even archaeological data. This is particularly true in Central America, an area that has served as a cultural meeting ground and has been used by tribes migrating from two important regions: the north and the south.

In the country now known as Honduras, historical documentation refers to a people called Xicaque or Jicaque. The name can be found in reports alluding to the Sula plain, to Olancho, and to the Segovia region (Stone, 1942). Unfortunately the term is a general one used to cover all pagan tribes in most of northern Honduras (Stone, 1941, p. 12), and is a Mexican word meaning "ancient inhabitants." It should not be forgotten that at the time of the Spanish arrival in northwestern Honduras, this region was under Maya domination and had important commerical connections with distant areas including Yucatán. It is also important to bear in mind that scattered throughout the rich sections of Central America were Mexican trading posts and settlements (Stone, 1941; 1949). In truth, something akin to a Mexican conquest of Central America was slowly taking place. To complicate matters even more, the Spaniards brought Mexican soldiers into Honduras. It is not surprising then that primarily the Mexicans should have been the ones to interpret the local situation and language to the Spanish invaders.

In spite of all this confusion, however, some "Jicaque" vocabularies from the western fringe of the Sula plain, the Lean and Mulia valleys, and the Department of Yoro, covering a time range from 1788 to the 20th Century have been preserved (see, e.g. Lehmann, 1920, pp. 654–666; Conzemius, 1923; von Hagen, 1943). They represent the same basic tongue but with certain sectional differences as the language spoken in 1955 by the Torrupán Indians in the Montaña de la Flor, municipality of Orica, department of Francisco Morazán, Honduras. In itself, the "Jicaque" speech has been linked with Chibcha, placed alone with the Paya and Lenca tongues, set apart as "unclassified," and recently related to the Hokan group (see Lehmann, 1920; Mason, 1940; Greenberg & Swadesh, 1953).

Location and Status.—The Torrupanes, whose name signifies "strong muscles" or "strong flesh" are popularly known as "Jicaques," a word which has no meaning whatsoever to the people to whom it is applied. There are about 200 Torrupanes within a reservation of 1,875 acres protected symbolically by a wooden stockade on the southern end, where approach from the outside world is easiest. Von Hagen (1943, pp. 62–66) has given an historical sketch of this territory. It suffices to say that the reservation became a legal reality on January 25, 1929.

Hispaniolized Torrupanes who remember little or nothing of their own language and whose customs relate them to the Ladino, are scattered in the Department of Yoro, principally in the hamlets of Jimia, Santa Marta, and Subirana, and a rapidly dwindling number are found in the hills of the upper Chamelecón River near El Palmar and the town of Chamelecón on the western edge of the Sula plain.

Von Hagen correctly recounts that the appearance of the Torrupanes in the Montaña de la Flor was caused through misuse of the Indians by local authorities in the Department of Yoro. Forced labor and similar persecutions took their toll, until finally an Indian, Pedro, according to von Hagen from the hamlet of Santa Marta, but according to the writer's informant from Jimia, killed some government soldiers sent to gather workers. This man accompanied by his wife, two sons, and another Torrupán, named Juan, with his wife fled to the region now made into a reservation (von Hagen, 1943, pp. 36–37). The original Pedro and Juan who started the Torrupán community in the Montaña de la Flor were known by the surname of Soto and Martínez respectively. What has not been told, however, is that two groups were formed in this area from their progeny. One is descended from Beltrán, a son of Pedro; and one from Fidelio, the son of Juan.

Social Organization.—Historical documentation brings out the fact that at least in the 18th century the "Xicaques" did not like to live in towns in the Spanish sense but preferred to have their dwellings separated, one from the other, in typical rain-forest fashion (Serrano y Sanz, 1908, pp. 389–399; in particular, pp. 394–395). Squier's statement, in 1858, which refers to communities of from 70 to 100 individuals spread over the Department of Yoro, could still signify the same type of settlement as he also writes: "Their huts are very rude structures, and are frequently abandoned on account of sickness, death, evil omens, or slighter causes" (Squier, 1858, p. 760). The writer has seen similar "settlements," if they can be so called, in Yoro in 1932, although with fewer inhabitants. They cannot in the least be classified by the word town. This same statement is true of the Torrupán in the Montaña de la Flor. Here, Honduran authorities take into consideration what they term "caseríos," and include eight: San Juancito, Acapulco, La Lima, Casa Quemada, Hierba Buena, Quebrada de los Latos, Tamagazapa, y La Laguna. These are not towns but scattered dwellings, usually of family groups, within the reservation.

Both Squier and Bancroft note that each "Xicaque" community was governed by a chieftain who was elected for life (Squier, 1858, pp. 760–761; Bancroft, 1882, p. 728). Von Hagen's account is contradictory as first he says only in case of "a war that affected the whole tribe" (1943, p. 56) was a chief or elder elected and that once the conflict was over, the individual again was no more than an elder in his habitation. Then later he writes that in the Montaña de la Flor an elder is appointed with full power over all the people in his group until his death (ibid) when he himself appoints his successor. The writer found this last statement to be true in 1955, although for the sake of the Honduran authorities, an *"alcalde," comandante,* and aid-de-camp are named by the community. There is also a council of elders (Agüero Vega, 1950, p. 36).

The line of succession from the original founders, Pedro and Juan, has been the following: Pedro's son Beltrán named his son Leonor head of his group. Juan appointed his son Fidelio who died in January 1955 but who named a nephew, Doroteo, about 55 years old as chief of his group. Fidelio's own son was about 28 years at the time of the succession, and it is said that his father felt he was too young. Mateo, a brother of Fidelio, might have acquired the post, but he suffered an accident which made him impotent and could not, therefore, be named.

Group Honor.—The Torrupán pride themselves on their honor, and it is difficult to find a people more honest and non-corruptible. This has made them easy prey to unscrupulous traders and to some of their Ladino neighbors who have placed an avaricious eye on reservation land. One of the reasons given for the untimely death of Fidelio is an accusation made by a mestizo, Marcial Martínez Chavarría, against some of Fidelio's group. The claim was that the Indians had stolen and eaten certain of his cattle. The chieftain himself said in court that he offered to pay the accuser for the animals not because his people had been guilty of the crime, "but so that Martínez Chavarría doesn't go around saying that the Indians rob cattle."[1] The court record continues with: . . . "this is why he offered to pay them and save the honor of his Indians. That this is all that he has dictated and can declare. His declaration was read to him and he said, 'Thus it is.' He did not sign as he does not know how."[2]

The significant part of this is that Fidelio was so disturbed at the idea that people would believe the Torrupán capable of such a fault that he himself, a relatively poor man, offered to pay for a crime not committed with the naive credence that this would halt false accusations! Authorities in Orica and the Indians themselves hold that the reason Fidelio died was not a sore throat which seemed to have grown worse during the trial, but the spiritual blow his morale suffered at such injustice. In connection with this it is interesting that the Indians of the Montaña de la Flor will not accept baptism nor allow a priest within their reservation. Their own manner of expressing this refusal is: "We do not rob. We do not drink. We are not bad men. Baptizing seems to whet the appetite and one can be bad."

In truth, no intoxicating drink is known to the Torrupán nor do they permit their members to partake of it outside the reservations. The fact that they have a word for drunkenness is possibly due to a carry-over from before the formation of the two groups cited above. Another interesting characteristic which points to their moral independence is that a Torrupán will not accept something for nothing, not even a present. If one offers, for example, gunpowder and lead which are esteemed more than gold by these people, they will offer something in return and will not accept money for their own possessions which might be desired by the visitor. "You gave me gunpowder. I give you this," is the usual commentary.

Houses.—Torrupán homes are plank houses tied with vines and roofed with

---

[1] . . . "sino, porque Martínez Chavarría no ande diciendo que los indios roban ganado."
[2] . . . "que por eso es que le ofreció pagárselas y salvar el honor de sus indios. Que esto es todo lo que él ha dicho y puede declarar. Le fué leída su declaración, y dijo, 'así es'. No firmó por no saber."

suyate (*Brahea dulcis* H.B.K.) palm leaves. The walls are from six to five feet high and the structure itself is usually large and rectangular with two doors and with room for from two to four hearth fires to accomodate each wife and her offsprings.

The fires are made by three tree trunks placed in the shape of a Y on the earthern floor.

They are covered with ash to keep them burning when the family leaves. When they go out, they are lighted with a flint and wick, or if outside, with sun and a piece of glass. There is no evidence nor memory of rubbing stones or of a wooden fire drill. At night, pine (*ocote*) torches are used generally for journeys through the woods, but at times within the house. Formerly, it is said that people slept on the floor with their feet towards the fire. In most houses today there are two or three-sided beds similar to wooden bins. These are raised off the ground by logs or boards. Hides and bark cloth serve as covers. Recently one or another person has bought a cloth hammock, an item hitherto foreign to them, from the ladinos. Occasionally logs or planks are placed horizontally for use as stools, although in most of the houses the floor is the only seat. Sometimes, but very rarely, a vertical plank partition separates one living quarter from the other. A half mezzanine used for keeping fishing poles, blow-guns, and odds and ends is common. There are also innumerable bins of construction cane and wood which are used to store pumpkins, gourds, and the like. In some houses a low wooden table made of a single plank and with a small raised rim serves for food preparation. The rare times a *metate* is needed it is placed on this table. Both iron and crude clay pots, all brought from traders, are near the various hearths. Often a half gourd, hung upside down over food on a kind of mescal fiber net rimmed with a vine hoop, is suspended from the ceiling and serves to keep off rats.

Baskets, carrying nets, hunting pouches of small animal or deer hide, gourds, bee's wax shaped as a disc, cloth bundles, fiber ropes or the material for making them, bird feathers, and hunting trophies hang from most of the available space of the walls, roof posts, or on *agave* strings strung across the room. The trophies consist of skulls and bones of deer, monkeys, agouties, etc., and are arranged in impressive hanging piles without covering of any kind. Occasionally, deer bones are put in corn shucks and attached to the outside walls of the house. They are supposed to assure success in the chase.

Agriculture and Land Tenure.—The Torrupán are primarily tuber eaters. Their two cash crops, corn and coffee, are grown almost entirely for the commercial value. Only recently has corn formed any part of their diet, and at that it is not important. Coffee is still not used at all. One of the tasks of the chief is to pick a spot for the community corn field and to distribute the work of clearing, sowing, etc. This labor is done by men, the women taking no part whatsoever. The produce of the corn field is divided among the men by the chief.

Apart from this each household has its own agricultural plot where the principal cultivation is starch tubers. These include white, yellow, and purple *yuca* (*Manihot esculenta* Crantz), sweet potatoes (*Ipomoea batata*), potatoes, malanga

(*Xanthosoma violaceum* Schott), and yams. In addition, beans, chile, bananas, plantains, pumpkin, tobacco, onions, and garlic are cultivated. The last two items are considered important as a cure for intestinal parasites.

Coffee is grown on the hillsides or between many of the houses. Near each dwelling, gourd trees, some cotton bushes, and occasionally orange and cacao trees are seen.

Pumpkin seeds are wrapped in corn husks and kept in baskets until needed. Seed corn is kept on the cob in the husk and wrapped in cloth. When ready to sow, all seeds are carried in a gourd tied to the waist. The wooden digging stick is used for planting. Women take no part in any agricultural work.

Wild Foods.—A number of non-cultivated fruits, berries, and palm nuts are eaten. Among these can be listed the wild alligator pear, a type of date, small corozo nuts, blackberries, and *zapotes*.

The fresh water snail, *jute*, commonly found in connection with graves in archaeological sites, are highly prized. They are eaten for pleasure and to cure fevers. Deer, wild pigs, monkeys, and other forest animals as well as birds, and fish all form part of their diet. Various kinds of wild honey are consumed. The favorite seems to be from a bee called in Torrupán, *aspennee*, and in Spanish, *muhuy*.

Food Preparation.—To boil or to stew, everything together in one pot, is the preferred method of preparing food. When there is a scarcity due to a bad winter or similar cause, and there is only corn to be had, it is prepared by grinding on rough stone slabs without legs, obvious crude copies of *metates*. A coarse *tortilla* is made with the corn but only when necessity demands, and occasionally for visitors, a drink borrowed from the mestizos of cooked corn (*posole*), hot chile, and honey is passed. Bananas and plantains are usually cooked in the ash with their skin, but are sometimes boiled or added to stews. Food is served in gourds and eaten with the fingers.

Food Storage.—Food stored in quantity is for sale and consists of corn and coffee. Corn is stored in a raised plank house or bin without any entrance except by removing the plank roof. Coffee is kept in a covered wooden trough within the dwelling. Other foodstuffs are really not stored but kept within the house in very small amounts hanging in net bags, baskets, gourds, or from the roof posts. It should be noted that tubers do not keep for any length of time and must be dug up not too many days before use or they will both sprout and rot. Honey, often together with wild bees, is kept in logs hanging from the outer wall of the house.

Hunting.—The favorite method of hunting small game and birds is with the blowgun and clay pellets. The blowgun is made from a branch of the *mogotillo* (*Saurania englesingii* Standl.) and hollowed with the aid of two vines: *Mimosa hondurana* Britton and *Equisentum giganteum* L. (see Von Hagen, 1943, pp. 50–52). The pellets are either baked or sun dried. When lead is not available to make bullets, the bow and arrow, either with a pointed palm point or a stunning rounded bee's wax head is used. Two forms of traps for birds are common. One is in the shape of a small cage or box of wood and the other is a bent piece of wood with a fiber twine attached. This has a loop at one end and when the bird steps within this loop after food, the wood snaps back and the bird is caught.

Fishing.—Three different kinds of poison are known for fishing, the most common being the bark of *P. grandifolia* (D.S.M.) Johnston (see Von Hagen, 1943, pp. 52–55). Women and men whose wives are menstruating or pregnant are not allowed at this kind of fishing. Hooks are sometimes brought from the Ladinos and used on a pole as the government tries to discourage the use of fish poisons.

Method of Labor.—The custom of group labor, a *junta* or gathering of men to work on a common project, is practiced by the Torrupán for forest clearing, house building, or communal planting. In addition, arrangement is sometimes made by nearby ladinos through the local chief for *juntas* to do some special job on their farms. The Torrupán *junta* differs from those common to the rest of indigenous Central America in that no alcoholic beverages nor food are served. If the work is done for outsiders, the payment, either in the form of food such as a steer, etc., or in money is made to the chief who is also responsible for dividing the recompense.

The task of keeping up the road to the reservation is carried out by the *junta* system. It is interesting psychologically that the Torrupán keep up two roads, even though they are legally obliged to work one. The first is a regular-sized mule path with bridges of tree trunks with earth on top at the low or possibly muddy places, and is for the use of all non-Indians, although the Torrupán themselves may go here if they want. The other approach is a narrow foot trail that follows the opposite side of the Guayape river. Only Indians use this, passing silently with their loads of corn, coffee, or tobacco hanging down their backs in carrying nets suspended from a tumpline.

Manufacturers.—Cordage of mescal (*Agave* Sp.), bark cloth made from some tree of the ficus family, boring a hole through certain seeds (see Dress) and the stringing of these and glass beads are all men's tasks. Mescal is used to make carrying nets, arrow bindings, etc., and for rope and string. Men also fashion different shaped baskets out of *carrizo* (*Arthostylidium racemiflorum* Stend.), a bamboo-like plant, and make pipes from the root of the *arrayán* (*Inga* Sp.) adorning them with incised designs and a metal rim on the bowl made from melted coins or lead. Both men and women clean the varied shaped gourds to serve as containers. Women alone make cotton thread to sew or to mend.

Narcotics.—The only vice the Torrupán has is the incessant use of tobacco. This includes men, women, and children. Formerly, green tobacco was chewed with the shell of the fresh water clam, *jute*, (Serrano y Sanz, 1908, pp. 394–395; 408) as a safeguard to colds and fevers. In 1955, tobacco both nearly green and ripe is powdered and carried in small gourds, usually decorated with a cross or round ball as a stopper, and smoked in the little pipes already mentioned, or is rolled into cigars.

Dress.—The women wear a sheath of cheap cotton cloth tied in at the waist and reaching to the ankles, or a blouse and skirt in the style of the past century.

The hair is usually parted in the center and worn in two braids. All go barefooted, but some wear a small necklace of bought beads mixed with seeds.

Most men wear a tunic of bark cloth or of blue and occasionally black cotton drill tied around the waist with a bark cloth belt or a vine and reaching below the knee. Sometimes a bought handkerchief or piece of material is worn over the bottom part of the tunic as an apron or additional decoration. The machete and the animal skin hunting pouch with its contents of tobacco, lead, etc., always dangle from the waist, the pouch hanging over one shoulder. When work is to be done in the bush, the bottom of the tunic is gathered around the legs and tied up, loin cloth fashion. The hair is worn in a short bob, at times touching the back of the shoulder, and a thin moustache on the upper lip with a beard on the chin is affected. Almost all men go barefooted, although occasionally one sees a hide sandal with the thong passing between the big and second toe and fastened around the ankle.

Recently, some men, particularly in Leonor's group, dress in the ladino manner even to hat and shoes. Practically every man, however, wears a short string of beads, either of glass mixed with seeds known as *lágrimas de San Pedro* (*Coix Lacryman Jobil.* Sp.) or only of these seeds. Many of these necklaces have an extra portion hanging loose in front. These adornments are called *rosarios* and are used as a "protection" against snake bites.

Domestic Animal Distribution.—Some cattle, pigs, fowl, and a few goats are owned within the reservation. The fowl includes chickens, ducks, and turkeys, but only the chickens and their eggs are consumed to any extent by the owners, and at that not daily. All are kept more as a bank account to be used for sale in an emergency or when something special such as cloth or ammunition is needed.

Time Count.—The year is divided into moons, the big division being "before the water (rain)" or in other words equivalent to summer, and after the rains. The Torrupán use the following terms when talking to non-Indians to denote certain periods in the day: "When babies are born" stands for early morning; "at the hour of prayer" for evening or late afternoon.

Curing and Magic.—There is no trace of a *curandero* or medicine man. A few remedies for intestinal parasites such as taking mustard in water and eating onions and garlic are common property. Likewise all Torrupán use the same cure for snake bite. They take the leaves of the *Acanthaceae*, "curarin" (*Justicia pectoralis*), mash them in milk, and both drink this and put it on the bite. This may be an importation from the Ladino as most botanists do not concede important medicinal properties to this plant. For the very prevalent cold or grippe, which they have feared from earliest times (Serrano y Sanz, 1908, p. 594), they have no remedy, and it is from fear of this that they do not like to accept food or money from a stranger without taking it in a leaf or having it placed aside so as to avoid direct contact with an outsider. This terror of colds is aggravated by the psychological attitude of the Indian who believes that with a cold he will die. So great is this conviction that only recently have the Torrupán consented to take aspirin bromo-quinine, or other similar medicines for the common cold.

Just as the few remedies for sickness are known to all the group, so is a curious form of divination known as the *Cabuya* or *Tapua*, and which at least the elder men all seem to practice. The process itself is known as "throwing the *cabuya* or cord." The *tapua* is a mezcal cord with two knots at either end. Its function reminds one of the *sabara* or swishing wood of the Guatuso Indians of Costa Rica (Sapper, 1902, p. 232). It is used to answer questions such as the whereabouts of a stray animal or lost article, how long a journey will take, etc. The man who "throws the cord" assumes a stooping position and takes an end in each hand. Then he doubles it over performing something akin to what a child does when he starts to make a Jacob's ladder with a string. As he makes more knots in the center, he murmurs some magical words and mumbles an incantation to himself. When he has finished working the cord, he stops and reads the knots telling the answer to the inquirer. More often than not his interpretation is correct.

Religious Beliefs.—Around the middle of the nineteenth century was the last time a Roman Catholic priest succeeded in gaining the confidence of these people. This was Father Manuel de Jesús Subirana, and the effect of his teachings still is reflected in the curious mixture of beliefs evidenced by the Torrupán. Von Hagen mentions two young gods, Hívaro and Kastariyus, who live in the sky but only look down on the world (von Hagen, 1943 p. 60), and correctly suggests that a confused conception of Jesus Christ is responsible for at least one of these deities, Kastariyus. In 1955, however, only one old man could remember the two names. All the Torrupán acknowledge the sun as the supreme being, and admitted respect or fear for an evil female goddess, Tsii, who dwells in large rocks accompanied by other though lesser devils (see, e.g., von Hagen, 1943).

Life Cycle

Birth.—Menstruating and pregnant women are considered unclean and at times dangerous. There are definite tabus in connection with both physical states which take the form of special diets. Women give birth stooping. Today a steel knife is sometimes used to cut the umbilical cord, although the preferred manner is with a knife made from a type of wild bamboo or the tender part of wild cane. The end of the cord is burned with a hot nail, and the afterbirth and the cord are buried.

Names.—The Torrupán do not give their children Spanish names until they reach the age of 12. Then they call the child after someone who has visited the reservation or whom they have heard, for example, a president or a general.

Marriage.—These people are polygamous, having when possible up to four women. Unfortunately, there seems to be a scarcity of females so not every man has several wives and some are without a wife. Marriages are prearranged at birth. Girls are taken at an early age, from 11 to 14 or even younger, to the house of the man and kept there.

Death.—The very sick are always abandoned in a little house apart and water or food shoved to them on long sticks. The exception was the death of the chieftain Fidelio in 1955. He was allowed to remain in his home and died on his wooden platform bed. Formerly, an entire dwelling was deserted if someone fell ill there. When a person dies, there is a wake for one night with food but nothing alcoholic. At Fidelio's death, a black tunic was worn by the men in his immediate family, the influence undoubtedly of the Ladino. Dead bodies are wrapped in bark cloth when available, or if not in cotton cloth and placed on a hide. It is then taken to the cemetery which is a fenced-in plot far removed from the dwellings. At the foot of some graves there is a wooden cross, and here the resemblance of anything familiar ends. On top of each grave is a clay pot placed upside down with a hole punched in the bottom. The explanation given is to enable the dead to see God and the light of the sun.

REFERENCES

Agüero Vega, Raúl, 1950. Los Indios Xicaques de la Montaña de la Flor. In *La Pajarita de Papel*, Año II, Nos. 9 y 10, pp. 34–39. Tegucigalpa.
Bancroft, Hubert Howe, 1882. The Native Races. Wild Tribes, vol. 1. San Francisco.
Conzemius, Eduard, 1923. The Jicaques of Honduras. In *International Journal of American Linguistics*, vol. 2, Nos. 3 and 4, pp. 163–170.
Expediente relativo a la acusación contra los Indios Jicaques de la Tribu selvática que habitan en la Montaña de la Flor, 1954. In the *Secretaría del Juzgado de Paz*. Orica, Dept. of Morazán. Honduras.
Greenberg, Joseph H. and Swadesh, Morris, 1953. Jicaque as a Hokan Language. In *International Journal of American Linguistics*. Vol. 19, No. 3. pp. 216–222.
Lehmann, Walter, 1920. Zentral-Amerika. 2 Teil. Berlin.
Mason, J. Alden, 1940. The Native Languages of Middle America. In *The Maya and Their Neighbors*, pp. 52–87. New York.
Sapper, Karl, 1902. Ein Besuch bei den Guatusos in Costarica. In *Mittelamerikanische Reisen und Studien aus Jahren 1888 bis 1900*. pp. 222–237. Braunschweig.
Serrano y Sanz, Manuel, 1908. Relaciones Históricas y Geográficas de América Central. In *Colección de Libros y Documentos Referentes a la Historia de América*. t. VIII. Madrid.
Squier, E. G., 1858. The Xicaque Indians of Honduras. In *The Athenaeum*. No. 1624. pp. 760–761. London.
Stone, Doris, 1941. The Archaeology of the North Coast of Honduras. In *Memoirs of the Peabody Museum of Archaeology and Ethnology*, Harvard University. Vol. IX, No. 1. Cambridge.
———, 1942. A delimitation of the area and some of the archaeology of the Sula-Jicaque Indians of Honduras. In *American Antiquity*. Vol. VII, No. 4, pp. 376–388. April.
———, 1949. Los Grupos Mexicanos en la América Central y su Importancia. In *Antropología e Historia*. V. 1, No. 1, pp. 43–47. Guatemala.
Von Hagen, V. Wolfgang, 1943. The Jicaque (Torrupán) Indians of Honduras. In *Indian Notes and Monographs*. No. 53. Museum of the American Indian. Heye Foundation. New York.